bratton
&gold
5th edition

KT-529-055

human

resource

management

theory & practice

palgrave
macmillan

© John Bratton and Jeff Gold 1994, 1999, 2003, 2007, 2012

All rights reserved. No reproduction, copy or transmission of this publication may be made without written permission.

No portion of this publication may be reproduced, copied or transmitted save with written permission or in accordance with the provisions of the Copyright, Designs and Patents Act 1988, or under the terms of any licence permitting limited copying issued by the Copyright Licensing Agency, Saffron House, 6–10 Kirby Street, London EC1N 8TS.

Any person who does any unauthorized act in relation to this publication may be liable to criminal prosecution and civil claims for damages.

The authors have asserted their rights to be identified as the authors of this work in accordance with the Copyright, Designs and Patents Act 1988.

First edition 1994
Second edition 1999
Third edition 2003
Fourth edition 2007
Fifth edition published 2012 by
PALGRAVE MACMILLAN

Palgrave Macmillan in the UK is an imprint of Macmillan Publishers Limited, registered in England, company number 785998, of Houndmills, Basingstoke, Hampshire RG21 6XS.

Palgrave Macmillan in the US is a division of St Martin's Press LLC, 175 Fifth Avenue, New York, NY 10010.

Palgrave Macmillan is the global academic imprint of the above companies and has companies and representatives throughout the world.

Palgrave® and Macmillan® are registered trademarks in the United States, the United Kingdom, Europe and other countries.

ISBN: 978–0–230–58056–5

This book is printed on paper suitable for recycling and made from fully managed and sustained forest sources. Logging, pulping and manufacturing processes are expected to conform to the environmental regulations of the country of origin.

A catalogue record for this book is available from the British Library.

A catalog record for this book is available from the Library of Congress.

10 9 8 7 6 5 4 3 2 1
21 20 19 18 17 16 15 14 13 12

Printed in China

We presuppose labour in a form that stamps it as exclusively human. A spider conducts operations that resemble those of a weaver, and a bee puts to shame many an architect in the construction of her cells. But what distinguishes the worst architect from the best bees is this, that the architect raises his structure in imagination before he erects reality. At the end of every labour process we get a result that existed in the imagination of the labourer at its commencement.

Karl Marx
Capital, Volume One; cited in Tucker, 1978, p. 344

People are the only element with the inherent power to generate value. All the other variables offer nothing but inert potential. By their nature, they add nothing, and they cannot add anything until some human being leverages that potential by putting it into play.

Jac Fitz-enz
The ROI of Human Capital, 2000, p. xii

After a few years away from their MBA programs, most managers report that they wish they had focused more on people management skills while in school.

Margaret Wheatley
Leadership and the New Science, 1994, p. 144

Dear lecturer

Thank you for adopting *Human Resource Management: Theory and Practice*. This fifth edition incorporates new material on sustainability, 'green' HRM and leadership, and as well, we reflect on world events such as the 2008 financial meltdown and the critical reflection exercise in management education and pedagogy. We have also taken account of comments from the many anonymous users and non-users of the fourth edition, as well as 11 more lecturers from all over the world who looked in detail at the manuscript for this new edition. If you are not familiar with previous editions of the book, the preface provides a complete explanation of our approach to teaching HRM and the structure and content of the text.

This fifth edition has been thoroughly updated, including new material on sustainable work systems, corporate social responsibility, ethics and HRM, dignity at work, diversity and equity, downsizing, 'target' cultures, and violence and bullying in the workplace. In the shadow of Japan's 2011 nuclear disaster, and vitriolic criticism and a promise to 'kill off the health and safety culture' from David Cameron, Britain's Prime Minister, a new extended discussion on occupational health and safety seems highly relevant. Reflecting the growing interest in creating sustainably oriented organizational cultures and in analysing the human resources causal chain, particularly the *mediating* effects of key variables, this fifth edition features two new chapters: 'Organizational culture and HRM' (Chapter 5) and 'Leadership and management development' (Chapter 10). For a more detailed description of changes in this edition, see 'New to the fifth edition' in the Preface.

More than ever, *Human Resource Management: Theory and Practice* in its fifth edition now not only teaches students, but also elicits their responses. Reflective questions and review questions prompt them to consider key concepts and implications. In addition, we are cognisant of rising tuition fees and the need to offer students greater value for money when they purchase textbooks. Thus, the companion website offers skill development exercises and other web resources that encourage students to discover more about HRM on their own. Finally, in the context of what has been called a post-crisis critical reflection on business schools, we hope this rewritten edition can help management faculty and students to reflect more deeply and critically on the purpose and content of HRM studies.

This new edition includes a variety of supporting materials to help you prepare and present the material in the textbook. The website at www.palgrave.com/business/bratton5 offers downloadable teaching supplements including lecturer notes, teaching tips and lecture enhancement ideas, PowerPoint lecture slides for each chapter and a comprehensive testbank of multiple choice questions for use in exams, quizzes and tests.

To give your students additional value when using this new edition, we suggest that you make reference to the book during your lecture, for instance identifying relevant sections of the chapter, referring to the 'HRM in practice' and 'HRM and globalization' features, encouraging students to log on to the companion website and watch the video interviews as part of 'HRM as I see it', and pointing them to the further reading suggestions. In addition, ask students to attempt the end-of-chapter case studies in preparation for your seminar or in-class discussion.

We would welcome any feedback on these new features or any suggestions on how we can improve the next edition. Please contact us via the email address on the companion website.

Best wishes

John Bratton   Jeff Gold

contents in brief

contents

VI the global context of human resource management   499

list of figures

list of tables

about the authors

John **Bratton** is Adjunct Professor in the Centre for Work and Community Studies at Athabasca University, Canada, and a Visiting Professor at Edinburgh Napier University Business School, Edinburgh, UK. His research interests and publications have focused on the sociology of work, leadership and workplace learning. John is a member of the editorial board of *Leadership*, the *Journal of Workplace Learning* and the *Canadian Journal for the Study of Adult Education*.

In addition to co-authoring the present text, he is author of *Japanization of Work: Managerial Studies in the 1990s* (1992) and co-author of the following books: *Workplace Learning: A Critical Introduction* (2003, with J. Helm-Mills, J. Pyrch and P. Sawchuk), *Organizational Leadership* (2004, with K. Grint and D. Nelson), *Capitalism and Classical Sociological Theory* (2009, with D. Denham and L. Deutschmann) and *Work and Organizational Behaviour* (2nd edn) (2010, with M. Callinan, C. Forshaw, M. Corbett and P. Sawchuk).

Jeff **Gold** is Professor of Organization Learning at Leeds Business School, Leeds Metropolitan University and Visiting Professor at Leeds University, UK, where he coordinates the Northern Leadership Academy. With Professor Jim Stewart, he is the founder of the HRD and Leadership Research Unit at Leeds Business School. He has designed and delivered a wide range of seminars, programmes and workshops on change, strategic learning, management and leadership, with a particular emphasis on participation and distribution. He is the

co-author of *Leadership and Management Development* (2010, with R. Thorpe and A. Mumford), *The Gower Handbook of Leadership and Management Development* (2010, with R. Thorpe and A. Mumford) and *Human Resource Development* (2009, with J. Beardwell, P. Iles, R. Holden and J. Stewart).

Chiara Amati is Lecturer in HRM at Edinburgh Napier University, UK. Chiara is a chartered occupational psychologist who joined Edinburgh Napier University Business School in 2010; she teaches on the MSc in HRM and on related undergraduate courses. Her main area of expertise is the emotional experience of individuals and leaders at work, which includes interest in aspects of job satisfaction, motivation, engagement and workplace stress. Chiara joined the university after a number of years working in a successful commercial psychology consultancy firm, primarily in the area of psychological health and well-being at work.

Chris Baldry is an Emeritus Professor of the Stirling Management School at the University of Stirling, UK. He has taught several courses, including introductory HRM, international HRM, work and employment, and organizational behaviour. Chris's recent research interests have focused on the changing world of work and employment, including the area of work–life balance. His work on occupational health and safety has led to publications looking at ill-health in offices and call centres, and safety trends for trackside rail workers. On the basis of his work in the latter area, he was called as an expert witness to the Cullen Inquiry on the Ladbroke Grove rail disaster. His other long-standing interest, in the interface between technological change and work organization, is reflected in his editorship of the journal *New Technology, Work and Employment*.

Norma D'Annunzio-Green is Subject Group Leader (HRM) at Edinburgh Napier University Business School, UK. She has significant experience in teaching and learning at both undergraduate and MSc levels and is currently programme leader for the part-time MSc in HRM (CIPD-accredited). Her main research interests focus on employee resourcing, performance management and talent management for HRM specialists and line managers. She has had over 20 publications in a range of academic journals including *Personnel Review*, *Employee Relations*, *Human Resource Development International* and the *International Journal of Contemporary Hospitality Management*. She co-edited the book *Human Resource Management: International Perspectives in Hospitality and Tourism* and is on the Editorial Board of the *International Journal of Contemporary Hospitality Management* and *World Wide Hospitality and Tourism Trends*.

Karen Densky lectures in English as a second language and ESL teacher education at Thompson Rivers University, Kamloops, Canada. Her research and teaching interests include curriculum theory and methodology. She has worked in teacher training programmes in Chile and Greenland. She is the author of *Creativity, Culture and Communicative Language Teaching* (2008), and has written the Vocab checklists for ESL students in this book, as well as comprehensive notes on ESL teaching and learning on the companion website.

Lois Farquharson is a senior lecturer in HRM and Faculty Director of Research Degrees at Edinburgh Napier University, UK. Lois is working on research projects focusing on leadership behaviours, actions and development interventions as evidenced within Investors in People organizations. In addition, she has an ongoing interest in the health sector and is engaged in developing knowledge exchange projects and delivering work-based learning programmes tailored to this context. Lois teaches employee resourcing and research methods, and supervises research students in the HRM, leadership and change management fields.

Helen Francis is Professor and Director of the People Management and Organisational Development Division, Edinburgh Institute, at Edinburgh Napier University, UK. Since her early practitioner experience in personnel management, she has developed a strong profile in the areas of HR transformation, organizational change, management learning, critical discourse analysis and more recently employer branding, and has published extensively in these areas. She is currently leading the development of a forthcoming CIPD-commissioned textbook on organizational effectiveness with Dr Linda Holbeche and Dr Martin Reddington.

Lesley McLean (née Craig) is lecturer in HRM and Programme Leader of the CIPD-approved MSc in HRM at Edinburgh Napier University, UK, as well as being a member of the CIPD. She joined Edinburgh Napier University in 2004, taking on the role of Programme Leader and teaching at both undergraduate and postgraduate levels, with a focus on international HRM and workplace ethics. Lesley's recent academic research focuses on professional learning and development, and she has further interests in the areas of sustainable leadership and employer branding. Lesley has previously worked in the luxury retail sector in a senior operations management role.

David MacLennan is an Assistant Professor in the Department of Sociology and Anthropology at Thompson Rivers University, Kamloops, Canada. One of his main research interests is the transition from craft to bureaucratic ways of organizing work and learning. The geographical focus of his work is small cities. His most recent publication is a co-authored paper on how small cities support child development. He is also involved in research on real estate development in the small city.

Anne Munro is the Business School Director of Research and Professor of Work and Industrial Relations at Edinburgh Napier University, UK. Anne is a member of the Employment Research Institute and Edinburgh Institute in the Business School, working on research projects in the HR, work-based learning and equalities areas. She teaches employment relations and research methodology, and supervises research students in the HR field. Anne is a member of the British Sociological Association, the British Universities Industrial Relations Association (BUIRA), the Higher Education Academy and the British Academy of Management, and is a Fellow of the CIPD.

Martin Reddington runs his own consultancy and is an Associate of the Edinburgh Institute, Edinburgh Napier University, UK. Martin's co-authored book, *HR Transformation: Creating Value Through People* (2nd edn), was published in 2010, and he is now co-editing a forthcoming work, commissioned by the CIPD, which reimagines the role of HR and organizational development in support of organizational effectiveness (scheduled to be published in 2012).

Lori Rilkoff is Human Resources Manager at the City of Kamloops in Canada. She has an MSc in HRM and Training and is a Certified Human Resources Professional. For her work on the City of Kamloops Wellness Works program, she was selected as part of the City's Innovation Committee in 2008, having 4 years earlier been awarded a Senior Management Award of Excellence for Wellness Works Program Leadership. As a 2010 Innovation Award finalist, Lori was also recognized by the British Columbia Human Resources Management Association for the encouragement and promotion of employer-based wellness programmes in the community. She was recently selected to be a member of the Excellence, Innovation and Wellness Advisory Committee for Excellence Canada (formerly National Quality Institute of Canada).

Human Resource Management: Theory and Practice has been written specifically to fulfil the need of introductory undergraduate and graduate courses for an accessible but critical, comprehensive analysis of contemporary HRM.

Overview

It is almost 20 years since the first edition of *Human Resource Management: Theory and Practice* was published, yet the management of people in the workplace continues to present challenges to managers and attract considerable research interest and research funding. As one would expect, the context has changed: 20 years ago, for example, there was no widespread use of the Internet, and today it is considered normal behaviour for people to take off their shoes when going through airport security.

Since 1994, HR practices and the HRM academic discourse have responded to ongoing developments, and it is a common cliché to say we live in 'turbulent' times. In the 1990s, privatization, deregulation and European integration seemed to define the decade. The quintessential 1990s corporate leaders, such as Kenneth Lay of Enron and Bernard Ebbers of WorldCom Inc. in the United States, were portrayed as 'visionaries' and risk-takers. After the dotcom crash, with the global financial crisis and in the wake of corporate scandals, which saw a few of the most egregious fraudsters sent to jail, competence, probity and managerial professionalism were again in high demand. A decade ago, the attacks on New York and Washington led to the ensuing 'global war on terror' and the invasion of Iraq and Afghanistan.

Ten years on, while writing this new edition, we witnessed seismic political and economic changes that have reverberated worldwide. In early 2011, the Arab Spring was the equivalent of the 1917 Russian Revolution as pro-democracy revolts stunned North Africa and the Arab world. We experienced the equivalent of the 1929 Great Crash as in 2008 the global financial sector imploded and was put on life-support by government bailouts – to the tune of £737 billion in the case of the UK. Today, public outrage over bankers' bonuses continues, Fred Goodwin of Royal Bank of Scotland in the UK has been stripped of his knighthood, and the spectre of a double-dip recession and sovereign default is stalking European economies. Add it all up, and economies are at best fragile, with most a long way from economic recovery. And if that were not enough, we witnessed in 2011 a nuclear disaster in Japan equivalent to the worst nuclear catastrophes in modern times and England, the most serious bout of civil disorder in a generation. The anti-capitalist Occupy movement that surfaced in many large cities around the Western world in 2011 was undeveloped, but it spoke to a growing disillusion with precarious free-market capitalism.

The deep economic recession is itself a complex phenomenon to analyse. Many theories try to explain it and, depending on our own life experiences and perspectives, we all have our favourite. Some would argue that the challenge ahead is nothing less than replacing Britain's broken economic model. That the so-called 'casino economy' which enabled the City to thrive is an unreliable engine of prosperity. That structural mismanagement of the economy, in particular the abandonment of manufacturing by successive governments, has left Britain poorly placed in the low-carbon, sustainability-tech revolution (indeed, Britain's abandonment of its traditional manufacturing capacity is certainly one of the big existential questions future leaders are going to have to confront). That the financial and economic crisis was a failure of markets, but also a failure of sovereign government to regulate in most Western states and so protect the public from capitalism's destructive greed. That it represents, as Henry Mintzberg (2009) argues, a monumental failure of management.

Others, however, have argued that the 2008 financial crash is fundamentally a crisis of management education and pedagogy. For years, critics have maintained that North American and European business schools have been teaching an excessively quantitative, socially detached style of management that uncritically accepted the axiomatic notion underpinning neo-liberalism that a sovereign government cannot defy the markets and that, left alone, business can take care of itself.

The thesis that business schools are complicit in the current economic crisis was perhaps best captured by *The Economist*, a venerable bastion of free-market ideology, when in 2009 it asserted that 'This has been a year of sackcloth and ashes for the world's business schools'. The years since 2008 have been a time for some soul-searching among academics responsible for teaching the disgraced bankers and financiers who caused the crisis. In a timely edition of the *British Journal of Management*, Graeme Currie and his colleagues (2010) provided a scathing account of what others have described as 'a fundamental intellectual failure' to subject neo-liberal inspired business models to critical analysis. Nobody in academia, in public institutions or in the trade union and environmental movements has yet offered a convincing narrative of how humanity can deal with the litany of economic and environmental catastrophes.

Approach

So, as we publish this fifth edition of *Human Resource Management: Theory and Practice*, what is the established consensus on HRM in the early twenty-first century? The emerging *zeitgeist* is critical reflexivity in management education and pedagogy. This approach would take it as given that the practice of management can only be understood in the context of the wider social, economic and political factors that shape or determine organizational life.

The application of C. Wright Mills' *The Sociological Imagination* (1959/2000) – the ability to connect local and personal problems to larger macro and global forces – has obvious and current resonance with HRM education. It would suggest, for example, that an employee's personal troubles caused by job loss resulting from downsizing should be linked to the broader public issue of the contraction of the welfare state, or how work and capital generally is being relocated offshore in a context of a globalization. It would also suggest linkages when a manager is faced with implementing a strategic reconfiguration of a work system into which she has had no input. For Mills, to make connections of this kind, workplace scholars have to develop an ability to change from one perspective to another, and in the process to construct a view of a total market society and its workings. It is the possession of this capacity that differentiates the social scientist from the 'mere technician'. Our aim here is thus to encourage students to ask tough questions about work and employment practices – to educate and not merely train students.

The notion of critical analytical HRM reflects recent contributions to the HRM literature. An approach concerned with the 'what', the 'why' and the 'how' of HRM. A concern with questions of: *What* do managers or HR professionals do? *Why* do they do it, and what affects what they do? *How* are HR practices enacted, and with what effect on employers, employees and society at large? This critical analytical approach to HRM echoes the belief that the contemporary workplace mirrors capitalist society at large, a market society characterized by creativity, innovation and immense material wealth, but also a society that exhibits constant change, strategic variation, social inequality and contradiction. Students need to develop a complex and context-sensitive understanding of contemporary HRM. The basis for this approach is influenced by recent commentaries from academics such as Peter Boxall, Rick Delbridge, Tom Keenoy and Tony Watson, on 'analytical' and 'critical' HRM, and the ongoing and relevant debate on critical reflexivity in management education and pedagogy.

We do, however, acknowledge that, in an introductory text, there needs to be an opportunity for students to engage in skill development related to HR. This new edition, therefore, still retains a practical element – the 'how to' activities of HRM – and more of this type of material has been placed on the book's companion website. Students and lecturers will find there, for example, activities on how to recruit and select and how to design training programmes.

More broadly, we aim to provide a more critical, nuanced account of the realities of the workplace in market societies, one that encourages a deeper understanding and sensitivity with respect to employment and HR-related issues. We hope that *Human Resource Management: Theory and Practice* captures the range of change evident in today's workplaces and will moreover lead to the kind of sensibilities that encourage the reader to question, to be critical and to seek multicausality when analysing contemporary HRM. This fifth edition of *Human Resource Management: Theory and Practice* has been written for students *looking to be managers in the local or increasingly global arena*, and therefore draws examples of and literature on HRM from Europe, Canada, the USA, China, India, Japan and other countries. This should help students to compare international developments in HRM and to develop a broader understanding of HRM issues and practices.

New to the fifth edition

Users of previous editions of *Human Resource Management: Theory and Practice* will find that we have retained the overall teaching and learning objectives of the previous versions. However, all the material retained from the fourth edition has been updated and has also been substantially edited to enhance readability and to allow for a seamless integration of new content.

Despite environmental degradation becoming a major concern for all humankind and there being a continuing interest in sustainability, the texts and discourses of mainstream HRM are largely shaped by entrenched orthodox economic growth models. Indeed, few texts mention, let alone incorporate, HR strategies for creating more sustainable workplaces. In 2012, *sustainability* is an opportunity – a hallmark for organizational change. In this edition, we have therefore included some of the emerging literature on *green HRM*.

The following is a list of the key changes and additions we have made to this new edition:

Chapter 2 incorporates emergent literature on corporate sustainability and outlines the **four pillars of sustainability** and the links to corporate-level and business-level strategy.

Chapter 3 has been significantly reworked, which reflects the interest in evaluating the outcomes of HRM. The new chapter examines some of the techniques for assessing the HRM function, and explores possible causal paths illuminating the **HRM–performance relationship**.

Chapter 4 has been renamed and rewritten to provide a more thorough discussion of work design trends and sustainable work systems.

Chapter 5, 'Organizational culture and HRM', is new to this edition. It explains different theoretical perspectives on organizational culture and the role of HRM in changing culture, and discusses the role of HRM in creating low-carbon sustainable workplaces.

Chapter 6 covers developments in workforce planning, along with a discussion of talent management.

Equality, diversity and equal opportunities in European workplaces are also new in **Chapter 7** on recruitment and selection.

Chapter 8 examines new developments in performance appraisal, while **Chapter 9** gives an extensive coverage of workplace learning and e-learning, including **new material on skills**.

Chapter 10, 'Leadership and management development', is new to this edition. It outlines the latest research and practices in organizational leadership and management development.

Chapter 11 has been thoroughly restructured and includes an expanded discussion of **variable payment schemes** in UK workplaces, explaining some paradoxes and tensions in pay systems in relation to managing the employment relationship.

Chapter 12 has been renamed and updated and also includes a discussion on trade unions and sustainable workplaces.

Chapter 13 has been rewritten to include new research and developments in **employee relations**.

Chapter 14 has been renamed and rewritten to introduce new issues such as **workplace bullying and violence**.

Finally, **Chapter 15** has been rewritten to introduce new developments in **globalization and international HRM**, and our **concluding chapter**, 'Recession, sustainability, trust: the crisis in HRM', takes a more controversial look at the debate on management education and pedagogies and the future of HRM as a discipline.

This edition includes new **HRM in practice** features that illustrate the link between HRM theory and practice in workplaces. The examples take contemporary themes such as sustainability, target culture and workplace violence, from a diverse range of organizations.

This edition also introduces two other new features, one of which is **HRM and globalization**. In this feature, examples of employment practices and management are taken from BRIC countries, as well as South Africa and North America.

The other new feature is **HRM as I see it**. This consists of video interviews with HR practitioners at companies such as Sky and Bupa (accessible on the book's companion website), in which they talk about key topics such as recruitment, organizational culture and talent management. These are accompanied by questions in the textbook for students to answer after watching the videos.

Designed specifically to meet the learning needs of international students, this new edition contains **Vocab checklists for ESL students**. This new feature helps students to comprehend HRM-related terminology and more sophisticated vocabulary used to talk about HRM, with links to explanations online and the Macmillan Dictionary, as well as learning tips.

The fifth edition contains all-new chapter **case studies**, which are international in scale and accompanied by assignments.

In addition, we have increased the interactive nature of the book, with more opportunities for students to check or reinforce their learning and to expand their knowledge outside the printed text. The reflective questions and HRM web links have all been extended to enhance the learning experience, and there are study tips and practising HRM features online.

We believe that this new edition of *Human Resource Management: Theory and Practice* and its companion website at www.palgrave.com/business/bratton5, with two new chapters, an emphasis on sustainability and 'green' HRM, a greater focus on gender and diversity, new features focusing on globalization and practitioners' views and, of course, reference to the most recent research and thinking throughout, will help students of HRM to make sense of these exciting developments.

Content

This book is divided into six major parts, which are summarised below. These parts are, of course, closely interconnected with the external and internal contexts, but, at the same time, they explore the core theories and practices that help the reader to understand the complexities of managing people in the contemporary workplace.

Part I introduces the whole arena of contemporary HRM. Chapter 1 discusses the nature and role of HRM and addresses some of the controversial theoretical issues surrounding the debate on HRM. Chapter 2 examines the notion of corporate sustainability and strategic HRM. Chapter 3 reviews the empirical studies on HRM outcomes and critically evaluates the HRM–performance relationship.

Part II examines the micro context of HRM. Chapter 4 reviews changes in job design and work systems, whereas Chapter 5 introduces the complex notion of organizational culture, considers the role of HRM in changing culture and finishes by examining the role of HRM in creating low-carbon sustainable workplaces. Chapters 1–5 provide the context of HRM and prepare the groundwork for Part III.

Part III introduces the topic of employee resourcing. Chapter 6 examines key HR practices, including HR planning and talent management. Chapter 7 examines recruitment practices to enable organizations to attract a high-quality pool of job applicants, as well as the use of multiple methods of assessment, all designed to select talented people.

Part IV covers employee performance and development. Chapter 8 examines the practice of performance appraisal and provides a critical review of some of the key developments in performance management and appraisal. Chapter 9 explains the link between corporate strategy and human resource development, discusses how human resource development may be implemented and examines the favoured theories of adult learning and HR development practices. Chapter 10 examines organizational leadership and explores the favoured theories of leadership and management development practices.

Part V focuses on the employment relationship. Chapter 11 presents a model of rewards in order to help the reader examine the complexities and practices associated with reward management. Research suggests that employers have been moving towards a more individualist approach to the wage–effort bargain, with variable pay systems increasingly replacing traditional wage schemes, and that these new pay practices go hand in hand with a more precarious employment and new work configurations, which demand more flexibility.

Chapter 12 highlights the major changes in industrial relations that are taking place at worksite and national levels, including collective bargaining and partnership strategies. Chapter 13 examines employee involvement and 'voice' and considers the context in which employee voice has changed over time.

Workplace health and safety has long been a neglected area of HRM. We seek to help to shift the balance in Chapter 14, which aims to explore why occupational health and safety is – or ought to be – a central pillar in HRM. It explains the benefits of a health, safety and wellness strategy and examines some common hazards in the modern workplace, for example occupational stress, violence and workplace bullying, one of several occupational health and safety issues that has jumped in importance in recent years.

Part VI looks at the global context of HRM. Chapter 15 examines international HRM within the context of globalization, while Chapter 16 considers the standing of HRM in a post-crisis era.

Supporting teaching and learning resources

The textual material is complemented by a number of features to help student learning. These include:

Chapter outlines and *chapter objectives* guide the student through the material that follows and allow them to check their progress.

HRM in practice examples illustrate current developments or practices in HRM. These are taken from a range of organizations in the EU to reflect the breadth of application of HR theory.

HRM and globalization examples illustrate the practices in HRM in companies outside the EU, which help students to understand the 'convergence' and 'divergence' debate in the comparative HRM literature.

HRM as I see it features give some interesting personal views from practitioners in the HRM field in videos on the book's companion website, with accompanying questions in the textbook. See page xxxvi for more details.

Reflective questions challenge the student to think analytically and critically, and to consider the broader relationships and interactions of the topics under discussion.

HRM web links enable students to download statistical information, follow current international developments in HRM practice and even monitor the job market in HRM.

Chapter summaries provide an abbreviated version of the main concepts and theories, which students may find useful for revision and also for checking their understanding of the key points.

Vocab checklists for ESL students help international students comprehend the HRM-related terminology and sophisticated vocabulary that they can use to talk about the discipline.

Discussion questions test students' understanding of core concepts and can be used to promote classroom or group discussion of different perspectives.

Further reading suggestions provide an elaboration of the key topics discussed in the text.

Chapter case studies demonstrate the application of theoretical material from the text and help the student to appreciate the challenges of managing people at work.

Chapter review questions test how much students have learned on completion of the chapter and are useful for revision.

The *reference list* provides the student with a comprehensive list of the sources and works cited in the text.

Indexes at the end of the book provide an author index and a subject index to help readers search easily for relevant information or references.

Companion website

Lecturers who adopt this textbook for student purchase have access to materials on the password-protected section of the book's companion website. Log on to find out more at www.palgrave.com/business/bratton5. The website offers downloadable teaching support and other resources, including:

- Lecture notes for each chapter that expand the content in the book and provide advice for teaching each topic. These include lecture enhancement suggestions providing new ideas for adding further dimensions to lectures, notes to accompany skill development exercises, tips on teaching ESL students and guideline answers to case study questions
- PowerPoint lecture slides for each chapter, including key points and definitions, learning objectives and relevant figures and tables, which you can edit for your own use
- A comprehensive testbank of multiple-choice and essay questions for use in exams, tests and quizzes
- Quick reference grids to readily locate both 'HRM in practice' articles and case studies in terms of context and topic coverage.

  Students also have free access to:

- A collection of videos with HR practitioners talking about key topics in the discipline from their point of view, recorded especially for this edition, and with accompanying questions in the textbook
- Extensive web links to further resources around the world to help them research topics in more depth
- Summary lecture notes to accompany each chapter topic
- Skill development exercises to improve their professional competencies

- Extra case studies and 'HRM in practice' features
- Study tips and 'practising HRM' features
- A searchable online dictionary and glossary to check definitions of key terms
- Learning tips for ESL students.

Overall, we are confident that the incorporation of new chapters, new material and student-focused features will continue to make *Human Resource Management: Theory and Practice* a valuable learning resource. We are also confident that this book will promote critical reflection so that readers will use multiple perspectives, question, doubt, investigate, be sceptical and seek multiple causes when analysing the problems and challenges of managing people in the workplace. We would welcome any feedback on the text or any suggestions on how we can improve the next edition. Please contact us via the email address listed on the companion website.

John Bratton   Jeff Gold
May 2012

authors' acknowledgements

No book is ever simply the product of its authors. This book was originally inspired by the teaching and research in which we were involved at Leeds Business School, UK, and Thompson Rivers University, Canada. We continue to be inspired by our students, but we are also indebted to our past and current colleagues at Leeds Business School, the University of Calgary and Thompson Rivers University for their ideas and encouragement in the writing of five editions of the book.

The fifth edition of *Human Resource Management: Theory and Practice* has been improved by the comments and suggestions of colleagues, anonymous reviewers and students. We have endeavoured to incorporate their insights and criticisms to improve this edition. We are particularly indebted to the following reviewers for their detailed comments: Peter Ayuk at Milpark Business School, South Africa; Marian Crowley Henry at the National University of Ireland, Maynooth, Ireland; Geraint Harvey at Swansea University, UK; Nina Kivinen at Åbo Akademi, Finland; Samantha Lynch at the University of Kent, UK; Robert McMurray at Durham University, UK; Willem de Nijs at Radboud University, Netherlands; Ciara Nolan at the University of Ulster, Northern Ireland; Patrick O'Leary at Ballarat University, Australia and Anisha Ramsaroop at the University of KwaZulu-Natal, South Africa.

We are also indebted to Peter Sawchuk, University of Toronto, for his insight into historical trajectories and some of the historical links between HRM and informal learning, expanded on in Chapter 16.

John Bratton would like to acknowledge Christine MacDonald, formerly an undergraduate student at Thompson Rivers University, for her research assistance, and Amy Bratton for her help proofreading most of the chapters. He would also like to thank Keith Grint, Les Hamilton, Sue Hughes and Norma D'Annunzio-Green in the UK; Esa Poikela and Annikki Järvinen in Finland; and Lori and Edward Rilkoff and Bernard Igwe, Bruce Spencer and Albert Mills in Canada for their friendship and support. Special thanks also to my children, Amy, Andrew and Jennie, and to Carolyn Forshaw, my wife and partner, who has provided unstinting support with all five manuscripts, and others, over the years.

Jeff Gold would like to thank colleagues and friends who have provided support in the completion of this book. In particular, thanks go to Professor Jim Stewart and partners of the HRD and Leadership Research Unit at Leeds Metropolitan University, Bupa, Unilever Supply Chain Academy, Morrisons, Hallmark Cards, LBBC Ltd, Webanywhere Ltd, TheWorksRecruitment Ltd, Skipton Building Society and members of Business Alliance. Thanks also to Professor Richard Thorpe at Leeds University and associates of the Northern Leadership Academy. But the most important mention must go to my family, my lovely wife Susan and the families of Katy and Graham, with a special mention to grandson Matthew (aged 5). I would like also to dedicate this edition to my dear mother, who passed away peacefully in October 2011.

Finally, we are grateful for the professional advice and support shown by our publisher, Ursula Gavin, Amy Grant and Helen Bugler, throughout the project.

Chapter outlines and objectives
Guide you through the material in each chapter and allow your progress to be checked

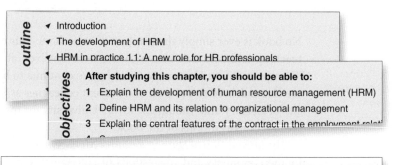

outline
- ◄ Introduction
- ◄ The development of HRM
- ◄ HRM in practice 1.1: A new role for HR professionals

objectives

After studying this chapter, you should be able to:
1 Explain the development of human resource management (HRM)
2 Define HRM and its relation to organizational management
3 Explain the central features of the contract in the employment relati...

Reflective questions
Challenge and encourage you to think critically about the broader relationships and interactions between the topics under discussion

reflective question
Based upon your reading or work experience, how important is HRM performance at work or to organizational success?

HRM web links
Enable you to download statistical information, follow current international developments in HRM practice and even monitor the job market in HRM

HRM web links
Go to the website of the HR professional associations (for example, Au... com; Britain www.cipd.co.uk; Canada www.hrpa.org; and USA www.sh... click on the 'Mission statement' or 'History'. Evaluate the information you... to the history of personnel management. Wh...

HRM in practice
Illustrate the link between HRM theory and practice in workplaces, covering contemporary themes and a diverse range of organizations in the EU

158

HRM in practice 5.1

Management surveillance: someone's watching you ...

Management have always felt the need to observe and monitor employees' work – a management function that can be traced from the 'overseers' in the first factories of eighteenth-century Britain to the foremen and supervisors of the twentieth century. Since the last two decades of that century, however, the rapid diffusion of information technology has created systems of monitoring and surveillance that seem, to many, to be all-embracing.

As a recent newspaper account put it:

From 'mystery shoppers' to swipe cards, from CCTV to phone, email and Internet monitoring, today's workforce is under constant surveillance. ('Work' Supplement, The Guardian, May 7, 2011)

The article goes on to report that such surveillance can even extend outside the workplace, with some organizations ...

Bentham. In a panopticon, the subject – in Bentham's example, the prisoner – never knows whether he is being watched or not but, because he *might* be, he suitably modifies his behaviour. One can see how the spread of CCTV and the electronic counting of throughput at supermarket checkouts seems to validate Foucault's claim.

However, as part of their long-standing work on call centres, Peter Bain and Phil Taylor (Bain and Taylor, 2000) showed that this model ignores the agency of both employees and managers. The call centre in their case study was characterized by intensive, repetitive and often acutely stressful work. The agents' performance was monitored in a variety of ways, including supervisors listening in and the recording of calls (remote observation), in addition to 'mystery shopper' calls ...

HRM and globalization
Provide examples of employment practices and management in BRIC countries, as well as South Africa and North America, and problematize them

HRM and globalization

A warm welcome to the kooky and the wacky

One of the biases of traditional HR practice is the tendency to see employees as somehow subsumed by their work role rather than being people with a broad range of passions, interests and abilities. This narrow view of the employee goes hand in hand with a narrow view of EI. 'He never asks me about myself, my family or my life outside of work' is a complaint that captures an employee's dismay at not being recognized as a person.

At the other end of the continuum is a workplace where workers are recognized as persons who do have lives and interests outside of work, and sometimes this recognition goes even further. Rather than maintaining the traditional sharp boundary bet...

great place to work if you are particularly green or have a penchant for mountain biking!

Dogfish Head Brewery celebrates its culture – an approach to life that is 'off-centered' but also socially responsible and, it is reasonable to expect, that would enhance work involvement, reducing barriers between employers and employees, and allowing workers to feel comfortable about raising concerns. One could imagine that the spirit of solidarity would improve ...

HRM as I see it

Consist of video interviews with HR practitioners on the book's companion website, accompanied by a summary of the interviewees' qualifications and experience, and questions to think about after watching the videos

HRM as I see it

Helen Tiffany
Managing Director, Bec Development
www.becdevelopment.co.uk

Bec Development is a people development consultancy firm, working with clients to implement growth in their organizations. It specializes in learning and development and offers:

- Training, delivered via workshops, seminars and courses
- Management development, to embed new behaviours and bring about change
- Leadership development through 360-degree feedback, psychological profiling, assessment centres and strategy days
- Coaching, including team, one-to-one and executive coaching
- Facilitation, by brainstorming and strategizing with clients
- Organizational development, including staff surveys, training needs analysis, talent development and competency frameworks.

Helen and her team work closely with each of their clients and their board of directors to help implement change through staff development, in line with the strategic aims of their clients' organizations. She is a Fellow of the CIPD, sits on the Council for the Association for Coaching and is a member of the executive board for Mentoring Digital Minds.

Chapter summaries

Provide an abbreviated version of the main concepts and theories, useful for your revision and checking understanding of the key points

summary

- In this introductory chapter, we have emphasized the importance of managing people, individually and collectively, over other 'factor inputs'. We have examined the history of HRM and emphasized that, since its introduction, it has been highly controversial. The HRM phenomenon has been portrayed as the historical outcome of rising neo-liberalism ideology, closely associated with the political era of Thatcherism.
- We have conceptualized HRM as a strategic approach, one that seeks to leverage people's capabilities and commitment with the goal of enhancing performance and dignity *in* and *at* work. These HRM goals are accomplished by a set of integrated employment policies, programmes and practices within an organizational and societal context. W...

Vocab checklists for ESL students

Help ESL students to understand HRM-related terminology and more sophisticated vocabulary used to talk about the discipline by linking to online explanations and learning tips

vocab checklist for ESL students

- cause (v) (n), causality (n), causation (n), causal (adj), causational (adj)
- construct (v), constructivist (n), construction (n)
- correlate (v), correlation (n), correlational (adj)
- empire (n), empirical (adj)
- generalize (v), generalization (n), general (adj), generalizable (adj)

- object (v) (n), objective (adj)
- perceive (v), perception (n), perceptive (adj)
- perform (v), performance (n), performativity (n)
- positivism (n), positivist (n), positive (adj)
- produce (v), product (n), productivity (n), productive (adj)

Chapter review questions

Test how much you have learned on completion of the chapter and are useful for revision

review questions

1 What forces are driving the added-value movement in HRM?
2 To what extent do you agree or disagree with the statement that 'the least important HR practices are measurable, whereas the most important HR practices are not.' Discuss.
3 Explain the statement that 'all evaluation methods require the measurement of some set of variables.'
4 What are the strengths and weaknesses of (a) the survey approach and (b) the case study approach to HR–performance research?
5 How can the effect of HR strategy on organizational performance be explained?

Further reading to improve your mark

Offer references that provide an elaboration of the key topics discussed in the text and can be used to help gain a better mark in essays

further reading to improve your mark

Reading these articles and chapters can help you gain a better understanding and potentially a higher grade for your HRM assignment.

- The changing role of HRM is explored in R. Caldwell (2001) Champions, adapters, consultants and synergists: the new change agents in HRM. *Human Resource Management Journal*, **11**(3): 39–52.

Critical studies are also found in the following:

- Delbridge, R. and Keenoy, T. (2010) Beyond managerialism? *International Journal of Human Resource Management*, **21**(6): 799–817.

Case studies

Demonstrate the application of theoretical material from the text and facilitate an understanding and appreciation of the challenges of managing people at work

case study

Canterbury Hospital

Setting

In the twenty-first century, New Zealand is tackling environmental issues similar to those of many countries: the more sustainable use of water, managing marine resources, reducing waste and improving energy efficiency. The country is particularly concerned about the decline of its unique plants, animal...

Companion website

www.palgrave.com/business/bratton5

See the section on the companion website in the preface for full details

bratton & gold
human resource management
5th edition

home | About this book | Lecturer zone | Student zone | HRM as I see it

About this book

What makes this book so special?

What is new for the 5th edition?

Guided tour of the book

Welcome to the companion website for Human Resource Management
Fifth edition
by John Bratton and Jeff Gold

human resource management
theory & practice
&gold

HRM as I see it: video and text feature

Video interviews with HR practitioners on the companion website at www.palgrave.com/business/bratton5, linked to chapter content

This exciting feature, new to the fifth edition, enables you to learn about how HRM operates *in practice.* In a series of video interviews, HR managers and directors from organizations such as Bupa, Sky, Unite the Union and telecommunications company Huawei discuss their activities in the workplace, providing invaluable insights into the 'real world' of HRM. Emphasis is given to HRM's involvement in business strategy, in other words to how it shapes the future direction of organizations, *making a sound knowledge of HRM essential for every future business person.*

Each interview starts with a discussion of why the practitioners decided to work in HR and how they got to where they are now. This is followed by a consideration of selected key topics such as partnership, diversity, organizational culture, trade union relations and recruitment from their point of view, and ends with the HR practitioner giving their advice to those who wish to pursue a career in HR.

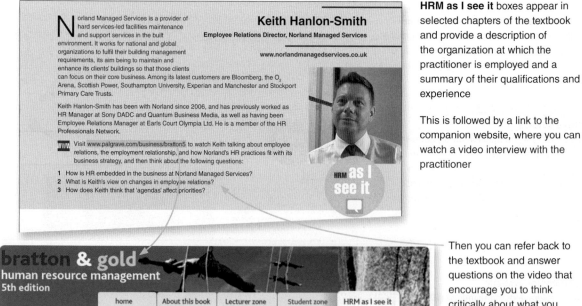

Keith Hanlon-Smith

Employee Relations Director, Norland Managed Services

www.norlandmanagedservices.co.uk

Norland Managed Services is a provider of hard services-led facilities maintenance and support services in the built environment. It works for national and global organizations to fulfil their building management requirements, its aim being to maintain and enhance its clients' buildings so that those clients can focus on their core business. Among its latest customers are Bloomberg, the O₂ Arena, Scottish Power, Southampton University, Experian and Manchester and Stockport Primary Care Trusts.

Keith Hanlon-Smith has been with Norland since 2006, and has previously worked as HR Manager at Sony DADC and Quantum Business Media, as well as having been Employee Relations Manager at Earls Court Olympia Ltd. He is a member of the HR Professionals Network.

Visit www.palgrave.com/business/bratton5 to watch Keith talking about employee relations, the employment relationship, and how Norland's HR practices fit with its business strategy, and then think about the following questions:

1 How is HR embedded in the business at Norland Managed Services?
2 What is Keith's view on changes in employee relations?
3 How does Keith think that 'agendas' affect priorities?

HRM as I see it

bratton & gold
human resource management
5th edition

home | About this book | Lecturer zone | Student zone | HRM as I see it

About this book
What makes this book so special?
What is new for the 5th edition?

HRM as I see it

Video interviews with HR practitioners

HRM as I see it boxes appear in selected chapters of the textbook and provide a description of the organization at which the practitioner is employed and a summary of their qualifications and experience

This is followed by a link to the companion website, where you can watch a video interview with the practitioner

Then you can refer back to the textbook and answer questions on the video that encourage you to think critically about what you have seen, and relate it back to the topics under discussion in the chapter

There are eight of these features in the book, linking to eight videos online. Here is a list of the practitioners and which chapter you can find them in.

Chapter 5: Keith Stopforth, Head of Talent and Development at Bupa Health and Well-being, talks about the organizational culture at Bupa and how this is implemented, how talent management works in the company, and how Bupa views diversity in the workplace.

Chapter 6: Sarah Myers, Director of Talent Management at Sky, discusses how talent management operates in the company, how the recession has impacted on this, and how their approach is firmly tied to the business strategy.

Chapter 7: Tania Hummel, Group Human Resources Director at the publisher Macmillan, gives her thoughts on the challenges facing recruitment, particularly with regard to diversity, and issues faced by HR in the publishing industry.

Chapter 9: Helen Tiffany, Managing Director of HR consultancy firm Bec Development, talks about the importance of human resource development and coaching.

Chapter 11: Ruth Altman, an experienced freelance HR practitioner, discusses the challenges faced by HR departments in universities and how higher tuition fees will impact on the reward system at universities.

Chapter 12: Ray Fletcher, Director of Personnel and Development at Unite the Union, considers trade unions in the contemporary workplace, their contribution to workplace learning, and possibilities for union–green coalitions.

Chapter 13: Keith Hanlon-Smith, Employee Relations Director at facilities maintenance company Norland Managed Services, discusses employee relations, the employment relationship and HR as a strategic partner (the Ulrich model).

Chapter 15: Lesley White, Human Resources Director UK and Ireland for Huawei Technologies, discusses the challenges of working in a UK-based HR department for a company headquartered in China, cultural differences in working and management styles, and the place of HR in Huawei's business strategy.

bratton & gold
human resource management
5th edition

home | About this book | Lecturer zone | Student zone | HRM as I see it

About this book

What makes this book so special?
What is new for the 5th edition?
Guided tour of the book
Contents list
Preface
Sample chapter
About the authors
Endorsements
Website outline
Samples
Overview of case studies

Lecturer zone

PowerPoint slides
Figures
Case study answer guides

Student zone

HRM as I see it

Video interviews with HR practitioners

Welcome to the HRM as I see it zone. This section of the website enables you to learn about how HRM operates in practice. In a series of video interviews, HR managers and directors from a range of organizations discuss their activities in the workplace, providing invaluable insights into the 'real world' of HRM.

Click on the photos below to access each video. You can then refer back to the textbook and answer the questions for each feature.

Visit the HRM as I see it zone at www.palgrave.com/business/bratton5 to watch these video interviews and learn about HRM from the point of view of a variety of experienced practitioners

publisher's acknowledgements

The authors and publishers are grateful to the following for permission to reproduce figures, tables and extracts of text:

The Academy of Management (NY) for permission to reproduce Table 3.1, 'The two dimensions of high-performance HR practices', from Huselid, M. A., The impact of HRM practices on turnover, productivity and corporate financial performance. *Academy of Management Journal*, **38**(3): 635–72. Copyright 1995.

The Chartered Management Institution for permission to use Figure 10.3, 'How leadership and management development links to organisation performance', from Mabey, C., *Management Development Works: The Evidence* (The Chartered Management Institution, 2005).

Claire Gubbins and Thomas Garavan for permission to use Figure 9.4, 'Changing HRD roles', from Gubbins, C. and Garavan, T. (2009), Understanding the HRD role in MNCs: the imperatives of social capital and networking. *Human Resource Development Review* 2009, **8**: 245.

Emerald Publishing for permission to use Figure 10.8, 'Concentration and Distribution in LMD', from Ross, L., Rix, M. and Gold, J. (2005) Learning distributed leadership, part 1. *Industrial and Commercial Training*, **37**(3): 130–7.

The *Globe and Mail*, for permission to use the extract featured in HRM and globalization, 'Multiculturalism's magic number', on p. 149, from Ingrid Peritz and Joe Friesen (2010) Multiculturalism's magic number. *The Globe and Mail*, October 2, pp. A14–15.

Great Place To Work ® Institute UK for permission to use the quotation in HRM in practice 5.2, 'Can we measure changes in organizational culture?' on p. 164.

Hugh Scullion for permission to reproduce Table 15.1, 'Examples of training and development interventions in multinational corporations', from Caligiuri, P. M. et al. Training, learning and development in multinational organizations. In Scullion, H. and Linehan, M. *International Human Resource Management*, p. 77. Reproduced with permission of Palgrave Macmillan.

The Institute for Employment Studies, for permission to use Figure 10.2, 'A model of impact on organisation performance', from Tamkin and Denvir, *Strengthening the UK Evidence Base on Management and Leadership Capability*. Research and Evidence Publications URN 06/2117, Department of Trade and Industry (2006). www.employment-studies.co.uk/pdflibrary/dti2117.pdf.

Palgrave Macmillan for permission to reproduce Figure 5.1, 'The dynamics of culture', from John Parker, Leonard Mars, Paul Ransome and Ms Hilary Stanworth, *Social Theory* (2003).

John Wiley & Sons, Inc. for permission to reproduce Figure 7.2, 'An attraction-selection-attrition framework' from Schneider, B. The people make the place. *Personnel Psychology*, **40**: 437–53. Copyright 1987.

The Management Standards Centre for permission to reproduce Figure 10.6, 'Functional areas of management and leadership standards', from www.management-standards.org.

Michael Beer for permission to reproduce Figure 1.5, 'The Harvard model for HRM', from Beer, M. et al. *Managing Human Assets* (The Free Press, 1984).

The Ministry for the Environment, New Zealand, for permission to use the figure depicting the CEF funding process in the case 'Canterbury Hospital' on p. 33, from www.mfe.govt.nz/withyou/funding/community-environment-fund/, Ministry for the Environment (New Zealand, 2011).

Morrisons PLC for permission to use the extract on p. 219.

Oak Tree Press for permission to use Figure 10.10, 'Holistic Evaluation', from Thorpe, R., Gold, J., Anderson, L., Burgoyne, J., Wilkinson, D. and Malby, R. *Towards Leaderful Communities in the North of England* (2009).

Pearson Education Inc., Upper Saddle River, NJ, for permission to reprint Figure 9.7, 'Experiential Learning Cycle', from Kolb, David A., *Experiential Learning: Experience as a Source of Learning & Development*, 1st edn, © 1984, p. 42.

Personnel Publications for permission to use the cartoon in Figure 14.4 'Stress caused by dual role syndrome'. *Personnel Management Plus* (1992) April.

Sage Publications for permission to use Figure 9.4, 'Changing HRD Roles', from Gubbins, C. and Garavan, T. Understanding the HRD Role in MNCs: the imperatives of social capital and networking. *Human Resource Development Review* (2009) **8**: 245.

Wiley Blackwell Publishing Ltd., for permission to reproduce Table 1.3, 'The Storey model of human resource management', from Storey, J. *Developments in the Management of Human Resources*. Copyright 1992.

Professor William Ouchi and The Institute for Operations Research and the Management Sciences (INFORMS), for permission to reprint Figure 8.5, 'Contingencies in performance management' from Ouchi, W. G. A conceptual framework for the design of organizational control mechanisms. *Management Science*, **25**(9): 833–48. Copyright 1979, The Institute for Operations Research and the Management Sciences (INFORMS), 7240 Parkway Drive, Suite 300, Hanover, MD 21076 USA.

For their permission to use photographs, the publishers would like to thank:

Barclays Group, Dreamstime, iStockphoto, Fotolia, Mat White, Shutterstock, Morrisons PLC.

Every effort has been made to trace all the copyright holders but if any have been inadvertently overlooked the publishers will be pleased to make the necessary arrangements at the first opportunity.

key topics grid

Key topic	Relevant chapter(s)	Other relevant material
Ethics, corporate social responsibility and environmental sustainability	Chapter 16: Recession, sustainability and trust: the crisis in HRM	• Chapter 1, p. 4, 'HRM in practice 1.1: A new role for HR professionals' • Chapter 1, pp. 33–4, 'Case study: Canterbury Hospital' • Chapter 2, pp. 44–50, 'Ethics and corporate social responsibility' • Chapter 2, p. 46, 'HRM in practice 2.1: Killer chemicals and greased palms' • Chapter 2, p. 52, 'HRM and globalization 2.1: Business urged to keep on eco-track' • Chapter 2, pp. 65–6, 'Case study: Zuvan Winery' • Chapter 4, pp. 131–5, 'Work redesign, sustainability and HRM' • Chapter 4, p. 139–40, 'Case study: Currency, Inc.' • Chapter 5, pp. 162–7, 'Sustainability and green HRM' • Chapter 15, p. 510, 'HRM in Practice 15.1: We are disposable people …'
Diversity, gender management and equal opportunities	Chapter 5: Organizational culture and HRM Chapter 6: Workforce Planning and Talent Management Chapter 7: Recruitment and Selecting Employees	• Chapter 1, p. 30, content on the feminist paradigm and gender analysis • Chapter 2, p. 54, 'HRM in practice 2.2: More women leaders: the answer to the financial crisis?' • Chapter 5, pp. 144–8, content on diversity, culture and the workplace • Chapter 5, p. 149, 'HRM and globalization: Multiculturalism's magic number' • Chapter 5, p. 153, 'HRM as I see it: Keith Stopforth, Bupa Health and Wellbeing' • Chapter 5, p. 159, content on feminist perspectives on workplace culture • Chapter 6, pp. 201–4, 'Diversity management' • Chapter 6, p. 202, 'HRM and globalization: What to do about macho?' • Chapter 7, p. 227, 'HRM in practice 7.2: Trapped in the marzipan layer' • Chapter 9, p. 287, 'Diversity and HRD' • Chapter 10, p. 334, 'HRM in practice 10.1: Much too macho?' • Chapter 11, pp. 388–90, 'Equal pay legislation' • Chapter 12, p. 426–7, 'Case study: Rama Garment factory'
Health, safety and wellness	Chapter 14: Health and Safety Management	• Chapter 5, pp. 165–7
Globalization and international HRM	Chapter 15: International HRM Chapter 16: Recession, sustainability, trust: the crisis of HRM	• Chapter 1, p. 24, 'HRM and globalization 1.1: The HRM model in advancing economies?' • Chapter 9, p. 315, 'HRM and globalization: Learning in a global context' • Chapter 11, p. 373, 'HRM and globalization: Building a hybrid at Samsung'
The recession	Chapter 1: The Nature of Contemporary HRM Chapter 16: Recession, sustainability and trust: the crisis in HRM	• Chapter 1, p. 4, HRM in practice 1.1: A new role for HR professionals' • Chapter 2, p. 54, 'HRM in practice 2.2: More women leaders: the answer to the financial crisis?' • Chapter 3, pp. 100–1, 'Case study: Vogue Apparel'. • Chapter 5, pp. 167–9, 'Paradox in culture management' • Chapter 6, p. 182, 'Workforce planning' (content on Northern Rock and workforce planning) • Chapter 6, p. 197, 'HRM as I see it: Sarah Myers, Sky'

Key topic	Relevant chapter(s)	Other relevant material
Work–life balance	Chapter 5: Organizational Culture and HRM	• Chapter 4, pp. 107–9, 'The primacy of work thesis' • Chapter 4, p. 126, 'HRM in practice 4.2: The home office' • Chapter 6, pp. 186–201, material on flexible working and work–life balance • Chapter 8, p. 258, 'HRM in practice 8.2: Performance target culture: "I have been near breaking point …"' • Chapter 14, p. 477, 'HRM in practice 14.1: Juggling work and life'
Organizational culture	Chapter 5: Organizational Culture and HRM	• Chapter 1, pp. 13–16, 'Scope and functions of HRM' • Chapter 13, p. 442, 'HRM and globalization: A warm welcome to the kooky and the wacky' • Chapter 15, p. 513 , 'HRM as I see it: Lesley White, Huawei Technologies' • Chapter 15, p. 521, 'The convergence/divergence debate' (covering different organizational cultures in a global working environment)
Leadership management and development	Chapter 10: Leadership Management and Development	• Chapter 5, pp. 153–5, 'Managerially oriented perspectives' • Chapter 5, p. 158, 'HRM in practice 5.1: Management surveillance: someone's watching you …' • Chapter 5, p. 161, 'Leading cultural change'
The voluntary/ tertiary sector and HRM in small and medium-sized enterprises		• Chapter 8, p. 252, content on performance analysis in small and medium-sized enterprises • Chapter 9, p. 324–5, 'Case study: Volunteers Together' • Chapter 10, pp. 354–6, 'Developing leaders and managers in small and medium-sized enterprises' • Chapter 11, p. 365, material on volunteers and reward management
The public sector		• Chapter 3, p. 78, 'HRM in practice 3.1: HR can lower NHS death rates' • Chapter 4, p. 126, 'HRM in practice 4.2: The home office', material on working from home in the public sector • Chapter 6, p. 183, 'HRM in practice 6.1: Planning the headcount on the policy roller-coaster' • Chapter 6, p. 184, material on workforce planning and the UK National Health Service • Chapter 8, pp. 251–2, material on performance measurement and human resource management in the public and the tertiary sector • Chapter 10, p. 357–8, 'Case study: The City of Sahali' • Chapter 14, p. 494–5, 'Case study: The City of Kamloops'

part I

the arena of contemporary human resource management

1

chapter 1

the nature of contemporary HRM

objectives

After studying this chapter, you should be able to:

1 Explain the development of human resource management (HRM)

2 Define HRM and its relation to organizational management

3 Explain the central features of the contract in the employment relationship

4 Summarise the scope of HRM and the key HRM functions

5 Explain the theoretical issues surrounding the HRM debate

6 Appreciate the different approaches to studying HRM

introduction

This book is concerned with managing people, both individually and collectively, in the workplace. Emerging from the worst cyclical economic recession since 1945, human resource management (HRM) has assumed new prominence as concerns about global competitiveness, the demographics of ageing and climate change persist. It is argued that these global drivers of change require managers to adjust the way in which they manage in order to achieve innovation, sustainable growth and an effective use of employees. For some, HRM is associated with a set of distinctive 'best' practices that aim to recruit, develop, reward and manage people in ways that create what are called 'high-performing work systems'. For others, the HRM stereotype is simply a repackaging of 'good' personnel management practices – the 'old wine in new bottles' critique – or more fundamentally exposes enduring conflicts and paradoxes associated with labour management. As managers strive to reduce costs, most follow conventional wisdom – downsizing, restructuring and outsourcing work to ever cheaper labour markets – rather than looking to HRM in order to create competitive advantage or provide superior public services. Critical management theorists point to the need to address the conflict between the dual imperatives of competitiveness and control, and the cooperation and commitment of employees. Within the academic study of HRM, this conflict is often framed in terms of 'the rhetoric versus the reality' of HRM.

This chapter examines the complex debate surrounding the nature and significance of contemporary HRM. After defining HRM, we will examine the nature of the employment relationship and HRM functions. We will also explore some influential theoretical models that attempt to define HRM analytically. We will begin, however, by briefly examining the development of HRM.

reflective question   Based upon your reading or work experience, how important is HRM to individual performance at work or to organizational success?

The development of HRM

Despite the fact that 'human resource management' outwardly appears to be a relatively neutral management term, the language used to talk about it is imbued with ideologies that reflect radical changes in society over time. As understood in the approach we are taking here, innovations in management must be analysed within a framework of existing social relationships and interdependencies in society. The notion that HRM is *embedded* in society helps to capture and express the importance of culture, national politics, practising law and indigenous business-related institutions, for example employment tribunals, in explaining how work and people are managed. Thus, developments in HRM respond to and are shaped by changes in markets, social movements and public policies that are the products of the economic and political changes in society.

Keynesianism: collectivism and personnel management

The roots of people management can be traced back to the Industrial Revolution in England in the late eighteenth century. However, we begin our discussion on this history with the economic and political conditions prevailing after the Second World War. The

A new role for HR professionals

There has been increased awareness and understanding of the impact that business activity has upon social and political systems as a result of high-profile corporate scandals, such as the alleged phone hacking at News International and the politicians implicated. Awareness has also been raised by global development initiatives such as the Business Leaders Initiative on Human Rights (a business-led organization aiming to find practical ways of implementing the Universal Declaration of Human Rights in a business context). As a result, organizations are increasingly being pushed to develop their business practices in order to operate within socially acceptable parameters. The 'triple bottom line' (Elkington, 1998) of *profit, people* and *planet* provides a convenient manifesto for the 'social contract' now expected from business. There is little doubt that there is tension between social obligations and the demands of shareholders. But who is awarded the daunting task of integrating the economic, social and environmental objectives into an organization's strategy, thus dealing with the complex task of balancing ethics and income? The need to define, balance and carry out these objectives has been intensified as the effects of the economic downturn are felt around the globe. A recent *People Management* article highlights this growing expectation that businesses will accept such responsibility:

> *The fallout from the world financial crisis continues unabated. For the first time since the Great Depression of the 1930s, some of the most sacred tenets of Western capitalism are being questioned in mainstream debate. Chief among these is our most basic assumption that growth is the primary goal of economic activity. There seems to be a widespread acceptance of the need for corporations to be more responsible as global tenants, to pay more attention to the broader consequences of economic activity*

> *and to adopt more sustainable practices … While the recklessness of the financial services industry seems to have been pivotal, our research suggests that the crisis was the culmination of a far wider malaise affecting how organisations operate, what leaders do, and how they are developed … Businesses are increasingly seen as participants in a wider ecology with responsibility for minimising their environmental impact and improving their contribution to social welfare. (Casserley and Critchley, 2010, p. 21)*

Much is made of the wide-ranging responsibilities of the human resources (HR) function. Alongside the strategic influence of their new role as a business partner in many organizations, and the ongoing need for them to provide operational support, HR professionals are facing renewed and unrelenting pressure to act as moral and ethical compasses for organizations. This is rooted in the welfare role of the personnel function prior to the advent of HRM. The HR function has been awarded great responsibility as a guardian of the ethos and values that must be embedded in an organizational culture if HR specialists are to be successful. The changing expectations of organizational stakeholders can be attributed to notable cases of corporate mismanagement and stakeholders' growing awareness that their reputation could be damaged. This has led to a competitive need to justify not only what organizations do with their profits, but also how those profits are generated in the first place. Cross-border business and an emphasis on employee welfare and social, legal and philanthropic responsibilities have all forced organizations to nominate 'natural' leaders to be responsible for internal and external ethical responsibility.

Stop! Should corporations behave in an ethical manner because it is morally right or because there is a 'business case' for management ethics? Should HR professionals act as the 'moral compass' for organizations?

Sources and further information: For further information, see the Business Leaders Initiative on Human Rights website www.blihr.org. See also Casserley and Critchley (2010), Francis and Keegan (2005) and Watson (2007).

Note: This feature was written by Lesley McLean (née Craig) at Edinburgh Napier University.

THE GOVERMENT LIES THE BANKS STEAL THE RICH LAUGHS

Mat Coleman

years 1950–74 were the 'golden age' of the Keynesian economic doctrine, as evidenced by the post-war Labour government's commitment 'to combine a free democracy with a planned economy' (Coates, 1975, p. 46). It was a period when both Conservative and Labour governments, anxious to foster industrial peace through conciliation, mediation and arbitration (Crouch, 1982), passed employment laws to improve employment conditions and extend workers' rights, which also encouraged the growth of personnel specialists. The Donovan Commission (1968) investigated UK industrial relations and recommended, among other things, that management should develop joint (trade union–management) procedures for the speedy settlement of grievances. The idea that there were both common and conflicting goals between the 'actors' – employers and trade unions – and the state's deep involvement in managing and regulating employment relations provided the *pluralist* framework for managing the employment relationship.

HRM web links   WWW   Go to the website of the HR professional associations (for example, Australia www.hrhq. com; Britain www.cipd.co.uk; Canada www.hrpa.org; and USA www.shrm.org). Then click on the 'Mission statement' or 'History'. Evaluate the information you find in relation to the history of personnel management. What are the origins of the association?

Neo-liberalism: individualism and HRM

In the 1980s and 90s, there was a radical change in both the context and the content of how people were managed. Western economies saw the renaissance of 'market disciplines', and there was a strong belief that, in terms of economic well-being, too much government intervention was the problem. The new political orthodoxy focused on extending market power and limiting the role of the government, mainly to facilitate this laissez-faire agenda (Kuttner, 2000). The rise of the political ideology of Thatcherism in Britain represented a radical break from the consensual, corporatist style of government, which provided the political backcloth to this shift in managerial ideas and practices. Whereas it was alleged that traditional personnel management based its legitimacy and influence on its ability to deal with the uncertainties stemming from full employment and trade union growth, HRM celebrated the *unitary* philosophy and framework. Strongly influenced by the up-and-coming neo-liberal economic consensus, HRM subscribed to the idea that there was a harmony of goals and interests between the organization's internal members. The new approach was therefore to marginalize or exclude 'external' influences such as the state or trade unions.

The landmark publication *New Perspectives on Human Resource Management* (1989), edited by John Storey, generated the 'first wave' of debate on the nature and ideological significance of the normative HRM model. Debate focused on 'hard' and 'soft' versions of the HRM model. The 'hard' version emphasizes the term 'resource' and adopts a 'rational' approach to managing employees, that is, viewing employees as any other economic factor – as a cost that must be controlled. The 'soft' HRM model emphasizes the term 'human' and thus advocates investment in training and development, as well as the adoption of 'commitment' strategies to ensure that highly skilled and loyal employees give the organization a competitive advantage. For some academics, the normative HRM model represented a distinctive approach to managing the human 'input' that fitted the new economic order (Bamberger and Meshoulam, 2000); in addition, being much more concerned with business strategy and HR strategy linkages, it signalled the beginnings of a new theoretical sophistication in the area of personnel management (Boxall, 1992). For those who disagreed, however, the HRM stereotype was characterized as a cultural construct concerned with making sure that employees 'fitted' corporate values (Townley, 1994), even attempting to 'govern the soul' (Rose, 1999). In this way, the HRM model, among both its advocates and its detractors, became one of the most controversial topics in managerial debate (Storey, 1989). The displacement of personnel management by HRM can be seen as the outcome of neo-liberalism ideology, much as the 'social contract' of the 1970s was an outcome of Keynesian economic planning and the 'Old' Labour government–union partnership.

Management and HRM

HRM, in theory and in practice, encompasses a diverse body of scholarship and managerial activities concerned with managing work and people. An early definition of HRM by Michael Beer and his colleagues focuses on all managerial activity affecting the employment relationship: 'Human resource management (HRM) involves all management decisions and actions that affect the nature of the relationship between the organization and employees – its human resources' (1984, p. 1). Acknowledging HRM as only one 'recipe' from a range of alternatives, Storey (1995a, 2001) contends that HRM plays a pivotal role in sophisticated organizations, emphasizing the importance of the strategic dimension and employee 'commitment' in generating HR activities. In his view:

Human resource management is a distinctive approach to employment management which seeks to achieve competitive advantage through the strategic deployment of a highly committed and capable workforce using an array of cultural, structural and personnel techniques. (Storey, 2007, p. 7)

Conceptualizing HRM as a high-commitment management strategy limits the discipline to the study of a relatively small number of distinct organizations as most firms continue to provide low wages and a minimal number of training opportunities (Bacon and Blyton, 2003). In contrast, Boxall et al. (2008, p. 1) define HRM as 'the management of work and people towards desired ends'. These authors advance the notion of 'analytical HRM' to emphasize that the primary task of HRM scholars is to build theory and gather empirical data in order to identify and explain 'the way management *actually behaves* in organizing work and managing people' (Boxall et al., 2008, p. 4, emphasis added).

This approach to HRM has three interrelated analytical themes. The first is a concern with the '*what*' and '*why*' of HRM, with understanding management behaviour in different contexts and with explaining motives. The second is a concern with the '*how*' of HRM, that is, the processes by which it is carried out. The third is concerned with questions of '*for whom and how well*', that is, with assessing the *outcomes* of HRM. The third characteristic in particular implies a critical purpose and helps us to rediscover one of the prime objectives of the social sciences – that of asking tough questions about power and inequality. It also reminds all of those who are interested in studying the field that HRM is 'embedded in a global economical, political and sociocultural context' (Janssens and Steyaert, 2009, p. 146).

Almost 50 years ago, sociologist Peter Berger wrote that the first wisdom of sociological inquiry is that 'things are not what they seem' (1963, p. 23). A deceptively simple statement, Berger's idea suggests that most people live in a social world that they do not understand.

The goal of sociology is to shed light on social reality using what the late C. Wright Mills called the 'sociological imagination' – the ability to see the relationships between individual life experiences and the larger society, because the two are related (1959/2000, pp. 3–4). Sociologists argue that the sociological imagination helps people to place seemingly personal troubles, such as losing a job to outsourcing or local environmental degradation, into a larger national or global context. For Watson (2010), a critical approach to studying HRM provides inspiration and an invitation to apply Mills' 'sociological imagination' to matters of HRM 'outcomes' that have 'wider social consequences'. In the context of the post-2008 crisis and the search for the 'new economic philosophy', Delbridge and Keenoy (2010) provide a persuasive argument for critical HRM (CHRM), an intellectual activity, grounded in social science inquiry, that contextualizes HR practices within the prevailing capitalist society, challenges the maxims of what Alfred Schutz has called the 'world-taken-for-granted' and is more inclusive of marginal voices.

We need a definition of the subject matter that conceptualizes HRM in terms of employ-ment or people management, one that distinguishes it from a set of 'neutral' functional practices, and one that conceives it as embedded in a capitalist society and its associated ideologies and global structures. The following attempts to capture the essence of what contemporary HRM is about:

Human resource management (HRM) is a strategic approach to managing employment relations which emphasizes that leveraging people's capabilities and commitment is critical to achieving sustainable competitive advantage or superior public services. This is accomplished through a distinctive set of integrated employment policies, programmes and practices, embedded in an organizational and societal context.

Following on from this definition, CHRM underscores the importance of *people* – only the 'human factor' or labour can provide talent to generate value. With this in mind, it goes without saying that any adequate analytical conception of HRM should draw atten-tion to the notion of *indeterminacy*, which derives from the employment relationship: employees have a *potential* capacity to provide the added value desired by the employer. It also follows from this that human knowledge and skills are a *strategic resource* that needs investment and skilful management. Moreover, the emergent environmental manage-ment literature provides a role for HRM in improving an organization's performance in terms of overall *sustainability*. Also implicit within our definition is the need for radical organizational and social change. Another distinguishing feature of HRM relates to the notion of *integration*. A cluster of employment policies programmes and practices needs to be coherent and integrated with the organization's corporate strategy. Finally, the 2008 global financial implosion and the 2011 nuclear crisis in Japan remind us that the economy and society are part of the same set of processes, and that work and management prac-tices are deeply embedded in the wider sociocultural context in which they operate. The conception of CHRM put forward here resonates with analytical frameworks holding that HR practices can only be understood in the context of economic-societal factors that shape or direct those practices. The approach adopted can be summed up in the succinct phrase 'context matters'.

This book is oriented towards helping people manage people – both individually and collectively – more effectively, equitably and with dignity. It is plausible to argue that if the workforce is so critical for sustainability performance, HRM is too important to be left solely to HR specialists but should be the responsibility of *all* managers. Furthermore, human dignity *in* and *at* work is, or *ought* to be, at the heart of contemporary HRM (Bolton, 2007). The dignity dimension provides support for a reconceptualized HRM model of empowered, engaged and developed employees, the 'missing "human" in HRM' critique (Bolton and Houlihan, 2007). Recently, critics have voiced concerns regarding the 'moribund and limited' nature of mainstream HRM (Delbridge and Keenoy, 2010, p. 800). The demands for dignity in the workplace are a key dimension of CHRM that provides strong support for extending the analysis of HRM outcomes beyond employee performance and commitment to include the 'dignity' aspects of the employment relationship and equality. To grasp the nature and significance of HRM, it is necessary to understand the management process and the role of HRM within it. But before we do this, we should explain why managing people or the 'human' input is so different from managing other resources.

The meaning of 'human resource'

First and foremost, labour is not a commodity. It is people in work organizations who set overall strategies and goals, design work systems, produce goods and services, monitor quality, allocate financial resources and market the products and services. Human beings, therefore, become human capital by virtue of the roles they assume in the work organization. Employment roles are defined and described in a manner designed to maximize particular employees' contributions to achieving organizational objectives. Schultz (1981) defined human capital in this way:

Consider all human abilities to be either innate or acquired. Every person is born with a particular set of genes, which determines his [sic] innate ability. Attributes of acquired population quality, which are valuable and can be augmented by appropriate investment, will be treated as human capital. (Schultz, 1981, p. 21; quoted in Fitz-enz, 2000, p. xii)

In management terms, 'human capital' refers to the traits that people bring to the workplace – intelligence, aptitude, commitment, tacit knowledge and skills, and an ability to learn. But the contribution of this human resource to the organization is typically variable and unpredictable. This indeterminacy of an employee's contribution to her or his work organization makes the human resource the 'most vexatious of assets to manage' (Fitz-enz, 2000, p. xii) and is helpful in understanding Hyman's (1987) assertion that the need to gain both *control over* and *commitment from* workers is the *leitmotiv* of HRM.

Managing people in a democratic market society extends beyond the issue of control. If the employer's operational goals and the employee's personal goals are to be achieved, there must necessarily be *cooperation* between the two parties. This reciprocal cooperation is, however, often accompanied by different forms of *resistance* and *conflict*. The nature of employment relations reminds us that people differ from other resources because their commitment and cooperation always has

These chefs provide an example of human capital in the context of a restaurant.

©istockphoto.com/Huchen Lu

to be won: they have the capacity to resist management's actions and join trade unions to defend or further their interests and rights. At the same time, employment entails an economic relationship and one of control and cooperation. This duality means that the employment relationship is highly *dynamic* in the sense that it is forged by the coexistence of control, cooperation and conflict in varying degrees (Brown, 1988; Edwards, 1986; Watson, 2004). Thus, HRM is inevitably characterized by structured cooperation and conflict.

The meaning of 'management'

The word *manage* came into English usage directly from the Italian *maneggiare*, meaning 'to handle and train horses'. In the sixteenth century, the meaning was extended to include a general sense of taking charge or directing (Williams, 1976).

The answer to the question 'Who is a manager?' depends on the manager's social position in the organization's hierarchy. A manager is an organizational member who is 'institutionally empowered to determine and/or regulate certain aspects of the actions of others' (Willmott, 1984, p. 350). Collectively, managers are traditionally differentiated horizontally by their function activities (for example, production manager or HR manager) and vertically by the level at which they are located in their organizational hierarchy (for example, counter manager or branch manager).

Management has been variously conceptualized as 'the central process whereby work organizations achieve the semblance of congruence and direction' (Mintzberg, 1973), as 'art, science, magic and politics' (Watson, 1986) and as a process designed to coordinate and control productive activities (see, for example, Thompson and McHugh, 2009). In his seminal work, Fayol (1949) envisioned management as a science. For Fayol, management is primarily concerned with internal planning, organizing, directing and controlling – known as the 'PODC' tradition. The creation of a formal organizational structure and work configuration is, therefore, the *raison d'être* for management. This classical stereotype presents an idealized image of management as a rationally designed system for realizing goals, but there are competing theoretical perspectives, as we will explain later in this chapter.

The nature of the employment relationship

The nature of the social relationship between employees and their employer is an issue of central analytical importance to HRM. The employment relationship describes an asymmetry of reciprocal relations between employees (non-managers and managers) and their work organization. Through the asymmetry of the employment contract, inequalities of power structure both the economic exchange (wage or salary) and the nature and quality of the work performed (whether it is routine or creative). In contemporary capitalism, employment relationships vary: at one end of the scale, they can be a short-term, primarily but not exclusively economic exchange for a relatively well-defined set of duties and low commitment; at the other, they can be complex long-term relationships defined by a broad range of economic inducements and relative security of employment, given in return for a broad set of duties and a high commitment from the employee.

The employment relationship may be regulated in three ways: unilaterally by the employer; bilaterally, by the employer and the trade unions, through a process of collective bargaining; and trilaterally, by employers, trade unions and statutes, through the intervention of the government or state (Kelly, 2005). What, then, is the essence of the employment relationship? Research into the employment relationship has drawn attention to economic, legal, social and psychological aspects of relations in the workplace.

At its most basic, the employment relationship embraces an *economic relationship*: the 'exchange of pay for work' (Brown, 1988). When people enter the workplace, they enter into a pay–effort bargain, which places an obligation on both the employer and the employee: in exchange for a wage or salary, paid by the employer, the employee is obligated to perform an amount of physical or intellectual labour. The pay–effort bargain is relevant for understanding how far the employment relationship is structurally conflictual or consensual. In the capitalist labour market, people sell their labour and seek to maximize their pay. To the employer, pay is a cost that, all things being equal, reduces profit and therefore needs to be minimized. Thus, as Brown (1988, p. 57) states, 'Conflict is structured into employment relations' as the benefit to one group is a cost to the other.

The 'effort' or 'work' side of the contract also generates tensions and conflict because it is inherently imprecise and indeterminate. The contract permits the employer to buy a potential level of physical or intellectual labour. The function of management is therefore to transform this potential into actual value-added labour. HR practices are designed to narrow the divide between employees' potential and actual performance or, in Townley's (1994, p. 14) words:

Personnel practices measure both the physical and subjective dimensions of labour, and offer a technology which aims to render individuals and their behaviour predictable and calculable … to bridge the gap between promise and performance, between labour power and labour, and organizes labour into a productive force or power.

The second component of the employment relationship is that it involves a *legal relationship*: a network of contractual and statutory rights and obligations affecting both parties to the contract. Contractual rights are based upon case law (judicial precedent), and the basic rules of contract, in so far as they relate to the contract of employment, are fundamental to the legal relationship between the employer and the employee. It is outside the scope of this chapter to provide a discussion of the rules of contract. But, to use Kahn-Freund's famous phrase, the contract of employment, freely negotiated between an individual and her or his employer, can be considered to be the cornerstone of English employment law (Honeyball, 2010).

Statutory rights refer to an array of legislation that affects the employer–employee relationship and employer–union relationship: the 'right not to be unfairly dismissed' or the 'right to bargain', for example. Statutory employment rights provide a basic minimum or 'floor' of rights for all employees. A complex network of UK and European Union statutory rights regulates the obligations of employers and employees even though these are not (for the most part) formally inserted into the employment contract itself. If they are violated, legal rights can be enforced by some compulsory mechanisms provided by the state, for example a tribunal or the courts. Table 1.1 provides an overview of how UK employment legislation has helped to shape the legal regulation of employment relations. In broad terms, the employment laws of the 1979–97 Conservative government sought to regulate the activities of trade unions. Cumulatively, the changes marked 'a radical shift from the consensus underlying "public policy" on industrial relations during most of the past century' (Hyman, 1987, p. 93). The changes in the law tilted the balance of power in an industrial dispute towards the employer (Brown et al., 1997).

The influence of European Union (EU) law increased steadily during the same period. Although it is not a comprehensive body of employment legislation, EU employment law does draw on the Western European tradition, in which the rights of employees are laid down in constitutional texts and legal codes. Under the 1997 'New Labour' government, a plethora of legislative reform in employment law facilitated trade union organization and collective bargaining and extended protection to individual employees. For example, the 2006 Work and Families Act gave additional protections in relation to pregnancy – the right to maternity leave, time off for antenatal care and the right to maternity pay (Lockton, 2010).

Table 1.1 Selective UK Employment Statutes and Statutory Instruments, 1961–2007

Year	Act	Year	Act
1961	Factories Act (Safety)	1993	Trade Union Reform and Employment Rights Act
1963/72	Contract of Employment Act	1996	Employment Rights Act
1965	Industrial Training Act	1996	Employment Tribunals Act
1968	Race Relations Act	1998	Employment Rights (Disputes Resolution) Act
1970	Equal Pay Act	1998	National Minimum Wage Act
1971	Industrial Relations Act	1999	Employment Relations Act
1973	Employment and Training Act	2002	Employment Act
1974	Health and Safety at Work etc. Act	2003	National Minimum Wage (Enforcement) Act
1974/76	Trade Union and Labour Relations Act	2003	Employment Equality (Sexual Orientation) Regulations
1975/86	Sex Discrimination Act	2003	Employment Equality (Religion or Belief) Regulations
1975	Employment Protection Act	2004	Gender Recognition Act
1978	Employment Protection (Consolidation) Act	2004	Employment Relations Act
1980	Employment Act	2005	Disability Discrimination Act
1982	Employment Act	2006	Employment Equality (Age) Regulations
1984	Trade Union Act	2006	Work and Families Act
1986	Wages Act	2006	Equality Act
1988	Employment Act	2007	Corporate Manslaughter and Corporate Homicide Act
1989	Employment Act		
1990	Employment Act		
1992	Trade Union and Labour Relations (Consolidation) Act		

reflective question Based on your own work experience or that of a friend or relative, can you identify three statutory employment rights?

The third distinguishing component of the employment relationship is that it involves a *social relationship*. Employees are not isolated individuals but members of social groups, who observe social norms and mores that influence their actions in the workplace. This observation of human behaviour in the workplace – which has been documented since the 1930s – is highly relevant given the increased prevalence of work teams. Furthermore, unless the employee happens to be an international football celebrity, the employment relationship embodies an uneven balance of power between the parties. The notion in English law of a 'freely' negotiated individual agreement is misleading. In reality, without collective (trade union) or statutory intervention, the most powerful party, the employer, imposes the agreement by 'the brute facts of power' (Wedderburn, 1986, p. 106).

Inequalities of power in turn structure the nature of work. Most employees experience an extreme division of labour with minimal discretion over how they perform their tasks or opportunity to participate in decision-making processes. Thus, the social dimension is concerned with social relations, social structure and power – *people with power over other people* – rather than with the legal technicalities between the parties. As such, employment relations are deeply textured and profoundly sociological (Bratton et al., 2009). Looking at the development of the mainstream HRM canon over the last 25 years, it can be seen how little these inherent inequalities figure, despite the fact that they can be readily observed in the contemporary workplace.

In recent years, mainstream HRM scholarship has focused on another component of the employment relationship: the *psychological contract.* This is conceptualized as a dynamic two-way exchange of perceived promises and obligations between employees and their employer. The concept has become a 'fashionable' framework within which to study aspects of the employment relationship (Guest and Conway, 2002; Rousseau and Ho, 2000). The 'psychological contract' is a metaphor that captures a wide variety of largely unwritten expectations and understandings of the two parties about their mutual obligations. Rousseau (1995, p. 9) defines this as 'individual beliefs, shaped by the organization, regarding terms of an exchange agreement between individuals and their organization.' Guest and Conway (2002, p. 22) define it as 'the perceptions of both parties to the employment relationship – organization and individual – of the reciprocal promises and obligations implied in that relationship.' At the heart of the concept of the psychological contract are levers for individual commitment, motivation and task performance beyond the 'expected outcomes' (Figure 1.1).

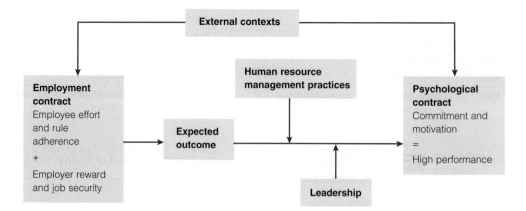

Figure 1.1 *The employment and psychological contract between employees and employers*

The psychological contract has a number of important features that employers need to appreciate. First, ineffective practices may communicate different beliefs about the reciprocal promises and obligations that are present (Guest and Conway, 2002). Thus, individuals will have different perceptions of their psychological contract, even when the legal contract is identical. Managers will therefore be faced with a multitude of perceived psychological contracts (PPCs) within the same organization (Bendal et al., 1998). Second, the PPC reaffirms the notion that the employment relationship is thought to be one of exchange – the promissory exchange of offers and the mutual obligation of the employer and employee to fulfil these offers. Third, PPCs are shaped in particular contexts, which includes HR practices. Rousseau argues that HR practices 'send strong messages to individuals regarding what the organization expects of them and what they can expect in return' (Rousseau, 1995, pp. 182–3). In the current post-crisis era, 'downsizing' has become a ubiquitous fact of organizational life (Datta et al., 2010; Mellahi and Wilkinson, 2010). Research suggests that those organizations downsizing can reduce the likelihood of psychological contract violation by ensuring that HR practices contribute to employees' perceptions of 'procedural fairness' (Arshad and Sparrow, 2010).

On any reading, the essence of the PPC thesis is the idea that a workforce is a collection of free, independent people, as though individual beliefs are fixed features of an employee's day-to-day behaviour. However, this addresses concerns of individual motivation and commitment within a *unitary* ideological framework. In doing this, in total contrast to critical paradigms, it neglects a well-established body of research grounded in sociology showing that people's beliefs and expectations about employment form *outside* the workplace. The work experiences of parents, for instance, shape the attitudes and career aspirations of their teenage children. The idea that family members and peer groups can influence expectations about career opportunities and the everyday reality of work is called 'orientation to work' (Goldthorpe et al., 1968; Hyman and Brough, 1975).

reflective question What do you think of the concept of the psychological contract? Why does there appear to be more interest now in managing it? How important is it to manage the psychological contract for (1) non-managerial employees, and (2) managerial employees?

Scope and functions of HRM

HRM is a body of knowledge and an assortment of practices to do with the organization of work and the management of employment relations. The mainstream literature identifies three major subdomains of knowledge: micro, strategic and international (Boxall et al., 2008).

The largest subdomain refers to *micro HRM* (MHRM), which is concerned with managing individual employees and small work groups. It covers areas such as HR planning, job design, recruitment and selection, performance management, training and development, and rewards. These HR subfunctions cover a myriad of evidence-based practices, training techniques and payment systems, for instance, many of them informed by psychology-oriented studies of work (see, for example, Warr, 2008). The second domain is *strategic HRM* (SHRM), which concerns itself with the processes of linking HR strategies with business strategies and measures the effects on organizational performance. The third domain is *international HRM* (IHRM), which focuses on the management of people in companies operating in more than one country.

Drawing on the work of Squires (2001), these three major subdomains help us address three basic questions:

- What do HRM professionals do?
- What affects what they do?
- How do they do what they do?

To help us answer the first question, the work of Harzing (2000), Millward et al. (2000) and Ulrich (1997) identifies the key *MHRM* subfunctions of HR policies, programmes and practices that have been designed in response to organizational goals and contingencies, and have been managed to achieve those goals. Each function contains alternatives from which managers can choose. How the HR function is organized and how much power it has relative to that of other management functions is affected by both external and internal factors unique to the establishment. A regulation-oriented national business system, with strong trade unions, employment laws on equity and affirmative action, and occupational health and safety regulations, elevates the status of the HR manager and strengthens the corporate HR function. In contrast, a market-oriented corporate culture, with employee pay based on going market rates, minimum investment in employee training and shorter employment contracts, is associated with outsourcing and decentralization of the HR function, which weakens the corporate HR function (Jacoby, 2005).

The size of the organization also appears to negatively affect the extent to which HR services are provided internally by HR specialists from the central HR unit. Klass et al.'s (2005) study, for example, found that an increasing number of small and medium-sized organizations – defined as those with 500 or fewer employees – have established a business relationship with a professional employer organization that assumes responsibility for delivering their HR services and interventions, a process usually referred to as 'outsourcing'. Klass et al. argue that the choice is not between an internal HR department and outsourcing the HR services, but is one in which limited resources mean that it is a case of either obtaining HR expertise and services externally or foregoing such services. In addition, an increasing number of European organizations have transferred responsibility for their HR functions from the central HR department to line management. This process of 'decentralization' has occurred as HR has assumed a more strategic role (Andolšek and Štebe, 2005; CIPD, 2006a).

SHRM underscores the need for the HR strategy to be integrated with other management functions, and highlights the responsibility of line management to foster the high commitment and motivation associated with high-performing work systems. SHRM is also concerned with managing sustainability, including, for example, establishing a low-carbon work system and organization, communicating this vision, setting clear expectations for creating a sustainable workplace, and developing the capability to reorganize people and reallocate other resources to achieve the vision. As part of the integrative process, all managers are expected to better comprehend the strategic nature of 'best' or better HR practices, to execute them more skilfully, and at the same time to intervene to affect the 'mental models', attitudes and behaviours needed, for instance, to build a high-performing sustainable culture (Pfeffer, 2005). Furthermore, national systems of employment regulation shape SHRM: 'the stronger the institutional framework ... the less [sic] options a company may have to impose its own approach to regulating its HRM' (Andolšek and Štebe, 2005, p. 327).

HRM web
links

Go to the website of the 2004 Workplace Employment Relations Survey (www.dti. gov.uk/employment/research-evaluation/grants/wers/index.html) for data on the job responsibilities of HR specialists. Has there been any change in the functions performed by HR specialists over the past decade? Are HR specialists involved in all the key areas of activity described in the text?

The peculiarities of national employment systems and national culture shape the employment relationship, and these forces and processes create different tendencies in HR practice operating across national boundaries. As such, they relate to the second question we posed earlier – what affects what managers and HR professional do? The HR activities that managers perform vary from one workplace to another depending upon the contingencies affecting the organization. These contingencies can be divided into three broad categories: external context, strategy and organization. The external category reinforces the notion that organizations and society are part of the same set of processes – that organizations are *embedded* within a particular market society that encompasses the economic and cultural aspects (see Chapter 5). The external variables frame the context for formulating competitive strategies (see Chapter 2). The internal organizational contingencies include size, work, structure and technology (see Chapter 4). Global as well as local factors can affect what managers do. For those managers in companies that cross national boundaries, *micro* HR policies and practices relating to global and local recruitment and selection, training and development, rewards and the management of expatriates will be affected by a particular country's institutional structure and cultural setting. These micro HR functions, when integrated with different *macro* contexts and overall strategy considerations, define the subdomain of *IHRM* (see Chapter 15).

It is important, therefore, to recognize that HR policies and practices are contingent upon external and internal contexts and are fundamentally interrelated. For example, a company responding to competitive pressures may change its manufacturing strategy by introducing 'self-managed' teams. This will in turn cause changes in recruitment and selection (for example, hiring people perceived to be 'team players'), and training and reward priorities (for example, designing crossfunctional training and designing a reward system that encourages the sharing of information and learning). HR practices, therefore, aim to achieve two objectives: to produce a synergy that improves employee performance and to enhance organizational effectiveness.

The third of our three basic questions – how do managers and HR professionals do what they do? – requires us to discuss the means or skills by which managers accomplish their HRM goals. Managers and HR specialists use technical, cognitive and interpersonal – such as mentoring and coaching – processes and skills to accomplish their managerial work (Agashae and Bratton, 2001; Senge, 1990; Squires, 2001; Yukl, 2005). Power is important because it is part of the influence process, as are legal procedures. In addition, communication practices and skills convey the formal and psychological contract to employees (Guest and Conway, 2002). Managing people is complex, and individual managers vary in terms of their capacity or inclination to use established processes and skills. These processes and skills therefore concern human relationships and go some way to explaining different management styles and the distinction between a manager and a leader (Bratton et al., 2004a). The micro, strategic and international domains, the contingencies influencing domestic and international HR policies and practices, and managerial skills are combined and diagrammatically shown in a three-dimensional model in Figure 1.2.

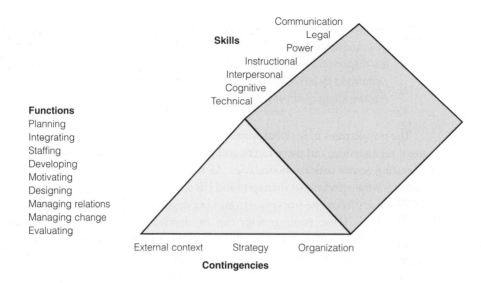

Figure 1.2 *HRM functions, contingencies and skills*
Source: *Adapted from Squires (2001)*

The model implies not only that HRM is a multidimensional activity, but also that its analysis has to be multidirectional (Squires, 2001). We might, for that reason, examine the effect of new technology (a contingency) on HR functions, such as training and development, and how HR functions are translated into action, such as learning processes. The model is useful in other ways too: it serves as a pedagogical device that allows its users to discover and connect a specific aspect of HRM within a consistent, general framework. It also helps to develop an 'analytical conception' of HRM by building theory and generating data based on managers' *actual* social actions in managing work and people across workplaces, sectors and different market societies (Boxall et al., 2008) – the classic rhetoric–reality gap notably highlighted by Legge (1995, 2005). It also offers HR specialists a sense of professional 'identity' by detailing professional functions, processes and skills. Finally, it helps HR specialists to look beyond their immediate tasks and to be aware of the 'totality of management' (Squires, 2001, p. 482).

HRM web links 🌐 Go to the website of the HR professional associations (for example Australia www. hrhq.com; Britain www.cipd.co.uk; Canada www.hrpa.org; or the USA www.shrm. org). Click on the 'Accreditation and/or certification' button. Using the information you find, compare the practices that HR professionals are formally accredited to practise with those practices listed in Figure 1.2. Does the information on the website give a comprehensive picture of 'What HRM specialists do'?

Theoretical perspectives on HRM

[Practice without theory is blind. (Hyman, 1989, p. xiv)

So far, we have focused on the meaning of management and on a range of HRM practices used in the contemporary workplace. We have explained that HRM varies across

Twenty-first-century senior HR leaders have a changing role

Early debate on HRM centred on the question 'How does HRM differ from personnel management?' For some, HRM represents a new approach to managing people because, in theory at least, it was envisioned to be integrated into strategic planning. HRM models also make reference to performance outcomes, predicting that a coherent 'bundle' of HR practices will enhance employee commitment and improve performance. To meet the challenges of the twenty-first century, it is argued, organizations therefore need a new senior manager, the chief human resources officer (CHRO). As one writer put it:

> The modern CHRO is required increasingly to act as both strategist and steward. Jeff Schwartz, of Deloitte Consulting, said: 'The requirements and perception of HR are changing dramatically as this function's leadership is now expected to play a central role in building and shaping – not just staffing – the enterprise strategy.' 'The role of the CHRO as an enterprise business leader is still evolving – but this transformation has never been more timely or relevant.' 'This is an environment that HR leaders have longed for – where their executive peers would view HR as a business partner, rather than as a back-office administrator.'[1]

In contrast, detractors argue that HRM is more a matter of repackaging 'progressive' personnel management. They emphasize that relatively few organizations have integrated HRM planning into strategic business planning, a central element in the HRM model. They also point to the incontrovertible evidence of a shift towards 'individually oriented' cultures that is symbolized by the growth of contingency pay, as well as the fact that a large proportion of UK firms are still preoccupied with traditional cost-focus strategies. The empirical evidence therefore suggests a lack of fit between knowledge of the normative HRM model and actual management practice.

Stop! Debates on HRM offer an interesting perspective on the issues of state intervention in a market society. Among academics, HRM is highly contentious, and its antecedents, its defining characteristics and its outcomes are much disputed. What is your view? Is HRM different from personnel management?

Sources and further information: [1]Deloitte Consulting's *Strategist and Steward* report, available at www.deloitte.com/us, and search for 'Strategist and Steward'. For a discussion on employee commitment and HRM, see Guest (1998); for evidence of the growth of 'individualism', see Kersley et al. (2005); and for further insight into the HRM debate, see Legge (2005).

Note: This feature was written by John Bratton.

©istockphoto.com/Daniel Laflor

organizations and market societies depending upon a range of external and internal contingencies. In addition, we have identified the skills by which managers accomplish their HRM goals. We will now turn to an important part of the mainstream HRM discourse – the search for the defining features and goals of HRM – by exploring the theoretical perspectives in this area.

Over the past two decades, HRM scholars have debated the meaning of the term 'human resource management' and attempted to define its fundamental traits by producing polar or multiconceptual models. A number of polar models contrast the fundamental traits of HRM with those of traditional personnel management, while others provide statements on employer goals and HR outcomes. These models help to focus debate around such questions as 'What is the difference between HRM and personnel management?' and 'What outcomes are employers seeking when they implement a HRM approach? Here, we identify six major HRM models that seek to demonstrate in analytical terms the distinctiveness and goals of HRM (Beer et al., 1984; Fombrun et al., 1984; Guest, 1987; Hendry and Pettigrew, 1990; Storey, 1992). These models fulfil at least four important intellectual functions for those studying HRM:

- They provide an analytical framework for studying HRM (for example, HR practices, situational factors, stakeholders, strategic choice levels and HR and performance outcomes).
- They legitimize HRM. For those advocating 'Invest in People', the models help to demonstrate to sceptics the legitimacy and effectiveness of HRM. A key issue here is the distinctiveness of HRM practices: 'it is not the presence of selection or training but a *distinctive approach* to selection or training that matters. It is the use of high performance or high commitment HRM practices' (Guest, 1997, p. 273, emphasis added).
- They provide a characterization of HRM that establishes the variables and relationships to be researched.
- They serve as a heuristic device – something to help us discover and understand the world of work – for explaining the nature and significance of key HR practices and HR outcomes.

The Fombrun, Tichy and Devanna model of HRM

The early HRM model developed by Fombrun et al. (1984) emphasizes the fundamental interrelatedness and coherence of HRM activities. The HRM 'cycle' in their model consists of four key constituent components: selection, appraisal, development and rewards. In terms of the overarching goals of HRM, these four HR activities are linked to the firm's performance. The weaknesses of Fombrun et al.'s model are its apparently prescriptive nature and its focus on four HR practices. It also ignores different stakeholder interests, situational factors and the notion of management's strategic choice. The strength of the model, however, is that it expresses the coherence of internal HR policies and the importance of 'matching' internal HR policies and practices to the organization's external business strategy (see Chapters 2 and 15). The notion of the 'HRM cycle' is useful as a heuristic framework for explaining the nature and significance of key HR practices that make up the complex field of HRM.

The Harvard model of HRM

As was widely acknowledged in the early HRM literature, the 'Harvard model' offered by Beer et al. (1984) provided one of the first comprehensive statements on the nature of

HRM and the issue of management goals and specific HR outcomes. The Harvard framework (Figure 1.3) consists of six basic components:

1 Situational factors
2 Stakeholder interests
3 HRM policy choices
4 HR outcomes
5 Long-term consequences
6 A feedback loop through which the outputs flow directly into the organization and to the stakeholders.

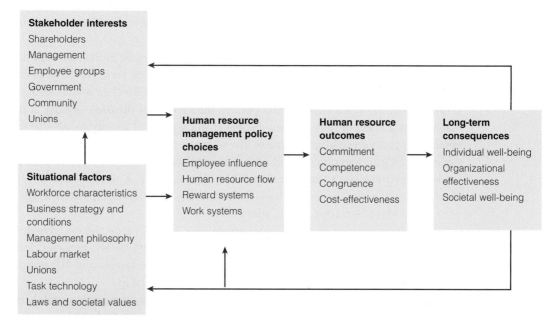

Figure 1.3 *The Harvard model of HRM*
Source: Beer, M. et al. (1984), Managing Human Assets, The Free Press

In the Harvard model of HRM, the *situational factors* influence management's choice of HR strategy. This normative model incorporates workforce characteristics, management philosophy, labour market regulations, societal values and patterns of unionization, and suggests a meshing of 'product market' and 'sociocultural logics' (Evans and Lorange, 1989). Analytically, both HRM scholars and practitioners will be more comfortable if contextual variables are included in the model because this reflects the reality of what they know: 'the employment relationship entails a blending of business and societal expectations' (Boxall, 1992, p. 72).

The *stakeholder interests* recognize the importance of 'trade-offs', either explicitly or implicitly, between the interests of business owners and those of employees and their organizations, the trade unions. Although the model is still vulnerable to the charge of 'unitarism', it is a much more pluralist frame of reference than is found in later models.

HRM policy choices emphasize that management's decisions and actions in HR management can be fully appreciated only if it is recognized that they result from an interaction between constraints and choices. The model depicts management as a real actor, capable of making at least some degree of unique contribution within the environmental and organizational parameters present and of influencing those parameters itself over time (Beer et al., 1984).

In terms of understanding the importance of management's goals, the *HR outcomes* of high employee commitment and competence are linked to longer term effects on organizational effectiveness and societal well-being. The underlying assumptions built into the framework are that employees have talents that are rarely fully utilized in the contemporary workplace, and that they show a desire to experience growth through work. Thus, HRM is indivisible from a 'humanistic message' about human growth and dignity at work. In other words, the Harvard framework takes the view that employment relations should be managed on the basis of the assumptions inherent in McGregor's (1960) classic approach to people-related issues, commonly called 'Theory Y', or, to use contemporary parlance, in conditions of human dignity at work.

The *long-term consequences* distinguish between three levels: individual, organizational and societal. At the level of the individual employee, the long-term HR outputs comprise the psychological rewards that workers receive in exchange for their effort. At the organizational level, increased effectiveness ensures the survival of the firm. In turn, at the societal level, as a result of fully utilizing people at work, some of society's goals (for example, employment and growth) are attained. The strength of the Harvard model lies in its classification of inputs and outcomes at both the organizational and the societal level, creating the basis for a critique of comparative HRM (Boxall, 1992). A weakness, however, is the absence of a coherent theoretical basis for measuring the relationship between HR inputs, outcomes and performance (Guest, 1997).

The sixth component of the Harvard model is a *feedback loop*. As we have discussed, situational factors influence HRM policy and choices. Conversely, however, long-term outputs can influence the situational factors, stakeholder interests and HR policies, and the feedback loop in Figure 1.3 reflects this two-way relationship.

As was observed by Boxall (1992), the Harvard model clearly provides a useful analytical basis for the study of HRM. It also contains elements that are analytical (that is, situational factors, stakeholders and strategic choice levels) and prescriptive (that is, notions of commitment, competence, and so on).

The Guest model of HRM

In David Guest's (1989, 1997) framework, different approaches to labour management are examined in the context of goals, employee behaviour, performance and long-term financial outcomes. According to this HRM model, managers are advised to consider the effects of a core set of integrated HR practices on individual and organizational performance.

For Guest, HRM differs significantly from personnel management, and he attempts to identify the major assumptions or stereotypes underpinning each approach to employment management. Personnel management seeks 'compliance', whereas HRM seeks 'commitment' from employees. In personnel management, the psychological contract is expressed in terms of a 'fair day's work for a fair day's pay', whereas in HRM it is 'reciprocal commitment'. In the area of employee relations, personnel management is said to be pluralist, collective and 'low trust', whereas HRM is unitarist, individual and 'high trust'. The points of differences between personnel management and HRM are also reflected in the design of organizations. Thus, organizations adopting the personnel management model exhibit 'mechanistic', top-down and centralized design features, whereas firms adopting HRM are allegedly 'organic', bottom-up and decentralized. Finally, the policy goals of personnel management and HRM are different. In the former, they are administrative efficiency, standard performance and minimization of cost. In contrast, the policy goals of HRM are an adaptive workforce, an improvement in performance and maximum utilization of human potential.

According to these stereotypes, HRM is distinctively different from personnel management because: (1) it integrates HR into strategic management; (2) it seeks employees' commitment to organizational goals; (3) the HR perspective is unitary with a focus on the individual; (4) it works better in organizations that have an 'organic' structure; and (5) employer goals prioritize the full utilization of human assets.

Implicit in the contrasting stereotypes is an assumption that the dominant HRM model is 'better' (allowing enhanced commitment and flexibility) within the current more flexible labour markets and in decentralized, flexible, empowering and organic organizational structures. However, as Guest correctly states, 'variations in context ... might limit its effectiveness' (1987, p. 508). The central hypothesis of Guest's (1997) framework is that managers should adopt a distinct set or 'bundle' of HR practices in a coherent fashion; the outcome will be superior individual and organizational performance.

Guest's model has six components:

1 An HR strategy
2 A set of HR policies
3 A set of HR outcomes
4 Behavioural outcomes
5 Performance outcomes
6 Financial outcomes.

The model acknowledges the close links between HR strategy and the general business strategies of differentiation, focus and cost (see Chapter 2). The 'core' hypothesis, however, is that HR practices should be designed to lead to a set of HR outcomes of 'high employee commitment', 'high quality' and 'flexibility'. Like Beer et al., Guest sees high employee commitment as a critical HR outcome, concerned with the employer's goals of binding employees to the organization and obtaining the behavioural outcomes of increased effort, cooperation and organizational citizenship. 'Quality' refers to all aspects of employee behaviour that relate directly to the quality of goods and services. Flexibility is concerned with how receptive employees are to innovation and change. The model focuses on the link between HR practices and performance. Only when all three HR outcomes – commitment, quality and flexibility – are achieved can superior performance outcomes be expected. As Guest (1989, 1997) emphasizes, these HRM goals are a 'package': 'Only when a coherent strategy, directed towards these four policy goals, fully integrated into business strategy and fully sponsored by line management at all levels is applied will the high productivity and related outcomes sought by industry be achieved' (1990, p. 378).

Guest (1987, 1989, 1997) recognizes a number of conceptual issues associated with the dominant HRM model. The first is that the values underpinning the model are predominantly individualist-oriented: 'There is no recognition of any broader concept of pluralism within society giving rise to solidaristic collective orientation' (Guest, 1987, p. 519). The second concerns the status of some of the concepts, such as that of commitment, which is suggested to be 'a rather messy, ill-defined concept' (Guest, 1987, pp. 513–14). A third issue is the explicit link between HRM and performance. This raises the problem of deciding which types of performance indicators to use in order to establish the links between HR practices and performance (see Chapter 3). It has been argued elsewhere that Guest's model may simply be a polar 'ideal type' towards which organizations can move, thus proposing unrealistic conditions for the practice of HRM (Keenoy, 1990, p. 367). It may also make the error of criticizing managers for not conforming to an image constructed by academics (Boxall, 1992). Furthermore, it presents the HRM model as being inconsistent with collective approaches to managing the employment relationship (Legge, 1989).

In contrast, the strength of the Guest model is that it clearly maps out the field of HRM and classifies its inputs and outcomes. The model is useful for examining the key employer goals usually associated with the normative models of HRM: strategic integration, commitment, flexibility and quality. The constituents of the model hypothesizing a relationship between specific HR practices and performance can be empirically tested by research. Guest's constructed set of theoretical propositions can also provide a framework for a critical dialogue on the precise nature, tensions and contradictions of HRM.

The Warwick model of HRM

The Warwick model emanated from the Centre for Corporate Strategy and Change at the University of Warwick, UK, and with two particular researchers: Hendry and Pettigrew (1990). The Warwick framework extends the Harvard model by drawing on its analytical aspects. The model takes account of business strategy and HR practices, the external and internal context in which these activities take place and the processes by which such changes take place, including interactions between changes in both context and content. The strength of the model is that it identifies and classifies important environmental influences on HRM. It maps the connections between the outer (wider environment) and the inner (organizational) contexts, and explores how HRM adapts to changes in context. The implication is that those organizations achieving an alignment between the external and internal contexts will experience superior performance. A weakness of the model is that the process whereby internal HR practices are linked to business output or performance is not developed. The five elements of the model are as follows:

1 Outer context – socioeconomic, technical, political-legal, competitive
2 Inner context – culture, structure, leadership, task-technology, business outputs
3 Business strategy content – objectives, product market, strategy and tactics
4 HRM context – role, definition, organization, HR outputs
5 HRM content – HR flows, work systems, reward systems, employee relations.

The Storey model of HRM

The Storey framework attempts to demonstrate the differences between what John Storey terms the 'personnel and industrials' and the HRM paradigm by creating an 'ideal type'. He devised the model by reconstructing the 'implicit models' conveyed by some managers during research interviews. We should note that the usage of an 'ideal type' is a popular heuristic tool in the social sciences. It is a 'mental image' and cannot actually be found in any real workplace. Its originator Max Weber wrote in *The Methodology of the Social Sciences*, that 'In its conceptual purity, this mental construct [*Gedankenbild*] cannot be found empirically anywhere in reality' (Bratton et al., 2009, p. 216). An ideal type is not a description of reality; neither is it an average of something, or a normative exemplar to be achieved. It is a *Utopia*. Its purpose is to act as a comparison with empirical reality in order to establish the differences or similarities between the two positions, and to understand and explain causal relationships.

Storey posits that the HRM model emerged in the UK as a 'historically situated phenomenon' and is 'an amalgam of description, prescription, and logical deduction' (Storey, 2001, p. 6). The four main elements in his HRM framework (Table 1.2) are:

- Beliefs and assumptions
- Strategic aspects
- Role of line managers
- Key levers.

Table 1.2 *The Storey model of HRM*

Personnel and industrial relations (IR) and human resource management (HRM): the differences		
Dimension	**Personnel and IR**	**HRM**
Beliefs and assumptions		
Contract	Careful delineation of written contracts	Aim to go 'beyond contract'
Rules	Importance of devising clear rules/mutuality	'Can do' outlook; impatience with 'rules'
Guide to management action	Procedures/consistency/control	'Business need'/flexibility/commitment
Behaviour referent	Norms/custom and practice	Values/mission
Managerial task vis-à-vis labour	Monitoring	Nurturing
Nature of relations	Pluralist	Unitarist
Conflict	Institutionalised	De-emphasised
Standardisation	High (for example 'parity' an issue)	Low (for example 'parity' not seen as relevant)
Strategic aspects		
Key relations	Labour–management	Business–customer
Initiatives	Piecemeal	Integrated
Corporate plan	Marginal to	Central to
Speed of decision	Slow	Fast
Line management		
Management role	Transactional	Transformational leadership
Key managers	Personnel/IR specialists	General/business/line managers
Prized management skills	Negotiation	Facilitation
Key levers		
Foci of attention for interventions	Personnel procedures	Wide-ranging cultural, structural and personnel strategies
Selection	Separate, marginal task	Integrated, key task
Pay	Job evaluation; multiple fixed grades	Performance-related; few if any grades
Conditions	Separately negotiated	Harmonisation
Labour–management	Collective bargaining contracts	Towards individual contracts
Thrust of relations with stewards	Regularised through facilities and training	Marginalised (with exception of some bargaining for change models)
Communication	Restricted flow/indirect	Increased flow/direct
Job design	Division of labour	Teamwork
Conflict handling	Reach temporary truces	Manage climate and culture
Training and development	Controlled access to courses	Learning companies

Source: Storey (1992)

Contemporary globalization is the defining political economic paradigm of our time. In terms of HR strategy, HRM policies and practices have to be aligned to the global activities of transnational enterprises, and must be able to attract and retain employees operating internationally but within different national employment structures. The word 'globalization' became ubiquitous in the 1990s. It was, and still is, a thoroughly contested concept depending on whether scholars view it as primarily an economic, a political or a social phenomenon.

In the economic sphere, globalization is understood as a worldwide process of integration of production and consumption resulting from the reduction of transport and communication costs – a global system of economic interdependences. Arguments that build only on these technical conceptions emphasize the positive aspects of globalization, and draw attention to the outsourcing of manufacturing jobs to China and India from high-wage Western economies. The economic argument is captured by this extract from a Foresight2020 research report:

On a per-capita basis, China and India will remain far poorer than Western markets and the region faces a host of downside risks,' Laza Kekic, director of forecasting services at the Economist Intelligence Unit, says. 'Asia will narrow the gap in wealth, power and influence, but will not close it.' The report assumes that world economic growth depends on the pace of globalization. Labour-intensive production will continue to shift to lower-cost countries but the report concludes that fears of the death of Western manufacturing are premature. Workers in the low-cost economies will benefit but Chinese average wages, for example, will rise only to about 15% of the developed-country average in 2020 compared with today's 5%.

Writers who conceptualize globalization in terms of politics and power argue that 'big business' has relegated national

HRM and globalization

governments to being the 'gatekeepers' of free unfettered markets. Because there is little competition from alternative ideologies, twenty-first century capitalism 'is more mobile, more ruthless and more certain about what it needs to make it tick' (Giddens and Hutton, 2000, p. 9). Modern capitalism has been called a 'febrile capitalism' that is serving the needs of Wall Street and the financial and stock markets.

Stop! Critics charge that national governments have lost power over their own economies as a handful of large corporations are being permitted to control natural resources and social life. In other words, civil society is perceived principally through the 'prism of economics'. Take a moment to assess critically the various standpoints in the globalization debate. What economic and political forces encourage outsourcing? What are the implications of outsourcing for HRM?

Sources and further information: See Giddens and Hutton (2000), Hoogvelt (2001), Chomsky (1999), and Gereffi and Christian (2009). To download Foresight2020 free of charge, visit www.eiu.com/foresight2020.

Note: This feature was written by John Bratton.

The HRM model in advancing economies?

©istockphoto.com/Jessica Liu

According to the stereotypes depicted in Table 1.2, the HRM 'recipe' of ideas and practices prescribes certain priorities. In this framework, the most fundamental *belief and assumption* is the notion that, ultimately, among all the factors of production, it is labour that really distinguishes successful firms from mediocre ones. It follows logically from this that employees ought to be nurtured as a valued asset and not simply regarded as a cost. Moreover, another underlying belief is that the employer's goal should not merely be to seek employees' compliance with rules, but to 'strive' for 'commitment and engagement' that goes 'beyond the contract' (Storey, 2001). The *strategic qualities* contained in Storey's framework show that HRM is a matter of critical importance to corporate planning. In Storey's words, 'decisions about human resources policies should ... take their cue from an explicit alignment of the competitive environment, business strategy and HRM strategy' (p. 10).

The third component, *line management*, argues that general managers, and not HRM specialists, are vital to the effective delivery of HRM practices (Purcell et al., 2009). Research evidence from 15 UK 'core' organizations suggests that line managers have emerged in almost all cases as the crucial players in HR issues (Storey, 1992).

The *key levers* element in the model focuses on the methods used to implement HRM. In researcher–manager interviews on HRM, Storey found considerable unevenness in the adoption of these key levers, such as performance-related pay, harmonization of conditions and investment to produce a work-related learning company. What is persuasive about the HRM narrative, observes Storey (2007), is evidence of a shift away from personnel procedures and rules as a basis of good practice, to the management of organizational culture as proof of avant-garde practice.

Ulrich's strategic partner model of HRM

To overcome the traditional marginalization of the personnel function and to strengthen the status of the profession, the UK Chartered Institute for Personnel and Development (CIPD) has long sought to demonstrate the added value of HR activities in business terms. Such a position requires a transition from the functional HR orientation, with the HR department primarily involved in administering policies, towards a partnership orientation, with the HR professional engaged in *strategic* decisions that impact on organizational design and organizational performance. In the last decade, the HRM model most favoured to support such a move has been provided by David Ulrich's (1997) 'business partner' model. Ulrich presents a framework showing four key roles that HR professionals must accomplish in order to add the greatest value to the organization (Figure 1.4). The two axes represent focus and activities. HR professionals must focus on both the strategic and the operational, in the both the long and the short term. Activities range from managing processes to managing people. Therefore these two axes delineate four principal roles:

- *Strategic partner* – future/strategic focus combined with processes
- *Change agent* – future/strategic focus combined with people
- *Administrative expert* – operational focus combined with process
- *Employee champion* – operational focus combined with people.

A later variant of the model integrates the change agent role into the strategic partner role, and gives greater emphasis to HR professionals playing a leadership role (Ulrich and Brockbank, 2005). As such, the first two roles require a strategic orientation; for example,

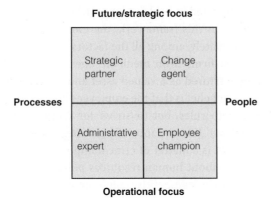

Figure 1.4 *Ulrich's human resources business partner model*

as a strategic partner, HR professionals work with other managers to formulate and execute strategy, and as a change agent, they facilitate transformation and significant change. During the 2000s, the Ulrich business partner model was widely espoused in the mainstream HRM literature, partly because of the perceived increase in status and prestige of HRM, because the strategic partner and change agent roles proved highly attractive to many ambitious HR practitioners, and because of its rhetorical simplicity (Brown et al., 2004). Furthermore, the administrative role provides for processes to 're-engineer' the organization towards great efficiency, while the employee champion relates to listening to employees and providing resources for employees. Research shows, however, that, of the small sample surveyed, few HR practitioners considered their primary roles to be those of the 'less trendy' employee champion and administrative expert (Guest and King, 2004; Hope-Hailey et al., 2005).

Although it has been influential, the way in which this model has been implemented would suggest a degree of pragmatism, probably to reduce cost, with the four roles being combined into three, but with implications for how HR departments are structured (Reilly et al., 2007). For example, administrative roles would be structured into a shared services centre, with the task of providing cost-effective processes to run transactional services such as payroll, absence monitoring and simple advice for employees. Centres of excellence provide specialist knowledge and development to produce innovations in more complex areas such as talent, engagement and leadership and management development. Strategic business partners take on the work with managers and leaders, influencing and helping the formation of strategy, perhaps as members of a management team.

Perhaps inevitably, the role of the strategic business partner attracts most attention, while the employee champion role, which concerns the well-being of staff, tends to be left to line managers and is therefore likely to be neglected (Francis and Keegan, 2006). With the recession following the 2008 financial crisis, there has been concern with sustaining organizational performance through leadership, shared purpose, engagement, assessment and evaluation, agility and capacity-building (CIPD, 2011). It is, however, suggested that none of these can be achieved without a good process of learning and development for HR practitioners. Despite the popularity of the business partners' model, a survey of managers revealed that only 47 per cent polled believed that Ulrich's model was successful in their organization, and 25 per cent said the model was ineffective (Pitcher, 2008).

HRM web
links

For more information on Ulrich's HRM model, go to: http://hrmadvice.com/hrmadvice/hr-role/ulrichs-hr-roles-model.html.

reflective
question

Reviewing the six models, what beliefs and assumptions are implied in them? What similarities and/or differences can you see? How well does each model define the characteristics of HRM? Is there a contradiction between the roles of 'change agent' and 'employee champion' as outlined in Ulrich's model? Is it realistic to expect HR professionals to be 'employee champions'?

Studying HRM

It has become commonplace to point out that HRM is not a discipline in its own right, but a field of study drawing upon concepts and theories from core social science disciplines including anthropology, psychology, sociology, law and political science. This provides relatively elastic boundaries within which to analyse how the employment relationship is structured and managed. In addition, these elastic boundaries generate multiple ways of making sense of the same organizational phenomenon or the differing standpoints found in the HRM canon. How we understand work and HRM is very much influenced by key social discourses, a discourse being a number of ideas that together form a powerful body of thought that influences how people think and act. Management in the twenty-first century is being influenced by multiple social discourses that include globalization, environmental destruction, social injustice and fundamental neo-liberal economic failure. We should also note that management research and education is going through a process of post-crisis reflexivity (Currie et al., 2010).

In understanding the recent debate that management education and pedagogy should be more reflexive and critical, it is crucial to develop a knowledge base of competing ideological perspectives or paradigms. For our purposes here, we will define paradigms as established frameworks of interrelated values, beliefs and assumptions that social science scholars use to organize their reasoning and research. Each paradigm in the social sciences makes certain bold assertions about the nature of social reality and, in turn, provides legitimacy and justification for people's actions (Babbie and Benaquisto, 2010). When people ask, 'What paradigm are you using?' they might just as well be asking, 'What is your own bias on this aspect of social life?', as each paradigm has a particular bias based on a particular version of knowing about social reality (Hughes, 1990). Paradigms are a 'lens' through which we view the world of work. Thus, when we refer to a particular paradigm to study the HRM phenomenon, we are speaking of an interconnected set of beliefs, values and intentions that legitimize HR theory and practice. For the purpose of developing a critical, analytical conception of HRM, we will in this section compare and contrast three major paradigms – *structural-functionalism, conflict* and *feminism* – that have emerged to make sense of work, organizations and HRM.

The intellectual roots of the *structural-functional paradigm* can be traced to the work of the French philosopher Auguste Comte (1798–1857) and French sociologist Emile Durkheim (1858–1917). Comte believed that society could be studied and understood logically and rationally, and he used the term *positivism* to describe this research approach.

Durkheim studied social order and argued that the increased division of labour in modern societies created what he called 'organic solidarity', which maintained social harmony: 'The division of labour becomes the chief source of social solidarity, it becomes, at the same time, the foundation of moral order' (Durkheim, 1933/1997, p. 333).

The popularity of the structural-functionalist approach is commonly attributed to the US sociologist Talcott Parsons (Mann, 2011). For Parsons, organizations can function in a stable and orderly manner only on the basis of shared values. In his words: 'The problem of order, and thus the nature of the integration of stable systems of social interaction ... thus focuses on the integration of the motivation of actors with the normative cultural standards which integrate the action system' (1951, p. 36). Although there are variations and tensions, the structural-functional paradigm takes the view that a social entity, such as a whole market society or an organization, can be studied as an organism. Like organisms, a social system is composed of interdependent parts, each of which contributes to the functioning of the whole. A whole society or an organization is held together by a consensus on values, or a value system. The view of an organization as a social system thus looks for the 'functions' served by its various departments and members and the common values shared by its members.

It is frequently assumed that managerial functions and processes take place in organizations that are rationally designed to accomplish strategic goals, that organizations are harmonious bodies tending towards a state of equilibrium and order, and that the basic task of managers is to manage resources for formal organizational ends. Thus, the structural-functionalism paradigm, sometimes also known as 'social systems theory', becomes inseparable from the notion of efficiency. The focus of much of the research and literature on management using this 'lens' is about finding the 'winning formula' so that more managers can become 'effective' (Thompson and McHugh, 2009). Common to all variations of structural-functionalism, which is often seen as the dominant or mainstream perspective, is a failure to connect management processes to the 'master' public discourse on market-based societies and globalization.

The intellectual roots of the *conflict paradigm* are most obviously found in the works of the German philosopher Karl Marx (1818–1883). The German sociologist Max Weber (1864–1920) also devoted much research to work and organizations within advanced capitalist societies. In his early manuscripts of 1844, Marx analysed the fundamental contradiction of capitalism that arose from structured tensions between capital (employers) and labour (employees). Specifically, he made the assumption that these two social classes have competing interests. For Marx, the relationship between capitalists and workers was one of contradiction. Each is dependent upon the other, and the two must cooperate to varying degrees. Yet there is a fundamental conflict of interest between capital and labour: the capitalist seeks to minimize labour costs; the workers seek the opposite. As a result, economic forces compel employers and employees to cooperate, but also there are forces that simultaneously cause conflict between the two groups.

Equally importantly, workers experience alienation or 'estrangement' through the act of labour. Marx describes alienation explicitly as an absence of meaning or self-worth. Alienated workers are people 'robbed' of the unique characteristic or the 'essence' of human beings – their ability to be creative through productive work. Marx's analysis of alienation continues to inform contemporary studies of work and the prerequisites for dignity *in* and *at* work (see, for example, Bolton, 2007).

Similar to Marx, Weber's analyses of advanced capitalist societies centre on work and organizations, especially large bureaucracies. Two themes within Weber's work are especially relevant to understanding contemporary theories of work and management. One is the notion of *paradox* in market societies. In *The Protestant Ethic* (1904–05/2002), Weber pessimistically warns of creeping rationalization and of the tendency of people to experience a debilitating '*iron cage*'. The process of rationalization is, according to Weber, unremittingly paradoxical (Bratton et al. 2009). He, and subsequent writers in the Weberian tradition, focused on the notion of '*paradox of consequences*' – two or more positions that each sound reasonable yet conflict or contradict each other. For example, an organization invests in new technology and achieves higher levels of efficiency, and ultimately rising profits. However, the performance benefits of the technology are accompanied by behaviours that reduce long-term efficiency as work becomes increasingly devoid of meaning or dignity for the employees. Thus, a paradox of consequence results when managers, in pursuit of a specific organizational goal or goals, call for or carry out actions that are in opposition to the very goals the organization is attempting to accomplish.

A second theme that lies at the centre of Weber's sociology is his analysis of *power* and domination by social elites (Bratton et al., 2009, p. 235). In *Economy and Society* (1922/1968), Weber stresses that power is an aspect of virtually all social relationships. However, Weber was primarily interested in legitimate forms of domination or power, or what he called 'legitimate authority', which allocates the right to command and the duty to obey. He argued that every form of social elite attempts to establish and cultivate belief in its own legitimate authority. For example, *legal-rational* domination, which Weber defined as 'a belief in the legality of enacted rules and the right of those elevated to authority under such rules to issue commands' (Weber, 1922/1968, p. 215), is exercised through bureaucracy, itself a product of the systematic rationalization of work and society. Weber viewed bureaucratic domination with some apprehension. The more perfectly bureaucracy is developed, 'the more it is 'dehumanized' (p. 975) as it 'reduces every worker to a cog in this [bureaucratic] machine and, seeing himself in this light, he will merely ask how to transform himself from a little into a somewhat bigger cog' (p. iix).

Critical scholars draw heavily on the works of Marx, and to a lesser extent Weber, to explain management activities in terms of basic 'logics' underlying capitalist production and society: goods and services are produced for a profit; technology and bureaucratic principles provide new opportunities for increasing both the quantity and the quality of work; and the agents acting for the capitalists – the managers – decide how and where goods and services are to be produced within the context of powerful economic imperatives that do not allow for substantial differences in management style or approach. Thus, managerial control is a *structural* imperative of capitalist employment relations, causing what Edwards' (1986) calls '*structural antagonism*'. Labour process analysis is part of the conflict school of thought. It represents a body of theory and research that examines 'core' themes of technology, skills, control and worker resistance, as well as, more recently, new 'postmodern territories' with a focus on subjectivity, identity and power (Thompson and Smith, 2010). The conflict paradigm, when applied to work organizations, sets out to discover the ways in which power, control, conflict and legitimacy impact on contemporary employment relations. It emphasizes that HRM can only be understood as part of a management process embedded within the wider sociocultural and political economy order of a capitalist society, which determines the nature of work and employment practices. The various critical approaches to HRM attempt to demystify and contextualize the situation of HRM by focusing on the interplay of economic, social and political forces, power and systematic inequality, and structured antagonism and conflict (see Delbridge and Keenoy, 2010; Thompson and Harley, 2008; Watson, 2010).

The third social science paradigm examined here, the *feminist paradigm*, traces its intellectual roots to eighteenth-century feminist writings, such as Mary Wollstonecraft's *A Vindication of the Rights of Woman* (1792/2004) and, in the 1960s, to Betty Friedan's *Feminine Mystique* (1963). Whereas Marx chiefly addressed the exploitation of the working class, the early feminist writers provided a 'sophisticated understanding into gender-based, persistent, and pervasive injustices that women continue to experience in all areas of life' (Bratton et al., 2009, p. 11). Researchers looking at the market society from a feminist perspective have drawn attention to aspects of organizational life that are overlooked by other paradigms. In part, feminist scholarship has focused on gender differences and how they relate to the rest of society. Over the decades, gender has become a concept to be wrestled with, but here we use the word to refer to a set of ideas that focuses on the processes of gender roles, inequalities in society and in the workplace, problems of power, and women's subordination and oppression.

Theoretically, one of the most important consequences of gender analysis is its power to question the research findings and analysis that segregate studies of HRM from those of gender divisions in the labour market (Dex, 1988), patriarchal power (Witz, 1986), issues of workplace inequality (Phillips and Phillips, 1993) and 'dual-role' and work–life issues (Knights and Willmott, 1986; Platt, 1997; Warhurst et al., 2008). More importantly, however, including the dimension of gender in the study of contemporary HRM has the potential to move the debate forward by examining the people who are deemed to be the 'recipients' of HRM theory and practice (Mabey et al., 1998a). For example, Dickens (1998) has noted that the equality assumption in the HRM model, which emphasizes the value of diversity, is part of the rhetoric rather than the reality. Reinforcing this observation, a large-scale Canadian study showed that women face a gender bias when it comes to career advancement. In addition, women from visible minorities face a 'double bias' favouring white men at all levels, from entry-level to middle managers right up to chief executive officers (Yap and Konrad, 2009). The feminist paradigm takes it as self-evident that gender inequality in the workplace can only be understood by developing a wider gender-sensitive understanding of society and employment practices.

reflective question It is important to explore your own values and views and therefore your own perspective on HRM. What do you think of these social science paradigms? How do they help us to explain the actions and outcomes of behaviour in organizations? Which perspective seem to you to be more realistic, and why? How do these paradigms help us to understand the uncertainties and conflicts evident in contemporary workplaces?

Critique and paradox in HRM

Since Storey's (1989) landmark publication, the HRM canon has been subject to 'external' and 'internal' criticism (Delbridge and Keenoy, 2010). The external critique has come from academics within the broad field of critical management studies and labour process theory. These critics include Alvesson and Willmott (2003), Godard (1991), Thompson and McHugh (2009) and Watson (2004). They expose structured antagonisms and contradictions, and contend that HR practices can only be understood in the context of the wider cultural and political economy factors that shape or direct those practices. Critical management theorists also argue that mainstream HRM researchers have routinely neglected or marginalized those most directly impacted by HR practices – the employees. Generally, there has been an intellectual failure to engage in the process of 'denaturalization' – of questioning 'taken-for-granted' beliefs and assumptions and 'unmasking' the questionable results of HRM research. Finally, critics hold that most HRM researchers have largely failed to subject employment practices to a critical scrutiny of 'unintended consequences', 'contradictions' or the 'collateral damage' resulting from their application (Delbridge and Keenoy, 2010, p. 803).

The principal 'internal' critics of HRM include Karen Legge (2005), who provides a sustained critique with respect to the divide between what she describes as the 'rhetoric' and the 'reality' of HRM. Similarly, Barbara Townley (1994) offers a sustained Foucauldian analysis and critique of HRM, and Winstanley and Woodall (2000) present a sustained ethical critique of HRM. More generally, Keenoy and Anthony (1992) have sought to explore the ambiguity associated with the term 'human resource management' itself. This relates to the question of where the emphasis of strategic management policy is placed: is it on the word *'human'* or on *'resource'* in management? This ambiguity generated the notion of 'soft' and 'hard' HRM and, more recently, provoked a collection titled *Searching for the 'H' in HRM* in the 'moral' market society (Bolton and Houlihan, 2007).

Analytically, critical commentaries of the HRM phenomenon echo the belief that the contemporary workplace mirrors the capitalist society at large: a social entity that may be characterized by creativity, innovation, wealth, but also one that exhibits constant change, strategic variation, human degradation, inequality, social power, differential interests, contradiction and paradox. Charles Dickens (1859/1952), in *A Tale of Two Cities*, nicely captures the existence of paradox in modernity: 'It was the best of times, it was the worst of times, it was the age of wisdom, it was the age of foolishness ...'. This duality of creativity and wealth alongside degradation and inequality in the workplace is neatly captured by a well-known drawing found in first-year psychology textbooks, an image that can be seen at the same time as a beautiful young woman and an old crone.

Drawing upon Weber's work, the 'internal' critics of HRM have used the paradox of consequence to encourage their audiences to view the reality of HRM differently. For example, new job and work designs (see Chapter 4) were promoted to revitalize organizations in order to enlist workers' knowledge and commitment, but what have emerged are downsizing and work intensification. A similar contradiction emerges in new reward systems (see Chapter 11) with the introduction of variable pay arrangements, but what can emerge is a 'bonus culture' that undermines other espoused employer goals such as loyalty and commitment, or, as the 2008 banking crisis attests, risk-aversion. Legge's incisive critique identifies the basic paradox that the dominant HRM model simultaneously seeks both control over and the commitment of employees, the tensions in the 'soft' and 'hard' schools of HRM, and the rhetoric that asserts 'we are all managers now'. Paradoxically, the inclusion of the HR director in the strategic management team, the process of 'decentralization' or the act of 'giving away HR management' to line managers, as well as the outsourcing of HR activities, might ultimately lead to the demise of the HR professional, thereby undermining the ongoing quest of HRM specialists for centrality and credibility (Legge, 2005).

Critical accounts of HRM also suggest a paradox of consequence arising from new networked organizational designs (Rubery et al., 2002). The short-lived nature of multiemployer networks, differentiated by employer, business contracts and employment contracts, encourages subcultures that may counter any efforts to create a 'high-commitment' culture and/or violate the psychological contract. As Legge explains, in discussing interfirm relationships: 'When flexibility is the justification and watchword … pragmatism … is likely to moderate, if not supplant, a truly strategic approach to HR' (2007, p. 54). Furthermore, when employers are urged to adjust to Britain's ageing workforce (Brindle, 2010), investment in work-based learning is at odds with the reality of 'HRM's organizationally sponsored ageism' (Lyon and Glover, 1998, p. 31).

In our view, studying HRM remains relevant. The global and environmental drivers of change that are reshaping Western economies and societies will cast a long shadow over contemporary organizations as managers struggle to control work and employment activities. Analytical HRM is, therefore, highly relevant given that its *raison d'être* is, using a variety of approaches or styles, to leverage people's knowledge and capabilities and manage employment relationships. In particular, given the need for organizations to develop sustainably oriented strategies, a reflexive, critical analysis of HRM is increasingly important to understanding organizational life.

Furthermore, with regard to concerns about an absence of reflexive critique in business schools, Delbridge and Keenoy's (2010) contribution elaborating what constitutes CHRM is both important and timely. In writing this text, we have found concepts from the social science paradigms to be highly relevant, albeit through the lens of our own cultural bias. As in previous editions of *Human Resource Management: Theory and Practice*, we are concerned with developing a context-sensitive understanding of work and practices of HRM. Throughout the book, we emphasize that paradox and antagonism is structured into the employment relationship. Many mainstream HRM writers have not been realistic about the nature of capitalism (Thompson and Harley, 2008). From our perspective, it goes without saying that different work systems and HR strategies and practices can only be understood in the context of the wider cultural-political economy, technological, environmental and market factors that direct or influence work regimes.

We are aiming to provide a more critical, nuanced account of the realities of the workplace in market societies, one that encourages a deeper understanding and sensitivity with respect to employment and HR-related issues. We hope that *Human Resource Management: Theory and Practice* captures the range of change evident in today's workplaces, and will moreover lead to the kind of sensibilities that encourage the reader to question, to be critical and to seek multicausality when analysing contemporary HRM.

case study

Canterbury Hospital

Setting

In the twenty-first century, New Zealand is tackling environmental issues similar to those of many countries: the more sustainable use of water, managing marine resources, reducing waste and improving energy efficiency. The country is particularly concerned about the decline of its unique plants, animals and ecosystems. The country is striving to build a positive image of New Zealand through exporting environmentally sensitive products and maintaining a reputation of being sustainable at home and abroad. The government has therefore recognized that there is a need to increase reporting on sustainable practices among New Zealand businesses in order to raise the profile of New Zealand globally on this important issue.

For the last few years, the Ministry for the Environment has promoted several grant-funding programmes to support environmental initiatives. In an attempt to control administration costs and improve the evaluation of the programme's outcomes, a decision was recently made to combine the funds supporting environmental initiatives at the community level. It is hoped that merging these funds will mean that the programme will be more streamlined and that there will be more flexibility to meet government priorities.

The combined funding programme, called the Community Environment Fund (CEF), aims to support community groups, businesses and local government in taking environmental actions. To be eligible for funding, applicants have to demonstrate that their projects will support one or more of the following objectives:

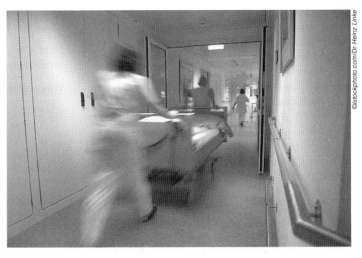

- Raise awareness of environmental damage
- Support and strengthen partnerships between community, industry, Maori populations and local government on practical environmental initiatives
- Involve the community in practically focused action for the environment
- Empower the community to take action that improves the quality of the environment
- Increase community-based advice, educational opportunities and public information about environmental legislation.

Eligible environmental projects will be considered for a minimum of $10,000 and up to a maximum of $300,000 of funding per financial year.

The problem

Canterbury Hospital, located near the city of Christchurch, provides a wide range of complex medical, surgery and mental health services, and is not only one of New Zealand's largest healthcare centres, but also its oldest. The hospital has a poor reputation in terms of its HRM and struggles with adversarial union relations. Workers are given low autonomy in their jobs, and the organizational structure contains several layers of management. Decision-making is primarily centralized.

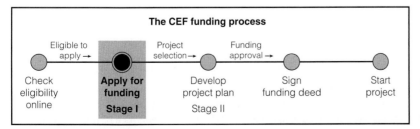

The CEF funding process

Eligible to apply → | Project selection → | Funding approval →

Check eligibility online | **Apply for funding** **Stage I** | Develop project plan Stage II | Sign funding deed | Start project

Source: www.mfe.govt.nz/withyou/funding/community-environment-fund/; Ministry for the Environment (New Zealand) (2011)

34

The hospital's administration recently became aware of the funding provided by the government's new environmental initiative. Subsequently, in a public meeting, Chief Executive Officer Heather Nicol announced the creation of an Environmental/ Sustainability Innovation Committee, made up of staff members chosen by management from the various hospital departments: 'Environmental stewardship is a key component of our hospital's strategic and operational planning, and through this new committee we will be contributing to our organization's and the country's goals to become more sustainable.' The committee, she said, would recommend and develop projects that would meet the funding criteria outlined by the government.

This new and revolutionary approach by the hospital administration took most of the staff by surprise. Although many were eager to learn about the environmental issues and contribute their ideas through this experience, others were suspicious of management's motives in involving staff members when they had never been asked to participate in such a public initiative before. Shortly before the initial meeting of the selected group, the HR department received an angry call from the union executive questioning why they had not been asked to sit on the committee and asking what criteria had been used to select the employees who were to participate. The union demanded a meeting with management to discuss how workloads and jobs would be impacted by the employees' involvement.

Assignment

Working either alone or in a study group, prepare a report drawing on this chapter and other recommended material addressing the following:

1 Using one of the five major HRM models, identify which aspects of the case illustrate traditional personnel management and HRM approaches.
2 What contribution can a set of 'best' HR practices make to this organization?
3 Reflecting upon the national business system, discuss how the effectiveness of HR practices depends on the context of an organization.

Note: Your report may be written to fit your own national business and legal context.

Essential reading

Dunphy, D. C., Griffiths, A. and Benn, S. (2003) *Organizational Change for Corporate Sustainability: Understanding Organizational Change*. London: Routledge.

Enhert, I. (2009) Sustainability and human resource management: reasoning and applications on corporate websites. *European Journal of International Management,* 3(4): 419–38.

Jones, G. (ed.) (2011) *Current Research in Sustainability*. Prahan: Tilde University Press.

Tyler, M. and Wilkinson, A. (2007) The tyranny of corporate slenderness: 'corporate anorexia' as a metaphor for our age. *Work, Employment and Society,* 21(3): 537–49.

For more on New Zealand's Community Environment Fund, go to: www.mfe.govt.nz/withyou/funding/community-environment-fund.

Note: This feature was written by Lori Rilkoff, HR Manager at City of Kamloops, BC, Canada.

WWW Visit the companion website at www.palgrave.com/business/bratton5 for guidelines on writing reports.

summary

◀ In this introductory chapter, we have emphasized the importance of managing people, individually and collectively, over other 'factor inputs'. We have examined the history of HRM and emphasized that, since its introduction, it has been highly controversial. The HRM phenomenon has been portrayed as the historical outcome of rising neo-liberalism ideology, closely associated with the political era of Thatcherism.

◀ We have conceptualized HRM as a strategic approach, one that seeks to leverage people's capabilities and commitment with the goal of enhancing performance and dignity *in* and *at* work. These HRM goals are accomplished by a set of integrated employment policies, programmes and practices within an organizational and societal context. We suggest that the HRM approach as conceptualized here constitutes CHRM, extending the analysis of HRM outcomes beyond performance to include equality, dignity and social justice.

◀ To show the multiple meanings of the term 'human resource management', we have examined five theoretical models. We have discussed whether HRM now represents a new orthodoxy; certainly, the language is different.

◄ We have explained that tensions are omnipresent. These include tensions between profitability and cost-effectiveness and employee security; between employer control and employee commitment; and between managerial autonomy and employee dignity. Throughout this book, we illustrate and explain some of these tensions and inevitable paradoxes to encourage a deeper understanding of HR-related issues.

◄ Finally, workplace scholars use a variety of theoretical frames of reference or paradigms – here the focus has been on structural-functionalism, conflict and feminist paradigms – to organize how they understand and conduct research into HRM.

vocab checklist for ESL students

◄ analyse (v), analysis (n), analytical (adj)

◄ arbitrate (v), arbitrator (n), arbitration (n)

◄ bureaucrat (n), bureaucracy (n), bureaucratic (adj)

◄ capitalize (v), capital (n), capitalist (n), capitalism (n)

◄ conflict (n), conflict perspective (n)

◄ contract (v), contract (n), contractor (n), contractual (adj)

◄ controversy (n), controversial (adj)

◄ criticize (v), critic (n), critical (adj)

◄ downsize (v), downsizing (n)

◄ economize (v), economics (n), economy (n), economist (n), economical (adj)

◄ employ (v), employee (n), employer (n), employment (n)

◄ equity (n), equitable (adj), equal (adj)

◄ globalize (v), globe (n), globalization (n), global (adj)

◄ idea (n), ideology (n), ideological (adj)

◄ interdepend (v), interdependencies (n), interdependent (adj)

◄ international human resource management (IHRM) (n)

◄ liberalize (v), liberalism (n), liberal (n) (adj)

◄ manage (v), manager (n), management (n), managerial (adj)

◄ mediate (v), mediator (n), mediation (n)

◄ micro human resource management (MHRM) (n)

◄ norm (n), normative (adj), normal (adj)

◄ oblige (v), obligation (n), obligatory (adj)

◄ outsource (v), outsourcing (n)

◄ paradigm (n)

◄ paradox (n), paradoxical (adj), paradoxically (adv)

◄ recruit (v), recruit (n), recruitment (n)

◄ restructure (v), restructuring (n)

◄ rhetoric (n), rhetorical (adj)

◄ sociology (n), sociologist (n), sociological (adj)

◄ stakeholder (n)

◄ stereotype (v), stereotype (n), stereotypical (adj)

◄ strategic human resource management (SHRM) (n)

◄ strategize (v), strategy (n), strategist (n), strategic (adj)

◄ sustain (v), sustainability (n), sustainable (adj)

◄ theorize (v), theory (n), theorist (n), theoretical (adj)

◄ unionize (v), union (n), unionization (n)

Note: some words are denoted as nouns (n) when in fact the word is a gerund; for example, 'restructuring' is in the gerund form; however, gerunds function grammatically as nouns, so the general term of noun (n) is used.

Visit www.palgrave.com/business/bratton5 for a link to free definitions of these terms in the Macmillan Dictionary, as well as additional learning resources for ESL students.

review questions

1 What is 'human resource management' and what role does it play in work organizations?

2 To what extent does the emergence of HRM reflect the rise and ideology of neo-liberalism?

3 To what extent is HRM different from conventional personnel management – or is it simply 'old wine in new bottles'?

further reading to improve your mark

Reading these articles and chapters can help you gain a better understanding and potentially a higher grade for your HRM assignment.

◀ The changing role of HRM is explored in R. Caldwell (2001) Champions, adapters, consultants and synergists: the new change agents in HRM. *Human Resource Management Journal*, **11**(3): 39–52.

Critical studies are also found in the following:

◀ Delbridge, R. and Keenoy, T. (2010) Beyond managerialism? *International Journal of Human Resource Management*, **21**(6): 799–817.

◀ Dickens, L. (1998) What HRM means for gender equality. *Human Resource Management Journal*, **8**(1): 23–45.

◀ Kochan, T. (2008) Social legitimacy of the HRM profession: a US perspective. In P. Boxall, J. Purcell and P. Wright (eds) *The Oxford Handbook of Human Resource Management* (pp. 599–619). Oxford: OUP.

◀ Legge, K. (2005) *Human Resource Management: Rhetorics and Realities*. London: Palgrave Macmillan.

◀ Storey J. (ed.) (2007) Human resource management today: an assessment. In J. Storey (ed.) *Human Resource Management: A Critical Text* (pp. 3–20). London: Thompson Learning.

◀ Thompson, P. and Harley, B. (2008) HRM and the worker: labour process perspectives. In P. Boxall, J. Purcell and P. Wright (eds) *The Oxford Handbook of Human Resource Management* (pp. 147–65). Oxford: OUP.

◀ Watson, T. (2010) Critical social science, pragmatism and the realities of HRM. *International Journal of Human Resource Management Studies*, **21**(6): 915–31.

 Visit www.palgrave.com/business/bratton5 for lots of extra resources to help you get to grips with this chapter, including study tips, HRM skills development guides, summary lecture notes, and more.

part I

the arena of contemporary human resource management

chapter **2**

corporate strategy and strategic HRM

objectives

After studying this chapter, you should be able to:

1 Describe the characteristics of strategic decisions and define what is meant by strategy and strategic management

2 Appreciate the meaning of 'quadruple bottom line' as a firm or organization strategy for sustainable work systems

3 Describe how strategic priorities vary by level – corporate, business and operational – and comment on the links between business strategy and human resource management (HRM)

4 Explain three models of human resources (HR) strategy: control, resource and integrative

5 Comment on the limitations of the literature on strategic HRM and HR strategy

A browse through the business section of any quality newspaper will reveal a ubiquitous use of the word 'strategy'. Writers use it both freely and dotingly. Strategy is the essence of managerial activity. The idea that employees' creative assets can play a strategic role in achieving competitive goals has led to a field of research labelled 'strategic' human resource management, or SHRM. Just as the term 'human resource management' has been contested, so too has the notion of SHRM. A strategic approach to the management of work and people is concerned with developing and implementing human resources (HR) policies and practices that will enable the organization to achieve its strategic objectives. A stream of empirical research has explored the performance effects associated with SHRM (for example, Guthrie et al., 2009; Martín-Tapia et al., 2009). As a subfield of study, SHRM represents a junction between the literatures on strategic management and HRM (Allen and Wright, 2008). The SHRM debate focuses on several important questions: First, what determines whether an organization adopts a strategic approach to HRM? Second, can we identify distinct bundles of HR activities with different competitive models? And finally, can SHRM enhance competitive advantage or improve services?

This chapter will examine the strategic management process and will introduce a new dimension into the debate – the notion of a 'green strategy'. It will then examine different 'models' of HR strategy and the degree to which these types of HR strategy vary systematically between organizations. We will then address a number of questions that relate to SHRM and performance, leadership, organizational structure and culture, and trade unions. There is a common theme running through this chapter – that much of the literature reveals structural constraints attesting to the complexity of implementing different HRM strategies in the contemporary workplace.

Strategic management

The word 'strategy', deriving from the Greek noun *strategos*, meaning 'commander in chief', was first used in the English language in 1656. The development and usage of the word suggests that it is composed of *stratos* (army) and *agein* (to lead). In a management context, the word 'strategy' has now replaced the more traditional term 'long-term planning' to denote a specific pattern of behaviour undertaken by the upper echelon of the organization in order to accomplish its performance goals. Hill and Jones (2010, p. 4) define strategy as 'an action a company takes to attain superior performance'. Johnson et al. (2005, p. 9) define it more broadly as 'the direction and scope of an organization over the long term, which achieves advantage in a changing environment through the configuration of resources and competencies with the aim of fulfilling stakeholder expectations'. Grant (2010) argues that strategy is simply 'about winning' (p. 4). Traditionally, a competitive strategy is developed by the organization's top executives. In learning organizations, in contrast, the accumulated actions of informed and empowered employees contribute to strategic development (Daft, 2010). In addition, a collaborative strategy can emerge from business partnerships with suppliers and customers, non-profit and environmental agencies and groups.

A strategy need not necessarily be made explicit or be equated with a formal plan. A strategy is best understood as a pattern of decision-making based on a clear understanding of the 'game' being played and a keen awareness on the part of the players of how to manoeuvre into a position of advantage (Grant, 2010). A successful strategy is consistent with the organization's external environment and with its internal goals, resources, capabilities and shared values. Strategic management is therefore best defined as a continuous process that requires the constant adjustment of three major, interdependent poles: the environment, the resources available, and the values of senior management (Figure 2.1).

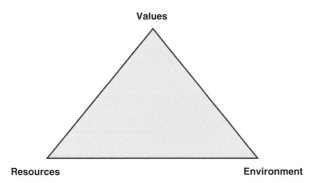

Figure 2.1 *The three traditional poles of a strategic plan or 'game'*

Model of strategic management

In the descriptive and prescriptive management texts, strategic management appears as a cycle in which several activities follow and feed on one another. The strategic management process is typically broken down into five steps:

1 Mission and goals
2 Environmental analysis
3 Strategic formulation
4 Strategy implementation
5 Strategy evaluation.

Figure 2.2 illustrates how the five steps interact. At the corporate level, the strategic management process includes activities that range from appraising the organization's current mission and goals, to strategic evaluation.

The first step in the strategic management model begins with top senior managers evaluating their position in relation to the organization's current mission and goals. The mission describes the organization's values and aspirations; it is the organization's *raison d'être* and indicates the direction in which senior management is going. Goals are the formally stated definition of the business scope and outcomes the organization is trying to accomplish (Daft, 2010).

Environmental analysis looks at the organization's internal strengths and weaknesses and at the external environment for opportunities and threats. The factors that are most important to the organization's future are referred to as 'strategic factors' and can be summarised by the acronym SWOT – **S**trengths, **W**eaknesses, **O**pportunities and **T**hreats.

Strategic formulation involves senior managers evaluating the interaction between strategic factors and making strategic choices that enable the organization to meet its business goals. The process, as described here, draws on the 'strategic choice' perspective (Child, 1972). Some strategies are formulated at the corporate, business and specific functional

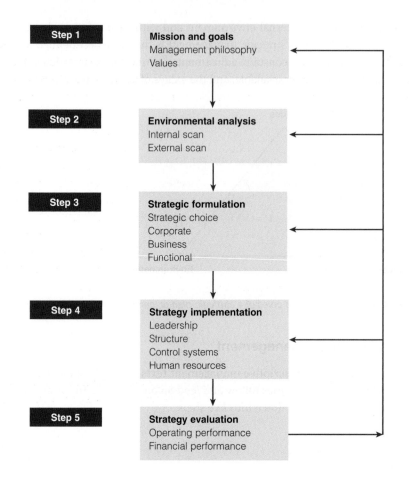

Figure 2.2 *The strategic management model*

levels. The concept of 'strategic choice' underscores the importance of asking such questions as who makes the decisions and why they are made. It also draws attention to strategic management as a 'political process' whereby decisions and actions on issues are taken by a 'power-dominant' group of managers within the organization. In Child's words:

[W]hen] incorporating strategic choice in a theory of organizations, one is recognizing the operation of an essentially political process, in which constraints and opportunities are functions of the power exercised by decision-makers in the light of ideological values. (Child, 1972, quoted in McLoughlin and Clark, 1988, p. 41)

In a political model of strategic management, it is necessary to consider the distribution of power within the organization: 'where power lies, how it comes to be there, and how the outcome of competing power plays and coalitions within senior management are linked to employee relations' (Purcell and Ahlstrand, 1994, p. 45). The strategic choice perspective on organizational decision-making makes the discourse on strategy 'more concrete' and provides important insights into how the employment relationship is managed.

Strategy implementation is an area of activity that focuses on the techniques used by managers to implement their strategies. In particular, it refers to activities that deal with leadership style, the design of the organization, the information and control systems, and the management of HR (see Figure 1.2). Prominent academics emphasize that leadership (for example, Westley and Mintzberg, 2007) and HR policies and practices (Schuler et al., 2001) are crucial components of the strategic implementation process (see Table 2.1, p. 53). Finally, *strategy evaluation* is an activity that determines to what extent the actual change and performance match the desired change and performance.

The strategic management model depicts the five major activities as forming a rational and linear process. It is, however, important to note that it is a normative model, that is, it shows how strategic management should be done rather than describing what is actually done by senior managers. Mintzberg (2009) believes that the model, uncritically taught to business students, tends to promote an 'excessively analytical, detached style of management' and underestimate the strategic role and contribution of HRM. Strategic management is a practice, learned in context. Divorcing the two helps to elucidate the Bank of England's monumental failure of management when 'the collective imagination of many bright people' failed to foresee the timing, extent and severity of the financial crisis occurring in 2008/09 (Stewart, 2009). As we have already noted, the idea that strategic decision-making is a political process implies a potential gap between the theoretical model and economic and social reality.

Hierarchy of strategy

Another aspect of strategic management in the multidivisional business organization concerns the level to which strategic issues apply. Conventional wisdom identifies different levels of strategy – a hierarchy of strategy (Figure 2.3):

- Corporate
- Business
- Functional.

Corporate-level strategy

Corporate-level strategy describes an organization's overall direction in terms of its general philosophy towards the growth and the management of its various operating units. The term 'corporate' is used in this book because the term 'corporate strategy' denotes the most general level of strategy in an organization and in this sense embraces other levels of strategy in both large and small business enterprises, non-profit organizations and public services. Corporate strategies determine the types of business a corporation wants to be involved in and what business units should be acquired, modified or sold. This strategy addresses the question 'What business are we in?' Devising a strategy for a multidivisional company involves at least four types of initiative:

- Establishing investment priorities and steering corporate resources into the most attractive business units
- Initiating actions to improve the combined performance of those business units with which the corporation first became involved
- Finding ways to improve the synergy between related business units in order to increase performance
- Making decisions dealing with diversification.

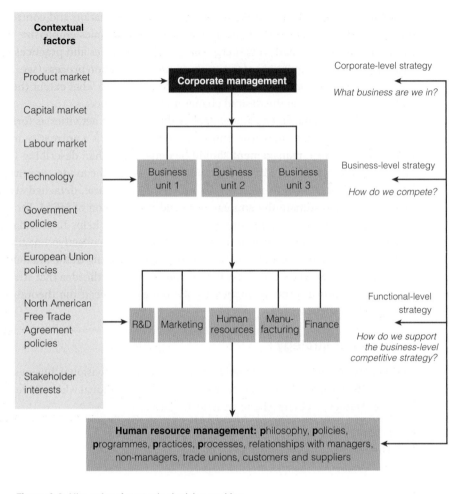

Figure 2.3 *Hierarchy of strategic decision-making*

Business-level strategy

Business-level strategy deals with decisions and actions pertaining to each business unit, the main objective of a business-level strategy being to make the unit more competitive in its marketplace. This level of strategy addresses the question 'How do we compete?' Although business-level strategy is guided by 'upstream', corporate-level strategy, business unit management must craft a strategy that is appropriate for its own operating situation. In the 1980s, Porter (1980, 1985) made a significant contribution to our understanding of business strategy by formulating a framework that described three competitive strategies: cost leadership, differentiation and focus.

The *low-cost leadership* strategy attempts to increase the organization's market share by having the lowest unit cost and price compared with those of competitors. The simple alternative to cost leadership is the *differentiation strategy*. This assumes that managers distinguish their services and products from those of their competitors in the same industry by providing distinctive levels of service, product or high quality such that the customer is prepared to pay a premium price. With the *focus strategy*, managers focus on a specific buyer group or regional market. A *market strategy* can be narrow or broad, as in the notion of niche markets being very narrow or focused. This all allows the firm to choose from four generic business-level strategies in order to establish and exploit a competitive advantage within a particular competitive scope:

- *Low-cost leadership*, for example Walmart
- *Differentiation*, for example Nudie Jeans
- *Focused differentiation*, for example Mountain Equipment Co-operative
- *Focused low-cost leadership*, for example Rent-A-Wreck Cars.

Miles and Snow (1984) have identified four modes of strategic orientation: defenders, prospectors, analysers and reactors. *Defenders* are companies with a limited product line and a management focus on improving the efficiency of their existing operations. Commitment to this cost orientation makes senior managers unlikely to explore new areas. *Prospectors* are companies with fairly broad product lines that focus on product innovation and market opportunities. This sale orientation makes senior managers emphasize 'creativity over efficiency'. *Analysers* are companies that operate in at least two different product market areas, one stable and one variable. In this situation, senior managers emphasize efficiency in the stable areas and innovation in the variable areas. *Reactors* are companies that lack a consistent strategy–structure–culture relationship. In this reactive orientation, senior management's responses to environmental changes and pressures thus tend to be piecemeal strategic adjustments. Competing companies within a single industry can choose any one of these four types of strategy and adopt a corresponding combination of structure, culture and processes consistent with that strategy in response to the environment. The different competitive strategies influence the 'downstream' functional strategies.

Functional-level strategy

Functional-level strategy pertains to the major functional operations within the business unit, including research and development, marketing, manufacturing, finance and HR. This strategy level is typically primarily concerned with maximizing resource productivity and addresses the question 'How do we support the business-level competitive strategy?' Consistent with this, at the functional level, HRM policies and practices support the business strategy goals.

These three levels of strategy – *corporate, business* and *functional* – form a hierarchy of strategy within large multidivisional corporations. In different corporations, the specific operation of the hierarchy of strategy might vary between 'top-down' and 'bottom-up' strategic planning. The top-down approach resembles a 'cascade' in which the 'downstream' strategic decisions are dependent on higher 'upstream' strategic decisions (Wheelen and Hunger, 1995). The bottom-up approach to strategy-making recognizes that individuals 'deep' within the organization might contribute to strategic planning. Mintzberg (1978) has incorporated this idea into a model of 'emergent strategies', which are unplanned responses to unforeseen circumstances by non-executive employees within the organization. Common to definitions of corporate strategy is the notion that strategy is focused on achieving certain goals and that it 'implies some consistency, integration, or cohesiveness of decisions and actions' (Grant, 2010, p. 16).

Ethics and corporate social responsibility

The previous sections have discussed decision-making at the three levels of strategy formulation, but have given little consideration to whether that decision-making is ethical or unethical. Neither have we considered how societal expectations impact on a firm's or organization's strategies. These considerations are the province of business ethics and corporate social responsibility (CSR). A series of high-profile cases, including those of Bernard Ebbers at WorldCom, Fausta Tonna at Parmalat and Bernard Madoff, former chair of the NASDAQ Stock Market, has drawn public attention to *white-collar crime*. The recognition that shocking and unethical behaviour has calamitous consequences, from a loss of jobs and savings to government indebtedness, has generated collective national anger and a distrust of corporate elites. In July 2011, the phone-hacking scandal or 'Hack-ingate' at News International (UK) also brought into sharp focus the unethical behaviour of senior executives in the pursuit of profit. In 2011, collective national anger focused public attention on the need for businesses to define their standards of ethical behaviour, for new CSR strategies and, moreover, for greater government regulation. This section, therefore, follows naturally from the discussion of strategic decision-making.

> **HRM web links**   WWW   Check the website www.businessethics.com, from which you will be able to download information on ethics in business.

Business ethics

Ethics are a set of moral principles and values that influence the decisions and actions of individuals within the organization. Any set of ethical principles does not emerge in a vacuum, but instead reflects the cultural values and norms of society (see Chapter 5). For example, bribing officials for contracts is regarded as bad in most cultures. *Ethical dilemmas* arise when two or more values conflict, for example when a pharmaceutical company has to meet profit targets but this involves testing a new drug on animals. The degradation of the environment is another classical illustration of an ethical dilemma. Petroleum companies extracting 'dirty oil' from the oil sands in Alberta, Canada, or drilling in the Gulf of Mexico satisfy shareholder interests in preference to reducing pollution.

The regulatory context determines the minimum obligations of an organization towards its various stakeholders, and ethical decision-making is mainly legally driven. That is, compliance-based codes guide the actions of managers in terms of the improper use of the organization's resources or conflicts of interest. The *ethical stance* is the extent to which an organization will exceed its minimum obligations to stakeholders and society at large (Johnson et al., 2005). In an evermore globalized economy, Carroll (2004, p. 35) argues that there is evidence of more organizations undergoing 'a program of moral reform' that involves writing value-based ethical policies that are compatible with cross-global operations. The aim is to help managers make informed decisions when faced with new ethical situations.

> **reflective question**   ⧉   Do you believe that organizations should act ethically or maximize shareholder return? How do ethics impact on the employment relationship?

Ethics permeate the employment relationship. The debate on whether HR practitioners can be a source of moral authority speaks to the growing interest in 'ethical stewardship' in decision-making and the role of the HR professional as 'a guardian of ethics'. However, with much of the research focusing on strategy and efficacy, ethics has been largely left out of the HRM discourse (Ashman and Winstanley, 2006). The centrality of ethics in the employment relationship is evident in the core HR processes. Ethics impacts on the recruitment and selection of employees (for example, in avoidance of discrimination), on rewards (for example, through notions of fairness), on training and development (for example, in terms of equal opportunities), on health and safety (for example, by the full disclosure of harmful chemicals, including any harmful long-term effects) and on the protection of whistleblowers (Winstanley and Woodall, 2000).

Corporate social responsibility

Ethics underscores the notion of *corporate social responsibility*, which is concerned with the ways in which managers' behaviour and actions exceed minimum compliance-based regulations. It concerns the ethical principle that an organization should be accountable for how its corporate strategy might affect local communities, society at large and the planet. Twenty-three years after the disastrous oil spillage from the *Exxon Valdez* on 24 March 1989, there is evidence that the concept of CSR is increasingly gaining popularity in advanced market societies (Koleva et al., 2010). In 2001, the European Commission defined CSR as 'a concept whereby companies integrate social and environmental concerns in their business operations and in their interactions with their stakeholders on a voluntary basis' (quoted by Koleva et al., 2010, p. 274). It is a concept whose time has come (Yakabuski, 2008).

HRM web links | For more information on CSR, visit the websites of UK-based Business in the Community at www.bitc.org.uk and the US-based Business for Social Responsibility at www.bsr.org/en.

The intellectual roots of CSR can be found in the *stakeholder theory* of the firm, which contends that firms should be managed not purely in the interests of maximizing shareholder return, but also in the interests of a range of stakeholders that have a legitimate interest in the organization, including employees, customers, the local community, suppliers, the environment and society in general (Donaldson and Preston, 1995).

The concept of CSR is problematic because it is people and not organizations who engage in unethical behaviour. And, of course, only people and not inanimate objects, such as organizations, can be responsible for unethical actions. Examples of corporate social *irresponsibility* abound. In Bhopal, India, for example, a chemical plant owned by the US global company Union Carbide operated under conditions considered illegal in the USA. On 3 December 1984, the plant experienced a major leak. Within hours, 3000 people were dead, with 15,000 dying more in the aftermath; 200,000 were seriously injured, and 500,000 still carry special health cards. Eventually, Union Carbide paid out just $470 million in compensation (Saul, 2005). See also HRM in practice 2.1 for another example of corporate irresponsibility.

The Corporate Manslaughter and Corporate Homicide Act came into force in the UK as a result of concerns over the difficulties of obtaining prosecutions of individual

Killer chemicals and greased palms

Managers may agonize over what is 'the right thing to do', whether the issue is the duty to accommodate an employee (for example, because of disability, or knowingly exposing employees or members of the public to a carcinogen. Corporate decisions often 'favour one stakeholder over another' (Beatty et al., 2003). There is evidence that individual values play a central role in predicting ethical decision-making at work (Giacalone et al., 2008). American-based Enron Energy Services, Canadian-based Bre-X, Italian-based Parmalat and UK-based Octel are iconic examples of unethical corporate decision-making. In the case of the UK-based company Octel, *The Guardian* newspaper reported:

> *The former chief executive of a British chemical company faces the prospect of extradition to the United States after the firm admitted $1 000 000 bribes to officials to sell fuel additives to Iraq. Paul Jennings, until 2009 chief executive of the Octel chemical works near Ellesmere Port, Merseyside, and his predecessor, Dennis Kerrison, exported tonnes of tetra ethyl lead (TEL), to Iraq. It is believed that Iraq is the only country that still adds lead to petrol.*
>
> *TEL is a killer chemical, banned from automobiles in Europe and the United States because of its links with brain damage to children. TEL is so toxic that workers went mad and died during the first attempt to manufacture the colourless, oily liquid commercially, at the Bayway refinery in New Jersey in 1924. American newspapers called it 'loony gas'. After that scandal, double-skinned rubber gear and goggles became de rigeur in its manufacture.*
>
> *In 2010, the company admitted that, in a deliberate policy to maximise profits, executives from Octel – which since changed its name to Innospec – bribed officials in Iraq and Indonesia with millions of dollars to carry on using TEL, despite its health hazards. In Iraq, bribes were paid in 2007 to sabotage field trails of MMT, a non-lead alternative additive. In Indonesia, money was poured into a 'defence of lead' campaign to pay off local politicians. Kerrison says these are 'false accusations'. And said: 'I have not authorized any bribes, backhanders, or other illegal or dubious payments'. (Leigh et al., 2010)*

The growing importance of understanding and preventing unethical corporate behaviour is evidenced by the enormity of its consequences, from collective national distrust of corporations (Bank of Scotland) to loss of life (Union Carbide and Octel). Decision-makers should understand five ethical principles. The *individual rights* principle reflects the belief that people have the right to free speech, to privacy, to freedom of conscience and to the due process of the law; it asserts that 'What is right for one individual is right for all.' The *distributive justice* principle declares that decisions should be based on fairness, equity and impartiality, and asserts the maxim 'Do unto others as you would have them do unto you.' The *utilitarian* principle emphasizes outcomes, and advises individuals to make decisions that result in the 'greatest good for the greatest number of people' as being the most moral. The *stakeholder* principle reflects the belief that the most moral decision takes into account the interests of a wide range of people, including employees, suppliers and shareholders. The *care* principle determines the most morally correct action to be the one that is sensitive to the relationships between co-workers and the needs of the situation.

Stop! Is it the competitive context or individual traits that are the root cause of unethical decisions? What relevance do the five ethical principles have for HRM?

Sources and further information: See Leigh et al. (2010). See also Beatty et al. (2003), Slapper and Tombs (1999), Giacalone et al. (2008) and Winstanley and Woodall (2000).

Note: This feature was written by John Bratton.

FOR USE AS A
MOTOR FUEL ONLY
CONTAINS
LEAD
(TETRAETHYL)

©istockphoto.com/Katie Roberts

executives when serious mismanagement had led to the death of either an employee or a member of the public. In response to this, the 2007 Act created organizational liability for when the actions of an organization fell far below what could reasonably be expected (Lockton, 2010).

reflective question Is it socially responsible when corporations encourage host countries to overlook health and safety or deregulate employment standards as a price for relocating?

Ethical behaviour and CSR are a function of the individual's values, the organizational culture in which the decision-making process is occurring and power resources. Managers who lack a strong moral commitment are much less likely to make unethical decisions if they are constrained by a societal and organizational culture that disapproves of such actions. Conversely, a manager with integrity can be corrupted by an organizational culture that 'turns a blind eye' or permits or encourages unethical action. In the UK, the act of *whistleblowing* as a practice that exposes unethical or illegal processes and practices has been given some protection by the 1999 Public Interest Disclosure Act. Early evidence suggests that the Act has helped to improve ethical standards in the workplace and reduce the number of cases of injustice to whistleblowers (Weale, 2000). The balance of *power* between employees and employers increases the propensity of whistleblowing. Skivenes and Trygstad (2010) note that the more equitable power balance found in the Norwegian model of industrial relations has illustrative effects because 'Norwegian employees, to a great extent, perceive their whistle-blowing activity as positive and effective' (p. 1091).

The existence of a website that encourages whistleblowing – WikiLeaks – may cause corporations to act accountably. In newly released cables, for example, US diplomats around the world are found to have lobbied for genetically modified crops as 'a strategic government and commercial imperative' in response to moves by France to ban a genetically modified Monsanto corn variety in 2007 (Vidal, 2011). The release of confidential and embarrassing US diplomatic and corporate documents by WikiLeaks has carried with it some uncomfortable lessons, not least for open government and corporate accountability and transparency (Gilmore, 2010; Saunders, 2010). The full implications of WikiLeaks for corporate whistleblowing are beginning to be realized. This twenty-first-century Jeremy Bentham-style 'Panopticon' may do what legislation has only partially succeeded in doing – actually provoking universal transparency and corporate citizenship.

CSR, however, has its critics. For some, corporate 'greening' strategy initiatives, for instance, represent a form of 'green-washing' the marketing or rebranding of goods to capitalize on a new *zeitgeist*, or it may be a public relations ploy to deflect public criticism away from environmentally irresponsible corporate practices. CSR activities can placate politicians and discourage regulatory controls, or can be characterized as a marketing strategy that misleads consumers into believing that they are helping the planet by buying 'green products'. In an era of largely unfettered global capitalism, the idea of good corporate citizenship is a self-regulatory response to public concerns that is still too marginal to make a real difference to irresponsible unethical corporate behaviour. A more effective response to flagrantly dishonest action will occur through greater scrutiny, transparency and regulation. For example, a reformed global financial system undertaken by the Group of 20 countries would have profound consequences for corporate- and business-level strategies.

Exploring corporate sustainability

The search for a strategy that provides competitive advantage is not straightforward. It is typical for competitive advantage or superior services to be explainable by identifying resources and human capabilities that competitors find difficult to obtain or imitate. Strategic capability, however, is increasingly predicated on CSR and complex linkages rooted in organizational culture and corporate sustainability (Garavan et al., 2010). This is unsurprising given that environmental destruction has become a major concern for all humankind (Jabbour et al., 2010). For business strategist Paul Shrivastava, 'sustainability is an opportunity – a touchstone for change' (2011, p. 3). The concept of 'green organizational identity' (Chen, 2011) is a response to a variety of political and social pressures to develop an integrated corporate strategy to enhance 'green competitive advantage' (Chen, 2011, p. 399). Here, we briefly explore the notion of corporate sustainability.

The term 'sustainability' has been in use in the English language since the late thirteenth century. It has its roots in the Latin word *sustinere*, meaning 'to support'. In the early twenty-first century, sustainability is arguably 'the word of the decade' (Sumner, 2005, p. 78). But in spite of its contemporary popularity, the concept of sustainability is controversial and elastic, and the emergent literature frequently contains many contradictory interpretations.

It has been acknowledged that the 1987 World Commission's publication *Our Common Future*, commonly known as the Brundtland Report, gave the concept of sustainability a legitimacy that had previously eluded it (Sumner, 2005). In essence, *Our Common Future* envisioned sustainable development as:

> a process of change in which the exploitation of resources, the direction of investments, the orientation of technological development, and institutional change are all in harmony and enhance both current and future potential to meet human needs and aspirations. (Sumner 2005, p. 81)

Since its publication, it has been subject to several major criticisms, not least of which is that it affirms the orthodox economic growth model. Arguably, this affirmation explains the reason for the Report's mainstream acceptance and the ease with which the notion of sustainability has been coopted into many corporate-level mission statements.

Since the publication of the Brundtland Report, the term 'sustainability' has entered management parlance, spawning such terms as 'sustainable business strategies' and 'sustainable work systems'. Unsurprisingly, critics warn that the acceptance and omnipresence of the term 'sustainability' has come at 'the price of conceptual vagueness, fluidity and co-option' (Sumner, 2005, p. 84). The literature identifies four main approaches to studying sustainability: economic, environmental, social and cultural. The *economic* perspective can be divided into two schools of thinking: neoclassical and ecological. The core premise of neoclassical economics is that firms seek to maximize their profits, reinvesting profits to increase output, in order to sell more and thus further increase profits, *ad infinitum*. Sustainability is defined in terms of money values and assumes the necessity and inevitability of economic growth. As far as the ecosystem is concerned, it is meant to serve that accumulation and cannot be seen as a value in itself. In contrast, the ecological economic school recognizes that orthodox growth models are responsible for the sustainability crisis. Adherents believe that sustainability involves 'handing down to future generations' local

© istockphoto.com/Brian Jackson

What role do you think HR plays in a sustainable business strategy?

and global ecosystems that largely resembles our own' (Goodstein, 1999, p. 109).

The incessant drive for bigger profits also means an accumulation of capital equipment: bigger and bigger plants and machinery, to make more and more cars, lorries and aeroplanes and so on. It is not only that we are consuming non-renewable mineral resources, such as oil, but that we are destroying the basis of the renewable resources – for example, forests, rivers and oceans – from which we draw our food. This is at the heart of the *environmental* critique of orthodox economic models. The imperative of capital accumulation means reducing costs by exploiting labour, exploiting all natural resources and exploiting the ecosystem. The environmental perspective defines sustainability in terms of 'the continued productivity and functioning of the ecosystem' (Brown et al., 1987, p. 716). Humanity overstepping an ecological limit may well cause a global collapse triggered by the ever-growing emissions of greenhouse gases (Randers, 2008).

The *social* perspective underscores the importance of human society. It involves 'improving the quality of human life while living within the carrying capacity of supporting ecosystems' (Farrell and Hart, 1998, p. 7). The *cultural* perspective, however, sees cultural enrichment as integral to sustainability: the continued satisfaction of basic human needs, as well as 'higher-level' cultural necessities (Brown et al., 1987). In terms of values, the environment, social and cultural perspectives move away from orthodox monetary values towards life values. Furthermore, by questioning private capital accumulation, they begin to champion the need to protect the global and local public spaces, or what some writers call the 'civil commons' (Sumner, 2005, p. 109).

In 2002, the Melbourne Principles were developed during a United Nations-sponsored international conference to provide guidance on how cities could be more sustainable. The Principles incorporated the divergent approaches to studying sustainability and outlined four interdependent and mutually reinforcing aspects of sustainable development: *economic growth*, *protection of the environment*, *social equity* and *cultural vitality*. These 'four pillars of sustainability' are expressed as an image in Figure 2.4.

The Melbourne Principles can guide creative thinking and provide a strategic framework for planning corporate-level and business-level strategy. First, corporate strategy should promote sustainable production and consumption, through the appropriate use of environmentally sound technologies and effective demand management. Furthermore, corporate leaders should recognize the intrinsic value of biodiversity and natural ecosystems, and act to protect and restore them. Also, a sustainable corporate strategy recognizes the need for social equity and social change. In addition, the Principles encourage leaders to recognize and build on the distinctive cultural characteristics, including the shared values, of the cities and communities where their organizations are embedded. These four articulated streams of thinking on sustainability suggest that a successful 'green',

Figure 2.4 *The four pillars of sustainability*

low-carbon, sustainable corporate strategy can be expressed as an axiom, the pursuit of *quadruple bottom line* performance – a balance of economic, environmental, social and cultural goals. The strategy literature affirms the need to integrate business strategy and HRM strategy, and it is to this debate that we now turn.

HRM web links WWW | For a definition of a 'green' economy, see the televised interview 'Achim Steiner: Ontario and the Green Economy' at: www.tvo.org/cfmx/tvoorg/theagenda/index. cfm?page_id=7&bpn=109158&bpn_segment_id=10072&ts=2011-05-10%2020:00:00.0

Strategic HRM

The SHRM literature is rooted in 'manpower' (sic) planning, but it was the influential work of Ouchi (1981) and Peters and Waterman (1982) that encouraged US academics, for example Beer et al. (1984), to develop models of HRM emphasizing its 'strategic' role. Interest in attaching the prefix 'strategic' to the term 'human resource management' can be explained from both the 'rational choice' and the 'constituency-based' perspective. From the 'rational choice' perspective, there is a managerial logic in focusing attention on people's assets to provide a competitive advantage when technological superiority, even once achieved, can soon erode (Barney, 1991). Consistent with Barney's resource-based model (RBM), many mainstream HRM writers go along with the view that 'For a variety of reasons related to changing markets, demands for greater speed and flexibility, and the growing attention to "intangible assets," HR ... has the potential to influence firm performance in a way that was not possible 20 years ago' (Huselid and Becker, 2001, quoted in Guthrie et al., 2009, p. 112). From a 'constituency-based' position, it is argued that HR academics and practitioners have embraced SHRM as a means of securing greater respect for the discipline as a field of study and, in the case of workplace practitioners, of enhancing their status among their peers by appearing more 'strategic' (Bamberger and Meshoulam, 2000).

reflective question | Is there a strong business case for the strategic approach to HRM, or is it more the case that academics and HR professionals have embraced SHRM out of self-interest? What do you think of these arguments?

The precise meaning of 'strategic HRM' and 'HR strategy' remains problematic. It is unclear, for example, which one of these two terms relates to an outcome or a process (Bamberger and Meshoulam, 2000). For Snell et al. (1996, p. 62), 'strategic HRM' is an outcome: 'as organizational systems designed to achieve sustainable competitive advantage through people'. For others, however, SHRM is viewed as a process, 'the process of linking HR practices to business strategy' (Ulrich, 1997, p. 89). Similarly, Bamberger and Meshoulam (2000, p. 6) describe SHRM as 'the process by which organizations seek to link the human, social, and intellectual capital of their members to the strategic needs of the firm'. According to Ulrich (1997, p. 190), 'HR strategy' is the outcome: 'the mission, vision and priorities of the HR function'.

Consistent with this view, Bamberger and Meshoulam (2000, p. 5) conceptualize HR strategy as an outcome: 'the pattern of decisions regarding the policies and practices asso-ciated with the HR system'. The authors go on to make a useful distinction between senior management's 'espoused' HR strategy and their 'emergent' strategy. The espoused HR strategy refers to the pattern of HR-related decisions made but not necessarily imple-mented, whereas the emergent HR strategy refers to the pattern of HR-related decisions that have been applied in the workplace. Thus, 'espoused HR strategy is the road map ... and emergent HR strategy is the road actually travelled' (Bamberger and Meshoulam, 2000, p. 6). Purcell (2001) has also portrayed HR strategy as 'emerging patterns of action' that are likely to be much more 'intuitive' and only 'visible' after the event.

We begin the discussion of SHRM and HR strategy with a focus on the link between strategy formulation and strategic HR formulation. A range of business–HRM links has been classified in terms of a proactive–reactive continuum (Kydd and Oppenheim, 1990) and in terms of environment–HR-strategy–business-strategy linkages (Bamberger and Phillips, 1991). In the 'proactive' orientation, the HR professional has a seat at the strategic table and is actively engaged in strategy formulation. In Figure 2.3 above, the two-way arrows on the right-hand side showing both a downward and an upward influence on strategy depict this type of proactive model.

At the other end of the continuum is the 'reactive' orientation, which sees the HR func-tion as being fully subservient to corporate-level and business-level strategy, and organiza-tional-level strategies as ultimately determining HR policies and practices. Once the business strategy has been determined, an HR strategy is implemented to support the chosen competitive strategy. This type of reactive orientation would be depicted in Figure 2.3 above by a one-way downward arrow from business-level to functional-level strategy. In this sense, an HR strategy is concerned with the challenge of matching the Philosophy, Policies, Programmes, Practices and Processes – the 'five Ps' – in a way that will stimulate and reinforce the different employee role behaviours appropriate for each competitive strategy (Schuler, 1992).

Here we draw on Schuler et al.'s (2001) work to emphasize the strategic 'reactive' role and contribution of HRM. Strategic management plans at corporate and business level provide the context within which HR plans are developed and implemented. HR plans provide a map for managers to follow in order to fulfil the core responsibilities of the HR function, which are to ensure that:

- The organization has the right number of qualified employees
- Employees have the right skills and knowledge to perform efficiently and effectively

52

Business urged to keep on eco-track

When companies make strategic decisions about what they can produce and at what price, they are acting as rational entities, motivated exclusively by profit. The more a company can drive its costs below those of its competitors, the greater the profits it stands to make. Take the example of US corporate giant McDonald's. The greenhouse gas footprint produced from the 550 million Big Macs sold in the USA every year is estimated to be 2.66 billion pounds of carbon dioxide equivalent (Patel, 2009; Rees, 1995). And there are the hidden health costs of treating diet-related illnesses. These social costs are paid for not by McDonald's, but by society. Thinking about food brings together the common valuation of the ecosystem, the need for responsive governments and the need for sustainable corporate strategies.

The Conference Board of Canada proclaims that sustainability is 'a strategy of choice' on the part of business leaders. Despite the fact that the recession and the issue of climate change are fading from public discourses, it is reported that Canadian companies are developing 'new growth strategies'. As Shawn McCarthy (2010) reports:

Companies face increasing pressure from rising energy costs and new regulations to cut pollution, while many of their traditional markets remain mired in the economic doldrums ... The Canadian Manufacturers and Exporters Association encourages its members to make new 'green' investments – not only to comply with rules and cut costs, but also to position themselves strategically in a more demanding, environmentally sensitive marketplace ... [Although] the urgency of climate change issues has faded from the public agenda ... in issuing its 'call to action,' the CMEA warned business executives that they 'should still expect to face greater demands for environmental improvements from governments, investors, customers and the public at large. ....

What we have to think about in terms of business strategy is how we can turn all these requirements [into] more

than just a cost factor, and how can we see it as a business opportunity ... We have environmental issues all around the world ... and there are major requirements on the part of your customers and major expectations on the part of your customers' customers for better environmental practices .... So if you can be a part of that solution, then you are able to carve out a new type of market niche that is going to help you differentiate yourself from a lot of your competitors,' Jayson Myers, president of the CMEA, said in an interview.

The rationale and business strategy outlined by the Canadian CMEA was also articulated by Chris Huhne, Secretary for Energy and Climate Change, at the TUC Climate Change Conference, held in London on 11 October, 2010: 'Our first priority is to build a new kind of economy; One where green growth leads to green jobs. A low-carbon economy that will help us recover at home and compete abroad'.

Stop! Using Figure 2.4 as a starting point, what kinds of corporate strategy should organizational leaders be developing? How do local and national attitudes about climate change influence national governments, business strategies and practices? How should 'sustainability' be defined? Who should be responsible for regulating carbon emissions? And, in times of a recession and amidst fears of job losses, should governments relax national emission regulations?

Sources and further information: See Patel (2009), Rees (1995) and McCarthy (2010).

Note: This feature was written by John Bratton.

The greenhouse gas footprint produced from the 550 million Big Macs sold in the USA every year is estimated to be 2.66 billion pounds of carbon dioxide equivalent.

- Employees exhibit the appropriate behaviours consistent with the organization's culture and values
- Employees meet the organization's motivational needs.

These four core activities are the *leitmotiv* of HRM and, according to Schuler et al. (2001), constitute the four-task model of HRM. The four core HR tasks provide the rationale that guides the strategic choice of HR policies and practices (Table 2.1).

Table 2.1 *Strategy implementation and the four-task model of HRM*

HR tasks	Major strategic decisions
Employee assignments and opportunities	• How many employees are needed? • What qualifications will the employees need? • What pay and conditions will attract people to the firm?
Employee competencies	• What competencies do employees have now? • What new competencies will be needed in the future? • How can new competencies be purchased or developed?
Employee behaviours	• What behaviours does the firm value? • What behaviours are detrimental to the strategy? • What behaviours need to be modified or eliminated?
Employee motivation	• How much more effort are employees able and willing to give? • What is the optimal length of time for employees to stay with the firm? • Can productivity be improved by reducing absence and tardiness?

The importance of context as a determinant of HR strategy has been incorporated into some 'best-fit' or contingency models. Extending strategic management concepts, Bamberger and Phillips' (1991) model suggest connections between three poles: the *environment*, the *HR strategy* and the *business strategy*. In the hierarchy of the strategic decision-making model (see Figure 2.3), the HR strategy is influenced by contextual variables such as markets, technology, national government policies, European Union policies and trade unions. Purcell and Ahlstrand argue, however, that those models which incorporate contextual influences as a mediating variable of HR policies and practices tend to lack 'precision and detail' in terms of the precise nature of the environment linkages, and that 'much of the work on the linkages has been developed at an abstract and highly generalized level' (1994, p. 36).

Drawing on the concepts of 'strategic choice' and 'hierarchy of strategy', John Purcell (1989) identified what he called 'upstream' and 'downstream' types of strategic decisions. Upstream or 'first-order' strategic decisions are concerned with the long-term direction of the corporation. If a first-order decision is made to take over another enterprise, for example a French company acquiring a water company in southern England, a second set of considerations applies concerning the extent to which the new operation is to be integrated with or separate from existing operations. These processes are classified as downstream, or 'second-order', strategic decisions. Different HR strategies are called 'third-order' strategic decisions because they establish the basic parameters for managing people in the workplace. In Purcell's words, '[in theory] strategy in human resources management is determined in the context of first-order, long-run decisions on the direction and scope of the firm's activities and purpose … and second-order decisions on the structure of the firm' (1989, p. 71).

The strategic choice perspective defines an organization's strategy as 'sets of strategic choices', which includes critical choices about 'means and ends' (Boxall and Purcell, 2003,

More women leaders: the answer to the financial crisis?

Governments have spent much time dealing with the recession that has resulted from the near-collapse of the financial system. The role of the financial sector in triggering the economic crisis has brought the key decision-makers into focus and highlighted the lack of women in prominent leadership positions. This has spurred the UK government on to comment on the role of women in the City (HM Treasury Committee, 2010):

> *Strong and effective corporate governance of the UK financial sector will be an important factor in ensuring the sector's long-term stability, enabling it to help businesses and households in the wider economy ... there is a risk of group-think if boards continually recruit individuals who share the same backgrounds and experiences. At the same time, as the economy recovers, it is imperative that businesses are drawing from the widest possible pool of talent, and that means ensuring that women's skills and experiences are utilised to the full. Concern about the under-representation of women on boards can be about business performance as much as fairness. There is a consensus that an effective challenge function within a board is required in financial institutions, and that diversity on boards can promote such challenge. While it is impossible to know whether more female board members would have lessened the impact of the financial crisis, the arguments for fairness, improved corporate governance, a stronger challenge function and not wasting a large proportion of talent seem more than sufficient to conclude that increased gender diversity is desirable.*

The European Commission also recently published a report emphasizing that women in senior positions are the key to economic stability and growth. It suggests that the persistent gender gap has developed from differing perceptions of the roles of men and women in life and work. However, the transformation in attitude and culture necessary to support change seems to be slow in the corporate world, and it can be difficult to change the status quo.

So how do organizations move to changing attitudes and perceptions? There are many methods of promoting the advancement of women, such as training opportunities, flexible working, networks, role models and mentors. However, more quantitative methods can also be used – in Norway, for example, quotas were introduced for the number of female directors of listed companies in 2005 because there was a perception that male-oriented boards did not effectively represent companies themselves or the markets they operated in. However, does this quota-based approach result in leadership roles as a 'right' for women rather than being the result of evidenced competence? The case of the public downfall of Lehman Brothers' female chief financial officer is attributed to the company's aggressive HR strategy to improve the representation of women, sexual orientation and ethnic groups; it was found that she did not have the requisite qualifications for the role. On the other hand, the CEO of PepsiCo highlights her hard work and determination in becoming a prominent woman in corporate America without the assistance of quotas.

Stop! What action might HR professionals take to develop a fair and diverse approach to promoting employees to senior leadership roles? What advice would you give organizations about the use of quotas to increase diversity at senior levels?

References and further reading: See HM Treasury Committee (2010) and Hofman and Hofman (2010).

Note: This feature was written by Lois Farquharson at Edinburgh Napier University.

p. 34). Case study analysis has highlighted the problematic nature of strategic choice model-building. A study of HRM in multidivisional companies, for example, found that HR strategy is determined by decisions at all three levels and by the ability and leadership style of local managers to follow through goals in the context of specific environmental conditions (Purcell and Ahlstrand, 1994). It is argued, therefore, that the strategic choice perspective might exaggerate the 'choice' in 'strategic choice' – the ability of managers to make strategic decisions independent of the market and the national settings in which they do business. In other words, the extent to which managers have 'choice' is 'variable' in different market society settings (Boxall and Purcell, 2003; Hyman, 1999; Paauwe and Boselie, 2003).

Another part of the SHRM debate has focused on the integration or 'external fit' of business strategy with HR strategy. This call for the HR function to be 'strategically integrated' is depicted in Beer et al.'s (1984) model of HRM. The authors espoused the need to establish a close two-way relationship or 'fit' between the external business strategy and the elements of the internal HR strategy: 'An organization's HRM policies and practices must fit with its strategy in its competitive environment and with the immediate business conditions that it faces' (Beer et al., 1984, p. 25). The concept of integration has three aspects:

- Linking of HR policies and practices with the strategic management process of the organization
- A need for line managers to internalize the importance of HR
- Integration of the workforce into the organization to foster commitment to or an 'identity of interest' with the strategic goals.

Not surprisingly, this approach to SHRM has been referred to as the 'matching' model.

The matching model

Early interest in the 'matching' model was evident in Devanna et al.'s (1984, p. 37) work: 'HR systems and organizational structure should be managed in a way that is congruent with organizational strategy.' This is similar to Chandler's (1962) often-quoted maxim that 'structure follows strategy'.

The notion of congruence or 'fit' between an external competitive strategy and an internal HR strategy is a central tenet of Beer et al.'s (1984) HRM model. Beer and his colleagues emphasize the need to analyse the linkages between the two strategies and how each strategy provides goals and constraints for the other. In their words, there must be a 'fit between competitive strategy and internal HRM strategy and a fit among the elements of the HRM strategy' (1984, p. 13). In the case of a subsidiary discount leisure airline (Jang, 2011), for example, consistent with the 'matching' or 'fit' model of HRM, the airline would need to create a low-cost structure of employment relations, which would be quite different from that of the parent airline company. The two distinctive business models would therefore create two systems of employee relations: the 'high road' and the 'low road' (Harvey and Turnbull, 2010).

The relationship between business strategy and HR strategy is said to be 'reactive' in the sense that HR strategy is subservient to 'product market logic' and corporate strategy; the latter is assumed to be the independent variable. As an observer put it, 'HRM cannot be conceptualized as a stand-alone corporate issue ... it must flow from and be dependent upon the organization's (market oriented) corporate strategy' (Miller, 1987, cited in Boxall,

1992, p. 66). There is some theorization of the link between product markets and approaches to people management. Thus, for example, each of the Porterian 'generic strategies' described earlier in the chapter involves a unique set of responses from workers and a particular HR strategy designed to develop and reinforce a unique pattern of expected behaviour. HRM is therefore seen to be 'strategic' by virtue of its 'fit' with business strategy and its internal consistency (see, for example, Boxall and Purcell, 2003; Schuler and Jackson, 1987).

Human resources strategy models

This section examines the link between corporate strategy and HR strategy. 'HR strategies' are here taken to mean the patterns of decisions regarding HR policies and practices that are used by management to design work and select, train, develop, appraise, motivate and control workers.

Researchers have studied HR strategies using the notion of typologies. By using conceptual frameworks or typologies, academics are able to compare and contrast different configurations or clusters of HR practices and further develop and test theories. This method of analysis is a derivative of Max Weber's (1903–1917/1949) methodological canon called 'ideal type' (see Chapter 1). Weber built his influential theory of bureaucracy, for example, through the use of an abstraction or ideal type. The function of the ideal type is to act as a comparison with complex social realities in order to establish their divergences or similarities, to describe them, and to understand and explain them causally. An ideal type is not a description of reality, nor is it an average of something, or a normative exemplar to be achieved: ideal types are logical hypothetical constructs (Bratton et al., 2009). The same is true of HR typologies – they are hypothetical constructs that do not necessarily exist in the workplace, but they simplify the multiple complexes of organizational life and help us to understand the nature of HR strategies.

Since the early 1990s, three models for differentiating between 'ideal types' of HR strategy have been proposed: the *control-based model*, the *resource-based model* and the *integrative* model, which combines the first two typologies.

The control-based model

This approach to modelling different types of HR strategy focuses on the complex hierarchy of managers and subordinates and control imperatives, and more specifically on managerial action to direct and monitor subordinates' role performance. According to this perspective, management structures, processes and HR strategy are instruments and techniques to control all aspects of work in order to secure a high level of labour productivity. This focus on monitoring and controlling employee behaviour as a basis for distinguishing different HR strategies has its roots in the labour process theory, a research programme inspired by Harry Braverman's (1974) *Labor and Monopoly Capital*. Adopting a Marxist framework of analysis, Braverman argued that managerial control, primarily through the application of scientific management techniques and controls embodied in machinery, had tightened in the twentieth century.

In the discourses of control strategies, the core premise is that labour's input is indeterminate. This assertion is derived from Marx's analysis of the capitalist labour process and what he referred to as the 'transformation of labour power into labour'. Put simply, when employers hire people, they have only a *potential* or a capacity to work. To ensure that each worker exercises her or his full capacity, the employer or agent (the manager) must organize the tasks, space, movement and time within which workers operate. Workers, however, have divergent interests in terms of pace of work, rewards and job security, and engage in formal (trade unions) and informal (restrictions of output or sabotage) behaviours to counteract management job controls.

Since the late 1970s, critical workplace scholars have sought to unmask the formal realms of workplace employment relations and conflict to explore the dynamics of managerial control, consent and workers' resistance at the point of production (Thompson and Smith, 2010). They have argued that, as a set of processes and practices that regulates work and people, control strategies bear the imprint of conflicting interests between the employer and employee, a conflict that reflects the nature of the capitalist employment relationship. In an insightful review of managerial control strategies and techniques, Thompson and McHugh state that 'control is not an end in itself, but a means to transform the capacity to work established by the wage relation into profitable production' (2009, p. 105).

What alternative HR strategies have managers used to render employees' behaviour measurable and controllable? Using the core premise of indeterminacy as a framing device to guide their enquiry, researchers have identified several alternative HR strategies. Friedman (1977) articulated the control orientation through the idea of *direct control* and *responsible autonomy*. These contrasting HR strategies reflect differing logics of control depending upon the nature of the product and the labour markets. Edwards (1979) identified dominant modes of control that reflect changing competitive conditions and worker resistance. An early system of individual control by employers exercising direct supervision was replaced by more complex structural forms of control: bureaucratic and technical. Bureaucratic control includes written rules and procedures covering work. Technical control includes machinery or systems – assembly line, surveillance cameras – that set the pace of work or monitor workers' performance. Edwards also argued that managers use a 'divide and rule' strategy, using gender and race, to foster managerial control. Burawoy (1979), another critical workplace scholar, categorized the development of HR strategies in terms of the transition from despotic to hegemonic regimes. The former were dominated by coercive manager–subordinate relations; the latter provided an 'industrial citizenship' that regulated employment relations through grievance and bargaining processes. The growth of employment in new call centres has recently given rise to a renewed focus of interest in the use of technical control systems: the electronic surveillance of the operator's role performance (Callaghan and Thompson, 2001).

The choice of HR strategy is governed by variations in organizational form (for example, size, structure and history), competitive pressures on management and the stability of labour markets, mediated by the interplay between superordinate and subordinate relations, the transmitter and the recipient of the control strategies involved, and resistance on the part of subordinates (Thompson and McHugh, 2009). Moreover, the variations in HR strategy are not random but reflect two management logics (Bamberger and Meshoulam, 2000). The first is the logic of direct, process-based control, in which the focus is on efficiency and cost containment (managers needing within this domain to monitor and control workers' performance carefully). The second is the logic of indirect outcomes-based control, in which the focus is on actual results (within this domain, managers need to engage workers' intellectual capital, commitment and cooperation). Thus, when managing people, control and cooperation coexist, and the extent to which there is any ebb and flow in intensity and direction between types of control will depend upon the 'multiple constituents' of the management process.

Implicit in this analysis of management control is that the logic underlying an HR strategy will tend to be consistent with an organization's competitive strategy. We are thus unlikely to find organizations adopting a Porterian cost-leadership strategy with an HR strategy grounded in an outcomes-based logic. Managers will tend to adopt process-based controls when means–ends relations are certain (as is typically the case among firms adopting a cost leadership strategy), and outcomes-based controls when means–ends are uncertain (for example, differentiation strategy). These management logics result in different organizational designs and variations in HR strategy, which provide the source of inevitable structural tensions between management and employees. In the British sociology of work literature, therefore, it is contended that HR strategies contain inherent contradictions.

reflective question

Thinking about your own experience, how have managers attempted to control you? Was each task closely monitored, or was the focus on actual outcome? What do you think of the argument that each type of competitive strategy requires a different HR strategy? Again, based on your experience, to what extent were different types of control mechanism related to the organization's product or service?

The resource-based model

The genesis of the RBM can be traced back to Selznick (1957), who suggested that companies possess 'distinctive competence' that enables them to outperform their competitors, and to Penrose (1959), who conceptualized the firm as a 'collection of productive resources'. She distinguished between 'physical' and 'human' resources, and drew attention to issues of learning, including the knowledge and experience of the management team. Penrose further emphasized what many organizational theorists take for granted – that organizations are a crucible of diversity. More than 20 years ago, Barney (1991) argued that '*sustained* competitive advantage' (emphasis added) is achieved not through an analysis of a company's external market position, but through a careful analysis of its skills and capabilities, characteristics that competitors find themselves unable to imitate. Barney identified four characteristics of resources and capabilities – value, rarity, inimitability and non-substitutability – as being important for sustainable advantage. When advanced technology is readily available to competing companies, Cappelli and Singh's (1992) argument is that the sum of people's knowledge and expertise, as well as the social networks that ensure reliable labour, has the potential to provide non-substitutable capabilities that serve as a source of competitive advantage or superior services.

HRM web links

An increasing number of US companies are establishing 'corporate' universities to help to build 'core' competencies. Examples of US corporate universities are Intel University (www.intel.com/lifeatintel/lifework/index.htm) and Motorola University (www.motorola.com/motorolauniversity.jsp).

The RBM impulse underscores the importance of a learning culture in the workplace (Foley, 2001; Rebelo and Gomes, 2011). Reflecting this orientation, 'organic' organizational structures, in terms of utilizing employees' capabilities, flexibility, communications and shared responsibility, are associated with culture-oriented learning (Rebelo and Gomes, 2011). We should note that training, the main form of interface between HRM and environmental management – the management of the interaction and impact of human societies on the ecosystem (Jabbour et al., 2010) – is insufficient to promote a learning culture. In fact, Rebelo and Gomes (2011, p. 187) state that 'many training programs did not involve leadership and the promotion of a culture stimulating the transfer and application of newly acquired knowledge in the workplace'. Studies, however, have empirically demonstrated how, all other things being equal, distinctive internal organizational capabilities forming high-performance work systems may potentially account for differences in labour productivity (Guthrie et al., 2009), export performance (Martín-Tapia et al., 2009), product innovation (Wei et al., 2011) and the organization's financial performance (Wei and Lau, 2010).

Jacoby's (2005) engagement in the debate is insightful in that he asserts that investment in competency-building varies between employers depending on whether or not senior management are insulated from shareholder pressure demanding a short-term growth in shareholder value. The more that top managers are insulated from shareholder pressure, the higher the likelihood that they will invest in the resource-based approach to HRM. Putting it in terms of a simple SWOT analysis, this approach calls attention to the strategic importance of harnessing internal 'strengths' and neutralizing internal 'weaknesses' (Barney, 1991). The RBM has been around for over 20 years, during which time it has been both widely adopted in the SHRM discourse and subjected to considerable criticism (Paauwe and Boselie, 2003). The notion of value inherent in the RBM and the fact that the idiosyncratic nature of the resource value is further shaped by the specific institutional context of a particular organization has been subject to broad and effective criticism (Kraaijenbrink et al., 2010). Figure 2.5 summarises the relationship between resources and capabilities, strategies and sustained competitive advantage.

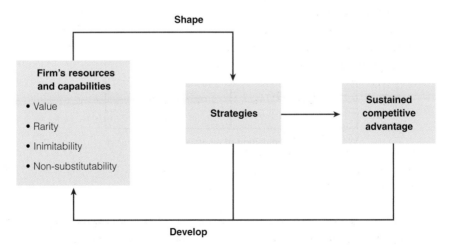

Figure 2.5 *The relationship between resources and capabilities, strategies and sustained competitive advantage*

reflective question Based upon your own work experience, or upon your studies of organizations, is continuous learning in the workplace more or less important for some organizations than others? If so, why?

An integrative model of human resources strategy

Bamberger and Meshoulam (2000) have attempted to synthesize elements of both the control and the RBM, believing that HR strategy must be explained in terms of a framework that encompasses the ebb and flow of the intensity and direction of HR strategy. They have built a model that characterizes the two main dimensions of HR strategy as involving 'acquisition and development' and 'locus of control'.

Acquisition and development is concerned with the extent to which the HR strategy develops internal human capital, as opposed to the external recruitment of human capital. It therefore develops a psychological contract that nurtures social relationships and encourages mutual trust and respect (Rousseau, 1995). Thus, organizations can lean more towards 'making' their workers (by a high investment in training) or more towards 'buying' their workers from the external labour market. They call this the 'make-or-buy' aspect of HR strategy.

Locus of control is concerned with the degree to which HR strategy focuses on monitoring employees' compliance with process-based standards. The focus here is on controlling the outcomes (the ends) themselves. This strand of thinking in HR strategy can be traced back to the ideas of Walton (1985), who made a distinction between commitment and control strategies (Hutchinson et al., 2000). As Figure 2.6 shows, these two main dimensions of HR strategy yield four different 'ideal types' of dominant HR strategy: *commitment, traditional, collaborative* and *paternalistic*.

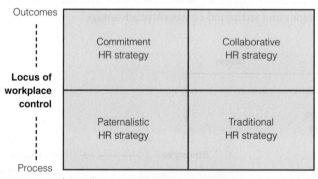

Figure 2.6 *Categorizing HRM strategies*
Source: Based on Bamberger and Meshoulam (2000)

The *commitment* HR strategy is characterized as focusing on the internal development of employees' competencies and on outcome control. In contrast, the *traditional* HR strategy focuses on the external recruitment of competencies and on behavioural or process-based controls. The *collaborative* HR strategy involves the organization subcontracting work to external independent experts (for example, consultants or contractors);

this provides for greater autonomy and performance evaluation primarily by measurement of the end results. The *paternalistic* HR strategy offers learning opportunities and internal promotion to employees in return for their compliance with process-based control mechanisms. Each HR strategy represents a distinctive HR paradigm, or set of beliefs, values and core assumptions, that guides managers' actions. Similar four-cell grids have been developed by Lepak and Snell (1999). It is reported that the HR strategies in the diagonal quadrants 'commitment' and 'traditional' are likely to be the most prevalent in contemporary North American workplaces (Bamberger and Meshoulam, 2000).

In summary, research affirms that an organization's HR strategy is strongly related to its competitive strategy. So, for example, the traditional HR strategy (the bottom right quadrant in Figure 2.6) is most likely to be adopted by management when there is certainty over how inputs are transformed into outcomes and/or when employee performance can be closely monitored or appraised. This dominant HR strategy is more prevalent in firms with a highly routinized transformation process, low-cost priority and stable competitive environment. Under such conditions, managers use technology to control the uncertainty inherent in the labour process and insist only that workers enact the specified core standards of behaviour required to facilitate undisrupted production. Managerial behaviour in such workplaces can be summed up by the managerial edict 'You are here to work, not to think!' Implied by this approach is a focus on process-based control in which 'close monitoring by supervisors and efficiency wages ensures adequate work effort' (MacDuffie, 1995, quoted by Bamberger and Meshoulam, 2000, p. 60). The use of the word 'traditional' to classify this HR strategy and the use of a technological 'fix' to control employees should, however, not be viewed as a strategy only of 'industrial' worksites. Case study research on call centres, workplaces that some organizational theorists label 'post-industrial', reveal systems of technical and bureaucratic control that closely monitor and evaluate their operators (Sewell, 1998; Thompson and McHugh, 2009).

The other dominant HR strategy, the *commitment* HR strategy (the top left quadrant in Figure 2.6), is most likely to be found in workplaces in which management lacks a full knowledge of all aspects of the labour process and/or the ability to monitor closely or evaluate the efficacy of the worker's contribution to the final product or service (as seen, for example, with R&D and healthcare professionals). This typically refers to 'knowledge work'.

©istockphoto.com/kristian sekulic

A teacher is one example of a knowledge worker.

In such organizational contexts, managers must rely on subordinates to cope with the uncertainties inherent in the labour process and can thus only monitor and evaluate the final outcomes. This HR strategy is associated with a set of HR practices that aim to develop highly committed and flexible people, internal markets that reward commitment with promotion and a degree of job security, and a 'participative' leadership style that forges a commonality of interest and mobilizes consent to the organization's goals (Hutchinson et al., 2000).

As others have noted, workers experiencing such a work regime and HR strategy do not always need to be overtly controlled because they effectively 'control themselves' (Bratton, 1992; Thompson and McHugh, 2009). To develop cooperation and common interests, an effort–reward exchange based upon investment in learning, internal promotion and internal equity is typically used (Bamberger and Meshoulam, 2000). In addition, such organizations 'mobilize' employee consent through culture strategies, including the popular notion of the 'learning organization'. As one of us has argued elsewhere:

For organizational controllers, workplace learning provides a compelling ideology in the twenty-first century, with an attractive metaphor for mobilizing worker commitment and sustainable competitiveness ... [And] the learning organization paradigm can be construed as a more subtle way of shaping workers' beliefs and values and behaviour. (Bratton, 2001, p. 341)

Critiquing SHRM and models of human resources strategy

In the last decade, the discourse of SHRM and HR strategy has been 'problematized'. Existing conceptualizations of SHRM are based upon the mainstream rational perspective of managerial decision-making – definable and coherent acts of linear planning, choice and action. Critical workplace scholars have challenged these core assumptions, arguing that strategic decisions are not necessarily the outcome of rational calculation. The assumption that a firm's business-level strategy and HR system have a logical, linear relationship is questionable given the evidence that strategy formulation is informal, politically charged and subject to complex contingency factors, and that key decision-makers often lack information, time and 'cognitive capacity' (Bamberger and Meshoulam, 2000; Mintzberg et al., 1998; Monks and McMackin, 2001; Whittington, 1993). As such, the notion of consciously aligning business strategy and HR strategy applies only to the 'classical' approach to strategy (Legge, 2005). Those who question the classical textbook account of strategic management argue that the image of the corporate manager as a reflective planner and strategist is a myth. Management's strategic actions are more likely to be uncoordinated, frenetic, ad hoc and fragmented (see, for example, Hales, 1986).

Another area of critique is the focus on the connection between external market strategies and the HR function. It is argued that contingency analysis relies exclusively on external marketing strategies (how the firm competes) and disregards the internal operational strategies (how the firm is managed) that influence HR practices and performance (Purcell, 1999). Work motivation and commitment are, as ever, central to managing employment relations, but strategizing 'best fit' disregards 'employee interests'. In coping with internal contradictions, the organization not only has to fit HR practices to competitive strategy, but must also integrate business and employee needs (Boxall and Purcell, 2003). In an industry in which a flexible, customized product range and high quality are the key to profitability, a firm can adopt a manufacturing strategy that, via 'high-performance work systems', allows for far fewer employees but within a commitment HR strategy regime. This was the strategy at Flowpak Engineering (Bratton, 1992). In this particular case, the technology and manufacturing strategy became the key intervening variable between the overall business strategy and the HR strategy. Furthermore, a simple SHRM model privileges only one step in the full circuit of industrial capital (Kelly, 1985). To put it another way, conceptions of SHRM look only at the realization of profitability within product markets rather than at the complex contingent variables that constitute the full transformation process.

Within the context of current economic globalization, we also need to view competitive posture as 'multidimensional', with resilient companies being agile at cost leadership and differentiation (Boxall and Purcell, 2003; Purcell, 1999). Furthermore, the sheer size of global markets and the rate of technological obsolescence encourage 'strategic alliances' between rival giants of industry, and between multinational corporations and complementary business partnerships (Hoogvelt, 2001), that can result in an unpredictable variety of control strategies not only between, but also within, organizations (Storey, 1983). In such contexts, managing people is less likely to be based on aligning HR practices to, in Porter's terminology, a 'single strategy' (Boxall and Purcell, 2003).

Social systems are inevitably open and frequently complex and messy (Sayer, 2000). In order to make sense of managerial actions, researchers have to rely on the abstraction and careful conceptualization of multiple practices and forces. But, as Sayer argues, if researchers 'divide what is in practice indivisible, or if they conflate what are different and separable components, then problems are likely to result' (p. 19). Unfortunately, in studies of SHRM, the conceptualization of managerial control can be problematic. The basic premise of the typologies of the HR strategy approach is that a dominant HR strategy is strongly related to a specific competitive strategy. Modelling suggests that the commitment HR strategy is most likely to be adopted when managers use a generic differentiation strategy. This might be true, but the idea that a commitment HR strategy follows from a real or perceived 'added-value' competitive strategy is more difficult in practice. It is misleading to conflate managerial actions and assume that they are not influenced by the indeterminacy of the employment contract and by how to close the 'gap' between an employee's potential and actual performance level.

Reflecting on this problem, Colling (1995, p. 29) correctly emphasizes that 'added-value [differentiation] strategies do not preclude or prevent the use of managerial control over employees ... few companies are able to operationalize added-value programmes without cost-constraints and even fewer can do so for very long'. Others have acknowledged that 'It is utopian to think that control can be completely surrendered' in the 'postmodern' work organization (Cloke and Goldsmith, 2002, p. 162).

Consistent with our focus on paradox, management's decisions and actions create potential 'strategic tensions' (Boxall and Purcell, 2003; Thompson and McHugh, 2009; Watson, 1999). Thus, one strategic decision and action might undermine another strategic goal. Acceding to the imperatives of a global free market, there is, for example, a tendency in a recession for corporate management to strive for profits by mass redundancies – so-called 'downsizing' – and by applying more intensive performance outcomes to those remaining at unit level. This pattern of action constitutes a strategy even though it manifests a disjunction between organizational design and employment relations. As Purcell (1989, 1995) points out, an organization pursuing a strategy of acquisition and downsizing might 'logically' adopt an HR strategy that includes the compulsory lay-off of non-core employees and, for the identifiable core of employees with rare attributes, a compensation system based on performance results. In practice, the resource-based approach predicts a sharp differentiation within organizations 'between those with key competencies, knowledge and valued organizational memory, and those more easily replaced or disposed of' (Purcell, 1999, p. 36). In such a case, the business strategy and HR strategy might 'fit', but, as Legge (2005, p. 128) points out, these HR practices are unlikely to engender employee commitment and will cause a misfit with 'soft' HRM values. Thus, achieving the goal of 'external fit' of business and HR strategy can contradict the goal of employee commitment and cooperation.

The 'best-fit' metaphor for SHRM contends that HR strategy is more effective when it is premeditated to fit specific contingencies in the organization's competitive or political context. It is important to emphasize that, however committed a group of managers might be to a particular HR strategy (for example, the commitment HR strategy), there are external conditions and internal 'structural contradictions' at work that will constrain management action (Boxall and Purcell, 2003; Streeck, 1987). All organizations are embedded in national cultures, and HR strategy will therefore be shaped by economic, technological, political and social factors. The kind of analysis explored here is nicely summed up by Hyman's pessimistic pronouncement that 'there is no "one best way" of managing these contradictions, only different routes to partial failure' (1987, quoted in Thompson and McHugh, 2009, p. 110). But reflecting on the SHRM discourse, whatever insights the different perspectives afford into the strategic management process, critical perspectives articulate that, as is the case with 'charismatic leadership', 'strategic' is no longer fashionable in management thought and discourse, having gone from 'buzzword to boo-word' (Bratton et al., 2009; Thompson and McHugh, 2009, p. 113).

case study

Setting

During the last decade, the wine industry has emerged as an important economic driver for South Africa. According to the South African Wine Industry Information and Systems, the wine industry adds 26.2 billion Rand (US$3.3 billion) to that country's gross domestic product every year. However, growth of this vital industry has raised concerns. Conservationists are worried that some of the region's most vulnerable natural habitats could be targeted in the quest for vineyard expansion.

Located in the Cape Province of South Africa, the Cape Floral Kingdom is one of these areas. As one of the richest plant areas on earth, it has earned international recognition as a global biodiversity hotspot and was recently established as South Africa's newest World Heritage Site. It is also where approximately 90 per cent of South Africa's wine production occurs. Following an initial study by the Botanical Society of South Africa and Conservation International, the wine industry and the conservation sector embarked on a pioneering partnership to conserve the rich biodiversity of the Cape Floral Kingdom. The programme they created, called the Biodiversity and Wine Initiative (BWI), aims to:

- Prevent further loss of habitat in critical conservation priority sites
- Increase the total area set aside as natural habitat in contractual protected areas
- Promote changes in farming practices that enhance the suitability of vineyards as a habitat for biodiversity and reduce farming practices that have negative impacts on biodiversity, both in the vineyards and in the surrounding natural habitat, through the sound management of all natural resources and the maintenance of functioning ecosystems.

Since 80 per cent of the Cape Floral Kingdom is privately owned, landowner participation in conservation efforts is essential. The BWI lays out specific criteria for wine producers to participate in the programme. The producers must have at least two hectares of natural or restored natural area on the farm that can be conserved, and new vineyards must not be developed in these areas. In addition, they must be registered with the Integrated Production of Wine scheme, which will require compliance with industry-prescribed environmental responsibilities. Although producers might not have

The Cape Floral Kingdom in the Cape Province of South Africa is one of the richest plant areas on earth.

implemented all of the required management techniques for retaining biodiversity (such as alien clearing, erosion control, rehabilitation of wetlands and rivers, appropriate fire management, etc.), they must have time-based plans and schedules in place to ensure a process of continual improvement.

The problem

South Africa's wine industry employs nearly 276,000 workers, with 58 per cent of employees considered unskilled, 29 per cent semi-skilled and 13 per cent skilled. While most employees receive fair and competitive compensation, training and skills development programmes are lacking, and more than half of the wineries in South Africa do not have any dedicated HR resources.

Kamali Masaku heads up the Zuvan Winery, with vineyards that have been owned by his family for several decades. Kamali is one of the landowners in the Cape Floral Kingdom that the BWI has targeted for participation in their programme. Kamali is interested in sustainability and wants to work towards his winery meeting the BWI's criteria. He is, however, concerned that, in order to comply with the BWI's environmental standards and to continue to succeed in the highly competitive wine industry, he will need to have employees with current technical knowledge and skills related to sustainable farming practices. With nearly 65 per cent of his workers considered to be unskilled, Kamali must now make the decision either to invest in the development of their skills or to recruit qualified help from outside his current labour force, although these new employees might demand higher wages. Kamali wants to be sure that his approach to this problem meets with the new business strategy he is about to embark on, with some promise of growth for his winery to cover his expected increased costs.

Assignment

Working either alone or in a study group, prepare a report drawing on this chapter and other recommended material that addresses the following:

1 For employees to be committed to the strategy, they need to understand the business case for sustainable wine production. Why is sustainability important to Zuvan Winery, and what can Kamali do to pursue sustainability for the company's and the community's good?

2 Which HR strategy (commitment, collaborative, paternalistic or traditional) is most likely to be used currently by wine producers in South Africa and other developing countries? Explain your answer.

3 Which HR strategy would be the most effective in helping Kamali with the challenges he will face in pursuing a sustainable approach to wine production? Why?

Essential reading

Browning, V. and Edgar, F. (2004) Reactions to HRM: an employee perspective from South Africa and New Zealand. *Journal of Management and Organization*, **10**(2): 1–13.

Budhwar, P. and Yaw, D. (2001) *Human Resource Management in Developing Countries*. London: Routledge.

Grobler, P. and Warnich, S. (2005) *Human Resource Management in South Africa*. Hampshire: Thomson Learning.

Kamoche, K., Debrah, Y. A., Horwitz, F. M. and Muuka, G. N. (2004) *Managing Human Resource Management in Africa*. London: Routledge.

Kidwell, R. and Fish, A. (2007) High-performance human resource practices in Australian family businesses: preliminary evidence from the wine industry. *International Entrepreneurship and Management Journal*, **3**(1): 1–14.

For more on the Cape Floral Kingdom and the BWI, go to www.sa-westcoast.com/general/bio-diversity-wine-initiative.html.

Note: This feature was written by Lori Rilkoff, HR Manager at the City of Kamloops, BC, Canada.

www Visit the companion website at www.palgrave.com/business/bratton5 for guidelines on writing reports.

summary

◀ This chapter has examined different levels of strategic management, defining strategic management as a 'pattern of decisions and actions' undertaken by the upper echelon of the company.

◀ Strategic decisions are concerned with change and the achievement of superior performance, and they involve strategic choices. In multidivisional companies, strategy formulation takes place at three levels – corporate, business and functional – to form a hierarchy of strategic decision-making. Corporate and business-level strategies, as well as environmental pressures, dictate the choice of HR policies and practices.

◀ Strategic management plans at corporate level and business level provide the context within which HR plans are developed and implemented. These HR plans provide a map for managers to follow in order to fulfil the core responsibilities of the HR function, which involves managing employee assignments, competencies, behaviours and motivation. These prime responsibilities of the HR function constitute the 'four-task model' of HRM.

◀ When reading the descriptive and prescriptive strategic management texts, there is a great temptation to be smitten by what appears to be the linear and absolute rationality of the strategic management process. We draw attention to the more critical literature that recognizes that HR strategic options are, at any given time, partially constrained by the outcomes of corporate and business decisions, the current distribution of power within the organization and the ideological values of the key decision-makers.

◄ A core assumption underlying much of the SHRM research and literature is that each of the main types of generic competitive strategy used by organizations (for example, the cost leadership or differentiation strategy) is associated with a different approach to managing people, that is, with a different HR strategy.

◄ We critiqued here the matching model of SHRM on both conceptual and empirical grounds. It was noted that, in the globalized economy with market turbulence, the 'fit' metaphor might not be appropriate when flexibility and a need for organizations to learn more quickly than their competitors seem to be the key to sustainable competitiveness. We also emphasized how the goal of aligning a Porterian low-cost business strategy with an HRM strategy can contradict the core goal of employee commitment.

◄ The resource-based SHRM model, which places an emphasis on a company's HR endowments as a strategy for sustained competitive advantage, was outlined. In spite of the interest in workplace learning, there seems, however, little empirical evidence to suggest that many firms have adopted this 'soft' HR strategic model.

vocab checklist for ESL students

◄ acquire (v), acquisition (n)

◄ analyse (v), analysis (n), analyser (n), analytical (adj)

◄ compete (v), competition (n), competitiveness (n), competitive (adj)

◄ competencies (n), competent (adj)

◄ congruence (n), congruent (adj)

◄ consume (v), consumption (n)

◄ corporate social responsibility (CSR) (n)

◄ differentiate (v), differentiation (n), different (adj)

◄ distribute (v), distribution (n), distributive (adj)

◄ diversify (v), diversification (n), diverse (adj)

◄ efficiency (n), efficient (adj)

◄ emerge (v), emergent (adj)

◄ ethics (n), ethical (adj)

◄ evaluate (v), evaluation (n)

◄ exploit (v), exploitation (n)

◄ formulate (v), formulation (n)

◄ hegemony (n), hegemonic (adj)

◄ implement (v), implementation (n)

◄ indeterminate (v), indeterminacy (n), indeterminist (adj)

◄ integrate (v), integration (n), integrative (adj)

◄ prospect (v), prospector (n), prospective (adj)

◄ resource-based model (RBM) (n)

◄ strategize (v), strategy (n), strategist (n), strategic (adj)

◄ Strengths, Weaknesses, Opportunities, Threats (SWOT) (n)

◄ sustain (v), sustainability (n), sustainable (adj)

◄ Utopia (n), Utopian (adj)

◄ whistleblow (v), whistleblower (n), whistleblowing (n)

Visit www.palgrave.com/business/bratton5 for a link to free definitions of these terms in the Macmillan Dictionary, as well as additional learning resources for ESL students.

review questions

1 What is meant by 'strategy'? Explain the meaning of 'first-order' and 'second-order' strategies.

2 Explain Purcell's statement that 'trends in corporate strategy have the potential to render the ideals of HRM unobtainable'.

3 What is meant by a 'green' or sustainable strategy?

4 Why must successful corporate strategies be consistent with the firm's external environment and with its internal environment?

5   Explain the link between business ethics and CSR. Can CSR stop the degradation of the environment?

6   'Business-level strategies may be constrained by human resource issues but rarely seem to be designed to influence them.' Discuss.

7. What does a 'resource-based' SHRM model of competitive advantage mean? What are the implications for HRM of this business strategy?

further reading to improve your mark

Reading these articles and chapters can help you gain a better understanding and potentially a higher grade for your HRM assignment.

◀ Mainstream notions of strategy are examined in Robert Grant's (2010) *Contemporary Strategic Analysis* (7th edn). Chichester: Wiley.

The link between SHRM and an organization's survival and sustainable competitive advantage is further explored in:

◀ Peter Boxall and John Purcell (2003) *Strategy and Human Resource Management*. London: Palgrave Macmillan.

◀ Boxall, P. (2003) HR strategy and competitive advantage in the service sector. *Human Resource Management Journal*, **13**(3): 5–20.

◀ Kamoche, K. (1996) Strategic human resource management within a resource-capability view of the firm. *Journal of Management Studies*, **33**(2): 213–33.

◀ Mathew Allen and Patrick Wright (2008) Strategic management and HRM. In P. Boxall, J. Purcell and P. Wright (eds) *The Oxford Handbook of Human Resource Management* (pp. 88–107). Oxford: OUP.

◀ John Storey (2008) What is strategic HRM? In J. Storey (ed.) *Human Resource Management: A Critical Text* (3rd edn) (pp. 59–78). London: Thompson Learning.

◀ Boselie, P. (2010) *Strategic Human Resource Management: A Balanced Approach*. London: McGraw-Hill.

 Visit www.palgrave.com/business/bratton5 for for lots of extra resources to help you get to grips with this chapter, including study tips, HRM skills development guides, summary lecture notes, and more.

chapter 3

HRM and performance

objectives

After studying this chapter, you should be able to:

1 Explain the importance of measuring the human resource management (HRM) contribution

2 Describe some variables used to measure the value added of HRM

3 Understand some techniques for evaluating the HRM function

4 Critically evaluate research on the HRM–performance relationship

introduction

stablishing a strong association between strategic human resource management (SHRM) and organizational performance has become a principal area of study over the past two decades. Indeed, this research agenda has been described as the 'holy grail' of HRM. Several explanations have been offered for why the SHRM and performance causal chain has become so fashionable. By demonstrating measurable outcomes, the position of the human resources (HR) practitioner within the organization is enhanced at a time when the HR function itself is being threatened with marginalization by outsourcing and delegation to line managers. Conclusive empirical evidence of the 'bottom line' contribution of HRM also locates the subject and HRM academics in business schools on a par with faculty teaching the more quantitatively oriented subjects.

The HRM–performance debate among academics has, however, been intense and often inconclusive. Some question the conceptual and methodological soundness of the research (see, for example, Legge, 2001; Wright and Gardner, 2003). Others contend that the research is too narrowly focused on measures of economic performance at the expense of employee well-being (Delaney and Godard, 2001), making the 'performative intent' of the research an 'ill-fated project' (Delbridge and Keenoy, 2010, p. 804). Others emphasize the importance of contingencies related to context, and the importance of analysing how the 'social relations of productivity' mediates the relationship between specific HR practices and workplace performance in particular contexts (Edwards et al., 2002).

Against this backcloth, the chapter begins by examining the rationale of linking the HR function with organizational performance. As a preliminary step towards understanding the effects of HR practices on performance, the chapter also discusses a variety of conceptual and methodological concerns. The final section critically reviews the evidence suggesting a causality between SHRM and performance and, in so doing, underscores the importance of workplace context when studying the relationship between HRM and performance.

Rationale for evaluating HRM

The current debate on the effects of SHRM on organizational performance has a long academic lineage that predates the modern HRM canon. Over the last five decades, employers and business pundits have bemoaned the low productivity of British workers and usually identified various 'restrictive practices' emanating from trade union as the main culprit behind poor performance (Ahlstrand, 1990; Nichols, 1986). The 'trade unions and productivity' debate was dominant during the 1960s and 1970s, but it was conceded that the relevant causal mechanisms were far from unambiguous.

The focus shifted in the 1990s to the impact on performance that potentially derives from usage of the HRM paradigm (Edwards and Sengupta, 2010). In Beer et al.'s (1984) canonical model, HR outcomes are seen as having longer term positive effects on individual well-being, organizational effectiveness and societal well-being. The interest in the SHRM–performance nexus also mirrors enthusiasm for the concept of the 'high-performance workplace' (HPW) and the 'high-performance work system' (HPWS). It is claimed that these new work models can deliver comparative advantage because an integrated 'bundle' of HR practices will have positive, synergistic effects on performance (MacDuffie, 1995). Narrowly conceived, bundling is a design issue within an HR system, making pay consistent with the adoption of team-based working, for example (Boxall and Macky,

2009). In terms of improving performance, designing a bundle or configuration of HR practices becomes *the* issue (Betcherman et al., 1994).

The drive to measure the effects of HRM on performance was given an added fillip when management commentators advocated that the HR function should move beyond its administrative role to a strategic 'added value' role (Boxall and Purcell, 2003; Fitz-enz and Davison, 2002; Paauwe, 2004; Ulrich and Beatty, 2001). According to Phillips (1996a), the adoption of HR strategies by organizations underscores the importance of measuring the contribution of individual, team and organizational variables towards organizational performance. As Pfeffer (1994, p. 57) argues, 'In a world in which financial results are measured, a failure to measure human resource policy and practice implementation dooms this to second-class status, oversight, neglect, and potential failure.' When HR services can be supplied by external business partners and when HR practitioners are increasingly trying to collaborate with line management, it is ever more apparent that HR specialists need to be able to evaluate in financial terms the benefits of different HR strategies. This rationale is captured by Fitz-enz's (2000, p. 4) blunt statement that 'if we don't know how to measure our primary value-producing asset, we can't manage it.' However, it is acknowledged that the challenges of measuring the contribution of 'human capital' to the firm's 'bottom line' is 'sometimes subtle, occasionally mysterious, and at times very convincing' (Phillips, 1996a, p. 6). We shall explore later in this chapter whether evidence on the positive effects on performance derived from strategic HR practices is convincing.

reflective question According to Peter Drucker, 'You can't manage what you can't measure.' At a time when so many people are engaged in so-called knowledge work, how valid is this maxim when strictly applied to managing people?

Modelling HRM and performance

The causal chain underlying SHRM and performance is a difficult relationship to disentangle because of a number of challenges. Simply put, there is a gap in knowledge in *how* bundles of HR practices can impact on the HR–performance relationship (Wei and Lau, 2010). Legge (2005) poses three basic questions that help to profile the methodological problems:

- What integrated bundle or configuration of HR practices produces superior performance results?
- What performance data do we use to measure the outcomes of HR practices?
- And how do we model the causal path between HR practices and performance outcomes?

We can examine how available research, from an epistemological position known as *positivism*, addresses (or fails to address) these basic questions using Figure 3.1. This depicts the HR–performance relationship as a theoretical framework with four major parts: (1) HRM; (2) employee performance measures; (3) organizational performance measures; and (4) other factors. Within each component, there are numerous concepts related to HRM and employee and organizational performance.

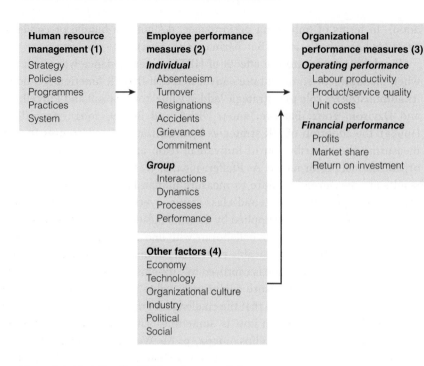

Figure 3.1 *Modelling the HRM–performance link*
Source: *Adapted from Phillips (1996a)*

Human resource management

To estimate the impact of HRM on organizational performance, the researcher has first to conceptualize HRM. Each concept has to be measured, and each can be either an independent or a dependent variable. The typical approach to HRM–performance analysis is to specify 'outcomes' – for example, absenteeism – as the dependent variable, the one to be explained, and a set of HR practices as the independent variables, the ones that have a causal impact upon absenteeism. Figure 3.1 shows that strategy, policies, programmes, practices and system of HR involved impact on employee and group performance, which in turn affect organizational performance.

Researchers typically identify a core number of HR practices that are considered to be prerequisites for the effective management of work and people across all work organizations. The debate surrounding the effects of a set of HR practices on performance can be grouped into the '*best practice*' and '*best fit*' schools. The former argues that a cluster of HR practices can be combined into a set that is applicable in a diverse range of workplaces and will boost performance; the latter posits that HR practices have to be consistent with both the internal and the external context of the organization.

Employee performance measures

The second challenge depicted in Figure 3.1 is the conceptualization and measurement of employee performance. Researchers have a number of options when it comes to measuring individual employee and group performance. Saks (2000) outlines three measurements: traits, behaviours and outcomes. For a positivist, a personal trait must be a precisely specified variable that is considered to be important in employees. A particular HR practice

© istockphoto.com/Alejandro Rivera

Poor time-keeping is an example of employee behaviour that can be observed and measured with more reliability than a trait.

may thus result in employees exhibiting key attributes, such as loyalty or commitment to the organization. Despite its popularity, making trait assessments is difficult because traits are not clearly defined entities.

In contrast, the measurement of data relating to behaviour focuses on what an employee does or does not do in the workplace. Examples include being absent from work, poor time-keeping and resigning from employment. Unlike traits, however, work-related behaviour can be observed and counted with some reliability.

The third approach is to measure outcomes, the things produced or accomplished during a specific period of time in the workplace. Outcomes can be the 'number of units completed', 'accidents' or 'customer complaints'. The advantage of using these 'intermediate' measures is the apparent objectivity involved. Whether it is commitment to the organization or absenteeism, turnover, accident or grievance rates, the problem of validity of the data and their reliability – as inconsistency will affect their generalizability – must be dealt with.

Organizational performance measures

Organizational performance, the third cluster of variables in Figure 3.1, is one of the most important constructs in HRM–performance research, but studies reveal multidimensional conceptions of this catch-all term, making it bothersome to pinpoint (Boxall and Macky, 2009). Any study analysing organizational performance must address two key issues. First is the dimensionality of performance, that is, establishing appropriate measures for the inquiry; second is the selection and combination of performance variables, that is, identifying which variables can be usefully combined and how this could be done (Richard et al., 2009). Both researchers and practitioners have tended to use relatively limited conceptualization, typically productivity ratios and financial ratios. Labour productivity, a popular measure, is usually defined as the quantity or volume of the major product or service that the organization provides and is expressed as a rate, that is, the productivity per employee or per unit of time; Huselid (1995), for example, measured productivity in terms of sales per employee. Another measure is quality, which usually refers to the attributes of the primary service or product provided by the organization. Although hard financial data are often used to measure organizational outcomes, researchers also use perceptual indicators to quantify performance. Examples include random surveys of passengers on an airline to obtain data on perceptions of the quality of the in-flight service, or healthcare sector surveys of patients to gather data on waiting times and perceptions of the quality of medical services.

Other factors

Disentangling the connection between HRM and organizational performance is further complicated by the fact that employee performance measures are only one set of variables that impact on organizational performance. Other variables, such as changes in the economy, technology, organizational culture, industry, government policies and social trends, the fourth part in Figure 3.1 above, can intercede to influence organizational performance, especially the financial measures; all this makes it highly problematic to isolate the effects of HR practices. Take, for example, sales per employee as a measure of performance. Other possible influences have to be controlled because, among other things, sales may fluctuate as a result of a sustained strengthening or weakening of a nation's currency. Further support for the 'other factors' caveat can be seen with the occurrence of catastrophic events such as the 11 September 2001 attack on the World Trade Centre, and the US subprime mortgage debacle in 2008, a crisis still reverberating in North America and Europe. These challenges underscore some major methodological and theoretical issues related to modelling the HR–performance relationship, issues we expand upon below.

reflective question Can the measurement of the HRM contribution be truly objective? How has the economic recession of 2008–12 impacted on the strategic HR–performance debate?

HRM web links Go to www.bbk.ac.uk/management for information on carrying out research on the relationship between HRM and organizational performance.

Demonstrating the HRM–performance relationship

The research agenda has focused on the search for causal relationships between clusters or bundles of best HR practices and competing performance outcomes (Arthur, 1994; Ashton and Sung, 2002; Becker and Gerhart, 1996; Betcherman et al., 1994; Boxall, 2003; Boxall and Macky, 2009; Buyens and De Vos, 2001; Delaney and Huselid, 1996; Den Hartog and Verburg, 2004; Edwards et al., 2002; Frege, 2002; Guest, 1997; Guthrie et al., 2009; Huselid, 1995; Hutchinson et al., 2000; Ichniowski et al., 1996; Konzelmann et al., 2006; Martín-Tapia et al., 2009; Paauwe and Boselie, 2003; Pfeffer, 1998; Purcell et al., 2009; Stavrou et al., 2010; Wright et al., 2003; Youndt et al., 1996) (see also HRM in practice 3.1). Establishing the validity of the hypothesized relationship between HR bundles and organizational performance is highly complex (Stavrou et al., 2010). Despite the fact that many studies have been performed, considerable ambiguity remains over the casual paths of that relationship, ranging from universalistic to contingency (Delery and Doty, 1996). In this section, we summarise the key studies to gain an understanding of the nature of the HRM–performance relationship and to assess the degree to which HR strategy may predict economic performance.

In North America, one of the earliest studies was that of Arthur (1994), who investigated the performance effects of two labour management taxonomies: 'control' (traditional personnel management) and 'commitment' (new HRM) in US mini-steel mills. His statistical regression results indicated that commitment-type HR practices were associated with both lower scrap rates (an indicator of production quality) and a significantly lower number of labour hours per ton of steel (an indicator of labour efficiency) than were control-type HRM practices. In addition, Arthur noted that integrated, and sets of, best HR practices had a greater impact than individual HR practices. Arthur's research, however, left major questions unanswered: What is the magnitude of the effect of HR strategy on economic outcomes? And how generalizable are the findings?

MacDuffie (1995) suggested that findings could be generalizable, at least to other manufacturing workplaces. MacDuffie's landmark publication found strong support for a positive relationship between commitment or high-performance HR practices and intermediate outcomes for individual workers (for example, turnover and sales) and the organization's financial outcomes (market value and profits). In fact, 'A one standard deviation increase in practices is associated with a relative 7.05 per cent decrease in (labour) turnover, and on a per employee basis, $27,044 more sales and $18,641 and $3,814 more in market value and profits, respectively' (MacDuffie, 1995, p. 667).

MacDuffie observed that 'high-performance' HR practices had two major dimensions (Table 3.1). The first dimension referred to worker skills, which included various practices to enhance workers' knowledge, skills and abilities. The second dimension referred to worker motivation, which included practices recognizing and reinforcing desirable workplace behaviours on the part of workers. The study also provided some insight into the 'best fit' theory, suggesting that although internal fit – the degree to which complementary HR practices are implemented as a cluster – does have a significant and positive effect on financial outcomes, external fit – the degree to which HR strategy is aligned with business strategy – does not (Bamberger and Meshoulam, 2000).

Table 3.1 *The two dimensions of high-performance HR practices*

Worker skills and internal processes	Employee motivation
Information-sharing	Performance appraisals to determine pay
Job analysis	Performance to determine promotion
Internal hiring	Qualified applicants per position
Regular attitude surveys	
Quality of work–life programmes	
Participation teams	
Profit-sharing	
Training	
Formal grievance procedures	
Employment tests for hiring	

Source: Huselid (1995)

Huselid's (1995) findings were replicated by Patterson's et al.'s (1997) UK study. In a later publication, Pil and MacDuffie (1996) provided further support for the 'internal fit' perspective, suggesting that when team working and complementary HR practices are introduced simultaneously, 'not only does new work practice induce an incremental improvement in performance, but so do the complementary practices' (Pil and MacDuffie, 1996, p. 428). This is shown in Figure 3.2. When a new work practice, such as self-managed work teams, is introduced, the greatest impact on performance over a period of time will occur when a complementary bundle of HR practices accompanies the new work regime – the so-called 'Huselid curve' (line B).

In another study, Delery and Doty (1996) identified seven strategic HR practices that have been linked to organizational performance: internal career opportunities, training,

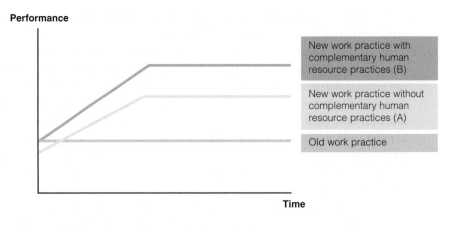

Figure 3.2 *Performance implications of complementary HR practices*
Source: Adapted from Pil and MacDuffie (1996), p. 428

results-oriented appraisals, profit-sharing, employment security, employee participation and job descriptions. They found that 'differences in HR practices are associated with rather large differences in financial performance' (Delery and Doty, 1996, p. 825). Youndt et al.'s (1996) research combined a cluster of HR practices into two indexes – labelled the 'administrative HR system' and the 'human-capital-enhancing HR system' – and found that these impacted positively on organizational performance when the HR practices were aligned with the organization's business strategy. Further evidence points to a positive association between a mix of HR practices and perceptions of organizational performance. As Delaney and Huselid (1996, p. 965) note in another study, 'progressive HRM practices, including selectivity in staffing, training, and incentive compensation, are positively related to perceptual measures of organizational performance.'

Betcherman et al. (1994) note a statistically significant association between 'new' HR practices and lower unit costs. Interestingly, the authors provide support for the idea that context is an important factor. What they call 'innovative' HR practices operate best in certain workplace 'environments'. The more intangible variables, such as 'progressive decision-making' and 'social responsibility', impacted more significantly on performance outcomes than did more tangible incentive-pay plans. Their results suggest (Betcherman et al., 1994, p. 72) that:

Innovative [HRM] practices and programs on their own are not enough to substantially improve performance. What seems more important is that they be introduced into a supportive work environment.

A study by Wright et al. (2003) found evidence that 'progressive' HR practices improve operational performance and profitability at least in part through enhanced employee commitment to the organization. Separate studies by Collings et al. (2010) and Peña and Villasalero (2010) support the contingency 'best fit' approach. In Peña and Villasalero's (2010) study of the Spanish banking sector, the relationship between HR and organizational performance was found to be moderated by the bank's business strategy: 'There is no one best way to manage human resources without considering the role of business strategy' (p. 2882).

Over the last two decades, interest in high-commitment-based HRM regimes has generated new management paradigms. This has generated a myriad of new acronyms such as HPW, HPWS, HPWP (high-performance work practice), HCM (high-commitment management) and HIWS (high-involvement work system) to refer to integrated, synergistic 'bundles' of HR practices that are said to enhance workplace performance. There is now a plethora of academic work on these variants of HPWSs (see, among others, Boxall and Macky, 2009; Danford et al., 2008; MacDuffie, 1995; Procter and Mueller, 2000; Ramsay et al., 2000). A key premise of the high-involvement workplace is that increased performance is a function of interactions between employee ability, informal learning, discretionary opportunities and multitasking. Findlay et al. (2000) found evidence that team working 'increased opportunities for creativity, responsibility and use of worker knowledge' (p. 238). They also found an 'abuse of flexibility' that caused work intensification.

The study by Konzelmann et al. (2006) argues that although securing full cooperation from employees is required if a cluster of better HR practices is to increase performance, the form of corporate governance under which managers operate might actually undermine a high-commitment-based HRM regime. Public limited companies, for instance, might have to give priority to shareholders' demands rather than employees' demands for greater consultation. The implications are profound: 'What secures positive HRM outcomes are, for workers, the quality of consultation and personnel policy [and in] securing these objectives corporate governance has an important part to play' (Konzelmann et al., 2006, p. 560).

Embedding performance

Reviewing some of the seminal studies on the HRM–performance relationship, Ichniowski et al. (1996) concluded that empirical evidence from intraindustry studies showed that high-performance work configurations and complementary bundles of HRM practices gave rise to superior output and quality performances, and that the magnitude of these performance effects was 'large'. Moreover, Ichniowski et al. (1996, p. 32, emphasis added) concluded that:

There are no one or two 'magic bullets' that are *the* work practices that will stimulate worker and business performance. Work teams or quality circles alone are not enough. Rather, *whole systems* need to be changed.

As we have already emphasized, the economy and society are part of the same set of processes, and work organizations are deeply 'embedded' in the wider national institutional environments in which they operate. This is where societal effects are most significant. The point here concerns the ways in which national institutions and culture establish a terrain on which HR strategies may have their effects. The findings from seminal US studies on the HRM–performance link may not be generalizable to a polyethnic Europe (Den Hartog and Verburg, 2004; Paauwe and Boselie, 2003). Arguably, in the post-banking crisis era, the effects of which continue to reverberate throughout the European Union, drawing attention to the need for government regulation strengthens the need for a change in HRM policies and practices.

Looking to European studies, Addison et al. (2000) demonstrated that employee involvement (EI) could be effective in increasing labour productivity and a firm's profits. Using data from Britain and Germany, Addison's et al. findings suggest that, in unionized

HR 'can lower NHS death rates'

The research focus on whether strategic HR practices can demonstrably contribute to the performance of an organization has been described as 'the HRM holy grail' (Purcell and Kinnie, 2008). In the context of changing demographics, the so-called 'grey tsunami' and rising healthcare costs, evidence of an unambiguous causal relationship between HR practices and hospital 'outcomes' would give greater legitimacy to HR professionals. UK researchers Carol Borrill and Michael West report a direct link between the quality of HR practices and patient mortality:

'The higher the levels of staff team-working, training, development and appraisals the lower the patient mortality … staff working in teams experienced higher levels of innovation and lower levels of stress.' The researchers surveyed 81 hospitals over a period of two years and gathered information on the quality of HR initiatives and on performance data. The results were consistent with an earlier teamwork survey, which found that staff working in teams experienced higher levels of innovation and lower levels of stress.

Andrew Foster, HR director for the NHS Executive, flagged up the importance of the results: 'Until now there has been no research that links current HR practices with a bottom-line output like patient mortality. This study shows a demonstrable link between HR and output in the NHS and I consider it to be the strongest weapon in my locker.' 'With a fixed budget you need an evidence-based case for investment in people issues,' Foster said.

This study is particularly interesting in that it uses outcomes different from those found in most other studies, but the method of collecting the observations needs to be carefully scrutinized. There is, for example, a tendency for researchers to rely on single indicators of outcomes, to ignore 'multiple' moderating variables, and to use performance indicators across dissimilar workplaces or departments with no regard for their appropriateness. A single hospital respondent may have incomplete knowledge of HR practices and health-related outcomes. In assessing the links between HRM and death rates, critical scrutiny would ask whether the researchers were able to control for social variables such as social class.

Stop! Why is this study considered important? What are the limitations of using a survey to gather data in order to explain the causal links between HR practices and health-related outcomes? Provide an example of variable(s) in a hospital that may cause you to question the research findings.

Many non-profit organizations have attempted to measure the effectiveness of HR practices. Why do you think they have done this? In your view, which HR interventions would be most effective in improving healthcare and why?

Sources and further information: For background information to help consider this study, see Gerhart (2008).

Note: This feature was written by John Bratton and is based on Zoe Roberts' report, 'HR can lower NHS death rates', *People Management*, October 11, 2001.

© istockphoto.com/DNY59

workplaces, the link between EI and financial performance is likely to be less clear-cut because EI arrangements reflect union power rather than a competitive response to external factors. Addison's et al. study predicts that EI in non-union regimes in Britain will yield positive economic results for the firm, but the union–EI nexus is associated with negative outcomes. Finally, the German evidence indicated that mandatory EI is associated with higher productivity in larger organizations (employing more than 100 workers) and lower productivity gains in smaller workplaces. Despite these interesting findings, the studies have limited value in demonstrating the relationship between HR strategy and performance because they examined only one HR practice and did not quantify the effect of coherent clusters of HR practices on overall organizational performance. The results therefore need to be read with some caution.

Statistical analysis can establish a causal connection between HR practices and outcome variables. Den Hartog and Verburg's (2004) study of high-performance HR practices in The Netherlands generated statistical data showing a correlation between HR practices associated with HPWSs and culture orientation. Basing their study on a questionnaire completed by senior HR managers and chief executives from 175 Dutch enterprises, the researchers noted increased commitment that resulted in Dutch workers doing more than was typically required in their contract or job description – going beyond contract – which increased economic outcomes. Importantly, work motivation was related to a specific set of HR practices fashioned to each specific context: 'The set of practices labelled "Employee skill direction" … were positively related to workers' willingness to go beyond contract and perceived economic performance of the firm and negatively to absenteeism' (Den Hartog and Verburg, 2004, pp. 74–5). Furthermore, autonomy showed a positive relationship with willingness to go beyond contract, and profit-sharing correlated positively with perceived economic performance, as did pay-for-performance. Den Hartog and Verburg found that employee skill and direction correlated positively with three out of four culture measures, especially 'innovation' and 'goal' (p. 69) (Table 3.2).

Table 3.2 *Correlations between HR practices, outcomes and cultural orientations*

	Firm performance	Beyond contract	Economic outcome	Employee turnover	Manager/ specialist turnover	Employee absenteeism	Manager/ specialist absenteeism	Supportive	Innovative	Rules	Goal
Employee skill/direction	.12	.31 **	.25 **	−.15	.03	−.20 **	−.24 **	.23 **	.41 **	.15	.42 **
Autonomy	.04	.27 **	.09	−.10	.02	−.04	−.05	.15	.06	−.30 **	.08
Reward	−.02	.10	.22 **	.11	−.02	−.09	−.19 **	.09	.21 **	−.03	.33 **
Profit-sharing	.07	.06	.17 *	−.08	−.03	.06	−.08	.00	.18	.01	.27 **
Performance evaluation	.03	.13	.15	−.15	−.17 *	.03	.12	.08	.16 *	.04	.11
Team performance	−.02	.14	.07	.02	−.08	−.10	−.04	.12	.12	−.05	.22 **
Information-sharing	−.02	.08	.01	−.17 *	−.02	−.14	−.01	.01	.04	.02	.06
Job evaluation	.14	−.02	.13	−.03	.09	−.03	−.10	.06	.21 **	.10	.11

Note: *p < .05; ** p < .01 (two-tailed)
Source: Adapted from Den Hartog and Verburg (2004), p. 69

HRM web links www Go to the 2005 Workplace Employee Relations Survey website www.dti.gov.uk/
employment/research-evaluation/grants/wers/index.html for more examples of
statistical techniques used to compute the mean differences and measures of
association between variables.

Den Hartog and Verburg's (2004) quantitative study demonstrated that national social institutions may moderate the effect of bundles of HR practices on an organization's performance. It emphasized the importance of the context in which companies and HRM systems operated. In The Netherlands, the employment relationship is highly regulated, trade union density and involvement is more extensive, unlike, for example, the situation in the USA, and Dutch labour laws ensure employee participation in workplace decision-making. Thus, the idea of a Dutch firm adopting a universal cluster of best HR practices to gain a competitive advantage is more problematic because these firms have less leeway to distinguish themselves from their competitive rivals. Although Dutch laws set the boundaries, the study provides evidence that managers can, within these boundaries, design HR practices to suit the specific needs of their organization. Moreover, a combination of HR practices with an emphasis on employee development, the strict selection of employees and an overarching philosophy in terms of HR strategy had significant positive effects on organizational performance. The authors, however, acknowledged that future research should focus more on hard economic data rather than on managers' 'perceptions' of performance, and should include data on workers' outcomes and voices.

Buyens and De Vos (2001) conducted a qualitative study to measure the added value of the HR function as perceived by managers in Belgian organizations. The study aimed to investigate how the value of the HR function was perceived by three groups of managers – top managers, HR managers and line managers – within the sample of 256 organizations. Qualitative data were gathered through interviews, focus groups and a questionnaire. The researchers found that, for top managers, the HR function added value through its change programmes following restructuring and downsizing. HR managers, on the other hand, most frequently mentioned 'management of the employee' as the area in which the HR function delivered value to the organization. The findings suggested that line managers had 'a rather traditional view of the HR function' (p. 81) because a majority most frequently mentioned functional HR activities such as selection and training as the domain in which the HR function added value. The authors acknowledged that the data were 'highly subjective in nature' and that the findings might be contingent on other factors such as size or industry. Another limitation of the study was the failure to quantify the magnitude of the value added by the HR function.

reflective question What are the strengths and weaknesses of using workplace surveys as a method for
collecting data to estimate the causal links between SHRM and performance?

Questioning research on the HRM–performance relationship

Demonstrable effects of HRM on organizational performance were summarised by Gerhart (2008), who wrote that 'the 20 per cent effect of HR on firm performance (for an increase in

1 standard deviation in HR practices) … once corrected … implies that the high firms have … 4.5 times higher performance' (p. 558). The size of the effect is so significant as to perhaps not be credible, comments the author. As some have argued, 15 or more years of extensive research have provided evidence of only a positive association, rather than causation. The research is 'riddled with error both with respect to data on HRM and on outcomes', writes Guest (2011, p. 10). The project to provide an evidence base for the hypothesized connections between HRM and organizational performance has received extensive criticism. Wright and Gardner (2003, p. 312) provide a bluntly critical assessment:

Methodologically, there is no consensus regarding which practices constitute a theoretical complete set of HR practices; how to conceptually categorize these practices; the relevance to business strategy; the appropriate level of analysis; or how HR-performance and firm performance are to be measured … Theoretically, no consensus exists regarding the mechanism by which HR practices might impact on firm outcomes.

Ultimately, there are two kinds of critique that have been made: those dealing with *research design* challenges, and those concerned with *causality*. A variety of research designs is used to study the workplace. In deductive theory construction and hypothesis-testing, designing a study to test the HRM–performance relationship involves specifying precisely *what* HR practices and performance indicators are to be measured, at what *level* (individual, establishment or corporate), and *how*. Explaining the process or mechanism by which a particular set of HR practices might enhance organizational performance comes down to understanding the logic of causation in social research. It is this process of theory-building and the systematic gathering of data that is said to define analytical HRM (Boxall et al., 2008).

Research design issues

Research design issues have been concerned with several aspects: (1) the conceptualization and scope of HR practices that constitute a theoretically coherent set of practices, (2) the appropriate level of analysis, (3) the conceptual construction and measurement of performance, and (4) the mode of data collection.

HR practices: concept, level and measurement

We introduced some of the research design issues when explaining Figure 3.1 above. For a positivist, there cannot be a meaningful study of the HRM–performance relationship, let alone agreement on causality, without precisely specifying the *HR practices* or variables. The researcher, on the basis of theory-derived considerations, has therefore first to specify what HR practices are to be studied and devise measures of these practices, a process referred to as *operationalization*. Conceptualization, then, should produce a specific, agreed-upon meaning for HR practice or a combination of practices for the purpose of the research.

There are a number of challenges in selecting the HR practices used in the analysis. First, there is no agreement on what constitutes core 'HR practices', and ambiguity surrounds which appropriate bundles, clusters or sets of practices have a positive effect on organizational performance. Whereas US academic Jeffrey Pfeffer (1994, 1998) identified 16 'best practices' in successful organizations, later consolidated into seven HR practices 'for building profits', European academics Den Hartog and Verburg (2004) isolated eight HR practices to test the HR–performance relationship (Table 3.3).

Table 3.3 Selective HR practices for enhanced performance according to Pfeffer and Den Hartog and Verburg

Pfeffer's (1998) seven practices	Den Hartog and Verburg's (2004) eight practices
1. Employment security	1. Employment skills
2. Selective hiring	2. Autonomy
3. Self-managed work teams	3. Pay-for-performance
4. High pay contingent on company performance	4. Profit-sharing
5. Extensive training	5. Performance appraisal
6. Reduction of differences in status	6. Team performance
7. Sharing of information	7. Information-sharing
	8. Job evaluation

The debate on what actually constitutes 'HR practice' echoes the early debate found in Storey's (1989) seminal text on whether 'HRM and personnel management are in fact so different', which noted 'the elasticity in the meaning of the term "human resource management"' (pp. 5–8). Twenty-three years on, the literature does not show an unambiguous conceptual agreement over what constitutes HRM (Purcell et al., 2009). Typically, studies report the mean number of HR practices per establishment, with some giving a mean as high as 6.9 (Bryson et al., 2007). Critical scrutiny of the findings, however, identifies only the general presence of HR practices (Purcell et al., 2009), and does not offer insights into the coverage of employees experiencing those practices. Findings do not always specify whether organizations use either individual or multiple HR practices for specific categories of employee. It is noteworthy that Wright et al.'s (2003, p. 32) results were based on data garnered from employees:

Using employees as the source of the HR practice measures ensures that the measure represents the *actual* practices rather than the espoused policies of the businesses.

A core theme in early industrial relations research is that managing employment relations involves choices between alternatives, resulting in different management styles and personnel practices for different categories of employee (Edwards, 1979; Fox, 1974; Friedman, 1977; Gospel and Littler, 1983). Those in lower positions in the organizational hierarchy are more likely to experience routine, relatively boring work and receive higher pay contingent on their performance. Managers and professional employees, on the other hand, tend to have decision-making powers and a high-trust relationship with their superiors, and are more likely to experience performance appraisal practices. The industrial relations literature shows general structural tendencies within which employees or groups of employees each have their own experience of work and HR practices. The choice and effectiveness of HR practices therefore depends on the coverage of the practices for particular employee groups, an important issue in the debate we examine below.

In research into the HRM–performance relationship, there are differences in terms of who or what should be studied, that is, the *unit of analysis*. In workplace research, the most typical units of analysis are individual employees, groups or teams, and organizations. Micro studies focus on the individual or work group, whereas the focal point in macro studies may be a corporation or a public sector establishment (Wright and Boswell, 2002). Although studies into the effects of a singular HR practice have been conducted on an individual's psychological contract (see, for example, Guest, 1998; Rousseau, 1995), the efficacy of recruitment and selection practices (Terpstra and Rozelle, 1993), rewards (McNabb and Whitfield, 1997) and training (Kalleberg and Moody, 1994), the researchers' emphasis has been on the effects of *multiple* or 'bundles' of HR practices at the organizational level, and various questions concern the conceptualization of these bundles of practices.

Researchers, and the respondents completing the researchers' questionnaire, might, for example, define a 'self-directed work team' in different ways, with or without a 'supervisor' or team 'leader'; similarly, they may define an 'EI' practice as employee 'participation' or as 'involvement' in corporate governance – the proverbial 'apples and oranges'. Subjective judgements of HR practice may be especially problematic when comparing multiple workplaces or work units within a single company. If the respondents to a questionnaire share a different meaning and definition of an HR practice, the veracity of the data estimating the effects will be seriously compromised. Ambiguity over the content of HPWSs has been noted (Danford et al., 2008), as have the serious difficulties related to specifying the independent variable in HPWSs (Boxall and Macky, 2009). Many studies rely on the measurement of the effects of 'too few practices'; alternatively, there may be 'a failure to operationalize HPWS sufficiently', or studies may lack robust evidence 'governing direction of causation' (Danford et al., 2008, p. 152).

Further criticisms concern the connections between such 'bundles' of HR practices. First, do these HR practices operate in a 'synergistic' way as a coherent, integrated cluster, or do they have independent effects? Ichniowski et al. (1997) argue that enhanced performance arises from their combination into a package. Others note that the number of cases on which the claim is based is small (Godard, 2004). Second, how do these HR practices combine in the workplace? The widespread debate on this question is between two schools of thought: 'best practice' and 'best fit'. The 'best practice' school argues that a cluster of HR practices can be combined into a set that is applicable in a diverse range of workplaces and will result in enhanced performance. The 'best fit' school posits that the HR practices have to be consistent with both the internal and the external context of the organization; an example of inconsistency here is the introduction of individual performance pay and self-managed work teams (Delery, 1998). Studies finding a common set of employment practices in 'successful' companies have a long history that can be traced back to the early 1960s (see, for example, McGregor, 1960; Purcell et al., 2009).

The best practice view has been subject to extensive critique. First, what constitutes 'best practice' is based on subjective judgements. Some researchers identify four core practices, whereas others have isolated as many as 16. To explore the HRM–performance relationship, researchers have used 26 general practices (Boselie et al., 2005). Although core HR practices relating to selection, appraisal, rewards and training are typically included, employee representation arrangements are often absent (Marchington and Grugulis, 2000). Second, as noted above, there is significant variation in how these best practices under scrutiny are *operationalized* and measured by workplace scholars. Suppose the researchers select 'training' as a key best HR practice. The response to the question 'Does your establishment undertake extensive training?' may become the operational definition of the concept of training. But training can also be operationalized as management development, formal workplace learning or skills training (Den Hartog and Verburg, 2004). In addition, respondents' interpretations of 'extensive' might be inconsistent.

Third, detractors argue that some degree of internal 'fit' is a necessary condition for workplace cooperation. A variant of early sociological research on hierarchical patterns of employment practices is provided by Kinnie et al. (2005). They argue the need to shape the HR practices to 'fit' with the expectations and needs of employees. For example, managers valued career development, rewards and recognition, participation, communication and work–life balance, whereas those employees lower in the hierarchy typically valued reward and recognition, openness, communication and work–life balance. These findings illustrate the importance of the social class–education–gender cluster of structural factors that influence employees' responses towards particular HR policies and practices. The heterogeneity of people means that what is considered 'best practice' for one group of employees can be bad practice for another, especially between men and women, young and old, and at different levels within the workplace settings. Furthermore, with the growth of non-standard employment, only 'core' employees might experience best HR practices, while 'peripheral' employees might experience something less than 'best' (Marchington and Grugulis, 2000).

Fourth, a degree of alignment between HR practices and business strategy is essential. HR practices that are effective in banking may be ineffective in hospitals: work motivation in the former may be driven by performance-related bonuses that are not transferable to healthcare providers. As John Purcell observes, the 'best practice' school leads into a 'utopian cul-de-sac', ignoring, among other things, business strategy (1999, pp. 36–8). These widespread criticisms of the 'best practice' (universalism) approach emphasize that the HR practices have to be consistent with both the internal and the external context of the organization: the 'best fit' (contingent) view. The latter view argues that HR practices are more effective when they are tailored to the 'external context' of the competitive strategy and, in turn, to the 'internal context' of the different kinds of employee behaviour necessary for the creativity, flexibility and quality differentiation that are needed to accomplish strategic goals (Jackson and Schuler, 1995). Others contend that HR practices need to fit employees' expectations (Edwards et al., 2002) and complement the manufacturing strategy (Boxall and Purcell, 2003) and the stages in the business life-cycle (Kochan and Barocci, 1985). For example, start-up organizations will need HR practices that encourage creativity and innovation, whereas mature organizations will need HR practices that restructure work and control costs (see Chapter 2).

The contingent, 'best fit' view is predicated on some uncertain assumptions, not least of which is that an organization has a competitive strategy with which HR practices can fit (Edwards et al., 2002; Legge, 2005; Ramsay et al., 2000). Furthermore, concern about the wisdom of advancing a contingency model of SHRM is, argues Purcell (1999), a 'chimera', restricted by the impracticality of modelling all the contingent variables. The way forward is to focus on appropriate 'HR architecture' and the processes that positively contribute to performance (Boxall and Purcell, 2003; Purcell and Kinnie, 2008). The 'best practice' and 'best fit' approaches need not be juxtaposed as binary alternatives (Edwards and Sengupta, 2010). In practice, there are a set of core 'best' HR practices that will benefit all work organizations. Although their adoption may not guarantee performance growth, their absence will impact negatively on employee rights, material well-being, dignity at work and commitment, resulting in a lower performance. In the context of global competitiveness and reduced government expenditure on public services, there is a need for what Wright and Snell (1998) call 'fit and flexibility', and for a set of best HR practices that fits the organizational context and strategy.

Performance: concept and measurement

The focus so far has been on issues concerning the independent variable – HR practices – in the HRM–performance model. We will now examine the problems concerning the *dependent* variable: performance. Performance variables have focused almost exclusively on financial measures (Boselie et al., 2005). Studies rely either on the hard 'objective' performance outcomes reported in published financial statements, or on the subjective assessment of outcomes of a single respondent, usually a senior HR manager. Respondents are asked to estimate the profitability or labour productivity of their organization relative to others in their sector. Both Cully et al. (1999) and Den Hartog and Verburg (2004) measure performance by requesting such information, relative to other firms, using a subjective scale ranging from 'a lot above average' to 'a lot below average'. Guest and his colleagues used both published accounting data and their respondents' evaluations of their companies' performance relative to that of their competitors (Guest et al., 2003). Other workplace scholars have used 'intermediate' or 'proximal' measures of performance (Betcherman et al., 1994; Harter et al., 2002). Typical examples here are the number of occupational accidents/ injuries, absenteeism rates, customer satisfaction, the number of formal grievances and complaints, sales per employee, scrap rates and voluntary resignations.

The notion of what constitutes 'superior performance' needs to be disaggregated, and, in order to gain a meaningful insight into what 'performance' means, the researcher and practitioner need to be able to 'compare and contrast performance measures at a variety of individual and organizational levels' (Truss, 2001, p. 1146). With these limitations in mind, numerous studies report that organizations implementing a package of internally consistent and mutually reinforcing HR practices experience 'significant' improvements in performance. Huselid (1995), for example, found that HR practices had a 20 per cent effect on a firm's performance. This suggests, however, an apparent paradox. If the pursuit of SHRM practices leads to improved performance, one would, from the perspective of economic rationality, expect such practices to be more widely used. This apparent paradox may result from the long-term investment costs associated with the resource-based approach to SHRM, the pressure on individual managers to achieve short-term financial results, or a disconnection between espoused strategic HR practices and their enactment by line managers (Whittaker and Marchington, 2003).

reflective question What do you think of this line of argument? If, indeed, strategic HR practices significantly improve performance, why do a relatively small proportion of workplaces adopt such an HR strategy?

Recent studies evince serious errors in the measurement of performance. As Saks (2000) notes, with the notable exception of Huselid's (1995) study, there is a tendency for researchers to rely on single indicators of performance, to ignore the relationships between 'multiple measures', and to use performance indicators across dissimilar workplaces with no regard for how appropriate they are, thus rendering comparisons meaningless. A common criticism is the sampling of 'informed' respondents (Gerhart, 2008). A single respondent may have incomplete knowledge of HR practices and performance, especially if she or he is located at the corporate office. Second, respondents may be unable or unwilling to disclose commercially sensitive information on performance indicators to an independent researcher. Third, research designs take no account of the 'lag effect'. It is not credible to argue that HRM drives performance when measurements of the *independent* variable (HR practices) and the *dependent* variable (performance) are conducted in the same time period. Overall, the reliability of the measures is 'frighteningly low' (Gerhart, 2008, p. 535; Wright and Gardner, 2003, p. 316). Finally, the focus on financial goals assumes that companies seek to design their HR systems to maximize short-term shareholder value, which does not acknowledge the goal priorities of different 'varieties of capitalism' (Godard, 2004; Jacoby, 2005; Paauwe, 2004; Sklair, 2002); financial performance is only one dimension of organizational effectiveness.

The assumption that financial performance is (or should be) the end goal of HRM under-scores attempts to 'legitimize' the field by placing a greater focus on the quest for causal connections between HRM and the 'bottom line' at the expense of the 'people' dimension of the equation – the missing 'human in HRM' (Bolton and Houlihan, 2007, p. 1). Arguably, the primary purpose of analytical HRM is to systematically research what, why and how HR factors affect organizational performance, but, in addition, it will analyse employees' experi-ences and responses to HR practices. Those employees experiencing HR practices are obli-gated to perform tasks designed to create profit for investment banking and corporate executives who make up a high proportion of the new global über-elite, or are compelled to provide public services at lowest cost. It is a world of structural inequalities.

Pay lies at the core of the employment relationship, yet despite its centrality to employee well-being, research shows that, parallel with the growth of the HRM paradigm, the inci-dence of low-wage work is 'stubbornly high', and 'gender discrimination is strongly entrenched in pay practices in the UK' (Grimshaw and Rubery, 2010, p. 357). Wilkinson and Pickett's (2010) *The Spirit Level* is the most recent study of a well-established body of research that demonstrates how income inequality is not only divisive, but also literally makes people less healthy. Critical workplace studies also draw attention to pervasive unfair discrimination on the basis of gender, disability and ethnicity (Carlsson and Rooth, 2008; Dean and Liff, 2010; Riach and Rich, 2002). Decent work is not an intellectual idea; it is a deeply felt aspiration of people in developed and developing societies. Tal's (2007) review of the quality of work finds little support for a growth in decent work in North America but notes a decrease in the index of work quality. The increasing use of non-standard employ-ment contracts engenders 'fear', anxiety and 'demoralization' for those whose choice is limited (Conley, 2008). Studies of cases of sets of HR practices commonly identified with the 'high-performance paradigm' have reported 'work intensification' (see, for example, Findlay et al., 2000) and higher stress levels (Danford et al., 2008; Godard, 2004).

HRM web links www Go to www.youtube.com/watch?v=cZ7LzE3u7Bw for more information on how income inequality impacts on health and other social problems.

Mode of data collection: survey or field interview

Having specified what HR practices and performance outcomes to study, and among whom, the researcher has to choose a method of collecting empirical data. In HR–performance research, the choice is often between the use of surveys or field interviews or a multi-strategy approach that uses a survey followed up by selective case studies and interviews with employees. Each research strategy has its strengths, weaknesses and sets of distinc-tions. Typically, survey-based research is characterized as being driven by theory-testing, whereas theory emerges from field-based research. A further basic distinction is between quantitative and qualitative data, which is essentially the distinction between numbers and words. Survey research makes observations of social reality more explicit using quantitative data; case study researchers, on the other hand, make observations using qualitative data. A related distinction is sometimes drawn between a quantitative focus on employee behaviour and a qualitative focus on interpretive meanings of employees' behaviour in terms of the values, work norms, culture and occupational community in question.

Traditional quantitative research emphasizes the measurement and analysis of causal relationships between variables rather than of processes – that is, *how* things happen. Quite aside from this limitation, there are other issues with survey research. The omniscient respondent does not exist, but many studies rely on the subjective assessment of the effectiveness of HR practices by a single respondent. With self-reported data, there is always the potential for bias (Saks, 2000), the obvious concern being that if only one response is received per establishment, 'any idiosyncratic opinions or interpretations of the questions can distort the results' (Ichniowski et al., 1996, p. 309). Thompson and McHugh (2009) argue that researchers often do not appreciate the important limitations of self-completed questionnaires, in particular when investigators rely on managerial informants for data on HR interventions and their effects when the respondent has a self-interest. The data are less than accurate because such informants, rather than reporting the reality (what *is*), may fall into a normative (what *ought to be*) mode (Guest, 1999; Thompson and McHugh, 2009).

In other words, the subjective assessment of a single respondent has the potential to induce 'socially desirable responses', responses that are intended to make the respondent look good in the eyes of the investigator or society at large (Saks, 2000). The investigator can check on the possibility of distortion in self-reports by surveying the views of relevant others. The value of talking to both managers and workers is emphasized by Nichols (1986, quoted in Bratton, 1992, p. 14):

> A study which systematically samples both managers and workers is always likely to provide at least some snippets of information that rarely surface in other accounts and to suggest different lines of interpretation.

In qualitative inquiry, researchers endeavour to interpret social phenomena in terms of the meanings people attach to them. They therefore stress the socially constructed nature of the workplace and social relations, and the situational constraints that shape the research. Such a research design is most useful when the researcher acknowledges nuances and wishes to study some complex process (Denzin and Lincoln, 2005), such as the causal processes underlying the HR–performance link. We should, however, note the problem of whether a researcher can ever give an objective account of organizational life, because all such accounts are 'linguistic reconstructions'. This is called the '*constructivist* model', which holds that the researcher and the researched create the data and ensuing analysis through an interactive process. Thus, the researcher's qualitative data do not 'discover' social reality; rather, this arises from the process and its cultural and structural contexts (Charmaz, 2000). The researcher is not simply a conduit for information but is instead deeply implicated in the production of knowledge (Schneider, 1999).

There has been a growing interest in using multistrategy research, combining quantitative, structured observations using questionnaires with qualitative, structured interviewing

Evaluating HR practices: the role of qualitative methods

Variable-based (or quantitative) research is a powerful way of determining whether desirable outcomes in work organizations are the result of HR practices. Those engaged in this kind of research typically begin by constructing a variable or performance indicator. They then attempt to determine whether a change in that variable is associated with – perhaps even caused by – a particular HR practice or set of practices.

But while variable-based quantitative research has it strengths, it has weaknesses as well. It forces us to select and preassign meaning to particular features of the social world. In situations where managing across cultures is the challenge, such selective attention, and the preassignment of meaning to behaviours, may lead to superficial or misleading accounts of what is actually going on.

Ideally, HR evaluations would employ mixed methods and bring both quantitative and *qualitative* approaches to bear on the work of evaluation. Qualitative methods start from the assumption that causality in the social world is different from causality in the physical or biological world. The power of a behaviour or verbal statement to bring about a certain outcome depends on the meaning attributed to that behaviour or statement. But the attribution of meaning varies across cultures: different cultures (or subcultures) will attribute different meanings to what, on the surface, appears to be the same behaviour or statement.

In a famous essay on qualitative methods, Clifford Geertz (1973) asks us to reflect on the difference between a blink and a wink. On the surface, both involve a closing and opening of the lid of one eye. However, whether this behaviour is seen as a blink or a wink depends on several factors: the context, the winker's skill at non-verbal communication, and a tacit cultural code that enables someone to distinguish between a blink and a wink. Getting the code wrong could cause a lot of confusion.

This simple example helps us think about how qualitative methods might complement quantitative methods in studying the effects of HR practices. Consider the claim that 'positive affect' boosts morale and motivation in an organizational setting. One could then argue that positive affect is a key leadership quality and refer to studies of US work organizations in which improved worker morale appears to be linked to managers who exhibit an upbeat demeanour.

But smiles and laughter mean different things in different contexts. Picture a young HR graduate assigned to work in an American bank in Moscow. His letters of reference are filled with superlatives: 'This young man has a winning personality: he motivates and inspires those who work alongside him.' Then imagine the surprise when reports from Russia are negative – there are just too many smiles, too much cheerfulness; the American HR graduate is considered superficial, and many find it hard to take him seriously. Others muse, 'Perhaps he is laughing at us?'

Stop! What does this example tell us about the importance of qualitative methods in the evaluation of HR practices? Are there situations, even in the US and UK, where 'positive affect' becomes a problematic rather than a desirable trait?

Sources and further information: See Geertz (1973) for a discussion of qualitative methods. Connelly and Ruarck (2010) provides an overview of the complex role of emotions in work organizations. For some insights into Russian views of the West, see the commencement speech delivered by Nobel Prize-winning author Alexander Solzhenitsyn at Harvard University in 1978. A pdf transcript of the speech may be found at harvardmagazine.com (July/August 1978) – page 24 of the transcript is especially revealing.

Note: This feature was written by David MacLennan at Thompson Rivers University.

©Marcin Balcerzak/Shutterstock.com

An interview is an example of qualitative research.

techniques, with the latter used to analyse the 'rhetoric' of survey research (Bryman et al., 2009). Although it should not be considered as a panacea, multistrategy research may provide a better understanding of mechanisms that cause or initiate performance changes following strategic HR practices.

reflective question   Given the number of variables affecting employment relations, do you think that qualitative, structured interviews can provide a reliable means of measuring the contribution of HR interventions in the workplace?

Theoretical issues: the logic of causality

Apart from the problems with respect to research design, there is theoretical controversy over the nature of the relationship between HRM and performance. Or put another way, *how* exactly does HRM increase performance? A key element of a theory is a causal mechanism, that is, some notion of how the independent and dependent variables are related. The causal mechanism can also be considered as the process, or chain of cause–effect linkages, that mediates the causal effect (Remler and Van Ryzin, 2011). The problem of identifying the intermediate variables or processes that would explain how HR practices cause their effects on work performance is hardly a novel problem. The eighteenth-century Scottish philosopher David Hume, for example, discussed at length the challenges of identifying the 'causal glue' in the cause–effect linkage (Hume, 1748/2007). There is no consensus, however, regarding the precise cause-and-effect linkages through which strategic HR practices generate long-term value (Wright and Gardner, 2003). The ambiguity surrounding the process is aptly called the 'HR black box': the mediating effects of core variables and processes that need to be present to produce such a relationship (Boselie et al., 2005). To understand this aspect of the debate, we need to appreciate the logic of causality in social research.

In social research, there are three main criteria for causal relationships:

- First, the variables must be correlated. A *correlation* seeks to assess the strength and direction of the relationship between the variables identified, and it exists when the variables are observed to be related. That is, changes in one variable are associated with changes in the other, or particular attributes of one variable are associated with particular attributes of the other. For example, height and weight are considered to be statistically correlated because of the association between increases in height and increases in weight. Statistical correlation in and of itself does not constitute a causal relationship between two variables, but it is one criterion of causality (Babbie and Benaquisto, 2010).
- Second, a causal relationship exists only when the cause precedes the effect in time. Clearly, the purchase of a BMW does not cause the owner to earn a high income in order to afford the purchase.
- Third, a causal relationship requires the variables to be non-spurious. That is, the observed empirical correlation between two variables cannot be explained in terms of some third variable. For example, the observed positive association (correlation) between ice-cream sales and deaths due to drowning is plausible enough, but a causal relationship between these variables would be spurious. A third variable, temperature, explains the observed correlation: most deaths by drowning occur in the warmer summer season, which is the peak period for ice-cream sales.

Thus, establishing that two variables tend to occur together is a necessary condition for demonstrating a causal relationship, but it is not itself a sufficient condition. For example, assume that a study of university students found a negative correlation between alcohol consumption (variable A) and grade point average (GPA; variable G). That is, those students who excessively consume alcohol tend to have lower GPAs than those who abstain, and the more alcohol consumed, the lower the GPA. A researcher might therefore claim that drinking alcohol lowers a student's grades, giving as an explanation, perhaps, that alcohol adversely affects memory, which would have detrimental consequences on examination grades. But as Bonney (2010) explains, if the inverse correlation (in symbol form A→G) is the only evidence, an alternative possibility exists. Achieving low grades is frustrating; frustration often leads to escapist behaviour; getting drunk is a popular means of escape; thus, low self-esteem as a result of low grades causes excessive alcohol drinking (G→A). Unless the researcher can establish which came first – the excessive drinking or the low grades – this explanation is supported by a correlation just as plausible as the first.

To complicate matters, suppose we introduce another variable: human emotion (variable E). Arguably, a student with an emotional problem, for example the break-up of a relationship, may exhibit escapist behaviour, including excessive consumption of alcohol. In addition, it seems plausible to suggest that emotional problems are likely to adversely affect grades. A correlation between alcohol consumption and low grades may exist but *neither* may be the cause of the other; rather, both are the consequences of a third variable – emotion. Put in symbol form:

Unless the researcher can rule out such third variables, this explanation is as equally supported by the data as are the first and second cases described.

In summary, when organizational researchers state that there is causal relationship between, say, pay and productivity, they mean that (1) there is a statistical correlation between the two variables, (2) a person's pay was established before the increase in productivity, and (3) there is no third variable, for example emotion, that could explain away the observed correlation as spurious. These are tough criteria to meet.

The implications of this look at causality suggest that HRM–performance analysis is inordinately complex. In effect, what appears to be a simple causal relationship between a configuration of HR practices (the *independent* variable) and performance or 'outcomes', such as profits (the *dependent* variable) only seems so because much of the discourse gives the illusion that the variables are controlled and explained. Although many peer-reviewed studies tend to underestimate the analytical challenges of proving causation (Guest, 2001a), it is commonly assumed that SHRM will improve organizational performance. Researchers, for example, can use data to demonstrate a positive correlation between clusters of 'participative' HR practices and performance outcomes. Table 3.2 above shows that employee skill and direction correlate positively with three out of the four culture measures, especially 'innovation' and 'goal' (Den Hartog and Verburg, 2004).

Employing deductive theorizing, mainstream positivists researchers might view the causal links between SHRM and performance like those shown in Figure 3.3. The line between A and B suggests a correlation between a set of HR practices and performance.

The obvious concern, based on the logic of causation, is establishing that changes in HR practices *cause* changes in performance.

(a) Cause   (b) Effect

HR practices ————————————→ Performance

Figure 3.3 *The positivist view of causation*

Purcell and Kinnie (2008) have done an excellent job of identifying the analytical problems here. The research has to satisfy the second criterion for causation – that the HR practices (cause) take place before the increase in performance (effect). A source of measurement error is reciprocal causation, in which researchers assume that causation runs one way but not in both directions. One of the key analytical limitations in the HR–performance literature is the inconsistency in establishing the direction of causality. It is a matter of debate whether high-performing organizations attribute their success to the adoption of strategic HR practices or whether high-performing organizations tend to adopt bundles of synergistic HR practices; the evidence is inconclusive (Guest et al., 2003; Patterson et al., 2004; Purcell et al., 2009).

It is also extraordinarily difficult to meet the third criterion for causal relationships in workplace research, the possible 'third variable' explanation. The sociological study by Bolton (2005, p. 1) emphasizes, for example, that employees are 'multiskilled managers of emotion', and that emotion management plays a significant role in organizational life. Evidence that there *is* a causal relationship between HR practices and performance assumes that nothing else has changed in the meantime. Indeed, there is persistent evidence that performance is 'multidimensional' (Ostroff and Bowen, 2000, p. 216) and is influenced by many variables both inside and outside the organization (Gerhart, 2008; Hitt et al., 2001).

The counterargument against the classic linear regression model is that HR practices have less influence on performance than do the various external economic and political variables. For instance, the implosion of the US building industry occurred not because of HR practices, but because of the 2008 subprime mortgage crisis. A similar argument can apply to the US auto industry and the case of the 'Detroit Three'. Their financial performance following 2008 depended not on SHRM, but on government bail-outs (Keenan, 2011a). In an extended causal model, the *external* causal mechanism could plausibly be the threat of downsizing that improves employee performance: high levels of unemployment in a recession three decades ago caused workers and their union representatives to become 'fearful' and more 'tractable in order to preserve jobs' (Bratton, 1992, p. 5). Exchange rates are another aspect of the HR–performance argument. Short-term volatility, as in the case of the 2010–12 European Union credit crises, for example, may significantly change overseas sales independent of SHRM.

The mediating effects of the wider external variables and the relational phenomenon make single-cause explanations of HRM and performance too simplistic. Guest (1997, p. 268, emphasis added) recognizes this problem when he states, 'We also need a theory about *how much* of the variance can be explained by the *human factor*'. Acknowledging nuances, the mediating effects of multiple key variables underscores the importance of *context* and studying employees and their values, attitudes and behaviour and social relations as factors contributing to performance.

Some scholars, even when the data establish the direction of causality, emphasize that 'what causes something to happen has nothing to do with the number of times we have observed it happening'. Hence, 'The conventional impulse to prove causation by gathering (quantitative) data on regularities ... is therefore misguided' (Sayer, 2000, p. 14). Although the researcher should not dismiss causal explanations, it is necessary, in order to better understand how the practice of HR influences performance, as well as its importance in assessing the causality of the relationship, to adopt 'a *wider* [emphasis added] conception of causation' than is customarily adopted by mainstream positivists. This epistemological position is called *critical realism*.

Adopting a critical realism approach to the study of causal inferences in HRM–performance research means that, in addition to establishing causal connections, researchers have to examine the deeper structures at work that lie beneath the observable patterns and generate those processes. A comprehensive explanation of the HRM–performance relationship therefore depends on looking 'inside the HR black box', that is, unmasking 'causal mechanisms and how they work, and discovering if they have been activated and under what conditions' (Sayer, 2000, p. 14). Critical realism's broader view of causation is shown in Figure 3.4.

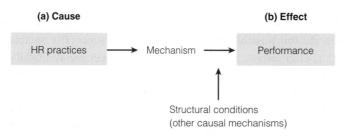

Figure 3.4 *Critical realist view of causation*

Boselie et al. (2005) acknowledge that the 'linking mechanism' between HR practices and performance and the *mediating* effects of other key variables are mostly ignored. The *internal* causal 'mechanism' could, for example, be that employees' work motivation increases performance, or that organizational culture increases employees' long-term commitment and flexibility. Other internal mechanisms could relate to the psychological contract. The work of Purcell and Kinnie (2008) lends credence to the view that we need to take account of employees' attitudes and behaviour, organizational culture, leaders, the behaviour of immediate managers as 'HRM agents', and work design systems in which the HR practices are embedded – in other words, the context.

Context, people and the social relations of performance

It is often difficult to establish what the context actually is and what different mixes of strategic HR practices are required for each situation; more problematically, quite different sets of HR practices have been effective in distinctly similar situations (Bowen and Ostroff, 2004; Grint, 2001).

'Context' can mean at least three things. The first relates to the social structures – meaning relatively stable patterns of social relations and human behaviour – at the macro and global levels. *Macrostructures* refer to the pattern of economic and political forces as well as social relations that lie outside the workplace but affect the realities of work and people management. Global structures are the patterns of worldwide economic and political relations between countries. The mix of strategic HR practices and employees' experiences of those practices are influenced by these social structures. The second sense of context relates to the *microstructures* at the organizational level, which shape the way in which work and people are organized and managed. At this level, the context can be organizational structure, technology, work design and a universal set of 'best practices' or a mix of HR practices that 'fit' a particular situation.

The third sense of context refers to often intangible aspects *of organizational* life, the patterns of shared assumptions, values and beliefs governing the way in which managers and other employees think about work, and how they act. Taking part in any social interaction are a transmitter and a receiver of word*s or actions*. What is important here is the employee's interpretation. Some employees can interpret that they are trusted and respected even though HR practices severely limit discretion and decision-making opportunities. Social phenomena are intrinsically meaningful, and meaning has to be understood – it cannot be simply counted or measured, and an inclusive causal explanation uses interpretative understanding (Sayer, 2000). Studies of causation in HR have to address complexities and nuances, not least that 'enduring multiple commitments and ties' are 'only partly formed by organizational scripts' (Clegg et al., 1999, p. 9). These views negate the idea that SHRM is a set of techniques that can simply be applied in the workplace, 'rather as an engineer selects tools from a box' (Edwards and Sengupta, 2010, p. 386).

The central argument here is that the contemporary workplace is an arena or 'space' in which social relationships shape the beliefs, expectations and behaviour and 'misbehaviour' (Ackroyd and Thompson, 1999) of individual employees that modifies and shapes the enactment of a whole range of HR policies and practices. This conceptualization of the contemporary workplace as open, compliant and, importantly, subject to acts of resistance and defiance against a management that denies employees the basic right to dignity (Bolton, 2005, 2007; Hodson, 2001), means that the positivist generalizations sought by statistical studies of the HR–performance relationship are 'inherently inappropriate' (Edwards and Sengupta, 2010, p. 387).

We discussed in Chapter 1 how people's contribution to the organization is typically variable. This indeterminacy of an employee's performance makes the 'human' in a theoretical model of HRM and performance the most difficult aspect to test and estimate. Improving our understanding of *how* HR practices increase performance requires us to take account of employees' attitudes, emotions, behaviours and 'misbehaviours', as well as how HR interventions are perceived by employees and their representatives (Edwards and Wright, 2001; Guest, 1997; Purcell and Kinnie, 2008).

Decades ago, research focused on possible determinants of 'good' employee behaviour. From this stream of research, there developed notions of 'economic man' and 'social man', and concomitant management practices called 'Theory X and Theory Y'. This genre of psychologically based literature is directed towards finding the 'motivation genie' for different organizational actors in different work situations, and to that end, the theories seek to tackle individual needs while meeting overriding organizational performance needs. Beer's et al. (1984) influential framework falls within a similar frame of reference that relies so much on a behavioural approach to work motivation, and thus recognizes the importance of human factors in predicting the efficacy of HRM. For Beer and his colleagues, HR policies and practices will contribute to the performance of the organization when, over the long term, managers strive to enhance employees' competence and commitment, as well as congruence and cost-effectiveness – the so-called 'four Cs' (p. 16); they go on to say, however that 'assessing HRM outcomes will not be solved easily' (p. 21).

The assumption that empowering workers increases their work motivation is hardly novel. The 'involvement–commitment cycle' is the reverse of the vicious circle of control discussed in the early 1980s. The 'AMO' theory, which states that performance is a function of employees' *a*bility, *m*otivation and *o*pportunity for employee voice, provides a theoretical rationale for a particular set of HR practices. When the opportunities in decision-making (O) change through high-involvement work practices, this leads to positive effects for ability (A), employee motivation (M) and performance (Boxall and Macky, 2009; Wright et al., 2003).

Theorists adopting a resource-based perspective argue that a diverse range of HR practices shape employees' intellectual and physical skills, enhance work motivation and provide the opportunity and the means for employees to contribute to operational decision-making (Bamberger and Meshoulam, 2000; Boxall and Purcell, 2003; Eisenhardt, 1989; Freeman and Lazear, 1995; Snell, 1992; Wright and McMahan, 1992). According to this view, employee *a*bility, *m*otivation and *o*pportunity for employee voice are used as behavioural indicators of employees' performance (Boxall and Purcell, 2003). Numerous studies provide support for the social constructs associated with HR practices and performance. This includes a well-established body of literature that recognizes the 'commercialization of feeling' (Hochschild, 1983) as a defining feature of service work, and the importance of emotion as a valuable resource to be harnessed and developed by management in order to gain employee commitment and competitive advantage (Ashkanasy et al., 2002; Bolton, 2005).

The connection between performance, workplace learning and employee commitment has also been explored in various ways (see, for example, Bratton et al., 2003; Foley, 2001; Garrick, 1998; Matthews and Candy, 1999). At the centre of the changed HR practices involving 'knowledge work' is the increased valuing of the organization's intangible assets, its people. This view holds that employees need to remain committed to the goals of the organization while simultaneously retaining a degree of autonomy that provides space for the 'internal dialogues' that encourage informal learning. But, as Garrick (1999, p. ix) observes, 'This rhetoric seeks fully to utilize workers' informal learning for productivity and efficiency gains.' The burgeoning research on informal workplace learning and communities of practice most certainly has implications for the links between employees' attitudes and behaviour commitment, and from there to performance, extending to the ways in which individual employees adapt and resist obligatory work roles and HR practices.

Positive employee attitudes and behaviours have the potential to reduce the gap inherent in the employment contract between the capacity to work and its exercise, and thus, in turn, to contribute to the value-added chain. The minutiae of human interactions, feelings and emotions have emerged as a new domain of the employment relationship that needs to be managed. Drawing on the pioneering work of Goffman (1959, 1961), Bolton's (2005) insightful study of the workplace as 'emotional arenas' draws attention to the complex motivations that lie behind employees' attitudes and behaviours. The presence of emotion management helps to avoid an overly deterministic picture of the links between

HR practices and employee behaviour and how, for example, 'communities of coping ... actually enable the organization to run smoothly' (Bolton, 2005, p. 151). This discussion of emotion management suggests that effective HR practices are a multidimensional management accomplishment. Moreover, research that focuses exclusively on a cornucopia of 'high-commitment' or 'high-involvement' practices has the effect of erroneously detaching HRM from organizational contexts.

Leadership theory has been applied to HRM–performance research (see Delery and Shaw, 2001; Guest and Conway, 2004; Purcell and Hutchinson, 2007; Purcell and Kinnie, 2008). Leadership is not a position, but a process (Bratton et al., 2004a; Grint, 2005). It is a 'relational' phenomenon residing in a particular context, implying that a 'leader affects and is affected by followers and the environment within which he or she operates' (Bratton et al., 2004a, p. 13). For Kotter (1996, p. 31), the driving force behind any successful change process is 'leadership, leadership, and still more leadership', which arguably suggest that standard HR practice indicators may be acting as proxies for wider 'social relations'.

As part of the HRM–performance debate, one particularly relevant approach is the leader–member exchange (LMX) model of leadership, which builds on German sociologist Georg Simmel's (1858–1918) work on forms of social interaction in a *dyad*, a term to describe a social group of two members. The central focus of LMX theory is the quality of the relationship between the immediate leader and the follower. It suggests that immediate leaders/managers direct their attention to the differences that might exist between the immediate manager and each of her or his subordinates, rather than treating subordinates as a homogeneous employee group (Bratton et al., 2004a). Studies have shown that high-quality LMX has important effects on employees' work behaviours, as evidenced by greater commitment and work performance (Liden et al., 2005).

In Purcell and Kinnie's (2008) HRM causal model, the quality of the leader–subordinate relationship strongly influences employees' perceptions of HR practices, and is thus likely to positively or negatively effect organizational performance. We should also note that 'toxic' behaviour – for example, ridiculing employees in public and promoting divisiveness between individuals or work groups – is related to decreased employee commitment, job satisfaction and performance. Pelletier's (2010) concept of, and empirical support for, 'leader toxicity' in the workplace draws attention to the limitations of the paradigm of positive, effective leadership by pointing out that human beings are imperfect individuals, and that 'good' (or 'bad') leadership is influenced by followers. The fact that HR practices are embedded in and interact with myriad other variables in the organization, and that leaders and a strong culture influence the strategic choice of employment practices, means

©Greg Epperson/Shutterstock.com

Leading from the front. Managers play a vital role in improving employee performance. It has been argued that front-line management and a high-quality relationship between the employee and employer lead to positive work attitudes and behaviours, with important consequences for organizational performance.

that generalizations about strategic HR practices may not bring the same positive results in another context.

Within the LMX theory of leadership, researchers have emphasized the important role that immediate managers play in enacting, modifying or obstructing HR practices (Hutchinson and Purcell, 2010; Liden et al., 2005; Purcell et al., 2009; Truss, 2001; Whittaker and Marchington, 2003). For example, Truss (2001, p. 1136), observes that 'managers act as a powerful mediator between the individual and HR practices'. For Purcell and his colleagues (2009), line managers are central to the causal chain in HR; their role is 'to implement and bring to life' HR practices (p. 182).

Most recently, a study of the role of immediate managers in the UK National Health Service (NHS) found that they are critical to the enactment of HR policies and practices, and thereby strongly influence service delivery (Hutchinson and Purcell, 2010). The notion of 'reciprocal exchange', in which employees engage in work-related behaviours that benefit the organization in return for rewards and support provided by the employer, is central to Liden's et al. (2005) premise that immediate managers act as socialization agents. They argue that a high-quality relationship between the employee and employer, as evidenced by greater obligations and performance, is developed through interactions with the immediate managers. The perceived amount of support that new employees receive from their immediate managers, and the perceived degree to which the new employee feels an obligation to reciprocate, in turn leads to positive work attitudes and behaviours, with important consequences for organizational performance.

This notion of a reciprocal exchange resonated with Agashae and Bratton's (2001) observation that immediate leaders can, through mentoring and coaching (perceived organizational support, 'POS'), facilitate informal workplace learning (perceived obligation to reciprocate, 'POR') and, as such, be change champions. This message is also reinforced by Armson and Whiteley's (2010) study of workplace learning; their data illustrate the reciprocal nature of the immediate manager–employee nexus: employees indicated a willingness to 'have a go' to learn 'outside the box' due to complex reciprocal human responses (p. 422).

The immediate manager mediating effects are, however, far from straightforward. Arthur (1994, p. 673) justified his results on the HRM–performance relationship by citing cost savings arising from an empowered workforce with *fewer* line managers: 'the resources required to monitor employee compliance ... can be reduced'. Similarly, other studies report a *fall* in the number of line managers by as much as 50 per cent following the introduction of self-directed work teams (Bratton, 1992; Edwards et al., 2002). According to Immen (2011), line management 'misbehaviour', left too long, can become contagious and impact negatively on employee engagement, turnover and, ultimately, the 'bottom line'.

The notion that the enactment of HR practices is connected to the relational facets of HPWSs is reinforced by academic research on team-based work regimes, traversing the fields of labour relations and job design. The studies by Findlay et al. (2000) and Edwards et al. (2002) underscore the importance of context and the 'social relations of productivity'. Support for innovatory team-based HR practices is likely to 'shrink' if the efficiency gains of high-involvement workplaces lead management to increase workload or decrease numbers in teams (Findlay et al., 2000). The ethnographic study by Edwards and his colleagues (2002) reported that the support of employees and their union for the '*pacte social*', which stressed cooperation between management and workers, was a key element in securing efficiency improvements. This cooperation was, however, built over an extended time period and within a context of relative job security, existing skills and the expectations of employees.

In Danford's et al. (2008) study, the high-involvement workplace–job satisfaction–employee commitment link was 'tenuous'. Traditional employee concerns with pay and working conditions have greater influence over employees' sense of job satisfaction and commitment to work. With regard to social relations, the other salient point to emerge is that, notwithstanding the emasculation of trade unions, 'most union members ... tended to believe conventional oppositional stances were more effective for placing constraints on managerial prerogatives and securing a degree of protection from work-intensifying pressures of HPWS' (Danford et al., 2008, p. 164). High-involvement HR practices do not automatically lead to 'positive levels of trust, satisfaction and commitment' (Boxall and Macky, 2009, p. 17), or result in 'mutual gains' for workers and employers (Danford et al., 2008, p. 164).

Purcell and Kinnie's (2008, p. 544) causal chain of **Intended** → **Actual** → **Perceived** practices → **Attitudinal** outcomes → **Behaviour** outcomes provides both context and nuance to the HR–performance debate. Their model provides a clear theoretical rationale for HR practices by starting with organizational values, the AMO framework (described earlier in the chapter) and work structure. It specifies the linkages from HR practices to processes to attitudinal and behavioural outcomes within the 'black box' of HR.

We have drawn upon the current HR–performance literature to develop an alternative causal HR–performance model, as shown in Figure 3.5. Here causation is *not* understood as regular successions of linear actions (Sayer, 2000). Our development of Purcell's et al. model puts forward an expanded multicausational explanation of how planned HR practices might affect sustainable organizational performance. The model identifies the following key factors: the ability, motivation, expectations, attitudes, emotions, and behaviours of individual employees; the leadership process; work-related learning; and organizational culture. These may nurture creativity, learning and innovation, and a sense of 'shared values', all of which are more likely to persuade employees to go 'the extra mile' and contribute to performance outcomes (Bowen and Ostroff, 2004; Bratton et al., 2003; Purcell et al., 2009).

These complex human processes, located within the wider context of a sustainable work system and a national and global political economy, suggest how HR practices are enacted – a look inside the metaphorical HR 'black box'. There are limits to what can be reasonably portrayed in a diagram, but Figure 3.5 is meant to convey to the reader the complex, interdependent and mutually reinforcing causal mechanisms that the classical causal model conflates.

Placing the mediating variables within overlapping circles avoids the tendency to view the HR 'black box' as series of linear causal steps. Conceptualizing the causal chain as a relational construct has several implications for the way we understand how strategic HR practices influence employee attitudes such as work commitment, and employee behaviours such as performance. First, power is integral to the employer–employee relationship. This means that the causal chain between planned HR practice and performance outcomes is mediated by power between the parties. The balance of power is dynamic, multidimensional and influenced by numerous variables. In particular, it is influenced by labour market conditions, product market competition, employees' skills, and organizational

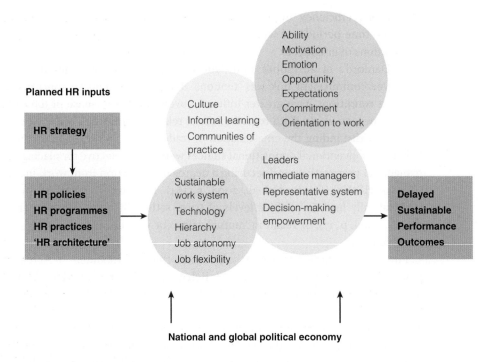

Figure 3.5 *Social relations, HRM and organizational performance*
Source: Adapted from Purcell and Kinnie (2008), p. 544.

bodies such as trade unions or professional associations, or government intervention such as employment and labour laws.

Second, the relation between a manager, a key agent of the organization, and an employee is inherently cooperative and consensual, or defiant and conflictual. The indeterminacy of the employment contract focuses attention on the importance of the relational nature of the exchange. Employees' performance will be influenced by the socioeconomic context, will be the subject of formal and informal negotiation, and will be significantly affected by the quality of the manager–employee relationship.

Most LMX approaches to understanding workplace leadership suggest that the immediate manager/leader plays an integral role as a purveyor of resources and support that extends beyond the formal job description, and, importantly, acts as a potential champion (or spoiler) of HR policies, practices and programmes. This has resonance with Grint's (2005) alternative leadership model, which proposes that, to be effective, leaders must achieve 'buy in' to their own 'version' of the context in order to authenticate their chosen management strategies in handling it. Thus, following Grint's thesis, workplace scholars should, if they are to understand the metaphorical HR 'black box', focus more of their research endeavours on 'the persuasive mechanism that decision makers use to render situations more tractable and compliant to their own preferred form of authority' (Grint, 2005, p. 1492).

Third, if organizational life is recognized as an arena of complex reciprocal human relations that are socially constructed and embedded in an organizational and national culture, SHRM is more appropriately configured not simply as a 'toolbox' from which a set of practices can deterministically improve performance, but rather as planned practices that *might* be enacted as envisioned. It seems plausible, therefore, that the analytical focus on the causal path between planned HRM and organizational performance has to incorporate issues often neglected in the HRM canon, such as conflicts of interest, power, human interactions and employment relations. Thus, the model signals a more inclusive research agenda and a wider definition of HRM, which is why, in this edition of the book, we have chosen to include new chapters on organizational culture and leadership.

reflective
question

Does this causal model predict a particular research design? Can organizational phenomena be understood only by statistical analysis, or is there scope for what Weber called '*verstehen*', or interpretive understanding?

Critical workplace scholars emphasize that organizational life is a world of structural inequalities, indeterminacy, indignities and often tyranny – workplace life as it is, in other words. Therefore HRM researchers must be attuned to these realities. The primary purpose of analytical HRM is to research what, why and how HR factors contribute to organizational performance, but, additionally, analysis needs to extend to largely neglected employee experiences and responses to HR practices. To evade or minimize the reality of structural inequalities and employee experiences of work and HR practices is to falsify workplace life and impoverish the notion of analytical HRM. Research into HRM–performance links will be more legitimate therefore when inquiry extends to the evaluation of HRM 'outcomes' beyond employee commitment and profitability and includes critical areas such as employee reactions, income inequality and employee well-being, matters of 'wider social consequences' (Watson, 2010, p. 918). Such is the richness and landscape of critical HRM analysis.

Vogue Apparel

Setting

The global financial and economic meltdown of 2008–10 shifted retail dynamics in Europe and North America. Recently, Twitter feeds were abuzz about plans by the North American companies Target Corporation and Loblaw to launch new discount apparel stores. Persistently high levels of unemployment in the USA have forced retailers to cut costs and prices, and the competitive UK retail clothing industry has seen discount chains increase their share of the $51 billion market. Such chains as Matalan and Primark Stores offer brands demanded by an increasingly value-focused consumer. Although continued growth in the market will come from the success of these retailers, it is expected that depressed demand and the prevalence of discounters will result in only a modest expansion over the next few years.

As UK clothing suppliers have lower productivity than their leading European competitors, opportunities for the low-cost foreign clothing suppliers of these discount chains have increased. This has resulted in imports making up an estimated two-thirds of the value of the UK clothing market. Traditional sources, primarily Hong Kong and India, are now facing competition from countries such as Morocco and new European Union members such as Romania.

Vogue Apparel is one of the largest discount chains, with 215 stores located in Ireland, Holland, Spain, Portugal, Germany, Belgium and the UK. It employs more than 27,500 people, and ranks as Great Britain's second largest clothing retailer by volume and the leading retailer in value clothing. It is expanding more rapidly than any other British retailer. Its primary customer base is those under 35 years old who are fashion-conscious and want high-quality clothing at reasonable prices.

Vogue Apparel prides itself on being a member of the Ethical Trading Initiative, which is an alliance of companies, trade unions and non-profit organizations that aim to promote respect for the rights of people in factories and farms worldwide. Vogue Apparel's commitment to monitoring and improving the working conditions of its 400 suppliers is reflected in its Code of Conduct, which stipulates, among other standards, that the suppliers must pay living wages and ensure working hours are not excessive.

The problem

An undercover investigation by the BBC recently revealed that workers in a Manchester factory owned by one of Vogue Apparel's suppliers were on duty up to 12 hours a day, earning only £3.50 an hour. Some workers were employed illegally and were working in poor conditions. As the BBC had previously revealed that Vogue Apparel contractors in India had employed children in slum workshops, Vogue Apparel took these new allegations seriously. It immediately commenced an investigation of the supplier, conducted by auditors and senior Vogue Apparel personnel.

The results of the audit were not positive – inaccurate records of rates of pay, fabricated payslips understating the hours worked, excessive working hours and cash payments made to the employees, among other things. During the investigation, Vogue Apparel agreed to remove all references to the Ethical Trade Initiative from 140 of its storefronts. A Vogue Apparel representative remarked: 'There are no excuses. We are absolutely committed to ensuring that the factories who sell to us treat their workers fairly and equitably.'

Over the next 12 months, Vogue Apparel recruited a new Director of Human Resources and Sustainability, as well as putting into place a wide-ranging ethical trade action plan that was acknowledged by the Ethical Trading Initiative. The intervention also included recruiting ethical trade staff in sourcing countries, developing new ethical trade policies and practices, and delivering awareness-raising training for buying staff and suppliers. Vogue Apparel assured its customers that it remained wholly committed to its ethics and its values. The training programme emphasized the importance of the connection between an employee's understanding of his or her work and Vogue Apparel's strategic objectives. Line manager training has now also emphasized that employee emotion is a valuable resource to be harnessed in order to foster commitment and boost sales per employee.

But despite these efforts, Vogue Apparel's employees increasingly have to pacify irate customers at the till about the company's ethical practices. In effect, this emotion in labour performed by front-line employees as a means of coping with difficult customers, and the emotional work used in normal interaction with customers is impacting negatively on employees' performance. They are uncertain how to respond to the

Forcing a smile. The emotional labour required by front-line staff in order to deal with irate customers had a negative impact on employee performance at Vogue Apparel.

questions and complaints from angry customers. The 'emotional zone' that encompasses staff–customer interactions at the till has affected the front-line staff, and turnover, already notoriously high in the retail sector, has now become the company's focus.

Assignment

Working either alone or in a study group, prepare a report drawing on this chapter and other recommended material addressing the following:

1 How do emotion and other factors mediate the relationship between HR practices and Vogue Apparel's financial performance? What is the significance of emotion management in this case?

2 Read the article 'The employee–customer–profit chain at Sears' by A. J. Rucci, S. P. Kirn and R. T. Quinn (1998, January–February, *Harvard Business Review*, pp. 82–97). How is the experience at Sears related to what has happened with employees at Vogue Apparel?

Ask yourself:

1 As a possible member of Vogue Apparel's target customer base, what decision would you make about purchasing their products in light of the revelations by the BBC?

2 Would the company's recent attempts to rectify the situation persuade you to resume shopping at Vogue Apparel?

Essential reading

Becker, B., Huselid, M. A. and Ulrich, D. (2001) *The HR Scorecard: Linking People, Strategy and Performance*. Boston: Harvard Business Publishing.

Bolton, S. (2005) *Emotion Management in the Workplace*. Basingstoke: Palgrave Macmillan.

Cohen, E. (2010) *CSR for HR: A Necessary Partnership for Advancing Responsible Business Practices*. Sheffield: Greenleaf Publishing.

Fineman, S. (2003) *Understanding Emotion at Work*. London: Sage.

Kennedy, V. (2010) 'Role of HR in catalyzing CSR policy to practice' January 10. Available at: www.articlesbase.com/human-resources-articles/role-of-hr-in-catalyzing-csr-policy-to-practice-1801505.html (accessed November 2011).

Kline, J. (2010) *Ethics for International Business: Decision-Making in a Global Political Economy*. New York: Routledge.

For more information on the UK retail clothing industry, visit www.infomat.com/research/infre0000282.html.

To learn about the Ethical Trading Initiative, go to www.ethicaltrade.org/.

Note: This feature was written by Lori Rilkoff, HR Manager at City of Kamloops, BC, Canada.

 Visit the companion website at www.palgrave.com/business/bratton5 for guidelines on writing reports.

summary

◀ We began this chapter by reviewing some of the literature, arguing that the HRM function is going through a transition in which the evaluation of HRM is being recognized as both fundamental and necessary.

◀ A review of the research undertaken in this chapter shows a substantive body of literature demonstrating that SHRM can and does make a positive and, in some cases, significant impact on organizational outcomes. The 'best practice' and the contingency 'best fit' perspectives are competing approaches to achieving superior performance. Both have their limitations.

▼ We examined the methodological and theoretical concerns relating to HR–performance research. Critics argue that the effectiveness of strategic choices in HR is difficult to measure due to major problems of measurement and meeting the criteria of causality. We have suggested that the social 'mechanisms' that impact on the causal chain in HR may be better analysed using a multistrategy research design.

▼ This chapter has examined the neglected dimension of analysing precisely *how* strategic HR practices improve performance. Our model has a heuristic purpose: it is designed to identify and magnify the influential social processes that shape employees' attitudes, behaviour, social relations and thence performance. Through this lens, social interactions, within definable social structures, play a central role in applying and scaffolding strategic HR policies, programmes and practices.

vocab checklist for ESL students

▼ cause (v) (n), causality (n), causation (n), causal (adj), causational (adj)

▼ construct (v), constructivist (n), construction (n)

▼ correlate (v), correlation (n), correlational (adj)

▼ empire (n), empirical (adj)

▼ generalize (v), generalization (n), general (adj), generalizable (adj)

▼ global structure (n)

▼ govern (v), government (n), governance (n), governmental (adj)

▼ hypothesize (v), hypothesis (n), hypothetical (adj)

▼ indicate (v), indication (n), indicator (n)

▼ macrostructure (n)

▼ marginalize (v), marginalization (n), marginal (adj)

▼ microstructure (n)

▼ object (v) (n), objective (adj)

▼ perceive (v), perception (n), perceptive (adj)

▼ perform (v), performance (n), performativity (n)

▼ positivism (n), positivist (n), positive (adj)

▼ produce (v), product (n), productivity (n), productive (adj)

▼ qualify (v), quality (n), qualitative (adj)

▼ quantify (v), quantity (n), quantitative (adj)

▼ rationalize (v), rationale (n), rational (adj)

▼ rely (v), reliability (n), reliable (adj)

▼ subject (v) (n), subjective (adj)

▼ subordinate (v), subordination (n), subordinate (adj)

▼ universal (adj), universally (adv), universality (n)

▼ validate (v), validity (n), validation (n), valid (adj)

Visit www.palgrave.com/business/bratton5 for a link to free definitions of these terms in the Macmillan Dictionary, as well as additional learning resources for ESL students.

review questions

1 What forces are driving the added-value movement in HRM?

2 To what extent do you agree or disagree with the statement that 'the least important HR practices are measurable, whereas the most important HR practices are not.' Discuss.

3 Explain the statement that 'all evaluation methods require the measurement of some set of variables'.

4 What are the strengths and weaknesses of (a) the survey approach and (b) the case study approach to HR–performance research?

5 How can the effect of HR strategy on organizational performance be explained?

further reading to improve your mark

Reading these articles and chapters can help you gain a better understanding and potentially a higher grade for your HRM assignment.

◄ Boxall, P. and Macky, K. (2009) Research and theory on high-performance work systems: progressing the high-involvement stream. *Human Resource Management Journal*, **19**(1): 3–23.

◄ Danford, A. Richardson, M., Stewart, P., Tailby, S. and Upchurch, M. (2008) Partnership, high performance work systems and quality of working life. *New Technology, Work and Employment*, **23**(3): 151–66.

◄ Guest, D. (2011) Human resource management and performance: still searching for some answers. *Human Resource Management Journal*, **21**(1): 3–13.

◄ Purcell, P. and Kinnie, N. (2008) HRM and business performance. In P. Boxall, J. Purcell and P. Wright (eds) *The Oxford Handbook of Human Resource Management* (pp. 533–51). Oxford: Oxford University Press.

◄ Wright, P. and Gardner, T. (2003) The human resource–firm performance relationship. Methodological and theoretical challenges. In D. Holman, T. Hall, C. Clegg, P. Sparrow and A. Howard (eds) *The New Workplace: A Guide to the Human Impact of Modern Work Practices* (pp. 311–29). London: John Wiley.

www Visit www.palgrave.com/business/bratton5 for lots of extra resources to help you get to grips with this chapter, including study tips, HRM skills development guides, summary lecture notes, and more.

the micro context of human resource management

chapter 4

work and work systems

objectives

After studying this chapter, you should be able to:

1 Explain the nature of paid work
2 Understand how management decisions concerning job and work design affect employee commitment, well-being and performance, employment relations and organizational and societal outcomes
3 Define job design and describe specific work organization strategies
4 Understand the theoretical arguments underpinning current job and work design practices
5 Explain the main elements of a sustainable work system
6 Understand the relationship between different job and work designs and human resources strategies

introduction

The study of the design of work and work systems is inseparable from the study of the management of the people doing the work. The way work is organized is a critical internal contingency affecting both micro and strategic human resource management (HRM). Management are the architects of job and work design, and different strategies have created a myriad of contrasting types of jobs and work systems. For example, there are jobs that provide employees with no variation in the tasks performed, and their work activities are closely supervised. In contrast, other jobs may require employees to perform a wider range of tasks within a self-managing team. There is a well-established body of research traversing organizational behaviour, labour relations and HRM that explores how different work design systems have important consequences for employee outcomes such as job satisfaction, skills and work-related stress, for organizational outcomes such as performance, as well as for societal outcomes such as social stability and sustainability. There is also another body of academic work, known as labour process theory, that focuses on the dynamics of managerial control, employee consent and resistance at the point of service or production, and emphasizes the continuity and limited effects of new work systems.

In this chapter, we define work and explore its significance in contemporary Western society. The social context of work should be seen as providing essential background knowledge for managers concerned with contemporary work and organizational paradigms. We explain how different work design strategies have different effects on employee commitment and performance. We then examine the implications of different work design configurations for managing the employment relationship. We conclude by examining evidence of tension and paradox in work redesign that questions the widespread claims that fashionable high-involvement work systems (HIWSs), for example, can truly reconcile the 'needs' of both the employees and the organization.

reflective question What is your own experience of work? Have you or your friends had jobs in which you were expected to 'check your brains at the door'? Have you experienced work in a team? How do you feel about working at home? What are the implications of new ways of working for (1) young people, women and ethnic minorities, and (2) HRM?

The primacy of work thesis

The centrality of work to capitalist modernity was acknowledged in the eighteenth century by Enlightenment thinkers. In Adam Smith's *Wealth of Nations* (1776), dividing work tasks within an occupation and the specialization of work into trades and occupations was linked to economic prosperity. As Smith explains:

> The greatest improvement in the productive powers of labour, and the greater part of the skill, dexterity, and judgement with which it is anywhere directed, or applied, seem to have been the effects of the division of labour. The effects of the division of labour, in the general business of society, will be more easily understood by considering in what manner it operates in some particular manufactures ... The work can often be collected into the same workhouse, and placed at once under the view of the spectator. (1776/1982, p. 109)

In this passage, Smith is giving his opinion that the factory and the division of labour are the best way to organize and manage work.

In Volume 1 of *Capital*, Karl Marx details the many work design strategies used by factory owners to increase profits. His analysis foreshadows the genesis of management in modern capitalism. Following Smith, Marx recognized that the division of labour was central to the development of capitalism; in addition, his identification of capitalism with the exploitation of labour relied, in part, on using such a division of labour and technology to secure the efficient extraction of surplus value (what is now called labour productivity), and the levels of profitability that it secures. In Marx's inimitable prose: 'Division of labour within the workshop implies the undisputed authority of the capitalist over men that are but parts of a mechanism that belongs to him' (Marx, quoted in Bratton et al., 2009, p. 126).

Marx believed that work, and how it is organized and managed, is central to social life. President Barack Obama's 2011 New Year's resolution 'To do everything I can to make sure our economy is growing' summarises Marx's central thesis that work profoundly conditions social, political and intellectual life processes far beyond the task-related activities performed in the workplace. Social scientists studying work have contributed to a lively debate on the centrality of work in the contemporary life experience. Against a backcloth of globalization, an inherent deskilling of work and precarious non-standard employment, some scholars prophesize the 'end of work' (Rifkin, 1996), while others argue that the centrality of work has diminished (Beck, 2000; Sennett, 2004). Other workplace scholars challenge the 'end of work' thesis and contend that work retains its role as a source of identity and an essential source of intrinsic worth, value and social affiliation (Doherty, 2009). In other words, despite seemingly constant change, 'work matters', and the work people do is crucial for their social life experience (for example, Bolton and Houlihan, 2009; Doherty, 2009; Edgell, 2012; Pupo and Thomas, 2010; Vallas et al., 2009; Watson, 2003).

This is what we mean here by the 'primacy of work thesis', an important axiom which holds that the relations into which men and women enter as they join the workforce have significant effects on their individual lives and on contemporary society in general. At the individual level, we can identify at least three factors that underscore the primacy of work. First, for the majority of adults, the income derived from their employment is their sole source of income. In the UK, approximately 75 per cent of household income is derived from paid employment. There is, however, a yawning gap between rich and poor households. In 2008–09, after distribution through taxes and benefits, the income of the top 20 per cent of households in the UK was four times greater than that of the bottom 20 per cent (Office for National Statistics, 2011a). The income derived from paid work strongly influences an individual's and family's overall 'life chances' (Weber, 1922/1968), by which Weber means the ability to gain access to scarce resources and valued resources such as property and education.

Second, for those people in full-time employment, work is a dominant waking activity. Over the last three decades, the restructuring of work has caused many households to depend on two incomes, with both parents and single-parent households increasingly 'juggling' work and child-care commitments. Such developments have generated research and debate on 'shift-parenting' (Edwards and Wajcman, 2005) and the 'work–life boundary' (Warhurst et al., 2008). Although it is a contested term, 'work–life balance' practices in the workplace are those which increase the flexibility and autonomy of employees in negotiating their time and presence in the workplace (McKie et al., 2009). However, work–life balance decisions made by individuals are constrained by a range of economic factors and are also circumscribed by prevailing national gender cultures and social norms and mores (Gregory and Milner, 2009).

Third, work is important because it has a personal dimension (Sayer, 2005). It is valued for the sense of social *identity* that it offers (Giddens, 2009). The term 'master status' (Hughes, 1945) is used to signify the status of an individual that dominates all his or her other statuses in most social contexts, and plays a pivotal role in the formation of the individual's social identity. When introduced to a stranger, he or she may ask, 'What do you do?' And during the conversation, one may say, 'I love my work. I am my work.' This implies that a person's work is his or her master status. Work can potentially be fun, creative and rewarding, and can embed us within a network of friends. It is the means through which human beings can realize the full potential of their humanity (Bratton et al., 2009), but it can also be 'miserable, toxic, soul destroying, inadequately rewarded, at times dangerous' (Bolton and Houlihan, 2009, p. 3).

At the society level, work and work systems are transformational – for over 250 years, work activities have left indelible imprints on the fabric of human societies. The factory system transformed society as people migrated from rural areas to the new urban centres. The ensuing social division of labour into trades and occupations transformed the social class structure, which provided the basis for new social movements. New work structures also instilled into people another phenomenon of modernity: 'time discipline'. The routine of daily life became increasingly measured in hours and minutes and, to satisfy the demands of contemporary work systems, cultural attitudes, values and customs changed (Thompson, 1967).

The restructuring of work is also critically important for the state. The British government established a system of mass elementary education in 1870 and state secondary education in 1902, and expanded university education in the twentieth century to meet the demands for suitably skilled workers and graduates willing to be engaged in new forms of work. The central significance of work systems to the ecosystem forms part of the public discourse on sustainability (see, for example, Docherty et al., 2009; Laszlo, 2009).

Finally, global capitalism has redistributed work as multinational corporations have focused on 'branding' (Klein, 2000) and have outsourced work to the emerging economies of India and China, with consequences for the social fabric of European and US cities and for social stability. The demonstrations in France in spring 2006 against non-standard or precarious employment – under the slogan 'Non à la précarité!' – further amplifies the centrality of work, as does the contagion of revolution in North Africa and the Arab states that occurred in 2011. With Egypt's youth unemployment rate at over 25 per cent, the pro-democracy uprising was led by the young, unemployed or underemployed educated elite, demanding jobs and taking advantage of their social network communications (Freeland, 2011; Grant, 2011).

reflective question   What role has the British (or your own) state played in the development of work in the new economy?

The debt crisis in Europe and the USA has propelled the issue of work onto the political agenda (Heyes and Nolan, 2010). Recent developments remind us that the economic and the social are part of the same set of processes, 'immutable and symbiotic and interdependent' (Bolton and Houlihan, 2009, p. 2). Capitalism has always depended on society to lubricate its wheels, which is why the rhetoric of 'too big to fail' when applied to banks, for instance, simply means 'so big that they can depend on society to pick them up when they topple' (Patel, 2009, p. 19). The immediacy of debt-choked economies can easily distract us from more persistent trends and features of the workplace: downsizing, an unprecedented growth in non-standard employment, a decline in trade union influence, inequity, work intensification and consequential work-related stress. Work-related issues are examined throughout this text.

The nature of work

Filling in the forms to apply for a student loan is not seen as work, but filling in forms may be part of a clerical worker's job. Similarly, when a mature student looks after her or his own child, this is not seen as work, but if she or he employs a child-minder, it is, for the minder, paid work. We can see from these examples that work cannot be defined simply by the content of the activity. So when we refer to the term 'work', what do we mean? Work is not just an activity, something one *does*, but something a person *has* (Gorz, 1982). We can begin to understand the complexity of work and its social ramifications by exploring the following definition:

> Work refers to physical and mental activity that is carried out to produce or achieve something of value at a particular place and time; it involves a degree of obligation and explicit or implicit instructions, in return for a wage or salary.

This definition draws attention to some central features of work. First, the most obvious purpose of work is an economic one. The notion of 'physical and mental' and 'value' suggests that the activities of both a construction worker and a computer systems analyst can be considered to be work. 'Mental activity' also includes the commercialization of human feeling, or what is called 'emotional work' (Bolton, 2005; Hochschild, 1983). The form and applicability of the concept of emotional work are contested (see Bolton, 2009; Brook, 2009), but the fact that the service sector provides the most employment in Britain (Nixon, 2009) emphasizes how important it is to analyse the full array of emotional work that takes place in the workplace, as well as the processes by which emotional labour is extracted and exploited (Bolton, 2009).

Second, work is structured spatially – geographically – and, by time and people's spatial embedding, shapes work and management practices (Herod et al., 2007). Throughout most of the twentieth century, work was typically carried out away from home and at set periods of the day or night. Thus, 'place and time' locates work within a social context. With the BlackBerry symbolizing the 'work anywhere' culture of our

©istockphoto.com/melhi

The mass timetable of the '8 to 5' factory world and the '9 to 5' office world, has given way to a complex flexi-place, flexi-time world and a 'work anywhere' culture.

times (Donkin, 2010), it is the 'flexibilization' (Atkinson and Hall, 2009) of the UK labour market that provides the backdrop to new expectations of flexible working, spatial mobility and temporal flexibility (see, for example, Coyle-Shapiro et al., 2005; Kelliher and Anderson, 2010). In term of employee well-being, current research has identified a range of mixed outcomes from flexible working arrangements. Some studies have found higher levels of job satisfaction, while others have documented evidence of work intensification in circumstances where flexible workers are working reduced hours without suitable adjustments of their workload in line with their paid hours (Kelliher and Anderson, 2010). The mass timetable of the '8 to 5' factory world, and the '9 to 5' office world, has given way to a complex flexi-place, flexi-time world.

> **WWW** Visit www.palgrave.com/business/bratton5 to read an HRM in practice feature on employees' experience of 'decent work'.

Third, work always involves social relations between people: between employer and employee, between first-line manager and other employees, between co-workers, and between manager and trade union representatives. The 1859 *Preface* is Marx's canonical text that served as a 'guiding thread' in his analysis of capitalism: 'In the social production of their life, men [sic] enter into definite relations that are indispensable and independent of their will, relations of production' (Marx, quoted in Bratton et al., 2009, p. 94). Social relations in the workplace can be cooperative or conflictual, hierarchical or egalitarian. When a parent cooks dinner for the family, he or she does tasks similar to those performed by a cook employed by a hospital to prepare meals for patients. However, the social relations involved are quite different. Hospital cooks have more in common (in this sense) with factory or office workers than with parents, because their activities are governed by rules and regulations. They accept 'instructions' from the employer or the employer's agent, a manager. Obviously, then, it is not the nature of the activity that determines whether it is considered 'work', but rather the nature of the social relations in which the activity is embedded. Thus, to be 'in work' is to have a definite relationship with some other who has control of the time, place and activity.

The fourth element of work is a reward. Rewards are of two types: *extrinsic* and *intrinsic*. The employee provides physical effort and/or mental application, and accepts fatigue and the loss of control over her or his time. In return, the extrinsic work rewards that he or she usually receives consist of (primarily) a wage or salary and possibly bonuses. The intrinsic rewards the worker might get from the job include status and peer recognition.

Although our definition helps us to identify key features of work, it is too narrow and restrictive. First, not all work, either physical or mental, is remunerated. We cannot assume there is a simple relationship in which 'work' means a paid employment or occupation, 'real' work that is recompensed – our definition obscures as much as it reveals. Most people would agree that some activities that are unpaid count as work. This work can be exhilarating or exhausting. Some of it is household-based work – cooking, child-rearing, cleaning and so on – and some of it is done voluntarily, for the good of society, for instance, working for the Citizen's Advice Bureau. The activities that are done in the course of this unpaid or 'hidden' work are identical to those in some paid jobs, such as working in a nursery or advising people on their legal rights. So is it fair to exclude this area simply because it is not paid?

Furthermore, whether an activity is experienced as work or non-work or leisure is dependent on social relations, cultural conditions and social attitudes, and on how various activities are perceived by others. So, for example, 'an active woman, running a house and bringing up children, is distinguished from a woman who works: that is to say, takes paid

Emotion at work

The link between work and employee emotion has been at the heart of human resources (HR) since the human relations movement of the 1930s, mainly captured as the 'happy productive worker' hypothesis. This offers an apparent win–win situation for organizations and individuals as it suggests that, if jobs or work is correctly designed, individuals will feel better and perform better.

However, this framework for interpreting how employees feel at work has tended to eclipse the more critical debates on emotion at work. These highlight that, beyond the more visible efforts aimed at reshaping jobs and job characteristics to achieve the desired emotions in employees, there are more subtle, indirect but still pervasive attempts to manage employees' feelings. As described in the now classic *The Managed Heart* (Hochschild, 1993), there is an exchange between the organization and the individual with regard to employees' feelings at work; feeling at work itself becomes a form of labour, referred to as 'emotional labour':

> What was once a private act of emotion management is sold now as labor in the public-contact jobs. What was once a privately negotiated rule of feeling or display is now set by the company's Standard Practices Division … All in all, a private emotional system has been subordinated to commercial logic and it has been changed by it. (Hochschild, 1983, p. 186)

Hochschild's publication sparked the start of extensive research in the area of 'emotional labour' and the management of private, individual feelings to achieve the outcome the organization requires. This suggests that each organization, or group within it, will have a set of either implicit or explicit rules for displaying emotion, akin at times to job requirements, that regulate when and how

©istockphoto.com/Phil Date

Service with a smile. Why is it that some job roles require an external display of happiness, while others don't?

certain emotions should or should not be displayed. For example, waiters are expected to smile, to externally display happiness, when taking a customer order, but a surgeon is expected not to display any emotion, even when communicating potentially distressing news to a patient. In this way, the display, or otherwise, of certain emotions becomes part of the job role and is expected, and therefore managed, by the organization. It has also been argued that organizational intervention can change not only what individuals display, but also what they feel at or about work – hence the suggestion that the organization intrudes into the regulation of individuals' private emotions, as in the quote above.

Since the 1980s, our understanding of emotional labour has become more detailed and more sophisticated. Initially argued to apply especially to jobs that involve high levels of direct contact with the public, emotional labour is currently considered to be relevant in many other job types and roles, even within leadership and management. Much of the original research into emotional labour argued for an inevitable adverse impact of employees 'faking' certain emotions at work; more recently, however, it has been suggested that this process might manifest itself differently across different situations, with the impact also depending on the individuals concerned and their specific job circumstances. The core importance of understanding aspects of how the organization manages the display of feelings and emotions remains, however, unchallenged, and this is still considered essential for gaining insight into emotion at work.

Stop! Hochschild's original research was conducted within the airline industry. Consider your own experiences of interacting with flight attendants. What emotions do they typically display in interacting with passengers? To what extent can these be considered authentic, and what display rules might they be following? How might these rules be learnt and managed?

Sources and further information: For further information, see Diefendorff et al. (2006), Fineman (2003) and Hochschild (1983).

Note: This feature was written by Chiara Amati at Edinburgh Napier University.

 Visit the companion website at www.palgrave.com/business/bratton5 for a bonus HRM in practice feature on employees' experience of 'decent' work.

employment' (Williams, 1983, p. 335). Historically, unpaid work is undertaken dispropor-tionately by one-half of the population: women. This book concentrates on paid work, and as a consequence we largely omit the critically important area of women's unpaid work in the household, although that is not to suggest that we see it as unimportant.

Second, our definition of paid work says little about how employment opportunities are shaped by gender, ethnicity, age and abilities or disabilities. For example, when women do have access to paid work, they tend to receive less pay than men doing similar work. Women are disproportionately represented in paid work that involves tasks similar to those they carry out in their domestic life – catering, nursing, teaching, clerical and retail employment. Ethnic and racially defined minorities experience chronic disadvantage in paid work because of racism in organizations and in recruitment. The likelihood of partici-pating in paid work varies with age and certain types of work. For example, young people are disproportionately represented in more physically demanding paid work. Disabled adults, especially disabled young adults, experience higher levels of unemployment and underemployment than do those who are able-bodied (Barnes, 1996).

Third, work can be dangerous and unhealthy, but the hazards are not distributed evenly. Manual workers face more work-related hazards, and have more accidents at work, than do (for example) office workers. It has been argued that this unequal distribution of work-related accidents is not only related to the risks the individuals face – it is also influenced by values and economic pressures. Our approach to understanding the issue of inequality surrounding work involves an analysis of the differential treatment of people based on class, gender and race. We need to look at who does what job, analysing the social and sexual division of labour. We need to consider what sort of occupations there are, and who exercises power or control over the social institutions.

reflective question   How has work in the new economy transformed gender roles?

Since the 1990s, social scientists have argued that there is indeed a 'new economy', concluding that new forms of knowledge production, Internet communications and major technological innovations have redefined capitalism and the global economy. In this context, the restructuring of organizations and work systems is intertwined with processes of economic and consumer globalization (Pupo and Thomas, 2010). A charac-teristic feature of the new economy is the notion of mobility. Work itself has relocated around the globe as multinational corporations search for low-cost labour. In turn, the global economy has swelled the flow of migrant workers searching for work. A popular image of the contemporary workplace is of a sophisticated computerized space where 'knowledge workers' connect to clients and customers around the globe. In this contem-porary context, the new 'flexible' or 'networked' organization replaces old bureaucratic hierarchal structures, and 'employment flexibility' is presented as an ideal for employees and employers alike. Overall, advanced technologies, a highly educated, creative and flex-ible workforce, and sophisticated management and HR practices define the new economy paradigm. An enduring issue for management, however, is deciding how work-related tasks are to be divided into various jobs and how will they relate to other tasks and other jobs, contingent upon the business's strategy, operating environment, technologies and organizational culture.

Job design

A job comprises one or more tasks that an employee performs in the workplace, and job design and redesign has been one of the most regularly researched topics in the field of work motivation and organizational behaviour (Fried et al., 1998). The design of jobs for individual employees or work teams has emphasized improved performance outcomes for the organization and a reversal of the negative effects of division of labour (Linstead et al., 2009). The critical literature on job design has questioned the view that job redesign is primarily motivated by a management ideology of improving the quality of work (Thompson and McHugh, 2009). Job design focuses directly on work-related tasks or activities that employees undertake to design, produce and deliver a good or service for the organization. In the literature, *job design* refers to the actual 'content and method of jobs' that employees perform in their jobs (Wall and Clegg, 1998, p. 337). Job design itself is at the core of a *work system*, defined here as a particular configuration of job tasks and the overarching relationships between these job tasks and the operational exigencies, leadership style and management policies and practices found in the organization (Beer et al., 1984; Cordery and Parker, 2008).

A myriad of different approaches can be taken in designing jobs. At its most basic level, job design decisions produce low or high levels of horizontal and vertical job-related tasks or activities. The core dimensions of job design are shown in Figure 4.1.

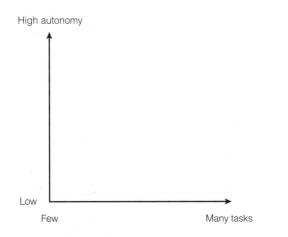

Figure 4.1 *The core dimensions of job design for individual employees*

The horizontal axis in Figure 4.1 represents the functional or technical tasks that are required to produce a product or service. Job design choices can entail only one simple task or a series of tasks combined in one job, depicted as a movement along the horizontal axis. Horizontal job enlargement has the effect of increasing cycle times and creating more complete and, hopefully, more meaningful jobs. The technical dimension, then, is concerned with the range of tasks undertaken by employees and raises issues of multi-skilling and functional flexibility. The vertical axis, on the other hand, represents the decision-making aspects of work activities, and shows the extent of employees' autonomy in the job. The extent to which the job allows employees to exercise choice and discretion in their work runs from low to high.

The two core dimensions enable us to contrast two jobs, shown as A and B in Figure 4.2. The characteristics of job design A limit the content or scope of the job, giving minimal, if any, discretion over how work-related tasks are performed. The focus is on a rapid completion of tasks and close supervision.

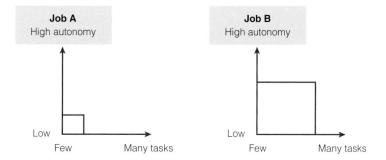

Figure 4.2 *Alternative job designs for an employee*

In contrast, job B is designed with more tasks and offers the employee more autonomy over how those tasks are performed. The focus is on improving job satisfaction by allowing the worker to complete several tasks with some self-supervision. During the last millennium, these core job design concepts have been central to the work redesign process in North America and Western Europe. Here, we trace the innovations in job and work systems from the eighteenth century.

Classical work systems: scientific management

We begin by studying what others call 'classical' approaches to designing work systems. These are considered classical partly because they are the earliest contributions to management theory, but partly because they identify ideas and issues that keep occurring in contemporary literature, albeit using a different vocabulary (Grey, 2005).

Innovations in how work is designed interested Adam Smith (1723–90), as mentioned above. Smith argued that the division of labour leads to an improvement of economic growth in three ways: output per worker increases because of enhanced dexterity; work preparation and changeover time are reduced; and specialization stimulates the invention of new machinery. Smith's early example of job design was taken from the production of nails. He wrote:

Man draws out the wire; another straightens it; a third cuts it; a fourth points it; a fifth grinds it at the top for receiving the head ... the important business of making a pin is, in this manner, divided into eighteen distinct operations. (1776/1982, p. 109)

In the nineteenth century, Charles Babbage pointed out that the division of labour gave the employer a further advantage: by simplifying tasks and allocating fragmented tasks to unskilled workers, the employer could pay a lower wage, and thus 'dividing the craft cheapens its individual parts' (Braverman, 1974, p. 80).

Marx gave a more critical interpretation of the division of labour. While not disagreeing with Smith that breaking complex tasks down into a series of simpler tasks increased labour productivity, Marx argued that it also stultified human creativity and that, as such, the division of labour was the locus of 'alienated labour'. Marx contended that workers experience four discrete but related types of alienation: from the product they produce, from their own work activity, from the human species, and from other human beings (Bratton et al., 2009, p. 92).

The influence of Smith's and Babbage's theories on the design and management of work is difficult to estimate (Parker and Wall, 1998). At the dawn of the twentieth century, however, interest in job and work design intensified when various kinds of trade union 'restrictive practice' were identified as causes of poor productivity (Edwards and Sengupta, 2010), and when Frederick Taylor's book *The Principles of Scientific Management* was published in 1911.

Scientific management

The American Frederick W. Taylor (1856–1915) pioneered the scientific management movement. This approach to job design, referred to as Taylorism, was also influenced by Henry L. Gantt (1861–1919) and Frank B. Gilbreth (1868–1924). Taylor developed his ideas on employee motivation and job design techniques at the Midvale Steel Company in Pennsylvania, USA, where he rose to the position of shop superintendent. Littler (1982, p. 51) has argued that 'Taylorism was both a system of ideological assertions and a set of management practices'. Taylor was appalled by what he regarded as inefficient working practices and the tendency of workers not to put in a full day's work, what Taylor called 'natural soldiering'. He saw workers who did manual work to be motivated by money – the 'greedy robot' – and to be too stupid to develop the 'one best way' of doing a task. The role of management was to analyse scientifically all the tasks to be undertaken and then to design jobs to eliminate time and motion waste.

Taylor's approach to job design was based on five main principles:

- Maximum job fragmentation
- The divorce of planning and doing
- The divorce of 'direct' and 'indirect' labour
- The minimization of skill requirements and time for learning the job
- The reduction of material-handling to a minimum.

Thus, the centrepiece of scientific management was the separation of tasks into their simplest constituent elements (the first principle). Most manual workers were viewed as sinful and stupid, and therefore all decision-making functions had to be removed from their hands (the second principle). All preparation and servicing tasks should be taken away from the skilled worker (direct labour) and performed by unskilled and cheaper labour (indirect labour in the third principle); according to Littler, this is the Taylorist equivalent of Babbage's principle and is an essential element of more work intensification (Littler, 1982). Minimizing the skill requirements for performing a task reduces labour's control over the labour process (the fourth principle), and finally, management should ensure that the configuration of machines minimizes the movement of people and materials to shorten the time taken (the fifth principle). Taylor's approach to job designs, notes Littler (1982, p. 52), embodies 'a dynamic of deskilling' and offers to organizations 'new structures of control'.

Some writers argue that Taylorism was a relatively short-lived phenomenon that died in the economic depression of the 1930s. Rose suggests that scientific management did not appeal to most employers – 'Some Taylorians invested a great effort to gain its acceptance among American employers but largely failed' (1988, p. 56) – but this view underestimates the diffusion and influence of Taylor's principles on job designers. In contrast to Rose, Braverman (1974, pp. 86–7) believes that 'the popular notion that Taylorism has been "superseded" by later schools of "human relations", that it "failed" … represents a woeful misreading of the actual dynamics of the development of management'. Similarly, Littler and Salaman (1984, p. 73) have argued that 'In general the direct and indirect influence of Taylorism on factory jobs has been extensive, so that in Britain job design and technology design have become imbued with neo-Taylorism'.

reflective question

Can you think of jobs in the retail and service sector that support the charge that work systems in the modern workplace continue to be imbued with neo-Taylorism?

Fordism

Between 1908 and 1929, Henry Ford applied the major principles of Taylorism, but also installed specialized machines and perfected the flow-line principle of assembly work; this kind of job design has, not surprisingly, come to be called Fordism. The classical assembly line principle should be examined as a technology of control over employees and as a job design to increase labour productivity, both job fragmentation and short task-cycle times being accelerated. Fordism is also characterized by two other essential features. First is the introduction of an interlinking system of conveyor lines that feed components to different work stations to be worked on, and second is the standardization of parts and products to gain economies of scale and lower unit costs. Speed of work on the assembly line is determined by the technology itself rather than by a series of instructions.

Management's control over the work process was also enhanced by a detailed time and motion study inaugurated by Taylor. Work-study engineers attempted to discover the shortest possible task-cycle time. Ford's concept of people management was simple: 'The idea is that man … must have every second necessary but not a single unnecessary second' (Ford, 1922, quoted in Beynon, 1984, p. 33). Recording job times meant that managers could monitor more closely their subordinates' effort levels and performance. Task measurement therefore acted as the basis of a new structure of control (Littler, 1982).

Ford's production system was, however, not without its problems. Workers found the repetitive work boring and unchallenging, job dissatisfaction being expressed in high rates of absenteeism and turnover. In 1913, for example, Ford required about 13,500 workers to operate his factories at any one time, and in that year alone the turnover was more than 50,000 workers (Beynon, 1984). The management techniques developed by Ford in response to these HR problems serve further to differentiate Fordism from Taylorism (Littler and Salaman, 1984). Ford introduced the 'five dollar day' – double the pay and shorter hours for those who qualified. Benefits depended on a factory worker's lifestyle being deemed satisfactory, which included abstaining from alcohol. Ford's style of paternalism attempted to inculcate new social habits, as well as new labour habits, that would facilitate job performance. Taylorism and Fordism became the predominant approach to job design in vehicle and electrical engineering – the large-batch production industries – in North America and Britain.

Bureaucracy

Bureaucracy is something everyone loves to hate. And with good reason. Everyday life presents us with a never-ending sequence of bureaucratic encounters that tax our patience and leave us speechless. The state of frustration many people feel when reflecting on their encounters with bureaucracy is a good starting point for thinking about work and work systems. But if we are seeking to understand the challenges of work design in a globalizing world, we have to proceed cautiously. Whatever the faults of the thing itself, the idea of bureaucracy has served as a useful conceptual reference point for thinking about organizations and the work processes situated within them. As we enter the pre-bureaucratic and post-bureaucratic worlds associated with globalization, this conceptual reference point will serve as a valuable navigational tool.

What is the meaning of pre- and post-bureaucratic in this context? With regard to pre-bureaucratic worlds, we can recall the work of Max Weber, who wrote the classic analysis of bureaucracy. For Weber, bureaucracy was to be understood in contrast to patrimony, the organization of social activities based on one's personal relationships to powerful people (usually men). In societies where patrimony is the dominant organizing principle, it is not what you know, but who you know, that determines your position in various organizations. In many traditional societies, patrimonial values continue to exert a strong influence on people's thinking, and HR professionals may find themselves working in these pre-bureaucratic societies.

With regard to post-bureaucratic worlds, Andrew Abbott has recently argued that what we have traditionally designated as organizations are being altered in fundamental ways. As a result in part of the changes we associate with globalization, 'organizations are responding not so much by changing organizational policies as by dismantling and reassembling what in mid-twentieth-century-terms we would have called the organization itself' (Abbott, 2009, p. 419). Abbott's analysis suggests we may be entering a post-bureaucratic era, and some people consider that this a good thing. But we must be careful not to lose sight of certain desirable features of bureaucracy, features (like the obligation to hire the most qualified person for the job) that classical bureaucratic theory helped to identify.

The point is that we must recognize that bureaucracy is not just a thing: it is also a conceptual model or 'thinking tool' that for many decades served as a basic reference point in discussions about organizations. The idea of bureaucracy helped people to think about the organizational settings of work processes and about optimal ways of linking the setting and the work process. In a period of globalization and rapid social change, when HR practitioners are likely to encounter both pre- and post-bureaucratic environments, it will be helpful to have a clear understanding what bureaucracy was.

Stop! Consider the phrase 'use your discretion'. How would the meaning of this phrase vary depending on whether one was working in a bureaucratic or a non-bureaucratic setting? As an HR professional, you typically urge your co-workers to 'use your discretion' when dealing with unforeseen circumstances on the job. How might your co-workers misinterpret your advice if they were not familiar with the organizational norms of bureaucratic settings?

Sources and further information: For more information, see Abbott (2009) and also Swedberg (2005).

Note: This feature was written by David MacLennan at Thompson Rivers University.

To many of us bureaucracy is a frustrating maze of rules and regulations, but this is exactly why it makes a good starting point for a discussion of work and work systems.

©istockphoto.com/ YinYang

As a job design and labour management strategy, scientific management and Fordist principles had limitations even when the workforce accepted them. First, work simplification led to boredom and dissatisfaction, and tended to encourage an adversarial climate in terms of industrial relations. Second, Taylor-style job design techniques carried control and coordination costs. With extended specialization, indirect labour costs thus increased as organizations employed an increasing number of production planners, controllers, supervisors and inspectors. The economies of the extended division of labour thus tended to be offset by the dis-economies caused by management control structures.

Third, there are what might be called cooperation costs. Taylorism increases management's control over the quantity and quality of workers' performance, but, as a result, there is increased frustration and dissatisfaction, leading to a withdrawal of commitment on the part of the worker. In both the USA and Britain, Taylorism created considerable industrial strife. An example of this was the 1917 engineering strikes against the introduction of time and motion practices, and the consequent 'dilution' of skilled labour. Quality control can also become a major problem for management. The relationship between controller and controlled can deteriorate so much that a further increase in management control is needed. The principles of Taylorism and Fordism thus reveal a basic paradox, 'that the tighter the control of labour power, the more control is needed' (Littler and Salaman, 1984, pp. 36–7). The adverse reactions to Taylorism led to the emergence of new approaches to job design that focused on designing work to achieve high performance without incurring the debilitating human costs associated with routinized work.

Sociotechnical work systems: the neo-human relations movement

In the 1920s, Harvard Business School professor Elton Mayo (1880–1949) applied the insights of psychiatry and sociology to the design of work and to management practice. He criticized F. W. Taylor for focusing solely on the engineering aspects of work and for believing that employees were solely motivated by extrinsic rewards.

In 1928, Mayo was invited by the Western Electric Company to set up an experiment in the relay assembly room at the Hawthorne Works in Chicago, USA. The experiment involved testing the effects on productivity of variations in working conditions (lighting, temperature and ventilation). The research team found no clear relationship between any of these factors and productivity. They then developed, after the fact, concepts that might explain the factors affecting worker motivation, concluding that not only economic incentives, but also the working environment motivated workers – recognition and social cohesion were important too. The message for management was also quite clear: rather than depending on management controls and extrinsic rewards, management needed to influence the work group by cultivating a climate that met the social needs of workers. The human relations movement advocated various techniques such as worker participation and non-authoritarian first-line managers, which would, it was thought, promote a climate of good human relations in which both the quantity and quality of the service or the goods demanded by the organization could be met.

The research at the Hawthorne Works ceased in 1932, a victim of the Great Depression (Gillespie, 1998), but under Mayo's direction a definitive account of the experiments was published in Roethlisberger and Dickson's book *Management and the Worker* (1939). Human relations detractors claimed managerial bias and the fact that the human relations theory played down the basic economic conflict of interest between the employer and employee. Critics also pointed out that when the techniques were tested, it became apparent that workers did not inevitably respond as predicted. Finally, the human relations approach to work design has been criticized because it neglects wider socioeconomic factors (Thompson, 1989).

During the 1960s and early 1970s, job design was guided by what Rose (1988) refers to as the 'neo-human relations' school and the wider-based 'quality of working life' movement. The neo-human relations approach to job design emphasized the fulfilment of social needs by recomposing fragmented work tasks. Advocates put forward five principles of 'good' job design that challenged the core principles of scientific management (Littler and Salaman, 1984):

- The principle of closure, whereby the scope of the job is such that it includes all the tasks to complete a product or process, thus satisfying the social need of achievement
- A good design incorporating control and monitoring tasks, by which the individual or group assumes responsibility for quality control
- Task variety, whereby the worker acquires a range of different skills so that job flexibility is possible
- Self-regulation of the speed of work
- That the design should encompass a job structure allowing some social interaction and a degree of cooperation between workers.

Competitive pressures in the 1970s compelled an increasing number of Western companies to reassess Taylorism and consider ways to redesign jobs. The earliest suggested antidote to Taylorism was the use of *job rotation*, which simply involves the periodic shifting of a worker from one work-simplified task to another (Figure 4.3). The advantage of job rotation is, it was argued, that it reduces the boredom and monotony of doing one simplified task by diversifying a worker's activities. An alternative approach involved the horizontal expansion of tasks, referred to as *job enlargement* (Figure 4.4). Instead of only grilling hamburgers, for example, a griller's job could be enlarged to include mixing the meat for the burger or preparing a side salad to accompany the order. With a larger number of tasks per worker, the time-cycle of work increases, thus reducing repetition and monotony.

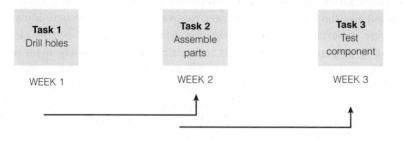

Figure 4.3 An example of job rotation

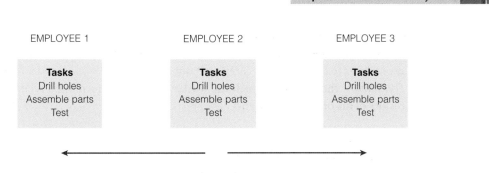

Figure 4.4 *An example of job enlargement*

A later and more sophisticated effort to overcome some of the major shortcomings of Taylorism was the vertical expansion of jobs, often referred to as *job enrichment*. This approach takes some authority from the immediate supervisors and adds it to the job (Figure 4.5). Increased vertical scope gives the worker additional responsibilities, including planning and quality control. For example, the fast-food worker from our previous example might be expected not only to grill the burgers and prepare the salad, but also to order the produce from the wholesaler and inspect the food on delivery for its quality.

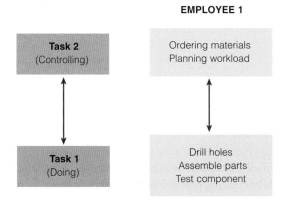

Figure 4.5 *An example of job enrichment*

Hackman and Oldham's (1980) seminal model of job enrichment – the *job characteristic model* – is an influential approach to job design. This model focuses on several measurable characteristics of jobs and assumes that employees may respond differently to these job characteristics. Hackman and Oldham propose that five core job characteristics result in the worker experiencing three favourable psychological states, which in turn lead to positive outcomes (Figure 4.6). The five core job characteristics are:

- *Skill variety* – the degree to which the job requires a variety of different activities in carrying out the work, requiring the use of a number of the worker's skills and talents
- *Task identity* – the degree to which the job requires the completion of a 'whole' and identifiable piece of work
- *Task significance* – the degree to which the job has a substantial impact on the lives or work of other people

- *Autonomy* – the degree to which the job provides the worker with substantial freedom, independence and discretion in terms of scheduling the work and determining the procedures to be used when carrying it out
- *Feedback* – the degree to which the worker possesses information related to the actual results of his or her performance.

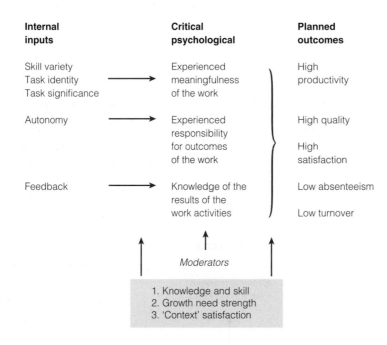

Figure 4.6 *The job characteristic model*

Source: Adapted from Hackman and Oldham (1980)

The chef/manager of a small restaurant would, for example, have a job high on skill variety (requiring all the skills of cooking plus the business skills of keeping accounts, and so on), high on task identity (starting with raw ingredients and ending with appetizing meals), high on task significance (feeling that the meals have brought pleasure to the customers), high on autonomy (deciding the suppliers and the menus) and high on feedback (visiting the customers after they have finished their meals). In contrast, a person working for a fast-food chain grilling hamburgers would probably have a job low on skill variety (doing nothing but grilling hamburgers throughout the shift), low on task identity (simply grilling burgers and seldom preparing other food), low on task significance (not feeling that the cooking makes much of a difference when the burger is to be covered in tomato ketchup anyway), low on autonomy (grilling the burgers according to a routine, highly specified procedure) and low on feedback (receiving few comments from either co-workers or customers).

Hackman and Oldham's framework suggests that the more a job possesses the five core job characteristics, the greater its motivating potential. The existence of 'moderators' – knowledge and skill, and the degree of need for growth and context satisfactions – explains why jobs theoretically high in motivating potential will not automatically generate a high level of motivation and satisfaction for all workers. This means that employees with a low growth need are less likely to experience a positive outcome when their job is enriched.

The job characteristic model has been tested by theorists and, according to Robbins (1989, p. 210), 'most of the evidence supports the theory'.

As part of the 'control debate' (Thompson and van den Broek, 2010), some theorists offered a more critical and ideological evaluation of the job enrichment approach to job redesign (Bosquet, 1980; Burawoy, 1979; Edwards, 1979; Friedman, 1977). Each of these scholars sought to locate the capitalist 'control imperative' in a more complex and organizationally sensitive context. Bosquet, for example, argues that modern management is being forced by labour problems to question the wisdom of the extreme division of labour and factory 'despotism'. Job enrichment (Bosquet, 1980, p. 378) 'spells the end of authority and despotic power for bosses great and small'; this should in turn lead workers liberated from boring jobs to demand total emancipation.

Friedman's (1977) influential study argues that although job enrichment techniques may increase job satisfaction and commitment, the key focus remains managerial control. He maintains that job design strategies such as job enrichment result in individuals or groups of workers being given a wider measure of discretion over their work with minimum supervision, and that this relative 'responsible autonomy' strategy is a means of maintaining and augmenting managerial decision-making and control (Friedman, 1977) or is a 'tool of self-discipline' (Coriat, 1980, p. 40) for workers. Much of the control debate thus emphasized that changing corporate regime practices needed senior management to entrust more decision-making to others. Thompson and van den Broek (2010) underscore management's dilemma: '*Who* to trust is the problematic of managerial agency' (p. 3).

reflective question How has public-sector work in Britain (or your own country) been transformed in the past decade? What is your own experience of using call centres in the UK and elsewhere?

Within the 'control' genre, one of the most penetrating early critiques of job redesign techniques is offered by Thompson (1989). Drawing upon the contributions of various theorists and the empirical evidence, he argues that many job enrichment schemes 'offer little or nothing that is new, and are often disguised forms of intensified [managerial] control' (1989, p. 141).

A significant body of research has focused on the diffusion of task fragmentation and 'rational' rules into interactive service work (Fuller and Smith, 1991; Ritzer, 2004). Drawing on Weber's (1922/1968) concept of rationalization, Ritzer (2004) is best known for applying the four elements of formal rationality – efficiency, quantity, predictability and control – to his investigation of service work in contemporary fast-food chains. Efficiency relates to the streamlined movement in time and effort of employees and products. The efficiency or performance of the operation is measured by the completion of a large number of quantifiable work tasks. Predictability means that managers, workers and customers all know what to expect. So a 'Big Mac' in Edinburgh is the same as a 'Big Mac' in New York or Shanghai. The fourth element in Ritzer's 'McDonaldization of society' thesis is control over workers by task fragmentation and bureaucratic rules. The power of the division of labour to control the labour input in captured in this passage:

Bureaucracies emphasize control over people through the replacement of human judgment with the dictates of rules, regulations, and structures. Employees are controlled by the division of labor, which allocates to each office a limited number of well-defined tasks. Incumbents must do the tasks, and no others, in a manner prescribed by the organization. They may not, in most cases, devise idiosyncratic ways of doing those tasks. Furthermore, by making few, if any, judgments, people begin to resemble human robots or computers. Having reduced people to this status, leaders of bureaucracies can think about actually replacing human beings with machines. (Ritzer, 2000, p. 24)

Interactive service fast-food work is characterized as low-paid, low-skilled, low-autonomy and poor career prospects. The term 'McJob' (Etzioni, 1988) embodies the worst elements of service sector employment. In spite of the research indicating that 'McJobs' are boring, unchallenging and controlling, some scholars have suggested that fast-food work and HR practices are a more nuanced phenomenon that allows for unambiguously negative outcomes, but also offers positive outcomes as a potential 'stepping-stone' to a rewarding career (Daniels, 2004) and 'job security' to younger and older employees (Gould, 2010, p. 799).

In the past two decades, the 'call-centre discourse' has been part of the dominant rhetoric of the new economy. With the growth of call or contact centres, critical research has drawn attention to the communications-driven routinization of much of the service work. An array of evidence has generated an interesting debate on the nature of service work and Taylorist-type surveillance, focusing on employers' desire to specify and script their employees' interactions with callers. The call-centre model has emerged as a dominant work design form that has been established in the realm of nursing and social work and has resited the loci of interactive customer servicing, especially to India (Smith et al., 2008; Taylor, 2010). It is alleged that sophisticated electronic communication and employee-monitoring systems, electronic eavesdropping on sales–client conversations and peer group scrutiny have created ever-tighter control regimes. Various metaphors have been used to capture call-centre work: 'electronic sweatshops' or the 'electronic panopticon', the 'assembly-line in the head' and the often-quoted 'electronic Taylorism' (for example, Callaghan and Thompson, 2001; Sewell, 1998; Taylor and Bain, 1998; Thompson and McHugh, 2009). Such arguments echo earlier debate on deskilling in manual and routine clerical work.

Despite, however, its resemblance to fragmentary and closely monitored manual work, it is argued that labelling all call-centre work as unskilled is misleading. This is because of the assortment of social competencies and emotional demands of the work (Thompson and McHugh, 2009). As with manual work, job expansion has occurred in much interactive service work. Workplace scholars documenting the tendency for employers to incorporate emotion into their job requirements have argued that such jobs increasingly demand standardized verbal scripts, disciplined displays of feelings, and other forms of body posture as part of the employee's performance (for example, Bolton, 2005, 2010; Warhurst et al., 2008). Indeed, many well-known companies have built their competitiveness advantage on the 'delivery of routinized niceness' (Bolton, 2010, p. 217).

©istockphoto.com/Johann Helgason

In the past two decades, the call-centre model has emerged as a dominant work design form.

Post-bureaucratic work systems: the self-management movement

Contemporary, post-bureaucratic approaches to job and work design grow out of, draw upon and sometimes react against classical approaches to work practices (Grey, 2005). For many scholars, the paradigm shift in work redesign that has occurred over the past two decades is team-based working. For example, Cloke and Goldsmith (2002, p. 138) argue that 'In the new organizational paradigm, the fundamental unit of structure is not the isolated individual but the collaborative self-managing team.' In Britain, successive Workplace Employee Relations Surveys have reported an increased adoption of team working or 'high-involvement' work practices (Boxall and Macky, 2009; Cully et al., 1999; Danford et al., 2008; Kersley et al., 2006; McBride, 2008; Millward et al., 2000; Procter, 2006). Consistent with the resource-based view of strategic competitive advantage (see Chapter 2; for example, Barney, 1991), team-based work practices take advantage of internal human skills and capabilities. The last 20 years have been marked by a thriving and prolific debate on different versions of team-based work and HR practices, including 'flexible specialization' to 'lean production' and to 'high-performance work systems' (HPWSs). Such new methods of work organization that depart from the 'rational' Fordist model are the focus here and in the next section.

reflective question

You have probably experienced group working as part of your business programme. Have you enjoyed the experience? What are the advantages/disadvantages of group projects? Why have 'team' projects become common practice in many business schools?

Team-based systems

If corporate giants, such as the Ford Motor Company, had once been the model of mass production – captured by Henry Ford's famous marketing slogan 'You may have any colour you wish, so long as it's black' – Toyota became the model for redesigning assembly lines. The early discourse on the limitations of Fordism is well captured by Piore and Sabel in their book *The Second Industrial Divide* (1984); according to these US authors, the Fordist model is incapable of responding quickly in highly competitive consumer industries. The alternative to Fordism was *'flexible specialization'*, which presented a revival of the 'craft paradigm'. This neo-romantic perspective on job and work redesign is described as:

A strategy of permanent innovation: accommodation to ceaseless change, rather than an effort to control it [based] on flexible – multiuse – equipment; skilled workers; and the creation, through politics, of an industrial community that restricts the forms of competition to those favoring innovation. (Piore and Sabel, 1984, p. 17)

The flexible specialization model was the antithesis of Taylorism; it had the following features:

- The small-scale production of a large variety of products for differentiated markets
- The utilization of highly skilled workers exercising considerable control and autonomy over the labour process

The home office

In 2011, British Transport Secretary Philip Hammond suggested that Londoners might consider working at home during the 2012 Olympics to ease congestion in the capital. This gives a political spin to a long-running debate on 'teleworking'. In the popular discourse, employers have claimed that having employees working at home saves on overheads, and that employees also take fewer sick days. Employees see it as giving them more flexibility over their time (often promoted as a way of combining work and domestic care responsibilities), but have also reported problems of loneliness and social isolation and, for women workers, an extension of the 'double shift' of paid work and domestic work.

Home-working is not something new but was previously mainly confined to manual work. The widespread diffusion of networked information technology in the last two decades has, however, opened up IT-based home working to a whole range of white-collar and managerial employees. Confederation of British Industry figures report that the number of employers offering at least some home-working rose from 14 per cent in 2006 to 46 per cent in 2008. In addition, mobile technologies now mean that there is a growing intermediate group of mobile workers who are not tied to an office but are in communication with their organization from a range of locations (BBC News Magazine, 2011).

A useful definition of telework is that it involves 'the decoupling of work activity from one material workplace such as "the office" … as well as from prescribed working hours, work schedules, scripts and practices' (Tietze, 2002, p. 385). This clearly poses a challenge to traditional models of management control over employees' work (which often rely on being able to *see* the workers) and the usual person-to-person collaboration that is the basis of most work.

To illustrate the contingent variables that can lie behind the success or failure of teleworking, Taskin and Edwards (2007) looked at two Belgian public sector organizations that had introduced it. The first was characterized by routinized and hierarchical white-collar work with a management culture emphasizing strict time-keeping and minimizing absenteeism. At the time of the research, the organization had just moved to a new open-plan office building (a structure based on visual supervision). The management had proposed telework as a 'reward' for meeting performance standards, and it was attractive to the employees as a means of removing themselves from a disliked work situation. Despite this, the project was abandoned because only some employees did work that fitted performance measurement and because of the clash with the dominant organizational culture of direct control. The authors concluded that this seems to confirm previous research indicating that 'strong hierarchies militate against telework by generating a lack of trust in employees when away from physical oversight'.

The second organization was also a public sector bureaucracy, but it had successfully introduced telework as a way of improving working conditions and making the work more attractive. Management exercised control through the development of a high-trust culture and the use of electronic communications. Employees, for their part, increased their number of emails and other e-contacts to maintain 'visibility' with management and co-workers. The two cases suggest that culture may be more important than structure in determining the success of teleworking, although the workers in the second organization were also more skilled than those in the first. Telework thus seems most likely to be applied to groups such as knowledge workers and managers rather than employees with little autonomy.

Stop! What do you see as the advantages to a company of its employees working from home? What would be the disadvantages?

Sources and further information: For further information, see Bryant (2000), Taskin and Edwards (2007) and Tietze (2002).

Note: This case was written by Chris Baldry at the University of Stirling.

- The use of process and information technology
- Strong networks of small producers that achieved flexibility and efficiency through collaboration (Appelbaum and Batt, 1994; Piore and Sabel, 1984).

In this work configuration, the flexible firm model developed by Atkinson (1984) provoked extensive attention from European policy-makers, management theorists and practitioners. The analysis surrounding the flexible firm model also became *de facto* British government policy in the late 1980s and 90s (Sisson and Storey, 2000). The flexible firm model is important in the new economy discourse because it gave theoretical legitimacy to flexible employment arrangements and thereby contributed to the growth of non-standard labour. In Europe, particularly in the UK, the flexible firm model has been linked with the post-bureaucratic agenda of promoting 'fluidity' by creating 'looser organizational boundaries' that tolerate 'outsiders' coming into the organization (Felstead and Jewson, 1999).

Japanese work systems

The 'Japanese threat' so challenged traditional manufacturing strategies three decades ago that influential management consultants proclaimed the need for Western companies to embrace the 'art of Japanese management' (Grey, 2005). The adoption of Japanese management practices set off a process of job and work redesign, and concomitant changes in managing the employment relationship (Bratton, 1992; Thompson and McHugh, 2009; Womack et al., 1990). In the 1980s, the 'Japanization of work' attracted considerable attention from North American and European academics and managers. Two important questions can be raised here: What are the major characteristics of the Japanese model of management? And do these characteristics constitute the basis of a new phase in job design?

In addressing the first question, stereotypical Japanese job and work systems involved both horizontal and vertical job enlargement. Machines are arranged in a group or 'cell' – cellular technology – and multiskilled workers have flexible job boundaries including self-inspection, which means that the team completes a whole component from start to finish. The team makes production and quality-improvement decisions. In other words, the form of job design resembles job B shown in Figure 4.2 above.

Turning to the second question, academics differ over whether or not the Japanese model constitutes a significant departure from traditional job design principles (for example, Elger and Smith, 1994). The work system is distinctive, it is argued, because it creates a complex web of *dependency relationships* that calls for adroit management (Oliver and Wilkinson, 1988). The practice of zero or low inventory – just-in-time production, in the approach known as *kaizen* – is vulnerable to delays and stoppages. This vulnerability was clearly demonstrated in spring 2011 when Toyota Motors and Honda Motors corporations announced the closure of their North American factories because of a supply shortage following the earthquake, tsunami and nuclear disaster that hit Japan from March 11 (Keenan, 2011b).

A further distinctive feature is the 'normative' dimension, which emphasizes the social and psychological aspects of the employment relationship. HR practices and management processes aim to generate a 'moral commitment' to common organizational goals (Dore, 1973; Etzioni, 1988; Findlay et al., 2000; Grey, 2005; Guest, 1987). Critics argue that the Japanese model constitutes a sophisticated control system designed to influence expectations and obligations beyond the formal effort–reward contract. Studies show that peer-group pressure or 'clan' control in team-based regimes creates a culture that reproduces the conditions of their own subordination (Bratton, 1992; Burawoy, 1979; Grey, 2005; Wells, 1993).

HRM web links　Go to the following websites: the Centre for the Study of Work Teams (www. workteams.unt.edu), DaimlerChrysler AG (www.daimler.com), Amicus (www. unitetheunion.org) and the Canadian Autoworkers Union (www.caw.ca). How do these different companies and unions view the introduction of work teams? Do teams improve performance? Are there any negative outcomes of team working for managers or workers?

High-performance work systems

The Japanese model is no longer avant-garde, but numerous US and European studies show that team-based work systems have become the dominant reality (for example, Fröbel and Marchington, 2005). For example, data from the 2004 Workplace Employee Relations Survey revealed that 72 per cent of workplaces had some core employees in formally designated work teams (Kersley et al., 2006, p. 90). Recent contributors to the 'team debate' use a myriad of new acronyms such as 'HPWS' and its conceptual companions 'HCM' (high-commitment management) and 'HIWS' to describe self-managed work teams designed to enhance organizational performance as well as employee voice.

The notion of HPWS appears to dominate the extant studies. Although there are conceptual and measurement issues associated with the research (Boxall and Macky, 2009; Nijholt and Benders, 2010), broadly speaking, HPWS refers to work and HR practices involving:

- Teams of between eight and 20 members performing a task that amounts to a 'rounded-off' product or service
- Team members performing multiple skill enhancement tasks
- Team members participating in operational decision-making.

The most important characteristic of a HPWS is that it 'possesses autonomy in the performance of its daily work activities' (Nijholt and Benders, 2010, p. 381). One interesting observation is that HPWS practices provide a 'soothing balm' to the more abrasive versions of 'lean' team-based regimes (Stewart and Danford, 2008, p. 147).

Some scholars have presented HPWSs as generally positive for workers in that they provide for more skills, a degree of autonomy and enhanced order and predictability, thereby contributing to job satisfaction and commitment while simultaneously enhancing organizational performance (for example, Harley et al., 2010; Ichniowski et al., 1997; Ramsay et al., 2000). Others, however, have argued that HPWS work and employment practices are commonly associated with work intensification. Heywood and his colleagues (2010) go further, arguing that by eliciting a discretionary effort from team members, HPWSs create a 'time squeeze' with negative repercussions for the work–life balance. Critical accounts of HPWSs are exemplified by Danford et al. (2008) and Godard (2004). Bratton's (1992) study of teams reminds us of the need to develop a context-sensitive understanding of self-managed teams. This suggests that HPWS work and HR practices do not have universally 'positive' or 'negative' outcomes for workers. Outcomes vary depending on contingencies such as on the batch size and added value of the work, social relations within the workplace and the presence and power of a trade union (for example, Edwards et al., 2002).

Business process re-engineering

A 'repackaged' version of the Japanese model business process re-engineering (BPR) falls within the post-bureaucratic genre (Albizu and Olazaran, 2006; Champy, 1996; Hammer, 1997). The BPR job redesign movement declares that work systems have to be 'radically' changed so that the re-engineered organizations can become adaptable and oriented towards continuous change and renewal. According to the re-engineering guru James Champy (1996, p. 3), BPR is 'about changing our managerial work, the way we think about, organize, inspire, deploy, enable, measure, and reward the value-adding operational work. It is about changing management itself.' Re-engineered organizations allegedly have a number of common characteristics (Table 4.1).

Table 4.1 *The re-engineered organization*

Characteristic	Traditional model	Re-engineered model
Market	Domestic	Global
Competitive advantage	Cost	Speed and quality
Resources	Capital	Information
Quality	What is affordable	No compromise
Focal point	Profit	Customer
Structural design	Hierarchical	Flattened
Control	Centralized	Decentralized
Leadership	Autocratic	Shared
Labour	Homogeneous	Culturally diverse
Organization of work	Specialized and individual	Flexible and in teams
Communications	Vertical	Horizontal

Central to re-engineered work systems, argues Willmott (1995), is the 'reconceptualization of core employees' from being considered a variable cost to being represented as a valuable asset capable of serving the customer without the need for a command and control style of leadership. With the ascendancy of 'customer democracy', employees are encouraged to exercise initiative in creating value for customers and thereby profits for the company. According to Hammer (1997, pp. 158–9):

Obedience and diligence are now irrelevant. Following orders is no guarantee of success. Working hard at the wrong thing is no virtue. When customers are kings, mere hard work – work without understanding, flexibility, and enthusiasm – leads nowhere. Work must be smart, appropriately targeted, and adapted to the particular circumstances of the process and the customer ... Loyalty and hard work are by themselves quaint relics ... organizations must now urge employees to put loyalty to the customer over loyalty to the company – because that is the only way the company will survive.

This passage is most revealing. It presents the debate on employee commitment, shared commitment and reciprocity in a different light. Furthermore, in the re-engineered organization, responsibility for the fate of employees shifts from managers to customers. In Hammer's (1997, p. 157) opinion, 'The company does not close plants or lay off workers – customers do, by their actions or inactions.'

Unlike earlier movements in work system redesign, re-engineering is market-driven. In essence, it views the management of people through an economic prism focusing on the relationship between the buyer and the seller of services or goods rather than between the employer and employee. In contrast to Beer's et al. (1984, p. 153) 'four Cs', consisting of commitment, competence, cost-effectiveness and congruence, Hammer and Champy (1993) emphasize only 'three Cs' – customers, competition and change. Moreover, reflecting the rhetoric of 'free markets', they emphasize that a government policy of 'tough love' towards business has created the need for BPR. For Champy (1996, p. 19), using a mixture of language discarded by the political 'old Left' and terminology of the 'new Right', 'a dictatorship of the customariat or ... a market democracy ... is the cause of a total revolution within the traditional, machine-like corporation'.

Some workplace scholars have, however, been highly critical of re-engineering. Grint and Willcocks (1995), for example, offer a scathing review of BPR, arguing that it is not new and pointing out that it is essentially political in its rhetorical and practical manifestations. Willmott is similarly scornful of BPR, emphasizing that re-engineering is 'heavily top-down' and pointing out that the re-engineered organization, using information technology, while creating fewer hierarchical structures, also produces 'a fist-full of dynamic processes ... notably, the primacy of hierarchical control and the continuing treatment of employees as cogs in the machine' (Willmott, 1995, p. 91). In his case study analysis of BPR in a hospital, Buchanan (1997) observes that the lack of clarity of BPR terminology and methodology offers 'considerable scope for political maneuvering' by politically motivated actors. A case study of BPR in the public sector found that conflict arose from 'very human needs to justify one's role in the new organization, or individual managers' needs to maintain their power bases within the organization' (Harrington et al., 1998, p. 50). Moreover, BPR does not obviate the inherent conflict of interest between employers and employees. When examined in the context of employment relations, BPR can be interpreted 'as the latest wave in a series of initiatives ... to increase the cooperation/productivity/adaptability of staff' (Willmott, 1995, p. 96).

HRM web links   Go to www.teamtechnology.co.uk/business-process-reengineering.html for an introductory guide to BPR.

Knowledge-based work systems

The final quarter of the twentieth century witnessed, alongside the feminization of employment, the emergence of so-called 'knowledge work', in which work was no longer about the mass production of tangible commodities but was concerned with the organization's intangible assets – knowledge (Sveiby, 1997). Indeed, as a dominant theme in the 'new economy' rhetoric, it is argued that knowledge is the principal asset of the corporation and of countries (Drucker, 1993). The nature of knowledge work is fundamentally different from what we have traditionally associated with the 'machine age' and mass production and marketing, the alleged differences between the nature of traditional work and knowledge work being illustrated in Table 4.2.

Table 4.2 The nature of traditional work and knowledge work

	Traditional work	Knowledge work
Locus of work	Around individuals	In groups and projects
Focus of work	Tasks, objectives, performance	Customers, problems, issues
Skill obsolescence	Gradual	Rapid
Skill/knowledge sets	Narrow and often functional	Specialized and deep, but often with diffuse peripheral focuses
Activity/feedback cycles	Primary and of an immediate nature	Lengthy from a business perspective
Performance measures	Task deliverables	Process effectiveness
	Little (as planned), but regular and dependable	Potentially great, but often erratic
Employee's loyalty	To organization and his or her career systems	To professions, networks and peers
Impact on company	Many small contributions that support business strategy	A few major contributions of strategic and long-term importance

Source: Adapted from Despres and Hiltrop (1995) and Boud and Garrick (1999)

Conventional wisdom says that if an organization's wealth and ability to compete exists 'principally in the heads of its employees, and, moreover, that it effectively "walks out the gates" every day' (Boud and Garrick, 1999, p. 48), greater attention needs to be given to those HR practices that recruit, motivate and retain core knowledge workers. Similarly, Quah argues that sustainable competitiveness depends not on 'having built the largest factory ... [but] on knowing how to locate and juxtapose critical pieces of information, how to organize understanding into forms that others will understand' (1997, p. 4, quoted in Thompson and Warhurst, 1998, p. 1). This realization that knowledge work is fundamentally different has led managers to change business strategies, patterns of interaction, HR practices and 'delayer' organizational structures. Some organizational theorists have described these anti-hierarchical characteristics in organizational design as a shift from 'modernist' to 'postmodernist' organizational practices (Clegg, 1990; Clegg and Hardy, 1999; Grugulis et al., 2003; Hassard and Parker, 1993; Heckscher and Donnelon, 1994).

Work redesign, sustainability and HRM

We started this chapter by examining the meaning of work in contemporary Western society and then proceeded to evaluate three contrasting and significant work system designs: the classical Taylorism and Fordism, the sociotechnical HIWS and the Japanese/ US self-management models. These broad job and work design systems are summarised in Table 4.3. Research shows that these models of flexibility are best understood in the particular cultural-economic context in which senior managers make strategic decisions; there is little to support the notion that they are of universal application (Procter, 2006, p. 479). Furthermore, an analytical approach that is context-sensitive emphasizes that work regimes do not have uniform outcomes but are likely to be contingent on a number of variables, such as business strategy and the historical legacy of social relations in the organization (Bratton, 1992; Edwards et al., 2001; Geary and Dobbins, 2001).

Table 4.3 Four approaches to work system design

	Motivation assumptions	Critical techniques	Job classification	Issues
Classical work system	Motivation is based on the piecework incentive system of pay. The more pieces the worker produces, the higher the pay	Division of tasks and responsibilities Task analysis 'one best way' Training Rewards	Division of tasks and of 'doing' and 'control' leads to many job classifications	Criteria of motivation may be questioned No role for unions Cooperation costs Product inflexibility
High-involvement work system	Motivation is based on social needs and the expectations of workers. To increase performance, focus on achievement, recognition and responsibility	Combine tasks Increase accountability Create natural work units Greater responsibility	Some supervisory tasks are undertaken by workers as the 'control' is shifted downwards	Criteria of motivation may be questioned Undefined union role
Japanese work system	Motivation is based on teamwork or 'clan-like' norms and the organizational culture. Performance and motivation are social processes in which some workers try to influence others to work harder	Intensive socialization Lifetime employment Consensual decision-making Non-specialized career paths Seniority-based pay	Requires fewer job classifications because of flexibility and a degree of autonomy	Criteria of motivation may be culture-bound Collaborative union role Work intensification
US lean work system	Motivation is based on the need to serve the customer. Performance and motivation are social processes in which strong leaders enthuse workers to work harder	Organizational norms and traditions are abandoned Networking Strong top-down leadership Workplace learning Information technology enables change Processes have multiple versions	Multidimensional jobs Workers are organized into process teams Workers are empowered to make decisions	Criteria of motivation may be questioned Market-driven Undefined union role Work intensification

Despite the fondness of workplace scholars for characterizing changes in terms of polar opposites, for example between 'traditional' or 'Fordist' and 're-engineered' or 'post-Fordist' characteristics, this oversimplifies the analysis. As Jaffee (2001, p. 129) notes, the lists of binary opposite features 'conform more to conceptual elegance than empirical reality'. Work redesign is not a smooth transition from one Weberian ideal-type model to another, and new work configurations are most likely to resemble a hybrid configuration that welds elements from the old organizational design onto parts of the new.

Thompson's (1993) offers a persuasive critique of post-bureaucratic organizations. He argues that postmodern theorists have fallen victim to technological determinism and to mistaking the surface of work systems for their substance. Contrary to management parlance, he contends that the 'leaner' post-Fordist designs give more power to a few:

'Removing some of the middle layers of organizations is not the same as altering the basic power structure ... By cutting out intermediary levels [of management] ... the power resources of those at the top can be increased' (1993, p. 192). Legge (2007) cautions us against the tendency to be swept along with the narrative of a 'post-Fordist world'. Without doubt, she argues, there have been changes, but 'most people in the developed west still work in large, bureaucratic organizations with institutionalized internal labour markets that are *policed* by personnel departments carrying out much the same activities as their predecessors a generation ago' (2007, p. 39, emphasis added). That most workers are subject to ever-present bureaucratic control over their work tasks is especially the case for workers in emerging economies, as viewers of the film *China Blue* will attest.

In recent years, there has been a renaissance in the study of 'green' jobs and sustainable work systems (for example, Florida, 1996). During the 1970s, the European Green movement and its critique of dominant economic growth were driven by a concern to preserve natural resources and save the ecosystem. The 'green' alternative economic strategy identified capital accumulation, with its *leitmotiv* of cost reduction by exploiting labour, exploiting all natural resources as well as global ecosystems, as 'inherently deadly' (Bahro, 1979, quoted in Brown, 1984, p. 106). The logic of capital accumulation – more and more, bigger and bigger – creates tension between global capitalism and nature; the 'second contradiction' of capitalism (O'Connor, 1996). Moreover, the perpetual quest to minimize costs means that corporations are 'hardwired to wriggle out of paying social and environmental costs' (Patel, 2009, p. 48).

The goal of designing sustainable work systems is to ensure that all operating and management practices, whether in the manufacturing or the service sector, occur efficiently and within the carrying capacity of the supporting ecosystems. The emergence of the 'triple bottom line' business, which balances profit, planet and people in its strategic operations, is a significant development. In total, the burgeoning body of academic work on sustainability and environmental management is an influential narrative that will shape and direct work system design. Redesigning jobs so that workers engage in low-carbon sustainable management issues and extend their knowledge about sustainability is a work practice that could improve an organization's environmental performance (Jabbour, 2011).

The notion of 'green teams' has generated interest among some scholars (Beard and Rees, 2000). A green team has characteristics associated with the paradigm of the high-performance workplace, especially those involving groups of employees working together to solve environmental problems, fostering informal learning on green practices, developing and implementing a sustainability-oriented work system, and resolving conflicts based on the best options of sustainable management practices (Beard and Rees, 2000). Numerous writers have espoused principles to 'de-carbon' work systems, including 'travel smart' programmes, sustainable purchasing, waste prevention and reduction, and pollution and toxin reduction, and these reap immediate rewards. The creation of a new 'green-collar economy' will, it is argued, create decent, productive work while helping to restore the health of the planet's ecosystems (Jones, 2009). The green building movement also offers immediate rewards by incorporating materials and design strategies that save energy and are in harmony with sustainability principles (Fosket and Mamo, 2009). Others, however, argue that in order to fully respond to sustainability challenges, organizations will have to develop a sustainability-oriented organizational culture (Crane, 1995; Linnenluecke and Griffiths, 2010), a central idea that we examine in Chapter 5.

**reflective
question**

How can organized labour play a more significant role in the restructuring of the economy towards more sustainable work systems and employment practices?

**HRM web
links**

Go to http://www.sustainableworkplaces.ca for information on promoting sustainable workplace practices.

Work systems often flow from corporate decisions to 'externalize' or 'globalize' work activities. In the twenty-first century, the modus operandi of public and private sector organizations is to be competitive by being embedded in complex networks that outsource and insource functions and activities across organizational boundaries and interorganizational relations (Flecker and Meil, 2010; Legge, 2007). The concept of 'value chains' captures the 'disintegration' of functions that occurs when work tasks are outsourced and relocated (Flecker and Meil, 2010). These value chains are dynamic and are reconfigured on an ongoing basis; they contain power relations as the dominant organizational coordinates and control the chain of suppliers or service providers. This restructuring across value chains is an important driver of changes in both work design and HR practices. Take the outsourcing of an organization's IT services, for example. This reconfiguration can impact on work practices in the IT service provider by reducing employees' autonomy as a result of higher degrees of formalization and work intensification, caused by penalty clauses in service agreements. HR practices, in particular pay and conditions, may be inferior in the service provider company, reflecting different systems of employment regulation – union versus non-union – in the public and private sectors (Flecker and Meil, 2010).

The debate on globalization has primarily focused on the emergence of a global structure for the manufacture and consumption of products. One nascent development that is underanalysed is a global structure for professional services (Yu and Levy, 2010). Scholars depict the relocation of relatively low-skill service work in call centres to Mumbai, for example, as a low-wage threat to jobs in Western Europe. A bout of media reporting recently focused on the 'outsourcing' of diagnostic radiology, accounting and legal services. In 2010, Thomson Reuters acquired Pangea3, a legal-process outsourcing company with most of its lawyers in India. For $30 an hour, the Indian lawyers perform the routine work that has traditionally been assigned to junior lawyers in North America for a fee of $300 an hour (Wente, 2011). Yu and Levy (2010) argue that these reports are 'highly exaggerated' for the North American market and fail to develop a nuanced institutional, culturally sensitive understanding of professional work. The structure of knowledge in professional work, professionals' embedded agency in national institutions, and the nature of communication between the client or patient and the professional, means that, in the foreseeable future, Yu and Levy expect 'the world to be less flat' in terms of the global outsourcing of professional work (2010, p. 776).

Globalization and its mantra of flexibility are, however, predicated on cheap transportation costs. In an age of energy scarcity and tighter carbon emissions, the so-called 'boundaryless' organization may be eclipsed by a shift away from global to local supply chains. The 'reverse globalization' thesis argues that distance is money, and therefore corporations need to have national or regional supply chains – in essence, they must go back to a local economy (Rubin, 2009). These developments suggest the need for a significant rethinking, far wider than popular 'green culture fix' strategies, of job and work system design (Fineman, 1996; Florida, 1996; Harris and Crane, 2002).

Changes in work system design and work practices clearly place HRM centre stage. At a strategic level, understanding the close connection between work redesign and HR practices helps to locate HRM in a strategic context (Boxall and Purcell, 2003). Furthermore, as Guest (1990) emphasizes, the high-involvement HR strategy is premised on the assumption that job and work systems should be designed using the ideas inherent in McGregor's (1960) Theory Y. That is, when workers are given challenging assignments and autonomy over their work assignments, they will respond with high motivation, high commitment and high performance. Beer and his colleagues (1984, p. 153) optimistically contend that 'well-executed changes in work system design can broaden employee responsibilities and result in a substantial improvement in all "four Cs"'. In the more critical language of labour process theory, the reintegration of conception and execution becomes a source of employee empowerment and improved productivity (Sewell, 2005). In practice, however, there is much concern and debate over the rupture in the psychological contract resulting from organizational restructuring, particularly from 'delayering' and 'downsizing' (Edwards, 2000).

In the domain of micro HRM, work design may impact all key HRM activities, including recruitment and selection, learning and development, rewards and employee relations. A company that produces small-batch, high value-added products using a team-based system will clearly have different recruitment and selection priorities from those of a company whose business strategy is dependent on large-batch production using dedicated machines that are operated by closely supervised, semi-skilled operators. Work design also affects workplace learning. As one of us has noted elsewhere, high-quality workplace learning is contingent upon the quality of job design (Bratton, 2005).

Closely related is Bolton's (2007) work, which serves to remind us of the centrality of work system design to human dignity *in* and *at* work. The ways in which work is organized and managed can all operate to promote or deny dignity. According to Bolton, the notion of dignified work is about much more than escaping routine and mundane work or attaining a state of 'self-actualization'. Neither is it an individual thing. Instead, it is a multifaceted phenomenon that embodies both objective factors (for example, job security) and subjective factors (for example, respect). As such, job and work designs that offer a degree of responsible autonomy and social esteem and respect provide 'dignity *in* work'; work configurations that offer, among other things, 'voice' and safe and healthy working conditions, afford 'dignity *at* work' (Bolton, 2007, p. 8).

Tension and paradox

Paradox is evident in work system design, and there are a number of ways in which to think about and conceptualize this paradox. Here we use a simple model presented by Jaffee (2001) and illustrated in Figure 4.7. The model shows that paradox stems from what is called 'differentiation–integration tension'. This refers to the inherent tension between management strategies for achieving a rational division of economic activities and, simultaneously, ensuring that these activities are coordinated and integrated. Differentiation

Technology and HR

Different forms of technology and technological change have been at the heart of many of the issues concerning the management of people and the work of HR professionals for a good number of years. In more recent times, however, these issues have emanated from the role of newer technologies in transforming societies, economic progress and how we work.

These more macro and intellectual concerns have been accompanied by the actual influence of technologies on the *practice* of HRM. For example, Sparrow et al. (2004) singled out technology as a transforming force, especially in the e-enablement of HRM and its impact on the creation and transfer of knowledge. With the new knowledge-based technologies advancing at a rapid pace, people management becomes an important mechanism for enabling organizations to translate investments more rapidly into better performance. This HRM–performance perspective has a focus on high-performance employment practices, leading to 'smarter working' and 'best practice' (Boxall and Mackay, 2009).

However, this focus assumes a universalist bundle of practices that somehow result in mutual gains for both employer and employee. Analysts from a critical HRM perspective have called for practitioners and researchers to reflect more carefully upon the shrinking 'human face' of HR from its customer base, and the implications for HR professionals themselves in terms of career opportunities and the development of new capabilities. Practitioners and researchers are also being encouraged to focus on identifying the *processes or pathways* that lead to sustainable individual, team and organizational performance. The emergence of social media technologies provides an opportunity to do this; these represent a move away from technology mostly operating on prescriptive, organization-centred systems to collaborative, web-based applications.

There are, of course, concerns on the part of organizations for their reputation in relation to employee 'misbehaviour' on blogs and social networking sites, and critical HRM analysts draw attention to the 'tyrannical dimension' of new technology, such as its role in enabling people to work longer hours and intensify their work. There is, however, growing evidence that these media have enormous potential to change the way in which people collaborate, communicate, organize their work and give voice to their opinions and expectations, especially when they are physically dispersed across time and space (Martin et al., 2009a). Used in this way, they can help to unlock the nature of people management tensions associated with the need to maintain control *and* seek commitment from workers, and there is also a need for more skilled and pragmatic approaches to managing these at the workplace.

Examples of this approach can be found that help us to understand the tensions associated with the economic and social exchange processes underpinning the employer and the corporate brand (Francis and Reddington, 2012) – an area of increasing interest to HR professionals.

Stop! There are many opportunities for academics and practitioners to collaborate in finding out how different organizations innovate and effectively exploit new HR technology. What is your view on how this might be done?

Sources and further information: For further information, see Boxall and Macky (2009), Francis and Reddington (2012), Martin et al. (2009a) and Sparrow et al. (2004).

Note: This feature was written by Martin Reddington, Associate of Edinburgh Napier University.

and the division of labour are fundamental management principles that underscore organizational goals to control costs and the quality of their products or services. As organizations increase in size and complexity, integration becomes an issue. How do different workers, departments and managers coordinate and integrate their interdependent activities?

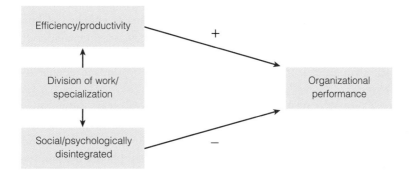

Figure 4.7 *The work design–human factor paradox*
Source: Adapted from Jaffee (2001)

The tension between differentiation and integration within the organization can be illustrated by a familiar manufacturing strategy: that management initially redesigns work involving a rigid division of labour and highly specialized tasks (for example, Fordism). The intended consequence is to rationalize the business and make the workers more efficient and productive. The unintended consequence, however, is a work experience that produces low levels of job satisfaction, motivation and commitment. This, as we discussed earlier, can limit the positive contribution made by the specialization of labour. Delbridge and Turnbull (1992) have detailed the limitation and potentially negative outcomes for workers in a just-in-time system, such as work intensification:

The brinkmanship of just-in-time production creates *extraordinary pressures* on employees and work organization. Such pressures may drive out HR support activities … needed to sustain employee motivation and morale. (Scarbrough, 2000, p. 16, emphasis added)

The crux of this problem is the managerial 'control' of labour's input. Management, as Geary and Dobbins (2001, p. 5) remind us, is not simply about controlling the labour process; it is also about enlisting workers' knowledge, creativity and discretionary efforts:

Management remains caught between two opposing imperatives: attempts at regulating employees too tightly run the risk of endangering the employees' creativity and commitment to management goals, while empowering employees runs the risk of reducing management control.

This fundamental paradox at the heart of the employment relationship becomes even more acute when managers redesign organizational structures and introduce flexible non-standard work patterns – sometimes called 'precarious employment' – that create a disadvantaged and marginalized workforce. This casualization of labour, it is argued, is unethical because it shifts some of the operational risks from the organization onto the most vulnerable employees (Rubery, 1996; Stanworth, 2000).

The notion of tension and paradox in work system design is apparent in the debate on team-based designs. While many scholars (see, for example, Piore and Sabel, 1984) consider that self-managed teams reverse Taylorism, others note that new post-bureaucratic designs have, paradoxically, revitalized Weber's typology of bureaucracy. New performance-related incentives, for example, have generated behavioural rules that reinforce bureaucratic control: 'Thus, intriguingly, the use of bureaucratic control emerges as the main element of labour control in this type of workplace' (Pulignano and Stewart, 2006, p. 104).

Legge's (2007) analysis of the networked organizational configuration identifies the tension that occurs when employers strive for both control *and* commitment. Organizational fragmentation resulting from national and global supply chains and interorganizational business arrangements are, she deftly observes, likely to 'inhibit the development of commitment to a common organizational culture and often involve the disruption of the psychological contract' (Legge, 2007, p. 53). Work team 'empowerment' does not eliminate worker resistance, and managerial control continues to be contested (McKinlay and Taylor, 1998).

Currency, Inc.

Setting

In today's modern office, employees generate over half a kilogram of waste paper per employee per day, and this is increasing by 20 per cent each year. Although it was originally believed that the use of computers would decrease the reliance on paper, the networked access to the Internet and company intranet typically results in more documents being printed. It is estimated that digital documents are being copied onto paper an average of 11 times. The introduction of an email system alone can cause a 40 per cent increase in paper use. Nearly half of the paper being used is considered to be high grade, which can easily be recycled.

The environmental impacts caused by a paper-hungry society are astounding. Over 40 per cent of the solid mass in landfills is created by paper and paperboard waste, and the paper industry ranks fourth in contribution to greenhouse gas emissions, with more than 100 million trees destroyed each year to produce junk mail. If the USA could cut office paper use by just 10 per cent, it would prevent the emission of 1.6 million tons of greenhouse gases, which is the equivalent of taking 280,000 cars off the road. Eliminating paper waste in landfills would almost double the lives of current landfill sites.

In their book *The Myth of the Paperless Office*, authors Abigail Sellen and Richard Harper say that organizations have increasingly striven to become 'paperless' in the hope of not only reducing the costs directly associated with paper, but also achieving greater efficiency, to 'move forward' and motivate change. However, Sellen and Harper caution that concentrating on a goal to eliminate paper can prevent organizations from identifying organizational work practices and value systems that really should be the focus of change.

The problem

Currency Inc., a medium-sized financial firm located in the City of Johannesburg, South Africa, had gone through tremendous changes in the past year: a merger with another company, a new CEO and lay-offs caused by a decline in the country's economy. Many of those affected by the lay-offs had been with Currency for most of their careers, and their abrupt departures caused fear and distrust among the employees who had remained. Absenteeism due to stress leaves suddenly became commonplace.

©istockphoto.com/René Jansa

At the first stakeholder meeting of the year, the company's new CEO, Kagiso Maree, introduced herself to the audience as an 'environmental champion'. Her inaugural presentation focused on the 'green' strategies she intended to implement in the company, proclaiming that 'financial firms are the "watchdog" of the business world and we need to set an example in South Africa by demonstrating environmentally friendly practices.' She laid out a corporate programme targeted at saving energy and conserving resources, with an initial focus on eliminating paper use. Currency, she said, would be a paperless organization within 2 years.

Once she had identified the areas of the business involving the most paper use, Kagiso assigned to several managers the task of implementing the new policies and processes targeted at eliminating paper use. Foremost on the agenda was the implementation of an electronic records retention system to reduce paper usage and the installation of scanners to discourage the printing of documents. This was followed by the roll-out of a new corporate policy allowing only double-sided printing for any company documents that had to be produced in hard copy. Photocopiers and printers were adjusted to default to this setting.

Such policies and attempts to implement the new 'green' initiatives were quickly met with uncertainty, cynicism and scepticism on the part of the workers. The new systems were left untouched or were underused because employees found either the hardware or the applications too confusing and even difficult to use. Employees quickly figured out ways around using the new technology and returned to their previous use, and waste, of paper.

Jokes about the next policy mandating 'paperless toilets' began to circulate throughout the offices. Returning to work after a holiday weekend, several managers found their office floors covered in hundreds of documents, with single-sided printing, produced by photocopiers that had been left to run continuously until depleted of paper. Kagiso, shocked at the workplace response, quickly assembled her management team for an urgent meeting to review why the new corporate programme had failed to gain acceptance by the employees.

Assignment

Working either alone or in a study group, prepare a report drawing on this chapter and other recommended material addressing the following:

1 How might the rise in staff absenteeism have been an indication of how the workers would react to the new 'green' strategies?

2 Although minimum waste is also a component of Japanese management techniques, which aspect of the Japanese approach is obviously lacking at Currency and might have increased the likelihood of the employees accepting the company's new 'green' initiatives?

Essential reading

Ackroyd, S. and Thompson, P. (1999) *Organizational Misbehaviour*. Thousand Oaks, CA: Sage.

Alvesson, M. (1996) *Communication, Power and Organization*. Berlin: Walter De Gruyter.

Maclagan, P. (2008) Organizations and responsibility: a critical overview. *Systems Research and Behavioral Science*, **25**(3): 371–81.

Sellen, A. and Harper, R. (2002) *The Myth of the Paperless Office*. Massachussetts: Massachussetts Institute of Technology.

Thompson, P. and McHugh, D. (2009) Power, conflict and resistance. Chapter 9 in *Work Organisations*. Basingstoke: Palgrave Macmillan.

Note: This feature was written by Lori Rilkoff, HR Manager at City of Kamloops, BC, Canada.

www Visit the companion website at www.palgrave.com/business/bratton5 for guidelines on writing reports.

---

summary

◀ We started this chapter by examining the primacy of work thesis and by defining work as a physical and mental activity performed to produce or achieve something of value at a particular place and time, under explicit or implicit instructions, in return for a reward.

◀ Research testifies that management's mantra is 'flexibility'. The current literature is couched in the language of 'high-involvement' and 'learning', but it appears that, in most cases, the 'quality' of work requiring extensive training an/or workplace learning does not match the rhetoric, and 'non-educative work is systemic' (Bratton, 1999, p. 491).

◀ Critical workplace scholars argue that 'new' work regimes embody neo-Taylorist principles and a technical mode of managerial control. The research on non-standard employment, the 'McDonaldization of work' and 'emotional labour' suggest both change and continuation in work design.

◀ We have cautioned against conceptualizing new work systems as a smooth transition from one ideal-type model to another. The tendency to compress the specific into categories of general trends not only compresses variations in work design, but also attaches a false coherence to emerging work forms. Change is sporadic and subject to constant renegotiation.

◀ Team-based systems are a complex 'interlocking' arrangement of technical, behavioural and cultural dimensions. In the context of capitalist employment relationships, tension and unintended consequences will arise with each new work system.

◀ We concluded by suggesting that, when organizing and managing work activities and systems, managers need to take steps to eliminate the carbon footprint, as well as to understand how new forms of work can change employees' perceptions of the content of the psychological contract.

vocab checklist for ESL students

◀ authority (n), authoritarian (adj)

◀ autocrat/autocracy (n), autocratic (adj)

◀ autonomy (n), autonomous (adj)

◀ business process re-engineering (BPR) (n)

◀ commercialization (n), commercial (n) (adj)

◀ enrich (v), enrichment (n)

◀ extrinsic (adj)

◀ flex (v), flexibilization (n), flexible (adj)

◀ flexible specialization (n)

◀ Ford/Fordism/Fordist (n)

◀ fragment (v) (n), fragmentation (n), fragmentary (adj)

◀ high-commitment management (HCM) (n)

◀ high-involvement work system (HIWS) (n)

◀ high-performance work system (HPWS) (n)

◀ intrinsic (adj)

◀ job design (n)

◀ just-in-time production (n)

◀ labour process theory (n)

◀ lean production (n)

◀ locus (n)

◀ migrate (v), migrant (n) (adj), migration (n)

◀ modernity (n), modern (adj)

◀ multinational companies (n)

◀ opining (v), opinion (n), opinionated (adj)

◀ paradox (n), paradoxical (adj), paradoxically (adv)

◀ paternity (n), paternal (adj)

◀ rationalization/rationality (n), rational (adj)

◀ spatiality (n), spatial (adj)

◀ sustainable work system (n)

◀ symbiosis (n), symbiotic (adj)

◀ Taylorism/Taylorist (n)

◀ transform (v), transformation (n), transformational (adj)

◀ work–life balance (n)

◀ work system (n)

Visit www.palgrave.com/business/bratton5 for a link to free definitions of these terms in the Macmillan Dictionary, as well as additional learning resources for ESL students.

review questions

1 Why define 'work' by its social context rather than by the content of the activity itself?

2 Explain the limits of Taylorism as a job design strategy.

3 'Job rotation, job enlargement and job enrichment are simply attempts by managers to control individuals at work.' Do you agree or disagree? Discuss.

4 Students often complain about doing group projects. Why? Relate your answer to autonomous work teams. Would you want to be a member of such a work group? Discuss your reasons.

5 'McJobs' is a term often used by critics of the 'new economy' to capture the realities of workplace life confronting young people today. What kinds of job does the term 'McJobs' refer to? How do the job design concepts discussed in this chapter help you to understand the term 'McJobs'? Is it an accurate description of employment today?

6 Why does capitalism always seem to produce new work systems, and what are some of its features today?

further reading to improve your mark

Reading these articles and chapters can help you gain a better understanding and potentially a higher grade for your HRM assignment.

◀ Baldry, C., Bain, P., Taylor, P. and Hyman, J. (2007) *The Meaning of Work in the New Economy*. Basingstoke: Palgrave Macmillan.

◀ Bolton, S. C. (ed.) (2007) (ed.) *Dimensions of Dignity at Work*. Amsterdam: Elsevier.

◄ De Menezes, L. and Wood, S. (2006) The reality of flexible work systems in Britain. *International Journal of Human Resource Management*, **17**(1): 106–38.

◄ Docherty, P., Kira, M. and Shani, A. (2009) *Creating Sustainable Work Systems* (2nd edn). London: Routledge.

◄ Edgell, S. (2012) *The Sociology of Work* (2nd edn). London: Sage.

◄ Flecker, J. and Meil, P. (2010) Organizational restructuring and emerging service value chains: implications for work and employment. *Work, Employment and Society,* **24**(4): 680–98.

◄ Ritzer, G. (2004) T*he McDonaldization of Society*. Thousand Oaks, CA: Pine Forge Press.

Visit www.palgrave.com/business/bratton5 for lots of extra resources to help you get to grips with this chapter, including study tips, HRM skills development guides, summary lecture notes, and more.

part II

the micro context
of human
resource
management

chapter 5

organizational culture and HRM

outline

- ◄ Introduction
- ◄ Culture and modernity
- ◄ Organizational culture
- ◄ HRM and globalization: Multiculturalism's magic number
- ◄ HRM as I see it: Keith Stopforth, Bupa Health and Wellbeing
- ◄ Perspectives on organizational culture
- ◄ HRM in practice 5.1: Management surveillance: someone's watching you …
- ◄ Managing culture through HRM
- ◄ Sustainability and green HRM
- ◄ HRM in practice 5.2: Can we measure changes in organizational culture?
- ◄ Paradox in culture management
- ◄ Case study: Big Outdoors
- ◄ Summary, Vocab checklist for ESL students, Review questions and Further reading to improve your mark

objectives

After studying this chapter, you should be able to:

1 Explain the relationship between national culture and organizational culture

2 Define organizational culture and be aware of notions of dominant culture, cultural diversity, subcultures and countercultures

3 Explain different theoretical perspectives on organizational culture

4 Understand how senior managers strive to change the culture of their organization and the role of human resource management (HRM) in the change process

5 Explain the role of HRM in creating low-carbon sustainable work systems

introduction

n 2010, the consultancy company Baringa Partners won Britain's Best Workplace Award largely because of its organizational culture, which emphasized open communications and the nurturing of talented employees. In the same year, research reported increased incidences of a 'binge-working culture' (Campbell, 2010), a 'long-hours culture' in which employees regard 'busyness' as 'voluntary' behaviour or overtime, and long hours as 'a badge of honour' (Chatzitheochari and Arber, 2009). And in 2011, a report by the UK House of Commons Justice Select Committee reported that their probation officers spent 75 per cent of their time on form-filling and responding to centrally driven emails, which they described as a 'tick-box culture' (Travis, 2011).

Workplace norms of work and leisure activities can be seen as an expression of organizational culture and power. The work–life balance discourse can illustrate that the different ways in which we *experience* work are shaped by a form of hegemony, and by what we believe, what we value and what we see as legitimate (Kärreman and Alvesson, 2009; Schneider, 2000). These intangible informal structures or 'ways of doing' work can be thought of as 'organizational culture'. Culture management is becoming important for thinking in strategic human resource management (HRM) because it is increasingly perceived to be a 'key lever' to release consensus, flexibility and commitment (Storey, 2007). Culture can also create a context in which employees 'follow the flow', where 'compliance is not only desirable: it is almost irresistible' (Kärreman and Alvesson, 2009, p. 1141). In the HRM canon, organizational culture has been described as a transformation process to unlock the 'holy grail' of commitment by appealing to employees' desire to contribute to 'goals beyond immediate self-interest' (Beer et al., 1984, p. 181). Critical management scholars, however, are highly sceptical about claims of managing cultures, regarding such claims as naive and as doing little to remove the 'structured antagonism' found in the employment relationship (Edwards, 1986, 1995).

To understand the contemporary workplace, we must consider not only job design and underlying structure, but also cultures related to the workplace. This chapter begins by introducing the concept of national culture and discusses its relevance to the contemporary workplace. We will then explore the complex concept of organizational culture – what it is, and how it manifests itself within the modern workplace. We examine different theoretical perspectives on organizational culture, and finally we will take a critical look at the clusters of HRM practices that are used to change and manage culture. This analysis then provides us with the opportunity to take a critical look at the organizational culture–performance relationship, with particular reference to sustainable low-carbon work cultures.

reflective question Based upon your own experience of work or of being a customer of an organization, is it possible to recognize a different tone or 'feel' within organizations? How do the intangible 'ways of doing' things at your university compare, for instance, with your employment experience?

Culture and modernity

The word 'culture' is one of the most complicated words in the English language (Williams, 1983). In everyday language, the word 'culture' is loaded with evaluative connotations related to social class, power and status (Parker et al., 2003). The complexity of its modern usage can be appreciated when, in everyday speech, we refer to rock music as 'popular culture' and opera as 'high culture'. In the latter case, culture is associated with the arts, refinement and a privileged education. When anthropologists and sociologists use the term 'culture', it includes such social activities, but it also emphasizes that a national culture has a 'collectivizing effect' and creates differences between populations.

A 'culture' refers to an imperfect collection of interrelated understandings and behaviours shared by a people, which are shaped by ways of thinking and acting, by identities and by the material artefacts that together shape a people's way of life. As such, culture includes all the things people learn while growing up among a particular group: attitudes, beliefs about how people should act in particular situations, how females and males should interact, perceptions of reality and so forth. By definition, culture is collective, it is shared by a group of people, and it is socially learned and transmitted from one generation to the next (Giddens, 2009; Macionis and Gerber, 2011). You might think of culture as a societal tapestry of woven threads that makes each society unique or, on a larger scale, as a national characteristic such as 'Englishness'. The central implication for human resources (HR) practice is that culture constrains and enables social action, conditioning social structure or relatively stable patterns of individual behaviour and motivations (Figure 5.1).

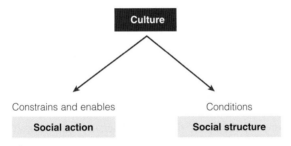

Figure 5.1 *The dynamics of culture*
Source: *Adapted from Parker et al. (2003)*

HRM web links Visit www.new-paradigm.co.uk/Culture.htm for a description of organizational culture, and www.tnellen.com/ted/tc/schein.html for an article on culture and leadership.

Cultural scholars contend that the culture of a human society is a manifestation of a complex interplay of symbols, laws, values, beliefs and practices that are learned and exhibited by its members (Adler and Gundersen, 2008). In the postmodernism discourse, now that the sacred and the 'spiritual' seem to be extinct, it is plausibly argued that culture has become material or materialistic in terms of its structures and functions (Jameson, 1991).

Symbols, for example, in languages, intellectual life and religion, are ideas that convey meaning between individuals and groups. One important aspect of culture is language. Words and utterances can have different meanings depending on the context. In Japan, for example, some utterances may be lost in translation. When government officials or business people say that they will take something 'into serious consideration', they mean 'no' (Buruma, 2011), but this is not always understood by expatriate managers. Take also the

©istockphoto.com/Anthony Seebaran

Symbols come in all shapes and sizes. What does this well-known symbol mean to you?

symbol of the cross, which has a powerful meaning for Christians but little for Buddhists. The Confederate flag, however, has a powerful meaning for Christians and non-Christians alike, as a searing symbol of the nineteenth-century American slave-holding states (Manji, 2010).

Symbols also influence the essential *values* that people hold about society and the world around them. Values have profound, although partly unconscious, effects on people's behaviour in different situations. A *norm* is a shared ideal (or rule) about how people ought to act in certain situations, or about how particular people should act toward particular other people. The different ways in which people act and interact with others, and the tendency for people to view their own way of life as 'natural', can cause personal disorientation or 'culture shock' for tourists and immigrants experiencing a new country (Macionis and Gerber, 2011). Shared symbols, values and behaviour, however, change over generations. The process by which each generation or other new members of society learn the way of life of their society is called *socialization*.

A mixture of factors distinguish 'capitalist modernity'. This term has come to define the vast and largely unregulated expansion of the production and consumption of commodities, their related national markets, individualism and secularization over the last 200 years (Sayer, 1991). Late modernity is associated with the production of information, conspicuous consumption, especially in the area of leisure, global markets and social networks. The dynamics of late modernity, it is argued, have brought an 'extensification of contemporary culture' (Lash, 2010, p. 2). Take, for example, the iconic coffee chain Starbucks: there are many stores not just in every European capital, but in seemingly every district of Beijing, Delhi, Johannesburg and Buenos Aires too. This growing extensification of contemporary urban life is being driven by multinational corporations and global intergovernmental organizations such as the International Monetary Fund, the United Nations and the World Bank, as well as non-governmental organizations such as Oxfam. Moreover, 'time' and 'space' have taken on a new meaning in contemporary culture with today's global capitalism. City-dwellers increasingly face the choices and uncertainties of a globalized market society, with experiences that cut across all spatial boundaries of social class and nationality or ethnicity, of religion and ideology, and whose reference point is both global and local (Giddens, 1990; Harvey, 1994).

In this context of seismic shifts in how contemporary societies are organized and an increasing extension of social structures – the patterns of social relations that bind people together and give shape to their lives – people acquire new values, beliefs and practices from the groups to which they belong. A national culture has a number of essential features: it is *collective, socially learned, transmitted, shared* and a product of human socialization and social interaction. These defining aspects of national culture are important in understanding the complexity of culture and how people seek to assert their social uniqueness over time and place; moreover, they help us to see how a society's beliefs and values can guide and shape the employment relationship.

Europe, North America and Asia are culturally diverse. Within their borders lie many cultures and subcultures formed by divisions such as social class, ethnicity and gender, this tapestry of multiple subcultures being in turn locally differentiated. A stream of studies describes the cultural traits found in Eastern and Western societies, perhaps the best known being Hofstede's (2010) study, which measured national culture in 64 countries. Hofstede's data, based on one global corporation, IBM, initially identified four independent dimensions of national cultural differences:

- *Power distance* – the extent to which those who are less powerful accept that power is distributed unequally
- *Individualism* versus *collectivism* – the degree to which members of society are integrated into communities
- *Masculinity* versus *femininity* – the general acceptance of sex-biased values and the sexual division of labour
- *Uncertainty avoidance* – society's tolerance for ambiguity and uncertainty, which ultimately deals with the search for truth.

HRM web links   Visit Geert Hofstede's website – http://geert-hofstede.com/website – which includes his publications and a link to a symposium video. Also visit http://tinyurl.com/2ndzbj, which includes critiques of Hofstede's work.

Since early modernity, the moral values of societies on both sides of the Atlantic have had a strong influence on the management of people. The value-loaded notion of 'fairness', for example, underwrites the structure of rewards and work obligations. This is illuminated by the maxim 'A fair day's wage for a fair day's work' (Hyman and Brough, 1975). Changing 'life' values have also changed participation rates in the labour market and challenged traditional gender roles in the workplace. In addition, different national cultures have influenced Western scholars' thinking on the best way to motivate employees, and on how to close the 'commitment gap' (see Chapters 1 and 3). In Maslow's theory of work motivation, for instance, higher order self-actualization is seen as the supreme human need. But this assumption presupposes an *individualist* culture in which the ties between individuals are loose and everyone is expected to look after themselves and their immediate families.

Renewed interest in the culture–performance link has generated studies comparing North American and East Asian cultural values. Faced with reports of superior Japanese management practices, researchers examined whether the 'commitment gap' between North American and Japanese workers can be attributed to differences in cultural values and national character (Lincoln and Kalleberg, 1992). In some national cultures, the values of *collectivism* and sharing are cited as a defence against an ideology seeking to lower taxes and privatize public services:

It's the difference between being human beings and animals. With animals, when one of them gets old, they let it die, they eat it. We want to take care of our people, our youths, our students, our elderly. We are the most egalitarian society [Quebec] in North America and we want to keep it that way. (Séguin, 2010, p. A16)

Hofstede's argument for cultural homogeneity has attracted considerable criticism. The empirical basis for his proposal is a statistical averaging of his quantitative data – survey responses from IBM's employees. But an average of personal values claiming to measure the values of a national culture is about as meaningful as an average of personal income. As has been well established elsewhere, in the same way as there is a wide variance in personal income in any population, so there is a wide dispersion in the personal values of that population (McSweeney, 2002).

Among the developed countries in the global economy, few are likely to exhibit a singular culture, being more likely to be plural, with hyphenated identities such as African-American, Chinese-Canadian, French-Canadian, Anglo-Indian and so on. In support of the cultural diversity argument, experts document almost 7000 languages worldwide, suggesting the existence of that many distinct cultures (Macionis and Gerber, 2011). In the countries located in the Asian region, there are at least seven major official languages, and the people believe in widely different religions and philosophies, ranging from Buddhism and Hinduism to Islam and Christianity. Within the European Union, there are 23 official and working languages. And within the UK, the question of whether or not Scotland, Wales, Northern Ireland or England has its own distinct culture evokes strong responses. Scotland, for example, as a land of lochs, mountains and tartan, forms a compelling image that transmits 'potent resonances for culture' (McCrone, 2001, p. 37).

The empirical evidence at the centre of Hofstede's argument for a 'national culture' contains contradictions and paradoxes. In reality, people live and work in multiple cultures. The quest for a 'unified' culture is therefore doomed to ignore the fragmentation and complexities of contemporary society. To argue that research on the relationship between national values and organizational cultures is 'loose' (Hofstede et al., 2010) is not to imply that cultural undercurrents do not structure human behaviour in subtle but highly regular ways, or that as citizens and as employees, we do not carry our cultural heritage and social identities into the workplace. We talk and act in a particular way that reflects both our collective unconsciousness and our ethical standards (Saul, 2008). In other words, cultural plurality does not mean that Western societies do not function without national or regional norms. Amidst the plurality, national culture translates into organizations by influencing the core values and beliefs that constitute their organizational cultures (see, for example, Zhang and Begley, 2011).

reflective question The problem of identifying a national culture is soon apparent when we examine values. Take Britain, for example. Just what are core 'British values'? How do we complete the phrase 'as British as …?' Is it possible to identify Indian or Canadian values?

Organizational culture

In the current organizational literature, the word 'culture' is used to capture various 'ways of doing' and employees' interactions, as in 'bonus culture', 'binge-working culture' or 'masculine culture'. When academics and executives debate the merits of transforming or managing 'organizational culture', what exactly is it that they are trying to change or manage? The notion of organizational culture is equally as complex as that of national culture, and equally it lends itself to very different uses. In the literature, the terms 'corporate culture' and 'organizational culture' are common. The distinction between the two is that the former is devised and transmitted downwards to subordinates by senior management as part of a strategy of mobilizing employee commitment and portrays the workforce as 'culture-takers'.

Multiculturalism's magic number

HRM and globalization

In the first decade of the new millennium, questions have been raised about the so-called multiculturalism experiment. In Europe, Chancellor Angela Merkel has claimed that German multiculturalism has 'utterly failed', and The Netherlands, the UK and France have all, to differing degrees, blamed multiculturalism for weakening their national social cohesion. Even in Canada, one of the world's most multicultural societies, 'its reality remains complex and at times volatile' (Peritz and Friesen, 2010, p. A14).

High levels of immigration in the last three decades have transformed Canada from a bilingual – English and French – two-culture society to a cultural mosaic. Immigration statistics reveal just how much Canada has changed. Before 1961, about 91 per cent of immigrants to Canada came from Western Europe, especially the UK, and less than 5 per cent came from Asian and Middle Eastern countries. Canadians celebrated their European cultural inheritance but gave 'scarcely a nod, let alone a meaningful nod, in the direction of the First Nations, the Métis, the Inuit' (Saul, 2008, p. 4).

Between 1991 and 2001, however, European immigrants constituted 20 per cent of total immigration, while immigrants from Asia and the Middle East made up 58 per cent. This change in the pattern of immigration was the result of a deliberate change in public policy. Now Canadian society is officially multicultural in that this aim is embodied in government social policy designed to encourage ethnic or cultural heterogeneity. Quebec has become the crucible for a Canadian debate over identity, values and how far newcomers should be accommodated at work and in other areas of life. In 2008, Quebec established a telephone 'hotline' to tackle matters of linguistic, ethnic and religious accommodation. The following three cases provide a window into managing the multicultural workplace:

©kbrowne41/Shutterstock.com

- *Case 1* – A Sikh employee in a food warehouse wants to wear a kara – a bangle-type metal bracelet that represents an expression of the Sikh faith. The warehouse has a ban on jewellery for employees who handle food, for hygiene purposes. The company wants to know if it should accommodate the employee's request.
- *Case 2* – A college student wears a Muslim face veil, or niqab, that covers her entire body except for a slit for her eyes. She has agreed to pose for her student ID bare-faced, but does not want the image to be entered into a college-wide computer database. The college is seeking a policy that will balance its security needs with the student's wishes.
- *Case 3* – A Muslim schoolteacher requests each Friday afternoon off to attend prayers at his mosque. The school board wants to know how to accommodate him.

Multiculturalism has generated controversy because people need to rethink their core values and norms. The issue of reasonable accommodation in multicultural workplaces has become a microcosm of the diversity dilemma: it affects the psychological contract, it is linked to the topic of dignity at work (Bolton, 2007), and it has repercussions for HRM.

Stop! If you were the HRM manager employed at these three workplaces, what advice would you give to each? What types of cultural knowledge might be common in a workplace in your home country? How would you react if you were asked by an employer to remove an article of faith, for example a cross or a kara?

Further reading and other resources: See Peritz and Friesen (2010), Saul (2008) and Taylor and Bain (2005). View the film *Slumdog Millionaire* (2009) for an insight into culture training at Indian call centres. And go to this book's website for information on how Quebec's Multiculturalism Commission advised the three organizations mentioned in this feature.

Note: This feature was written by John Bratton.

Organizational culture, on the other hand, is a product of employees' creativity and portrays the participants as 'culture-makers' (Linstead and Grafton Small, 1992).

The terms *culture* and *climate* are used interchangeably by some culture researchers (Schneider, 2000). These are complementary constructs, but they reveal overlapping nuances in the social and psychological life of complex organizations. Culture scholars tend to use qualitative methodology derived from anthropology to examine symbolic and cultural forms of organizations. Climate researchers, however, attempt to measure individuals' perceptions of workplace conduct and the meaning they assign to it using quantitative methods, such as regression analysis. The distinction between culture research and climate research therefore lies in the different methodology traditions, what they consider to be significantly meaningful and the agenda underlying each approach. More critical interpretations contend that the psychological treatment of culture largely reflects 'a neo-human relations agenda' (Parker, 2000).

The different approaches generate different definitions of organizational culture. An early definition by Smircich focuses on values that guide employees' conduct at work and shape their interactions. Organizational culture (Smircich, 1983, p. 344) is the:

Social or normative glue that holds an organization together … The values or social ideals and the beliefs that organization members come to share. These values or patterns of beliefs are manifested by symbolic devices, such as myths, stories, legends and specialized language.

In contrast, a definition focusing on shared meanings and symbolism is articulated by Alvesson (2002, pp. 3–4):

For me values are less central and less useful than meanings and symbolism in cultural analysis … Culture is not primarily 'inside' people's heads, but somewhere 'between' the heads of a group of people where symbols and meanings are publicly expressed, for example, in work group interactions, in board meetings but also in material objects. Organizational culture then is central in governing the understanding of workplace interactions, events and processes. It is the context in which these phenomena become comprehensible and meaningful.

A synthesis of the definitions captures the essential elements of organizational culture. It concerns the importance of shared values, beliefs and language that shape and perpetuate organizational reality, so that employees' work conduct is more predictable and governable.

reflective question Reading the two definitions of organizational culture, does your university have a culture? How does this differ within and between the different faculties, schools or departments of the university?

To understand organizational culture, we must examine its parts, even though any organizational culture is greater than the sum of its parts. Drawing on the work of Edgar Schein (2010), Figure 5.2 shows three fundamental levels of organizational culture: *artefacts*, *values* and *basic assumptions*. These can be imagined as an iceberg. The uppermost subtriangle might be viewed as the 'tip of the iceberg', representing the observable parts of organizational culture, which are embedded in shared values, basic assumptions and beliefs that are invisible to the human eye. Each level of culture influences another level.

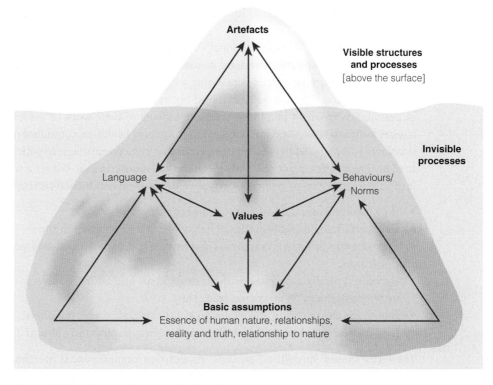

Figure 5.2 *The three levels of organizational culture*

The first level comprises the visible, the *artefacts* and material objects such as buildings, technology, art and uniforms that the organization 'uses' to express its culture. For example, when a company uses only email for internal communication, the cultural message is that IT is a highly valued resource. Displaying art on office walls signals to members and visitors that creating a stimulating cultural context in which employees can explore ideas and aesthetics is highly valued (Harding, 2003). Other examples are the wearing of professorial apparel, the doctor's white coat in the National Health Service (NHS) and the black gown worn by academics at official university ceremonies. The visible culture also includes *language*.

How managers describe other employees is an example of using symbols to convey meaning to each other. For example, Walmart refers to its employees as 'associates', and at Disneyland they are known as 'cast members'. Social *behaviour* is another aspect of observable organizational culture, including rituals and ceremonies. *Rituals* are collective routines that 'dramatize' the organization's culture. For example, the office party can be viewed as a ritual for *integrating* new members into the organization. *Ceremonies* are planned and represent more formal

©istockphoto.com/Luca Cepparo

Leather, tattoos and long hair could be considered an expression of this motorcycle club's visual culture.

social artefacts than rituals, as in, for example, the 'call to the bar' ceremony for graduating lawyers.

The second level of organizational culture comprises perceived shared work-related *values*, which are invisible. Previous studies suggest that perceived organizational ethical values refer to workers' beliefs concerning what practices are acceptable or appropriate in their organization (Biron, 2010). Perceived organizational values are therefore the standards of desirability by which employees evaluate aspects of their work or profession and make choices between options (Warr, 2008). For example, in healthcare, standard medical practice is influenced by a belief in evidence for practice or by a commitment to patient-centred care. In many universities, practice is influenced by the espoused value 'We are a teaching-centred institution'. Employment-related espoused values possess six characteristics (Warr, 2008):

- They involve a moral or ethical statements of 'rightness'.
- They pertain to desirable modes of behaviour at a given point in time.
- They directly influence employees' behaviour and experiences, and act as significant moderators.
- They are typically associated with strategic goals and address questions such as 'What are we doing?' and 'Why are we doing this?'
- They guide the selection and evaluation of the organization's members.
- They may vary with respect to male/female, demographic and cultural differences.

The term 'shared' in cultural analysis implies that organizational members are a whole. Each member has been exposed to a set of dominant values, although not every member may internalize and endorse these. Despite the substantial evidence that perceived organizational values influence the behaviour of workers, the practical application of the insights generated by this research has been limited (Biron, 2010).

The third level of organizational culture relates to *basic assumptions*, which are invisible, unconscious, taken for granted, difficult to access and highly resistant to change. These are the implicit and unspoken assumptions that underpin everyday choices and shape how members perceive, think and emotionally react to social events. For example, in the NHS, assumptions about the relative roles of doctors and nurses, about patients' rights or about the sources of ill-health underpin everyday decisions and actions (Davies, 2002). The basic assumptions or beliefs about human nature, human relationships, relationships to nature and how the world works form the base from which employees, who enter the workplace as social beings with life histories and experiences, build their values of how the world *should* be. Assumptions and values then guide employees' workplace conduct and shape their interactions, as do the artefacts with which members surround themselves. Organizational culture manifests itself most clearly through the organization's policies and practices (Zhang and Begley, 2011).

HRM web links   www   Visit http://web.mit.edu/scheine/www/home.html, which is Schein's official website.

reflective question   PS   Thinking about your own university or college, does the culture manifest itself through policies or practices? For instance, do you expect *and* experience a student-centred focus? Do teaching staff primarily focus on their teaching or their research interests? Is there a 'publish or perish' culture? Try to assess your answer at three levels: observable artefacts, shared values and basic assumptions of the culture.

Keith Stopforth

Head of Talent and Development, Bupa Health and Wellbeing

www.bupa.co.uk

Bupa is an international private healthcare company with bases on three continents and over 10 million customers in over 200 countries. Bupa provides health insurance, care homes, health assessments, occupational health services and child care, and runs its own hospital, Bupa Cromwell Hospital, in London. The company also owns several healthcare companies overseas, including Sanitas in Spain and IHI Danmark in Denmark.

Keith Stopforth has been with Bupa since 2001. He now works in Bupa Health and Wellbeing in the UK, having previously worked as a sales manager and then branch training manager at Prudential. Keith is currently developing his skills in executive coaching and mentoring. He is a member of the Talent Forum 2011.

Visit www.palgrave.com/business/bratton5 to watch Keith talking about talent management, organizational culture and diversity at Bupa, and then think about the following questions:

1 What is Keith's view of organizational culture and the role of the HR department in 'shaping' culture?
2 What are the role of competencies in this process?
3 How does BUPA embrace diversity? What opportunities are provided to encourage prospective employees, and how do you think these could be applied in other companies?

HRM **as I see it**

Perspectives on organizational culture

The family tree of the different perspectives on organizational culture is rooted in classical sociological theory. The work of the German sociologist Max Weber is representative of the canonical literature on understanding employees' work conduct as a cultural phenomenon: individuals behave 'not out of obedience, but either because the environment approves of the conduct and disapproves of its opposite, or merely as a result of unreflective habituation to a regularity of life that has *engraved itself as a custom*' (Weber, 1922/1968, p. 312, emphasis added). Much contemporary writing in culture analysis can be divided into two schools of thought: managerialist and critical.

Managerially oriented perspectives

This body of writing examines culture from the premise that it can play a role in building organizational consensus and harmony, and can improve performance. From this viewpoint, organizational culture is a *variable* – an attribute that an organization possesses or '*has*' and, as such, can be created by corporate managers.

This standpoint is associated with the *structural-functionalist* approach to cultural analysis. Its theoretical roots date back to Auguste Comte (1798–1857) and Emile Durkheim (1858–1917) and, in the twentieth century, to the US sociologist Talcott Parsons (1902–1979) (see Chapter 1). The central premise of the structural-functionist approach is that cultural processes can create organizational stability and consensus. The task of senior management is therefore to focus on how culture can be managed and disseminated downwards to organizational members.

Within this genre, Peters and Waterman's influential book *In Search of Excellence* is probably the best well-known example of the 'has' school. These gurus view culture as an elixir that binds together the specific human qualities that lead to a maximizing of employees' commitment to providing a high-quality service or product – what is sometimes called a 'commitment-excellence organization'. Thus, mainstream theorists are said, in Martin's (1992) words, to follow an *'integration'* perspective. In this sense, management-inspired cultural processes and interventions attempt to alleviate the many forms of the ever-present conflict that arises from managing the labour process. This approach focuses on building a culture that binds members together around the same core values, beliefs and norms, which are considered to be prerequisites for achieving the organization's strategic goals. For integration or functionalism theorists, culture is conceptualized as 'organization-wide agreement with values espoused by top management' (Martin and Frost, 1996, p. 600). The notion of 'cultural engineering' – creating the 'right' kind of culture to align with strategic goals – is seen as a 'lever' for fostering commitment and loyalty in the workforce.

What constitutes the 'right culture' for excellence is, however, a matter of debate. A popular approach is the contingency theory, which is based on the belief that senior managers need to consider both external and internal variables when deciding what kind of culture best fits their organization. Deal and Kennedy (1982), for example, identify important contingencies such as the level of risk, the size and design of the organization, ownership and governance, technology and the need for innovation. In the leadership literature, a connection between leadership, culture and employees' commitment to the organization has often been theoretically proposed. Employee organizational commitment is the degree to which employees identify with the organization's goals and values, their willingness to exceed a minimum level of effort on behalf of the organization, and their intention to remain with the organization.

Specifically, recent studies have found that 'transformational' leadership behaviour is an antecedent variable in regard to employee commitment. For example, Simosi and Xenikou (2010, p. 1611) conclude that both transformational leadership behaviour and contingent reward were found to be 'significantly and positively related to affective and normative commitment' as well as to employees' feeling of obligation to remain in the organization. Champy contends that 'values are our moral navigational devices' and that, for real change to occur, leaders need 'cultural warriors' at every level of the organization to communicate new values to their peers (1996, p. 79). Whereas management gurus such as Peters and Waterman, Deal and Kennedy, and Champy focus on values that foster 'strong' corporate cultures, researchers have in recent years argued that cultural diversity and the changing nature of the employment relationship have heightened how important it is to understand the dynamics of employee commitment as a potential determinant of motivation (see, for example, Becton and Field, 2009; Mathew and Ogbonna, 2009; Su et al., 2009).

Contingency studies do draw attention to cultural heterogeneity, and Martin (1992) refers to these as the *differentiated* perspective. An organization such as the NHS might have one dominant culture expressing its core values, but it also has sets of *subcultures* defined by professions, function and space. An image of professional groups with strong norms and values potentially challenging aspects of the organization's core values is associated with Ouchi's (1980) concept of the 'clan', itself drawn from Durkheim's theory of mechanical solidarity. A study of healthcare providers revealed that 'complex multiple cultural values are often hierarchical and are commonly interpreted in ways that ascribe differentiated, fragmented and collective meaning' (Morgan and Ogbonna, 2008, p. 61). Healthcare professionals may collectively interpret the espoused value of providing the 'best possible care' for patients, but that 'care' will be delivered differently by the various professional groups. For doctors, this may mean eradicating the cause of illness, whereas for occupational therapists it may mean helping patients achieve greater mobility (Fitzgerald and Teal, 2004). In contrast, a macho and aggressive subculture might exist among male workers doing mundane or unpleasant work (Ackroyd and Crowdy, 1990).

Subcultures help to bind workers together, to cope with shared frustrations and to preserve a distinctive identity (Bolton, 2005). The analyses of subcultures reveal a wide variation in values, work conduct and assumptions – these are, however, a normal part of organizational life.

reflective question Do you think a complex organization like the UK's NHS has subcultures? What are the implications for HRM practices if core subcultures exist?

A sociologically informed analysis of culture also acknowledges the existence of *countercultures* in work organizations. These create their own form of organizational reality through a subculture that actively opposes the dominant values and norms (Martin and Siehl, 1983). For example, a policy change focusing on 'putting customers first' may produce countercultures as some staff may be reluctant to abandon professional or trade norms and may strongly reject service-oriented values. Mergers and acquisitions may also produce countercultures. There may be a 'clash of corporate cultures' when the values, beliefs and norms held by members of an acquired organization are inconsistent with those of the acquiring organization. The debate on the existence of subcultures and countercultures emphasizes the complexities and interwoven character of organizational culture and avoids an overly static and monolithic picture of everyday organizational life.

Critically oriented perspectives

Critical cultural scholars share a similar view that values and norms are deeply embedded in society. In contrast to the structural-functionalist perspective that understands culture as something an organization 'has', critical workplace theorists proceed from the idea that the organization 'is' a culture. The central premise is that, at its roots, the work organization is a manifestation of human consciousness, a source of power, a socializing and controlling force. Moreover, adherents of the 'is' view of culture are likely to play down any outcomes in terms of efficiency that result from changes in the culture (Alvesson, 2002). Here, three critically oriented perspectives – symbolic-interactionist, conflict and feminist – will serve as alternative lenses through which to understand organizational culture.

The *symbolic-interactionist* approach understands organizational culture as the sum of all the employees' interactions. In this school of thought, culture plays the role of a 'carrier' for shared meaning (hence 'symbolic') and is produced by workers and managers in face-to-face encounters (hence 'interactionist') as they go about their everyday workplace activities. The culture of the organization is created by its members and reproduced by the networks of symbols and meanings that employees share and that make shared work conduct possible. The analysis of organizational culture can therefore occur through studying observable artefacts, language, action and the beliefs and values of organizational members.

©iofoto, 2011. Shutterstock Images

The office water cooler is a well-known location for sharing workplace stories.

In the realm of shared *artefacts*, displayed mission statements, framed photographs of individuals and ceremonies, technology and displayed art are all manifestations of culture. *Language* is explored to see how it is used to communicate effectively in order to make work conduct possible. Story-telling touches all of us, reaching across cultures and generations (Fulford, 1999). In workplaces, shared *stories, myths* and *legends* serve to construct a common ground for understanding work behaviour. For example, an account of a dramatic event in the past history of the company serves to create a shared meaning of how workers are expected to handle problems in the present.

Also scrutinized is shared work *action.* Rites commonly found in the workplace are those of recognition (for example, an employee of the month award) and of conflict (for example, a disciplinary hearing). Shared *beliefs* and *values* are examined too. In workplace talk, the espousal of 'values' or perceived 'ethical values' is omnipresent; this can concern either legislative provisions that are not always heeded (for example, antidiscrimination laws) or values that are not adequately supported or funded by the organization. Employee groups will wrap their proposals around a 'values' rhetoric to elevate these demands over more pedestrian ones. By highlighting day-to-day social interaction, this analysis explains why organizational cultures are enduring. However, research suggests that a lack of organizational support and mistreatment and indignity at work can undermine the normative influence of perceived ethical values (Biron, 2010). Furthermore, a common critique of this approach relates to its underemphasis of how larger social structures cause disagreement on meanings.

Unlike the integration perspective, the *critical perspective* explores how values, beliefs and norms develop to sustain inequalities and the power of employers. It sets out to develop an understanding of organizational culture by situating it in the context of capitalist relations of domination and control. The intellectual roots of this analysis are found in the canonical text written by Karl Marx and Friedrich Engels. In the 1859 preface to *The Critique of Political Economy,* Marx wrote: 'The mode of production of material life conditions the social, political and intellectual life process in general. It is not the consciousness of men that determines their being, but, on the contrary, their social being that determines their consciousness' (Tucker, 1978, p. 4). For Marx, cultural knowledge is socially produced on the basis of particular structures of economic relationships. Furthermore, in *The German Ideology,* Marx and Engels (1998) reiterate the point that ideas about how the world works, perceptions of reality and so forth are cultural constructs that reflect constellations of class interests – typically those of society's most powerful social elite. Moreover, dominant ideas in society are directly interwoven with the economy and with work-related activities. Many conflict theorists agree with Marx's assertion that social elites use *ideology*, a non-material element of culture, to shape the thoughts and actions of other social classes, as, for example, in the popular idea that markets can best decide society's economic priorities because 'governments cannot pick winners'. Public discourse often supports these views, since no alternatives are debated or offered.

Conflict perspectives call attention to the perpetual tension, conflict and resistance that exists between different employee groups. The structured antagonism between capital and labour, and, in tandem with this, managerial control, focuses on the '*who*' of power over other people and the '*how*' of employee commitment. Here, the focus is on 'strong' corporate cultures as an employment strategy to develop a sense of 'community' and to activate employee emotion, which might lead to enhanced loyalty and commitment to the company (Ray, 1986; Thompson and McHugh, 2009). Around this thesis, a body of literature has developed which argues that cultural control overlaps and exists alongside, rather than replaces, more traditional forms of management control strategies, such as bureaucracy, technology and the more traditional HRM policies and practices, for example completing forms or 'punching in' at the start of a working day. In this sense, systems of cultural hegemony do not replace but instead *complement* other employment strategies adopted over time that aim to increase the loyalty and control of employees, and ultimately their efficiency.

reflective question   What national (macro) and global forces drive the development of employment strategies? To what extent have the reverberations of the 2008–12 economic crises caused managers to change the mix of employment strategies, including cultural control, with which they experiment?

The picture represented by critical workplace scholars is one that represents contradictory and unstable organizational cultures. Drawing on the postmodernist discourse, this approach has been referred to as the *fragmentary* perspective (Martin, 2002). As such, organizational culture is characterized by ephemerality, ambiguity and change, and exposes claims of unified corporate cultures. Culture is 'a loosely structured and incompletely shared system that emerges dynamically as cultural members experience each other, events, and the organization's contextual features' (Martin, 1992, p. 152). The value of this fragmentary approach lies in its exposure of the naivety of using a culture metaphor to describe the organization – it is naive to think that there is no ambiguity in what cultural members believe and do. For example, it might expose claims of truth such as 'We are an equal opportunity employer' while masking the gender or race inequality arising from a male-dominant or white-dominant workplace (Martin, 2002).

The *feminist perspective* argues that gender is a central aspect of work and organizations. Why, 35 years after the passing of the UK Sex Discrimination Act, and in an age of alleged equality of opportunity (in developed economies at least), is the gender gap so enduring in the workplace? Understanding the gender problem in organizational culture analysis is important for at least four reasons:

- First, virtually every human culture known to exist has been dominated by the men, and *external* societal values associated with notions of masculinity and femininity are often reflected in work-related processes. For example, it is common to find processes that privilege the rationality and 'objectivity' associated with masculine attributes while suppressing emotion, which is associated with family and other feminine attributes.
- Second, gender inequality is supported by ideology that seeks to 'naturalize' gender roles. As Eagleton (1983, p. 135) remarks, 'Ideology seeks to convert culture into Nature'. The idea that a woman's place is in the home, or a woman is incapable of performing the duties of a firefighter, illustrates the existence of this ideology.

Management surveillance: someone's watching you …

Management have always felt the need to observe and monitor employees' work – a management function that can be traced from the 'overseers' in the first factories of eighteenth-century Britain to the foremen and supervisors of the twentieth century. Since the last two decades of that century, however, the rapid diffusion of information technology has created systems of monitoring and surveillance that seem, to many, to be all-embracing.

As a recent newspaper account put it:

> From 'mystery shoppers' to swipe cards, from CCTV to phone, email and Internet monitoring, today's workforce is under constant surveillance. ('Work' Supplement, The Guardian, May 7, 2011)

The article goes on to report that such surveillance can even extend outside the workplace, with some organizations hiring private investigators to check up on cases of suspected employee absenteeism.

In addition to the long-standing management desire to monitor actual performance, it is clear that there is a perceived need to monitor employee time-use to avoid what has in the USA been termed 'cyberloafing'. There is a rather fuzzy line here between management prerogative and employee privacy: under human rights legislation, employees are entitled to a 'reasonable' amount of personal communication, although they should not expect to be able to use company equipment for this purpose. If the line is crossed, it can be costly: the European Court of Human Rights awarded more than £6000 to an employee of a Welsh college whose emails, telephone and Internet usage had been secretly monitored.

The apparent omnipresence and scope of electronic monitoring led in the 1990s to a renewed interest in French philosopher Michel Foucault's claim that contemporary society had become characterized by surveillance. Foucault resurrected the term 'panopticon' ('all-seeing'), first invented for the design of a model prison by the eighteenth-century economist Jeremy Bentham. In a panopticon, the subject – in Bentham's example, the prisoner – never knows whether he is being watched or not but, because he *might* be, he suitably modifies his behaviour. One can see how the spread of CCTV and the electronic counting of throughput at supermarket checkouts seems to validate Foucault's claim.

However, as part of their long-standing work on call centres, Peter Bain and Phil Taylor (Bain and Taylor, 2000) showed that this model ignores the agency of both employees and managers. The call centre in their case study was characterized by intensive, repetitive and often acutely stressful work. The agents' performance was monitored in a variety of ways, including supervisors listening in and the recording of calls (remote observation), in addition to 'mystery shopper' calls in which the responses of customer service agents were assessed. Bain and Taylor found that experienced customer service agents knew when they were being monitored and often manipulated the call flow, logging on and off to get small breaks. There were also variations in the degree to which individual managers pursued remote observations, since overintensive monitoring led to stressed and demoralized employees who could not deliver a good quality of service. Also, as the supervisors' bonuses were calculated on their team's performance, they did not want the team to have too many 'red' observations. Finally, during the period of the research project, the call-centre workers successfully took the issues of working conditions and health and safety to the trade union, and the union was subsequently able to contest many of the daily instances of management control.

Stop! Count the number of ways in which your actions are known to others who are not your direct acquaintances (for example, when using your cash card, shop loyalty card or Internet log-on, or being seen on a town-centre CCTV). If our general social privacy is being eroded, how much privacy should we expect in the workplace?

Sources and further information: See Bain and Taylor (2000), Sewell (1998) and Sewell and Wilkinson (1992).

Note: This feature was written by Chris Baldry at the University of Stirling.

- Third, *inside* the workplace, practices involved in recruitment, selection and appraisal often conform to and extend the sex-biased societal values that reinforce job segregation – the tendency for men and women to work in different occupations – as well as systemic discrimination against women.
- Finally, some organizations (for example, schools and the media) play a direct part in the socializing processes by which people acquire gender identities (Aaltio-Marjosola and Mills, 2002). For example, the social association between masculinity and physical hazards contributes to the gendered nature of 'the way things are done' in an organization, justifying 'masculine occupations'.

Feminist perspectives have brought about a major shift in our ways of thinking about culture and knowledge, and also about the way in which the political impinges upon and permeates all of our ways of thinking and acting, both public and private. The argument is that, with notable exceptions, mainstream analysis has generally reflected dominant social beliefs about gender roles that men inhabit the 'public' domain of action, decision-making, power and authority, while women inhabit the 'private' domestic world. Thus, critical feminist scholars have contended that the standard treatment of organizational culture neglects how gender, a patriarchal system, subtle stereotyping, social networks that unintentionally exclude women, systemic discrimination, female-hostile banter and sexuality, that is, sexual characteristics and sexual conduct in the workplace, profoundly shape work cultures. Although sexuality serves to affirm men's sense of shared masculinity, it can serve to make women feel uncomfortable, and leaving the organization is often seen as the only alternative (Brewis and Linstead, 2000). Organizational culture is often a crucial determinant of sexual harassment (Chamberlain et al., 2008) that can be an entrenched feature of workplaces through pornographic pin-ups, taunting and innuendo, and predatory conduct.

National culture, with its societal value system and norms, is deeply intertwined with organizational culture in a dialectical relationship, each being fashioned and refashioned by the other. Including the gender-sexuality paradigm in the study of organizational culture has pushed the boundaries of the differentiation approach by addressing concerns of inequality and discriminatory workplace practices. As sociologist Judy Wajcman observes, the contemporary workplace is not gender neutral; indeed, 'gender is woven into the very fabric of bureaucratic hierarchy and authority relations' (Wajcman, 1998, p. 47). In broad terms, work cultures can be studied from three perspectives, those of *integration, differentiation* and *fragmentation*. Joanne Martin (1992) argues that all three are necessary to fully understand how culture operates in the workplace. Each of the major perspectives we have examined can be used as a theoretical compass for navigating through the myriad and competing views found in the organizational culture and HRM literature.

reflective question Which of these perspectives do you consider most useful for understanding the nature of contemporary organizations and why?

Managing culture through HRM

Organizational cultures are amazingly stable and enduring. From an integrationist perspective, a strong culture can produce a common value system that is consistent with organizational goals such as higher productivity. From this point of view, corporate culture functions as the ultimate form of management control – a self-controlled, committed workforce dedicated to management's expectations and goals. Thus, developing a 'strong' culture in which members of the organization develop a fierce loyalty to the organization offers the possibility to close the 'commitment gap' in the employment relationship, thereby releasing the workers' creative and productive capacity).

As was noted in Chapter 1, an important goal of HRM is to manage the psychological contract, to change the employment relationship from a binary *low-trust* and *low-commitment* relationship to a participatory *high-trust* and *high-commitment* relationship, as well as to capture, manage and control emotion in the organization (Bolton, 2005; Legge, 2005). Contemporary workplace scholars, drawing heavily on Erving Goffman's (1967) work comparing human interactions with drama, argue that a robust corporate culture provides normative and behavioural 'scripts' for employees to follow. The 'scripts' are written by management and reflect the big issues of productivity, organizational flexibility, social legitimacy and 'strategic tensions'. The scripts may also provide clear expectations of work behaviour for new initiatives such as high-performance work systems, or may be used to capture and manage employees' emotional labour (du Gay, 1996).

The role of HRM in translating and crafting an organization's culture has received substantial attention in both the popular and the academic HRM literature. It has been argued, for example, that 'the HR professional must recognize, articulate, and shape a company's culture' (Brewster et al., 2008, p. 312). Several researchers have examined the phenomenon of organizational culture in multinational corporations. The issue they have focused on is whether the subsidiaries of multinational corporations generate 'third cultures', that is hybrid versions of their home and host country cultures (Hui and Graen, 1997; Zhang and Begley, 2011). Amid culturally diverse environments, although an organizational culture may be partly crafted by senior managers, it is not effortlessly manipulated by them. Indeed, as HRM is one of the main transmitters of company policies and practices, changes in HR policies and practices that run counter to, or do not blend with, perceived organizational values will usually meet with resistance from managers and other employees, and may fail (Biron, 2010; Gahan and Abeysekera, 2009; Zhang and Albrecht, 2010). In this context, leadership and HRM theorists have tried to identify effective ways to change manifestations of organizational culture: visible *artefacts*, including language and shared behaviour; work *values*, which are invisible, but can be espoused; and various sets of HRM practices that reinforce the culture. This section reviews strategies of planned culture change:

- Leadership processes that create the motivation to change behaviour, with a particular emphasis on their symbolic content
- Reframing social networks of symbols and meanings through artefacts, language, rituals and ceremonies
- Initiating new HRM practices to change work conduct.

A careful review of the literature shows that all three strategies implicitly adhere to Lewin's (1951) three-stage model of planned change, which involves 'unfreezing' present inappropriate employees' work conduct, 'changing' to new behaviour patterns and positive reinforcement to 'refreeze' the desired change.

Leading cultural change

The role of leadership in generating employees' support for cultural change is rooted in the leadership literature (see, for example, Bass and Riggio, 2006). There are, however, socio-logically informed writers who recognize that cultures can be changed to match strategic goals. In contrast to the crudely prescriptive functional approach, Morgan (1997, p. 152) cautiously argues that:

Managers can influence the evolution of culture by being aware of the symbolic consequences of their actions and by attempting to foster desired values. But they can never control culture in the sense that many management writers advocate.

The guiding maxim for implementing successful strategies for cultural change is that of meeting 'complexity with complexity' (Bate, 1995, p. 5). One mainstream approach acknowledging complexity is John Kotter's (1996) sequential model, which focuses on what specific work behaviours leaders should engage in when managing change, typically involving Lewin's 'unfreezing', 'changing' and 'refreezing' stages. Kotter's model attempts to change culture through an empiricist-rational strategy, that is, by assuming that employees make rational choices if provided with the 'correct' information. In an economic crisis, Canadian writer Naomi Klein (2007) reminds us that 'unfreezing' and organizational change may occur through 'shock therapy', as witnessed by the 2008 banking crisis, as well as by skilful management.

Reframing of social networks and meanings

One strategy to change an organizational culture is by reframing social networks of symbols and meanings in order to increase the commitment that individual employees show to their organization's mission. This can be done by changing physical artefacts, for example displaying a framed copy of the organization's new mission statement, or by rede-signing work systems, such as creating work teams that have greater autonomy. Many organizations have reframed shared symbols and meanings by changing the language to promote high levels of discretionary employee behaviour. Stories and story-telling are pervasive in culture management. Stories often contain, both explicitly and implicitly, arguments for and against work-related values; they help members to locate work experi-ences and develop new insights, which in turn promote sense-making or sense-giving and new ways of behaving (Boyce, 1997; Gold et al., 2002).

Notable examples of language and narrative strategies to achieve cultural change can be seen with British Airways and their mission of 'Putting People First', as well as in 'corporate' universities, where students are increasingly conceptualized as 'clients', and professors as 'service providers' who must 'brand' their institutions and sell their 'products', as do car and beer manufacturers, for example. The general gist of this cultural change strategy is that, if it is properly introduced, the reframing of cultural artefacts is potentially very effec-tive in disconfirming the appropriateness of employees' present behaviours, providing employees with new behavioural models and affirming new ways of doing things.

HRM practices to change culture

People are key carriers of values into the workplace. Thus, one way to change or reinforce a particular culture is through the 'individual–organizational fit' (Purcell et al., 2009, p. 23).

Evidence suggests that a strong culture can be created by a galaxy of HR practices directed towards individual employees. HR *selection* practices are an important means of 'knowing' and managing a culture change (Townley, 1994). Personality- and competency-based tests represent the psychological calculation of suitability and enable managers to find talented individuals who seem to 'fit' the new culture. Changing and managing culture involves formal and informal work-related learning, a process sociologists call *socialization*. By means of socialization, employees learn the symbols and meanings and shared practices of an organization.

In addition, the performance appraisal system is a systematic HR practice used to classify and rank employees hierarchically according to how well they integrate the newly defined set of beliefs, values and actions into their normal ways of doing things. The newly espoused values are incorporated into the appraisal system to enable employees to be compared with each other, to render them 'known' and to reinforce the desired cultural change. HR *reward* practices can have a reinforcing or 'refreezing' effect when the appraisal system connects desired work behaviours with rewards. For example, given the general *commodification* of education, new contracts in universities reinforce a 'research culture' in which promotion and pay are tied to research productivity rather than teaching excellence. Administrators or managers can furthermore reinvigorate the culture change process and increase discretionary behaviour with new formal *training* and, importantly, the informal learning of organizational values and routines.

Drawing upon leadership and HRM studies, the three strategies of planned culture change are shown in Figure 5.3. Steps 1 and 2 represent Lewin's 'unfreezing' stage, steps 3 and 4 represent the 'changing' stage, and step 5 represents the 'refreezing' or consolidation process. The cluster of HR practices mentioned above is a conduit through which dominant shared values can be both carried into the organization and enacted (Purcell et al., 2009). The most sceptical detractors claim that HR practices can help to sustain 'cultural doping' so that individual employees exhibit shared values and routines – how work is performed – congruent with those of their organization (Alvesson and Willmott, 1996). In strong cultures, a metaphorical 'glue' therefore bonds employees and encourages each to internalize the organization's culture because it fulfils their need for social affiliation and identity.

Sustainability and green HRM

The meaning of sustainability was explored when we examined the concept as part of a corporate strategy (see Chapter 2). In this chapter, we have explained that values pervade all areas of human life and strongly influence the way in which work and people are managed. The different ways of thinking about sustainability vie for legitimacy in the public discourse and also challenge human values both outside and inside the workplace. In mainstream management, economic sustainability is defined in terms of maintaining the expansionist economic cycle, an approach based on money values. On the other hand, broader definitions underscore a variation of what is called the 'quadruple mix'. In management parlance, this refers to the pursuit of *quadruple bottom line* performance, which is a balance of economic, environmental, social and cultural goals. This perspective represents a shift away from economic values towards life values.

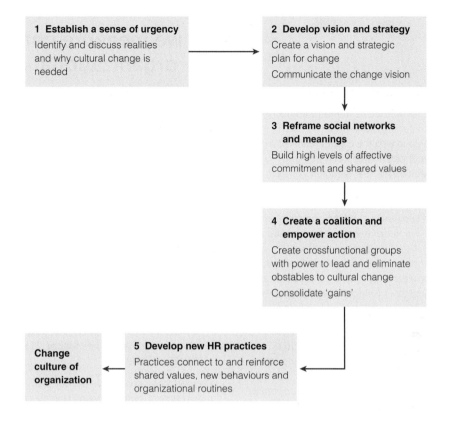

Figure 5.3 A strategy for changing organizational culture

The debate that shapes much of what we hear, think and decide about sustainability is, by and large, dominated by economists, partly because of the money-value logic of our market society, but also, it is argued, because 'economists are clear and ecologists are muddled' on the meaning of sustainability (Sumner, 2007, p. 92). Unsurprisingly, then, it is the economic perspective that tends to influence patterns of organizational decision-making.

In mainstream definitions of the term, sustainability is seen as a strategic goal or mission that is underpinned by values and a strong culture expressing what the organization is and its relationship with its customers and employees. To borrow from Purcell et al. (2009), it can be the 'Big Idea'. If long-term sustainability is to go beyond quaint rhetorical notions of 'going green', several scholars maintain that organizations have to develop a 'sustainability-oriented organizational culture' (see, for example, Chen, 2011; Jabbour et al., 2010; Linnenluecke and Griffiths, 2010). The concept of a sustainable culture involves developing a set of values consistent with sustainability that are 'embedded' into all activities, such as purchasing, work systems, distribution and HR management. As part of a move towards corporate sustainability, sustainability-based values should 'interconnect' the relationships between suppliers and customers and the organizational culture. Sustainability-based values should be 'enduring' to provide a stable base for both the achievement of flexibility and the management of performance. It is a form of organizational learning in which a series of interrelated behaviours create a collective sense-making (Weick, 2001).

A sustainable workplace is a 'collective endeavour' and has the same attributes as strong corporate cultures where the culture acts as a metaphorical 'glue' that bonds employees

Can we measure changes in organizational culture?

Much cultural analysis is framed within a workforce commitment–performance relationship in which a configuration of a 'strong' culture produces a loyal workforce and superior performance. The new recognition that in order to provide superior services, especially in service-oriented, team-based workplaces, managers need to enlist the know-how of all their employees places a premium on interpersonal communication (Guirdham, 2011). A culture that emphasizes communication and trust helped Baringa Partners, a management consultancy firm, to win the top award of Best Workplace in Britain (Widget Finn, 2010). In one employee's inimitable words:

> 'I love this place and I love the job I do. I believe we are all exceptionally proud to work for such a unique, encouraging and fair company.' According to Mohamed Mansour, managing partner, Baringa has a company culture that focuses on supporting and growing talented and motivated staff: 'All our senior people are involved in every recruiting decision we make. We use personal networks, selecting the best people we have worked with, alongside more traditional methods of finding new talent.' Recruiting in this way makes a difference to the psychological contract Baringa has with its employees: the emphasis is not just on ensuring staff are suitable for the organization, but also that the organization is suitable for staff.
>
> Communication and trust are essential to Baringa's success, claims Mr Mansour. 'We have no big central office where everyone gets together round the coffee machine. Our consultants spend most of their time at client sites, so we use regular company meetings every six weeks to catch up with

colleagues, meet new joiners, get up to date with strategy and achievements, and give everyone an opportunity to have their say.' The meetings contribute to the open, honest and consistent communication needed to build trust. As one staff member says: 'Everyone is open, honest and approachable, with a can-do attitude to getting things done as a team. Nobody is left to do things on their own, which is excellent and a vast improvement on previous places I have worked.'

> Celebrating success is a key way to motivate staff. The company gives a quarterly award of £500 to an employee who has demonstrated an exceptional contribution to the company's core values, with annual awards for Team of the Year, the Star Player, One to Watch and Cheerleader. (Great Place to Work® Institute UK)

Despite these impressive accounts of culture management, demonstrating a relationship between a 'strong' culture and superior performance is not without its problems. Ideally, the methodology would permit a calculation of how different cultures – 'weak' versus 'strong' – affect performance, while controlling the other factors influencing performance. The data must demonstrate the extent to which the staff internalize new core values, using a particular set of performance variables over a period of time.

Stop! What HR practices did Baringa use to create a successful culture? How can we be confident about the culture–performance link? What credible evidence do we need to explain the impact of culture on performance?

Sources and further information. See Widget Finn (2010). Also review Chapter 3, 'HRM and Performance', and look at Ashkanasy et al. (2000).

Note: This feature was written by John Bratton.

and work processes together. As Purcell and his colleagues observe, although ad hoc HR practices can easily be replicated, 'it is the mix of these practices with well-developed routines underpinned by values collectively applied and embedded which is so hard to imitate' (2009, p. 26). Scholarship on organizational sustainability affirms the importance of the efficient management of finite natural resources, the need to consult and 'engage' the entire workforce, and the effective management of people (Quaddus and Siddique, 2011). Moreover, it confirms the importance of convergence between low-carbon sustainable strategies, an organizational culture based on ecological values and integrated HR practices (Bratton, 2009; Fernandez et al., 2003). The established use of HR processes in workplace health and safety, lean regimes, minimum waste production and cultural management makes HRM well positioned to coordinate the goal of a green, sustainable strategy (Jabbour et al., 2010).

A cluster of HR practices is both a carrier through which dominant values are expressed and enacted and also, by their outcomes, an expression of deep-rooted values (Purcell et al., 2009). The extant literature on organizational culture and business strategy highlights how important it is for the prevailing business strategy and organizational culture to be consistent with each other – 'internal fit' – and with the wider operation of the organization – 'external fit' (see, for example, Hau Siu Chow and Liu, 2009). Extending the 'best fit' debate, a 'green' HR strategy should coincide with the organization's business strategy and create an appropriate culture to enhance sustainable organizational performance. The emergent literature on 'green HRM' emphasizes that a set of integrated HR practices covering recruitment, performance management and appraisal, learning and development, rewards and employment relations can build a more sustainable workplace culture (Renwick et al., 2008). Broadly speaking, the role of green HRM in sustainable strategy is to develop and support the organization's low-carbon and sustainable initiatives (Wehrmeyer, 1996). Figure 5.4, an extension of Fombrun et al.'s (1984) model, suggests five broad categories of HRM functions in which the role of green HRM in sustainable management can be analysed.

An obvious way to build a low-carbon workplace is through self-selection by prospective employees. Given a choice, people are attracted to 'green' employers that are keenly attuned to climate change issues and have a strong ecological approach (Philips, 2007) . Environmentally sensitive job previews combined with an accurate portrayal of the organization's culture can attract talented people with values that match and sustain sustainability (Jabbour, 2011; Wehrmeyer, 1996). Another obvious way to embed a new 'Big Idea' based on ecological values in the workplace is through the *selection* process. Employment selection tests based on attitudinal and behavioural profiling can be used to screen applicants for green values. However, the validity and predictive power of these assessment techniques have all been subject to challenge (see Chapter 7). Emergent studies in environmental management suggest that, in those organizations with proactive sustainability programmes, the sustainability criteria are systematically integrated further than just in the recruitment and selection process, reaching into employee performance appraisal and the rewards and training dimension.

The reward system is a good indicator of the seriousness of an organization's commitment to sustainability management (Wehrmeyer, 1996). Employee *performance appraisal*, for example, can incorporate low-carbon performance standards related to material and energy waste, recycling and air and water emission indicators. A shift to ecological values and sustainable processes can further be reinforced when employee

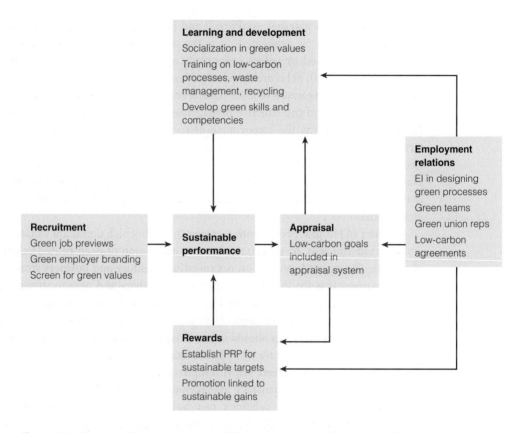

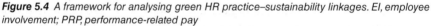

Figure 5.4 *A framework for analysing green HR practice–sustainability linkages. EI, employee involvement; PRP, performance-related pay*

rewards are linked to low-carbon and sustainable performance goals. For example, monetary rewards can be related to acquiring designated green skills and competencies, and ecological knowledge, meeting energy-saving or waste reduction targets and achieving sustainable performance goals.

Non-union and union employee voices can be heard via *employment relations* practices designed to allow employees or their representatives some 'say' in how their workplace is managed. Employee voice mechanisms such as suggestion schemes, employee involvement teams and self-managed teams are seen by many observers as a major element of the green HRM strategy, largely because they provide workers with an opportunity to use their intimate knowledge *of* work and discretion *at* work to generate creative ecofriendly initiatives rather than rely solely on managers. The rationale for employee voice processes can be partly explained by the necessary human input into a successful sustainable strategy, a strategy based on low levels of carbon emissions, product differentiation and high levels of value added and quality.

Sustainability *training* and *workplace learning* are considered to be the main HR interventions that work towards developing a low-carbon work system (Garavan and McGuire, 2010; Jabbour, 2011; Jabbour et al., 2010; Sarkis et al., 2010). Much of this training is related to improving employee health and safety, saving energy and waste management. For example, the US company 3M has encouraged employees to find creative ways to reduce pollution through their Pollution Prevention Pays (3P) programme, which has already saved the company close to $300 million (Renwick et al., 2008, p. 7). European trade unions have extended their traditional occupational health and safety concerns by strongly supporting environmental improvements and green skills training. In the UK, the Trades Union Congress (TUC) has included the environmental and sustainability issue in its training for union representatives, and has called for investment in training as a cardinal principle in creating decent and green jobs. The TUC position is nicely summed up by Frances O'Grady (2010): 'Without green skills, there can be no decent green jobs; without decent green jobs, no flourishing green industries; and without these green industries, we will not – cannot – build a green economy'.

In the European Union, trade unions have attempted to strengthen engagement in sustainable work at workplace level by calling for major investments in energy efficiency and renewable technologies, asking for mandatory environmental audits and bringing sustainability issues forward into 'mainstream' bargaining agendas (Trades Union Congress, 2010). For trade unions, the low-carbon agenda is rooted in their long-standing aspirations for healthy working conditions, social justice, high-skill jobs and decent work (Mayer, 2009; Storey, 2004). The link between green working conditions and social justice is perhaps not self-evident. But, as analysis suggests, exposure to toxic health hazards disproportionately affects blue-collar workers. As Mayer (1996) reminds us, workers are on the front line of the fight to remove toxic substances that threaten the health of workers *inside* the workplace and members of local communities *outside* it.

Conflict between environmental groups and trade unions is not, however, uncommon. For example, in North America, Keystone XL, the proposed 2673 kilometre pipeline that would carry oil sands crude from Canada to US refineries on the Gulf Coast, has stirred fierce emotion between local communities and US unions. Opponents fear that leaks from the pipeline will endanger the underground water reservoir beneath the Nebraska Sandhills, which lie in the proposed path of Keystone XL. Local unions, on the other hand, support the project because it will generate jobs: 'The message is jobs. That's pretty much as simple as it is,' said Ron Kaminski, representative for Laborers Local 1140 (Vanderklippe, 2011).

Overall, a review of the environmental management literature notes the importance of aligning HR practices: 'companies that are able to align practices and human resource dimensions with the objective of environment management can be successful in the organizational journey towards environmental sustainability', writes Jabbour (2011, p. 104). This section has offered a potentially fruitful framework for examining HR interventions to create sustainable workplaces. Future research may provide insight into whether green HRM theory is matched with green HRM action and improved eco-performance.

HRM web links Go to www.tuc.org.uk and search for 'green jobs and green skills', which will bring up TUC policy statements on these issues.

Paradox in culture management

Is the Big Idea always a Good Idea? And assuming that top managers are able to change to a strong one-culture organization, is this necessarily desirable? If the central premise of the 'has' theory is that ideas within a social work group are homogeneous, unified and uncontested, a strong one-culture organization can have unintentional consequences. It can give members an organizational identity, reinforce complex friendship networks and employee engagement, and strongly influence designated behaviour without the need for costly bureaucratic controls. However, if fundamental changes are needed, a strong corporate culture can be an impediment to a management mantra of creative thinking, informal learning and innovation. Although the prescriptive literature presents organizational culture as a variable that can be easily manipulated to produce ideal types of coherence and integration to 'fit' new organizational goals, careful consideration should be given to the unintended or paradoxes of such a strategy.

These tensions surface in the relevant literature. Management scholars, who primarily understand the one-culture phenomenon as a unifying force, focus on the counterforces that challenge strong corporate cultures. The lay-off of workers in response to the recession and deep cuts in government expenditure are, however, a compelling reinforcement of the two-culture, or 'us and them', organization. Employment laws legitimating workplace unionism and collective bargaining have a similar unintended consequence of reinforcing the adversarial duo or multicultures (Beer et al., 1984). The rationales for investing in training and enlisting employees' tacit knowledge to create sustainable workplaces have a similar unintended consequence for managers. Fernandez et al. (2003), for example, argue that green initiatives stem from the synergy between an empowered, engaged and creative workforce and a new context of unsustainable growth and business practices. The learning-creativity paradigm as a source of competitive advantage and high-quality services is based upon critical reflection and open dialogue activities that might be considered to be deviant behaviour (Coopey, 1996). Eco-initiatives are often the result of workers challenging conventional ideas and solutions and effectively 'rule-breaking'. In other words, the creation of green initiatives requires a nurturing and celebration of the creative potential of deviant thinking and action (Bratton and Garrett-Petts, 2008) and can, as such, be viewed as a counterforce to cultural homogeneity.

Despite attempts by the trade union movement in Britain to build alliances to produce sustainable, low-carbon growth, there is evidence that many employers consider union involvement as a challenge to the one-culture system and management prerogative. The 'green bargaining agenda' based on ecofriendly principles and insights is not without contradiction. The trade union movement can potentially act as the pivotal agency of environmental and social change (Mayer, 2009; Storey, 2004), but unions face barriers to playing this role because they can find themselves representing workers on opposite sides of conflicts related to environmental protection and job security. For environmental movements, for example, the generation of nuclear energy and the importation of hazardous waste is unsustainable, yet job security is a major issue for the unions representing workers at nuclear power plants and at incineration plants processing imported toxic waste (Oates, 1996; Storey, 2004).

Organizational culture is embedded in powerful informally shared social interactions and norms. For this reason, the most sceptical detractors argue that culture *as a whole* cannot be 'created, discovered or destroyed by the whims of management' (Meek, 1992, p. 209). Willmott (1993) notes a potentially manipulative intent of corporate agendas for culture change, and details the resistance to strong cultures, or what he calls 'corporate culturalism', found among powerful professional groups. For example, a 'Big Idea' that expected professional engineers to 'sell their services to clients' caused many to resist and threaten resignation (Schein, 2010). Similarly, in the public sector domain, it is suggested that professionals, may 'evade commercial feeling rules' (Bolton, 2005, p. 108). Sociological studies describe all kinds of unusual and idiosyncratic employee conduct that creates small spaces of 'uncolonized terrain, a terrain which is not and cannot be managed' (Gabriel, 1995, p. 478). The scope for employees to offer 'empty performances' and to be indifferent to officially sponsored values is nicely captured by Goffman's classic study (1961, p. 267; also quoted in Bolton, 2005, p. 138):

> Whenever we look at a social establishment ... we find that participants decline in some way to accept the official view of what they should be putting into and getting out of the organization ... Where enthusiasm is expected, there will be apathy, where loyalty, there will be disaffection; where attendance, absenteeism; ... where deeds are to be done, varies of inactivity.

Furthermore, Ackroyd and Thompson's (1999) concept of 'misbehaviour' emphasizes not only the messy reality of conflict in the workplace, but also the fact that employee resistance to new 'Big Ideas' can be less overt, less familiar, less observable and barely manageable.

Not surprisingly therefore, critical workplace scholars tend to be highly sceptical about claims of managing cultures, regarding such claims as naive. In particular, the preoccupation with culture obscures enduring structural inequalities, antagonism and conflict (Edwards, 1995). As demonstrated in the recent recession, culture does nothing to remove the need for top management to try to reduce labour costs, intensify the pressure of work and render employees redundant. The binary conflict of interest between capital and labour that exists within a 'negotiated order' of mutual cooperation suggests that the significance of organizational culture cannot be grasped unless it is related to structures of power – *power over other people* – within a context of market exigencies.

These arguments stress that the work values of managers and other employees are shaped by outside variables such as class, gender, race and profession or trade. Furthermore, that culture can never be wholly managed because it emerges from complex processes involving how employees construct their sense of identity in ways that are beyond management's control. At the very best, culture-change interventions are only successful at the observable behavioural level rather than the subconscious level (Ogbonna, 1993). Finally, adding to the complexity of managing culture is the omnipresent Internet. It has, for example, been argued that the Internet adds a 'space dimension' that may undermine a prevailing configuration of norms and values or culture in new ways (Ogbonna and Harris, 2006).

Big Outdoors

Setting

Despite being one of the largest and most developed markets in the world, the retail industry for sports and camping goods in the UK has faced several challenges in recent years. This has come as a result of rising consumer debt, unemployment and demographic shifts causing a movement away from traditional competitive sports. However, the consumer's continued focus on recreational activities, as well as the development of 'extreme' sports such as rock-climbing, ice-climbing and caving, has helped to maintain growth levels. The rising participation of retirees in hill-walking has also helped to protect the market from more serious reversals. Many retail outlets are now offering specialized services and specific brands to attract this new demographic and lure back their cautious loyal customers.

The problem

Established in 1984, Big Outdoors is an outdoor and sporting goods retail firm specializing in hiking and camping equipment. It currently employs 13 full-time workers with an additional 18 part-time workers to assist

©istockphoto.com/Juanmonino

with increased sales on weekends. As the firm sells to the low end of the market, most of the employees are students supplementing their income to pay for their education who have very little training or experience in the activities the store sells supplies for. The majority of the staff are between the ages of 18 and 23 years old. The hourly pay rate is only slightly more than the minimal wage, and staff turnover is high.

Recently, Big Outdoors was sold to a new owner, Jonathan Tempest, an avid rock-climber, who plans to introduce better quality merchandise with a focus on the high end of the market. His personal business philosophy is 'Focus on high-quality merchandise and excellent customer service, and profit will take care of itself.' With his strong background in the recreational retail industry, Jonathan recognizes that this will require a new business plan as well as a shift in the organization's culture. As the firm is too small to have an in-house HR department to help make these changes, Jonathan decides to hire a local HR consulting firm. He also creates a team of the most experienced employees to provide input into any changes that will be made.

At the first meeting with the consultant Kelly Maynard, Jonathan introduces the team members and lays out his plan to change the firm's merchandise and market focus. However, he admits he is struggling over how to approach changing the overall culture to fit the new direction of the company. Jonathan stresses he wants the team to take a lead role in this aspect. Kelly asks to have some time to study the firm's current HR practices, including its recruitment, training and reward processes, before she makes any recommendations to Jonathan.

Assignment

Acting as the consultant, prepare a report drawing on the material from this chapter addressing the following:

1 What change interventions can Jonathan introduce in order to create a culture at Big Outdoors that is more aligned with the new strategic vision?
2 What do you think of Jonathan's decision to create an employee team? What role, if any, should members of that team play in implementing a cultural change in the organization?

Essential reading

Burke, W. (2011) *Organizational Change: Theory and Practice*. Los Angeles: Sage.

Schein, E. (2010) *Organizational Culture and Leadership*, 4th edn. San Francisco:Jossey-Bass.

Tushman, M. and O'Reilly, C. (1996) Ambidextrous organizations: managing evolutionary and revolutionary change. *California Management Review*, **38**(4): 8–30.

To learn more about the role of leadership in culture change in a retail environment, go to www.icmrindia.org/casestudies/catalogue/Human%20Resource%20and%20Organization%20Behavior/HROB063.htm.

Note: This case was written by Lori Rilkoff, HR manager at City of Kamloops, BC, Canada.

 Visit the companion website at www.palgrave.com/business/bratton5 for guidelines on writing reports.

summary

◀ In this chapter, we have explored the nature of organizational culture – a unique configuration of shared artefacts, common language and meanings and shared values that influences ways of doing things in the workplace. The culture of an organization influences what employees should think, believe or value.

◀ We have discussed how national culture and organizational culture are deeply intertwined – each influencing the other, with the latter embedded in society. Yet we have noted that standard accounts of organizational culture have tended to neglect how gender, patriarchy and sexuality in society and in the workplace profoundly influence the dynamics of organizational culture.

◀ We explained that culture analysis can be divided into different schools of thought. The functionalist perspective stresses that culture can play a role in building consensus and harmony, and emphasizes how this can improve performance. It views organizational culture as a variable – it is something that an organization '*has*' and can, as such, be produced and managed.

◀ The prescriptive literature tends to present too uniform a view of organizational culture. Alternative approaches point out the existence of subcultures and counterculture. These concepts are important if we believe that organizations consist of individuals and work groups with multiple sets of values and beliefs.

◀ The critical perspective focuses on a sociological concern to describe and critically explain cultural processes, how culture emerges through social interaction, power relations, communities of practice and norms. It also focuses on connections between social inequalities and patriarchal systems *outside* the workplace, and socialization processes and conduct *inside* it. Viewed through a sociologist's lens, culture is something that a work organization '*is*'.

◀ We have emphasized that a set of integrated HR practices is both a carrier through which dominant values are expressed and enacted and also, by their outcomes, an expression of deep-rooted values. The well-established use of HR practices to promote health and safety, minimize waste and manage culture makes HRM well positioned to lead and coordinate the goal of a green sustainable strategy.

◀ We make no claims of originality, but we do offer a potentially fruitful framework for exploring how a set of integrated green HR practices – covering recruitment, performance management and appraisal, learning and development, rewards and employment relations – can help to build more sustainable work practices. Finally, we have emphasized that managers must be aware of the messy realities that shape complex organizations.

vocab checklist for ESL students

◀ appraise (v), appraisal (n)
◀ artefact (n)
◀ assume (v), assumption (n)
◀ binge (n)

◀ collectivize (v), collectivism (n), collective/collectivizing (adj)
◀ counterculture (n)
◀ culture (n), cultural (adj)

- diversity (n), diverse (adj)
- dominate (v), domination (n), dominant (adj)
- expatriate (v), expatriate (n)
- feminist (n) (adj), feminine (adj)
- heterogeneity (n), heterogeneous (adj)
- idealize (v), ideology (n)
- individualism/individual (n)
- integrate (v), integration (n)
- International Monetary Fund (n)

- multiculturalism (n), multicultural (adj)
- non-governmental organization (n)
- pluralism/plurality (n), plural/pluralistic (adj)
- ritualize (v), ritual (n), ritualistic (adj)
- secularize (v), secularization (n)
- socialize (v), socialization (n)
- subculture (n)
- United Nations (n)

Visit www.palgrave.com/business/bratton5 for a link to free definitions of these terms in the Macmillan Dictionary, as well as additional learning resources for ESL students.

review questions

1 How does national culture relate to organizational culture?
2 Review the functionalist and critical perspectives on organizational culture described in this chapter. Which perspective do you find most appealing and plausible? Why?
3 What impact do expectations about gender have upon workplace activities and HR practices? To what extent, if at all, do notions of masculinity and femininity reinforce or challenge traditional notions of organizational culture?
4 What role can HRM play in creating a more sustainable low-carbon work system?

further reading to improve your mark

Reading these articles and chapters can help you gain a better understanding and potentially a higher grade for your HRM assignment.

- Mats Alvesson's (2002) *Understanding Organizational Culture*. London: Sage emphasizes the importance of avoiding 'quick fixes' when it comes to organizational culture.
- The links between work values in countries with a different cultural heritage are explored in Peter Warr's (2008) article Work values: Some demographic and cultural correlates. *Journal of Occupational and Organizational Psychology*, 81: 751–75. See also H. de Cieri (2008) Transnational firms and cultural diversity. In P. Boxall, J. Purcell and P. Wright (eds) *The Oxford Handbook of Human Resource Management* (pp. 509–29). Oxford: OUP.
- For insight into 'green' workplaces, see P. Docherty, M. Kira and A. B. Shan (2009) *Creating Sustainable Work Systems* (2nd edn). London: Routledge; C. J. C. Jabbour (2011) How green are HRM practices, organizational culture, learning and teamwork? A Brazilian study. *Industrial and Commercial Training*, **43**(2): 98–105; and W. Wehrmeyer (1996) *Greening People: Human Resources and Environmental Management*. Sheffield: Greenleaf Publishing.
- More critical accounts of culture management can be found in Karen Legge's chapter, HRM: from compliance to commitment, pp. 209–40 in *Human Resource Management: Rhetorics and Realities* (2005), Basingstoke: Palgrave Macmillan; B. McSweeney (2002) Hofstede's model of national cultural differences and their consequences: a triumph of faith – a failure of analysis. *Human Relations*, **55**(1): 89–118; P. I. Morgan and E. Ogbonna (2008) Subcultural dynamics in transformation: a multi-perspective study of health care professionals. *Human Relations*, **61**(1): 39–65; and M. Parker (2000) *Organizational Culture and Identity*. London: Sage.

Visit www.palgrave.com/business/bratton5 for lots of extra resources to help you get to grips with this chapter, including study tips, HRM skills development guides, summary lecture notes, and more.

part III

employee resourcing

chapter 6

workforce planning and talent management

objectives

After studying this chapter, you should be able to:

1 Explain the place of planning in human resource management
2 Explain the difference between manpower planning, human resource planning and workforce planning
3 Give details of the use of ICT in workforce planning
4 Explain the various meanings of and approaches to flexible working
5 Understand developments in the idea and practice of talent management
6 Understand the requirements for diversity management
7 Outline key ideas in human resource accounting

introduction

How certain are you that you can make a plan for the future? What was the impact on your planning of the UK Government's announcement in October 2010 of spending cuts in the public sector, which will lead to the loss of 490,000 jobs in the public sector by 2014/15 (as quoted in the *Guardian*, October 19, 2010)? As you might imagine, similar questions need to be asked in organizations to ensure that the right number of people, with the right kind of talent and skill combinations, get into the right positions at the right time. A plan that achieves this is called a *workforce plan*, and its purpose is to provide some degree of certainty and control over future events. However, as we all know very well, plans do not always work out as intended.

The global economic crisis and the consequent recession in the late 2000s has made the process of planning for the recruitment and deployment of a workforce increasingly precarious (see Chapter 2). The decisions involved in making such plans rely on data that can be used to make forecasts about the future. First, there are forecasts relating to the demand for the workforce, based on the requirements of the organization in relation to its environment. Second, there are forecasts for the degree to which the supply of the workforce will match demand for it. In both instances, however, the ability to forecast with any kind of certainty will be reduced, and uncertainty and complexity will be increased. This could mean that plans made through an analysis of past data might become no more than a way of making sense of the past – in other words, they will fail to account for future events, and workforce planners will need to become more creative. The shocks and disturbances of the late 2000s have increased the need for planning to become both an analytical process for predictability and a creative process for working with unpredictability, unknowable shocks and complexity. It also needs to become a continuous process with as much emphasis on doing the planning as having a plan.

People and planning

At the start of the twenty-first century, it was claimed that the route to competitive advantage is achieved through people (Gratton, 2000). There was growing evidence that effective human resources (HR) practices could enhance a company's sustainability and profitability if there was integration with business purpose (Guest et al., 2003), although there was also evidence of a failure by many senior managers to recognize this (Caulkin, 2001). Furthermore, according to the resource-based view of the firm, an organization can derive competitive advantage from its resources through the development of human resource management (HRM) systems and routines that are unique to that organization (Barney et al., 2001). Thus, any organization could plan how it would deploy and combine a range of HR practices and achieve high commitment and enhanced performance (Wall and Wood, 2005).

At this time, prior to the economic downturn that started in 2008, there was a concern about skills shortages and competition between organizations to attract and develop people who could add most to an organization's performance. This became known as the 'war for talent' (Michaels et al., 2001), with many organizations adopting policies for *talent management* (TM). For HR practitioners, TM represents another opportunity to attain credibility and a status as professionals (Chuai et al., 2008) by presenting a rational and coherent argument for specific HR practices that contribute directly to the outcomes the organization desires. This supports the idea of 'HRM as a modernist project' (Legge, 2005,

p. 337), pushing to address the traditional weaknesses of personnel managers by constructing a 'hard' version of HRM that is more strategic. Finding a more strategic role has been a long-running feature of HR's story over the last 20 years, requiring a variety of approaches to achieve it (Tamkin et al., 1997). In some cases, this involves supporting business strategy by developing appropriate policies and procedures. In others, it means being proactive and playing a leading role in driving strategy.

The ability to formulate plans has been one of the requirements for joining strategic discussions and, as we will show in this chapter, this ability is connected to priorities for people in organizations. Thus, in times of relatively full employment, people and their skills were important because of their scarcity. For example, in the 1960s, the main concerns of manpower planning were an emphasis on the quantities, flows and mathematical modelling of people. During the years of recession in the 1970s and 80s and then the 1990s, manpower planning was used to reduce or 'downsize' the workforce. A more qualitative view of people underpinned *human resource planning* (HRP), which involved the development and provision of a framework that would allow an organization to integrate key HR practices so that it could meet the needs of its employees, enhance their potential and meet the performance needs of the business strategy. The uncertainty and complexity of organization and business conditions in the late 2000s is resulting in more varied approaches and methods relating to planning, which we will call *workforce planning*. This will include putting together TM strategies that aim to develop more people in house and retain key employees (Chartered Institute of Personnel and Development [CIPD], 2009a), as well as searching for new ways to reduce staffing numbers in the face of business recession and cuts in government funding.

reflective question From your experience or reading, how much importance do you think is given to plans for people in organizations? Can small organizations engage in workforce planning?

Manpower planning

What we now call workforce planning was originally referred to as 'manpower planning'. During the twentieth century, this represented a response by personnel and HR managers to ensure that the necessary supply of people was forthcoming to allow targets to be met. In theory at least, a manpower plan could show how the demand for people and their skills within an organization could be balanced by supply. The key stages of this approach are shown in Figure 6.1.

The idea of balance between demand and supply reflects the influence of the language of classical labour economics, in which movement towards an 'equilibrium' serves as an ideal. Such influences can be found in some of the definitions and explanations of manpower planning put forward over the past 50 years. For example, in 1974, the UK's Department of Employment defined manpower planning as a 'strategy for the acquisition, utilization, improvement and preservation of an organization's human resources'. Four stages of the planning process were outlined:

1 An evaluation or appreciation of the existing manpower resources
2 An estimation of the proportion of currently employed manpower resources that were likely to be within the firm by the forecast date

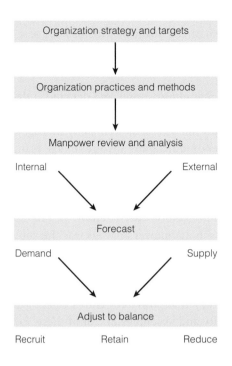

Internal

External

Demand

Supply

Recruit   Retain   Reduce

Figure 6.1 *Reconciling demand and supply*

3 An assessment or forecast of labour requirements needed if the organization's overall objectives were to be achieved by the forecast date

4 Measures to ensure that the necessary resources were available as and when required, that is, the manpower plan.

Stages 1 and 2 were linked in the 'supply aspect of manpower', with stage 1 being part of 'normal personnel practice' (Department of Employment, 1974). Stage 3 represents the 'demand aspect of manpower'. There were two main reasons for companies to use manpower planning: first, to develop their business objectives and manning levels; and second, to reduce the 'unknown' factor. Stage 4 requires an interaction between demand and supply so that skills are utilized to the best possible advantage, and the aspirations of the individual are taken into account (Smith, 1980).

Because of the complexity of interaction of these factors within a context that included aims of optimization and overall equilibrium, manpower planning became a suitable area of interest for operational research and for the application of statistical techniques (Bartholomew, 1971). In this process, organizations could be envisaged as a series of stocks and flows, and as part of an overall system of resource allocation. Models of behaviour could be formulated in relation to labour turnover, length of service, how quickly promotions occurred and age distribution. These variables could be expressed as mathematical and statistical formulae and equations that would allow solutions to manpower decisions to be calculated. With the growing use of computers, the techniques and models became more ambitious and probably beyond the comprehension of most managers (Parker and Caine, 1996). In large organizations, there was, however, a growth in the number of specialist manpower analysts who were capable of dealing with the complex processes involved.

reflective question Do you think a manpower system can be adequately represented as a series of stocks and flows?

Emphasizing statistical models of manpower supply and demand at the expense of the reality of managing and interacting with people was bound to be met with suspicion, certainly by employees and their representatives, as well as by managers 'forced' to act on the results of the calculations. Hence, during the 1970s and 80s, manpower planning acquired a poor reputation as a system with few benefits and only a few examples of when 'comprehensive and systematic manpower planning [was] fully integrated into strategic planning' (Cowling and Walters, 1990, p. 6). There were a number of attempts to make manpower planning techniques more 'user-friendly' to non-specialists. Thus, the fall-out from theoretical progress in manpower analysis was the application of techniques to help with 'real' manpower problems (Bell, 1989), for example why one department in an organization seemed to suffer from a dramatically higher turnover of labour, or why graduate trainees were not retained in sufficient number. Personnel managers were able to build up a 'toolkit' of key manpower measures relating to, for example, employee turnover, retention, stability and absenteeism. All of these could be relatively easily calculated, either monthly or quarterly, and expressed graphically to reveal trends and future paths.

Through the 1990s, such techniques were incorporated into PC-based computerized personnel information systems. As the software became more user-friendly, personnel departments were able to take advantage of this and make themselves more responsive to business needs. Most large and medium-sized organizations will now employ some form of computerized personnel system, and there are many providers of suitable software; we will explore such developments later in this chapter.

HRM web links Go to www.acas.org.uk/index.aspx?articleid=1183 for access to a booklet published in the UK by the Advisory, Conciliation and Arbitration Service – *Managing Attendance and Employee Turnover* – which provides assistance to organizations that have labour turnover and absenteeism problems. You will also find examples of formulae used to measure absenteeism and turnover. Go also to www.softwaresource.co.uk, a site established by the CIPD, which provides information on and access to many HR software products and suppliers.

Diagnosing manpower problems

The use of manpower planning techniques within computerized personnel information systems can be seen as part of a continuing search by the personnel function to find areas of expertise to legitimize its position and prove its value by 'adding to the bottom line'. Thus, there is an attempt to use manpower information as a way of understanding problems so that action can be taken as appropriate. In this way, HR managers have been practising what Fyfe (1986, p. 66) referred to as 'the diagnostic approach to manpower planning'. This approach built on and broadened the demand and supply approach outlined in Figure 6.1 in order to identify problem areas and understand why they were occurring. This is shown in Figure 6.2.

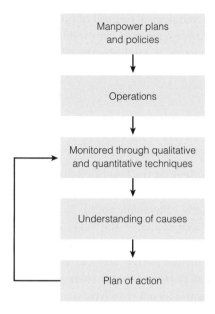

Figure 6.2 *The diagnostic approach to manpower planning*

The idea of an equilibrium between demand and supply can occur only on paper or on the computer screen; the more probable situation is one of continuous imbalance as a result of the dynamic conditions facing any organization, people's behaviour and the imperfections of manpower models. A diagnostic approach would mean becoming aware of manpower problems by monitoring statistics such as turnover and stability, as well as by obtaining qualitative data from interviewing staff. Such interviews might reveal concerns with job satisfaction and the career paths open to staff, reflecting the fact that aspirations they hold that are not being met by current practices. Rather than express these aspirations openly for fear of conflict with management, many staff may prefer to seek employment elsewhere. The loss of talented staff has important cost implications, and a diagnostic approach to retention can provide a significant pay-off.

Employee turnover

The reasons for employee turnover are based on complex factors often requiring solutions that are specific to the context of each organization. Morrell et al. (2001) suggested that explanations of voluntary employee turnover fall into two categories:

- *Economic or labour market reasons* – the emphasis being on external factors such as market conditions
- *Psychological reasons* – the emphasis being on feelings and perceptions relating to job satisfaction, involvement and commitment within the psychological contract.

Research on employee turnover has focused on the latter, seeking to explore more closely why voluntary turnover occurs, which is particularly important given the costs of replacing and recruiting new staff, as well as the pressure on the remaining staff to cover the work. For example, employee turnover may rise in times of organizational change; that is, the 'shock' of changes in patterns of work may lead to decisions to quit (Morrell et al.,

2004). A better understanding of the psychological features of turnover can allow for more focused interventions and avoid the unnecessary costs involved (see Chapter 1). Morrell et al. (2004) suggest the use of certain measures to minimize the effects of change, including:

- Surveys
- Consultation processes
- Intra- and extra-firm career guidance
- Exit interviews
- Leaver profiling.

In the 2000s, the loss of staff is also seen as the loss of intellectual capital and experience, and the replacement of 'knowledge workers' can be both expensive and time-consuming (Buckingham, 2000; Ton and Huckman, 2008). In addition, Des and Shaw (2001) highlight the importance of social capital – the value of relationships between people, embedded in network links that facilitate the trust and communication that are vital to an organization's overall performance. Social capital is reduced when people leave, with a negative impact on organizational performance (Shaw et al., 2005).

We would usually expect high employee turnover to have a negative impact on performance, but recent research has proved that this is not always the case. Siebert and Zubanov (2009) completed an analysis of employee turnover in a large retail organization in the UK and found differences in commitment among full-time core sales assistants compared with part-timers, these differences affecting the turnover–performance relationship. With the full-time staff, there was a negative relationship between turnover and performance, but with the part-timers, the relationship was positive. This suggested a need to consider differences between work systems for different groups in organizations. Thus, full-time or core staff would benefit from high-involvement approaches to their management including less monitoring and control of their performance and more training and career development; part-time or secondary staff would, however, be allocated more routine tasks, more control and less training and career development.

A similar result was found in Budhwar et al.'s (2009) study of high turnover in Indian call centres, where many staff were college graduates with little experience and little intention of staying, so their commitment to working in the organization was limited. Much of the work was considered 'monotonous' and, along with night shifts, affected 'quality of life' and 'work–life balance'. It is hardly surprising that such a work system results in high turnover, but presumably there is a ready supply of staff that can be recruited as substitutes, with only low levels of training needed.

Human resource planning

HRM seeks to make an explicit link between strategy, structure and people. During the 1990s, the plan to bring this about was referred to as the HR plan. This also symbolized the intention to link HR practices to superior performance at work. There has been an ongoing debate on the benefits of adopting a 'high-road' HRM strategy of high training, high involvement, high rewards and quality commitment (Cooke, 2000) versus a 'low-road' strategy characterized by low pay, low job security and work intensification. Furthermore, research suggested the importance of introducing HR practices together in a 'bundle' so that they would enhance and support each other. For example, a plan to introduce performance appraisal on its own will be far less effective without a consideration of training, reward, careers and the attitudes and styles of managers.

It is also important to coordinate the implementation (Hoque, 1999), although any plan to do this will be subject to local culture and everyday meanings, which support the 'strength' of the HRM system (Bowen and Ostroff, 2004). For example, if the organization is pursuing a strategy of increasing its exports, the staff's perception of what they feel the organization is like, based on such factors as policies, rewards and how managers behave towards the staff, will affect how HRM activities such as training and career development will affect overall performance. More recent research highlights how different pressures from both within and outside any organization will affect how HRM is implemented (Boon et al., 2009); in the UK, case study research has highlighted the need for an integrated system of HRM covering skills, recruitment, absenteeism, reward and encouragement to be innovative in order to achieve superior performance (Department of Trade and Industry, 2005a).

A high-road HRM strategy linked to a high-performing organization requires a belief by management that engagement with people represents the key source of competitive advantage because an organization's route to success is based on having a distinctive product and/or service quality as well as price (MacLeod and Clarke, 2009). Furthermore, the continuing development of those people will be a vital feature of both the formation and the implementation of a business strategy.

HRM web links WWW Go to www.bis.gov.uk/policies/employment-matters/strategies/employee-engagement. This is the UK's Department of Business site on Employee Engagement.

While there is evidence of a correlation between high-road HRM and business performance (Wall and Wood, 2005), such evidence may not always convince managers in their decision-making. A resource-based view of organizations would suggest that the distinctive expertise and skills of people are a first-order element of strategy-making and therefore a key element in planning (Liff, 2000). However, HRM is in many cases still a third-order strategic issue (Coleman and Keep, 2001), so that when difficulties arise, many organizations swiftly move towards a version of HRM in which HR activities are designed to respond to strategy, with people viewed as a resource whose cost must be controlled. We know from experience that, in sectors such as retail banking, when competition and deregulation created conditions of continuous flux, it became easier to adopt a low-road version of HRM resulting in branch closures and the loss of many jobs (Storey et al., 1997).

Another example can be found in the implementation of business process re-engineering (Hammer and Champy, 1993) during the 1990s. As discussed earlier (see Chapter 4), this involved a radical change in business processes by applying IT to integrate tasks and produce an output of value to the customer. As the change unfolded, unnecessary processes and layers of bureaucracy were identified and removed, and staff became more empowered to deliver high-quality service and products. Business process re-engineering has, however, almost always been accompanied by unemployment (Grey and Mitev, 1995), a fact that HRP may attempt, with difficulty, to disguise. Downsizing by reducing staff numbers is seen by many organizations as a means of improving their efficiency, productivity and overall competitiveness (Cross and Travaglione, 2004), but, as we will explore below, redundancy can also have many negative consequences for organizations.

WWW Visit www.palgrave.com/business/bratton5 for a bonus case study on downsizing at the Royal Bank of Scotland.

In the UK, specific historical, social, political and institutional contextual features make for a business environment that is largely incompatible with high-road HRM (Cooke, 2000). Thus, with the pressure to sustain or increase profits, employees are more likely to be treated as a 'number' in the quest to reduce costs. This has been a continuing pattern, so that HRP has become a framework to accommodate the 'multifarious practices' of 'pragmatic and opportunistic' organizations (Storey, 1995b). It is perhaps for these reasons that, during the 2000s, the term 'workforce planning' came to be preferred, particularly as organizations began to face growing uncertainty towards the end of the decade (Cappelli, 2009).

reflective question Can an organization claim a high-road approach to HRM while adopting low-road practices? What are the consequences of this?

Workforce planning

In 2008, the bank Northern Rock was nationalized as a consequence of a strategy that failed during the financial crisis. Around 6500 people worked for the bank in 2008, but by June 2010 this figure was close to 4000, with more job losses planned. Like many other organizations, the bank was seeking to plan for the future while facing uncertainty and unpredictability. So the notion of 'right people, right skills, right place and right time' was fraught with difficulty. The trade union suggested that the job cuts were 'short-termist' and likely to worsen unemployment in the UK's North East, where the bank was based. The then CEO, Gary Hoffman (who resigned in November 2010, intending to join another bank in 2011), said 'There is still a challenging economic environment and in order to meet our objectives, we must align our staffing level to match the smaller size of the business, increase efficiency and reduce our cost base' (as quoted in the *Guardian*, June 9, 2010).

But, of course, it had not been always like this, and pre-2008, Northern Rock, like many other organizations, had faced a different problem: that of finding the right kind of people to support its delivery of services and growth. The search was on to find 'high-potential' individuals in the so-called 'war for talent' (Michaels et al., 2001) as part of a growing interest in TM (see below). Workforce planning is the process of forecasting the supply and demand of skills against the requirements of future production and services delivery in a situation of uncertainty and change. It is a process that must be set in a particular context, and can cover many different activities, including the formulae involved in manpower planning such as employee turnover, and the diagnostic and strategic understanding of HRP (Curson et al., 2010); it can also be broader in scope than either of these.

Cappelli (2009) suggest two types of forecast. First, there are internal forecasts to consider the future workforce in terms of numbers and skills or competencies and how these will be affected by competition for staff and the requirements of the work. Any organization will need to understand the talent of its workforce, how such talent will occupy particular roles, and the relationship between roles. A future perspective will consider the preparation for and movement between roles, including succession planning and the management of careers. The second type of forecast is the prediction of demand, which has to be considered against the demand for products and services. The latter determines skill requirements for the future and is considered be significant in national efforts to move

Planning the headcount on the policy roller-coaster

In June 2011, the General Teaching Council for Scotland reported that only 1 in 5 of the 2009–10 cohort of newly qualified teachers had secured a permanent full-time job. All Scottish probationary teachers are guaranteed a post for 1 year after qualifying, but after that employment in the education sector is not guaranteed. The proportion of new teachers with no job at all had risen from 13.5 per cent to 16.2 per cent, and the numbers being offered full-time or part-time temporary and supply teaching had also risen (BBC News, 2011).

This is a good example of the difficulties of workforce planning in a large heterogeneous sector such as primary and secondary education, with the additional problem of the time lag between entering a programme of initial professional education and the state of the labour market on completion. The number of teachers required in any year is dependent on a range of factors such as the number and composition of the school-age population, policy decisions on maximum and minimum class sizes, the rate of teachers leaving the profession and the state of public sector finances. The teaching degree, like most initial degrees in Scotland, is a 4-year course, during which time any of these variables can change. In any part of the public sector, such changes are likely to be a direct result of fluctuations in policy – the 2010 cohort of new teachers had the misfortune to be looking for work at a time of impending cutbacks in public sector financing and of economic conditions that had led many older teachers to postpone early retirement.

Another example of how state policy directly affects workforce planning and composition is given by Stephen Bach's detailed analysis of the use of immigrant nursing staff in the NHS (Bach, 2010). This was driven by government's perception of a staffing crisis (in relation to policy targets set for the service) and a manipulation of immigration policy to meet the crisis. In the early years of the twenty-first century, the government of the day had pledged to increase the nursing workforce in England by 20,000 additional posts by 2004 and then, in a revised plan, by 35,000 by 2008. Because of the lags in bringing UK-trained nurses into employment, for similar reasons to those we have seen for teachers, the response was actively to step up recruitment from overseas. The government was thus susceptible to criticism that it was poaching trained nursing staff from developing nations.

However, by 2005, staff targets had been exceeded, after which policy priorities changed from staff expansion to curbing expenditure. In the meantime, the number of domestic nurse training places had expanded by a third, so overseas recruitment was drastically reduced. The government changed the immigration points system and removed most nursing grades from the shortage occupation list. This meant that an employer would have to prove it had a vacancy and had been unable to recruit UK or European Economic Area nurses. It also meant that existing work permit-holders were deterred from changing employer in case they lost the right to work in the UK.

Bach's study shows, first, that the supply of immigrant workers has not been the result of an inexorable process of globalization, as is often inferred by populist discussions of immigration. More importantly, it indicates that, in the public sector, workforce planning and the supply and demand of labour are inevitably going to be critically affected as much by state policy as by the normal labour market interplay of supply and demand for suitably qualified people.

Stop! What do you think public sector managers can do to secure a stable and suitably qualified workforce?

Sources and further information: See BBC News (2011) and Bach (2010) for background reading.

Note: This feature was written by Chris Baldry at the University of Stirling.

Visit the companion website at www.palgrave.com/business/bratton5 for bonus HRM in practice features on Ernst and Young's maternity coaching scheme, and flexible shifts and part-time staff at Kwik Fit.

towards high-value/high-skill production in the UK (UK Commission for Employment and Skills, 2009).

But it is not just organizations that undertake workforce planning. Governments, for example, are to a greater or lesser extent interested in the supply of skills to match forecasts in demand. Green et al. (1999) have shown how countries such as South Korea, Singapore and Taiwan – the 'tiger economies' – consider skill requirements against targets for growth, which in turn sets the direction for the supply of skills obtained in schools, colleges and universities. Information for planning is gathered systematically in combination with efforts to persuade employers to demand skills at higher levels.

In sectors such as the UK's National Health Service (NHS), workforce planning faces significant complexities due to the large variety of skill classifications and needs. Curson (2006) sees medical workforce planning as analogous to crystal-ball gazing, and Parsons (2010) views it as both a science and an art since predictions for the future, based on the analysis of trends, can hardly be relied upon when future requirements based on need rather than demand are likely to change so rapidly. Part of the art of workforce planning is the utilization of tools such as simulations and scenarios to create conversations between different stakeholders that then set the direction for action (Micic, 2010).

The use of ICT in workforce planning

As we indicated earlier, workforce planning can be supported through the use of information and communication technology (ICT). It is argued that human resource information systems (HRISs) can enhance a more systemic consideration of HR activities and their linkage with the organization's vision and goals (Mayfield et al., 2003). Indeed, generating, capturing, tracking and disseminating organizational knowledge, in all its manifestations in software packages and online, are key features of knowledge management and organizational learning, and both can be facilitated by a HRIS. HRIS has become a form of organizational intelligence, enabling the production of various forecasts and scenarios for future possibilities and unexpected shocks (Hurley-Hanson and Giannantonio, 2008).

During the 1990s, there was a widespread use of HRISs for transaction applications in operational areas such as employee records, payroll and absence control. This suggests that its primary use was as a means of collecting data for others to use in decision-making, and that it was used much less in expert systems and decision support applications (Kinnie and Arthurs, 1996). Ball (2001, p. 690) concluded at the end of this period that 'HRM still seems to be the laggard in running its own systems' to support decision-making and strategy.

A crucial element in any HRIS is how the information is used, especially in decisions concerning how people are employed at work. It is suggested (Liff, 1997a) that a HRIS can be seen from different viewpoints that in turn affect its use. These viewpoints are that its purpose is:

- To provide an objective view of an organization in which the information used is comprehensive and accurate, allowing the best decisions to be made
- To construct organization realities, including the categories and classifications determining the information that should be collected
- To make sense of what is going on within an organization and what needs to be done, according to how information is interpreted by each person, based on his or her view of life at work.

In three case studies, Liff (1997a) found that each view could be used to explain managers' use of a HRIS. Managers were most attached to an objective view of a HRIS and viewed the information it represented as neutral; that is, skills were defined from a 'rational reassessment of current labels' (Liff, 1997a, p. 27). In addition, there was a belief that the HRIS categories could construct a new approach to managing staff and play a role in 'serving dominant business strategy'. The third view could, however, also be found, especially in the way in which apparent discrepancies in information produced by the system could be understood on the basis of existing knowledge of life at work.

In the 2000s, there has been an extension of HRISs towards e-HR (Kettley and Reilly, 2003), with many HR departments using the Internet and web-enabled technologies to create an organizational network of HR data and information. In addition, there has been a development of new approaches to HR activities such as e-recruitment, e-learning and e-reward. Another approach is to allow staff to access information on HR issues, for example how much holiday they have left for the year, via a business-to-employee (B2E) portal. Advanced B2E solutions include attempts to influence ways of working and relationships, such as enhancing e-working by developments in telephony, shared collaboration spaces, online meeting rooms and shared access to intelligence and knowledge management applications. Furthermore, making such information available on the Internet allows it to be accessed by staff from a PC anywhere in the world.

Other ICT developments provide an opportunity for HR departments to work strategically with other functions. Many large and medium-sized organizations have, for example, attempted to integrate all information flows through enterprise resource planning (ERP) software – a typical HR module within ERP might include the items listed in Table 6.1 (see Jackson, 2010). Each heading in the module provides access to a database requiring data to be entered. Once entered, information can then be processed and re-presented for appropriate use. Furthermore, most ERP systems allow for an integration between modules and units within modules, which forms parts of an organization's knowledge management system (see Chapter 10). Jackson (2010) argues that ERP allows routine HR functions to be consolidated to support business processes, saving cost and securing competitive advantage. However, like all software and technology innovations, it is necessary to consider how change is implemented to secure the benefits and full use of ERP's functionality.

Table 6.1 Headings for a typical HR module within ERP

Application screening	Salary administration
Payroll	Work schedule
Planning	Travel expenses
Recruitment	Benefits administration
Compensation management	Personnel development
Funds and position management	Personnel time management
Time evaluation	Shift planning, training
Event management	

HRM web links You can examine ERP software for use in HR at the following web links: www.lawson.com/Solutions/Software/Human-Capital-Management and www.sageabra.com/products_and_services/why_sage_abra_hrms.

reflective question Do you think that all communications at work can be settled via e-HR and B2E? Is there a 'solution' for HR issues?

Flexibility

In planning how to respond to rapid technological and global change, and customer demands, many organizations invoke the idea of 'flexibility' (see Chapter 4). This is a term with a variety of different meanings and a variety of implications for workforce planning.

reflective question How many definitions of flexibility can you think of? As you consider these different definitions, examine the implications for skills, the hours and location of work, the type of contract and the overall motivation and satisfaction of people at work.

Stredwick and Ellis (2005) suggest some key advantages of flexible working. For businesses, there is the chance to exploit the 24-hour economy and open new labour markets that avoid traditional working patterns. Employees seem to like flexible working too, achieving 'far more in the flexible mode' with no 'desire to go back to traditional working patterns' (p. 5). Flexibility can also be seen by employees as means of achieving a more satisfactory work–life balance (Jones et al., 2007), allowing for greater control over their working time, especially for women and those with caring responsibilities (McDonald et al., 2005).

The ambiguity in the definitions of flexibility has allowed a number of interpretations to justify a variety of organizational activities. A key idea is Atkinson and Meager's (1985) model of a 'flexible firm', which identified four types of flexibility that could be implemented:

- *Functional* – 'a firm's ability to adjust and deploy the skills of its employees to match the tasks required by its changing workload, production methods and/or technology' (Atkinson and Meager, 1985, p. 2)
- *Numerical* – a firm's ability to adjust the level of labour inputs to meet fluctuations in output
- *Distancing strategies* – the replacement of internal workers with external subcontractors, that is, putting some work, such as running the firm's canteen, out to contract (now referred to as 'outsourcing')
- *Financial* – support for the achievement of flexibility through the pay and reward structure.

These flexibilities are achieved through a division of employees into the core workforce and the peripheral workforce. Flexibility here is something done *to* the workforce (Alis et al., 2006). The core group is composed of those workers expected to deliver functional flexibility and includes those with firm-specific skills and high discretionary elements in their work. The peripheral group is composed of a number of different workers, such as those directly employed by a firm as secondary workers to perform work with a low discretionary element, or those employed as required on a variety of contracts, for example part-time, temporary and casual workers. This category of employee might also include

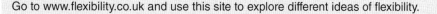

highly specialized workers such as consultants. The final category comprises trainees, some of whom may be being prepared for eventual transfer to the core group. It is important to remember, when considering the issue of flexibility, that organizations have a choice about the type of flexibility that can be adopted.

The idea of the flexible firm has been recognized for many years, although not without criticism (see Pollert, 1988), and is often accepted as a 'panacea of restructuring' as it combines different changes in the organization of work, such as multiskilling, job enlargement, teamwork, labour intensification and cost control (Pollert, 1991).

HRM web links WWW   Go to www.flexibility.co.uk and use this site to explore different ideas of flexibility.

©istockphoto.com/diego cervo

Working from home is one definition of flexibility. How many others can you think of?

Flexible working today

It has been argued that the hard HRM approach, with its emphasis on people as numbers within a framework of cost control, has held most sway in the practice of flexibility (Richbell, 2001). Thus, the 2004 Workplace Employment Relations Survey (Kersley et al., 2006) revealed that 30 per cent of workplaces had employees on temporary or fixed-term contracts in 2004, a similar proportion to that found in 1998 (32 per cent; Department of Trade and Industry, 2005b). The survey showed that 83 per cent of workplaces had part-time employees, a rise from 79 per cent in 1998 (Department of Trade and Industry, 2005b). Part-time employees made up more than half the workforce in 30 per cent of workplaces, and in 44 per cent of workplaces that employed part-time staff, women made up all the part-time staff.

Recent times have seen the acceptance of a range of terms and practices that come under the umbrella of the idea of 'flexibility', with all its definitions and implications. In the UK, partly as a response to European Union directives on working time, parental leave and part-time work, and partly as a stimulus to policies on work–life balance, parents of children under the age of 6 years and parents of disabled children have the legal right under the 2002 Employment Act to request more flexible working with respect to hours worked, time and possibly location. The Work and Families Act 2006 extended maternity, paternity and carers' rights. Thus, there has been a shift towards a more employee-friendly approach in the UK and to flexibility that allows more choice over where and when work can be done. This has resulted in a range of possible 'ways of working' such as:

- *Annualized hours* – working time is organized on the basis of the number of hours to be worked over a year rather than a week; it is usually used to fit in with peaks and troughs of work
- *Compressed hours* – which allows individuals to work their total number of agreed hours over a shorter period. For example, employees might work their full weekly hours over 4 rather than 5 days

- *Flexi-time* – employees have a choice about their actual working hours, usually outside certain agreed core times
- *Home-working* – either on a full-time basis or on a part-time basis where employees divide their time between home and office
- *Job-sharing* – involves two people employed on a part-time basis, but working together to cover a full-time post
- *Shift-working* – gives employers the scope to have their business open for longer periods than an 8-hour day
- *Staggered hours* – employees can start and finish their day at different times
- *Term-time working* – employees can take unpaid leave of absence during the school holidays.

Research by Kelliher and Anderson (2008) suggests that such practices are perceived by employees as enhancing job quality, particularly with respect to control, autonomy and work–life balance. There are, however, some downsides to these practices in relation to opportunities for learning and development because remote working means less visibility at work.

The onset of the financial crisis has meant a strong association of flexibility with short-term working, which has been shown to have played a key role in preserving jobs, especially among staff with permanent contracts. The effect of this has been to increase the labour market segmentation between permanent and temporary staff (Hijzen and Venn, 2011).

reflective question   Considering the next 10 years of your working life, which form of flexible working most appeals to you, and how do you expect employers to respond in terms of pay, conditions and opportunities for learning and development?

Visit www.palgrave.com/business/bratton5 to read HRM in practice features on Ernst and Young's maternity coaching scheme, and flexible shifts and part-time staff at Kwik Fit.

Teleworking

One of the most significant choices for flexible working has been teleworking, telecommuting and/or home-working. According to Duxbury and Higgins (2002, p. 157), such work is 'performed by individuals who are employed by an organization but who work at home or at a telecenter for some portion of their working time during regular business hours'.

Huws (1997) identified five main types of teleworking:

- *Multisite* – an alternation between working on an employer's premises and working elsewhere, usually at home, but also in a telecottage or telecentre
- *Tele-home-working* – work based at home, usually for a single employer and involving low-skilled work performed by people tied to their homes
- *Freelancing* – work for a variety of different clients
- *Mobile* – work carried out using communication technology such as mobile phones, fax machines and PC connections via the Internet, often by professional, commercial, technical and managerial staff who work 'on the road'
- *Relocated back functions (call centres)* – specialist centres carrying out activities such as data entry, airline bookings, telephone banking, telephone sales and helpline services.

The trend towards greater home-working and teleworking is being driven by a variety of factors: technology with the impact of email, the Internet and cheaper and faster ICT;

employees demanding and expecting more flexibility and a better work–life balance; and employer initiatives to use home-working to boost productivity, retention and loyalty, and to reduce costs (Dwelly and Bennion, 2003).

HRM web links Go to www.flexibility.co.uk/viewers/homeworkers.htm, a site that provides resources for individuals working (or wanting to work) from home. The home page of the Telework Association is www.telework.org.uk, which provides advice to workers and managers, and includes an online magazine, job information and a teleworking handbook.

It is claimed that there are a variety of benefits from teleworking, including a reduction or elimination of travelling to work accompanied by a reduction of stress, which can in turn increase productivity. As technology has moved from basic PC and telephones, home-workers can now teleconference and hold interactive problem-oriented meetings using advanced software such as Windows Meeting Space. One claim is that parents have more time for family responsibilities and so achieve a better work–life balance (Tremblay 2003), although many mothers would claim that time with children creates its own pressures and stresses (Hilbrecht et al., 2008). In addition, working at home can also mean an imbalance towards work because it is always present (Scott-Dixon, 2004).

Telework is inevitably mainly devoted to information and knowledge-based services, including professional work. Among such workers, there is the potential for feelings of isolation because there is not the constant presence of others to provide social contact, points of comparison and feedback. Golden et al. (2008) completed research on such workers but found that isolation was not related to lower commitment, intention to leave or loyalty to an organization, perhaps because of the benefits of being at home. There was, however, an impact on job performance, especially where workers spent significant time without face-to-face interactions, although some people are likely to benefit from the lack of distractions.

One significant feature of telework has been the growth of call or contact centres, which have been regarded as one of the 'success stories' of the UK economy, employing around 800,000 people (Department of Trade and Industry, 2004). Since 2008, however, call centres have also been the focus of significant job losses both in the UK and elsewhere. The operation of call centres is based on the idea that customers can be serviced at a lower cost through the use of telephones and other ICT links, with the possibility of also learning about customers in order to enable cross-selling.

Within this process, there are two key but usually contradictory aims – the needs to be cost-efficient but customer-oriented (Korczynski, 2002). Thus, customers may appreciate staff's time in dealing with their enquiries, but, simultaneously, the length of time taken to respond to customers is being monitored, with pressure to minimize cost. This can place stress on staff and has led to the view of call centres as opportunities for job intensification in which managers can tightly monitor and control staff performance and limit their autonomy (Stredwick and Ellis, 2005). One consequence of this is high rates of absenteeism and turnover, with terms such as 'sweatshop' and 'slave labour' frequently being applied (Deery and Kinnie, 2004). There is also evidence that long work hours can lead to fatigue and ill-health when balanced against domestic requirements (Bohle et al., 2011; Hyman et al., 2003).

HRM web links ▄▄▄ Go to www.bullyonline.org/related/callcntr.htm, which examines the problem of bullying in call centres.

Although there is concern about working conditions in call centres, alternatively, through attention to the design of jobs, call centres can become locations of high-performance work systems, which can positively affect motivation and performance. This allows staff more autonomy as there is less staff monitoring and more focus on team work and leadership (Russell, 2008). The potential here is that, as information and knowledge workers, call staff can significantly enhance the services that call centres provide, although the tension with cost savings can often limit customer interactions with actual employees.

HR practices can play a key role in supporting the creation of high-performance work systems in work cultures, but, as we have already suggested, the 'strength' of an HRM system is demonstrated in the everyday relationships between staff and management. As argued by Wood et al. (2006), there are significant links between the opportunity for relationship-building within call-centre work design and performance, and crucially management's orientation towards these. Interestingly, in comparisons across different countries, it was those countries with coordinated or 'social market' economies, such as Austria, Denmark, Germany, Sweden and The Netherlands, all with more regulated labour markets and institutions, that were associated with better quality jobs and lower turnover in call centres. In countries with liberal market economies, such as the USA and UK, there was a tendency for lower job discretion for workers in call centres (Holman et al., 2007).

HRM web links ▄▄▄ Go to www.ilr.cornell.edu/globalcallcenter for details of the Global Call Center Project.

Offshoring and outsourcing

Although call centres have been an apparent success, many organizations have in recent years sought even further cost savings from flexible working by moving their call centres to countries with low wages but similar or even higher skills. Once the customer is used to the lack of face-to-face contact, why not take the process a step further, removing the now irrelevant geographical boundary? This process is referred to as offshoring.

It is argued that offshoring can create wealth even when workers may lose their jobs in their home country. Farrell (2005, p. 68) argues that the 'price' of an organization's ability to cut costs and create new markets is 'continuous change and higher turnover for workers', which can cause 'pain and dislocation'. To avoid this, it is claimed, labour markets need to become more flexible so that workers can benefit from the gains of globalization as well as suffer the costs. Organizations can include training for re-employment, career guidance and reasonable severance packages in their HR plans. One argument is that although jobs may be lost to low-wage economies, displaced workers can retrain and move to higher valued-added jobs. Offshoring has, therefore, become linked to claims of increasing productivity (Amiti and Wei, 2009).

There is, however, some doubt that highly skilled jobs are safe when economies such as India also aspire to high value-added work (for example, in ICT development). Levy (2005) argues that organizations are developing the ability to integrate geographically dispersed operations, which can mean skilled workers in one location competing with skilled workers in different parts of the world. It is also possible that, where there are shortages of skilled and qualified staff, an organization may prefer to offshore some activities such as innovation to locations where qualified staff are more readily available (Lewin et al., 2009).

In addition to offshoring, an organization can seek to slice up or 'disaggregate' its value chain by outsourcing (Contractor et al., 2010); in this process, an organization seeks to source aspects of its production or service processes by setting up a contractual relationship with an external provider. This allows an organization to focus on its core capability and obtain supporting services such as sales, administration (including HR – see below) and ICT at a lower cost from providers who are in turn able to concentrate on their core capability. According to Harland et al. (2005), in addition to focusing on core activities, the principal drivers for outsourcing are freeing up assets, reducing costs and the potential benefits of working with a supplier or partner who is able to exploit advanced technologies. For example, in the pharmaceutical industry, specialist contract research organizations provide outsourced services in areas such as data management, medical coding and marketing, allowing companies to focus on high-value activities.

As a consequence, it has in many organizations become more difficult to speak of a unified entity; instead, in such companies, it is best to consider the working of relationships both internally and externally. Among these relationships will be those characterized by a tight specification of contracts with outsourced service providers, with low trust and pressure to lower costs and compete on price. Colling (2005, p. 95) refers to these as 'distanced' relationships that can also create difficulties for the contracting organization.

©istockphoto.com/DNY59

The effect on British Airways of strikes at catering supplier Gate Gourmet provides one example of the difficulties that can arise for the contracting organization in a distanced relationship.

An example here might be the relationship between British Airways (BA) and its outsourced catering supplier, Gate Gourmet. In 2005, under pressure to reduce costs in the UK, Gate Gourmet sought to make redundancies and change working conditions. This resulted in a dispute with the trade union, which escalated in August 2005 when the company attempted to bring in 130 temporary workers to cope with the peak travel season. This was followed by an unofficial or 'wildcat' strike by workers and the dismissal of 800 staff. There were a number of consequences for BA: first, they could provide no in-flight food; second, some flights were cancelled; and third, around 1000 BA staff, many of them friends and family members of the staff at Gate Gourmet, stopped work in solidarity with them – this led to the delay or cancellation of around 900 flights, at an extra cost of around £45 million.

In contrast, other relationships are more 'engaged', characterized by mutual trust and joint approaches to planning and working via projects and high value-added services in which the outsourced supplier can play a vital role in enhancing decision-making and performance capability through innovation and knowledge production – a typical claim of many consultancies involved in knowledge process outsourcing (Mudambi and Tallman, 2010). Because such relationships are based on a mutual recognition of the contribution of talented staff, it also becomes possible to consider more strategic possibilities for collaboration and cooperation.

HRM activities are among the services that have been outsourced in recent years. For example, since 2000, telecommunications company BT has outsourced significant HR services to Accenture (see Saunders and Hunter, 2007). Outsourcing in HR is based on the view that administrative work and operations can be carried out by outside suppliers, leaving HR staff to concentrate on strategic and high value-added work. Sako and Tierney (2005) examined the growth of HR outsourcing, finding that although operations such as payroll administration have been more susceptible to outsourcing, there have been more deals that have bundled processes together with moves towards a transformational view of HR outsourcing in which an organization seeks consulting and systems integration as part of the bundle. It is argued that because HR suppliers are outside the organization, they are more accountable, can take a more objective view and can gain a more complete understanding of performance.

Interestingly, research by Woodall et al. (2009) found that, especially in larger organizations, the decision to outsource HR was usually taken because of the success of outsourcing other activities. That is, it was not especially made on the basis of a full understanding of the costs and benefits. It was also found that reductions in core HR staff meant significant challenges in providing a quality service, partly because there was insufficient understanding of the role and activities of HR practitioners.

Attitudes to work

With a growing number of temporary, fixed-term and outsourced service contract workers, there has been some interest in the effect of employment status on motivation and commitment to work.

reflective question

What do you think would be the effect of being given a fixed-term contract? How would it affect your motivation and satisfaction at work?

Research by Guest et al. (1998) into the views of workers in a variety of different settings found that people on fixed-term contracts generally had a positive psychological contract. Reasons given for this were that employees on fixed contracts had more focused work to complete and did not have to engage in organizational politics or complete administrative duties. They might also face lower work demands than permanent staff, avoiding stress and taking less work home. Such employees perhaps benefit from a better work–life balance (Hogarth et al., 2001).

McInnis et al. (2009) explored different understandings of contracts and the relation to commitment. They suggested that staff on short-term contracts could be faced with contracts that were also organization-centred and set clear terms to define the work to be done – but such contracts had little connection to commitment. Evans et al. (2004), however, examined the work of highly skilled technical contractors in the USA over a period of two and a half years. It was observed that their work was cyclical, involving periods of contract work on projects, and often involved intense activity and pressures from contracting organizations to use their expertise to solve problems, at any time of day. There were also periods between contracts, or 'downtime' – sometimes referred to as 'beach time', 'bench time' or even 'dead time'. They did not consider themselves unemployed at such times – this was normal for contracting. It was found that contractors, even though they were free from normative pressure for permanent employment, did not necessarily enjoy a desirable flexible lifestyle. The contractors often worked longer hours when contracted, and when they were not, they had to continue working to ensure the next contract, using past work to promote their reputations. They had little time to relax.

One of the most persistent findings is the significance of the psychological contract for gaining commitment. How staff perceive their obligations affects their attitudes, motivation and feelings of justice (Battisti et al., 2007). Part of such perceptions relates to the way in which HR practices are employed in combination with an opportunity to innovate within a role. These findings reinforce the view that, in planning to become more flexible, organizations are faced with a choice. Taking an ad hoc approach that is nevertheless driven by cost reduction may produce improved short-term financial results, but is likely to have a negative impact on motivation, innovation and commitment. Although the use of outsourcing and temporary and fixed-term contracts may have positive results, a consistent finding in the research is, however, that high-road HR practices lead to a positive psychological contract and positive organizational outcomes. Organizations may be tempted by the 'wrong sort of flexibility' (Michie and Sheehan-Quinn, 2001, p. 302), which does not improve productivity or competitiveness. However, many organizations have during the 2000s been persuaded of the need to focus on their relationship with talented staff, even though the recession has put a different emphasis on such a stance, as we will now consider.

Redundancy

Workforce planning is always a contingent process and, clearly, one of the contingent factors is economic conditions. The CIPD (2010a) also identified this factor as a barrier to diversity management, and, in spite of claims that recession provides an opportunity to focus on the talent within organizations, the late 2000s have been characterized by job losses in all sectors, the emphasis shifting from the private to the public sector in the UK following the Comprehensive Spending Review in October 2010. However, redundancy, or 'employee downsizing' as it is sometimes referred to, has also been a feature of many economies in the face of global pressures, cost competition and shifts in demand. As Datta et al. (2010, p. 282) argue, it has 'become the norm in many countries'.

In the UK, the legal framework for redundancy provides for payments, introduced in 1965, and minimum standards set by the European Union relating to consultation, compensation, selection and periods of notice.

HRM web
links   Go to www.direct.gov.uk/en/Employment/RedundancyAndLeavingYourJob/
Redundancy/DG_10029835 for information on redundancy consultation and
notification.

Losing staff has negative consequences for organizations, as well as for those made unemployed. First, and perhaps most obviously, redundancy is a violation of the psychological contract based on a build-up of mutual expectations and obligations between employees and the organization, in which the greater the degree of employees' involvement in their work, the more negative is their feeling of violation (Stoner and Gallagher, 2010). Second, there is a loss of skill, knowledge, wisdom and social capital – the talent that employees accumulate over years of practice at work. The result of downsizing may thus be a loss of productivity (Yu and Park, 2006).

Third, there is an effect on those employees who remain at work after a period of downsizing. If they respond sympathetically towards those made redundant, they may experience effects such as guilt, lower motivation and commitment, mistrust and insecurity (Thornhill et al., 1997); this is referred to as 'survivor syndrome'. A further effect, according to Appelbaum and Donna (2000), is that compromising productivity by downsizing is detrimental to the survivors, leading to an increase in absenteeism (Travaglione and Cross, 2006). Managers may suffer, particularly when 'delayering' occurs, through 'burnout' as a consequence of changing workloads and loss of opportunities for progression (Littler et al., 2003). There might also be a decline in loyalty and 'even increases in white collar crime' (p. 226). Fourth, redundancy is stressful for those made unemployed, possibly due to the process of being made redundant itself and then through the experience of unemployment (Pickard, 2001; see also Richard Sennett's *The Corrosion of Character* [1998] for an extensive consideration of the debilitating effects of downsizing and job insecurity).

In their wide-ranging review of research, Datta et al. (2010) found that the negative outcomes of redundancy have as much to do with the manner of implementation as with the fact of having been made redundant itself. The way in which change is conducted during downsizing, along with contextual factors such as organizational culture and climate, will affect the outcomes (Self et al., 2007). Forde et al. (2008) explore the idea of 'socially responsible restructuring' during a period of mass lay-offs in the UK steel industry. This idea is based on the need to engage with the interests of all stakeholders during the process of restructuring and redundancy as part of an organization's corporate social responsibility agenda, as suggested by the European Union (European Commission, 2008).

It was found, however, that there were significant gaps between what was said and what was done about the process of restructuring. For example, socially responsible restructuring would suggest allowing time for access to job counsellors and external support agencies, but these were often found to be blocked by managers. In addition, fair and objective criteria for lay-off and redeployment might have been stated, but they were interpreted as inequitable and subjective by employees. It is suggested that HR has a key role to play to ensure 'ethical stewardship' (Forde et al., 2008, p. 22) in situations such as these.

HRM web links   ⚎   Read more about socially responsible restructuring at http://ec.europa.eu/ employment_social/equal/news/200708-cede1_en.cfm.

Talent management

During the 1990s and for most of the 2000s, there has been competition between organizations to find and develop 'high-potential' staff as part of a 'war for talent' (Michaels et al., 2001). As a consequence, TM has become a significant area of policy activity, accompanied by a growing list of books, conferences and techniques. More recently, focusing on the importance of knowledge workers and knowledge creation and sharing, Whelan and Carcary (2011) have suggested that organizations need to adopt a 'smart' version of TM in order to retain staff and their knowledge. There is, however, also a concern that TM is another repackaging of HR practices as 'old wine in new bottles' (Chuai et al., 2008).

There has been some evidence of how TM is practised in organizations and how recession has altered the focus (CIPD, 2009a; Tansley et al., 2007a) towards developing talent in house and concentrating on essential development. One response has been to strengthen relationships through TM. For example, at BT, a 'talent deal' sets out commitments to a 'talent pool' consisting of career planning, networking opportunities and mentoring.

reflective question　What is your understanding of talent? Is TM necessary in a recession?

TM policies need to be set against the context and situation of each organization. This can lead to variety of approaches, as shown in Figure 6.3. In this figure, the two dimensions of Exclusive/Inclusive and People/Position provide four possible patterns. First, the 'exclusive people' approach rests on the assumption that key individuals or stars are necessary for the organization's success (Groysberg, 2010). As a consequence, attention is given to those people considered to be 'high potential' and/or 'high performing' (Incomes Data Services, 2010). In contrast, an 'exclusive position' approach starts from the question, 'What key positions are needed to meet the strategy?' People with the right skills and attributes can then be found to fill those positions. Huselid et al. (2005) refer to strategically critical jobs as 'A' positions, filled by 'A' players. Such positions are supported by 'B' positions and 'C' positions – the latter might be seen as jobs that can be outsourced or eliminated. The crucial argument is that improving the performance of 'A' players in 'A' positions will have a more than proportionate impact on the overall performance of the organization. An example might be the performance of customer service staff who have direct interactions with customers.

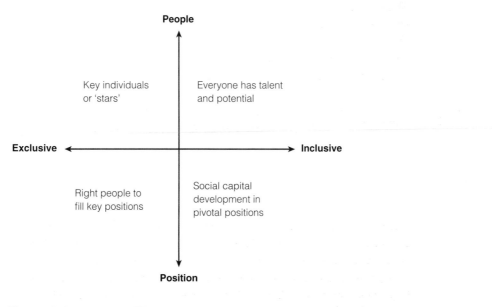

Figure 6.3 Approaches to TM

The 'inclusive people' approach is a recognition that everyone in an organization has talent and the potential for high performance. For example, according to the Learning and Development Manager of the restaurant chain Nando's, their approach to TM is based on the assumption that 'everyone who works for us is talented' and that everyone can 'grow and develop in their own environment' (quoted in *People Management*, May 3, 2007, p. 16). This approach also gives more attention to the relationships between people and to how work is often organized through teams, for example in legal work and software development. So giving attention to the 'stars' could actually reduce performance overall (Groysberg et al., 2004). The inclusive position approach highlights the importance developing relationships based on cooperation, trust and goodwill, and accessing networks – referred to as *social capital development* (McCullum and O'Donnell, 2009). Relationships with others both inside and outside an organization give strategic importance to pivotal positions in providing above-average impact (Collings and Mellahi, 2009).

Succession planning

Succession planning has traditionally been concerned with ensuring a smooth replacement for senior managers and leaders, so that there will be less disruption to performance (Giambatista et al., 2005). More recently, succession planning has been presented as the purpose of TM, although there may still be some disconnection between TM and succession processes (Tansley et al., 2007a) if both processes are completed without sharing information. The key link focuses on a plan that considers the organization's future direction and requirements against the capabilities and potential of those selected for a 'talent pool'. Membership of a pool is determined by a selection process including interviews, 360-degree feedback and other assessments. In larger organizations, there can be different pools for different levels. Tansley et al. (2007a, p. 26) identify four levels:

- Entry level
- Emerging talent
- Rising stars
- Executive talent.

The connections between the levels are referred to as the 'talent pipeline', and this provides an organization with a plan for flexible succession, as well as with a way of motivating internal staff (CIPD, 2009a). There can also be lateral movement between roles, departments and projects. Talent pools and pipelines allow a strategic view of a flow of the right people at the right time, what Ready and Conger (2007) refer to as a 'talent factory'. Part of the planning involves identifying who the right people are for each pool. Succession sometimes has to occur quickly, perhaps in response to an emergency or an absence. At such moments, Rothwell (2011) points to the importance of replacement plans carrying the implication that replacements are not needed on a permanent basis.

A typical approach might be to chart high performers against high potential, as shown in Figure 6.4. Each combination of performance and potential can be used to identify staff for talent pools. The top right corner identifies high performers with high potential, whereas the bottom right corner identifies high performers with low potential. This chart is frequently presented as a 3 × 3 matrix with nine boxes, allowing for more differentiation. Crucially, however, this allows a strategic view of talent from which a plan for succession and development can be made. There are also software solutions to help with this process.

Pollitt (2007) showed how one organization used software including functions for succession planning and identifying future blockages to track 300 managers in a global talent pool.

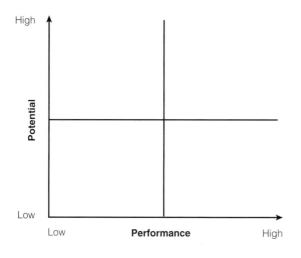

Figure 6.4 *A performance/potential chart*

reflective question What approach would you adopt for someone in the top left segment of the chart – that of low performance and high potential?

S ky entertains and excites more than 10.1 million homes through the most comprehensive multichannel, multiplatform television service in the UK and Ireland. It continues to break new ground with its own portfolio of channels, which includes Sky 1, Sky Living, Sky Arts, Sky Atlantic, Sky Sports, Sky News and Sky Movies.

Sky also works with dozens of other broadcasters on the satellite platform, online and mobile. Sky is now leading the UK into the age of high-definition television with Sky+ HD, and has launched Europe's first 3DTV channel, Sky 3D, as well as Sky Anytime+, its Internet-delivered video on-demand service. The company is also the UK's fastest-growing broadband and home phone provider.

Sarah Myers joined Sky in 2003. She is a Fellow of the CIPD and has an MSc in Human Resources from the London School of Economics. She is also a member of the HR Leadership Alliance for the Heads of Talent Management, an alumna of the School of Coaching and a member of the Editorial Board of *People Management* magazine.

WWW Visit www.palgrave.com/business/bratton5 to watch Sarah talking about TM at Sky, how it has been affected by the recession and its relationship to business strategy. Then think about the following questions:

1 What does Sarah mean by looking 'end to end' in TM?
2 How is development related to talent groups at Sky?
3 In Sarah's view, how is talent linked to succession?

Sarah Myers
Director of Talent Management, Sky

---

www.sky.com

HRM **as I see it**

Career management

TM strategies are increasingly required to take a more long-term view, which means focusing on the retention of committed staff, who in turn expect their careers to be considered (Scott and Revis, 2008). In the past, the term 'career' was one that was usually applied to managerial and professional workers, and HR practices provided support for career development along a 'well-made road' via which individual desires for status and fulfilment could be reached (Sennett, 1998, p. 120). Along the way, of course, many employees encountered blocks to their careers, such as a lack of opportunities and support and, for women, cultural and structural prejudices to career progress referred to as the 'glass ceiling' (Davidson and Cooper, 1992). Graduates too might find their aspirations unsatisfied as they experienced a gap between what they expected and what their organizations provided (Pickard, 1997). In addition, those from ethnic minorities might find themselves 'ghettoed' into certain sectors of work (Singh, 2002). For many employees, however, it was indeed possible to embrace the idea of an organizational career that could be planned for the course of a working life, and theoretical models supported a view that careers could be planned and managed (Grzeda, 1999).

Through the 1990s and into the 2000s, there were significant changes in the way in which careers were explained, understood and managed. Various tensions – such as competition, recession and short-term financial pressures, a breakdown in functional structures in favour of process structures such as project teams and even the loss of bureaucratic personnel systems that planned career moves – have combined, in some companies, to 'dump the basic idea of the corporate career' (Hirsh and Jackson, 1997, p. 9). Many employees still, however, regard their job as a career step (Taylor, 2002).

Adamson et al. (1998) suggested that there have been three changes in organizational career philosophy:

- An end to the long-term view of the employer–employee relationship
- An end to movement through the hierarchy being seen as career progression
- An end to logical, ordered and sequential careers.

One of the manifestations of these changes is that fewer organizations would now claim to offer careers for life, with some evidence that employees are unhappy with the ways in which their careers are developing (CIPD, 2003). If neither individuals nor organizations can plan for the long term, this suggests that the term 'career', with its implication of predictable progression, may have lost its commonly understood meaning. Instead, the career path becomes 'multidirectional' (Baruch, 2004).

An alternative view is that of the 'portfolio career' (Templer and Cawsey, 1999), in which individuals might expect, over the course of their working lives, to work for a variety of different organizations in a variety of positions; as a result of this, they will need a range of skills, learning new ones as required to enhance their employability. Included in the sequence might be periods of leisure, education and domestic tasks. A related view is that of the 'boundaryless career' (Arthur and Rousseau, 2000), during which individuals can consider movements between jobs, locations and occupations. Sullivan and Arthur (2006) also refer to psychological mobility, which considers how people perceive their abilities in making career choices in the light of current realities. This reflects an interest in what Khapova et al. (2007, p. 115) see as the 'subjective career' based on an 'individual's interpretation of his or her career situation at any given time'.

Similarly, it reflects the 'protean career' (Hall, 2002), in which individuals are proactive in directing their careers, using personal values to evaluate their success. These images are part of a general move towards all of us accepting responsibility for our own career development through acquiring employability skills and developing life-long learning (O'Donoghue and Maguire, 2005). Research by De Vos and Soens (2008) suggests that a 'protean career attitude' is related to career success, but this requires skills of career self-management, supported by organizational culture and HR practices including the development of career competencies (Ball, 1997) that should include a balance between work and non-work. Sturges et al. (2010) show the importance of perceptions of the organization's support for career management, especially relationships with managers and others, if staff are to be retained and developed. Furthermore, if such support is absent, staff are more likely to manage their careers in order to take them away from the organization.

These views of career learning are not, however, universally accepted. For example, Mallon and Walton (2005), in a study of career learning among local government and health workers in the UK and New Zealand, found that few were actively engaging in this. Furthermore, most still saw their careers in terms relating to their employment within their organizations (or previous organizations where workers were now working for themselves). It was still very much the case that definitions of careers were organizationally situated, and that this affected what was deemed relevant to learn. In addition and more generally – as a consequence of the expansion of higher education – there is a growing number of graduates with higher levels of knowledge and skills, but these do not automatically make them employable. Employability, skills and knowledge require a valued response from employing organizations (Elias and Purcell, 2003).

reflective question The notion of careers is subject to change and flux. Who do you think should be responsible for the development of people's working lives? How are you making yourself employable, and what are the skills of employability and life-long learning? To help you, examine the HRM web link www.ics.heacademy.ac.uk/Employability/index. htm, which will take you to a site devoted to employability.

These varying images of what constitutes a career point to a 'pendulum of ownership of career development' by which responsibility swings between the organization and the individual (Hirsh and Jackson, 1997, p. 9). Over the last 20 years, many organizations have engaged in restructuring activities that have led to 'delayering' and the removal of grades. The spread of career development initiatives could thus be seen as a way of empowering and motivating staff who have remained in place as part of a core workforce, and this extends now to TM strategies. Given the different approaches to TM we considered above, it is not entirely clear how these will affect patterns of career development. However, we can suggest a segmented pattern encompassing career development for everyone at work, but with different patterns for different work groups:

- Managers and 'high-potential/high performance' staff – careers managed by the organization, not always for life, but with succession-planning to fill senior positions
- Highly skilled workers – attempts to attract and keep key workers by offering career development paths

- The wider workforce – more limited development opportunities often caused by and resulting in uncertainty over career paths; there is an expectation that these workers should look after themselves.

Research suggests a mixed picture of career management practice. In the UK, the CIPD (2003) carried out a survey of over 700 organizations relating to their current and emerging practice on career management. There was good practice in some organizations, but fewer than one-half had a written strategy for career management, with only around a quarter having a strategy for all staff. The greatest focus was on developing and retaining managers and key staff, with only 9 per cent aiming to provide employees with a better understanding of career opportunities and expectation. There was, however, an overwhelming espousal of the philosophy of a partnership approach to career management for all employees, even though the reality suggested a focus on particular groups of staff.

Lips-Wiersma and Hall (2007) have provided a case study of careers in an organization during change, finding evidence that staff were taking more responsibility for careers but that this was shared with the organization. Thus, where staff were setting their own career goals and aiming to find opportunities such as secondments, HR either helped or initiated projects with secondments, seeking to link the individuals' career aspirations with the culture and direction of the organization. According to Lips-Wiersma and Hall (p. 789):

Career management and development has a significant role to play in achieving mutuality of organizational and individual interests.

For those selected into talent programmes and talent pools, it would seem that the benefits include development opportunities that enable career enhancement. Research by the CIPD (2010a) based on surveys and interviews showed, not surprisingly, that selection for such programmes was likely to increase engagement and help employees see a future with their organization, so a career path was clearer. In addition, coaching, mentoring and networking – thus increasing social capital – were more highly valued. The HR function was important in ensuring that the programme was well run and considered effective for the organization.

reflective question How do think those not selected for talent pools might respond, and what impact is there on their careers?

Finally, in this section, it is useful to consider Sullivan et al.'s (2007) kaleidoscope career model, which takes a lifespan approach and suggests that each person can seek a best fit of choices based on the parameters of:

- *Authenticity* – an alignment of internal values with those of the place of work
- *Balance* – between work and non-work demands, including family, friends and personal interests
- *Challenge* – of stimulating work and career advancement.

These parameters are interpreted differently over a lifespan and between generations in organizations. For example, those considered to be part of Generation X (born between 1965 and 1983) have a higher preference than baby-boomers (born 1946–1964) for authenticity and balance (Sullivan et al., 2009). We await further research on those born after

1983, or Generation Y, who appear to seek high rewards but want flexibility to do so, being very information-savvy and well networked. Will they seek more challenges but also more of a work–life balance, and will they therefore be difficult to satisfy?

Diversity management

One of the most important trends in recent years has been an interest in the benefits to be achieved by planning for a diverse workforce, known as 'diversity management', and its connection with business and organizational success (Tatli et al., 2007). Furthermore, it is argued that diversity and TM actually need to be completely integrated and should be seen as 'one and the same thing' (CIPD, 2010b, p. 19).

This move towards diversity can be seen as an extension of, but simultaneously a contrast to, the promotion of equal opportunities during the 1970s and 80s. Equal opportunities is the view that people should be treated equally regardless of race, ethnic origin, gender, sexual orientation and other social categorizations, so that 'individuals are enabled freely and equally to compete for social rewards' (Jewson and Mason, 1986, p. 307). Jewson and Mason set equal opportunities within a free-market tradition, and the purpose of legislation and policies was seen as removing obstacles within and distortions to the working of markets. They pointed to a liberal approach based on 'positive action' to ensure fair and meritocratic procedures in organizations, underpinned by antidiscrimination legislation. They contrasted this with a more radical view, highlighting the embedded nature of discrimination, which could not be corrected through fair procedures alone. Instead, disadvantaged groups would need 'positive discrimination' to achieve fairness, although this still remains unlawful in the UK.

There has, however, been a general recognition that equal opportunities based on 'sameness' has not fulfilled its promise, and that while overt discrimination has been largely removed, prejudice and stereotyping remain embedded within organizations and society at large. One of the crucial difficulties is that debates on equality are based on ethical arguments, often framed in terms of either social justice or a business case, which Gagnon and Cornelius (2000) suggest tends to produce sterility when it comes to practice.

Diversity, according to Schneider (2001, p. 27) is 'about creating a working culture that seeks, respects, values and harnesses difference'. The basic contrast with equal opportunities is an acceptance that there are differences between people, that such differences can be valued, and that they are the source of productive potential within an organization. It is suggested that diversity can provide an organization with a valuable resource in competing both globally and locally. Thus, Singh (2002) highlights a business case for diversity, claiming that inclusion and the development of people 'to the best of their abilities' (p. 3) will result in commitment, creativity and competitive advantage for

Courtesy of Barclays Bank PLC

For Barclays Bank, valuing the diversity of its employees is the key to success.

What to do about macho?

A basic assumption of HR theory is that the performance of a work organization is linked to its people, and that an individual's job performance is a function of his or her human capital (knowledge and skill). It follows that the link between human capital and earnings should be strong: those who possess human capital should be rewarded with good jobs and high earnings.

But what if a particular segment of the population were systematically excluded from good jobs and did not receive the earnings one would expect given their human capital? This is the situation of women in many parts of the world. While in some nations (or groups of nations), there has been significant progress in reducing work-related gender inequalities, in other parts of the world such inequalities persist.

Take the case of Latin America. Recent research by economist Hugo Nopo indicates that while the earnings gap between men and women has narrowed, it still favours men. The gap persists despite the gains that women have made in the acquisition of human capital. 'It is somewhat paradoxical' writes Nopo, 'that besides having more schooling, women still earn less than men' (2011, p. 80).

There are obviously many factors at work here. Traditional gender roles and gender discrimination may still exert a powerful influence in Latin American cultures. However, according to Nopo, gender biases diminish when employers have access to accurate information about productivity (2011, p. 81):

In the absence of information ... individuals use observable characteristics such as gender, skin colour, and height as proxies for productivity. When real information about productivity is revealed, individuals do not use these proxies anymore and base their decisions on the productivity data instead.

Rational arguments may be sufficient to alter the views of those who discriminate against women in the workplace. At home, however, in the private world of the family, things may be different. Nopo points out that the women devote 70–80 per cent of their time to domestic work in Latin American households – 'far more than women's contribution in other societies' (2011, p. 81). To free up the time necessary to complete this domestic work, women must look for flexibility in their paid work arrangements. Women therefore 'choose' 'part-time work, small firms, and informal jobs' (p. 81). This helps to explain the earnings gap and the fact that women are not adequately rewarded for their human capital. It also points to barriers that prevent work organizations from making optimal use of available human capital.

Stop! The word 'macho' captures some of the qualities associated with the masculine gender role in Latin America. What does macho mean to you? Is there a word that captures the qualities associated with the feminine gender role in Latin America?

Do HR professionals have any business thinking about the home life of their employees? And what could be done to change gender roles in Latin America, especially in households where traditional ways of doing things are taken for granted?

Are traditional gender roles uniformly strong or weak in countries such as the USA or UK, or is there some variation within these countries? Among which groups, or in which parts of the country, might the influence of traditional gender roles remain strong?

Note: This feature was written by David MacLennan at Thompson Rivers University.

the organization. For example, Barclays Bank (http://group.barclays.com/Citizenship/Diversity-and-our-people) declares the following:

> Our people are the foundation of Barclays success. It's as simple as that. We want the most talented, whatever their style, personality, age, race, gender, sexual orientation, or disability.

reflective question How do you think that Barclays can achieve such a vision of diversity?

Like Barclays, many organizations are seeking to manage diversity, and this requires organizations to recognize differences. According to Liff (1997b), there are four approaches to managing diversity based on the degree of commitment to social group equality as an organizational objective, and on the perceived relevance of differentiation between social groups for policy-making:

- The first approach might be to dissolve differences in order to 'stress individualism' (Liff, 1997b, p. 13) so that everyone's needs and desires for effective working are recognized. This tends to minimize differences, giving little recognition to the value of difference – rather like traditional equal opportunities approaches.
- In contrast, a second approach is to value differences. Crucial here is the recognition that past practices have reinforced inequalities and led to under-representation and disadvantage. This may mean that there needs to be a change in practice to create a culture reinforcing the fact that everyone has a valued role in an organization.
- The third approach of accommodating differences seeks not to waste talent but to ensure that everyone has an equal chance. This could mean, for example, targeting recruitment for under-represented groups that have the necessary qualifications.
- A fourth approach is to utilize differences, recognizing their usefulness and developing policies that value them. Liff uses the example of a career track for 'family' women with career breaks, gradual promotion and part-time work. The crucial feature of the policy would be that this track would be valued in the same way as the traditional track.

It might be argued that the idea of managing diversity is not a great deal more in advance of traditional approaches to equal opportunities. Indeed, many organizations espouse a commitment to equality and diversity that could easily be translated into a focus on 'sameness', rather than tackling the complexity of 'difference'. However, in contrast to the preventive stance of equal opportunities, managing diversity takes a more positive line in which an organization seeks to avoid accusations of treating people unequally (Kirton and Greene, 2000). There is also a widening of the coverage beyond traditional concerns with race and gender, and this echoes legislative and regulative support related to age, sexual orientation and disability.

Probably the most important feature is, however, the encouragement from senior management to put diversity at the forefront of its concerns. Some organizations, for example Ford and BT, have indicated this by the appointment of diversity directors or diversity champions. Thus, there is value to be gained from being diverse, in terms of both orientation towards the external context, by appreciating the diversity of cultures and ethnic backgrounds of staff and customers, and recognition of the variety within an organization.

Diversity needs to be seen strategically, as part of a cultural change process (Singh, 2002) and one that is good for organizational performance (Pilch, 2006). Recently, in the UK, the Confederation of British Industry, the Trades Union Congress and the Equality and Human Rights Commission all joined forces to argue that meeting legal and moral requirements on diversity can have clear business benefits (Confederation of British Industry, 2008). Research in Ireland for 132 companies clearly showed a link between high-performance working and organizational outcomes when factors such as diversity were managed in an integrated and cohesive manner (Flood et al., 2008).

There are, however, also doubts. Foster and Harris (2005), for example, identified that employers and employees are often confused by the simultaneous focus on equality and the valorization of difference in the workplace, and question whether diversity is just equality repackaged or genuinely represents something new. In addition, there is a critical engagement with the concept of diversity and its origins (Lorbiecki and Jack, 2000) and a warning against the dangers of a 'utilitarian' business argument (Western, 2008).

For diversity to be taken seriously, it has to be more than checking possible prejudice in the recruitment literature or expecting line managers to take responsibility for implementing plans. It needs to be recognized that historical tradition plays a vital role, usually below the surface of consciousness, in maintaining normative value sets that will prevent the agenda of diversity advancing. There needs to be a challenge to and a critique of the attitudes and background assumptions that individuals implicitly hold and that are also embedded in everyday objects and activities that form the commonality of our lives and to which we are bound (Wood et al., 2004). Thus, greater attention to socialization and the development of a culture of tolerance is required if the positive benefits of diversity are to be gained.

There is, however, also a potential for greater conflict based on the misunderstandings that are caused when people from different backgrounds and cultures have different points of view and different values; this can, in turn, lead to lower job satisfaction and higher staff turnover (McMillan-Capehart, 2005). The CIPD (2010b) found a range of barriers to integrating talent and diversity, such as unsuccessful previous experiences, an exclusive orientation towards talent and a lack of boardroom diversity. However, their research also pointed to some excellent examples of practice in managing diversity in such organizations as BT, the Guardian Media Group and the NHS in the London borough of Tower Hamlets. There is an argument for organizations to appreciate the value that can be provided through the talents of a diverse workforce. However, as Ford et al. (2009) found, such an argument needs to work with the interests of leaders and managers. Although compliance with the law is expected, many people do not like to be told what to do, and the area of diversity often falls into this category.

HRM web links   Go to www.nhsemployers.org/EmploymentPolicyAndPractice/EqualityAndDiversity/Pages/Home.aspx, which provides an overview of NHS strategy for equality and diversity. Also check out the Employers' Forum on disability at www.efd.org.uk, which provides guidance on recruiting and retaining disabled employees, and the Employers' Forum on Age at www.efa.org.uk.

Human resource accounting

Making people redundant would appear to contradict claims that 'people are our greatest asset' and the fact that people as human capital are a crucial asset in the knowledge economy (Pilch, 2000). However, the need to show the value of people has led to various attempts use the language of accounting to represent this value in an organization's financial statement. We refer to such efforts as *human resource accounting* (HRA), which we define as the process of identifying, quantifying, accounting and forecasting the value of human resources in order to facilitate effective HRM. HRM needs to be measured and expressed in financial terms to gain credibility (Toulson and Dewe, 2004), and a failure to do this has been a key factor in reducing the importance of decisions related to HR.

Unlike capital items and materials, people cannot be owned by an organization. They can, however, be said to 'loan' their abilities to perform in return for rewards from the organization (Mayo, 2002). Organizations will seek to obtain the most from such a loan by combining people's knowledge and skills with other resources to add value. Furthermore, such value-adding can increase over time through the knowledge and skills that employees develop from performing their work, and from specific activities such as training and development. An organization might therefore claim that it is important to include such value-adding capability on its balance sheet. There have for many years been attempts to account for the value of people in organizations, with a tendency to treat people in financial terms, 'the dominant image of HRA for many people' (Flamholz, 1985, p. 3) being putting 'people on the balance sheet'. Valid and reliable models of measurement have, however, been lacking, and HRA has 'progressed at something less than a snail's pace' (Turner, 1996, p. 65).

More enthusiasm for HRA has been found in Sweden, where many organizations have used its key ideas in decision-making, leading to a 'changed way of thinking' about the management of HR (Gröjer and Johanson, 1998, p. 499). HRA was, for example, integrated into the management control process of three companies researched by Johanson and Nilson (1996) in which managers were trained and information systems adjusted. Furthermore, HRA statements were included in the companies' annual reports. It was found that HRA techniques were useful as management tools, but management were also ambivalent towards HRA since the techniques could also be used to assess the efficiency of the managers themselves (Johanson, 1999).

As a tool that management can use to control costs, HRA can be accused of contributing to a narrow view of people in organizations as being an expense to be minimized and cut when necessary. This view can significantly underrate the value of people in terms of their accumulation of knowledge and understanding as they learn at work, which makes them difficult to replace as well as difficult to copy. People therefore have a value that is greater than simply the cost of their employment. Although that value is difficult to capture in financial terms, knowledge and understanding in an organization form part of its intangible assets or intellectual capital, which includes features such as brand names, as well as knowledge and understanding. Edvinsson and Malone (1997) suggest that intellectual capital in an organization is composed of two factors. First, there is structural capital, such as hardware and software, trade and brand names, and relationships with customers and suppliers – as Edvinsson and Malone (1997, p. 11) have put it, 'everything left at the office when the employees go home'. Second, there is human capital, which is the knowledge and skills of employees at work as well as their values and culture. In combination, human capital plus structural capital equals intellectual capital.

reflective question What is the intellectual capital of your course? How is this intellectual capital valued?

Mayo (2002, p. 38) suggests the use of a 'human capital monitor' to calculate the added value of people in an organization. The key idea is that added value, in the form of both financial and non-financial contributions, can be assessed by considering:

- *People as assets* – composed of employment costs, capability, potential, alignment of values and contributions

plus

- *People's motivation/commitment* – which is affected by factors in the work environment such as leadership, practical support, reward and recognition, and learning and development.

What is significant about intellectual capital is that, as the knowledge economy advances, more organizations will need to invest in knowledge-creating activities, in which the production of new knowledge is a vital differentiator between different organizations (Garvey and Williamson, 2002). However, the difficulty has always been how to value intangible assets within the accountancy profession (Cleary, 2010), although there have been moves to find such an understanding in recent years – albeit with limitations. In the UK, following the report of the Accounting For People Task Force (2003), a central recommendation was that organizations producing annual operating and financial reviews should include information on 'human capital management'. There was an acceptance that the lack of agreed measurements and definitions would require an evolutionary approach, and that this could, of course, be used as an excuse to avoid any effort to produce human capital information on management. Toulson and Dewe (2004) have called for HR managers to become familiar with a range of measurement practices and tools in order to enhance their understanding of different points of view.

The CIPD (2005a) has provided a guide on human capital reporting covering a range of measuring tools and methodologies, ranging from simple and subjective anecdotes about the value of people's performance to internal and external benchmarking, through to the identification of the human capital drivers of performance. Sánchez et al. (2009) recently developed a model for universities to enable the reporting of intellectual capital. However, there continues to be uncertainty over the requirement for organizations to provide a more wide-ranging report beyond finances. Verma and Dewe (2008), for example, found, in a survey of UK organizations, that there was recognition of the importance of measuring human resources, but that there had been little progress in doing so due to lack of support as well as uncertainty over what to measure.

HRM web links [www]

You may wish to consult Lev Baruch's work on the measurement of intangible assets at www.baruch-lev.com, where his research papers can be obtained. Go to http://www.iasplus.com/standard/ias38.htm for a summary of IAS 38, the International Accounting Standard for intangible assets. And look at http://annualreport. marksandspencer.com/financial-review/financial-review.aspx for the Operating and Financial Review of Marks and Spencer, with a report on 'People' at http:// annualreport.marksandspencer.com/financial-review/people.aspx.

case study

TNNB Ltd

Setting

TNNB is a family-owned engineering business producing electrohydraulic systems for a wide range of customers, mostly for export. It has won two Queens Awards for Export and is regarded as a leader in its sector. Each system is built to order, with a salesperson obtaining the initial details before a design engineer builds a portfolio of images that can be presented to the customer. On approval, which can take anything up to 6 months, a contract is established and the order is handed over to project managers.

The principal tasks of the project managers are to build a relationship with the customer, to draw up a plan with key dates for completion, to ensure safe delivery and check installation, and to make sure that resources are allocated at the right time in the right combination. Project management is complex work, and to ensure delivery against the terms of the contract with the customer, where delays can result in a loss of revenue, it is necessary to establish a strong network of relationships with everyone involved in the completion of an order. Although a project plan will contain the key details and requirements for completion, it is up to a project manager to track performance, often in parallel streams, so that any disconnections can be prevented or dealt with. As Lewis (2000) identifies, it is always necessary for a project manager to know:

- Where we are
- Where we should be
- How can we get on track again.

The problem

TNNB employs two project managers who can between them be responsible for several projects at a time, usually at different stages of completion. During a period when six projects were in process, it became evident early on that some key stages were not being completed against schedule, the company managers being alerted by the prospect of penalty clauses. Further evidence revealed that one of the project managers had a reputation for being too slow and measured, spending too much time in his office, apparently making a paper plan that seemed to be out of step with events on the ground. He could identify where the project should be, but could seldom identify the current status of the project. The second project manager was more likely to have the opposite problem – good on the live situation of

©istockphoto.com/endopack

the project but poor at planning, often resulting in reactive scheduling.

TNNB had two managers, cousins within the owning family, and after a brief meeting together, they decided to take a closer look at what was happening. It soon became clear that there were tensions between the systems engineers and the mechanical design and service engineers. In addition, the project managers were not dealing with this effectively, with the main systems engineer claiming he was 'being let down' and was feeling 'frustrated' through the 'incompetence' of the project managers. He argued that neither project manager seemed to have the necessary skills or talent for the job, and that both were associated with missed deadlines or crisis meetings to get things done at the last minute because no advance information had been provided.

The two project managers were defensive about their work, arguing that management had not prepared them sufficiently for the role. Furthermore, they said that the company's shift to project-based working had, despite its success in the market, not been properly thought through.

The family managers felt threatened by what they found. First, they believed that project-based working with good project managers was the only way they could ensure continued progress in the company. Second, systems engineering added a distinctive feature to the product, and any possibility of losing engineers from this section would cause difficulties. But losing any of their engineers would not be helpful since they were difficult

208

to find, had learnt a lot on the job, which took time, and had mostly been with the company for several years (with some not far from retirement).

Assignment

Working either alone or in a study group, prepare a report drawing on this chapter and other recommended material addressing the following:

1 How would a TM strategy help this company?
2 What perspective or approach to talent would be appropriate?
3 What policies and practices for talent development are needed now?

4 What policies and practices for talent development are needed in the future?

Essential reading

Lewis, J. P. (2000) The *Project Manager's Desk Reference: A Comprehensive Guide To Project Planning, Scheduling, Evaluation, and System.* New York: McGraw Hill.

Note: This feature was written by Jeff Gold.

 Visit the companion website at www.palgrave.com/business/bratton5 for a bonus case study on downsizing at the Royal Bank of Scotland, and for guidelines on how to write a report.

summary

◀ Manpower planning in the 1960s and 70s emphasized quantities, flows and mathematical modelling to ensure that the necessary supply of people was forthcoming to allow targets to be met.

◀ Personnel specialists were able to utilize manpower measures of labour turnover, absenteeism and stability to diagnose and solve problems, increasingly aided by PC-based software packages. Manpower planning could play a vital role in the management of the employment relationship.

◀ HRP could be seen to be a continuation and extension of this process, which fully recognizes the potential of people and their needs in the development of strategies and plans. Integrated systems of HR activities are associated with superior performance in high-performing organizations.

◀ Workforce planning is a process of forecasting the supply of and demand for skills against the requirements of future production and services delivery in a situation of uncertainty and change. It is a process supported by the use of ICT enabling the production of various forecasts and scenarios for future possibilities and unexpected shocks. Such systems can also be provided over the Internet as a feature of e-HR.

◀ In many organizations, the language of flexibility and a range of different practices have been employed, often without consideration for their effect on employment relations. There has been a growth in the number of part-time and tele-home-working employees, with government backing for flexible working, as well as in the outsourcing and offshoring of services. There is, however, little evidence of the overall impact on business performance and people's motivation.

◀ TM has become a significant area of policy activity accompanied by a growing list of books, conferences and techniques. Patterns of TM can vary according to inclusivity and the attention given to people or positions.

◀ Fewer organizations offer careers for life, and career planning has become more difficult. Each person will need a range of skills to develop a portfolio career, and there has been a growing emphasis on people accepting responsibility for developing their own careers and making themselves employable.

◀ There is growing interest in managing diversity at work. Diversity is a means of creating heterogeneity in the workforce, a variety of experiences, backgrounds and networks enhancing the ability to solve complex problems. Managing diversity needs to be seen as part of cultural change.

◀ The late 2000s have been characterized by job losses in all sectors. Negative outcomes of redundancy have as much to do with the manner of its implementation, and contextual factors such as the organization's culture and the climate will affect the outcomes.

◀ HRA has been advocated as presenting the value of people as assets, but there has been a lack of a valid and reliable model of measurement.

vocab checklist for ESL students

◀ business process re-engineering (n)
◀ business-to-employee (B2E) (n)
◀ corporate social responsibility (n)
◀ discretion (n), discreet/discretionary (adj)
◀ diversity (n), diverse (adj)
◀ enterprise resource planning (ERP) (n)
◀ equal opportunity (n)
◀ flexibility (n), flexible (adj)
◀ human capital (n)
◀ human resource accounting (HRA) (n)
◀ human resource infrastructure system (HRIS) (n)
◀ human resource planning (HRP) (n)
◀ information and communication technology (ICT) (n)
◀ intellectual capital (n)

◀ kaleidoscope career model (n)
◀ knowledge process outsourcing (n)
◀ manpower planning (n)
◀ offshoring (v), offshore (n) (adj)
◀ outsourcing (v) (n)
◀ redundancy (n), redundant (adj)
◀ retain (v), retention (n)
◀ second (v), secondment (n)
◀ social capital (n)
◀ succeed (v), succession (n)
◀ talent (n), talented (adj)
◀ talent management (TM) (n)
◀ telecommute (v),telecommuting (n)
◀ teleworking (n)
◀ turnover (n)

WWW Visit www.palgrave.com/business/bratton5 for a link to free definitions of these terms in the Macmillan Dictionary, as well as additional learning resources for ESL students.

review questions

1 'When an organization is mapping out its future needs, it is a serious mistake to think primarily in terms of number, flows and economic models.' Discuss.

2 How is workforce planning linked to strategic planning?

3 What would be your response to the publication of figures that showed an above-average turnover of students in a university/college department?

4 What are the various approaches to managing talent in times of recession?

5 Can negative outcomes associated with redundancy be avoided?

further reading to improve your mark

Reading these articles and chapters can help you gain a better understanding and potentially a higher grade for your HRM assignment.

◀ Peter Cappelli has written a range of papers and books on talent and workforce planning. In A supply chain approach to workforce planning, *Organizational Dynamics*, **38**(1): 8–15, he charts the decline of manpower planning but shows how, in the face of uncertainty, forecasts for supply and demand for talent are still very necessary.

▼ For a more critical perspective on flexibility based on extensive interviews in eight case studies around 60 organizations in various forms of interorganizational relationship, read M. Marchington, D. Grimshaw, J. Rubery and H. Willmott (eds) (2005) *Fragmenting Work: Blurring Organizational Boundaries and Disordering Hierarchies*. Oxford: Oxford University Press.

▼ A critical review of interest in TM is taken by Robert E. Lewis and Robert J. Heckman (2006) in Talent management: a critical review, *Human Resource Management Review*, **16**(2): 139–54.

▼ For a recent update on theories and practice of career management and development, the 4th edition of *Career Management* by Jeffrey H. Greenhaus, Gerard A. Callanan and Veronica M. Godshalk (2010), published by Sage, Thousand Oaks, CA, is recommended.

▼ Gill Kirton and Anne-Marie Greene (2010) provide a critical view of diversity management in *The Dynamics of Managing Diversity: A Critical Approach (3rd edn)*. Oxford: Butterworth-Heinemann.

 Visit www.palgrave.com/business/bratton5 for lots of extra resources to help you get to grips with this chapter, including study tips, HRM skills development guides, summary lecture notes, and more.

recruiting and selecting employees

objectives

After studying this chapter, you should be able to:

1   Understand the importance of recruitment and selection in the formation of the employment relationship

2   Understand the key features of recruitment and selection policies

3   Explain the nature of attraction in recruitment

4   Explain the effectiveness of various selection methods

introduction

' You're hired!' And with these words, on an annual basis, Lord Alan Sugar selects his latest recruit. Each year, a range of budding apprentices present themselves to Lord Sugar and his panel as part of the BBC's flagship recruitment and selection programme. Although it is clearly a balance between human resources (HR) practice and entertainment, and is presented as the job interview from hell, *The Apprentice* also covers some of the key features of recruitment and selection, effective or otherwise. First, a position is made available, to which apparently several thousand people are attracted. Whereas it is not entirely clear what is in the job description or personnel specification, suffice it to say that there is a six-figure salary. Then, through a series of 'auditions' as well as interviews, around 70 applicants are selected for a second round, followed by psychological tests, from which the short list of 16 are presented to Lord Sugar. In the following weeks, through a series of tasks, aided by the assessment of trusted colleagues, choices are made about the applicants – usually resulting in the immortal line 'You're Fired!' – until an appointment is made in the final week of the programme.

It is often the case that those who make it to the final are strikingly different in terms of their education, experience and personality characteristics. These are, however, less relevant than the chance for Lord Sugar and his panel to base their assessments on what they see so that they can predict how a potential employee might behave in the future and fit into the organization. Of course, whether the winner's job with the organization meets their expectations as part of an evolving employment relationship and a positive psychological contract based on a mutual and reciprocal understanding is something that is left to our imagination.

reflective question What are your expectations for employment? What attracts you to employment opportunities in the current economic climate?

Recruitment and selection policies

Recruitment and selection have always been critical processes for organizations. In earlier chapters, we discussed ethics in recruitment and selection practices (Chapter 2) and how such practices can change or reinforce a particular culture (Chapter 5). After a period during which recruitment difficulties had been reported in many organizations, and employer branding in terms of recruitment and selection was needed to stand out as a 'good employer' (Chartered Institute of Personnel and Development [CIPD], 2005b), the recession in the late 2000s led to a significant reduction in the number of vacancies. According to CIPD's (2010c) survey of over 480 organizations, fewer organizations were experiencing recruitment problems, and some had even cut or reduced their graduate schemes, although for many these remained the same (at 42 per cent). In circumstances where many applicants chase fewer jobs, just like in *The Apprentice*, employers clearly have more power, and therefore many approaches to recruitment and selection emphasize this power. Traditional approaches to recruitment and selection attempt to attract a wide choice of candidates for vacancies before screening out those who do not match the criteria set in the job descriptions and personnel specifications. Figure 7.1 shows an overall view of the stages of recruitment and selection, and the connection of these processes to workforce planning.

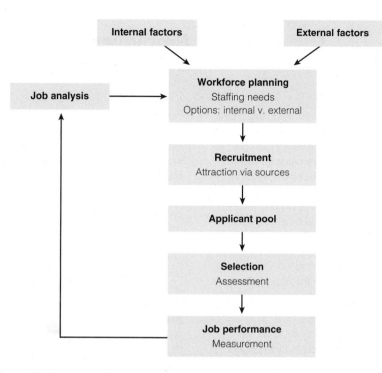

Figure 7.1 *The stages of recruitment and selection*

There are wide variations in recruitment and selection policies and practices, reflecting an organization's strategy and its philosophy of people management. In large multinational organizations, for example, there is a distinction between policies to attract those destined for international careers and policies suited to local conditions (Sparrow, 2007). Where indicated by the workforce plan (see Chapter 6), an organization will seek ways of attracting a pool of applicants and then differentiating between them, avoiding the costs of hiring the 'wrong' ones (Newell, 2005, p. 115). In recent years, there has been interest in the idea of an employer brand (Knox and Freeman, 2006), based on the image the organization wishes to project to potential applicants in order to attract them. Many larger organizations use their websites for this purpose or employ recruitment agencies to help them (CIPD, 2010c).

> **www**   Visit www.palgrave.com/business/bratton5 to read an HRM in practice feature on how Adidas attracts new staff.

The employer brand will also be reflected in the psychological and behavioural characteristics expected of employees, which are expressed through competency frameworks (Roberts, 1997); we will explore these below. Such frameworks have allowed organizations to adopt a range of sophisticated recruitment and selection techniques in order to identify and admit the 'right' people. In this way, as 'organizationally defined critical qualities' (Iles and Salaman, 1995, p. 204), a competency framework augments an organization's power. For example, one tool of assessment we will consider is personality testing, and a survey by Piotrowski and Armstrong (2006) found that popular qualities for testing included integrity and potential for violence. Such information can be used to make judgements about who to admit. Crucially, however, such models need to work within the constraints of a legal context and policies for diversity management (Daniels and Macdonald, 2005).

Employer branding and the employment 'deal'

Employer branding is now recognized as an important part of the HR 'toolkit', stimulated by a growing awareness of the application of marketing principles in attracting better applicants and leveraging employee engagement and retention. This places the spotlight on the employer's 'brand promise', which has been defined as the employee value proposition (EVP) or employment 'deal', initially promoted by recruitment consultancies since the 1990s as part of the 'war for talent'. This centres around promoting a positive image of the organization as a good place to work, as illustrated by Google's portrayal of the 'Top 10 Reasons' to work for the company, such as having fun, fulfilling work and a supportive workplace (Google, 2012).

Consultancy-driven recipes for 'employer of choice' strategies have become very popular, and employers are increasingly seeking more sophisticated means of linking their HR strategy and the corporate brand, beyond the aim of attracting job applicants. The challenge is to find a way of building employees' 'buy-in' to a new brand articulation in ways that enhances their engagement and performance, especially during periods of redundancy and cost-cutting. More active employee involvement is key, as shown by the Co-operative Group's attempts to reinvent its company brand during a time of declining performance. In the words of the Director for HR (MacLeod and Clarke, 2009, p. 45):

> The engagement strategy was a catalyst for re-building trust and confidence between individuals, their line managers and the organisation. We asked people how they felt about working here, why they felt that way and what should be done to change things.

Research into making and keeping an employer brand promise has been informed by exchange concepts, notably the idea of the psychological contract. This is commonly described in terms of a reciprocal relationship of inducements from employers in exchange for contributions from their employees – for example, meaningful work pay and benefits in return for the employees' initiative and discretionary effort.

Detractors have, however, pointed to the somewhat passive role accorded to employees in the current modelling of human resource management (HRM) and EVP, treating them essentially as *consumers* 'buying into' their employer's vision and brand, rather than as active *producers* of HR practices or employer brand. This is promoted by an over-reliance on statistical instruments concerned with the mechanistic cause-and-effect relationships between organizational 'drivers' and employees' performance. More research work needs to be done on how employers might reformulate the design process of EVPs in order to facilitate more authentic employee involvement and participation that are of mutual benefit to the stakeholders involved.

Stop! Academic debates about the emergent concepts of EVP and engagement have pointed to unrealistic *unitarist thinking* about the employment relationship, which assumes that what is good for the organization is always good for employees and vice versa. What is your view?

Sources and further information: See MacLeod and Clarke's (2009) report to the government, *Engaging for Success*, and for further insight into employee engagement, see Balain and Sparrow (2009). An examination of how linkages between social exchange, EVP and engagement can be applied in practice is contained in Francis and Reddington (2012).

Note: This feature was written by Professor Helen Francis and Dr Martin Reddington at Edinburgh Napier University.

www Visit the companion website at www.palgrave.com/business/bratton5 for bonus HRM in practice features on how Adidas attracts new staff, and on the Co-op's internship scheme.

reflective
question

How would an employer prove to you that it was seeking to develop its employer brand based on a positive psychological contract? Go to BP Global Careers at www.bpfutures.com. How has BP's image and brand been affected by the Gulf Oil Disaster?

Recruitment and attraction

Recruitment is the process of attracting the interest of a pool of capable people who will apply for jobs within an organization. In this definition, we can highlight three crucial issues. First, there is a need to attract people's interest in applying for employment. This implies that people have a choice about which organizations they wish to work for, even though during times of recession such choices might be limited. Second, people may be capable of fulfilling a role in employment, but the extent to which this will be realized is not totally predictable. Third, how capability is understood is increasingly determined by an organization's approach to talent management. As we saw in Chapter 6, there are some choices to be made, especially in terms of whether there should be an exclusive or an inclusive focus (Lewis and Heckman, 2006).

Under different labour market conditions, power in the recruitment process will swing between the buyers or sellers of labour – the employers and employees, respectively. It is therefore important to understand that the dimension of power will always be present in recruitment and selection, even in organizations that purport to have a high-commitment

Macmillan Publishers Ltd is one of the largest international publishing groups in the world, with 7000 staff operating in more than 80 countries. Macmillan publishes a variety of academic and scholarly, fiction and non-fiction books and online content, as well as STM (science, technical and medical) and social science journals, educational course materials and dictionaries, and higher education textbooks. Divisions of the company include NPG (Nature Publishing Group), Macmillan Education, Pan Macmillan, Picador and Palgrave Macmillan.

Tania Hummel joined Macmillan in 2006 as Personnel Manager for the London divisions, having spent many years in publishing, most notably with Rough Guides and Lonely Planet publications. She has an MSc in HRM, with a special interest in management development.

Visit www.palgrave.com/business/bratton5 to watch Tania talking about recruitment, diversity and the challenges faced by HR in the publishing industry, and then think about the following questions:

1 How does Tania describe the differences between personnel management and HRM?
2 What does she see as the role of HR in the business?
3 What issues are facing recruitment today? How do companies ensure diversity in the workplace?

Tania Hummel
Group Human Resources Director, Macmillan Publishers

www.macmillan.com

HRM **as I see it**

HR strategy. Thus, in conditions of recession, employers are likely to reduce recruitment budgets and costs, giving more attention to developing the talent that has already been employed (CIPD, 2010c).

Budgetary factors will also affect how recruitment channels are used, with more use of online recruitment, as we will consider below. Generally, there needs to be an intelligent use of recruitment channels in all circumstances. For example, the ageing profile of the workforce requires an adjustment of recruitment polices (Lyon and Glover, 1998). Henkens et al. (2005) found that the use of the Internet and agencies for recruitment reflected a bias towards younger applicants, whereas older workers were more dependent on formal channels of recruitment such as newspapers and journals.

In addition, since the early 1990s, there have been more graduates entering the labour market, but the number of 'graduate' jobs has not kept pace, with a consequent reduction in the power of many new graduates to find employment on advantageous terms (Brannie, 2008). This means that many graduates will take longer to find employment that matches their skills and aspirations. It might also affect the perceptions of value to be gained from studying for a degree against the price of a degree. Among today's graduates are those referred to as Generation Y (those born between 1977 and 1994), who are said to be confident and thrive on challenging but flexible work, expecting quick feedback and reward while maintaining a balanced lifestyle (Broadbridge et al., 2009).

HRM web links www Go to www.ashridge.org.uk/Website/Content.nsf/wFARCRED/ Generation+Y?opendocument to find out about Ashridge's Generation Y research project.

reflective question Do you consider yourself as part of Generation Y? What are your expectations for working, and what do you expect in recruitment?

Fitting the person to the environment, organization and job

Effective recruitment depends on the extent to which the overall management philosophy supports and reinforces an approach to HRM that focuses on the utilization and development of new employees once they have joined an organization. Although HR policies will be designed to achieve particular organizational targets and goals, those policies will also provide an opportunity for individual needs to emerge and be satisfied. This view assumes that a fit between a person and the environment can be found so that their commitment and performance will be enhanced (Kristof, 1996). Some commentators doubt that such mutuality could ever occur on an equal basis, and believe that organizational needs, as determined by senior management, will always take precedence; however,

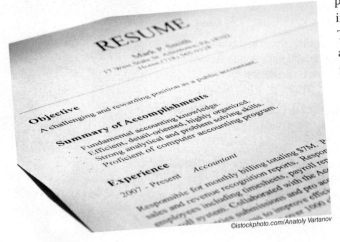

©istockphoto.com/Anatoly Vartanov

Recruitment is a process of attracting the right people to apply for the job.

individual needs may, through HRM activities, influence how the organization's needs are perceived. Recruitment and then selection processes will therefore aim to attract and admit those whom management view as the 'right' people for such an approach. In one sense, an organization already knows who the right people are for its vacancies since they are the very people who are already employed and are present in the company's talent pool. Such internal recruitment might be based on performance assessment and the decisions of senior managers, whose choices could be made on the basis of candidates' similarity to themselves (see Mäkelä et al., 2010).

Taking a strategic view of recruitment requirements starts with the strategic plan. Research by Tyson (1995) found that although there were many differences between organizations, HRM could help to shape the direction of change, influence culture and 'help bring about the mindset' that would decide which strategic issues were considered. HR considerations, including the results of a review of the quantity and quality of people, should thus be integrated into the plan (see Chapter 6). The goals, objectives and targets that then emerge set the parameters for performance in an organization and for how work is organized into roles and jobs. A key role for HR is to align performance within roles with the organization's strategy, so recruiting the right people for a role depends on how that role is defined in terms relating to the performance needed to achieve the strategy (Holbeche, 1999). Once a recruitment strategy has been formed, an organization might outsource its implementation, especially where there are a large number of staff to be recruited (Tulip, 2004), although recent moves to focus on the talent already employed might reduce this tendency (Ordanini and Silvestri, 2008).

Traditionally, creating a specification containing the requirements for a particular role has required the use of *job analysis techniques*; these may include a range of interviews, questionnaires and observation processes that provide information about work carried out, the environment in which it occurs and, vitally, the knowledge, skills and attitudes needed to perform the job well. In recent years, information derived from the analysis of work performance has been utilized to create a taxonomy or framework of either criterion-related behaviours or standards of performance referred to as *competencies*. Although most frameworks are developed within organizations and are based on the meanings of behaviour that exist within an organization, there are also frameworks that can be applied more generally or to specific groups in different organizations. According to the CIPD (2010d, p. 1), competencies are 'the behaviours that employees must have, or must acquire, to input into a situation in order to achieve high levels of performance'. (This definition, focusing on behaviour patterns, differs from the idea of competence used with Vocational Qualifications, which are related to performing activities within an occupation to a prescribed standard. You can read more about the development of Vocational Qualifications at www.qcda.gov.uk/qualifications/60.aspx.) Competency frameworks are concerned with behaviour that is relevant to the job and the effective or competent performance of that job, although factors such as equipment and the behaviour can also have an impact.

Competency frameworks are widely thought to help an organization to align its objectives with the various HR activities of recruitment and selection, appraisal, training and reward (Holbeche, 1999). In addition, competencies enhance a common understanding of effective behaviour at work and provide a basis for more consistency in assessment practices (Whiddett and Hollyforde, 2003).

HRM web links www

SHL is one of the main suppliers of job assessment software that can be used to develop competencies. Details of its Universal Competency Framework can be found at www.shl.com/WhatWeDo/Competency/Pages/UniversalCompetencyFramework. aspx. SHL also provides a useful book on job analysis techniques, which you can download at www.shl.com/assets/resources/Best-Practice-Job-Analysis.pdf.

Table 7.1 shows how one large financial services organization in the UK sets out its competencies. Each competency is defined and described by a range of indicators that enables assessment and measurement. The competency of 'creating customer service' is, for example, indicated by:

- Anticipating emerging customer needs and planning accordingly
- Identifying the customers who will be of value to the company
- Recommending changes to current ways of working that will improve customer service
- Arranging the collection of customer satisfaction data and acting on them.

Table 7.1 *Competencies in a financial services organization*

Personal focus	Self-control Self-development Personal organization Positive approach
Customer focus	Creating customer service Delivering customer service Continuous improvement
Future focus	Delivering the vision Change and creativity
Business focus	Delivering results Providing solutions Systemic thinking Attention to detail
People focus	Developing people Working with others Influencing Leading

The analysis and definition of competencies should allow the identification and isolation of dimensions of behaviour that are distinct and are associated with competent or effective performance. Competencies can therefore be used to provide, at least from an organization's point of view, the behaviours needed at work to achieve the business strategy. On this assumption, the assessment of competencies is one means of selecting employees, as will be discussed below. Competencies will enable organizations to form a model of the kinds of employee they wish to attract through recruitment.

HRM web links www

Competency frameworks are now widely established in all kinds of organization. Check how the British Medical Association advocates the use of its framework at www.bma.org.uk/about_bma/bma_jobs/HRCompetencies.jsp?page=1. Note how this framework is used in recruitment.

Whatever the model constructed, an organization's commitment to its HR processes will form part of its evolving value system and make it even more attractive to those seeking employment. Many organizations seek to express their values by statements of visions and missions. For example, the following can be found at www.morrisons.co.uk/Corporate/Corporate-responsibility-2011/Responsible-retailing/Our-values.

Our values are at the heart of everything we do, defining what we expect of each other and what our customers can expect of us as we aim to deliver our vision of becoming the 'Food Specialist for Everyone'.

CAN DO

Can do is about making things happen. It's about getting the job done and delivering results. It's about being positive and rising to a challenge.

ONE TEAM

One team is about working together to reach a common goal. It's about keeping our promises, building trust and respect, and valuing each other's contribution.

BRINGING THE BEST OUT OF OUR PEOPLE

Bringing the best out of our people is about developing ourselves and those around us. It's about constantly learning so we can improve the way we work and the experience we give our customers.

GREAT SELLING AND SERVICE

Great selling and service is about delivering a great experience for our customers. It's about sharing our knowledge and know-how and always striving to do better.

GREAT SHOPKEEPING

Great shopkeeping is about setting high standards and taking care of every detail. It's about having pride in our work and making quality our top priority.

FRESH THINKING

Fresh thinking is about finding new and better ways of working. It's about greater awareness, asking questions and coming up with bright ideas that give us the edge.

Courtesy of Morrisons PLC

Such statements form part of the image, or 'brand' in talent management terms, that is projected by the company. Projected images, values and information on espoused goals will be made sense of by people in external labour markets, including both those employed and those unemployed. This interaction will determine how attracted potential recruits feel to an organization.

reflective question Think about an organization you would like to work for. What images, values and information related to that organization come into your mind? What is the brand of that organization?

The image projected by an organization and the response from potential employees provide the basis for a compatible person–organization (P–O) fit, a variant of the person–environment fit referred to earlier (in addition to P–O fit, person–vocation fit, person–job fit, person–preferences for culture fit, and person–team fit; see Barber, 1998; Wheeler et al., 2005.) Schneider (1987), using a theory of interactional psychology, proposed an attraction–selection–attrition framework to explain the workings of this process and the differences between organizations that are caused by the attraction of people to the organization's goals, their interaction with those goals and the fact that 'if they don't fit, they leave' (Schneider, 1987, p. 437). The proposed framework is shown in Figure 7.2. Schneider argued that people are attracted to an organization on the basis of their own interests and personality. Thus, people of a similar type will be attracted to the same place. Furthermore, the attraction of similar types will begin to determine the place. Following selection, people who do not fit, because of either an error or a misunderstanding of the reality of an organization, will leave, resulting in attrition from that organization.

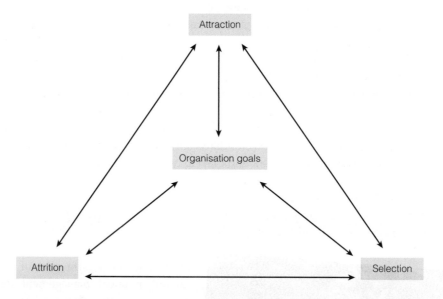

Figure 7.2 *An attraction–selection–attrition framework*
Source: Schneider (1987), p . 440. Reproduced with the permission of John Wiley & Sons, Inc.

At the heart of the framework lie organizational goals, originally stated by the founder and/or articulated by top managers, and out of these emerge the structures and processes that will form the basis of decisions related to attraction. This framework was supported by research conducted by Judge and Cable (1997), who found that applicants seek P–O fit, attempting to match their values with the reputation surrounding an organization's culture. Understanding the operation of P–O fit can prevent unnecessary and expensive attrition. As we said in Chapter 6, one area that suffers from high staff turnover is call-centre work. McCulloch and Turban (2007) considered P–O fit related to selection in 14 call centres in the USA and Canada among over 200 staff who stayed and those who left, showing that taking P–O fit into account during selection can play a key role in preventing high attrition.

Furthermore, P–O fit can be enhanced by an attention to socialization processes once new employees have been selected (Cable and Parsons, 2001), and in recent years, there has been growing interest in retaining talent through *onboarding* programmes (Dai and de Meuse, 2007). For example, Google's onboarding programme for software engineers includes face-to-face, online and on-the-job training, mentoring, membership of a support community and practice-based learning, all deemed to be successful in creating a congruence between Google's values and the values of those seeking sustained employment in the company (Johnson and Senges, 2010).

In addition to P–O fit, there is also interest in the extent to which there is a match between an individual's skills, knowledge and abilities and the requirements of a job, referred to as the 'person–job' (P–J) fit. Research by Carless (2005) found that both P–O and P–J fit were positively linked to attraction – the perception that an organization was a desirable place to work. However, P–J fit becomes more important in relation to a candidate's intention to accept a job offer, suggesting that once applicants move toward job acceptance, they become more concerned with how they will use their abilities than with working in an organization that matches their values. There is also the issue of person–team fit (Hollenbeck, 2000), which considers how people can be matched to variations in organizational structure. For example, in a decentralized structure in which the focus is on self-managing teams, different characteristics might be required compared with more centralized or departmental structures.

This analysis of attraction, based on images and congruence of values, and then use of abilities, has been complicated by recent concerns about attracting a more diverse workforce. Recent changes in legislation have also set limits on the expression of values. For example, images used in advertisements for recruits need to take into consideration possible discrimination against older applicants.

Recruitment channels

The main means of attracting applicants can be summarised as follows:

- Walk-ins
- Employee referrals
- Advertising
- Websites
- Recruitment agencies
- Professional associations
- Educational associations.

Advertising and other recruitment literature comprise a common means by which the organization's values, ethos and desired image are made manifest, often in the form of glossy brochures. The utilitarian approach that focused on specifying job details, terms and conditions has been superseded by advertising that attempts to communicate a message about the company image, possibly over a long period of time through 'low-involvement' advertisements that seek to create awareness of an organization rather than generate recruits (Collins and Han, 2004). A good example might be the series of adverts for BT broadband, which clearly advertises a product but maintains ongoing awareness of BT as a brand and an organization. There has been a marked shift towards recruitment advertisements that are creative and reflect the skills normally used in product marketing. Recruitment advertising is now fully established within mainstream advertising.

HRM web links [WWW] Go to www.makeupyourownmind.co.uk/quality-scouts-home.html to find out about McDonald's Quality Scouts. What are the various methods used to attract applicants?

Over the last decade, there has been a rapid growth in online recruitment, e-recruitment having become another facet of the rapid progression of e-HRM. As a result, organizations are advised to consider the design of their websites and the terms that applicants might use to carry out job and vacancy searches (Jansen and Jansen, 2005). It has also been shown that the usability of a company's website affects an applicant's perception of a job (Cappelli, 2001), and that content features such as testimonials by current employees, pictures, policies and awards can affect perceptions of the organization's culture (Brady et al., 2009). Some companies use websites combined with 'smart phone' apps in recruitment.

According to the CIPD (2010c), 63 per cent of organizations regard their own website as their most effective method of attracting applications. The survey also found that 33 per cent make use of commercial job boards such as Monster (www.monster.co.uk) and Step-Stone (www.stepstone.com), although evidence from other surveys suggests that such sites can also attract unsuitable applicants (Parry and Tyson, 2008). Further research also found different attitudes towards commercial job boards in comparison to company websites, including the potential of reaching a wider pool of applicants and the convenience of the method (Parry and Wilson, 2009).

In many cases, especially at a time when there are more applicants than vacancies, online applications via websites can be a way of saving costs in recruitment and also allowing a faster response and turnaround. Although cost saving is clearly a major benefit, some companies see online recruitment more strategically. For example, when Whitbread faced the problem of recruiting managers for its 400-site Brewsters and Brewers Fayre restaurant business, it developed its own recruitment website. The site was searched over 100,000 times in the first 4 months, with 1300 applications. This enabled the company to build a database and maintain contact with potential candidates. Another benefit to the company was its ability to establish consistency in its brand to potential employees (Smethurst, 2004).

As online recruitment has developed, it has been accompanied by the use of tools for filtering applicants and tools for starting the selection process (Parry and Tyson, 2008), probably much valued by employers during a recession when the ratio of applications to positions available will be high. Pollitt (2008) reports the approach of the mobile phone company 3, who work with a commercial e-recruitment operator that provides five online 'gateways' for both external and internal recruitment. Applicants can view video clips of employees talking about working for 3, as well as upload their details and create e-mail alerts for jobs that become available. They can also monitor the progress of any application made and receive messages on their mobile phone.

HRM web links   Check the services provided by ActiveRecruiter at www.taleo.com/solutions/recruiting and Real Match at www.realmatch.com.

reflective question   Go to either the British Airways website at www.britishairwaysjobs.com/baweb1, or that of investment company Merrill Lynch at www.totalmerrill.com/publish/mkt/campaigns/careers/index.aspx. How do you think these websites filter out those who do and do not wish to work for British Airways or Merrill Lynch? Did you take the interactive challenges? Does online recruitment increase the power of employers in the graduate labour market?

In the late 2000s, social networking sites such as Facebook and LinkedIn, and social media such as Twitter, have grown in popularity, and all of these allow information about vacancies in organizations to be shared. While informal 'word of mouth' information about jobs has long been recognized for its accuracy and effectiveness in employee referrals (Iles and Salaman, 1995), employees can quickly, through Web 2.0 social networking, refer their friends or contacts towards vacancies – although how useful this will be to an organization will depend on the value of those people's social networks (Casella and Hanaki, 2008). It is, of course, also possible for organizations to explore the public pages of network sites to assess the extent and value of a person's links or to find other applicants within a network. Research in Belgium suggests there is some interest among recruiters in the use of social networking sites, especially LinkedIn, but also the possibility that such interest will lead to biased decisions on selection based on profile pictures and personality as indicated by the person's presence on a site (Caers and Castelyns, 2010).

Internships or placements

One method of attracting applicants is through internships or placements, which are often used by students for work-based research as part of their programmes (Hynie et al., 2011), but also provide an opportunity for students to gain experience and increase their market-ability. If students then take up positions within the organization, the organization gains through the motivation of students to work and in terms of savings on training and induction. Research suggests that experience gained from internships increases employment prospects and starting salaries. Where internees perform well, employers place more value on such programmes (Gault et al., 2010). Because internships and placement offer employers an advanced opportunity to assess potential applicants, a selection process is increasingly used, involving some of the methods we will consider below.

HRM web links   Explore internship opportunities and the selection process at www.graduatesyorkshire.co.uk/internships.

Visit www.palgrave.com/business/bratton5 to read an HRM in practice feature on the Co-op's internship scheme.

Job descriptions

A further manifestation of the image projected by an organization to which recruits will be attracted is a description of the actual work that potential employees will be required to do. The traditional way of providing such information is in the form of a *job description*, usually derived from a job analysis and a description of the tasks and responsibilities that make up the job. Against each job description, there is normally a specification of the standards of performance. A typical format for a job description is given in Figure 7.3.

JOB DESCRIPTION

Job title

Department

Responsible to …

Relationships

Purpose of job/overall objectives

Specific duties and responsibilities

Physical and economic conditions

Figure 7.3 *Job description format*

In addition to a job description, there is, in the form of a *personnel or person specification*, some attempt to profile the 'ideal' person to fill the job. It is accepted that the ideal person for the job may not actually exist, and that the specification will be used only as a framework within which a number of candidates can be assessed. In the past, a format for a personnel specification has been the seven-point plan, based on the work of Rodger (1970) and shown in Figure 7.4. An alternative to the seven-point plan was Munro-Fraser's fivefold grading system (1971), as in Figure 7.5. In both forms of personnel specification, it was usual to indicate the importance of different requirements. Thus, certain requirements might be expressed as essential and others as desirable.

PERSONNEL SPECIFICATION

Physical characteristics

Attainment

General intelligence

Specific aptitudes

Interests

Disposition

Circumstances

Figure 7.4 *Rodger's seven-point plan*

Both job descriptions and personnel specifications have been key elements in the traditional repertoire of HR managers. Over the years, various attempts have been made to develop and fine-tune techniques and practices. One such development has been the shift of emphasis in job descriptions away from specifying tasks and responsibilities towards the results to be achieved (Plachy, 1987). There has, however, been a growing awareness of the

Figure 7.5 *Munro-Fraser's fivefold grading system*

limitations and problems of such approaches. Watson (1994) noted that job analysis, used to produce job descriptions and person specifications, relied too much on the analyst's subjective judgement in identifying the key aspects of a job and deriving the qualities that related to successful performance. In addition, the use of frameworks such as the seven-point plan may provide a 'cloak for improper discrimination' (Watson, 1994, p. 189). Current legislation on discrimination needs to be carefully considered in job descriptions and person specifications. For example, criteria set for physical characteristics might discriminate against applicants with a disability who in fact have the ability to do the job.

HRM web links In the UK, ACAS provides examples of job descriptions and personnel specifications at www.acas.org.uk/index.aspx?articleid=1393.

The move towards flexibility and changing work practices (see Chapter 6) has seen the appearance of new forms of work description. It is argued that traditional job descriptions are too narrow and may restrict opportunities for development and growth within jobs (Pennell, 2010). Some organizations have replaced or complemented job descriptions with performance contracts. These contain details of what a job-holder agrees to accomplish over a period of time, summarising the purpose of a job, how that purpose will be met over the time specified and how the achievement of objectives will be assessed. This approach allows job requirements to be adjusted by agreement between the job-holder and his or her manager. It also allows a clear link to other HR processes. Performance contracts signal to new recruits the expectation that their jobs will change and that they cannot rely on a job description as the definitive account of their work. Adler (Adler, N. J., 2002) refers to this reorientation as performance-based recruitment and selection.

As we have already discussed, competencies are used to create a specification of the characteristics of those sought for particular positions (Industrial Relations Services, 2003a; Roberts, 1997). It has been argued (Feltham, 1992) that the use of competencies allows organizations to free themselves from traditional stereotypes in order to attract applicants from a variety of sources. Stereotypes of the ideal person may be contained within personnel specifications, and organizations may, despite warnings, be reinforcing the stereotype in their recruitment practices. Competencies appear to be more objective, have a variety of uses in attracting applicants and allow an organization to use more reliable and valid selection techniques.

The test of success of a recruitment process is whether it attracts a sufficient number of applicants of the desired quality within the budget set (Connerley et al., 2003). Traditionally, applications are made by a combination of letter, a completed application form and/or a CV. Increasingly, such forms can be submitted by email or completed online (Parry and Wilson, 2009). Recruiters might reasonably expect a number of applicants per position available, referred to as the recruitment ratio, thus allowing a choice to be made. Too many applicants may reduce the cost per applicant but add further costs in terms of the time taken to screen the applications. Too few applicants may be an indication of a tight labour market but may also be an indication that the values, ethos and image projected by the organization onto the market, including information on the work, as provided by job descriptions and specifications, are poor attractors. Recruiters need to monitor the effect of such factors on the recruitment process. If there are insufficient applicants from particular ethnic groups, too few men or women or disabled applicants, the recruitment process may indirectly discriminate and/or fail to meet legal requirements.

Selection

As we have seen, it is usual for an organization that wishes to recruit new employees to define criteria against which it can measure and assess applicants. Increasingly, such criteria are set in the form of competencies composed of behavioural characteristics and attitudes. Rather than trust to luck, organizations are using more sophisticated selection techniques. Organizations have become increasingly aware of making good selection decisions, since selection involves a number of costs:

- The cost of the selection process itself, including the use of various selection instruments
- The future costs of inducting and training new staff
- The cost of labour turnover if the selected staff are not retained.

The CIPD's research (2010c) on selection methods used in UK organizations showed that competency-based interviewing was the most common approach (78 per cent), followed by interviewing following the contents of the CV/application form (that is, biographical; 64 per cent), structured panel interviews (61 per cent) and telephone interviews (47 per cent). Other methods being used were references before interviews, group exercises and tests for specific skills, general abilities, literacy/numeracy, attitudes and personality; in addition, 42 per cent also used an assessment centre.

The configuration of selection techniques chosen will depend on a number of factors. As argued by Wilk and Cappelli (2003, p. 117), it is not simply a case of 'more is better'. Selection methods will depend on the characteristics of the work and the level of pay and training. It is also crucial to remember that decisions are being made by both employers and potential employees, even during a recession, and that the establishment of mutually agreed expectations during selection forms part of the psychological contract (see Chapter 1), which will strongly influence an employee's attitudes and feelings towards the organization (Herriot et al., 1997). According to Hausknecht et al. (2004), there are good reasons why organizations need to consider the reaction of applicants to selection methods:

- If selection is viewed as invasive, the attraction of the organization may be diminished.
- Candidates who have a negative experience can dissuade others.
- A negative selection experience can impact on job acceptance.
- Selection methods are covered by legislation and regulations relating to discrimination.

Trapped in the 'marzipan layer'

The *Sex and Power 2011* report by the Equality and Human Rights Commission found that the rate of progress towards gender equality in senior management had remained extremely slow, and that the process had even reversed in some sectors. Despite women starting on their career ladder often better qualified than men, after some years women either drop out of management or remain trapped in 'the marzipan layer' below senior management, leaving the higher ranks to be dominated by men (as quoted in *Guardian*, August 17, 2011).

This phenomenon, often referred to as the 'glass ceiling', has been attributed to both continuing direct discrimination (which remains unlawful) and more subtle indirect discrimination such as an expectation to work long hours that clashes with family responsibilities (a clash still less likely to be experienced by men).

A good example of the way these pressures permeate a whole organizational culture is shown by Jacqueline Watts' examination of women civil engineers in the extremely male world of the construction industry (Watts, 2009). When newcomers who are different (in their gender or ethnicity) join an existing group, one response is what is called 'boundary heightening', in which the majority deliberately emphasize their group characteristics. Thus, when a woman enters predominantly male territory such as a building site, the amount of sexual innuendo and jokes or displayed pornography may actually increase. Similarly, in the

setting of the boardroom, the pre-business conversation may be devoted to male sports interests, effectively excluding the sole woman present.

Watts' women engineers all remarked on the expectation that they would work long hours (the general feeling that 'hard working means long working') and on the predominantly male management style; this was seen by the women respondents as authoritarian and top-down compared with their own preferred style of more inclusive, participative management. When on site and faced with the boundary-heightening behaviour described above, the women engineers felt compelled to defeminize their clothing and appearance (no make-up or heels) 'otherwise you'd never survive'. All, however, found the heightened visibility, sexual harassment and intimidation to be emotionally draining, and this had led one participant to leave the profession.

The chances of resisting these pressures were seen as slim to non-existent: to emphasize work–life balance in the face of the 'heroic narrative' of staying late would cast them as slackers and open them up to criticism. The women felt they had no option but to collude with the male style of management in choosing, for example, not to voice any concerns they might have over staff workloads in case they were seen as less committed.

Watts concludes that:

> Women managers experience challenges not faced by male counterparts because of the dominant masculinist ethos of corporate management culture that privileges men, ranks some men above others and places women on the periphery of the managerial class.

Stop! The continued exclusion of women from senior decision-making roles is clearly a huge waste of talent and expertise. How would you remedy this, given that the equality legislation has had relatively little effect on the cultural pressures indicated above?

Sources and further information: See Watts (2009) for more information of her study of women in engineering.

Note: This feature was written by Chris Baldry at the University of Stirling.

©istockphoto.com/Peter Close

- Mistreatment during selection will put off future applications and may also stop applicants from buying the organization's products or using their services.

reflective question How would you react to a negative experience in a selection process?

An important factor is the perception of fair treatment, and this applies to both the methods used and the process as a whole, referred to as procedural justice or fairness (Gilliland, 1993). Bauer et al. (2001) have sought to measure the reactions of applications for jobs using a procedural justice scale relating to selection. Items in the scale include the job-relatedness of tests, the 'opportunity to perform', which is the chance to demonstrate knowledge, skills and abilities, the provision of feedback and treatment with warmth and respect. The scale could be used by organizations to evaluate the fairness of their selection procedures and the correction of problems. Positive reactions to selection can result in greater efforts to perform, which can in turn help organizations to identify the best candidates (Hausknecht et al., 2004).

Underlying the process of selection and the choice of techniques are two key principles:

- *Individual differences* – Attracting a wide choice of applicants will be of little use unless there is a way of measuring how people differ. People can vary in many ways, for example intelligence, attitudes, social skills, psychological and physical characteristics, experience and so on.
- *Prediction* – Recognition of the way in which people differ must be extended to a prediction of performance in the workplace.

Selection techniques will, to a varying degree, reflect these principles of measuring differences and predicting performance. Organizations may increasingly use a variety of techniques, and statistical theory is used to give credibility to those techniques which attempt to measure people's attitudes, attributes, abilities and overall personality. Some commentators would suggest that this credibility is 'pseudoscientific' and that many limitations remain with selection techniques. Iles and Salaman (1995), for example, claim that this 'psychometric' model appears to value:

- *Individualism* – in which individual characteristics are claimed to predict future performance
- *Managerialism* – in which top managers define the criteria for performance
- *Utility* – in which the costs and benefits, in monetary terms, of using different selection techniques are assessed.

reflective question What do you think are the implications associated with individualist, managerialist and utilitarian values in the selection process?

We are once again reminded that power is an important consideration when making decisions about employing people. Selection instruments often seem to be neutral and objective, but the criteria built into such instruments that allow the selection and rejection of applicants make up a knowledge base that provides the organization and its agents with power.

Reliability and validity issues

Two statistical concepts – reliability and validity – are of particular importance in selection. *Reliability* refers to the extent to which a selection technique achieves consistency in what it is measuring over repeated use. If, for example, you were being interviewed by two managers for a job in two separate interviews, you would hope that the interview technique would provide data such that the interviewers agreed with each other about you as an individual. Alternatively, if a number of candidates were given the same selection test, you would want to have some confidence that the test would provide consistent results concerning the individual differences between candidates. The statistical analysis of selection techniques normally provides a reliability coefficient, and the higher the coefficient (that is, the closer it is to 1.0), the more dependable the technique.

Validity refers to the extent to which a selection technique actually measures what it sets out to measure. There are different forms of validity, but the most important in selection is criterion validity, which measures the results of a technique against set criteria; this may be the present success of existing employees (concurrent validity) or the future performance of new ones (predictive validity).

Validation is in practice a complex process, and studies involving a large number of candidates would be required in order to allow a correlation coefficient to be calculated – in testing with criteria, this is referred to as a *validity coefficient*. If the coefficient is less than 1.0, an imperfect relationship between the test and the criterion is indicated. Even if the coefficient indicates such a relationship, a selection technique may, however, still be worth using: that is, you would be better to use the instrument than not use it. In addition, different selection techniques can be assessed in relation to each other according to their validity coefficient results. One difficulty is that it usually takes a long time to conduct validity studies, and by the time such studies were completed, it would be highly likely that the work from which some of the criteria were derived would have changed. Validity is also related to the particular environment in which performance is carried out. Such problems have not, however, stopped many organizations using tests and other selection techniques that have been validated by the test designers in a range of organizations or situations. (Go to www.socialresearchmethods.net/kb/measure.php for more details on validity and reliability.)

CVs and biodata

For many positions, applicants will be asked to provide a CV (a curriculum vitae, called a résumé in the USA and Canada), which enables them to set out their experience, skills and achievements. Importantly, it also provides an early chance for the organization to screen the applicants before moving to the next stage of selection. There has been interest in how selectors make decisions on the basis of information contained in CVs, and whether such decisions are informed by the criteria set out in the job descriptions and specifications, or are subject to personal bias. For example, would an applicant who attended a particular university be more likely to be selected on the basis of their CV? Proença and de Oliveira (2009) examined the assessment of CVs in selection and the reasoning used by selectors. They found some interesting contradictions between the use of objective knowledge and criteria, as set out in the formal documentation, and more implicit knowledge and emotion.

In addition to CVs, there is growing interest in information about a person's past experiences and behaviours in particular situations. This can be gathered by questionnaires including several multiple-choice questions and/or scenarios seeking data that can be verified as factual. Such information is referred to as *biodata*. Items can then be scored to predict against aspects of future behaviour such as job performance and absenteeism, results that have been shown to have relatively high validity (see Becton et al., 2009).

Selection interviewing

Of all the techniques used in selection, the interview is the oldest and most widely used, along with application forms and letters of reference, referred to by Cook (1994, p. 15) as 'the classic trio'. In recent years, with the advent of secure technology, interviews can also take place by video. Various attempts have been made to classify selection interviews, and it may be useful to point out some of the categories that have been developed:

- *Information elicited* – interviews have a specific focus and require information at different levels:
  - An interview may focus on facts. The style of the interview will be direct, based on a question and answer session.
  - An interview may focus on subjective information once the factual information has been obtained.
  - There may also be a focus on underlying attitudes, requiring intensive probing techniques and usually involving qualified psychologists.
- *Structure* – interviews may vary from the completely structured, based on planned questions and responses, to the unstructured, allowing complete spontaneity for the applicant and little control for the interviewer. A compromise between the two extremes is most likely, the interviewer maintaining control by the use of guided questions but allowing free expression on relevant topics.
- *Order and involvement* – the need to obtain different kinds of information may mean the involvement of more than one interviewer. Applicants may be interviewed serially or by a panel.

The selection interview has been the subject of much review and research over the past 60 years. During much of that time, overall results on the validity and reliability of interviews have been disappointing. In 1949, Wagner carried out the first comprehensive review of research associated with the employment interview. Wagner noted that, in the 174 sets of ratings that were reported, the reliability ranged from a correlation coefficient (r) of 0.23 to one of 0.97, with a median value of $r = 0.57$. Validity, from the 222 results obtained, ranged from $r = 0.09$ to $r = 0.94$, with a median of $r = 0.27$ (Wagner, 1949). Wagner considered such results to be unsatisfactory. This pattern of low-validity results continued in other research for the next four decades. In their review, for example, Ulrich and Trumbo (1965) agreed that the interview seemed to be deficient in terms of reliability and validity, and they were forced to conclude that judgements about overall suitability for employment should be made by other techniques.

There have been two lines of research to examine the reasons behind such poor results for the selection interview. The first focuses on how interviewers process information that leads to a decision on acceptance or rejection. The second focuses on the skills of effective interviewing. Table 7.2 outlines a summary of this research.

HRM **and globalization**

Unpacking the meaning of credentials

In a fascinating new study of higher education in the USA, sociologist Ann Mullen writes 'we need to look not just at *who* goes to college, but at who goes *where* to college' (Mullen, 2010, p. 5). The main thrust of her argument is that even though more and more students are attending college and earning credentials, post-secondary education in the USA remains highly stratified. Even when students graduate with the same credential (the baccalaureate or bachelor's degree), its value and prestige will depend on the institution that awarded it.

Mullen's analysis alerts us to a challenge in employee recruitment. What do credentials stand for? At first glance, they appear to solve the problem of globalizing markets for educated labour. Employers seem justified in believing that knowledge and skill would be similar between similar credentials earned in different countries. But if the meaning of the same credential varies within a developed country such as the USA, as Mullen suggests, one must obviously proceed cautiously when attempting to evaluate the meaning of credentials earned in different countries.

As a starting point, it is helpful briefly to consider different theories of credentialism. Steven Brint provides an overview starting with a definition: 'By credentialism, I mean the monopolization of access to rewarding jobs and economic opportunities by the holders of educational degrees and certificates' (Brint, 2006, p. 166). He then proceeds to review various criticisms of credentialism. Many of these criticisms focus on the question of whether credentials are 'information-rich': does the possession of a credential tell us whether a person has the knowledge and skill that will enable them to perform the tasks and duties of a particular job? If the answer is 'yes', they are indeed information-rich.

But perhaps credentials are not information-rich in the way suggested above. Perhaps they just tell us that a person is trainable (or educable): the person has qualities of attentiveness and perseverance that will enable them to learn on the job. Or perhaps credentials are merely signals of a person's social background: an employer may believe that a particular university produces upper-class applicants who are a better 'fit' for the organization. Here, credentials are not

information-rich, at least not in the sense that they tell employers specific things about job-related knowledge and skill.

The question of whether credentials are information-rich becomes even more challenging when we are referring to situations in which HR professionals from one country are responsible for hiring credentialled workers from another country. This situation, which is becoming more common all the time, forces us to think critically about what credentials mean and what they tell us about the person who has earned them. To answer this question satisfactorily, we must know something about the education system in the country where the credential was earned, and this knowledge is often not readily available.

Stop! The credentials demanded for access to particular occupations sometimes seem unjustified. Provide one example of a situation where demands for higher entry-level credentials are justified, and one example of where they are not. If such increased demands are not justified, why are they made?

You have been accused of discrimination for your criticisms of the credentials earned in a developing country. As an HR professional, how would you respond? What institutions have been created to evaluate the meaning and value of credentials?

Sources and further information: See Brint (2006) and Mullen (2010) for more information on credentials.

Note: This feature was written by David MacLennan at Thompson Rivers University.

©stockphoto.com/ericsphotography

Table 7.2 *Reasons for poor results from selection interviewing*

Processing of information	
Pre-interview	Use of application forms to reject the applicant on grounds of sex, academic standing or physical attractiveness
First impressions	Decisions made quickly lead to a search during the rest of the interview for information to support those decisions. Negative information will be heavily weighted if the decision is rejection, but a positive early decision may lead to warm interviewer behaviour
Stereotypes	Interviewers may hold stereotyped images of a 'good' worker against which applicants are judged. Such images may be personal to each interviewer and are potentially based on prejudice
Contrast	Interviewers are influenced by the order in which applicants are interviewed. An average applicant who follows below-average applicants may be rated as above average. Interviewers may compare applicants against each other rather than against objective criteria
Attraction	Interviewers may be biased towards applicants they 'like'. This attraction may develop where interviewers hold opinions and attitudes similar to those of the applicant
Skills of interviewing	
Structure	Variations in interview structure affect reliability, low scores being gained for unstructured interviews
Questions	Interviewers may use multiple, leading, embarrassing and provocative questions
Listening	Interviewers may talk more than listen, especially if they view the applicant favourably. Interviewers may not be 'trained' to listen effectively
Retention and interpretation	Interviewers may have a poor recall of information unless guides are used and notes made. Interviewers may have difficulty in interpreting the information

By 1982, Arvey and Campion (1982) were able to report less pessimism about reliability and validity when interviews were conducted by boards (panels) and based on job analysis and job information. In particular, reference was made to the success of *situational interviews* (Latham et al., 1980). In these, interview questions are derived from systematic job analysis based on a critical incident technique (see Flanagan, 1954). Questions focus on descriptions of what an applicant would do in a series of situations. Responses are judged against benchmark answers that identify poor, average or excellent employees.

In addition to situational interviews, Harris (1989) reported on other developments in interview format that relied on job analysis. These included *behaviour description interviews*, which assess past behaviour in various situations, and *comprehensive structured interviews*, which contain different types of question, for example situational, job knowledge, job simulation and work requirements. Such developments have resulted in an enhanced effectiveness of the selection interview and improved scores for reliability and validity. To achieve the benefits of such improvements, organizations need to pay more attention to providing formal training on structured selection interviewing. This is, however, not always easy to achieve since untrained interviewers may believe they are doing a good job in predicting future performance (Chapman and Zweig, 2005).

The use of questions about past behaviour combined with competencies in selection interviews has enhanced effectiveness even further. Pulakos and Schmitt (1995) compared the validity results during the selection process for experience-based (or behavioural) questions and situational questions. The former are past-oriented questions and are based on the view that the best predictor of future performance is past performance in similar situations. Applicants are asked job-relevant questions about what they did in other situations. This contrasts with situational questions, in which applicants are asked what they would do in response to particular events in particular situations. Responses to both types of question can be scored on behaviour scales, but experience-based questions have shown better results with respect to predictions of job performance, that is, predictive validity.

These results can then be used by organizations with competency frameworks. An ICT company has, for example, a competency relating to 'managing meetings'. Interviewers could base their questions around an applicant's past behaviour in managing meetings by asking the applicant to explain what she or he did in managing a specific meeting. Follow-up questions can be used to reveal further features of the applicant's performance, which can then be assessed against the competency indicators. Research by Campion et al. (1997, p. 655) found that these were 'better questions' that enhanced the effectiveness of the interview.

Barclay (1999) found a rapid increase in the use of structured techniques as part of a more comprehensive approach to selection. In particular, it was found that behavioural interviewing was being used systematically, especially in combination with a competency framework. Further research by Barclay (2001) found that behavioural interviewing was referred to in a variety of ways in organizations, for example competency-based interviewing, criterion-based interviewing, skills-based interviewing, life questioning and behavioural event interviewing. It was claimed that, however it was referred to, behavioural interviewing had improved the selection process and decisions made, a finding supported by Huffcutt et al. (2001) in their study of the use of interviews for positions of high complexity.

However, these approaches to interviewing have not been without criticism. First, since behavioural or competency-based questions are based on past behaviour, there is an assumption that behaviour is consistent over time, allowing prediction into the future. This assumption can be challenged on the basis that people do learn from their mistakes and can learn new ways of behaving. Furthermore, it might be suggested that people also tend to behave according to contingent factors such as time, place and especially the presence of others. A second assumption is that the questions allow a fair comparison between different candidates. They might, however, disadvantage those candidates with more limited experience or a poor recall of their experience, even though they might possess attributes or ideas that are not revealed in an interview (Martin and Pope, 2008). Even though a structured approach provides a degree of control over the interview, it still might possible for applicants to prepare their answers in advance or distort their responses to create a desirable impression (Levashina and Campion, 2006).

It is interesting at this point to note that much of the progress in interviews as a selection technique has occurred where organizations have sought to identify behaviour and attitudes that match their models of employees to be selected. This has required an investment in more sophisticated techniques of analysis. It is agreed that traditional job analysis techniques allow the production of job models in terms of tasks and responsibilities; however, organizations faced with change and seeking to employ workers whose potential can be utilized and developed will increasingly turn to techniques of analysis producing inventories of the characteristics and behaviours, such as competencies, that are associated with effective performance in the present and the future.

One consequence of more structured approaches to interviewing, including the training of interviewers, is the impact on applicants' reactions. A review by Posthuma et al. (2002) reported growing research interest in such reactions, generally showing that applicants prefer interviews compared with other selection instruments – the interview had greater *face validity* – which concerns whether applicants judge selection techniques to be related to the job (Smither et al., 1993).

One interesting dilemma, however, emerges for organizations – should the interview focus on establishing a good relationship with an applicant to elicit a positive reaction from the candidate about the selection process, or should the interview be concerned with using good structure and sophisticated questions that have higher predictive validity? In their research, Chapman and Zweig (2005, p. 697) found that this tension exists, with some interviewers preferring less structure in favour of building a rapport that 'potentially contaminates an otherwise standardized procedure'. Organizations need to recognize that the interview is a source of anxiety for applicants, inevitably affecting their performance. The danger is that an anxiety-affected interview performance may mask an applicant's ability to perform the job (McCarthy and Goffin, 2004). In addition, applicants' self-evaluation can impact on their perception of fairness and reactions to interviews in selection. Applicants who evaluate themselves positively are more likely to view the interview as fair (Nikolaou and Judge, 2007).

HRM web links Selection interviews can be quite daunting for candidates. For particular guidance on competency-based interviews, try www.allaboutmedicalsales.com/competency.html.

Psychometric testing

Selection based on competencies and attitudes has been one result of the increased attention given to identifying psychological factors through testing, and to how such factors predict job performance. Testing, it would seem, offers organizations a cost-effective process in their search for the right people to match the company's personality. For example, during the expansion of the coffee house chain Costa, 1800 new 'team' members were sought. The company worked with a testing house to develop a team-member personality questionnaire based on the company's values that measured particular qualities, such as a person's achievement orientation (Dawson, 2005).

We can make the following distinctions between different kinds of test:

- *Ability tests* – these focus on mental abilities such as verbal reasoning and numerical power, but also include physical skills testing such as keyboard speeds. In such tests, there may be right/wrong answers or measurements that allow applicants for a position to be placed in ranked order.
- *Inventories* – these are usually self-report questionnaires about personality, indicating traits, intelligence, values, interests, attitudes and preferences. There are no right/wrong answers but instead a range of choices between possible answers.

Taken together, tests of personality and ability are referred to as *psychometric tests* and have a good record of reliability and validity. Most people have some fears related to any test, and this has caused confusion over the meaning, use and value of psychometric tests.

The 1990s saw a rapid growth in the number of organizations using such tests, which was the result of more people, especially HR practitioners, being trained to administer them (McHenry, 1997). The CIPD survey (2010c) indicated that 44 per cent of organizations used personality/attitude/psychometric questionnaires, 43 per cent used literacy and/or numeracy tests, and 27 per cent used general ability tests.

Both forms of test provide a set of norms, developed from the scores of a representative group of people (the 'norm' group) of a larger population, for example UK adult men or women in a sales role. Figures are then expressed in percentiles, which allows for standardization. Thus, a raw score of 120 on a personality test or a section of a test might be placed in the 60th percentile, indicating that the applicant's result is higher than that of 60 per cent of the norm group but less than the score obtained by 40 per cent of the group. If the test had good predictive validity, this would be a valuable indicator allowing a comparison to be made between different applicants. Inventories would also include some allowance for 'distortions' and 'fake' responses (Dalen et al., 2001) as personality tests are generally thought to be less reliable than ability tests. An important issue here is the extent to which a test might discriminate against particular groups of people, which can lead to legal challenges (Jackson, 1996).

reflective question   A personality questionnaire contains the item 'I think I would make a good leader.' This was answered 'true' by twice as many men as women, implying that men are twice as likely to become good leaders. What do you think of such an item and its implication?

Ability tests may be of a general kind, for example those relating to general mental ability or abilities such as verbal fluency and numerical ability. In addition, there are also tests for specific abilities, often referred to as aptitude tests, for example for manual dexterity and spatial ability. Furthermore, there are tests for specific jobs, such as computer aptitude and sales aptitude (Toplis et al., 2005).

For many years, there has been a great deal of interest in the extent to which general mental ability and cognitive abilities can be shown to be valid in terms of predicting performance and can be generalized across a range of occupations (see Schmidt, 2002). For example, Bertua et al. (2005) sought to examine whether general mental ability and cognitive ability tests were valid predictors of job performance and training success in UK organizations. They did this by completing a meta-analysis of 56 papers and books covering 283 samples of testing. The analysis showed that the tests were valid predictors of performance and training success across a range of occupations, including senior managers. This was also the case for changes in the composition of job roles. The authors claimed that the results provided 'unequivocal evidence for the continued and expanded use of general mental ability tests for employee selection in UK organizations' (Bertua et al., 2005, p. 403).

HRM web links   The Watson–Glaser test measures high-level verbal reasoning abilities and is often used in selecting managers and professionals. Go to www.talentlens.co.uk/select/watson-glaser-critical-thinking-appraisal.aspx#description for more details.

On the personality front, there has over the past 25 years been growing interest in what has been referred to as the five-factor model as an explanation of the factors that determine a person's personality (Wiggins, 1996). The five-factor model – sometimes called the 'big five' model of personality – proposes that differences between people can be measured in terms of degrees of:

- *Emotional stability (neuroticism)* – adjustment versus anxiety, level of emotional stability, dependence versus independence
- *Extroversion* – sociable versus misanthropic, outgoing versus introverted, confident versus timid
- *Openness to experience* – reflection of an enquiring intellect, flexibility versus conformity, rebelliousness versus subduedness
- *Agreeableness* – friendliness versus indifference to others, a docile versus a hostile nature, compliance versus hostile non-compliance
- *Conscientiousness* – the most ambiguous factor, seen as educational achievement, or as will or volition.

Salgado (1997) sought to explore the predictive validity of the five-factor model in relation to job performance through a meta-analysis of 36 studies that related validity measures to personality factors. It was found that conscientiousness and emotional stability showed most validity for job performance, and that openness to experience was valid for training proficiency.

There are, however, doubts about an over-reliance on personality tests with respect to their use in predicting future performance, especially in relation to complex tasks such as management. Within the five-factor model, for example, conscientiousness has been highlighted as a predictor of overall job performance. However, a study by Robertson et al. (2000) attempted to test the link between conscientiousness and the performance of 453 managers in five different companies. The results showed no overall statistical relationship, although there was a link with particular performance factors such as being organized and being quality-driven. It was also found that there might be an inverse relationship between conscientiousness and promotability. This result supports the view that suitability for complex work cannot be assessed on the basis of a narrow measurement of a psychological profile.

This situation also applies to the assessment of intelligence. Ceci and Williams (2000) suggest that the measurement of intelligence, although used in various ways by HR departments, does have drawbacks if such measurement is based on the assumption of intelligence as a fixed property of individuals. They argue that intelligent behaviour such as complex thinking is strongly connected to the setting, composed of the task, the location and the other people involved.

Limitations on the value of intelligence, as measured by intelligence quotient tests, as a predictor have led to a growing interest in the assessment of another kind of intelligence based on feelings, sensing others' feelings and the ability to perform at one's best in relationship with others. This is referred to as *emotional intelligence* (Dulewicz and Higgs, 2000), and there is mounting evidence that employers are attempting to utilize this view of intelligence in their competency frameworks (Miller et al., 2001). Emotional intelligence has been popularized by the work of Daniel Goleman (2006), who divides emotional intelligence into five emotional competencies:

- The ability to identify and name one's emotional states and to understand the link between emotions, thought and action

- The capacity to manage one's emotional states – to control emotions or to shift undesirable emotional states to more adequate ones
- The ability to enter into emotional states (at will) associated with a drive to achieve and be successful
- The capacity to read, be sensitive to and influence other people's emotions
- The ability to enter and sustain satisfactory interpersonal relationships.

Partly as consequence of the interest in emotional intelligence, efforts have been made to develop a test with valid and reliable psychometric properties. For example, Akerjordet and Severinsson (2009) describe the design of an Emotional Intelligence Scale and an Emotional Reactions and Thoughts Scale for use in maternity care. Interestingly, they suggested that self-reporting might pose difficulties.

HRM web links **www** Find out more about emotional intelligence tests at www.haygroup.com/ww/services/index.aspx?id=1566. You can try a test online at www.ivillage.co.uk/test-your-emotional-intelligence-eq/74101.

Self-reporting in the completion of tests is a key issue considered by Morgeson et al. (2007a), who provide a fascinating review of personality testing based on the author's considerable experience and expertise in the field. They conclude that, in view of the self-reporting process that most tests employ, faking should not only be expected, but could also actually be seen as an ability that could be useful in certain situations. They highlight the generally low validity figures for such tests, suggesting that measures which are more job-related carry greater face validity because the results can be explained more easily. They also suggest a need for an alternative to self-report measures.

An interesting finding about tests is that academics' debates on validity are not especially significant for practitioners, who tend to choose tests because they are well-known (Furnham, 2008). This means that the most popular tests are the:

- Myers–Briggs Type Indicator (www.myersbriggs.org/my-mbti-personality-type/mbti-basics)
- 16PF Questionnaire (www.ipat.com/about/16pf/Pages/default.aspx)
- Belbin Team Role (www.belbin.com/rte.asp?id=8)
- Occupational Personality Questionnaire (www.shl.com/assets/resources/OPQ-UK.pdf).

Online testing

©istockphoto.com/webphotographeer

Online testing is also being used for selection and other HR purposes, this being referred to as e-assessment. One feature of testing is to provide a filter for organizations in order to reduce the number of unsuitable candidates (Czerny, 2004), although such a process may also screen out good applicants. A CIPD (2010c) survey found

Online testing, or e-assessment, is a popular form of candidate selection, especially in the early stages of recruitment, when it can be used to filter out applicants.

that 32 per cent of organizations were using preapplication elimination/progression questions, and most of this would have occurred online. The banking organization Lloyds TSB, for example, has an online application form based on its competency framework; this acts as the first stage in filtering applicants. For the second stage, there is a 20-minute numerical reasoning test, also completed online (Pollitt, 2005). The results of this test are then scored electronically, and this feeds into the bank's recruitment management system.

It is claimed that online testing provides organizations with the ability to test at any time and any place in the world, with the added benefit of being able to process the applicants quickly (Lievens and Harris, 2003). Furthermore, as tests are taken, the results can be accumulated and used to improve the validity of the tests. There might even be a correlation between performance in online tests and successful learning at work. One difficulty, however, is that there is a loss of control over the administration of a test; thus, you can take a test at any time and in any place in the world – but also with anyone else to help. Toplis et al. (2005, p. 52) pose the question, 'How do you know who is responding to the test at the end of the line?' There is, however, interest in comparing Internet testing with traditional paper and pencil testing. One issue, for example, is whether a person has an understanding of computers, which can affect the perceptions of a test (Weichman and Ryan, 2003).

Potosky and Bobko (2004) compared the responses of 65 students to Internet and paper and pencil versions of untimed and timed tests. They also assessed the students' understanding of computers in advance of the process and their reactions at the end. One interesting finding was the issue of timing; that is, it was reported that time on the Internet (virtual time) was different from actual time. This affected the time to find and read the instructions or the time to download a test online. The appearance of a test is also affected online, with fewer items being seen compared with a full paper test. This may also affect the order in which items are responded to since it is easier to move around a paper test compared with its online counterpart. The results showed interesting differences in test performance between the Internet and paper and pencil versions on the timed test. For the untimed test, there was little difference.

Another issue is the perception of efficiency and user-friendliness of the website in taking tests online. For example, sites that are difficult to navigate will affect applicants' overall satisfaction , especially in the earlier stages of selection (Sylva and Mol, 2009).

reflective question How do you feel about taking a test online?

Whatever developments occur in the use of e-assessment in recruitments, all tests need to conform to the requirements of discrimination laws. In the UK, tests should be endorsed by the British Psychological Society, which will check for any sexual and ethnic bias within the test. In addition to this endorsement, the impact of tests needs to be followed up and monitored to ensure that a test does not result in discrimination in practice against one sex or particular ethnic groups.

HRM web links You can find many tests to take yourself – without applying for a job. Go to www.myskillsprofile.com/index.php?partnerid=2221. From there, for example, you can take an online emotional intelligence test at www.myskillsprofile.com/instructions/eiq16.

Assessment centres

In their examination of organizational selection practices, Wilk and Cappelli (2003) found that as the complexity and demands of work increased, there was a need for a variety of selection methods. The CIPD (2010c) found that 42 per cent of organizations used assessment centres during selections. Given the weakness of single measures, organizations can combine techniques and apply them together at an event referred to as an assessment centre. Such events may last for 1–3 days, during which a group of applicants for a post will undergo a variety of selection techniques. For example, in the case of Lloyds TSB referred to above (Pollitt, 2005), the last stage of the selection process is attendance at an assessment centre, lasting 24 hours (from 5 pm until 5 pm the following day). Candidates attend in groups of 12 or 24 and are observed by assessors as they complete an interview, a case study presentation, group exercises and a role play. They also complete a numerical reasoning test to verify the online test.

We can make a distinction here between development centres (see Chapter 9), which yield information to help identify development needs, and assessment centres, which are designed to yield information to help make decisions concerning suitability for a job. Assessment centres can also be used to select participants for training programmes, especially for leadership and management development (see Chapter 10), and to promote internal applicants to more senior positions (Thornton and Gibbons, 2009).

It is argued that it is the combination of techniques, providing a fuller picture of an applicant's strengths and weaknesses, that makes assessment centres so valuable. Woodruffe (2000) outlines four generalizations about assessment centres:

- Participants are observed by assessors who are trained in the use of measurement dimensions such as competencies.
- Assessment is by a combination of methods and includes simulations of the key elements of work.
- Information is brought together from all the methods, usually under competency headings.
- Participants can be assessed in groups.

Although there may be no such thing as a 'typical' assessment centre (Spychalski et al., 1997), the general methods used are group discussions, role plays and simulations, interviews and tests. The following activities were, for example, used in the assessment centre to select customer service assistants for European Passengers Services Ltd (Mannion and Whittaker, 1996, p. 14):

- Structured interview
- Perception exercise
- Communication exercise
- Personality inventory
- Customer service questionnaire
- Tests for clear thinking and numerical estimation.

The objectives for using these methods were to generate information about:

- The ability to work under pressure
- Characteristic behaviour when interacting with others
- Preferred work styles

- The ability to think quickly
- The ability to make quick and accurate numerical estimates
- Experience and aptitude for a customer service role.

The European Passengers Services assessment centre process was judged to be a success, underpinned by the objectives and standardized decision-making of the assessors. Candidates attending an assessment centre will be observed by assessors who should be trained to judge candidates' performance against criteria contained within the dimensions of the competency framework used.

There has been interest in assessment centres that measure dimensions of personality and/or behaviour, referred to as dimension-based assessment centres (Lance, 2008), based on the judgement of assessors while candidates complete the exercises. A common problem is that assessor ratings may be affected because there are too many people to assess at the same time during an exercise (Melchers et al., 2010), and this problem may become more difficult to solve when organizations attempt to save costs by reducing the number of assessors. One possibility is to focus more on interviews with higher validity possibilities that measure dimensions similar to those of an assessment centre, thus screening out applicants who score less well at the interview and reducing the number to measure at the assessment centre (Dayan et al., 2008). Another possibility is to use measurement dimensions that are more focused and specific to particular tasks, in contrast to measurements that are used across all exercises. This approach is a feature of task-based ACs, where attention is given to specific dimensions of behaviour for each task, which are observable in the outcomes of participating in that task (Jackson et al., 2010).

reflective question

Have any of your colleagues applying for graduate training programmes been put through an assessment centre? What was their reaction to this process?

If your colleagues were to relay negative reactions to you about their experience of selection techniques with one organization, this might affect your image of it. Again, the question of face validity is important – whether the applicants feel that the selection techniques are connected to the job. For example, in response to the problem that an assessment centre lacked realism and variety, the accountancy firm Ernst and Young ran its centre in real offices, having candidates answer emails and telephone calls. This apparently made the organization's expectations clearer (Trapp, 2005). Kolk et al. (2003) found no difference to the process in terms of validity when they made an assessment centre more transparent to candidates by revealing, prior to their attendance, the dimensions of assessment that would be observed and used to make judgements.

Pre-employment activities

During recruitment and selection, even in times of recession, both parties in the relationship are making decisions. It is therefore important for an organization to recognize that high-quality applicants, attracted by the organization's image, could be lost at an early stage unless they are supplied with realistic organization and work information. Applicants have expectations about how the organization will treat them, and recruitment and selection represent an opportunity to clarify these.

Realistic job previews (RJPs) provide a means of achieving this by offering 'accurate, favourable, and unfavourable job-related information to job candidates' (Templer et al., 2006, p. 158). RJPs can take the form of case studies of employees and their work, the chance to 'shadow' someone at work, job sampling and videos, the aim being to enable applicants' expectations to become more realistic. One possibility therefore is that expectations about work and an organization can be lowered, allowing applicants to deselect themselves; however, for those who continue into employment, organizational commitment, job satisfaction, performance and job survival are likely to increase (Phillips, 1998; Premack and Wanous, 1985).

A key feature of RJPs is their promotion of accurate pre-employment expectations that serve to 'vaccinate' employees for when they are faced with job demands once employed. RJPs also serve to communicate an organization's honesty about such demands (Hom et al., 1999). For example, if the work is located overseas, there is a need for information about living in another country, referred to as a realistic living conditions preview (Templer et al., 2006). Research in Canada by Richardson et al. (2008) highlighted the importance of realistic living conditions previews in revealing non-work factors such as the well-being of the partners and children of those employees who live abroad.

What is clear is that recruitment and selection provide an arena for engagement between organizations and potential employees in which both parties develop an 'image' of each other. If managers fail to understand the mutuality of this process, they endanger the attractiveness of the organization and thereby threaten the organization's ability to recruit good applicants (Hausknecht et al., 2004). In combination with RJPs, organizations such as Siemens and DaimlerChrysler provide applicants with a link to current employees who act as mentors (Spitzmüller et al., 2008), and this can play a role in increasing attraction.

Watson and Hamilton Lawyers

case study

Setting

In England and Wales, the provision of legal services has been slowly moving in the direction of increased competition between law firms, prompted by changes in the regulatory framework that seeks to remove restrictive barriers so that clients can benefit. Many law firms, especially those which operate in commercial law, have already sought to enhance their position in the market by embracing marketing expertise and placing more focus on the achievement of outcomes that satisfy client requirements.

Watson and Hamilton Lawyers (WHL) is a medium-sized firm of UK commercial lawyers, based in the Midlands. Within the firm, there are around 50 directors who have an equity stake in the firm, with a further 60 staff who are professionally qualified as lawyers, 50 staff who are qualified as legal executives and around 40 support staff including HR and marketing. WHL's strategy is to pursue a path of expansion and growth based on offering high-quality legal services to clients.

A key finding has been the recognition that around 80 per cent of fee income is generated from 20 per cent of clients, who are seen as crucial to the delivery of the firm's strategy in two ways: first, such clients need to be retained and, second, they also need to be the focus of the development of business relationships. Therefore, in a difficult market, the senior directors of the firm saw the retention of key clients and the development of opportunities for future business with clients as paramount. Following research, a number of crucial behaviours and actions that needed to be enacted were identified (see the table). Once such behaviours had been identified, it was recognized that they could be used in a variety of ways at WHL, such as:

- In selecting new staff
- In assessing the potential of lawyers for future development, including self-assessment and development

It is vital for WHL that its employees develop and maintain good business relationships with their clients.

- For senior staff coaching and developing more junior staff
- In setting targets and goals for development
- In reviewing progress against targets
- As a common language for the firm to talk about performance.

The problem

Soon after the development of these behaviours, it became obvious that recruitment and selection procedures would need to change. The firm had a poor history relating to these areas, particularly in relation to professional staff, who were essential for fee-earning. Applicants were most commonly attracted through informal contacts, and decisions for employment were made on 'feel'. While the strategy and senior directors provided the parameters for decisions on recruitment and selection, managers were then 'given free rein', and most recent staff had been recruited on the basis of 'word of mouth' information obtained informally using 'field knowledge'.

Job descriptions (and personnel specifications) were not always produced, and evidence suggested that there

Retaining clients		Developing opportunities for future business	
1.1	Establishing contact	2.1	Working in partnership
1.2	Attending to needs and requirements	2.2	Delivering a quality service
1.3	Making the relationship work	2.3	Nurturing
1.4	Building value	2.4	Seeing the opportunities
1.5	Adding value	2.5	Exploiting those opportunities

was little involvement on the part of HR. There was no information on selection methods, questions used, criteria for assessing responses or judgements made on suitability. There was a 'perception of secrecy', with a strong possibility that decisions were biased towards the status quo and towards reinforcing the culture within a department.

There was apparent confusion over responsibility for determining vacancies for fee-earning staff and over how potential applicants were identified, especially with respect to the use of 'field knowledge'. Given the importance of behaviours relating to retaining clients and developing opportunities for future business, those involved in selection seemed to have little understanding of such requirements for fee-earners, nor were they using selection methods to make such assessments.

Assignment

Working in a group or on your own, prepare a report that argues for changes to the recruitment and selection policy incorporating the crucial behaviours of retaining clients and developing opportunities for future business. Explain how the 'perception of secrecy' can be tackled through a more effective assessment process based on these behaviours.

Note: This feature was written by Jeff Gold.

Visit the companion website at www.palgrave.com/business/bratton5 for guidelines on writing reports.

summary

◀ This chapter has examined the nature of recruitment and selection in organizations.

◀ The attraction and subsequent retention of employees is crucial to an employment relationship, which is based on a mutual and reciprocal understanding of expectations. Employers have, however, significant power in recruitment and selection. The overall approach taken will reflect an organization's strategy and its philosophy towards people management.

◀ Recruitment and selection practices are bound by the law of the land, especially with respect to discrimination in terms of sex, race, disability, age and sexual orientation. In the UK, the Equality Act 2010 provides a simplification of discrimination legislation. Unless exempted by the provisions of occupational requirement, discrimination is against the law directly, indirectly or by harassment or victimization. The antidiscrimination legislation set forward over the past 35 years provides the foundation for a growing interest in diversity at work.

◀ It is essential that organizations see that, whatever the state of the labour market and their power within it, contact with potential recruits is made through the projection of an 'image' that will impact on and reinforce the expectations of potential recruits.

◀ Competency frameworks have been developed to link HR practices to the key requirements of an organization's strategy. Competencies can be used to form a model or 'image' of the kinds of employee that an organization is seeking to attract and recruit. The response to the image provides the basis for a compatible P–O fit. Images or the 'brand' will feature in recruitment literature and, increasingly, on the Internet via e-recruitment.

◀ There has been a growth in online recruitment as a form of e-recruitment, with recent surveys showing that 63 per cent of organizations regard their own website as the most effective method of attracting applications. Features on websites such as testimonials by current employees, pictures, policies and awards can affect perceptions of an organization's culture. Social networking sites now allow a sharing of information about vacancies and applicants.

◀ Key documents in recruitment and selection are job descriptions and personnel specifications, although there is a growing awareness of the limitations of traditional approaches to their construction. Some organizations have switched to performance contracts, which can be adjusted over time. In addition, personnel specifications may be stated as competencies, which appear more objective.

◀ Selection techniques seek to measure differences between applicants and provide a prediction of future performance at work. Techniques are chosen on the basis of their consistency in measurement over time – reliability – and the extent to which they measure what they are supposed to measure – validity. Applicants' experience of selection methods, especially perceptions of fair treatment, strongly influences feelings their towards the organization.

◄ There are a range of selection techniques, the most common of which is the interview, and this has been the subject of much research. Recent years have indicated that a structured approach and the use of behavioural interviewing based on competencies increase the effectiveness of interviews in selection. The use of competencies in selection is a reflection of the current interest in assessing personality and abilities by the use of psychometric tests. Techniques of selection may be combined in assessment centres to provide a fuller picture of an applicant's strengths and weaknesses.

◄ Online testing allows organizations to process applicants more quickly. This may, however, filter out good applicants as well as unsuitable ones.

◄ Applicants have expectations about how the organization will treat them, and the recruitment and selection process represents an opportunity to clarify these. The use of RJPs can increase commitment and job satisfaction by clarifying expectations and communicating an organization's honesty.

vocab checklist for ESL students

◄ aptitude (n)
◄ assessment centre (n)
◄ attrition (n)
◄ coefficient (n)
◄ competencies (n), competent (adj)
◄ competing framework (n)
◄ curriculum vitae (CV) (n)
◄ discriminate (v), discrimination (n), discriminatory (adj)
◄ face validity (n)
◄ flagship (n)
◄ opportunity to perform (n)

◄ person–job (P–J) fit (n)
◄ personnel specification (n)
◄ person–organization (P–O) fit (n)
◄ pessimism (n), pessimist (n), pessimistic (adj)
◄ procedural justice (n)
◄ pseudoscientific (adj)
◄ realistic job preview (RJP) (n)
◄ realistic living conditions preview (n)
◄ recruitment ratio (n)
◄ reliability (n), reliable (adj)
◄ validity (n), validation (n), valid (adj)

WWW Visit www.palgrave.com/business/bratton5 for a link to free definitions of these terms in the Macmillan Dictionary, as well as additional learning resources for ESL students.

review questions

1 Who holds the power in recruitment and selection?
2 How can recruitment and selection support an organization's diversity strategy?
3 How can the predictive validity of the employment interview be improved?
4 Should job descriptions be abandoned in recruitment and selection?
5 'Appeal to their guts instead of just their brains.' How far do you agree with this view of graduate recruitment?
6 Are assessment centres a fair and valid way of selecting employees?

further reading to improve your mark

Reading these articles and chapters can help you gain a better understanding and potentially a higher grade for your HRM assignment.

◄ Selection techniques and methods have always been subject to criticism at a variety of levels, including measurement criteria, validity and reliability, decision-making and applicant reactions. For a broad-ranging review of the research in this area, see P. Sackett and F. Lievens (2008) Personnel selection. *Annual Review of Psychology,* **59**: 419–50.

◄ A key issue in selection is the perception of fairness of the methods used. A very interesting cross-national comparison of procedural justice can be found in N. Anderson and C. Witvliet (2008) Fairness reactions to personnel selection methods: an international comparison between the Netherlands, the United States, France, Spain, Portugal, and Singapore. *International Journal of Selection and Assessment,* **16**(1): 1–13.

◄ Diversity issues are increasingly important in recruitment and selection. M. Van den Brink, M. Brouns and D. Waslander, D. (2006), in their article Does excellence have a gender? *Employee Relations,* **28**(6): 523–39, consider the recruitment of professors in The Netherlands, finding gender differences in terms of selection and recruitment procedures.

◄ There is an interesting debate about the value of personality tests in selection. An argument in favour of tests is presented by D. S. Ones, S. Dilchert, C. Viswesvaran and T. A. Judge (2007) In support of personality assessment in organizational settings. *Personnel Psychology*, **60**: 995–1027. A response is provided by F. P. Morgeson, M. A. Campion, R. L. Dipboye, J. R. Hollenbeck, K. Murphy and N. Schmitt (2007b) Are we getting fooled again? Coming to terms with limitations in the use of personality tests for personnel selection. *Personnel Psychology*, **60**: 1029–49.

 Visit www.palgrave.com/business/bratton5 for lots of extra resources to help you get to grips with this chapter, including study tips, HRM skills development guides, summary lecture notes, and more.

part IV

employee performance and development

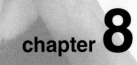

part IV

employee
performance and
development

chapter **8**

performance management
and appraisal

objectives

After studying this chapter, you should be able to:

1 Explain the purpose and uses of performance management, assessment and appraisal

2 Provide a model of performance management

3 Assess various approaches to understanding performance at work

4 Understand contrasting approaches to assessment and appraisal

5 Explain the use of performance management and appraisal in employee development

6 Understand the use of different performance-rating techniques

introduction

Ever since you arrived at university or college, you knew that there would at some point be an assessment of your work performance. Whether in the form of examinations, assignments, group activities and so on, you have had the chance to demonstrate your capabilities and develop your potential. The results of the assessment are used in an appraisal of what you will do next. So, as in a workplace, your life as a student has to be connected to a performance management system (PMS) in which assessment and appraisal are crucial activities.

Of course, any information you receive about your performance rating as a student will depend on your response to feedback, which in turn will depend on the judgements you make about your own performance, or self-appraisal. Consider for a moment your reactions to the feedback you received on your last assignment. Did you regard the judgement as a valid measurement of your performance? Perhaps you might see more value in receiving feedback from people other than your tutors. You can make use of multisource feedback (MSF) from other students in group work, employers in job placements or even your parents so you get a 360-degree appraisal of your performance. And obviously it is not just students whose performance is assessed. In recent years, through the National Student Survey (see www.heacademy.ac.uk/ourwork/supportingresearch/nss), students have been able to provide feedback on the performance of their university or college as a form of upward appraisal.

Because performance management and appraisal are often seen as key features of an organization's drive towards achieving competitive advantage and high performance, such information can be used in goal-setting as part of a performance and development plan (PDP). In this chapter, we will explore the working of PMSs, especially appraisal and assessment, and seek to explain some of the contentious features that have, in the past, failed to find respect among employers and employees alike. The chapter will, however, also explore how performance management has the potential to reverse the negative images of its past so that it can become the source of continuous dialogue between an organization's members.

reflective question How well does the PMS operate in your university or college?

Performance measurement and human resource management

Performance management refers to the set of interconnected practices designed to ensure that a person's overall capabilities and potential are appraised, so that relevant goals can be set for work and development, and so that, through assessment, data on work behaviour and performance can be collected and reviewed. This has in many organizations resulted in the development of an integrated PMS, often based on a competency framework (Strebler et al., 1997) (see Chapter 7).

At the centre of the PMS is work performance, in which the key ideas are that the principal dimensions of a person's work can be defined precisely in performance terms, allowing measurement over agreed periods of time that also takes account of particular constraints within the performance situation (Furnham, 2004). Measurement yields data that become information, allowing rational, objective and efficient decision-making that can be used in performance appraisals, objective-setting, assessment of development needs, regular feedback to individuals and regular review meetings (Chartered Institute of Personnel and Development [CIPD], 2009b). Through the use of assessment metrics that connect to business objectives, appraisal and performance management provide the possibility of matching human resources (HR) practices with organizational strategy. Performance management forms the nub of the strategic link between HR inputs and practices and organizational performance (Ferguson and Reio, 2010); it is also a vital feature of the development of high-performance work systems (Macky and Boxall, 2007) and the intent of sustained organizational performance (CIPD, 2009b).

Significant attention has been paid to setting organizational goals and directions so that business performance can be improved, and, importantly, to how such improvements can be measured. Based on the well-known dictum that 'if you can't measure it, you can't manage it', finding ways of measuring performance has become a major preoccupation in many organizations in both the public and the private sectors. All organizations have some means of measuring performance, and whichever methods of measurement are chosen, they are considered to play a key role in the efficient and effective management of the organization (Kennerley and Neely, 2002). Both now and in the future, performance data and indicators that can be quickly produced by information and communication technology are likely to affect decision-making in all sectors (Hatry, 2010), with a direct impact on how performance is managed and goals are set (Kagaari et al., 2010).

It is argued that measurement of performance is an indication of an organization's culture and the strategic thinking of its managers (Pun and White, 2005). Indeed, measurement is a crucial determinant of culture and what managers consider in their thinking. If, for example, turnover and costs are the key measures, these will form the indicators used in setting objectives for others and deciding how achievement is judged. Traditionally, of course, performance measurement has been based on accountancy models, with embedded assumptions relating to turnover, costs and especially profit – the bottom line. This provides an underpinning rationale for a 'control approach' to an organization's activities, including performance management and appraisal. It is argued that the control approach is an outcome of the drive towards rationality and efficiency found in our organizations, and in recent years perhaps simply of the drive towards survival, especially in small and medium-sized enterprises (SMEs). Such beliefs may certainly become part of a set of taken-for-granted assumptions that dominate life in organizations and may also be difficult to challenge. This is certainly the case for the HR profession, who have sought to provide a clear link between their activities and organizational outcomes, usually expressed in financial terms (Prowse and Prowse, 2010).

Organizational leaders, managers and employees are often unaware of the ways in which such beliefs are embedded in their actions. For example, much of the language of organizations, and many of the processes developed, can be related back to such a mechanical assumption of organizing. Mintzberg (1989, p. 339) argued that the form of structure called 'machine bureaucracy' has dominated thinking on how organizations should be constructed, and that terms such as 'getting organized', 'being rational' and 'achieving efficiency' represent evidence of this domination. As Mintzberg (1990, p. 340) wrote: 'I believe that to most people, what I am calling machine bureaucracy is not just a way to organize, it is the way to organize; it is not one form or structure, it is structure.'

reflective
question Does a mechanical assumption of organizing underpin how people talk about work?
What effect does such talk have in terms of how judgements and decisions are made?

As we saw in Chapter 6, there have been growing efforts to prove the special value of *people* in organizations by measuring and expressing human resource management (HRM) in financial terms (Toulson and Dewe, 2004). This is a partial acceptance of the control approach that is implied in traditional accountancy models. There has, however, been interest in developing alternatives to a financial measure. An example of this is return on investment, which aims to identify value-drivers in organizations (Scott, 1998), such as customer satisfaction and loyalty, and intellectual capital – although the intangibility of these can make some value-drivers more difficult to develop. There are, however, measurement models that take a wider view, perhaps more strategic and long term, which encompass a range of values rather than just financial, and can stimulate continuous improvement (Pun and White, 2005). For example, the total quality management (TQM) movement, which emerged in the 1980s and is still prevalent in many organizations, provides tools and measurements to bring about lasting change. The idea of continuous improvement in TQM is referred to as *kaizen*, and there is a close connection to another system of continuous improvement and measure called Six Sigma – find out more at www.isixsigma.com.

The European Foundation for Quality Management (EFQM) 'excellence model' provides a way of understanding how the whole organization works based on nine elements of 'excellence', including people. Each element can be judged on a range of criteria, and improvements can then be planned accordingly. For example, one of the criteria for people is that 'people are involved and empowered'. Another holistic measurement framework is Kaplan and Norton's (2000) 'balanced scorecard', in which a variety of perspectives are considered under the headings of customer, financial, internal business, and innovation and learning. Measures can be set for each, and these can then be aligned with strategy. Managers and employees can subsequently develop their own measures in response.

Over the last 15 years, there have been significant efforts to reconfigure the value-drivers in the public sector through more measurement against targets. In the late 1990s, there was a shift towards a more a customer-oriented approach to performance measurement (Mwita, 2000), referred to as 'new managerialism'. A Best Value framework was introduced in England in 1997, followed by five dimensions of performance indicator:

- *Strategic objectives* – why the service exists and what it seeks to achieve
- *Cost/efficiency* – the resources committed to a service and the efficiency with which they are turned into outputs
- *Service delivery outcomes* – how well the service is being operated in order to achieve the strategic objectives
- *Quality* – the quality of the services delivered, explicitly reflecting users' experiences of the services
- *Fair access* – ease and equality of access to services.

The overall aim of Best Value was to encourage a reorientation of service delivery towards citizens and customers, and to produce a quality-driven organization (Sheffield and Coleshill, 2001). By 2008, the Best Value performance indicators had been replaced by nearly 200 National Indicators used to monitor and measure local government performance, but by 2010 these had been abolished as they were seen by the new UK government to be too much micromanagement. In parallel, Scotland, Wales and Northern Ireland had their own policies for local authority performance management – for Scotland, go to www.scotland.gov.uk/Topics/Government/PublicServiceReform/14838/564; for Wales go to www.wlga.gov.uk/english/wales-programme-for-improvement; and for Northern Ireland, go to www.doeni.gov.uk/index/local_government.htm. However, local authorities and the public sector as a whole then faced large cuts in budgets from 2010 while still being required to meet some standards on front-line services.

A 'not-for-profit' social enterprise is a business that measures performance against social objectives, and reinvests profits or 'surpluses' into projects that help the community or environment.

© Lisa F. Young/Fotolia.com

Although the public sector is facing significant flux, some attention is being given to community and voluntary groups, of which there are many thousands throughout the UK. Even though such groups are also likely to face funding difficulties, there is interest in how volunteerism as performance can help to meet some of society's needs. One part of what is called the 'third sector' of businesses measures performance against social objectives, in which profits or 'surpluses' are reinvested in projects that help the community or environment. Such social enterprises have been seen as a source of creativity and responsible work that raise the standards of ethical and socially responsible business (Cabinet Office, 2007).

SMEs, usually understood as any business with between 10 and 249 staff (along with businesses with fewer than 10 staff, which are referred to as microenterprises), make up over 95 per cent of all organizations. For many years, there has been concern about their performance and their potential for growth (see Gold and Thorpe, 2010). Research suggests that most SMEs have little time for an analysis of performance, and that measurement is mostly responsive to problems as they emerge. This, for the most, means a basic profit and loss measurement to ensure survival (Garengo et al., 2005). It has been suggested that, by close attention to helping managers of SMEs deal with their immediate problems and concerns, more complex measures of performance can be introduced (Gold and Thorpe, 2008).

HRM web links 📶 There are a variety of approaches and frameworks for setting performance measures. Try www.som.cranfield.ac.uk/som/cbp, the home page of the Centre for Business Performance, which researches the design and implementation of performance measurement and management systems. You can find out more about the balanced scorecard at www.balancedscorecard.org. There is more about the EFQM excellence model at www.bqf.org.uk/performance-improvement/about-efqm-excellence-model.

The purpose and processes of performance management

There is considerable pressure on organizations to show that they are organized and systematic in their approach to the management of employee performance, and that there is a clear link between such performance and the organization's goals. The recent interest in talent management policies (see Chapter 6) highlights the importance of ensuring that employees are able to use their talents effectively in the performance of work (Baron, 2009). In addition, effective performance management can result in increased employee engagement (Mone et al., 2011).

Activities such as appraisal and assessment have traditionally been completed in isolation and have not always been able to demonstrate their value to organizational performance. Therefore, during the 1990s, there was a growing interest in performance management to ensure that HRM could be seen as being vital to an organization's concerns, leading to performance improvement and competitive advantage (Armstrong and Baron, 2004). The adoption of a PMS represents an attempt by an organization to show a strategic integration of its HRM processes, which can together be linked to the goals and direction of an organization. However, this move relies very much on the role of managers and the quality of their relationships with employees (Sparrow, 2008), and it therefore represents something of a conundrum for HR managers. That is, the activities of a PMS, designed and assembled by HR, require the serious attention and commitment of other managers for their effective operation, and this cannot always be assured (Rao, 2007).

It is a strategic focus on business objectives that gives performance management its distinctive position in HRM (Baron, 2009), providing the link between the organization's values, performance and competitiveness (Boudreau and Ramstad, 2009). However, the degree to which strategic aims and a PMS are integrated is open for discussion, creating a gap between the rhetoric and the reality of claims for the contribution of performance management to organizational effectiveness (Stanton and Nankervis, 2011).

For example, according to a survey by the CIPD (2009b) of over 500 companies in the UK, there was a high level of agreement regarding the importance of performance management and the inclusion of regular review meetings (90 per cent), objective-setting (82.5 per cent), regular feedback to individuals (83 per cent), performance appraisals (82.8 per cent) and assessment of development needs (75.1 per cent). However, in reality such activities were not always completed – for example, only 62.7 per cent completed regular review meetings to assess their progress against targets and only 75.3 per cent set objectives or targets. Performance appraisal was more likely, at 81.3 per cent. The survey found a trend towards greater integration by incorporating talent management, developing potential, planning careers and providing coaching or mentoring as part of a PMS, although we can see the working of the conundrum that we referred to above in the responses on the impact and benefit of a PMS. For example, only 20 per cent replied that performance management had had a positive impact on individual performance, and only 19 per cent replied that line managers benefitted most from performance management. Just 37 per cent thought that performance management would help line managers to develop the capability to manage people better.

reflective question Why do you think there is so much variation in the impact and benefits of PMSs in organizations?

A key feature of a PMS is its attempt to provide a link between all levels of an organization through goals, critical success factors and performance measures. An organization's goals will thus be derived from business strategy and translated into sector goals, departmental goals, manager goals and employee and/or team goals respectively.

Visit www.palgrave.com.business/bratton5 to read an HRM in practice feature on coaching for performance at Morrisons.

As Locke and Latham (2009, p. 22) have argued, 'Purposeful activity is the essence of living action', and people who commit to goals are likely to exert more effort and sustain it over time. At each stage, there will be an attempt to provide measurable performance indicators of the achievement of goals. Furthermore, in response to the dynamic conditions of globalization and technical change, there is a need to review and reset goals and targets through the year (Rose, 2000). A PMS will also provide a means of supporting performance through diagnosing development needs, providing ongoing feedback and review and coaching where required. In a PMS, the attitudes of line managers are crucial because they are the key actors in implementing the various HR processes in the cycle. The integrated nature of a PMS is outlined in the performance management cycle shown in Figure 8.1.

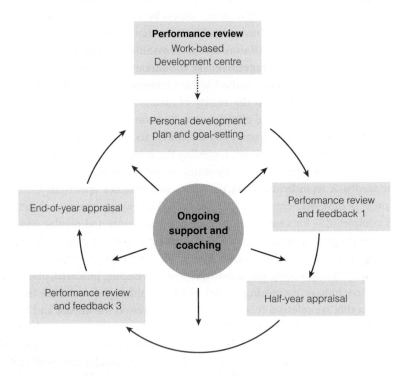

Figure 8.1 A performance management cycle

A PMS might incorporate, especially for managers, development centres, which are the same as assessment centres (see Chapter 7) in that assessment tests and exercises are used to provide a report on individual strengths and limitations. Development centres do, however, differ in their emphasis on diagnosing development needs, leading to suggested development activities and a PDP (Ballantyne and Povah, 2004). Although a range of activities may be used, a development centre usually involves psychometrics and feedback from a qualified occupational psychologist, MSF and a self-diagnosis against the organization's competency framework. A PDP also includes an attempt to link the overall business aim with key areas of responsibility, the competencies that are expected to be demonstrated in performing a role, and goal-setting with measurable objectives.

Although development centres are concerned with development needs, their similarity to assessment centres may make it difficult to escape the tension between judgement and development that is a feature of all processes concerned with assessing and appraising people at work. Carrick and Williams (1999) suggest that development centres may, for some participants, result in the diagnosis of many development needs and have a demotivating influence. Because this may be the expected outcome for some potential participants, this may influence their decision to participate, and their overall performance if they do. As Woodruffe (2000, p. 32) warned, 'Assessment centres masquerading as development centres are wolves in sheep's clothing.'

Overall, there is a need for considerably more research into the value of development centres. However, some research carried out by Halman and Fletcher (2000) highlights examples of the tensions inherent in development centres and performance management more generally. This relates to assessment and performance. In their research, 111 customer services staff attended a development centre. Prior to attending, each person self-assessed his or her performance and was then rated by assessors as part of the development centre. The research revealed a variety of responses to self-ratings depending on whether participants under-rated, over-rated or even accurately rated their performance. For example, those who over-rated their performance tended to make little adjustment in response to any feedback provided, possibly due to their view that they did not need to improve their performance. We will consider the issues of ratings, judgement and feedback in performance management in more detail below.

reflective question   How do you respond to critical feedback when you believe you have performed well?

HRM web links   SHL is of one of the UK's biggest providers of development centre methods – see www.shl.com/images/uploads/cs_CocaCola.pdf for a case study of the development centre provided for Coca Cola.

Once a PDP has been established, according to the performance management cycle, work is carried out to meet the objectives set. There should also be ongoing coaching from the immediate manager and support for any training and development needs identified (see Chapter 9). Over the last 10 years, coaching has become a key activity managers can use to support change and development in organizations. Such is the belief in the value of coaching that many organizations seek to develop a 'coaching culture' (Garvey et al., 2009).

Objectives and performance are reviewed, perhaps every quarter- or half-year, in order to monitor progress and make any adjustments. During the course of the year, feedback might be obtained from different sources, this being used to improve performance as well as being fed into the end-of-year review, at which an overall assessment and appraisal might also be carried out.

Performance, judgements and feedback

A PMS can be used for a variety of purposes, which can be broadly categorized as follows:

- To make administrative decisions concerning pay, promotions and careers, and work responsibilities – the *control purpose*
- To improve performance through discussing development needs, identifying training opportunities and planning action – the *development* purpose.

Both categories require judgements to be made. In the first category, a manager may be required to make a decision about the value of an employee both in the present and in the future, and this may cause some discomfort. For example, several decades ago, McGregor (1957, p. 89) reported that a key reason why appraisal failed was that managers disliked 'playing God', which involved making judgements about the worth of their employees. Levinson (1970) thought that managers experienced the appraisal of others as a hostile and aggressive act against employees that resulted in feelings of guilt related to any criticism given. Such views highlight the tension between appraisal as a process to control employees and appraisal as a supportive development process. It is a tension that has never been resolved and lies at the heart of most debates on the effectiveness of appraisal in particular and, as we will explain below, performance management more generally.

The ability to make judgements about employees' performance that can lead to decisions about their contribution, value, worth, capability and potential has to be considered as a vital dimension of a manager's relationship with those employees. Decisions will be interpreted by an employee as feedback, defined as 'actions taken by (an) external agent(s) to provide information regarding some aspect(s) of one's task performance' (Kluger and DeNisi, 1996, p. 254). Gilliland (1993) have pointed to the importance of feedback that is timely as well as informative for a perception of fairness. What is particularly interesting is the way in which individuals respond to feedback or how people perceive the accuracy of the feedback received, referred to by Anseel and Lievens (2009) as 'feedback acceptance', which is based on the extent to which feedback confirms how people see themselves.

There is no simple formula for how feedback can be used to motivate people, even though managers may be quite convinced, in their own minds, that there is. However, we do know that feedback has a definite influence in terms of demotivation (Coens and Jenkins, 2002). Figure 8.2 shows the range of responses from employees to feedback on their performance at work.

reflective question   What motivates you to work? Make a list of these factors, and then make another list of what demotivates you. It is likely that the latter will be longer, covering a wide range of factors.

As suggested, the response to feedback can result in two possibilities: validation if there is agreement with the judgement made, or a defensive posture when there is disagreement. The latter is especially likely when feedback is negative or critical, and the impact on subsequent performance can also be negative.

DeNisi and Kluger (2000) conducted a review of research considering the relationship between feedback and performance. They found that, in one-third of cases, feedback had a negative effect on performance. As DeNisi and Kluger highlighted, when feedback does

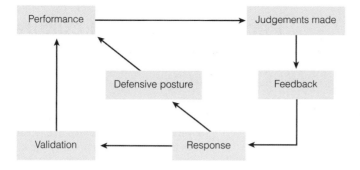

Figure 8.2 *Responses to feedback on performance at work*

have the potential to help someone focus on what is to be done in performing a task or learning details, performance usually improves. The main danger, however, occurs with feedback that can have a potentially strong impact on an employee's view of 'self', for example self-belief and self-esteem. The response to feedback, especially critical feedback, is likely to be affective or emotional, which can be detrimental to performance.

Because of the dangers of negative feedback, Kluger and Nir (2009) have suggested a positive approach, especially in appraisal interviews, called *feedforward*. A win-win approach is adopted that avoids a retreat into defensive emotions by focusing on stories of experience from work that can look forward to provide support so that performance can improve.

HRM web links   Kluger has set up a site devoted to feedforward at http://www.feedforward.co.il. The idea of feedforward is drawn from the technique of appreciative inquiry – see www.appreciative-inquiry.co.uk/?idno=4 for more details.

As well as feedback provided to employees on their performance, some might prefer to take a more proactive stance, seeking feedback themselves. Such behaviour may be undertaken in pursuit of a goal, as well as to provide protection for a person's image or ego (Anderson et al., 2003). Contextual factors such as the attitudes of managers and leaders can influence a person's approach to seeking feedback, and given the importance of feedback on each person's sense of self, there is growing interest in creating more open feedback environments (Anseel et al., 2007).

Particular problems for fostering a diversity agenda can arise from the basis on which many judgements are made in the various processes that form a PMS. PMSs are used for many purposes, including helping in decision-making regarding people's careers, the development they will undertake, the payment they will receive and their future direction in the organization. Well-documented patterns in organizations suggest that some groups suffer disadvantages in these areas.

For example, in the UK, around 40 per cent of the workforce, but only around 30 per cent of managers, are women, with far fewer women becoming senior managers or directors of organizations (Sealy et al., 2008). This is the so-called 'glass ceiling' for women, suggesting that there are limits on their progress in organizations. There is a similar problem for black, Asian and minority ethnic managers; figures here suggest that 10 per cent of the population, but only 6.8 per cent of managers, are classified within this grouping

HRM **in practice** ➡ 8.1

Performance target culture: 'I have been near breaking point …'

In February 2007, a 38-year-old employee at Renault's Technocentre came home from work while his wife and small son were on holiday and took his own life. His wife later told the French newspapers that her normally calm and poised husband had been pushed to exhaustion by his work to the extent that he was 'beyond sleep': 'he suffered from enormous pressure, bringing files home and waking in the middle of the night to work'. His was the third suicide at the centre in four months (*Guardian* Work Supplement, March 10, 2007).

Management has always felt the need to monitor employee performance, often setting desirable performance targets or offering target-based incentives such as bonus payments. However, when those targets become *minimum* performance standards rather than goals to be aimed for, the consequences of failing to reach them can be experienced by employees as coercive.

What is significant here is that the Renault suicides were not those of car assembly employees (where the stress and health consequences of intensified track-working have been well documented for several decades), but those of highly qualified engineers and technicians, working in a £700 million research and design plant set in 150 acres of countryside and with its own restaurants, bank and other facilities. The primary cause of the spate of suicides, according to the French unions, was Renault's application of quantitative production targets to the creative process.

It would seem that there has been a general increase in the spread of quantitative performance targets, first pioneered by F. W. Taylor over a century ago in the context of manufacturing, to areas of white-collar and professional work formerly characterized by a high degree of autonomy. Andrew Danford and his colleagues have examined the introduction of the so-called 'lean' management techniques used to achieve these quantitative targets into the UK Revenue and Customs Service (HMRC) (Carter et al., 2011). Lean essentially means 'doing more with less' – less time, less labour power and less materials.

When, however, these management techniques begin to diffuse into areas of white-collar work, problems can arise. In their study of HMRC, the researchers found that previous performance standards had shared normative understandings of how much case work could be completed in a given time period, and most staff enjoyed sufficient autonomy and job discretion to manage their own workloads within such broad parameters. The new 'lean' model meant the imposition of targets based on 'results' rather than on the quality of service delivery. Targets were generated by the introduction of 'time and motion studies', which involved lean advisers and line managers armed with clipboards and stopwatches, generating sets of optimum work cycle times. Line managers announced daily and hourly targets at team meetings and then conducted patrols, on the hour, to monitor individual performance against them.

Moreover, staff also had to meet quality targets. If one piece of work out of a large batch was found to be in error, the complete batch would be failed and the officer concerned could be publicly rebuked. When surveyed, just 1 per cent of respondents indicated they had felt 'very pressurized' prior to 'lean' management, whereas 63 per cent felt this way after 'lean' management had been introduced. One employee commented:

> The job now is very stressful and I have been near breaking point several times since working under Lean. I never ever felt like this before. I used to love my job; now I feel at times like an empty shell.

Stop! How useful are targets in boosting or maintaining output or service delivery? Is there any support for the view that although the negative consequences for employees are regrettable, they are necessary in order for an organization to stay competitive?

Sources and further information: See Carter et al. (2011) for more information on the HMRC case, and Bain et al. (2002) for a study of call centres.

Note: This feature was written by Chris Baldry at the University of Stirling.

 Visit the companion website at www.palgrave. com/business/bratton5 for bonus HRM in practice features on 720-degree feedback at Cadbury and coaching for performance at Morrisons.

©iStockphoto.com/courtyardpix

(Race for Opportunity, 2008). There are many reasons for this, largely relating to biased and stereotyped judgements about performance. As in selection decisions (see Chapter 7), distortions occur in how people and their performance are rated (Grote, 1996), such as when managers make judgements based on stereotypes and generalizations, demonstrate similarity bias (rating people who are similar to them more highly) and relying on first impressions or comparisons with others to make judgements.

One explanation for the occurrence of these distortions in judgement during PMS is provided by social role theory (Eagly, 1987). This suggests that social structures influence the roles that people can adopt and the behaviours expected. For example, if it is expected that women will become mothers, this will affect how the different genders are viewed in a PMS. As women leave work to care for children, this reinforces the consistent expectation of the social role of women (Diekma and Eagly, 2000), and even when women return to work, it is expected that there will be conflicts between family and work (Benschop and Doorewaard, 1998). As a consequence, women's performance at work may be less highly rated than men's. However, the recent trend of men taking time away from work for family has also been linked to a poor performance rating; that is, both men and women suffer the family care stereotype (Butler and Skattebo, 2004).

reflective question Have you ever felt your work performance to be judged unfairly against a social stereotype?

Appraisal interviews

We define 'appraisal' here as a process that provides an analysis of a person's overall capabilities and potential, allowing informed decisions to be made for particular purposes. It is a process that is central to the purpose of stimulating performance (Aguinis, 2009) and an important part of the process is assessment, whereby data on an individual's past and current work behaviour and performance are collected and reviewed. The process of appraisal is usually completed by means of an interview, once or twice a year, between an employee and his or her line manager.

As well as stimulating performance improvement, there are a variety of other declared purposes and desired benefits for appraisal, including:

- Improving motivation and morale
- Clarifying expectations and reducing ambiguity related to performance
- Determining rewards
- Identifying training and development opportunities
- Improving communication
- Selecting people for promotion
- Managing careers
- Counselling
- Discipline
- Planning remedial actions
- Setting goals and targets.

This potential list of purposes for appraisal has led to the view that appraisal is something of a 'panacea' in organizations (Taylor, 1998), although expectations and hopes are more often than not confounded. A recent development has been the link made in many organizations between appraisals as performance reviews and bonus payments.

reflective question   Why do you think it is difficult to meet the hopes for and expectations of appraisal systems at work?

When we consider the history of appraisal, it soon becomes apparent that, of all the activities comprising HRM, appraisal is arguably the most contentious and least popular among those who are involved. Managers do not seem to like doing it, and employees see no point in it (Heathfield, 2007). HR managers, as guardians of an organization's appraisal policy and procedures, often have to stand by and watch their work fall into disrepute. Although most organizations seek to complete appraisals in one form or another, often under the heading of Performance Development and Review, with normative guidelines and training available, there is evidence of a gap between such direction and what actually happens. For example, guidelines might emphasize a ratio of time to talk that is tilted towards the employee or appraisee, but research suggests that this ratio is in reality rarely achieved. Crucially, negativity is often the main feature of appraisal conversations, which makes the interaction difficult for the participants (Asmuß, 2008).

Remarkably, despite the poor record of appraisal within organizations, it is an accepted part of management orthodoxy that there should be some means by which performance can be measured, monitored and controlled (Barlow, 1989). Indeed, a failure to show that management is in control would be regarded as highly ineffective by those with an interest in the affairs of an organization. As a result, appraisal systems have for some time served to prove that the performance of employees is under control, or at least to give the appearance of its being so. As Barlow (1989, p. 500) has stated, 'Institutionally elaborated systems of management appraisal and development are significant rhetorics in the apparatus of bureaucratic control.' It is not surprising therefore that most appraisal schemes are underpinned by a 'performance control approach' (Randell, 1994, p. 235), which we present as Figure 8.3, with a focus on setting targets or key performance indicators linking individuals to an organization's strategic direction. As one manager in CIPD's (2009b, p. 14) survey stated:

Ultimately there is no point doing performance management if it does not deliver the business objectives. It should enable you to take action at the individual level if people are pulling in the right direction ... everyone whatever level they are knows where their personal [key performance indicators] fit.

The idea of control may perhaps lie at the heart of the problem of appraisal in organizations, and this stems from the key points we raised above about judgements and feedback. There is always a danger in any situation when a manager has to provide feedback to employees that the outcome will be demotivated employees. The seminal study that highlighted this was carried out by Meyer et al. (1965) at the General Electric Company. Although this work was carried out in the mid-1960s, it is remarkable how the lessons have been forgotten and how the mistakes uncovered then have been repeated many times over in many organizations since.

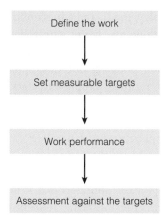

Figure 8.3 *Performance control in appraisal*
Source: Adapted from Randell (1994)

Meyer et al.'s study looked at the appraisal process at a large plant where appraisal was judged to be good. There were 92 appraisees in the study who were appraised by their managers on two occasions over 2 weeks. The first interview discussed performance and salary, the second performance improvement. The reactions of the appraisees were gathered by interviews, questionnaires and observation. It was discovered that although interviews allowed for general praise, criticism was more specific and prompted defensive reactions. Defensiveness on the part of appraisees involved a denial of shortcomings and blaming others. On average, 13 criticisms were recorded per interview, and the more criticism received, the more defensive the reaction of the appraisee. The study revealed that the defensive behaviour was partly caused by most appraisees rating themselves as above average before the interviews – 90 out of 92 appraisees in fact rated themselves as average or above. It was also found that, subsequent to the interviews, criticism had a negative effect on the employees' performance. A summary of some of the conclusions from this study is set out in Figure 8.4.

- Criticism often has a negative effect on motivation and performance
- Praise has little effect – one way or another
- Performance improves with specific goals
- Employees' participation in goal-setting helps to produce favourable results
- Interviews designed primarily to improve performance should not at the same time weigh salary or promotion in the balance
- Coaching by managers should be day to day rather than just once a year

Figure 8.4 *Summary of findings from Meyer et al.'s (1965) study*

Since this study, there has in many respects been a long search to find a way of appraising employees that reduces the negative; however, we should not be surprised therefore to find an attachment by many managers to the idea of control in appraisal

©istockphoto.com/Anna Bryukhanova

Some critics have argued that appraisal attempts to simplify a relationship between managers and employees that is ambiguous, complex and dynamic.

(Townley, 1994), and a perception by employees that they are being controlled by appraisal systems. Barlow (1989) took the argument further, pointing out that appraisal serves to make rational, simple and static a relationship between managers and employees that is ambiguous, complex and dynamic. Ambiguity, complexity and dynamism cannot be eliminated in reality, and therein lies the falseness of the experience of appraisal. For many employees, appraisal is just not seen as relevant. The following reflects the opinion of one manager about appraisal, gathered in a field study in a sector of the petrochemicals industry (Barlow, 1989, p. 505):

> If we were asked for a good man, we certainly wouldn't go hunting through appraisal forms. We'd do it by personal knowledge and I suppose, to some extent, by rule of thumb. Appraisal forms are no use. It's what's left out rather than what's put in that's important.

When an organization seeks to implement strategic changes to improve performance based on principles of learning, communication and employee involvement, there is an apparent contradiction when appraisal is part of performance management, as this is oriented towards control. For example, Soltani et al. (2005) studied a number of organizations that were seeking to utilize principles of TQM. It was found that although there was a recognition that appraisal should match the requirements of TQM, there was little evidence of this occurring. Indeed, appraisal was often characterized as ineffective, based on high subjectivity that ignored individual objectives, and managers unqualified in providing feedback. These factors tended to work against the changes sought through TQM.

Generally, appraisal as an informal and continuous process will make the formal appraisal less isolated and less prone to negativity. It must, however, be acknowledged that, given the importance of appraisal in making judgements and decisions that can have a significant bearing on a person's future, appraisal is bound to be perceived as a political process (Poon, 2004). Employees who believe that their appraisal is based on subjectivity or bias and subjects them to unfair punishments are likely to experience appraisal as being of low quality, resulting in less satisfaction at work, lower commitment and greater intention to leave (Brown et al., 2010) (although in times of high unemployment, they may remain under sufferance). There are concerns about how bias and prejudice, albeit implicit, might influence ratings during appraisal (Wilson and Jones, 2008). In addition, older employees may miss out on appraisal and on any opportunities arising (Grund and Sliwka, 2009).

It is important that appraisal is perceived to be fair and ethical (Ilgen et al., 1979; Sillup and Klimberg, 2010), particularly with respect to what is called 'procedural justice', which concerns perceptions of *how* appraisal is conducted and completed rather than the outcomes of appraisal (Cawley et al., 1998). Research completed in China by Chen et al. (2011), for example, found that perceptions of procedural justice moderated employees' responses to appraisals. They found that if procedural justice was high, this increased employees' acceptance of performance goals, even if the appraisal was negative.

There is still, however, a tendency to associate feedback with criticism even though most people do their work well most of the time (Swinburne, 2001). One suggestion is that employees may not have realistic expectations about appraisal and perhaps need training on how to use feedback and take action (Cook and Crossman, 2004). Another approach is to work with the feedforward principles referred to above. Bouskila-Yam and Kluger (2011) report on the development of a strength-based performance appraisal and a goal-setting process that focuses on the patterns of strengths of an employee and how these can be expanded in the future. Weaknesses are not ignored but are minimized, so that a ratio of three positives to one negative is maintained to ensure positive energy and emotions (Fredrickson and Losada, 2005).

It is also possible to widen the sources of feedback. In recent years, for example, there has been a growth in the popularity of MSF (Smither et al., 2008), during which individuals receive feedback from different people, including peers, subordinate staff, customers and themselves. Where feedback is received from 'all round' a job, this is referred to as 360-degree appraisal or feedback, or – with variations – 180-degree, 270-degree or 540-degree feedback (McCarthy and Garavan, 2001; see also below). The growth in such approaches is based on the view that feedback from different sources allows for more balance and objectivity than the does single view of a line manager. We will examine MSF and 360-degree appraisal in more detail later in this chapter.

A further development is the move to online appraisal, probably a feature of integrated human resources information system processes or talent management packages (see Chapter 6). The apparent value of such approaches is the way in which information about employees in particular positions is stored against their skills and competencies (see www.peopleadmin.com/position-management for an example). HR managers can also monitor the completion of appraisals and consider the pattern of ratings. Payne et al. (2009) compared employee reactions between those who completed online appraisals and those who used a more traditional paper and pencil approach. The results indicated greater participation in the process, in terms of completing self-ratings, by the online appraisees, but there was also a perception that the online process was of lower quality, perhaps because of the limited feedback, which lacked detail.

HRM web links Because of the difficult nature of appraisal, a plethora of resources and training programmes is available. For basic advice on appraisal interviewing, check the Advisory, Conciliation and Arbitration Service (ACAS) at www.acas.org.uk/media/pdf/o/q/B07_1.pdf. ACAS also publishes a booklet on appraisal-related pay at www.acas.org.uk/index.aspx?articleid=625.

Performance and development

It is highly unlikely that the pressure for rationality, efficiency and control in organizations will disappear as it is a powerful force that underlies any organized activity. However, for a PMS to be seen as a driver of organizational performance, it also has to include an alignment with the organization's talent management policies based on people first developing skills and then also being challenged to develop themselves (Baron, 2009). This view, of course, provides a contrast to the control orientation of a PMS and questions the underlying principles that are required to develop a culture supporting and reinforcing the ideas and practices of high-performance HRM based on employee engagement, commitment and trust. This can be a painful process. It may, for example, be difficult to resist the requirements of financial controllers seeking to control costs during a recession. It is therefore no surprise that surveys continue to show ambivalent support for performance management as a helpful process for skill development and careers (CIPD, 2009b).

In a seminal paper, Walton (1985) wrote about disillusionment with the apparatus of control that assumed low employee commitment and mere obedience, reporting on a number of organizations that had attempted to move towards a workforce strategy based on high employee commitment. Performance management and appraisal can serve as the fulcrum of such a movement, although considerable difficulties can arise (Wilson and Western, 2000). The contrast between control approaches and commitment could not be greater for managers: the former involves a concentration on techniques, the latter a shift towards attitudes, values and beliefs. The skill for HRM practitioners is to acknowledge the importance of the former while arguing for a greater place for the latter.

reflective question What particular skills are needed by HRM practitioners to argue for two potentially conflicting points of view, such as the need for control and the need for commitment?

A developmental PMS that attempts to harness potential would, for many organizations, mean a more inclusive approach to talent management (Iles and Preece, 2010). It has been accepted that discussions of potential and prospects for development have been confined to leaders and managers, thereby sending a strong message to the rest of the organization that only managers are worthy of such attention – with the implicit assumption that non-managers cannot develop.

More recently, attention has expanded to those doing key jobs in strategically key positions, referred to by Huselid et al. (2005) as the 'A' positions, but this still represents an exclusive approach to talent. Changes in employment conditions through the 1990s have meant that more employees are included in PMS and appraisals. This has also been brought about by changes in organizational structure in the 2000s that have sought to move decision-making to the point of interaction with customers and clients, and see such interactions as the source of creativity. This provides line managers with significant responsibility to ensure that effective communication and feedback are given to employees (Industrial Relations Services, 2003b).

In putting more emphasis on the development of potential, the suspicion that has surrounded control approaches may be reinforced, which should not be surprising as there has been pressure to shift the orientation for some time. As long ago as 1983, Harper suggested dropping the word 'appraisal' because it put employees on the defensive. He recommended instead a shift towards future-oriented review and development that actively involved employees in continuously developing ways of improving performance in line with needs, similar to Kluger and Nir's (2009) feedforward interview process referred to earlier. Moving in such a direction requires a more flexible approach on the part of line managers. It also results in inevitable tensions because such objectives might be concerned with immediate performance set against current tasks and standards, but employees and even their managers might also be concerned with a variety of work and personal changes such as a change of standards, task, job role or even career.

What are the roots of outstanding performance, and how can performance be improved? These basic questions lie at the heart of performance management and appraisal. How we answer these questions depends on how we view the relationship between skill, knowledge and ability.

The work of psychologist Carol Dweck provides provocative new insights into this topic. Dweck (2008) argues that thinking about ability and performance tends to fall into one of two categories or mindsets. The fixed mindset sees ability as something you either possess or fail to possess. The growth mindset sees ability as something that changes over time. Those who endorse this latter view believe that, with good 'coaching' and plenty of practice, individuals can improve their performance on any given task.

Obviously a manager's mindset will influence his or her approach to performance management and appraisal. The performance appraisals of managers who hold incremental (or growth) views of ability will produce better results than the performance appraisals of managers who hold entity (or fixed) views of ability. One could argue that the dominant trend is towards growth views of ability. Indeed, performance appraisals should be getting better all the time!

Although this claim about a dominant trend may be plausible, it is easy to imagine exceptions to the general rule. In situations where managers cling to stereotypes about particular groups or individuals, we would expect to encounter versions of the fixed view of ability. This would be the case even in developed nations where women seek access to non-traditional occupations. But fixed views of ability may be especially prevalent in developing nations where traditional gender roles persist to a greater degree and women have yet to attain legal protection against workplace discrimination.

Consider the case of videographers working for a British company undertaking PR and advertising for multinationals that operate in India and China. Women represent a rapidly growing segment of the workforce in these two nations, and the HR team is seeking to increase the number of female

videographers they employ. However, women who work with more experienced videographers (mostly men) typically receive low evaluations. The goal of increasing the number of female videographers seems out of reach. Questioned about the feedback and instruction they were receiving, the women made the following comments: 'Mostly he just criticizes me, pointing out the various things I am doing wrong. He never takes the time to show me what I might do to improve my performance. Often his tone of voice seems to suggest: "This is a waste of time; women are not suited for this kind of work."'

Stop! What is going on here? How could the experienced male videographers be encouraged to accept a growth mindset? Would a change in mindset lead to better quality performance appraisals? Explain why.

Sources and further information: For more information on Carol Dweck and her ideas, see Dweck (2008) and also check out the website www.mindsetonline.com.

Note: This feature was written by David MacLennan at Thompson Rivers University.

Mindset: how views of ability influence the quality of performance appraisals

HRM **and globalization**

Once employees have been encouraged to pay attention to their progress at work, the organization must be able to respond to their medium- and long-term aspirations (see the text in Chapter 6 on career management). The manager's role will be to resolve the inevitable tension that will result between individual goals and the manager's interpretation of organizational goals. But how can data about employees be gathered for such purposes? Of necessity, there has to be a shift in attention towards the performance of work. This will provide a link to the value of a PMS as a means of recognizing employees via feedback on what they have done, and engaging them in a dialogue about improving performance (Armstrong and Baron, 2004) that considers the importance of trust and perceptions of justice (Farndale et al., 2011). In such a context, it becomes possible to identify how learning and development can help employees to meet their needs and aspirations.

The performance of a work task can be presented as a relationship between means and outcomes (Ouchi, 1979). The means take the form of the attributes, skills, knowledge and attitudes (competencies) of individual employees that are applied to a task in a specific context. The outcomes take the form of results achieved, which may be measurable either quantitatively or qualitatively against an explicit or implicit standard or target. Between means and outcomes lies the behaviour of the individual in a transformation process, as shown in Figure 8.5.

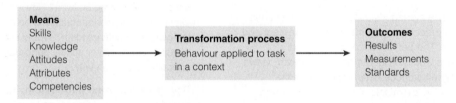

Figure 8.5 *Performance as a transformation process*

Although all phases of this process can form the focus of performance management, particular attention to behaviour in the transformation process will reveal how an individual has applied knowledge, skills and attitudes to practice when carrying out a task; this will include taking account of all aspects of the context, including time and place, machinery and equipment, other employees and other circumstances. For example, the presence of a manager might have an impact on an employee's performance. There is significant interest in this part of the transformation process, because it is in practice that new knowledge can be created (Newell et al., 2002). Research has partly focused on the importance of knowledge that people learn informally in practice, which is acquired intuitively and implicitly, often without intention (Sternberg and Horvath, 1999). Such knowledge is often referred to as 'tacit knowledge', a rather ambiguous term but one that is seen as key in knowledge creation as it emerges from practice (Nonaka et al., 2000a), and as a key feature of workplace learning (see Gold et al., 2010c and Chapter 10).

We must also remember that practice occurs in a context, that contextual factors can have a significant bearing on overall performance, and that these need to be considered in the various PMS processes of managing, measuring, assessing and rewarding performance (CIPD, 2009b). Thus, attention paid to how an employee performs will provide rich data on that employee's current effectiveness and potential for further development. If, for example, we assume that an employee has been trained to complete a basic task, attention to practice in the transformation process will provide data on a number of issues. The first time she completes the task, an assessment of her behaviour will reveal nervousness until completion, when the results achieved can be compared against a standard. This nervousness can be corrected by adjustments to the employee's skills and practice until she has gained confidence. Further study reveals that, once confidence has been gained, the employee will perform with some sense of rhythm and flow that achieves a perfect result.

Given static conditions and standards, this is as far as the employee can go in this task. She can continue to perform with confidence, but after some time this becomes too easy. This feeling prompts her to ask for some adjustment, possibly at first to the work targets and then to an extension of tasks within the job. The important point is that ease within the transformation process, assessed by the employee and others, leads to developmental adjustments. Continued attention to the process may eventually result in a further range of adjustments, such as increased responsibility through job enlargement and job enrichment, and a reconsideration of the employee's future direction within the organization. On the way, the organization may benefit from rising her efficiency and effectiveness, including better standards.

Through attention to the behaviour of an employee in the transformation process, data can thus be provided for a whole gamut of developmental decisions over time, starting with adjustments to reach minimum standards and then addressing career changes and progression. Individual employees are able to set targets, objectives and goals for each stage through appraisal.

The focus on practice as the starting point for PMS processes is brought into greater prominence when we consider that many people now perform tasks that are knowledge-intensive within what is recognized as a knowledge economy and a knowledge society (Rohrbach, 2007). Highly skilled jobs require significant and ongoing learning, or life-long learning. Furthermore, such work often requires a response to unusual or changing situations, where on-the-spot decisions are needed with little time for considered deliberation. This is not untypical of professional work or work requiring high levels of expertise (Beckett, 2000).

A number of techniques have been developed that allow for a consideration of practice against the various stages of the transformation process. The ability to employ various techniques in performance management will depend on a number of contingencies. Ouchi (1979) has provided a framework specifying these and allowing for a choice to be made; Figure 8.6 has been adapted from his work. This framework can be used to reconcile the dilemma that organizations may face in performance management and appraisal, that is, the dilemma between the desire to maintain control and the desire to foster a developmental emphasis. Forms of control depend on the feasibility of measuring desired performance – 'the ability to measure either output or behaviour which is relevant to the desired performance is critical to the 'rational' application of … bureaucratic forms of control' (Ouchi, 1979, p. 843).

In Ouchi's framework, if an organization either has high ability to measure outputs or behaviour, or has perfect knowledge of the transformation process involved in production, it could opt for a bureaucratic control approach and base appraisal on behaviour, output measurements or both. Thus, in cell 1, typical of traditional manufacturing and service organizations where work process steps can be clearly stated, both behaviour and output techniques can be used. Appraisal interviews or online measures can include ratings against dimensions drawn from a competency framework, with a focus on behaviour or outputs that can be assessed.

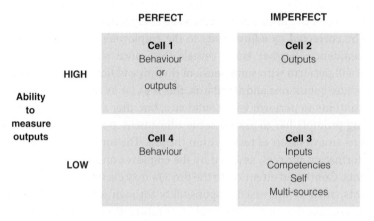

Figure 8.6 *Contingencies in performance management*
Source: Adapted from Ouchi (1979)

In cell 2, only outputs can be successfully measured, perhaps because work processes cannot be directly observed; this may occur with field sales workers, for example. The key issue here seems to be how such outputs are judged and the criteria utilized. Research by Pettijohn et al. (2001), for example, which sought to understand salespersons' perspectives of appraisal, found that although appraisal was a common practice within sales management, there was some dissatisfaction with the criteria used. In particular, salespersons preferred to be appraised with respect to customer satisfaction and the product knowledge that lay within their control. The failure to include such criteria had implications for morale, turnover and overall performance. Even if outputs provide more objective measurement criteria, it is still possible for subjective criteria to affect how sales staff are evaluated. Vilela et al. (2007) showed how factors such as physical attractiveness and being in favour with a supervisor can affect the judgement of a salesperson's performance.

Approaches are now moving from cell 1 to cell 2 in areas such as police work (Shane, 2010), where performance appraisal has traditionally been based on a model of compliance and control that fits a bureaucratic framework. Instead, it is argued that there could be a stronger focus on what the police achieve, as indicated by empirical measures.

In cell 4, employees' behaviour can be observed, but outputs are more difficult to discern; this may be the result of groups of employees producing group outputs or measurable outputs over a long period of time, for example in research work. Particular difficulties occur when appraisal, which is inherently an individual process, is applied to a group or team – you may already have had experience of group work and the problems that occur when a group mark is given for assessed work. In the workplace, there may be variations of effort and variations in the skill required. There is also variability in the life of teams, some teams coming together for a single project, others working together over several tasks. In addition, a team may increasingly have to operate over different locations.

All this suggests that the performance management of teams requires a consideration of relevant circumstances rather than a 'one-size-fits-all' prescription (Scott and Einstein, 2001), including the situations faced and the beliefs and motives of team members (Chang et al., 2008). Van Vijfeijken et al. (2002) suggest that effective group performance management requires a combination of goal-setting and rewards based on group performance. This needs to consider the degree of interdependence between tasks completed by group members, the complexity of tasks and the interdependence of goals, which considers how one person's goal is affected by or affects the attainment of goals by others.

HRM web links

Team appraisal is often a difficult process. You can view a short online video on team appraisal at www.staffs.ac.uk/about_us/university_departments/personnel/policies/team_good_example.jsp.

In all the above cases, the logic of control may be extended to some form of performance- or merit-related pay system. In cell 3, however, there is an imperfect knowledge of transformation and a low ability to measure outputs directly, making bureaucratic control more difficult. Ouchi refers to this cell as a 'clan' based on a ritualized, ceremonial or 'cultural' form of control arising from shared attitudes, values and beliefs. Cell 3 would include the work of professionals and knowledge workers, as well as most managers and, increasingly, forms of work organization in which higher levels of discretion and autonomy are granted to individual employees. It also includes teams within a network, where expertise must be used selectively and leadership shared between team members (Friedrich et al., 2009). Behaviour, although difficult to observe formally, can be observed by those present at the point of production.

A university can, for example, bureaucratically control who becomes a lecturer through its selection processes; hence it is possible to assess 'inputs' through qualifications and other attributes. Once the lecturer is in place, however, his or her performance is much more difficult to assess and appraise. Some universities have used competency frameworks. For example, one institution is seeking to base performance management on an 'assessment of the outcomes and competence requirements established during the Performance and Development Review'. The difficulty here is the attempt to measure outcomes when the work is non-standardized. Furthermore, the use of competencies has been widely criticized as a reduction and fragmentation of complex work, but one giving power to those who seek to control such work (Gold et al., 2010b).

Consider further the work of professionals in the public sector, in which performance management and appraisal have been seen as a shift towards managerialist language and techniques. In response to deregulation and competition, often sponsored by central government as part of the trend referred to as new managerialism or new public management (Pollitt, 2000), there have been various attempts to curtail the power of professionals within the public sector and remove or usurp their monopoly (Exworthy and Halford, 1999). Research so far suggests the emergence of new relationships and a reordering of professions and management: head teachers, for example, require leadership skills that include the assessment of their staff. In the UK, the National College for School Leadership has been established with the aim of ensuring 'that school leaders have the skills, recognition, capacity and ambition to transform the school education system into the best in the world' (for further details, see www.nationalcollege.org.uk).

In the UK's National Health Service (NHS), with over 1 million employees, many of whom are professionally qualified, appraisal was developed in the 1980s and has been seen as one of the tools necessary to bring about a change in culture. Research by Redman et al. (2000) found that, after several years of experience, appraisal was generally valued, with particular strengths being the setting of objectives, personal development planning and, where they occurred, having quarterly 'mini' reviews. There was, however, also evidence of 'patchy application' (p. 59). Although there remains little systematic evidence of PMS in the NHS, such evidence as does exist points to the importance of feedback and participation in setting goals (Patterson et al., 2010).

Generally, the performance management of people whose work is knowledge-based is difficult to observe and requires a longer timeframe for measurement. Reilly (2005) suggests that one cannot impose performance management in such circumstances. Furthermore, such workers tend not to want hierarchical career progression, and many will resist moves into managerial posts. Career-planning tools can help them to determine their own career paths.

Approaches to rating performance

We can see that there are a number of opportunities for performance rating to occur. The different approaches to rating can be classified as inputs, results and outcomes, and behaviour.

Rating *inputs* is a broad and potentially vague category that has traditionally been concerned with listing traits or personality attributes. Typical attributes are dependability, loyalty, decisiveness, resourcefulness and stability. Because such attributes may be difficult to define, there will be little agreement on their presence in employees between the different groups using lists of measures. The use of personality attributes in performance management and appraisal can lack reliability, giving rise to charges of bias, subjectivity and unfairness. This is normally the case when managers attempt to measure their employees in appraisal interviews. As indicated above, many organizations now prefer to use reliable and valid psychometric instruments as a way of helping employees to diagnose strengths and weaknesses for a development plan.

Ratings based on the *results and outcomes* of work performance provide the most objective technique for collecting data for appraisal. When available, measurements can be taken at different points in time and comparisons made with objectives. Typical measurements might relate to production, sales, the number of satisfied customers or customer complaints. The CIPD (2009b) survey clearly indicates the popularity of such an approach, with 85 per cent of respondents claiming the use of objective-setting and review as part of their PMS. Ratings might utilize the language of standards as set out in vocational qualifications (see Chapter 9). Such standards attempt to describe what competent people in a particular occupation are expected to be able to do. The outcomes achieved can be assessed against performance criteria for each standard. It is not surprising that most measurements are quantifiable, although many organizations will attempt to modify quantification with qualitative measurements or comments.

The attractiveness of results and outcomes as objective sources of data makes them a feature of many PMSs, but do such approaches reflect performance control or development approaches? Factors for consideration will relate to how objectives, targets and goals are set, how managers and employees interact in work towards their achievement, and the whether employees use the measurements as feedback in order to develop further. As Pettijohn et al. (2001) found, it is important that the criteria used to judge performance are controllable by those being judged: a failure here affects morale and overall performance.

During the 1960s, for example, there was a growth in schemes of management by objectives, which were designed to control the performance of managers and stimulate them in terms of their development. If this could be achieved, it was believed, the needs of managers and the organization could be integrated. Such schemes soon came under attack, however, and many fell into disrepute. Levinson (1970, p. 134) attacked the practice of management by objectives as self-defeating because it was based on 'reward–punishment psychology', which put pressure on individuals without there being any real choice of objectives. Modern approaches to objective-setting will face similar charges unless managers pay as much attention to the process by which objectives are set as to the content and quantification of objectives, and the environment in which employees work towards their achievement.

Attention to the *behaviour* of employees as practised in the transformation process will reveal how an individual has applied aptitudes, attitudes and competencies to the performance of work and will provide rich data on current effectiveness and the potential for further development. This attention can occur on a continuous basis, taking into account both subjective and objective data. Such an approach forms the foundation of a PMS concerned with the direction of performance and support for employees' continuing development. Once these processes have been established, employees may be more willing to accept more codified approaches to rating their behaviour. Frameworks of competencies associated with effective performance can, for example, provide the integrating link within a PMS between identifying key performance factors and setting objectives that can then be reviewed and rated; there is, however, evidence that the competencies identified are not always included in an appraisal process (Abraham et al., 2001).

Two kinds of ratings scale can be developed:

- *Behaviour-anchored rating scales* (BARSs) provide descriptions of important job behaviour 'anchored' alongside a rating scale. The scales are developed by generating descriptions of effective and ineffective performance from people who know the job; these are then used to develop clusters of performance and scales (Rarick and Baxter, 1986). Each scale describes a dimension of performance that can be used in appraisal. For example, in a scale developed for the behaviour of 'planning', the performance scale can vary between 'Excellent' and 'Unacceptable', and in between would lie a range of possible behaviours with varying degrees of effectiveness.
- *Behavioural observation scales* (BOSs) involve the people doing the rating assessing the frequency of specific job-related behaviours that are observable. Figure 8.7, for example, shows BOSs that have been derived from a financial services company.

Both BARSs and BOSs are based on specific performance and on the descriptions of employees involved in a particular job. Research by Tziner et al. (2000) provided a comparison between BARSs and BOSs with respect to the satisfaction of those being rated with their appraisal and with the setting of goals to improve performance. It was found that goals developed using BOSs were more specific than those set using a BARS since they were based on what a 'rater' actually observed rather than on evaluation. Furthermore, since BOSs require a rating of several behaviours rather than the identification of a single 'anchor', as in BARSs, this reduces bias and allows more specific feedback, with the formation of clearer goals. What is particularly interesting is the potential for such instruments to enhance self-appraisal and allow a dialogue between employees and others based on more objective criteria.

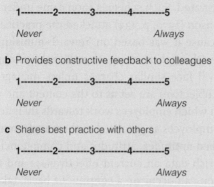

Developing people

a Gives praise where it is due to others in the team

1---------2---------3---------4---------5

Never   *Always*

b Provides constructive feedback to colleagues

1---------2---------3---------4---------5

Never   *Always*

c Shares best practice with others

1---------2---------3---------4---------5

Never   *Always*

Figure 8.7 *BOSs in a financial services company*

Self-appraisal

Referring back to our earlier analysis, we saw that have been significant problems associated with performance appraisal. These stemmed mainly from the way in which systems were put in place as a way of superiors evaluating employees for a variety of purposes, for example improving performance, pay and promotion. What cannot be escaped, however, is that all employees have an opinion on how well they are performing, the rewards they desire and deserve, and the training they require. That is, whatever techniques of appraisal are employed, self-appraisal and self-rating will always be there too. When the emphasis of PMS is on evaluation and control, it is only to be expected that differences will exist between an individual's self-appraisal and the appraisal of his or her superior. Campbell and Lee (1988) put forward a number of discrepancies between self-appraisal and supervisory appraisal:

- *Informational* – there is disagreement over the work to be done, how it is done and the standards to be used in judging the results.
- *Cognitive* – behaviour and performance are complex, and appraisers attempt to simplify this complexity. Different perceptions will result in disagreement between appraisers and appraisees.
- *Affective* – the evaluative nature of performance control appraisal is threatening to appraisees and triggers defence mechanisms, leading to bias and distortions in interpreting information. Appraisers also may find appraisal threatening.

All this suggests that self-appraisal in an environment of evaluation and control is not effective, which is not surprising. Campbell and Lee (1988, p. 307), however, suggested that 'such pessimistic conclusions did not rule out the possibility that self- appraisals can be used as important developmental and motivational tools for individuals'. We have already shown that employees are able to observe their own performance and obtain data for appraising strengths and weaknesses, and for identifying future goals, from the processes of working. Self-appraisal as a minimum condition allows the emergence of data for use in a discussion about performance, especially where the work is complex or knowledge-intensive (Ryan and Tipu, 2009). The extent to which employees are able to appraise themselves objectively becomes a question of how willing they are to seek and accept feedback from their work behaviour and the environment they are in. Employees can learn to appraise themselves and will treat this as part of their own development if they can see its value for themselves rather than viewing it as a manipulative management tool.

HRM web links   How good are you at seeking feedback? What are the skills needed for giving and receiving effective feedback? The following website may help you: http://tutorials. beginners.co.uk/feedback-skills.htm.

Multisource feedback

Self-appraisal for development will not occur unless it is set in an environment that facilitates and encourages such a process. If a positive experience is gained from self-appraisal, employees may then be willing to share their thoughts on the process with others. Many organizations have sought to increase the amount of feedback received and the number of sources of feedback. Kettley (1997) claimed that the popularity of MSF had arisen from a number of factors:

- It is a way of empowering employees and promoting teamwork by allowing employees to appraise their managers.
- It increases the reliability of appraisals and balance in 'flatter' (that is, less hierarchical) organizations.
- It reinforces good management behaviour by allowing people to see themselves as others see them.

The various sources of feedback might include:

- The immediate manager
- Staff (upward appraisal)
- Peers (peer appraisal)
- The manager and/or other staff (180-degree appraisal)
- The manager, staff and peers (360-degree appraisal)
- The manager, staff, peers, customer, suppliers and others (540-degree or 720-degree feedback).

   Visit www.palgrave.com.business/bratton5 to read an HRM in practice feature on 720-degree feedback at Cadbury.

As the number and range of MSF schemes have grown, so too has interest in their impact. The crucial factor is the extent to which self-rating is supported by the ratings of others. What do you think the outcome would be if a manager had a positive perception of his or her performance but was rated less well by others, for example staff and internal customers? Yammarino and Atwater (1997) have provided an examination of possible HRM outcomes based on the range of agreements between 'self' and 'other' ratings. For example, where self-ratings are higher than the ratings of others, this is likely to lead to negative outcomes, whereas self-ratings that are lower than the ratings of others will result in a mixture of positive and negative outcomes.

MSF is growing in popularity, although the CIPD's (2009b) survey found that only around 25 per cent of organizations used 360-degree feedback. There is evidence of both its benefits and its difficulties. For example, *upward appraisal* for managers leads to performance improvement where managers start from a low or moderate rating and the feedback process is sustained over time; there is less impact, however, on managers who already have a high performance rating (Reilly et al., 1995). Managers prefer feedback from people they can specify, although staff, understandably perhaps, prefer anonymity (Antonioni, 1994). Most importantly, upward appraisal provides a powerful message to managers that performance will be assessed and improvement is expected. Managers can prepare themselves by becoming aware of the behaviours being assessed.

However, managers can also treat ratings with ambivalence or worse. For example, Atwater et al. (2000) found that managers who faced feedback from staff during a period of organizational change demonstrated a low impact where the change had been cynically introduced. Research by Van Dierendonck et al. (2007) in the NHS suggested that upward appraisal had only a small positive effect but, more importantly, that there was a gap between the self-ratings of managers and those of their staff. This led to some reduction of ratings by managers but no change of behaviour. Perhaps one of the most valued features of upward appraisal is the opportunity for staff to express their views in a constructive manner, which adds to their sense of being included (Howe et al., 2011).

Peer appraisal appears to be especially suitable for professional and knowledge-based workers such as doctors, teachers and researchers. The responses can be unpredictable, but research suggests that some will undertake further learning as a consequence (Colthart et al., 2008), and that peer-led discussions about learning and development are more acceptable than other alternatives (Main et al., 2009). There are, however, some possible tensions, since peers in managerial roles are usually connected with each other through their work or more informal relationships, and may be unwilling to offer formal feedback or make comparisons between their peers. Within teams, peer feedback can lead to resistance and avoidance of blame if the team is not performing well (Peiperl, 2001).

reflective question   Do you review the performance of your group after any work completed? Do you provide feedback to each other?

Moving round from upward and peer appraisal, *360-degree appraisal* completes the circle of MSF. Such a move does, however, require confidence and trust in the way it works because the outcome can become demoralizing and negative for the target group of appraisees, usually managers and leaders. 360-degree appraisal usually requires ratings from a sample of relationships, probably no fewer than eight. The feedback is collected by questionnaire, increasingly completed online, which can speed up the process (Mason et al., 2009) and can be seen as a more objective approach.

As with all approaches to appraisal, there can be both positive and negative reactions. Where appraisees are open-minded and willing to use the views of others to assess their self-perceptions, the process can be positive (Taylor and Bright, 2011). Individuals can, however, be hurt by too much negative feedback, and there might be confusion over whether the process is for development or for judgement relating to pay or promotion (Handy et al., 1996). Recent research into leadership development in a university in Australia (Drew, 2009) suggests that responses range from 'no surprising feedback' (that is, just reinforcement and affirmation) to 'new insights' that lead to plans for change.

The value of the 360-degree appraisal will also depend on how the process is positioned in an organization, on how a climate of support is established and facilitated for its implementation, and on amelioration of the negative effects. In particular, organizations need to consider employees' willingness to give and receive feedback and to use the various rating techniques. Training programmes are crucial before the implementation of MSF schemes. It would also seem that such schemes have more value as development and performance improvement processes rather than as a judgement mechanism involved in pay and promotion (McCarthy and Garavan, 2001).

Smither et al. (2005) sought to explore the impact of MSF on performance over time by examining 24 studies. However, they found only small improvements in performance, suggesting that other factors were also important. Their research suggested that the following factors were important in determining how much performance improvement might result from MSF:

- The characteristics of the feedback
- Initial reactions to the feedback
- Personality
- The feedback orientation of those receiving feedback
- The perceived need for change
- Beliefs about change
- Goal-setting
- Taking action.

Each of these factors could have an impact ranging from the nature of the feedback, for example positive or negative, to beliefs about the ability to take action. There are no clear paths to performance improvement from MSF feedback. Instead, the process will benefit some employees and not others. In particular, an organization needs to assess the impact of any MSF feedback scheme, and provide support by developing a coaching culture (DeNisi and Kluger, 2000), especially as a common problem reported by managers is a lack of interest on the part of others (including the employees' immediate line managers) (Garavan and McCarthy, 2007). In addition, as we indicated earlier, perceptions of procedural justice are important in appraisal, and this is significant for the acceptance of MSF, as is the decline of cynical attitudes of managers towards MSF (McCarthy and Garavan, 2007). Smither et al. (2008) showed how wider features of context can affect the impact of MSF over time. They found that, 9 months after completing MSF, 145 managers tended to recall strengths rather than weaknesses, and there was little evidence of performance improvement. MSF needs to be supported by reviews, coaching and perhaps learning projects, especially since the process is often used with development programmes for leaders and managers (see Chapter 10).

HRM web links   Go to www.psytech.com/Documents/Guidelinesfor360Feedback.pdf for a free booklet on 360-degree feedback. https://www.leadingpeople.co.uk/leadership360-1.asp provides an example of an online approach to 360-degree feedback for leadership development. Notice how the findings are reviewed through one-to-one coaching that leads to an action plan.

Given the potential for tension between performance management and appraisal that is oriented towards judgements, in contrast to process oriented towards development, there needs to be some way of providing reconciliation. The development of competency frameworks, along with other measurement devices, has improved the reliability and validity of feedback on employees' attitudes, aptitudes and performance. This still does not, however, remove the underlying emphasis on control. Indeed, some would claim that the use of the various techniques within a PMS serves to enhance the 'manageability' of employees (Townley, 1994). PMSs also place a great deal of faith in the support of the management team as the assessors and facilitators of other people's development. There is no guarantee of either, and our understanding of what really happens in performance management and in organizations generally is still limited.

Importantly, so much of the literature concerning performance management and appraisal works from the neo-human relations assumption that all employees have an interest in achieving the objectives set or in responding to measurements when they have participated in the process (Newton and Findlay, 1996). Employees do, of course, have an interest in what they do at work, but they also have many other interests with only a tangential connection to workplace performance, possibly including many activities that work against management requirements for performance, such as gossiping and having fun, but also more serious forms of behaviours such as theft of the organization's property (Ackroyd and Thompson, 1999).

case study

Robertson Engineering

Setting

Robertson Engineering is a family-owned business that designs and manufactures equipment for mining. Based in the North-East of England, the company grew by serving local coal mines, but since the 1980s it has sought new customers. Having survived the demise of the UK market, the business has been successful in securing contracts for Chinese and Australian mining companies. There are currently 45 staff, but this is likely to grow over the next few years.

The company's MD is Bill Robertson. He is a third-generation owner of the business, and recognizes that more attention needs to be given to performance management. In particular, there needs to be a more systematic process so that talent can be identified to enable growth. Although he believes that things are happening informally, the MD is aware is that he needs to demonstrate, using objective data, that he has control of the business. This means that people's performance has been agreed against targets that are tied to business objectives.

The problem

Until recently, any assessment of performance had been undertaken rather informally. This is traditional in small businesses, and most of the staff were used to a 'friendly chat' with their line manager. There are four line managers, and they had all been appointed from within the business and therefore had close relationships with the people they managed. Owing to the size of the business, Bill ran 'a tight ship', with only the line managers between him and the rest of the staff, so performance management was very much left to the managers.

When action or changes were needed, such as promotions or replacements of staff, Bill relied on information from the managers to make a quick decision. It had always been the case that people were promoted from within, and that training needs could be identified 'as and when' needed. This did not please everyone, and Bill knew that some of the staff were not always happy with the way managers made judgements about work performance, or with their support (or lack of support) for training. Most of the time, however, any clear differences and variations in performance could be 'smoothed over', and the annual company profit share tended to satisfy the bulk of the workforce.

Until recently, Robertson Engineering had used an informal appraisal system with its employees.

There had been little attention given to setting goals, and hardly any attempt had been made to record and monitor targets. Because production tended towards fairly lengthy time scales, it was felt that as long as people knew when delivery was required, and that everyone had a 'rough' idea when their input was needed, goals could be 'loose'. As long as delivery was achieved on schedule, profit would be secured.

But some changes were needed, and Bill saw an increasing connection between the performance management of staff and the expansion of the business, although he did not want to lose the informality that had come from being a smaller business. He certainly did not want to create a bureaucratic process of unnecessary form-filling. He was also aware that many staff were very sensitive to feedback, and this could become difficult if judgements about performance were written down formally.

But there was an attraction in understanding more about staff performance, albeit through the eyes of line managers, and he wanted individuals to have their own development plans. Being an engineer, he could also see the logic of a talent pipeline and, as most staff were likely to stay with the company, some connection to career development. Indeed, he could see how performance management might provide him with the perfect process to move the business forward.

278

Assignment

Working as a group or on your own, prepare a report for Bill that outlines the way forward. You will need to consider:

- An appropriate approach to performance management in this organization
- The purpose of the exercise, and what skills would be needed by the managers

- The issue of staff sensitivity to feedback
- Whether training would be needed, and what methods would be used.

Note: This feature was written by Jeff Gold.

 Visit the companion website at www.palgrave.com/business/bratton5 for guidelines on writing reports.

summary

- ◀ The key idea of a PMS is that the principal dimensions of a person's work can be precisely defined in performance terms, allowing measurement over agreed periods of time, and also takes account of particular constraints within the situation of performance. Performance management forms the nub of the strategic link between HR inputs and practices and organizational performance.

- ◀ Through its link to measurement, performance management provides evidence that management is rationally, efficiently and effectively controlling an organization. There are, however, measurement models that take a wider view, perhaps more strategic and long term, which encompass a range of values (not just financial) and can stimulate continuous improvement.

- ◀ Research evidence shows the importance of performance management, with a wide range of activities featured. Different criteria are used to judge performance and to help diagnose development needs, providing a link to the organization's goals. A performance management cycle integrates various HR processes, including development centres, objective-setting and personal development planning, feedback and reviews. There is, however, often a gap between the rhetoric and the reality of claims for its contribution to organizational effectiveness.

- ◀ Performance management has a 'control' purpose to aid decisions about pay, promotion and work responsibility, and a 'development' purpose in improving performance, identifying training opportunities and planning action.

- ◀ A PMS might incorporate development centres, which are the same as assessment centres in that assessment tests and exercises are used to provide a report on individual strengths and limitations. However, they differ in their emphasis on diagnosing development needs, leading to suggested development activities and a PDP.

- ◀ Managers have a vital role to play in providing feedback, both formally as part of a PMS and informally as part of everyday work. The acceptance of feedback as valid will depend on its frequency as part of an ongoing relationship and on how well managers understand the perceptions of their staff.

- ◀ The performance control approach to appraisal is still seen as evidence of rationality and efficiency at work. Such beliefs often become taken-for-granted assumptions and difficult to challenge. Employees who believe that their appraisal is based on subjectivity or bias and subjects them to unfair punishments are likely to experience appraisal as being of low quality.

- ◀ A more developmental approach to performance management and appraisal has to include an alignment with talent management policies based on people developing their skills and being challenged to develop themselves.

- ◀ Performance can be rated in different ways. Inputs, in the form of personality attributes or traits, may lack reliability and may be seen as subjective and unfair. Results and work outcomes allow quantifiable measurement and are therefore seen as being more objective. Rating behaviour within performance allows the use of such techniques as BARSs and BOSs.

◀ Performance might be reviewed and appraised using a variety of MSF processes, including self-appraisal and feedback from managers, peers, subordinates and others as part of a 360-degree appraisal process.

vocab checklist for ESL students

◀ 360-degree appraisal (n)
◀ appraise (v), appraisal (n)
◀ behavioural observation scale (BOS) (n)
◀ behaviour-anchored rating scale (BARS) (n)
◀ cognition (n), cognitive (adj)
◀ feedback (n)
◀ feedforward (n)
◀ high-performance work system (n)
◀ key performance indicator (n)
◀ mentor (v), mentor (n), mentoring (n)
◀ multisource feedback (MSF) (n)

◀ panacea (n)
◀ peer appraisal (n)
◀ performance and development plan (PDP) (n)
◀ performance development and review (n)
◀ performance management system (PMS) (n)
◀ psychometrics (n), psychometric (adj)
◀ self-appraisal (n)
◀ tacit knowledge (n)
◀ total quality management (TQM) (n)
◀ upward appraisal (n)

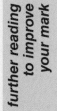 Visit www.palgrave.com/business/bratton5 for a link to free definitions of these terms in the Macmillan Dictionary, as well as additional learning resources for ESL students.

review questions

1 What should be the purpose of performance management and appraisal?
2 What is the role of 'objectives' in performance management? Can performance be 'managed by objectives'?
3 Does a PMS enhance strategic integration within HRM?
4 Can knowledge workers and/or professionals be performance-managed?
5 Do you think that students should have more say in appraising and assessing themselves and each other?
6 Do you think that appraisal and assessment techniques enhance the 'manageability' of employees?

further reading to improve your mark

Reading these articles and chapters can help you gain a better understanding and potentially a higher grade for your HRM assignment.

◀ It is argued that most research on PMS is intended to serve a managerialist agenda leading to prescribed behaviours. S. McKenna, J. Richardson and L. Manroop (2011) Alternative paradigms and the study and practice of performance management and evaluation. *Human Resource Management Review,* **21**(2): 148–57 call for more innovation in research using a variety of approaches or paradigms.

◀ A. Neely (2007) *Business Performance Measurement.* Cambridge: Cambridge University Press sets performance management in a wider context and considers connections to measurement frameworks and methodologies.

◀ B. Townley (1993) Performance appraisal and the emergence of management. *Journal of Management Studies*, **30**(2): 221–38 provides an analysis of appraisals based on the work of Michel Foucault.

◀ For a well-considered view of appraisal and feedback, based on research, try Clive Fletcher's (2004) *Appraisal and Feedback: Making Performance Review Work* (3rd edn). London: Chartered Institute of Personnel and Development.

◀ The importance of fairness and justice has been highlighted, and more research on this issue can be found in P. W. Thurston and L. McNall (2010) Justice perceptions of performance appraisal practices. *Journal of Managerial Psychology*, **25**(3): 201–28.

◀ The importance of ethics in performance management has been considered by Diana Winstanley and Kate Stuart-Smith (1996) Policing performance: the ethics of performance management. *Personnel Review*, **25**(6): 66–84.

 Visit www.palgrave.com/business/bratton5 for lots of extra resources to help you get to grips with this chapter, including study tips, HRM skills development guides, summary lecture notes, and more.

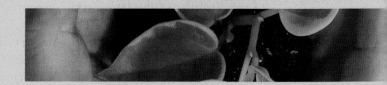

part IV
employee
performance and
development

chapter **9**

human resource development and workplace learning

outline

◄ Introduction

◄ The meaning of HRD

◄ Strategy and HRD

◄ National HRD

◄ Implementing HRD

◄ HRM as I see it: Helen Tiffany, Bec Development

◄ Workplace learning

◄ HRM and globalization: Learning in a global context

◄ Knowledge creation and management

◄ HRM in practice 9.1: Managing knowledge

◄ e-Learning

◄ Case study: Volunteers Together

◄ Summary, Vocab checklist for ESL students, Review questions and Further reading to improve your mark

objectives

After studying this chapter, you should be able to:

1 Understand the connections between human resource development (HRD) and strategy

2 Discuss the effectiveness of a national infrastructure for HRD

3 Explain how HRD may be implemented

4 Explain key ideas of workplace learning

5 Understand developments in knowledge creation and management

6 Explain key aspects of e-learning

281

introduction

Imagine you have finished your degree and have accepted a position as a graduate trainee in marketing at a leading pharmaceutical company. On the first day, you discover that the company sees human resource development (HRD) as an investment in the learning of its people, and not just training as a short-term cost. The company claims to embrace key aspects of the country's concern for increasing skills with a well-established apprenticeship system in which trainees work towards vocational qualifications. This sets your expectation that HRD is considered to be a strategic consideration in the organization. Soon afterwards, you meet with the marketing director, who outlines how you will access the company's learning resources, much of which are now available online as e-learning. He also tells you that your line manager has responsibility to help you complete a training needs analysis, so that measurable objectives can be set for any training undertaken, against which outcomes can be evaluated.

Soon after starting with the company, you meet with other graduates on a 3-day training programme. You learn a lot, but on your return to work, you find that no one is prepared to follow up and help you transfer your learning into work practice. In particular, your line manager takes little interest, whereas you soon find out that other graduates have benefited from their managers acting as coaches and helping trainees to integrate work and learning. However, your own experience suggests little support and, even more problematically, the work you are given does not provide sufficient challenge. Both these features provide barriers to further learning and development.

The meaning of HRD

In recent years, there has been significant interest in the link between a nation's skills base and the ability of that country to compete in the global economy. Further links are made between skills and such ideas as social mobility, engagement and sustainability (Department for Business, Innovation and Skills, 2010a). One important consequence is a growing interest in the profession of HRD, its theoretical development and its contribution to practice. After many years of low organizational awareness of their expertise (Gold et al., 2003), HRD practitioners now form a significant section of the Chartered Institute of Personnel and Development (CIPD) in the UK, where they are able to present themselves as the experts in the development of knowledge, skills and learning, and as proactive in their approach to change (Mankin, 2001). Accompanying this growth, there has been more focus on the theoretical basis of HRD (Woodall, 2001), new journals and conferences being devoted to HRD as a separate discipline rather than a subdiscipline of HRM.

Despite this interest, there are, however, differing views about the meaning of HRD and its purpose. For example, 'human resource development' as a term is seldom used by professionals in practice (Sambrook and Stewart, 2005) – they prefer terms such as 'training', 'development' or 'learning and development'. This tends to mean that HRD is seen as an academic subject, although there are some interesting efforts by academics in HRD to make connections to practice (see Gold and Stewart, 2011).

Most attempts to define HRD suggest that it has two purposes: first, to improve people's performance, and second, to help people learn, develop and/or grow. For example, in the 1970s, Nadler's definition of HRD (quoted in Nadler and Nadler, 1989, p. 4) seemed to imply both purposes:

HRD is organized learning experiences provided by employers, within a specified period of time, to bring about the possibility of performance improvement and/or personal growth.

The 'and/or' proviso in this definition has given rise to some debates over the last 35 years, and more recently has been subject to a more critical treatment in which the 'performative' focus is seen to dominate against a more empowering 'learning' focus (see Rigg et al., 2007). This critique might also point to the way in which definitions such as Nadler's explicitly suggest that it is employers who make the provision and *do* something *to* employees, so that employers might then expect outcomes serving the interests of the organization.

Others, such as Stewart (2007), have attempted to neutralize this connection by seeing HRD as 'constituted by planned interventions in organizational and individual learning processes' (p. 66). The value of this definition is the way in which learning processes can work at different levels, a theme we will explore more carefully later in the chapter; it also highlights that interventions are not owned by any particular group or person. For example, employees could provide their own interventions or access activities from outside the organization, perhaps via a social networking link, that are shared with others at work.

We might also suggest that some learning processes might not be planned at all but might emerge more informally through everyday work, problems and interactions. Crucially, it may be recognized that informal learning needs to be shared and utilized (Marsick and Watkins, 2001), but, as we will explore later, this is not a particularly straight-forward process. However, given such possibilities, we will suggest our own definition of HRD to be any intervention or activity that enables and results in learning at work. We might also add that some commentators, for example Lee (2004), would resist any attempt to define HRD because to do so in uncertain and unpredictable times would give 'the appearance of being in control' (p. 38).

reflective question   How much of your learning is achieved informally? Who influences such learning?

Strategy and HRD

Strategic work at whatever level of consideration – for a nation, an organization, groups within and between organizations or individuals – is concerned with considering the long term and the future, with survival and sustainability as the key purposes. As a result of strategic understanding, strategies, polices and plans can be made, which can then be assessed and reviewed. Increasingly, it is becoming recognized that what is significant is the quality of the practice of strategy-making and doing (see Chapter 2).

At a national level, there have been ongoing concerns about the UK's strategy for competing in knowledge-based economies based on high-level skills and talent (Leitch, 2006). The intent is that, in order to sustain the economy through and beyond the recession, we need a transformation based on skills and on employment practices that will utilize those skills (UK Commission for Employment and Skills, 2009). To achieve this, employers need, however, to have ambitious plans for the development of their products and services so that high-level skills are demanded. As argued by Keep et al. (2006), any strategy for skill use has to be seen in combination with innovative product and investment activities.

Although some improvement has been made in the UK, there is still concern over skills gaps and skill deficiencies, a problem that appears to be inherently 'systemic and cultural' (Bloom et al., 2004, p. 3). Furthermore, recession affects expenditure on training, with recent surveys pointing to a cut in funding in over 50 per cent of organizations (CIPD, 2010e); in addition, only 56 per cent of staff had received training in the previous 12 months in 2009, compared with 63 per cent in 2007 (National Employers Skills Survey, 2009).

HRD is a key feature of a 'high-road' HRM strategy (Cooke, 2000) based on high involvement, high rewards and quality commitment. HRD has a pivotal role in the integration of practices with links to high-performance working (International Labour Organization, 2000), in which high-level skills and high discretion in the performance of work allow decision-making to be decentralized to those people closest to the customers. Two important implications arise from this view. First, employees are recruited for a skilled working role that will require learning and change, rather than for a job that might soon become obsolete. Employees are expected to retrain, and indeed many employees undertake courses of self-study in order to continue their learning and remain 'employable'. Employees are therefore carefully selected as much for their ability to learn as for their current repertoire of skills. Once recruited, employees become worth investing in, although the form of this investment may be subtler than simply possessing a large training budget. That is, learning becomes embedded into workplace practice as an ongoing process.

Second, line managers are fully involved in their subordinates' development, to such an extent that the differentiation between learning and working becomes virtually impossible to discern (and include in a budget). There is an emphasis on informal learning and an appreciation of its value, which line managers regard as part of their job and a responsibility on which they will be assessed.

reflective question Do you recognize the image of line managers portrayed here? What factors might prevent its realization?

In earlier chapters, we briefly examined HRD and workplace learning. The emergent literature on low-carbon sustainable work systems, for example, emphasized the pivotal role of HRD (Chapter 2) and how both mainstream and critical scholars stress that both HRD and workplace learning can create a 'strong' corporate culture (Chapter 5). McGoldrick and Stewart (1996) have argued that HRD has a strategic function; they identified leadership as a key variable in linking strategy, culture, the commitment of employees, and approaches and responses to changed and changing internal and external conditions. They suggested that HRD can influence each of these factors by:

- Shaping organizational culture
- Developing current and future leaders
- Building commitment among staff
- Anticipating and managing responses to changed conditions.

Over the years, managers in organizations and writers have viewed the process of planning strategy as deliberate and purposeful. This has been labelled by Mintzberg (1990) as the 'design school' model of strategic work. The key features of this approach are a prescription to assess external and internal situations, uncovering threats and opportunities, strengths and weaknesses, and the declaration of an intent incorporating the values and visions of the strategy-makers. This is followed by an attempt to formulate strategies that simply and clearly reconcile the gap between perceptions of current reality and desires for the future.

It would thus seem that the extent to which HRD becomes a feature of strategy depends on the ability of senior managers to sense important environmental trends and signals in HRD terms, that is, in terms of learning for employees. In the same way, it is argued that HRD professionals can make their work strategic by integrating it into the organization's long-term planning, resulting in HRD plans and policies that seek to improve performance (Garavan, 2007). This view of strategic HRD (SHRD) is almost entirely responsive to organizational strategy. It is for others to define the needs relating to the work to be carried out and the skills and knowledge necessary for their implementation. Mayo (2004) argues that SHRD must be business-led in order to create value. This requires a recognition of the drivers in terms of:

- The medium- to long-term goals of the business, covering its mission, vision and values, principles and beliefs about people and their development, while maintaining core competencies
- Current goals and objectives relating to the strategies of various business units, manpower plans and change programmes
- Problems and issues that require an HRD response, such as waste, ineffectiveness, compliance with regulations and the needs of individuals and teams.

HRD specialists thus respond by providing solutions (Garavan et al., 1999a) through the development of a training system that involves employees in identifying their training needs. This view is very much tied to the idea that skills are quantifiable and measurable, allowing tasks to be defined in terms of the skills and people assessed against such definitions (Thursfield, 2000). An extension of this view is to incorporate competencies, expressed as either criterion-related behaviours or standards of performance (see Chapter 7). Organizational goals can be cascaded through to employees and expressed as performance expectations. HRD specialists can work as partners with line managers to set performance targets, and identify with the staff the competencies required for effectiveness. They also partner HRM to implement the performance management system (see Chapter 8; Tseng and McLean, 2008). The contribution of HRD will be judged on the benefits it brings in achieving the performance targets.

A contrast to this view of SHRD is again derived from Mintzberg (1987), who suggested that strategies can emerge from the actions of employees, such as a salesperson's work with customers. Through employees' interaction with production processes, customers, suppliers and clients, both internal and external to their organization, employees can monitor, respond to and learn from evolving situations. As a result of such interactions, employees develop what Yanow (2004) refers to as 'local knowledge', and if senior managers can value this more carefully, it can flow to create knowledge that will inform the organization's strategy.

Alternative versions of SHRD provide for a more reciprocal and proactive influence on organizational strategy. Boxall and Purcell (2003, p. 245) suggest that recruitment and selection should complement training and development:

It is important to learn how to balance HR practices that reinforce the execution of a given strategy with practices that help the firm to conceive of a completely different one.

HRD specialists could play an important role by developing new ideas that both match strategy and take it forward. They can also develop facilitating and change-management skills (McCracken and Wallace, 2000), which they are able to do because managers themselves appreciate the emergent features of strategy-making and provide support for learning activities.

Gold and Smith (2003) highlight the various ways in which senior managers can respond to external pressures for change. One such response is to see learning as the way forward. That is, the need for change includes HRD as a principal component in forming a strategic plan. This is accompanied by managers acting as key advocates of HRD, recognizing that people are more likely to be productive when they feel that their work is personally meaningful and not simply a means to another end (Boud and Garrick, 1999). One important effect is that management become more accepting of ideas from others within the organization, a culture that supports learning thus being developed.

Although such ideas can feature in any organization, they seem to have particular relevance to knowledge-based organizations, in which the production of new knowledge is a vital differentiator (Garvey and Williamson, 2002; Newell et al., 2002). For example, Watson and Harmel-Law (2010) show how workplace learning in a Scottish law firm can benefit the organization, although there is a need for support from others, and contextual factors such as structure and pressure to meet income targets can provide obstacles to learning.

In the UK, there continue to be doubts about how SHRD issues are considered. According to the UK Commission for Employment and Skills (UKCES; 2009), there are wide skill-level variations between regions and sectors that show some improvements internationally, although many people are seen as 'low' skilled. Furthermore, other countries have also been improving their skill levels, leaving the UK unchanged relatively. A recent large-scale audit of skills in England (UKCES, 2011) pointed to the importance of high, intermediate and generic skills such as management and leadership, professional skills and science and technology skills for economic growth, but recognized the likelihood of the persistence of low-skilled jobs in the economy, in addition to lack of demand.

Within organizations, even where strategic management is taken seriously, the focus in the UK is in most cases on profit maximization, cost minimization and marketing, which makes HRD and skills a fourth-order consideration (Coleman and Keep, 2001). Training is seldom considered either as an input or as a direct outcome of strategic considerations, and this confounds the drive towards high-performance working and high-road HRM. This often means that marketing and financial matters carry much greater importance over people issues (Guest, 2000).

This highlights a key point about strategy-making: even when strategy is given full consideration, there are a number of possible paths that may be taken – for example, cost, mergers, information technology and marketing – and using the skills and learning of the workforce is only one of these (Coleman and Keep, 2001). Choosing a path other than skills and learning lies at the core of a UK problem of low-priced, low-quality production and a low demand for skills. Thus, if an organization chooses a production process that implies a low product specification in terms of skills, this has a corresponding impact on the demand for skill (as products with a high specification tend to be more complex and need frequent updating and/or alteration to the specification) (Green et al., 2003). This maintains what Keep (2004, p. 16) refers to as an organization's 'low skills trajectory'. It is a problem with which successive governments, especially in the UK, have been concerned – without finding a solution.

HRM web links   The UKCES is seeking to provide strategic leadership on skills development in the UK. You can find out more at www.ukces.org.uk.

Diversity and HRD

The issue of diversity is prompting many organizations to find a training response, and it is one that needs to be considered strategically (Home Office, 2003). In addition, in the UK, especially in the public sector, there has been a growing awareness of the embedded nature of discrimination following the publication of the report from the Stephen Lawrence Inquiry (Macpherson, 1999). As we have already identified, a number of changes in the legal context (see Chapter 6) are widening the coverage of antidiscrimination legislation, and this is coinciding with a broadening of philosophies that seek to shift the idea of equal opportunities at work towards diversity, often emphasizing the business benefits. However, a CIPD (2007a) survey in the UK found a significant disconnection between policies for diversity and the reality, and little evidence that diversity was considered to be a 'mainstream business issue' (p. 3). Diversity is usually considered as conforming with the law and therefore as a cost.

This is inevitably a difficult issue, but a common view is that HRD and training activities have an important part to play, although such activities frequently 'hope' to raise awareness leading to a change of behaviour to eliminate discrimination (Tamkin et al., 2002, p. 29). Awareness programmes are a common form of diversity training, especially where information needs to be communicated to a large number of staff on issues such as changes in the law. Such programmes can, however, also be criticized for being too generalized and not focusing on the skills needed for changing behaviour. In contrast, skills-based training allows behavioural aspects to be considered, with particular attention to interactions between people that enable the promotion of diversity at work.

A particular issue to consider here, one to critique, is that many work interactions are concerned with performance and profit measures and improvement, often in what is seen as an instrumental manner. Diversity can be seen as challenge to such an approach (Bierma, 2009). Skills-based learning for improving interactions is often based on Bandura's (1986) social learning theory, in which behaviour change can occur by role modelling new behaviours. Participating in role play can sensitize participants to diversity issues within interactions, allowing practice in a relatively supportive and safe environment, with feedback from an experienced coach. However, it needs to be recognized that the shift towards diversity requires the adoption of a long-term view of cultural change – it is not a 'one-size-fits-all' or a 'one-off' effort but has to be continuous. The strategy needs to be problem-oriented by identifying the issues that need to be confronted so that it is clear what is being tackled; in this way, any learning can be matched to need.

Crucially, for such learning to have any chance of being effective, it requires a supportive learning climate (see below) and support from senior managers and leaders who are basing their support on a clear business case for diversity, this being communicated throughout the organization. Metcalfe (2010), for example, shows how the computer company HP made diversity central to its leadership development, with a focus on how diversity issues were communicated and represented, including questions of cultural values, beliefs and norms. Such processes can provide a space for a critical confrontation of deeply embedded prejudices, which Wood et al. (2004) argue is required if the aspirations of the diversity agenda are to be seriously considered. It is also apparent that HRD academics need to embrace diversity more seriously since it remains the case that the focus on performance is likely to squeeze out the complexity and critique needed to increase the attention being given to diversity (Bierma, 2010).

National HRD

As we have suggested, the Leitch report (2006) highlighted ongoing concerns over the UK's strategy for competing in knowledge-based economies based on high-level skills and talent. In response, the government emphasized its agreement that skills were a key reason why the country was lagging behind other successful economies (Department of Innovation, Universities and Skills, 2007). More recently, following a change in government in 2010, and with the intention of recovering from recession, the strategy for skills has also included an extension of social inclusion and building of the 'Big Society' (Department for Business, Innovation and Skills, 2010a). Through such moves, a national HRD (NHRD) agenda has been established; this, as we consider in this section, concerns how a country views the contribution of skills towards its economic and social life, finding expression in the policies and practices of the state, its agents and its organizations. McLean (2004) suggested that interest in NHRD arises from such issues as the need to alleviate poverty, improving the quality of people's lives, technological advances and globalization and labour shortages, so that more attention is paid to upskilling employees.

HRM web links ▓▓▓ Most UK government statements on these issues apply only to England, and the governments and assemblies of Wales, Scotland and Northern Ireland have their own plans. For Scotland, go to www.scotland.gov.uk/Publications/2007/09/06091114/0; for Wales, go to www.learningobservatory.com/uploads/publications/1723.pdf; and for Northern Ireland, go www.delni.gov.uk/index/successthroughskills.htm.

In the UK, decisions about HRD are taken principally by those in organizations in what is referred to as a voluntarist approach. The role of government in this approach is to encourage organizations to take responsibility for their own training and development and its finance. This can be contrasted with a more interventionist approach in which the government or its agents seek to influence decision-making in organizations and make decisions in the interests of the economy as a whole. There is often a combination of these two approaches, albeit usually with a preference for one against the other, as shown in Figure 9.1. In France, for example, there is a system of training levies supported by a range of other interventions that form a 'social partnership' between the government and organizations (Noble, 1997, p. 9). The levy is an annual sum of money set by the government as a proportion of payroll, which is then used as a grant to organizations to fund training. If an organization does not provide training, it pays the levy but does not receive any grant. In the UK, however, the voluntarist approach relies heavily on market forces for skills, and in particular on the views of decision-makers in organizations.

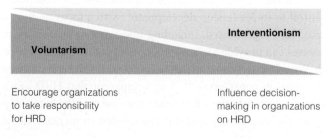

Figure 9.1 *Voluntarism versus interventionism in HRD*

reflective
question   Do you think a levy system is a fair approach to encouraging organizations to devote
resources to HRD?

One view, probably the dominant one, is that people are worth investing in as a form of capital. People's performance and the results achieved can then be considered as a return on investment (ROI) and assessed in terms of costs and benefits. This view is referred to as *human capital theory* (Garrick, 1999). Although this theory may be dominant, it may also obscure key processes such as how management can ensure successful performance, and how costs and benefits can be measured. Furthermore, it can present HRD in fairly narrow terms based on tangible and measurable benefits (Heyes, 2000), which may place a restriction on activities that have an uncertain pay-off over a longer time period. Investment can therefore become reduced to a cost.

Nowhere in the industrialized West is the restriction on development more in evidence than in the UK, where Taylorist–Fordist approaches to control (see Chapter 4), through job design and the deskilling of jobs in order to reduce training costs, continue to hold sway in many organizations. Marsick and Watkins (1999) suggest that, based on a metaphor of a machine, jobs are seen as parts coordinated by a rational control system, in which performance can be measured as observable behaviour that is quantifiable and criterion-referenced. A number of other implications can also be drawn:

- Attitudes are important only in so far as they can be manipulated to reinforce the desired performance.
- Each individual has a responsibility for his or her part, but no more, and has to work against a set standard.
- Learning is based on a deficit model, which assesses the gap between employees' behaviour and the set standard.
- Training attempts to close the gap by bringing employees up to, but not beyond, the desired standard or competence.
- There is little place for a consideration of personal development.

A further implication of the above ideal is a subservience of HRD to accounting procedures that measure the cause-and-effect relationships between programmes and output and profit in the short term. If a relationship cannot be shown, there will be pressure to provide the proof or cut the cost of the training. Even where organizations espouse an HRD approach, sufficient amounts of the machine ideal all too often remain in place, hidden from view, and present an effective and powerful barrier to organizational learning (OL). For example, many HRD professionals come under pressure to prove the 'bottom line value' of their work and show an ROI in evaluation (Burkett, 2005).

reflective
question   To what extent do the above features of the machine metaphor influence the learning
programmes in which you are involved?

Human capital theory (and the implied machine image) may be dominant in HRD but can be contrasted with a softer and more developmental view of people and their potential. Gold and Smith (2003), for example, found that some managers who were strong advocates of HRD took a *developmental humanistic approach* based on the personal empowerment of the workforce through learning. Achieving results is still important, but the key argument is that individuals are most productive when they feel that their work is personally meaningful rather than simply a means to an end. Furthermore, learning provides a way of coping with change and fulfilling ambitions. HRD can therefore move beyond the technical limitations of training and embrace the key ideas of learning and development implied in such concepts as the learning organization and life-long learning. The tensions between human capital theory and the developmental humanist view still, however, require those involved in HRD to present their arguments in appropriate terms.

These views provide a background against which the case for HRD is made at the different levels of individuals, the organization and the economy/society. Of particular concern in the UK has been what has been called the 'low-skills equilibrium', in which the economy becomes trapped in a cycle of low value added, low skills and wages, and high unemployment (Wilson and Hogarth, 2003). The main idea, first suggested by Finegold and Soskice (1988), is that products are specified in low skill terms because of the need to keep costs down. As Wilson and Hogarth (2003, p. viii) argue, 'Other things being equal, the lower the specification, the lower the skill intensity of the production process … [and therefore] the lower the demand for skill.' This problem has dogged many efforts to raise skills levels in the UK and is now recognized as a crucial factor to tackle (UKCES, 2011); however, it remains to be seen how this will happen.

Clearly, understanding skills and how skills are defined is central in NHRD. Felstead et al. (2002) suggest that 'skill' can mean:

- Competence to carry out a task
- A hierarchy of skill levels that are dependent on the complexities and discretions involved
- A variety of types, including generic skills applied in diverse situations, and specific skills suitable for particular contexts.

Most decisions on the definition of skills take place in organizations, exposed to factors such as the structure of domestic markets, short-term financial pressure, models of competitive advantage based on economies of scale, central control, cost containment and standardization (Wilson and Hogarth, 2003). These all combine to design tasks to a low specification, requiring low skills and providing low value added (Bloom et al., 2004). Even if an organization reports a deficiency in skills, these can easily be defined in low skills terms, in what Bloom et al. (2004, p. 12) call a 'latent skills gap', where organizations can accept and adjust to low skill requirements, losing awareness of the restriction that this imposes.

For over 20 years, there has been concern in the UK relating to the commitment to skills and HRD. Part of this concern has related to global competition, change and the impact of information and communication technology (ICT), and the transformation from industrial production to a knowledge-based society. The attention to skills and commitment to HRD can therefore be seen as part of a broader agenda pursued by UK governments. For example, during the 1990s, various White and Green Papers sought to set the vision for the twenty-first century (Department for Education and Employment, 1991) and a 'learning revolution' incorporating 'life-long learning' and the 'learning society' (Department for Education and Employment, 1998).

In 1998, the National Skills Task Force was set up by the government to develop a national skills agenda to 'ensure that Britain has the skills needed to sustain high levels of employment, compete in the global marketplace and provide opportunity for all' (National Skills Task Force, 1998, p. 38). The task force established skills priorities for basic skills, generic skills, intermediate skills, ICT specialist skills and mathematics, which resulted in further strategic declarations in 2003 (Department for Education and Skills, 2003) and 2005 (Department for Education and Skills, 2005); these sought to encourage employers to invest in training. However, even though some improvements were reported by Leitch (2006) and UKCES (2009), overall research suggested that the pattern of low skills remains.

HRM web links 🔳🔳🔳 The Department for Business, Innovation and Skills has responsibility for skill policy, mainly in England. Go to www.bis.gov.uk/policies/further-education-skills for more information.

There have been many attempts to prove that HRD has an effect on performance, but, as Machin and Vignoles (2001) suggest, this link is difficult to show. This is partly because research tends to examine the impact on intermediate factors such as labour turnover and productivity, rather than profitability. There is also the 'endogeneity problem' (Machin and Vignoles, 2001, p. 11), which means that the direction of causality may be reversed: instead of HRD being the cause of an improvement in production and profitability, it may be that more productive and profitable firms do more HRD. It has become a crucial feature of the case for HRD that there needs to be an association between skills and organizational performance (Tamkin et al., 2004). For example, Green et al. (2003) conducted a survey of over 1000 senior managers with respect to the relationship between product specification and skill requirements. They found an association between managers' perceptions of higher levels of product specification and higher levels of skills, and this was often connected with technical changes and computerization.

The crucial features of a high-performing firm are (Department of Trade and Industry, 2005a):

- Informality and dialogue that allow faster decision-making
- An open sharing of information between peers and networks of managers
- Visible and accessible leadership and management
- A focus on the long term and on outcomes
- Culture and employee relations characterized by pride, innovation and strong interpersonal relations.

These features are supported by a bundle of HR practices, including workforce development and skill levels, which relate to the overall direction of the organization and work changes. Further case investigations of high-performing firms (Sung and Ashton, 2005) suggest that skill development is focused on performance and is continuous. In addition, it is not just a matter of technical skills but of 'creating a work environment in which employees can learn all the time as part of their normal work and where they can take advantage of the system for performance and innovation' (Sung and Ashton, 2005, p. 26). However, doubts do remain over whether high-performance working can be equated with high skills (Lloyd and Payne, 2004), as low-skill work design and cost reduction remain a reality for many. In addition, for NHRD, there is a concern with polarization in the economy between those employed in high-skilled, often highly paid, work and those in low-skilled work (Holmes and Mayhew, 2010).

Although decisions on skills are made by organizations, it is recognized that there needs to be some degree of coordination between the supply of and demand for skills if a movement to higher skills levels is desired. Green et al. (1999) show how, in the 'tiger economies' of Singapore, Taiwan and South Korea, the state plays a strategic role in the transformation of skills by playing a 'matchmaking' role. In this process, the state takes a longer view of skill requirements in comparison to targets for the growth of the economy, setting the direction for the supply of skills through the education system, and stimulating demand by persuading employers to undertake workplace training, upgrading skills through targets and incentives. This has enabled these economies to move up the skills ladder. A similar pattern of NHRD has also been found in Australia (Learning and Skills Council, 2008).

<table><tr><td>reflective
question</td><td>Who should have responsibility for ensuring a supply of skilled people – the government, individuals or employers?</td></tr></table>

Investors in People

One aspect of policy that has sought to encourage organizations to consider how skills and training can be considered strategically, and even to pursue a high skills vision (Bell et al., 2004), is the UK award of Investors in People (IiP). Established in October 1991, IiP provides a set of standards for training and development requiring organizations to develop business plans that include schemes to develop all their employees and evaluate the results. There is some evidence that this initiative has had a degree of success. It has survived since 1991 and has been adopted by organizations in Australia and South Africa, with pilot schemes in Germany, France and The Netherlands (Bell et al., 2004).

It could be argued that IiP represents something of a spurious means of stimulating the demand for HRD within an organization. Down and Smith (1998), for example, found that many organizations achieving IiP had least to change because they were already doing what was required to achieve the award. There are also concerns of an uneven coverage of training, with a greater concentration being seen at managerial and professional level, and with low rates of accreditation among small businesses (Hoque et al., 2005). Furthermore, once the award has been gained, an organization may reverse its commitment on training provision (Hoque, 2003), leading to staff cynicism. As Bell et al. (2002, p. 1077) found, employees can easily be critical of management motives for implementing IiP – 'all managers wanted was a laurel wreath on the paperwork'.

However, recent evidence by Tamkin et al. (2008) shows that IiP helps to provide a framework for HRD and human resource management (HRM) policy generally, which can result in greater investment in skills and an impact on performance and profit. Furthermore, research by Bourne and Franco-Santos (2010) suggests that IiP enhances management capabilities, which improves businesses' performance in contrast with non-IiP organizations.

The link between IiP and performance cannot always be seen to be direct. Smith (2009) argues that organizations can recognize the need to change and then show alignment with the IiP standard. Gold and Smith (2003) suggest that awards such as IiP can play a special role in providing a rationale, a process and a positive language for HRD where managers are already convinced of its virtues. They suggest that the recommendations, ideas and exhortations relating to HRD and learning at work, plus the structures to support these, are a feature of what they term the 'learning movement'. The key point is that even though the learning movement provides the resources to support HRD, decision-makers still have a choice and can remain oblivious to pressures for more HRD, or sceptical about its benefits. Gold and Smith found that making a decision in favour of HRD was related to a recognition of the need to change and the fact that this could be achieved through HRD.

A further factor was, however, the background orientations of the decision-makers, which made them favourably disposed towards HRD; that is, the managers themselves had had positive experiences of HRD or espoused values of openness, trust and commitment, which they believed could be achieved through HRD. It was also found that, once a decision to pursue HRD had been made, it was usually then necessary to persuade others, which often required a great deal of discussion and action to keep HRD alive, especially where more sceptical views might block progress.

HRM web links 🌐 For more information, go to the IiP home page at www.investorsinpeople.co.uk.

Union learning

Recognition by trade unions may also lead to more effective HRD strategies (Green et al., 1998). Under provisions in the 2002 Employment Act, recognition can be granted to union learning representatives (ULRs), who can have paid time off to arrange learning for union members. Several particular purposes are allowed, the first being to promote the value of training and learning, including analysing training needs, giving advice to members and arranging events for training and learning. Second, ULRs consult with employers on issues concerning members' training and learning. ULRs are entitled to receive paid time off so they can be trained to carry out their role, attending courses with their union in order to develop the skills to analyse needs and negotiate with employers (Lee and Cassell, 2004).

ULRs can also seek to codify arrangements for learning and training at work through learning agreements and learning committees. This may cover the rights of individuals to learning, and resources for ULRs to their complete duties. Since April 2006, a union academy has sought to offer guidance to employers and employees on learning at work and to provide courses. Recent research on the Union Learning Fund suggests its value in helping unions to establish joint workplace training and learning committees with employers, which also improves relations and trust in responding to times of recession (Stuart et al., 2010).

HRM web links 🌐 The home page of the Union Learning Fund, which provides support to unions for learning at work, is at www.unionlearningfund.org.uk. A handbook on the role of ULRs can be downloaded at www.unison.org.uk/acrobat/17751.pdf.

The vocational education system

Within the voluntarist environment of the UK, employers have a choice about how much they can invest in HRD, and many choose to minimize this, leaving those outside organizations (the government and its agents) with little option but to offer a range of supply-side measures and an 'exhortation' to employers to provide more activities (Keep, 1999). Working on the basis of a voluntarist approach to HRD, successive governments in the UK have framed their policies around the idea of a market-led system for skills in which demand and supply determine the amount of training provided. Given the difficulties outlined above, the role of government and its agents within a market-led approach has been to improve the UK's training infrastructure and provide funding for interventions to support the smooth working of the system where markets fail. It should be noted again that overall policy is essentially an English policy, with policies for Scotland, Wales and Northern Ireland largely decentralized among the devolved authorities. There are, however, common links between all parts of the UK.

Governments have a key role to play in establishing a vocational education and training (VET) infrastructure that is accepted as credible in terms of the quantity and quality of trainees who are available for employment. A VET system will vary between countries, but the key elements are shown in Figure 9.2.

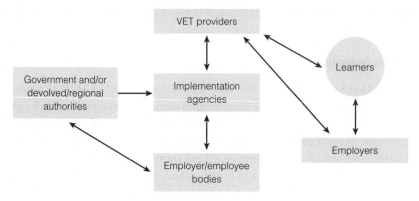

Figure 9.2 *Key elements of a VET system*

The main outcome from VET systems are learners who are educated and trained and ready to join the workforce. This may be measured by qualifications, even if significant training at work is often not accredited. Policies can be implemented by agencies who may also provide funding for supporting and stimulating VET. In Australia, for example, Australian Apprenticeship Centres contract with the government to engage with employers to support apprenticeship training. Agencies may also monitor quality assurance for qualifications and associated training. VET providers include schools, colleges and universities as well as a large number of training providers. Employers can play a role in setting the standards for qualifications, and employee groups such as trade unions can seek to ensure learning resources for employees.

The UK's VET system has been subject to considerable change in recent years but is essentially demand-led. The role of government has been to provide the foundations for a supply infrastructure, the main feature of which has been the establishment of a National Qualifications Framework that sets out levels for the recognition of qualifications in England, Northern Ireland and Wales. More recently, a Qualifications and Credit Framework has been set up, which contains vocational qualifications at these levels. There are nine levels, running from Entry to Level 8, with qualifications associated with a National Qualifications Framework level based on the demand placed on the learner. There is also a Framework for Higher Education Qualifications that shows the levels of degrees, doctorates and so on.

HRM web links   To see the relationships between the frameworks, go to www.ofqual.gov.uk/qualification-and-assessment-framework/89-articles/250-explaining-the-national-qualifications-framework.

We will focus our attention on vocational qualifications that are based on national standards, that is, National Vocational Qualifications (NVQs; in England, Northern Ireland and Wales) and Scottish Vocational Qualifications (SVQs). N/SVQs provide qualifications based on the required outcomes expected from the performance of a task in a work role, expressed as performance standards with criteria. These describe what competent people in a particular occupation are expected to be able to do and are usually referred to as 'competences'. It is worth noting here that NVQ competence refers to standards or outcomes to be achieved that can be assessed against performance criteria. This approach to competence contrasts with that considered in Chapter 6, which was concerned with behaviours.

It is claimed that NVQs and SVQs are directly relevant to employers' needs since they are based on National Occupational Standards set by employer-led standard-setting bodies. National Occupational Standards are developed by 23 employer-led Sector Skills Councils (SSCs), set up in 2002 and identified by Leitch (2006) as having a key role in stimulating the demand for skills in their sector. For example, SEMTA is the SSC for science, engineering and manufacturing, representing employers in the aerospace, automotive, bioscience, electrical, electronics, maintenance, marine, mathematics, mechanical, metals and engineered metal product industries. Research suggests that SSCs, while purporting to be employer-led, do have difficulty in engaging with employers, especially smaller organizations (Payne, 2008).

HRM web links Go to www.semta.org.uk/about_us.aspx for more details on SEMTA, and www.ukces.org.uk/ourwork/sector-skills-councils for information about licensing, measurement and performance in all 23 SSCs.

Competence-based NVQs and SVQs are well established but have been, since their inception in the 1980s, subjected to criticism. There have been concerns over the meaning of competence, with its emphasis on achieving outcomes and on assessment measured against standards in preference to attention to knowledge and understanding. In addition, short-term political pressures have, throughout the history of NVQs, tended to influence and distort their development (Williams, 1999), and there are doubts whether NVQs and SVQs provide a more effective framework for training than other approaches (Grugulis, 2002). A long-standing problem relates to the low levels of NVQ, especially Levels 1 and 2. These have recently been criticized as being of little use or value in the labour market, even though they are undertaken by large numbers of 16- and 17-year-olds (Wolf, 2011). This has put into doubt recent developments and attempts to remove an 'academic–vocational' divide by providing diplomas for 14–19-year-olds. Crucially, the report emphasized the importance of maths and English for future employment.

In terms of institutions to support the delivery of the government's strategy, there have been several changes of approach, including the level of operation – regional, subregional, local authority – and the responsibility of institutions. Until recently, the policy was based on regionalism, with Regional Development Agencies supplemented by a Learning and Skills Council, which provided regional contracts for Business Links. The Learning and Skills Council was closed in 2010, its funding responsibilities being transferred to a Skills Funding Agency, and the Regional Development Agencies are set to close in 2012. It is not clear how these will be replaced, but in some parts of England Local Economic

Partnerships are able to bid for funding to support local economic development, with some consideration for skill development.

HRM web links [WWW]   Business Links, which provide advice and support to businesses through regional offices, will also close by 2012 but will remain online at www.businesslink.gov.uk.

©istockphoto.com/Bart Coenders

Apprentices at work.

Apprenticeships

One criticism of the UK's vocational education system, based as it is on competence-based NVQs, is that, in contrast with other countries such as Germany, there is a lack of rigour. The German apprenticeship system is based on combining academic and technical skills with guidance from workplace experience, which results in workers of a higher status (Grugulis, 2002). It is partly to counter such criticisms that the UK government introduced a framework of work-based training that will lead to apprenticeship status, with plans to increase the number of apprentices (Department for Business, Innovation and Skills, 2010a), with the 2011 national budget announcing an extra 40,000 apprenticeship places at a time of high youth unemployment. The Apprenticeship system, previously referred to as Modern Apprenticeships, is composed of:

- *Entry to Employment* – a programme for school leavers not yet ready to take up apprenticeship or employment
- *Apprenticeships:* – 1-year programmes leading to an NVQ at Level 2, key skills and a technical certificate
- *Advanced Apprenticeships* – 2-year programmes leading to an NVQ at Level 3, key skills and a technical certificate.

HRM web links [WWW]   There are slight variations in the Apprenticeships scheme in Scotland, Wales and Northern Ireland. See www.apprenticeshipsinscotland.com for Scotland, http://wales. gov.uk/topics/educationandskills/skillsandtraining/apprenticeships/?lang=en for Wales, and www.delni.gov.uk/apprenticeshipsni for Northern Ireland.

It is not clear whether this attempt to return to quality-driven, work-based learning has succeeded. There are concerns about completion rates and, as argued by Fuller and Unwin (2003), the quality of the learning depends on the culture of the organization, including the learning opportunities made available, the degree to which there is breadth in the opportunities, and how far apprentices are allowed to participate in skilled practices. There is also concern that organizations such as restaurant chain McDonalds, which could take on around 10,000 apprentices each year, would use funding for training that they should provide anyway, such as induction training (James, 2010).

In 2005, the Apprenticeship Task Force (2005) reported that apprenticeships improved business performance and represented cost-effectiveness in terms of training in that apprentices were more productive over time. Furthermore, apprentices were more likely to stay with the organization and reinforce the company's values. However, not all employers value apprenticeships, instead preferring to upgrade the skills of existing staff (Lewis et al., 2008).

The UK government, in the face of rising youth unemployment, committed increased resources to apprenticeship, suggesting that by 2014 there could be over 300,000 extra places. This figure includes 10,000 adult apprenticeships, allowing retraining for new skills following redundancy.

HRM web links Find out more about Apprenticeships at www.apprenticeships.org.uk. The National Apprenticeship Service is the agency responsible for funding and coordinating apprenticeships; see www.apprenticeships.org.uk/About-Us/National-Apprenticeship-Service.aspx.

Visit www.palgrave.com.business/bratton5 to read an HRM in practice feature on BNY Mellon's advanced apprenticeships.

Implementing HRD

Although there are many recommendations to adopt a more strategic approach to HRD and make it more business-driven, there remains the crucial factor of how HRD is implemented. A number of uncertainties and tensions arise here. Who, for example, should take responsibility for HRD? Should it be HRD specialists, with their sophisticated repertoire of interventions and techniques? Or should it be line managers, who are close to work performance and are able to influence the way in which people learn and develop, and the environment in which this occurs? How should needs be identified, and whose interests should they serve: those of employees seeking opportunity and reward for the sacrifice of their effort, or those of the organization in the pursuit of goals and targets? What activities should be used, and do the activities add value? How does HRD relate to business goals? A crucial feature of HRD, given the claims made for its connection with high-performance working and knowledge creation, is the measurement and assessment of learning. In any organization, a range of factors influence learning, and HRD practitioners may not be the best people to make judgements about its impact (Clarke, 2004).

Overall, there may be still insufficient evidence about what is happening inside organizations when HRD is considered, which is compounded when we consider both formal and informal approaches to learning at work. For example, line managers seem to offer low support for formal training (CIPD, 2005c) but play a crucial role in what is learnt informally on an everyday basis. So although it is becoming clearer that the formal aspects of HRD, such as plans, policies and activities, can have a crucial impact, informal features may be of even greater importance.

reflective question How do your peers, colleagues and/or managers influence everyday learning where you are?

Formal models of implementation have shown a remarkable tendency to match the conventional wisdom of how organizations should be run. Depending on the resources committed to their activities, trainers have had to justify the commitment by an adherence to prescriptive approaches. Employees traditionally learnt their jobs by exposure to experienced workers who would show them what to do ('sitting by Nellie'). Much learning undoubtedly did occur in this way, but as a learning system it was haphazard and lengthy, and bad habits as well as good could be passed on. In some cases, reinforced by employers' tendencies to deskill work, employees were unwilling to give away their 'secrets' for fear of losing their jobs. Most importantly, line managers did not see it as their responsibility to become involved in training, thus adding to the forces that served to prohibit any consideration of valuing employee potential.

A systematic training model

The preferred routine is to adopt a systematic training model, an approach that emerged during the 1960s under the encouragement of the industrial training boards. The approach was based on a four-stage process, shown in Figure 9.3, and was widely adopted, becoming ingrained in the thinking of most training practitioners. Buckley and Caple (2007, p. 24) suggest it emphasizes 'logical and sequential planning and action'.

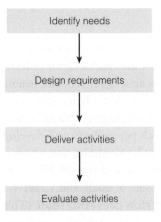

Figure 9.3 *A four-stage model of training*

This model neatly matches the conception of what most organizations would regard as rationality and efficiency, a consistent theme in many HRM processes. There is an emphasis on cost-effectiveness throughout: training needs are identified so that wasteful expenditure can be avoided, objectives involving standards are set, programmes are designed and implemented based on the objectives, and outcomes are evaluated or, more precisely, validated to ensure that the programme meets the objectives originally specified and the organizational criteria. There is a preference for off-the-job learning, partly because of the weaknesses identified in the 'sitting by Nellie' approach, and partly to formalize training so that it is standardized, measurable and undertaken by specialist trainers. The trainers can focus on the provision of separate training activities that avoid the complexity of day-to-day work activities and make evaluation all the easier.

In this systematic model, the assessment and analysis of training needs is concerned with identifying gaps between work performance and standards of work or performance criteria that have a training solution. Once these have been identified, clear and specific objectives can be established that can be used to design learning events and evaluate the outcomes. Training needs can exist and be identified throughout an organization. Boydell (1976) identified three possible levels for this: organization, job or occupation, and individual. Needs are in theory identified at the corporate or organizational level and fed through to the individual level. The approach reflects a mechanistic view of organizations and the people within them. In particular, there is an emphasis on the flow of information down the hierarchy to individuals, whose training needs are assessed against standards defined by others. Each person has a responsibility to perform against the standard and to receive appropriate training if they are unable to meet the standard.

Emerging from a consideration of needs will be plans for development activities. These may take the form of on-the-job or work-based opportunities supported by line managers and others, off-the-job courses run by specialists and, increasingly, open and distance learning or e-learning activities (see below). Evaluation occurs as the last stage of the model. Although a number of writers have pointed out the value of evaluation at each stage (Donnelly, 1987), the image of evaluation encompassed by many trainers is that of a final stage added on at the end of a training course. In such cases, evaluation serves to provide feedback to the trainers, so that small adjustments and improvements may be made to activities; evaluation can also provide data to prove that the training meets the objectives set, so that expenditure on training may be justified.

reflective question The four-stage model (Figure 9.3) may be rational and efficient, but is it a model of HRD?

Over the years, the basic elements of the four-stage training model have remained, and most organizations that claim to have a systematic and planned approach to training will have some representation of it. There have also been a number of refinements by advocates of a more realistic and more sophisticated model. Donnelly (1987) argued that senior management may, in reality, abdicate responsibility for training policy to training departments, with a consequent potential for widening the gap between training and organizational requirements. Essential prerequisites for any effort to implement a training model are a consideration of budgets, attitudes, abilities and culture or climate. A key requirement of training activity is that it should be relevant and 'reflect the real world'.

We can, however, easily see how training could become either isolated from organizational strategy or reactive to it. Bramley (1989) argued that the training subsystem may become independent of the organizational context. He advocated turning the four stages into a cycle that was open to the context by involving managers in analysing work situations to identify desirable changes, and then designing and delivering the training to bring the changes about. Evaluation occurs throughout the process, with an emphasis on managers taking responsibility for encouraging the transfer of learning that occurs during training into workplace performance. In this way, the model is made effective rather than mechanistically efficient. Garavan et al. (1999a, p. 171) suggest that a 'jug and mug' metaphor could be suited to the trainer role here, with a very passive involvement of learners at any stage.

Refinements to the basic form of the systematic model imply that a more sophisticated view of training is being taken. This essentially involves taking account of reality and organizational context. Implicit in such a view are the inherent limitations of organizational reality, which may prevent the basic model operating or may maintain training activity at a low level. The reality may thus be little consideration for training in relation to organizational strategy, but instead a culture that emphasizes short-term results against set standards. Organizational politics may interfere with decisions on training needs (Clarke, 2003), or managers may simply refuse to accept responsibility for supporting the transfer of learning where training is undertaken. These are all features of an organization's learning climate, a consideration of which is essential for implementing HRD.

Taylor (1991) argued that it is possible to present two views of why systematic training models may not match organizational reality. In the first, referred to as the *rehabilitative critique*, it is argued that the concepts of the systematic model are sound and can be used as an approximation of reality, serving to highlight the problems to be overcome at each stage by refining techniques. In identifying training needs, for example, trainers may not have access to the 'real' learning needs of the organization because of a lack of access to information and low credibility with senior managers. The refinement would be for trainers to raise the profile of training. However, the second view – the *radical critique* – argues that the systematic model is based on flawed assumptions and is merely a 'legitimizing myth' (Taylor, 1991, p. 270) to establish the role of the trainer and allow management's right to define skill within the employment relationship. It is often assumed, for example, that training is in everyone's best interest. In times of rapid change, however, the definition of skill and the redesign of work, which determine and are determined by employee learning, may lead to a divergence of interest between employees and management, and may unbalance the employment relationship between them.

Taylor (1991) concluded that although systematic models might have helped to professionalize the training activity and provide a simple and easily understood explanation of training procedures, such models were incomplete and really only suitable for organizations operating in stable environments where goals could be clearly set, outcomes measured and mere compliance obtained from employees. According to Taylor (1991, p. 273), however:

Continued adherence towards what is still essentially a mechanistic procedure may well prevent trainers tapping into the more nebulous but powerful organizational forces such as mission, creativity, culture and values.

Thus, in recent years, there has been greater interest in considering some of the key contextual issues that make training, and learning generally, more effective. This may include factors such as the motivation and interests of learners, the support from managers and supervisors, and the overall learning culture. Instead of being systematic, trainers need to become systemic in their thinking about the learning process at work (Chiaburu and Tekleab, 2005); that is, they need to understand the various factors that have an impact on HRD, the interdependence and tensions between the factors and how they combine to produce (or not) training, learning and development in all parts of the organization.

HRM web
links

There are many HRD resources available on the web. For a closer look at Learning Needs Analysis, try www.conted.ox.ac.uk/courses/professional/lnat. If you are looking for activities, try www.trainingzone.co.uk. You will have to join the site, but once you are logged on, you will have access to an amazing collection of resources and news. Go to www.mapnp.org/library/trng_dev/trng_dev.htm, the training and development page of the Free Management Library. If you are prepared to explore a little, you will find links to many HRD resources here too.

An integrated and systemic approach

In contrast to the mechanistic view of training implied by the systematic approach above, many organizations, especially those facing uncertain environments and the expectation of rapid and continuous change, have sought a more integrated and systemic approach in recent years. It is an approach that highlights key interdependencies within organizations, such as the link to strategy, the role of line managers, the link to team-based learning and knowledge transfer (Hirsh and Tamkin, 2005). It is therefore an approach to which the label 'human resource development' seems more suited.

Sloman (2005) suggested a shift from training, which is principally instructor-led and involves content-based interventions, to learning based on the self-direction of staff and learning from work, with managers taking responsibility to support this process. For HRD professionals, there is a need to engage with the reality of the organization at both the strategic and the operational level in order to provide value and enhance their credibility. The image is closer to that of what is called a 'business partner', in which HRD works alongside business units as an agent or facilitator of change. The notion of partnership is drawn from Ulrich's (1997) views on how human resources (HR) can add value and deliver results, and from more recent work for HR transformation (Ulrich et al., 2009). Gubbins and Garavan (2009) suggest a variety of HRD roles ranging from traditional trainer roles to those of a strategic business partner, as shown as Figure 9.4.

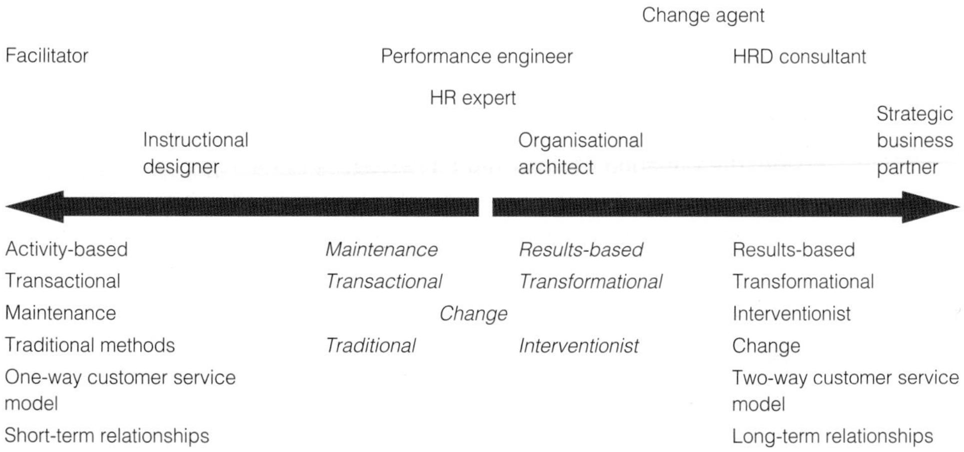

		Change agent	
Facilitator		Performance engineer	HRD consultant
		HR expert	
	Instructional designer	Organisational architect	Strategic business partner

←——————————————————————→

Activity-based	*Maintenance*	*Results-based*	Results-based
Transactional	*Transactional*	*Transformational*	Transformational
Maintenance		*Change*	Interventionist
Traditional methods	*Traditional*	*Interventionist*	Change
One-way customer service model			Two-way customer service model
Short-term relationships			Long-term relationships

Figure 9.4 *Changing HRD roles*
Source: Gubbins and Garavan (2009), p. 260

Following Ulrich (1997), HRD professionals have three possibilities:

- To provide routine transactional services such as traditional training programmes, as part of a *shared service* provision with other HRM professionals
- To become more specialist by providing leading and complex HRD processes that are valued by others within a *centre of excellence*, perhaps by using the latest research in collaboration with universities
- To become a strategic *business partner*, working with business leaders on the organization's agenda for the future.

In most cases, but especially as strategic business partners, HRD professionals have issues and possibilities similar to those of others in HRM. There is a need to develop a knowledge and understanding of how to add to value that meets the needs of key stakeholders. For some, this means HRD becoming what the CIPD (2010f) calls an insight- and business-driven discipline, possibly in contrast to a people-driven discipline. Others, however, would argue against such prioritization and the potential for this to drive out concerns for people and their development and well-being (Keegan and Francis, 2010).

The context of enacting an HRD role has a vital impact on its value. Any HRD policy has to be translated into the structures, systems and processes that might be called a learning climate or environment. The learning climate in an organization is composed of subjectively perceived physical and psychosocial variables that will fashion an employee's effectiveness in realizing his or her learning potential (Temporal, 1978). Such variables may also act as a block to learning. Physical variables cover the jobs and tasks that an employee is asked to undertake, the structure within which these are set, and factors such as noise and the amount of working space. Of particular significance is the extent to which the work carried out can be adjusted in line with employee learning, for example following the completion of an HRD activity.

Psychosocial variables may be more powerful; these include the norms, attitudes, processes, systems and procedures operating in the workplace. They appear within the relationships in which an employee is involved, for example with managers, work colleagues, customers and suppliers. Fuller and Unwin (2003, p. 46), drawing on their research of apprenticeship learning, have suggested that an organization's learning environment can be considered as expansive or restrictive – as two ends of a continuum. At the more expansive end, an organization is characterized by such factors as access to learning and a range of qualifications, a vision of workplace learning and career progression, the valuation of skills and knowledge, and managers as facilitators of development. In contrast, a restricted environment is characterized as having little or no access to qualifications, a lack of vision, recognition and support for learning, and managers as controllers of development.

reflective question Consider any organization you have worked in. Which end of the expansive–restrictive continuum most accurately describes its stand on learning?

At the heart of the learning climate or learning environment lies the line manager–employee relationship. HRD requires the integration of various activities such as identifying needs, choosing learning activities and supporting the application of new skills work, and the key to achieving this lies in the thoughts, feelings and actions of line managers.

Some organizations have recognized this and have included 'developing others' within their competency frameworks for managers (Industrial Relations Services, 2001). Gibb (2003) provides a number of advantages arising from the greater involvement by line managers in HRD:

- It will mean that development becomes possible for a wider range of staff, and encourages a proactive approach to life-long learning.
- There is likely to be a better link between organizational and individual needs because line managers are more likely to understand the requirements of work as well as the organizational goals.
- Helping the learning of others is a learning process for line managers too.
- It can lead to better relations and help to support change in organizations.

Of course, as identified by Gibb, there might also be some difficulties. For example, pressures of work may reduce the opportunities for HRD, and managers may not have the skills or positive attitudes for developing others. In addition, by giving responsibility to line managers, the role of specialist HRD practitioners may be reduced and the provision of resources outsourced. Nevertheless, there has been growing interest in how a line manager can support HRD, especially through coaching.

Coaching

Coaching has become a significant HRD activity, with recent survey evidence indicating its use in 82 per cent of organizations, where it is seen as a way of motivating and development talented staff (CIPD, 2010e), although only 36 per cent have a system to evaluate it. In addition, the responses of staff to being coached can vary since it is a practice linked to counselling and therapy and the provision of 'remedial' work for people who need 'fixing' (Western, 2008, p. 99).

Originally a development within the sporting field aimed at improving performance (Evered and Selman, 1989), coaching was adapted during the 1970s and 80s as a management activity to enhance employees' development, with particular emphasis on the transfer of learning from formal training courses into workplace activity. There has been a growth in interest in coaching, with conferences, books, journals and training materials devoted to coaching now more readily available. Coaching is mainly concerned with current performance and development issues, based on a relationship between a line manager and an employee, and structured around specific issues and goals (Gray, D.E., 2010). It can be contrasted with mentoring, which tends to focus on long-terms issues such as careers and personal development (see Chapter 11). There are also other variations in coaching such as peer and team coaching (Parker et al., 2008), as well as executive coaching and business coaching for managers in small and medium-sized enterprises (see Chapter 10).

The particular focus of attention in coaching is combining performance improvement with HRD (Megginson and Pedler, 1992), increasingly as part of a talent management agenda. The performance focus is not, however, without tension, and the quandary of being accountable for performance and HRD could lead to a regression into stereotyped management behaviour (Phillips, 1995). That is, managers may find it difficult to develop their staff when there is a need to meet performance targets, the latter usually taking precedence. Gold et al. (2010b) suggest that coaching provides two benefits for an organization: first, managers who are coached are more likely to improve performance, and second, managers who coach are more likely to learn about their staff and improve their performance. Other benefits include the relief of stress and increased leadership sustainability by experiencing how to show compassion to others (Boyatzis et al., 2006).

reflective question   Can coaching be both performance- and development-focused?

www   Visit www.palgrave.com.business/bratton5 to read an HRM in practice feature on coaching for performance at Morrisons.

Although the evidence on the value of coaching is still emerging, this has not prevented interest in the development of a coaching culture or coaching organization (Garvey et al., 2009). Based on their study of major organizations, Clutterbuck and Megginson (2005a, 2005b) have provided a framework for developing a coaching culture based on a consideration of:

- Coaching linked to business drivers
- Encouraging and supporting coaches
- The provision of training for coaches
- Reward and recognition for coaching
- A systemic perspective
- Management of the move to coaching.

Any attempt to bring about a change in culture is difficult, but coaching can itself support such changes (Stober and Grant, 2008). Research suggests that organizations are taking a variety of routes in embedding coaching. For example, Knights and Poppleton (2008) found three approaches in a study of 20 organizations:

- *Centralized and structured* – senior managers provide high support and formal structures to ensure consistency, as, for example, found in London's Metropolitan Police.
- *Organic and emergent* – based on informality and networks, coaching evolves slowly according to the context of practice, as in, for example, the international emergency assistance organization the Cega Group.
- *Tailored middle ground* – a blend of the previous two approaches, with some degree of direction for consistency but also a response to the particulars of the context. This can be seen in, for example, the BBC, where coaching started with a small group of committed coaches but grew, requiring structure and direction.

For a coaching culture to emerge, there needs at some stage in all cases to be momentum based on good practice, training for coaches and support from senior managers who see the value of coaching. As more coaches become involved, there is need for guidance from 'master-coaches' (Garvey et al., 2009, p. 62) and coaching supervisors, who provide an opportunity for coaches to share learning and problems. This also, however, requires care since coaching often involves revealing thoughts and feelings (Butwell, 2006).

A growing number of models and skills for coaches have been presented. Probably the most well known is Whitmore's (2002) GROW model, which provides a direction for a conversation between:

- *Goal* – establish a clear objective to be achieved
- *Reality* – establish the current performance and situation
- *Options* – finding ideas and alternatives
- *Will or Way Forward* – commitment to action.

Whitmore's model is particularly useful for introducing coaching into organizations, although it can be criticized for its lack of theoretical underpinning. Barner and Higgins (2007), for example, suggest that all coaching practice is implicitly based on a theoretical model and that these models need to be more clearly understood and articulated.

HRM web links Go to www.mentoringforchange.co.uk/classic/index.php for information about 14 models of coaching. What theories, if any, underpin the models? The Center for Narrative Coaching at http://narrativecoaching.com is based on narrative theories of making meaning through our connections to stories.

There are increasing efforts to specify those behaviours or competences needed for coaching. Anderson et al. (2009) identified the following coaching behaviours for managers:

- Shared decision-making
- Listening
- Making action plans
- Questioning
- Giving feedback
- Developing staff personally and professionally.

It has also been identified, as we have seen elsewhere, that any behaviour is performed in a context that can help or hinder its enactment. For example, priority for coaching has to be provided by senior managers.

Although models and skills do provide some degree of clarity for training programmes and qualifications, allowing a degree of prespecification of what is to be learned, there are also some doubts that coaches are in many cases faced by complex and ambiguous interactions with those they are coaching. It is a process that is inevitably dynamic and not easily captured by the abstractions of models or skills formed outside the process. As argued by Gold et al. (2010b), coaches are often required to respond spontaneously to the words of a coachee, with little time for deliberating or specifying a model. At such moments, coaches have to respond with what they have available – their experience and wisdom derived from such experience – a process referred to as *bricolage*, a term developed by the French anthropologist Claude Levi Strauss (see www.generation-online.org/p/plevistrauss.htm).

HRM web links The European Mentoring and Coaching Council has provided a set of standards for coaches (and mentors) as a part of a quality award. Details can be found at www.emccouncil.org. There is a resource centre for coaching at www.coachingnetwork.org.uk/ResourceCentre.htm and, very usefully, you can freely access a peer-reviewed journal on coaching at www.business.brookes.ac.uk/research/areas/coachingandmentoring.

HRM as I see it

Bec Development is a people development consultancy firm, working with clients to implement growth in their organizations. It specializes in learning and development and offers:

Helen Tiffany

Managing Director, Bec Development

www.becdevelopment.co.uk

- Training, delivered via workshops, seminars and courses
- Management development, to embed new behaviours and bring about change
- Leadership development through 360-degree feedback, psychological profiling, assessment centres and strategy days
- Coaching, including team, one-to-one and executive coaching
- Facilitation, by brainstorming and strategizing with clients
- Organizational development, including staff surveys, training needs analysis, talent development and competency frameworks.

Helen and her team work closely with each of their clients and their board of directors to help implement change through staff development, in line with the strategic aims of their clients' organizations. She is a Fellow of the CIPD, sits on the Council for the Association for Coaching and is a member of the executive board for Mentoring Digital Minds.

Visit www.palgrave.com/business/bratton5 to watch Helen talking about HRD, specifically about coaching, and then think about the following questions:

1 What is 'unique' about the sector in which Helen works? Does this affect the approach to HRD?
2 How does Helen's view of HR relate to business strategy? How can this be achieved?
3 According to Helen, why has coaching become so important? Why is it having such a large impact?

Evaluation and transfer of training

Coaching is a process that features HRD as a management responsibility. In particular, it can provide a link between HRD activities, transfer of skills to the work environment and evaluation. Figure 9.5 shows a model of the transfer within HRD adapted from the work of Baldwin and Ford (1988, p. 65). The framework specifies six crucial linkages, indicated by the arrows in Figure 9.5. We can, for example, see that new skills can be learnt and retained, but support and opportunity to use the learning must be provided in the work environment. The influence of the framework can be seen in the work of Holton et al. (2007) who have developed a Learning Transfer System Inventory that allows an organization to diagnose the factors affecting or preventing transfer of learning. The items in the inventory relate to:

- Motivational factors relating to the expectations that people have about applying new skills
- Secondary influences concerning the degree of preparedness of learners, and their belief or conviction in their ability to use their skills
- Environmental elements such as supervisor support or sanctions, and peer support
- Ability elements relating to the opportunity to apply new skills, the energy and workload of learners and the way in which training is designed to link to work performance.

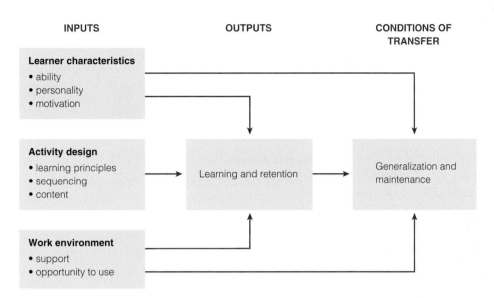

Figure 9.5 *A framework for the transfer of training*
Source: *Adapted from Baldwin and Ford (1988)*

Managers' support activities can include goal-setting, reinforcement activities, encouragement to attend and modelling of behaviours, all part of their role as coaches. Billett (2001, p. 213), for example, suggests that the successful development of workplace knowledge, particularly after HRD input, is underpinned by the degree to which 'affordances' are provided within the workplace, that is, opportunities for learners to engage with learning at work and be supported by managers as coaches. A culture of learning and support from managers has a direct effect on staff's motivation for training and learning (Chiaburu and Tekleab, 2005), and is therefore central to transfer and the overall learning climate.

The activities of managers to support transfer within HRD are also a key feature of the evaluation of HRD. As we indicated above, within the mechanistic view of training, evaluation often appears as the final stage. The key purpose of evaluation is to show how training input leads to particular outputs and outcomes. In a well-known model of evaluation (Kirkpatrick, 1998), for example, measurements could be taken at four stages to show a chain of causality in order to prove a result (Figure 9.6).

This view of evaluation matched the mechanistic view of training and became the orthodoxy for many years, with a number of adaptations to improve its working. For example, Phillips (1996b) added another stage beyond 'Results'. This stage would require an effort to assess the costs and benefits so that the programme's net benefits, or what is usually called the 'return on investment', could be measured, calculated by the ratio of programme benefits to programme costs, and expressed as a percentage (Phillips, 2005). Phillips gives an example a programme with a cost of £35,000, that produces benefits of £105,000. Here, the net benefit is £70,000, so the ROI is (£70,000/£35,000) × 100 = 200 per cent. Phillips points to the use of doing such calculations as evidence to prove the value of HRD and as a key part of the process of communicating to different audiences. Although HRD staff may not have the time to devote to data collection, it is increasingly possible to complete the process leading to the calculation of ROI by using specialized software (Burkett, 2005).

> **Level I: Reaction**
> of the learners following an activity

> **Level II: Learning**
> skills, knowledge gained as a result of the activity

> **Level III: Behaviour**
> the effect on the performance of the learner within the workplace

> **Level IV: Results**
> the effect of changes in performance on measurable results at work
> for example production/service figures, costs, and so on

Figure 9.6 *Levels of evaluation for training*
Source: Adapted from Kirkpatrick (1998)

Proving the worth of HRD by producing an acceptable ROI is certainly growing in importance (especially in the USA; see the ROI Network at www.roiinstitute.net/roi-network), but there have been persistent doubts about its efficacy and value when applied to many training and development activities (Guba and Lincoln, 1989); this is especially so in terms of the idea that the outcomes of training can be quantified and measured as if in a chain of causality. As we have indicated above, there are key factors in the organizational context, such as the support of others and opportunities for application, that affect employees' ability to use new skills and knowledge, and in turn affect overall work performance. Thus, whereas the mechanistic view of training will seek to use evaluation to prove the worth of training, ultimately to the organization in terms of cost savings and profit improvement, an integrated approach will seek to use evaluation to improve the quality of HRD activities and enhance the learning of participants in activities. It will do this by providing data for feedback and review discussions, especially between participants and their managers or peers, so that opportunities for application and continued learning can be identified.

Anderson (2007), for example, points to the need for any approach to evaluation to include the values of those receiving the learning and training. The task initially becomes one of developing the metrics that will reflect the needs of decision-makers so that they can assess whether investment in learning is contributing to organizational performance. As the metrics are formed, it becomes possible to employ a range of methods for evaluation, as well as to involve others in the process. Managers, for example, can indicate the value of HRD and how they are playing a role in evaluation and data generation to support action, but can also show why action is not occurring, for example, after a training event. Torres et al. (2005) suggest that evaluation can link HRD to ongoing learning through:

- Feedback from evaluation to make changes
- Integrating change with work activities and the organization's systems, culture, leadership and communication infrastructure

- An attempt to align meanings, values and feelings through questions, surfacing assumptions and allowing dialogue.

Linking HRD to its impact on work activities and beyond represents a shift from the linear reasoning of mechanistic models, because it becomes possible to raise important issues about what may be, or importantly may not be, occurring to allow HRD to have an impact on performance. Establishing the metrics strategically allows these to become part of the meanings made that will be evaluated by managers and those participating in HRD. It can identify any barriers to the use of learning and show how these can tackled with the support of managers and others (Mooney and Brinkerhoff, 2008). In this way, an organization engages in what Preskill (2008, p. 129) calls 'evaluation capacity building', so evaluation becomes purposeful and useful in improving the impact of HRD and enhancing the learning climate and workplace learning. We will now move on to consider this aspect.

HRM web links 🔲 Go to www.orau.gov/pbm/training.html for a set of links on evaluation and the impact of training, but if you wish to explore the technique of reviewing in learning, try www.reviewing.co.uk. This site also has a section on evaluation and transfer at http://reviewing.co.uk/reviews/evaluation-transfer.htm. For a broad view of evaluation and the latest ideas for practice, www.evaluation.org.uk is the site of the UK Evaluation Society.

Workplace learning

Learning in the workplace is seen as the crucial contributor to dealing with change, coping with uncertainty and complexity in the environment, and creating opportunities for sustainable competitive advantage (Antonacopoulou et al., 2005; Bratton et al., 2004a). As argued by Billett (2006), the workplace provides the space for learning where most people gain skills and knowledge every day of their working lives. Workplace learning has therefore become a key idea in recent years.

First, it casts a whole organization as a unit of learning, allowing managers to take a strategic view and others to think in terms of how their learning impacts on the wider context. Second, it is an idea that unifies an increasingly diverse set of influences and disciplines within HRD (McCormack, 2000), such as training and organizational development, knowledge and information systems. Some writers have extended the influences still further. Swanson (2001), for example, talks about HRD as an octopus that draws on a variety of different influences – anthropology, sociology, speech communications, music, philosophy and, in the future, chaos theory, a branch of mathematics concerned with non-linear dynamics (for more information, try http://hypertextbook.com/chaos). McGoldrick et al. (2001, p. 346), accepting the multidisciplinary character of HRD, argue that there is 'no single lens for viewing HRD research', that a variety of perspectives are being employed, and that this is leading to increasing sophistication in theorizing about and understanding learning at work. Third, workplace learning highlights the significance of HRD practitioners as people with specialist knowledge and skills, and contributes to the advancement of their professional status (Gold et al., 2003). Key ideas for application include, for example:

- The learning organization and OL
- Knowledge creation and management
- e-Learning.

We will first consider the idea of the learning organization.

The learning organization

The learning organization is seen as a strategy for performance improvement and competitive advantage (Weldy, 2009). In the UK, the idea was first developed by Pedler et al.'s (1988) learning company project report, which provided the following definition: an organization that facilitates the learning of all its members and continuously transforms itself. Pedler et al. (1991) went on to provide a list of dimensions of a learning company that could be used to differentiate it from a non-learning company. Among these were a learning approach to strategy, participative policy-making, 'informating' (that is, the use of information technology to inform and empower people), reward flexibility and self-development opportunities for all.

Another source of encouragement for the learning organizations was Senge's (1990) idea of five disciplines that were required as a foundation:

- Personal mastery
- A shared vision
- Team learning
- Mental models
- Systems thinking.

Still another view was presented by Watkins and Marsick (1996), who developed a model and a survey instrument, the Dimensions of the Learning Organization Questionnaire (DLOQ), which examined seven dimensions of the learning organization: continuous learning, dialogue and inquiry, team learning, embedded systems, empowerment, system connections, and leadership. What became clear was that such models represented an ideal of a learning organization but became difficult to implement. One survey (KPMG, 1996), for example, found that even where managers were in favour of learning organizations, they often faced difficulties in finding support for the idea: 'I have been trying to foster the learning concept for some time but with little success as the resistance to change is too great' (p. 2).

reflective question Why do you think the idea of the learning organization has been difficult to implement?

Part of the difficulty, as explained by Garavan (1997), was the idea that a learning organization was an ideal rather than a reality that could be achieved. In recent years, the idea has been compared to a journey, possibly one that is never completed. Learning organizations have retained some of their persuasive appeal as an influence on thinking about workplace learning. For Örtenblad (2004), the vagueness of the idea of the learning organization can also be a source of creativity, although he argues that there is a need for some clarity to avoid the concept of the learning organization becoming a mere fashion. He suggests that overly bureaucratic organizational structures might pose particular difficulties; as a result, some have suggested that smaller organizations might be more suited to the idea because their structures are relatively organic and flexible, with less bureaucracy (Birdthistle and Fleming, 2005), or that digital organizations may be appropriate because of their knowledge-based work and workforce (Cabanero-Johnson and Berge, 2009). Larger organizations can, however, also benefit through project-based learning (see below).

Part of the journey towards the image of a learning organization is to use instruments such as the DLOQ, whose dimensions were validated by Yang et al. (2004), as a form of organizational needs assessment to begin the journey. For example, Jamali et al. (2009) show its use in the IT and banking sectors in Lebanon. As Weldy and Gillis (2010) show, the DLOQ will highlight the different perceptions at different levels of an organization, as well as weaknesses such as lack of communication, involvement or participation, which are seen as necessary for enacting the learning organization.

Understanding learning

How we understand and explain learning in organizations is, of course, crucial. Throughout the twentieth century, there have been many ideas concerning learning, and a traditional distinction is usually made between *associative learning* (or behavourism) and *cognitive learning*, the main differences between the two traditions being summarised in Table 9.1.

Table 9.1 *Traditions of learning*

Associative learning or behaviourism	Cognitive learning
Learning in terms of responses to stimuli: 'automatic' learning	Insightful learning
Classical conditioning (Pavlov's dogs)	Thinking, discovering, understanding, seeing relationships and meaning
Operant or instrumental conditioning	New arrangements of previously learned concepts and principles

We can see how the nature of the work that employees are required to perform will lead to the acceptance of a particular view of learning. It will also underpin much of a manager's understanding of human behaviour and motivation. The reduction of work into low-skilled and repetitive tasks will therefore favour associative and behaviourist views of learning even where, in the initial phases of learning, knowledge and understanding are required. The main thrust of the learning is to produce behaviour that can be repeated time after time in relatively unchanging conditions. More complex work favours a need for knowledge, understanding and higher order cognitive skills, underpinned by cognitive learning theories. The work of writers such as Anderson (1981), for example, considers learning from an information-processing perspective in which learners seek to solve problems by seeking relevant information, and then matching and processing the information into a solution to provide knowledge and understanding before execution through action.

Behaviourist and cognitive theories of learning are viewed by Beckett and Hager (2002, p. 98) as representing a 'standard paradigm of learning'. The basic assumption here is that the 'human mind' is viewed as a 'stock room' that is at first empty but gradually becomes filled with knowledge. Both theories have value in HRD. For example, behaviourist theories underpin the importance of reinforcement and feedback in learning, including the opportunity to practise new skills. Coaching by managers has a part to play in this process.

Cognitive theories focus on how learners process information through thinking and memory, organized into patterns or schema to attend to what is happening (Sadler-Smith, 2006). Tests such as the Cognitive Styles Index (Allinson and Hayes, 1996) suggest that people process information between two preferences:

- *Analytical* – a preference for step-by-step models and structured decision-making
- *Intuitive* – a preference for less structure and more openness and creativity.

reflective question What is your preference for decision-making? Do you recognize different preferences among others when you work in a group?

Recent research suggests that it is possible to consider both analytical and intuitive processing together. For example, a high preference for both would indicate versatility and openness but also structured thinking (Hodgkinson and Clarke, 2007).

HRM web links Read more about other measures of how the brain processes information such as the Herrmann Brain Dominance Instrument at www.hbdi.com/WholeBrainProductsAndServices/thehbdi.cfm and the Kirton Adaption–Innovation Inventory at www.kaicentre.com. To examine your own style of learning, go to www.cdtl.nus.edu.sg/success/sl8.htm.

Although research on behaviourist and cognitivist learning is continuing, there is also interest in theories concerning the interaction of learners with their context, often referred to as *experiential learning*. Kolb (1984), for example, has provided an integrated theory of experiential learning in which learning is prompted through the interaction of a learner and her or his environment. The theory stresses the central role of individual needs and goals in determining the type of experience sought and the extent to which all stages of learning are completed. For learning to occur, all the stages of a learning cycle should be completed. Individual learners will, however, have an established pattern of assumptions, attitudes and aptitudes that will determine their effectiveness in learning. Kolb's learning cycle is shown in Figure 9.7.

Kolb's experiential learning model is one of a number that have led to the popularity of assessing the approach to learning through learning style questionnaires. If you would like to examine your own style of learning, try www.cdtl.nus.edu.sg/success/sl8.htm, which includes links to various online instruments. But take care – research by Coffield et al. (2004) examined 69 learning style instruments but found that many had psychometric drawbacks and were not recommended for use in education or training.

According to Kolb, learning occurs through grasping an experience and transforming it. Transformation of the impact of experience on the senses (CE), through internal reflection (RO), allows the emergence of ideas (AC) that can be extended into the external world through new actions (AE). Unless the process can be completed in full, learning does not occur, and individuals may not begin the journey to qualitatively finer and higher forms of awareness, which may be called development.

Kolb's model has been very influential for many HRD practitioners and has also heightened awareness of the factors that contribute to learning or prevent learning at work. Learning activities at work could thus be designed on the basis of individual and group

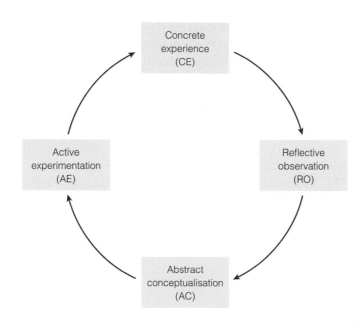

Figure 9.7 *Kolb's learning cycle*

Source: Kolb (1984). Reproduced with permission of Pearson Education Inc.

learning preferences. Learners might also attempt to overcome their blocks to learning. Individuals might, for example, lack the belief that they can take action in certain situations, or they might have negative feelings about certain activities. The important point about such blocks is that they are based on personal meanings, feelings and emotions towards learning, and this connects with other models of learning such as neurolinguistic programming, for example, which examines the way in which learners represent the world in their brains and order their thoughts by language to produce largely automatic actions (Tosey, 2010).

Learners can examine how such processes occur and how they can model themselves on the processes of others whom they see as more effective. Harri-Augstein and Webb (1995) presented an approach to learning based on uncovering personal meanings and myths that produce 'robot-like' performance and appear very difficult to change. It is suggested that, through critical awareness, learners can begin to experiment and change. Such views of learning link to a growing interest in adult learning and development, and the importance of reflection to examine behaviour and assumptions and premises about learning (Mezirow, 1991).

HRM web links   www.anlp.org is the home page of the Association of Neuro Linguistic Programming, but if you want to read a critical examination, try http://skepdic.com/neurolin.html. A key writer in adult learning has been Stephen Brookfield. If you want to read more about his views, go to www.stephenbrookfield.com/Dr._Stephen_D._Brookfield/Home.html. This site includes access to some of the key articles and tools of for critical thinking.

Although models of learning such as Kolb's cycle have been influential, they are not without criticism for being overly focused on individuals at the expense of their interaction and involvement with others (Holman et al., 1997). Others point to the importance of critical reflection allowing more attention to questioning assumptions relating to context, but also to considering more collaborative ways of learning (Bergsteiner et al., 2010; Reynolds, 2009). In addition, there has been growing interest in how people learn on an everyday basis, mostly with others in an informal manner, through their participation in practice.

There has been an increasing influence of the work of Russian psychologist Lev Vygotsky and his sociocultural theory of human development (Wells, 1999). Vygotsky (1978) suggested that learning occurs through participation in actions and interaction with others. The result of what happens socially is an internalization of understanding within the individual. This process from the outside to within is principally mediated through the use of 'tools' such as language and other social symbols. Vygotsky's work underpins much of the interest in social approaches to learning, especially in what are referred to as communities of practice (CoPs; see below). As we will see below, this view is particularly pertinent to the idea of OL.

Organizational learning

Although many organizations have attempted to pursue the vision of a learning organization, which by necessity requires attention to individual and group or team learning, there has also been significant interest in the idea of OL. The difference between a learning organization and OL is subtle but important: whereas the former is concerned with ideas and practices to enhance the learning of groups and individuals so that the organization can benefit, OL is an attempt to use the ideas of learning at an organizational level; that is, it relates to how learning occurs organizationally and to the barriers that can occur between organizational levels (Schilling and Kluge, 2009). There are links here between OL and organization culture (see Chapter 5).

Much of the interest in OL has occurred in academic circles, and it now constitutes a field of interest in its own right, with journals and conferences, along with a diverse body of knowledge, devoted to it (Easterby-Smith et al., 1999). It is not just, however, academics who have an interest: OL is also invoked as a response to cope with the challenges of global competition and technological change. The key idea is that if current ways of working (the organization's routines), which are the result of an accumulation of experience over time, are insufficient to remain or become competitive, the organization must change its practices and learn new ways of doing things (Antonacopoulou et al., 2005; Easterby-Smith et al., 1998). This may not, however, always be possible or even identified. The organization may accept its current ways of working and resist any attempts to change, apart from slight modifications to keep things as they are. This what is referred to as *single-loop learning* (Argyris and Schön, 1978). In contrast, an organization needs to challenge its current principles of work so that it can respond to changes in the environment and understand the reasons why it may fail to do so. Such a critical approach on the part of the organization is referred to as *double-loop learning*.

Much of the OL literature works from the assumption that an organization is a single and unified entity with the ability to learn. The difficulty here is that learning is clearly a human attribute, whereas the term 'organization' is used to understand a set of activities and processes carried out by people working with other resources. As pointed out by Weick and Westley (1996), organizations cannot be directly perceived, so explaining learning at an organizational level requires the invocation of particular metaphors, which

HRM **and** globalization

Learning in a global context

Any discussion of learning in a global context must be culturally sensitive. It must recognize that ideas about learning vary across cultures. This variation concerns the content of what is learned: what knowledge and skills are valued most? But it also concerns the form that learning takes: what is the best way to transmit or acquire the knowledge and skill necessary to do a job well?

One way to think about this question of the form of learning is to focus on the relation between research and practice. In the field of learning research, there has been considerable progress in the last decade, but it often takes a while for such progress to be reflected in the classrooms and workplaces where learning takes place. Even when a preponderance of evidence suggests that a particular approach to teaching and learning is superior, many practitioners will persist with traditional ways of imparting knowledge and skill to their students or, conversely, will advocate the new approach with evangelical zeal.

This presents certain challenges to the HR professional seeking to promote employee learning in another country. The HR professional from the West may be shocked to realize that learning practices in a middle-income nation are still heavily influenced by a traditional behaviourist approach. One might encounter, for example, a situation in which local workshop organizers appear to believe that learning works best when there is a regular schedule of positive and negative reinforcement. This is not to say that behaviourist approaches have nothing to offer, but the ideas about punishment that some people associate with behaviourism are problematic. Particularly troubling is the fact that the local workshop organizer does not hesitate to issue harsh reprimands to participants in front of their workmates when they fail to get the correct answer. When questioned about this practice, the organizer responds 'You Westerners are too soft. Your approach to learning is ineffective.'

At the other extreme, imagine you are collaborating with a colleague from the UK or USA. Both of you work with an international chain of high-end hotels. Statistics indicate that there are significant profit margins from coffee drinks and cocktails. Senior marketing people have asked to you to travel to various destinations in developing countries where you will conduct workshops in managing innovation. For your colleague, this is the chance of a lifetime. This is an opportunity, he insists, to introduce 'discovery learning' to people whose approach to everything is very traditional. 'We will have day-long sessions of brainstorming,' he continues, 'and will encourage participants to be creative, to try whatever comes to mind.' Unfortunately, your colleague fails to acknowledge that discovery learning works best when learning tasks are well structured and participants have regular coaching and high-quality feedback.

On the surface, this second scenario appears very different from the first. But what underlies both cases is a failure to appreciate that research on learning is an ongoing process, and that knowledge about learning is continually being revised and improved.

Stop! What is the best way to respond to scenario 1 and scenario 2? In which scenario do you think workshop organizers are most likely to reach a compromise on the question of workshop design? Explain. What kinds of argument would you use in an effort to reach a compromise?

Sources and further information: To see a summary of latest research on learning, check out the following website: http://psyc.memphis.edu/learning/whatweknow/index.shtml.

Note: This feature was written by David MacLennan at Thompson Rivers University.

©istockphoto.com/Maciej Laska

The HR professional from the West may be shocked to realize that learning practices in a middle-income nation are still heavily influenced by a traditional behaviourist approach.

is not equal to direct experience. A biological metaphor of the organization might, for example, suggest that organizations learn very much like humans – hence Dixon (1994) turns Kolb's learning cycle, an explanation of individual learning, into an OL cycle. However, there is still difficulty in showing how individual learning can be linked to the group and organizational levels of analysis.

One model of OL has been presented by Crossan et al. (1999), who argue that learning begins at the individual level, and then moves on to the group level before reaching the organizational level. There are four processes in a '4Is model':

- *Intuiting* – individuals see patterns in their experience that provide new insights, which they translate into metaphors for possible communication to others.
- *Interpreting* – individuals explain their insights to themselves and then others, through talk, and these then become possible ideas for application.
- *Integrating* – the group shares in the understanding and takes action as a consequence.
- *Institutionalizing* – the learning at individual and group levels becomes organizational through 'systems, structures, procedures and strategy' (Crossan et al., 1999, p. 525), with which others can work.

Crossan et al. (1999) suggest that these processes are unlikely to flow without difficulty. For example, power and politics are likely to play a role (Lawrence et al., 2005) in the way in which ideas are accepted, rewarded or rejected.

Another model, presented by Nonaka et al. (2000b), identifies how context can enable or inhibit knowledge conversion between people and levels. Their view of context is as a shared space for knowledge creation, referred to as 'Ba' which can be physical such as an office, or virtual such as an email or wiki, or mental such as shared experiences. Ba originates in a socialization phase in which face-to-face experiences are vital for the transfer of tacit knowledge (see below).

HRM web links WWW   Find out more about Nonaka's spiral and Ba at www.polia-consulting.com/A-Japanese-approach-of-KM-the-Ba.html.

One view of OL that has gained popularity in recent years is the cultural view (Yanow, 2000). The importance of this view is that it focuses attention on what groups practise and on the values, beliefs and norms that are shared between group members by talk, rituals, myths and stories. Thus, in any place we refer to as an organization, there will be a variety of groups, all practising or 'organizing' according to the meanings they have made within the group. OL is therefore concerned with what people do in their local situation. This also means that OL is not only concerned with change, innovation or finding new ways to compete. Because OL is based on the meanings made within groups, it can also be concerned with sustaining the group and its practices – which those outside the group may call 'resistance' to change and learning.

The cultural view supports some of the research that has been carried out, indicating that OL is mostly informal and improvisational, 'situated' in a particular context, and is a function of the activity that occurs at a local level (Lave and Wenger, 1991) within CoPs. Furthermore, learning within CoPs is likely to be at variance with what is supposed to happen, at least in the eyes of managers, who will have formed and espoused abstract versions of what should be learnt but will miss vital details in the process. Brown and

Duguid (1991) used the ideas of CoPs and situated learning to make a distinction between canonical practice and non-canonical practice, the former referring to what is supposed to be learnt, and the latter to what is actually learnt and practised in the working context. Learning is strongly related to becoming a practitioner within a CoP, with its own norms, stories and views about what is effective. This makes the task of achieving the benefits of OL even more complex. Brown and Duguid (1991, p. 53) argued that an organization needs to be conceived as a 'community-of-communities' and needs to 'see beyond its canonical abstractions of practice to the rich, full-bloodied activities themselves'.

Recent years have seen some attempt to harness the creative potential of CoPs. Thus, it is argued that managers can identify potential CoPs and provide an infrastructure of support so that they can be made 'a central part of their companies' success' (Wenger and Snyder, 2000, p. 145). There has been criticism of how far managers can form and manipulate CoPs (Roberts, 2006); we would, however, suggest that the ongoing and everyday processes that make up life within CoPs are not amenable to easy control by managers, nor are they easy to study, with the result that a wide variety of meanings and uses are attached to CoPs (Li et al., 2009).

reflective question   How far are students members of a CoP? Do they practise 'non-canonically'? What difficulties does this cause?

Nevertheless, there continues to be a desire to utilize informal learning to underpin improvements in organizational performance (Fuller et al., 2003). An example of this is the study of lawyers completed by Gold et al. (2007). This focused on the situations in practice when lawyers had to perform under pressure, for example in court, or with clients. Individual professionals were able to present their views of the events and derive learning, which they validated with others. The study showed that there were considerable opportunities for practice-based learning, which was shared with others, and that this stood in contrast to more formal and individualized approaches to learning. The process also revealed the importance of practice for knowledge creation and management.

Knowledge creation and management

There may be difficulties in applying models of OL, but this has not prevented the rapid growth of attempts to capture the knowledge that is generated by learning. The creation of knowledge and its management are now considered as a source of competitive advantage. The economy has become knowledge-based (Organization for Economic Co-operation and Development, 1996), the basic idea being that knowledge becomes the key ingredient of products and services. Differences between organizations and nations will therefore depend on the extent to which information can be obtained, turned into knowledge and applied to production.

This emphasis on knowledge has resulted in a plethora of new concepts, such as knowledge workers, knowledge-intensive organizations, knowledge networks and knowledge societies. There is also an emphasis on the skills of employees who are recast as knowledge workers. They are the owners of intellectual capital since it is people who are able to construct, manipulate and apply new knowledge, adding value to what is

Managing knowledge

In June 2011, a Work Foundation report concluded that Britain cannot pin its hopes for the future on finance or manufacturing, but must concentrate on developing a 'knowledge economy' for lasting growth. The report defines a knowledge economy as one in which value is created from exploiting knowledge and technology rather than from physical assets and manual labour (*Daily Telegraph*, 29 June 2011).

This theme has for over a decade underpinned the rise of the concept of knowledge management, on the grounds that, for a company to develop internal processes of constant innovation, the knowledge and ideas of its employees must be seen as an asset to be developed and diffused to everyone in the organization. This has been criticised as an attempt to capture workers' 'tacit knowledge' – the unwritten knowledge that they carry in their heads that is based on their cumulative experience of doing the job.

McKinlay (2002) examined attempts to create knowledge management systems in an international pharmaceutical company. Pharmaceuticals is seen as one of the key knowledge-based sectors, and more than two-thirds of McKinlay's survey respondents explicitly regarded themselves as 'knowledge workers'. The aim of the project was to diffuse small-scale and local innovations rapidly across the entire organization.

However, the approach taken by management was to use IT to create centralized databases of good ideas and lessons learned. McKinlay concluded that this had been fairly ineffective in developing innovative knowledge management processes. One reason was that workers actually developed their tacit knowledge through face-to-face interaction with other team members. 'In this sense, tacit knowledge was context-specific, generated and bounded by interpersonal relationships' (McKinlay, 2002, p. 79) – the complete

opposite of searching a central database for ideas or solutions. In practice, constructing the database simply became another item on project managers' check-lists in the drug development process. The database was validated by the number of hits registered by particular sites, and there was no qualitative measure of its impact on organizational performance.

The second reason why this was ineffective was the challenge to ownership of the expertise. On the one hand, knowledge management expected individuals voluntarily to hand over the very experience that defined them as experts, while on the other, searching the database could be seen as a sign that the individual's experience was inadequate.

However, one section of the technical workforce had developed their own knowledge management system, which operated more like a social network site. Members were encouraged to engage in dialogue and self-reflection, follow links to related sites, and above all take time – no short-term deadlines were involved. The objective was to deepen expertise within existing project teams and create and capture knowledge through a more organic process. But although this seemed to be both popular and successful, it remained limited to a minority of employees. In the main knowledge management programme, there remained a tension between the functional hierarchy in the organization, with its preference for centralized data, and the creation of genuine information networks that, by their very nature of open access, challenged the hierarchical structures.

Stop! Do you think that knowledge management is just another management technique, or does it require a whole new approach to management and organizational structure?

Sources and further information: See McKinlay (2002).

Note: This feature was written by Chris Baldry at the University of Stirling.

WWW Visit the companion website at www.palgrave. com/business/bratton5 for bonus HRM in practice features on coaching for performance at Morrisons and BNY Mellon's advanced apprenticeships.

Pharmaceuticals is seen as one of the key knowledge-based sectors.

©istockphoto.com/Amanda Rohde

produced. Human capital accumulation has therefore become one of the new reasons for an investment in HRD (Garavan et al., 2001) and a contrast to the previous narrow conceptions implied by human capital theory.

The key reason for such developments has of course been the advances made in the application of ICT, especially in combination with the Internet. ICT can be used to store, retrieve, analyse and communicate information, and involves a convergence of microtechnologies, computing, telecommunications, broadcasting and optical electronics in a revolutionary way (Castells, 1996). An important characteristic of this revolution is how knowledge is applied to knowledge-generating and information-processing/communication devices, with a feedback loop that enables knowledge and information to be viably accumulated and transferred.

Not all knowledge can, however, be captured by ICT, and this highlights the never-ending value of people, although, as argued by Scarbrough and Swan (2001), there has increasingly been more attention paid to the systems and technologies of knowledge management than to learning within the workplace, thereby 'glossing over the complex and intangible aspects of human behaviour' (p. 8). So much of what counts for knowledge is created and used in practice, so it becomes difficult to separate knowledge from what Tsoukas (2000) calls a 'knowing subject', who always exists in a place of action, in a social context.

In considering knowledge, it is common to distinguish between 'knowing-that' and 'knowing-how'. The former is concerned with knowledge about facts and explanations for facts that are explicit and communicable, whereas the latter refers to the ability to do something in a particular situation. Knowing-that is based on knowledge that has been codified, for example written into books, journals or papers on the Internet, and therefore becomes communicable. It is this knowledge that lies at the heart of the digital revolution. Knowing-how is, however, particularly important in the performance of skilled work.

Whereas performance may require knowing-that, dealing with the particulars of a situation, especially a new or unexpected situation 'cannot be accomplished by procedural knowledge alone or by following a manual' (Eraut, 2000a, p. 128). Such knowledge is personal, based on the requirements of the situation and the understanding of the person carrying out the performance. This is referred to as *tacit knowledge*; it is the ability to deal with different situations, known and unknown, often responding spontaneously to surprise through improvisation and without thought (Schön, 1983). To work out the difference between codified and tacit knowledge, think about riding a bike. Could you codify the explanation into a manual for riding bikes? It is more likely that it will be very difficult to explain the skill of riding a bike because the understanding is tacit and difficult to put into words (Polanyi, 1967).

Models of OL such as Nonaka et al.'s (2000b) rely to some extent on making tacit knowledge explicit, but there are different views on whether this is possible (Beckett and Hager, 2002). Collins (2001) suggests a range of possibilities for tacit knowledge ranging from 'Concealed knowledge' or 'the tricks of the trade', which is deliberately concealed and not passed on to others, to 'Uncognized/uncognizable' knowledge, in which humans do things such as speak acceptably formed phrases in their native language without knowing how they do it. Gourlay (2006), however, argues that the term 'tacit knowledge' is used where people cannot 'give an account' (p. 67) of an action or behaviour for which there is evidence. This connects more closely with learning and could relate to situations in which there are uncertainties, failures, surprises that Spender (2008) calls 'knowledge-as-practice' (p. 166) – which can be source of creativity but can also be constrained by situational factors.

HRM web links www Go to the online book on knowledge management at www.kmbook.com.

Although knowledge management is often seen as technical issue of data storage and dissemination, there is much interest in connecting knowledge management with learning as part of a process of knowledge creation and production (Kessels, 2001). According to Garvey and Williamson (2002), successful knowledge-productive organizations are proactive in learning new ways of doing things. They do this by going beyond formal knowledge management systems, attempting to work also with informal and tacit knowledge. There are clearly multiple opportunities for sharing knowledge between individuals and team members, across departments and even within networks of different organizations. But this means creating a climate of trust whereby people can share ideas both informally and formally. There is an acceptance that learning is a social activity, and this may not always be productive – competition between units can, for example, have a negative impact (Hansen et al., 2005). To promote knowledge-sharing, Von Krogh (2003) argues that three factors are necessary:

- *Opportunity structures* – which provide occasions for knowledge-sharing and depend on cues and interactions between members of the community. It is, however, acknowledged that a community of workers may not always have the same interests.
- *Care* – which involves empathy, help and trust.
- *Authenticity* – which involves sharing accurate and reliable knowledge.

Some organizations are now seeking to exploit social learning by becoming project-based. Consider, for example, the work of professional services in law, architecture or advertising, the work of the culture industries such as fashion, film-making or videos, and the work of those producing software and multimedia products (Sydow et al., 2004). These all require a project-based approach to enable a response to customers demanding differentiated goods and services that meet their particular requirements; such products need to be customized through negotiation rather than standardized. Although many organizations undertake some degree of project work, project-based firms do most of their work in projects and organize support for such work in response to project requirements rather than through traditional functional arrangements (Lindkvist, 2004).

reflective question ?S How do you think such functions as finance, marketing and HRD are affected by project-based working?

Because many projects are concerned with developing new or different products, they contain the potential to create new knowledge and learning. Taking advantage of this so that it can be shared elsewhere in the organization requires a range of learning devices, such as project reviews, logs of critical incidents and the informal sharing of ideas. In project-based organizations, there is need to explore learning within projects and to exploit learning between projects and within the organization as a whole (Brady and Davies, 2004). By managing the tension between exploitation and exploration, an organization can become what O'Reilly and Tushman (2004) call 'ambidextrous', creating versatile structures and configurations allowing independent units to develop innovations within an accountable framework.

Learning from both exploitation and exploration adds to an organization's ability to work with new information, especially from external sources such as customers, suppliers, regulatory agencies and others, and this can then be used to innovate by adapting and making changes to products and services. This quality in an organization is referred to as absorptive capacity (Cohen and Levinthal, 1990) and is seen as a key feature of OL (Sun and Anderson, 2010). In rapidly changing environments, in order to sustain or advance competitive advantage, it is argued that an organization needs dynamic capabilities (Teece et al., 1997) in order to respond. This requires learning about the use of resources in new routines and developing new configurations for practice, both of which are closely connected to knowledge creation and management (Easterby-Smith and Prieto, 2008).

e-Learning

One area in which the technology revolution is having a massive impact in HRD is the provision of e-learning. Until very recently, the term 'e-learning' would have been covered by a range of different activities involving the delivery of HRD activities, including computer-based training, web-based training and online learning. Preceding these terms were those of 'distance learning' and 'flexible learning'. Through the rapid investment in web facilities, all these terms have now been incorporated under the heading 'e-learning'. Indeed, on 24 March 2011, a search for 'e-learning' on Google returned 139,000,000 hits – the corresponding figure had been only 63,000,000 in 2006. It is difficult to define e-learning precisely, and any attempt to pin it down is likely to be superseded by events. The CIPD, however, uses the following (Sloman and Reynolds, 2002, p. 3):

Learning that is delivered, enabled or mediated by electronic technology for the explicit purpose of training in organizations. It does not include stand-alone technology-based training such as the use of CD-ROMs in isolation.

©istockphoto.com/Chris Schmidt

e-Learning is having a massive impact on HRD.

Research has suggested a number of benefits of e-learning (Pollard and Hillage, 2001), including the ability to learn 'just in time' at the learner's pace and convenience, the provision of updateable materials and a reduction in delivery costs. There is also the possibility of collaborative working, sometimes with learners spread over large distances, with tutor support, flexibility of access from anywhere at any time and monitoring of learner progress. Most computer-mediated conferencing systems enable a moderator to track participation and adjust provision as required. On the downside, a learner clearly needs access to ICT with an Internet or network connection. This can be expensive to set up and requires collaboration between IT and HRD/learning specialists. Furthermore, the material has to be digital, and must be made attractive and interesting to the learner.

The UK has a strong and vibrant digital and creative sector involved in the design and production of materials for e-learning, referred to as the 'stuff' of e-learning (Rossett, 2002). However, stuff still has to be engaged with or 'stirred' in a learning process. Although it is quite possible for such stirring to occur without intervention, a blended approach is recommended to ensure some effectiveness (Stewart, 2010), including support from coaches so that e-learning is focused on action and application to work. Blended learning was supported by 95 per cent of respondents in a survey by CIPD (2008) and research by Bonk and Graham (2006). However, research in higher education on e-learning suggests a variety of views on e-learning relating to issues such a demand from learners and quality, and this is likely to be replicated in other organizations (Kanuka and Kelland, 2008).

HRM web links WWW Moderation is a key skill in e-learning, and a well-known model of this is Salmon's five-stage model, details of which can be found at www.atimod.com/e-moderating/5stage.shtml.

Surveys by CIPD (2008, 2009c) found that e-learning was being used in 57 per cent of organizations and accounted for 12 per cent of training time, although this was likely to increase in the future. During the recession, it would appear that, as compensation for reducing external training, there has been a switch to e-learning, with 62 per cent of organizations reporting its use of (CIPD, 2010e).

Such figures are, however, very likely to underplay the unplanned and informal use of the technology and networks both at work and beyond. It is clear that everyone can join online groups, build networks and communities through social networking sites, add to and use wikis and even create new identities. They can also use smartphones and technologies as they move around. These forms of mobile learning, or m-learning (Stewart, 2010), are difficult to control by any organization. Control was a key factor found by Martin et al. (2009b) in their exploration of strategies for Web 2.0 technologies. It was suggested that control could be considered in terms of how far technologies allowed staff to collaborate and express their own views, requiring decentralization by the organization. A further factor was engagement, which relates to the ease with which staff could engage with technologies for sharing knowledge and collaborating.

Several larger organizations have attempted to use e-learning to recast their central HRD provision. There is an emphasis on employee self-service via company intranets, allowing staff to take responsibility for their choice of training. For example, at the Spanish company Telefónica, as part of a training policy to increase participation and interaction (Gascó et al., 2004), a distance learning system was installed to provide geographical and time flexibility; this was composed of self-study, technical and videoconferencing provision. An extension of this policy is the creation of corporate universities (CUs), such as the Heineken University at www.heinekenuniversity.com.

Cunningham et al. (2000) suggest that most CUs are simply rebadged training departments, but it also argued that a CU reflects an organization's strategic priority for learning, especially where staff are dispersed globally (Paton et al., 2007). Gibb (2008, p. 143) suggests that a CU reflects an aspiration to 'create a strategic learning organization that functions as the umbrella for a company's total education requirements.' The key features that make a CU distinctive are, according to Paton et al. (2007):

- *Corporate-level initiatives in large, highly complex and differentiated settings* – CUs will have a presence on the board. They may be distinct from the HRD function within large business units. They aim to deliver a specific corporate contribution, avoiding the replication or duplication of what is being managed or delivered at a local level.
- *The pursuit of continuing corporate alignment* – the CU is seen as a vehicle by which the control of HRD activities, broadly interpreted, can most effectively be aligned with strategic priorities, such as post-merger integration, customer loyalty and developing leadership.
- *Raising standards, expectations and impact* – the CU reflects the strategic priority afforded to learning. Issues might be ensuring the highest quality of provision, including harnessing the best available technology to create a virtual learning platform across global sites.

Further features of a CU include an influence on training and development for the entire value chain, including customers and suppliers and, of course, the use of the label 'university', with its implications of high standards and rigour. There are, however, bound to be doubts about how far these can be compared with more traditional universities (Walton, 2005).

HRM web links ▨▨▨ The e-Learning Centre provides links to articles and resources relating to e-learning; you can find it at www.e-learningcentre.co.uk. The eLearning Network acts as a source of information and best practice at www.elearningnetwork.org. www.capella.edu provides access to Cappella University, which offers 500 online undergraduate and postgraduate courses.

There are clearly more developments to come in e-learning, and technological developments, including improved access possibilities, will certainly continue apace. The role of HRD specialists will inescapably be affected as learners move from being present in training rooms to being members of virtual communities. A key issue will be how learning theories can be used in different aspects of e-learning environments. For example, behaviourist theories might be incorporated into staged learning and social learning theories for the development of support processes and communities online (Gillani, 2003). There will be many opportunities for knowledge-sharing through a variety of modes of contact and timings of interaction. Much will, however, depend, as we indicated earlier, on the nature of the demand for skills within organizations, which will have a knock-on effect on the supply of e-learning materials and activities.

Volunteers Together

Setting

The Third Sector consists of many thousands of community and voluntary sector groups that seek to serve a public or community purpose. These can range from well-known charities such as Oxfam and Barnardo's to smaller voluntary groups operating in local areas. A growing feature of the Third Sector includes businesses with social objectives, where profits or 'surpluses' are reinvested into community or environmental projects. Such social enterprises are seen as a sources of socially and environmental responsible work that can raise the standards of ethical business.

Volunteers Together (VT) is a coordinating body for the Third Sector in a large city in the north of England. Located in a converted primary school, close to the city centre, its status is guaranteed by a trust, although its day-to-day operations are in the hands of a Chief Officer (CO), two managers and five staff who all work on full-time contracts. In addition, there are around 30 volunteers. The overall task is to provide leadership and support for a wide range of Third Sector groups in the city, which before the recession numbered close to 5000. Since the recession, however, the number of groups has fallen to around 4000. The main reason for this has been a lack of funds and support, especially from the city council, which provides statutory funding. In addition, donations from private sources have suffered considerably.

The problem

At a recent strategic 'away day', all the staff worked on a new vision for VT – to ensure the development and sustainability of harmonious, thriving communities and neighbourhoods. This is to be achieved by:

- Ensuring that the value of the sector is recognized by strategic partners (both statutory and private) as being key to the development of a healthy, harmonious, sustainable city
- Striving to provide services that impact on the lives of the citizens by supporting and developing:
  - Community development, empowerment and engagement
  - Cooperative activity in neighbourhoods and communities

©istockphoto.com/Rick Rhay

- Environmental sustainability and respect for the local environment
- Community-led organizations aimed at meeting local needs
- Community ownership (of decisions and the allocation of resources)
- Volunteers and volunteering opportunities
- Supporting the development and sustainability of community anchors in all neighbourhoods as the 'hubs' for the local delivery of support services.

One of the main outcomes to be achieved relates to how value and impact can be shown. In the discussions that followed between the CO and his full-time staff, they realized that much of this had to be done through the volunteers, who tended to be 'clueless' on issues relating to proving the value of money spent or on responding to any formal mechanisms to share the ideas and knowledge that had been gained from working with the groups.

Volunteers tended to have their own way of working, based on lots of energy and goodwill towards the groups they favoured. In many cases, this meant spending more time with some groups and less time with others. It also meant avoiding any attempt to meet what they saw as 'time targets'; after all, they were volunteers and unpaid, so it should be left to them to decide how time should be allocated to the groups and which groups should benefit from their attention.

They also established deep affection and friendships within certain groups. They would see such relationships as vital to their work, but also were unwilling to reveal too much about a group beyond the confines of the relationship. While the full-time VT staff were entitled to know some basic information, because such information could also be used to decide which groups should and should not receive support for their activities, the volunteers recognized they had to take care how much was revealed. However, the CO knew that VT's survival would rely on creating a flow of knowledge between those who worked with Third Sector groups and VT's full-time staff.

Assignment

Working in a group or on your own, help the CO consider how he can enhance OL in VT and beyond. You might consider the following questions:

1 To what extent can OL ideas help this organization?
2 How can knowledge gained by volunteers from their interactions become organizational knowledge?
3 How can learning and development activities help this organization to show value and impact of its work?

Note: This feature was written by Jeff Gold.

◀ Most attempts to define HRD suggest that it has two purposes – first, to improve the performance of people, and second, to help people learn, develop and/or grow.

◀ There have been ongoing concerns about the UK's strategy for competing in knowledge-based economies based on high-level skills and talent. The intent is that, in order to sustain the economy through and beyond the recession, we need a transformation based on skills and employment practices to utilize those skills.

◀ For HRD to become a feature of organizational strategy, senior managers must incorporate the need for learning into their consideration of trends and signals in the environment, such as changes in markets and technology. A strategy for HRD can often respond to organizational strategy by using competencies to set performance expectations and targets.

◀ HRD and training activities have an important part to play in implementing diversity policy through awareness programmes and skills-based development.

◀ NHRD concerns how a country views the contribution of skills towards its economic and social life, finding expression in the policies and practices of the state, its agents and organizations.

◀ Decision-makers in organizations determine the demand for skills, taking a broadly human capital view that may lead to a restricted approach to HRD. In contrast, some organizations adopt a developmental humanist approach, which can lead to a greater focus on the potential of people for learning.

◀ The understanding of skills and how skills are defined is central in NHRD. Low skill levels among many workers remains a problem in the UK.

◀ Governments have a key role to play in establishing a VET infrastructure that will be accepted as credible in terms of the quantity and quality of trainees who are available for employment.

◀ A systematic approach to training is still the preference in many organizations; this emphasizes the need for cost-effective provision. Recent years have seen attempts to develop a more integrated approach that recognizes interdependencies with organizations, the importance of line managers and HRD professionals as business partners.

◀ The learning climate or learning environment in an organization greatly influences the effectiveness of its HRD policies, especially the relationships between managers and employees.

◀ To support HRD, managers have been encouraged to become coaches with a growing interest in developing the idea of a coaching culture or coaching organization. Coaching can provide a link between HRD activities, transfer to work and evaluation.

◀ Workplace learning casts a whole organization as a unit of learning and unifies the diverse set of influences and disciplines within HRD, such as training and organization development, knowledge and information systems.

◀ OL has become a key field of interest. Some explanations assume that organizations learn like people, but there are also attempts to provide different explanations by focusing on the culture of groups and how learning occurs in the context of their practice.

◀ The creation of knowledge and its management are now considered as a source of competitive advantage. The economy has become knowledge-based, the basic idea being that knowledge becomes the key ingredient of products and services.

◀ e-Learning materials and approaches may need to be blended with more traditional approaches for effectiveness. Mobile learning, or m-learning, is difficult for organizations to control.

vocab checklist for ESL students

◀ analyse (v), analyst (n), analysis (n), analytical (adj)

◀ apprentice (v) (n), apprenticeship (n)

◀ barrier (n)

◀ bricolage (n)

◀ coach (v) (n), coaching (n)

◀ developmental humanist approach (n)

◀ dimensions of learning questionnaire (DLOQ) (n)

◀ double-loop learning (n)

◀ e-learning (n)

◀ endogeneity problem (n)

◀ human capital theory

◀ implement (v), implementation (n)

◀ infrastructure (n)

◀ intervene (v), intervention (n), interventionist (n) (adj)

◀ intuition (n), intuitive (adj)

◀ latent skills gap (n)

◀ national human resource development (NHRD) (n)

◀ National Qualifications Framework (n)

◀ neurolinguistic programming (n)

◀ obsolete (adj)

◀ psychosocial (adj)

◀ return on investment (ROI) (n)

◀ sceptic (n), sceptical (adj)

◀ Sector Skills Council (SSC) (n)

◀ single-loop learning (n)

◀ strategic human resource development (SHRD) (n)

◀ union learning representative (ULR) (n)

◀ vocation (n), vocational (adj)

◀ vocational education and training (VET) (n)

◀ volunteer (v) (n), voluntary (adj)

www Visit www.palgrave.com/business/bratton5 for a link to free definitions of these terms in the Macmillan Dictionary, as well as additional learning resources for ESL students.

review questions

1 What is meant by SHRD and how is it connected with organizational strategy?

2 What should be the role of government in HRD?

3 What are the requirements for effective learning at work?

4 Learning is a 'good thing' for everyone. Discuss.

5 What should be the role of managers in HRD?

6 How can e-learning benefit organizations and individuals?

further reading to improve your mark

Reading these articles and chapters can help you gain a better understanding and potentially a higher grade for your HRM assignment.

◀ HRD is still a relatively new field of study, which draws its ideas from a variety of disciplines. Different views and definitions are covered in D. McGuire (2011) Foundations of human resource development. In McGuire, D. and Jorgenson, K. (eds) *Human Resource Development*. London: Sage, pp. 1–11.

◀ While there is growing interest in the idea of NHRD, G. Wang (2008) National HRD: a new paradigm or reinvention of the wheel. *Journal European Industrial Training*, **32**(4): 303–16 shows its historical links to development economics.

◀ The UK has had a problem of skills that government policy has sought to address. A critical view of the narrow focus of policy is provided by E. Keep and K. Mayhew (2010) Moving beyond skills as a social and economic panacea. *Work Employment & Society*, **24**(3): 565–77.

◀ There is significant interest in the role of line managers in HRD, which is considered by A. Ellinger and R. Bostrom (2002) An examination of managers' beliefs about their roles as facilitators of learning. *Management Learning*, **33**(2): 147–79.

◀ D. Clutterbuck and D. Megginson (2005a) *Making Coaching Work: Creating a Coaching Culture*. London: Chartered Institute of Personnel and Development uses case material to develop framework for a coaching culture.

◀ OL is often seen as a way to improve performance but a more critical view can be found in A. Örtenblad (2002) Organizational learning: a radical perspective. *International Journal of Management Reviews*, **4**(1): 87–100.

◀ Critical HRD as an emerging concept is considered by S. Sambrook (2008) Critical HRD: a concept analysis. *Personnel Review*, **38**(1): 61–73.

 Visit www.palgrave.com/business/bratton5 for lots of extra resources to help you get to grips with this chapter, including study tips, HRM skills development guides, summary lecture notes, and more.

chapter 10

leadership and management development

objectives

After studying this chapter, you should be able to:

1 Understand the meanings of leadership, management and leadership and management development (LMD)

2 Assess the requirements for strategic LMD

3 Explain various models of leadership and management for development purposes

4 Explain key approaches to implementing LMD

5 Understand how LMD can be used with leaders and managers in small and medium-sized enterprises

With the current economic difficulties, as well as their consequences, such as the opening of London Heathrow airport's Terminal 5 going 'belly-up' (House of Commons Transport Committee, 2008) and vital services such as hospitals failing (Healthcare Commission, 2009), who shall we blame? Leaders and managers, of course. It has been a long-standing issue in the UK that there are not enough leaders and managers, nor are they of the right quality. There has subsequently been much research interest in considering what leaders and managers do, the meaning of leadership and management, and how those who become leaders and managers should behave. In Chapter 3, as part of the review of the human resource management (HRM)–performance debate, we examined the role of organizational leadership in understanding the HRM 'black box'.

Of course, everyone has their own model of leadership and management, often based on prejudiced experience. In addition, most people who manage or lead learn from experience, especially in organizations such as small and medium-sized enterprises (SMEs), where few resources are available for formal development events or a strategic approach. If you talk to anyone who works as a leader or manager about their learning, you will often find that most learning occurs at work, and that they are made aware of this learning process through reflection on practice. Learning and development also often relies on the support of others through coaching and mentoring, or by working in an action learning group with other leaders and managers on problems that they face. However, this also makes leadership and management development (LMD) less formal and more difficult to evaluate.

Meanings of leadership, management and LMD

In the UK and elsewhere, a job title usually provides an indication of the role to be enacted and the level of responsibility. This would suggest that someone called a 'Leader' might be more senior than someone called a 'Manager', but this is not always the case. For example, in one organization we know of, there are Team Leaders who are junior to Department Managers, who are in turn junior to the Chief Operating Officer. It is therefore difficult to generalize from titles about what people do as managers and leaders, or to be precise about the number of managers and leaders (Burgoyne et al., 2004). However, figures calculated at a national level in the UK, as part of the Economic and Labour Market Review, suggested that there were in December 2010 4.5 million 'Managers and Senior Officials' out of a workforce of over 29 million. But this figure works from a particular classification of work and would exclude others who manage and lead in their work, such as professionals and those who have discretion for planning and decision-making in knowledge-based and service organizations (Moynagh and Worsley, 2005).

HRM web links   Key data on the labour market are published regularly in the UK and can be found at http://www.ons.gov.uk/ons/taxonomy/index.html?nscl=Labour+Market.

If we consider what leaders and managers actually do, one starting point might be to refer to various studies of the work of those who lead and manage. For example, the work of F. W. Taylor, recognized as the founder of scientific management, in the early part of the twentieth century, and of Henri Fayol, who identified the basic functions of planning, organizing, coordinating, commanding and controlling, are often invoked as the foundations of what leaders and managers are supposed to do. Taylor sought to define the role of managers by analysing work tasks so that those managers could find the 'one best way' to control work and reduce waste. Such studies, albeit influential, have not always been useful for leaders and managers in helping them to decide what to do and how to learn what to do in the particular circumstances they face. These challenges, which continue to the present day, have not, however, prevented the formation of a continuous stream of ideas and models that seek to overcome them. It is not our intention to cover such developments, but suffice it to say that many of theories about management and leadership exist and form the basis of leadership and management qualifications such as the Master's in Business Administration (MBA) or other training programmes.

<table>
<tr><td>reflective
question</td><td>PS</td><td>What do you understand by human relations theories? What has been the influence of such theories on how leaders and managers motivate others or on what styles of behaviour they need to learn?</td></tr>
</table>

The reality of leadership and management at work

Although much effort is expended in forming *theories* about leaders and managers, other studies have focused more carefully on what leaders and managers *actually do* at work. For example, Rosemary Stewart (1975) studied the work of hundreds of managers in the UK and found that most:

- Worked at a brisk pace with little free time
- Spent a lot of time interacting with people
- Based a lot of their work on personal choice
- Did not work according to neat, well-organized models.

In the USA, John Kotter (1982) studied those in general management positions and found that they spent a lot time dealing with issues through conversations. Managers seldom had a formal plan but worked with an informal 'agenda' to build a network so that they could achieve their objectives.

Another study by Henry Mintzberg (1973), of senior managers, also found fragmentation and variety in the way they worked, with an emphasis on verbal rather than written communication and a high use of networks. Mintzberg suggested a range of roles for managers:

- *Interpersonal* – such as figurehead, leader or liaison
- *Informational* – such as monitor, disseminator or spokesperson
- *Decisional* – such as entrepreneur, disturbance-handler, resource allocator or negotiator.

Mintzberg suggested that 'leader' was just one role within management and so raised the crucial question of whether leadership is in fact different from management. Certainly, since the 1970s when Mintzberg completed his work, there has been growing attention to this matter, with much discussion on how leaders deal with flux, fast

©istockphoto.com/Pali Rao

Dealing with issues through conversations.

change and transformation, while managers deal with day-to-day operations and transactions (Bennis and Nanus, 1985). Questionnaires have even been developed which allow the assessment of leaders and managers as transformational and transactional (see Bass and Avolio, 1990).

HRM web links   Consider the uses of the Multifactor Leadership Questionnaire at www.mlq.com.au.

Rather than there being a separation between leadership and management, especially in terms of roles, we would suggest that, in practice, aspects of the two are found together. There is a tendency, however, in uncertain and difficult times, for leaders to be given prominence, with the expectation that they will provide direction and maintain engagement (Holbeche, 2008a). Nevertheless, even this tendency can be misleading since it can result in particular individuals being identified as 'leaders' – as Alimo-Metcalfe and Alban-Metcalfe (2005) showed, leadership can instead be found at all levels of an organization. In fact, there is now significant interest in how leadership, as a process of influence and mutual working, becomes distributed across teams and groups, and whole organizations (Thorpe et al., 2011).

This factor has implications for developing leaders and managers, as does the variety of work contexts in which leading and managing occur. For example, although most attention is given to work in larger organizations, where roles can be clearly defined, most work units in the UK are SMEs or microbusinesses, and many of these are family owned. In such organizations, the term 'leadership' seems to have little meaning or value (Kempster and Cope, 2010). We need to remember that there are also differences between leading and managing in the public sector, the professions and the Third Sector, and across boundaries between organizations, both physically and virtually. In addition, given the variety of purposes in organizations, there are sure to be different values at work, along with different perspectives on the ethical and moral considerations of decision-making (Robinson, 2010) and the impact of decisions on the environment (Western, 2008).

Defining LMD

Burgoyne et al. (2004) suggested that it is difficult to generalize about developing leaders and managers because of the variations in context and situations faced. As we have suggested, there are debates about meanings of leadership and management, as well as about the meanings of such terms in different work contexts. Nevertheless, some generalization is possible, even if some accuracy is lost in application. For example, Gold et al. (2010b) suggest two possible definitions of LMD. The first of these is applicable where it is believed possible to specify a 'correct' or 'best way' to lead or manage:

> A planned and deliberate process to help leaders and managers become more effective. (p. 19)

Planning and deliberation is based on the existence of specified ideas, models and theories that leaders and managers need to learn in order to practise. Such a definition underpins many of the LMD courses and programmes available, including those that provide accreditation.

Leadership at Starbucks

HRM and globalization

In 2000, Howard Schultz, the founder of Starbucks, left his position as CEO. By 2007, Starbucks was losing market share, and Schultz was invited to return to his position as leader of the company. Within just over a year after he had returned in 2008, Schultz had turned the company around and Starbucks' stock had more than doubled in price. But what does Schultz's success tell us about the qualities of good leaders? To what extent are the qualities of good leaders 'universal', and to what extent do those qualities vary across cultures?

As a tentative response, we can begin with a working definition of what makes someone a good leader. Although there is no consensus on this, many people would agree that good leaders persevere. Their actions demonstrate a sustained commitment to core values. It is reasonable to suggest that this quality of perseverance would be valued in many cultures. People all over the world want their leaders to 'stay the course' in troubled times and to uphold core values despite pressures to compromise. Schultz demonstrates this commitment to core values, which comes across clearly in interviews and articles on him, and in his own account of his professional struggles and victories.

If we look closer, however, we can begin to appreciate the culturally variable dimension of leadership. Schultz clearly demonstrates his sustained commitment to the core values. He also upholds these core values even when there is some tension between them and the values of society at large. He emphasizes this point in a recently published autobiography (Schultz, 2011), in which he writes of the values he tried to reaffirm when he took the helm of Starbucks for the second time: 'Above all, I refused to compromise on the employee health insurance plan and the quality of Starbucks coffee.' Perhaps proclaiming a commitment to quality coffee might be construed as a heroic act of defiance in almost any country of the world, but the question of employee health insurance is especially controversial in a county such as the USA, where health insurance lies at the heart of very heated political debates.

In this example, we see how the universal and the culturally specific dimensions of leadership overlap. A sustained commitment to core values might be recognized universally as a quality of good leadership. But if we define good leadership with reference to a leader's willingness to uphold values, even when those values are controversial, there is a good chance we will be touching on culturally specific values. Thus, the definition of a good leader may have both a universal and a culturally variable dimension.

The example of Howard Schultz demonstrates the difficulty of formulating a single, universally accepted definition of a good leader. Rather than aspire to such a definition, it is perhaps more appropriate to recognize that definitions of what makes a good leader will have universal and culturally specific attributes. In recognizing this duality, we are more likely to appreciate the complexities of leadership in a globalizing world.

Stop! Some cultures value the rebel more than others. It could be argued that the USA is such a culture. To what extent will cross-cultural variations in how the non-conformist or 'rebel' is viewed influence prevailing definitions of good leadership? The phrase 'innovate or perish' has recently emerged as the new wisdom of leadership theory. How might one reconcile this phrase with the suggestion that leaders must be willing to stay the course in troubled times? (Starbucks' experiment with instant coffee might be relevant to this question.)

Sources and further information: Read Schultz (2011) for Howard Schultz's fascinating story.

Note: This feature was written by David MacLennan at Thompson Rivers University.

©istockphoto.com/Daniel Laflor

In contrast, a second definition gives more prominence to how leaders and managers really work and how learning can occur within their work:

A process of learning for leaders and managers through recognised opportunities. (p. 19)

This definition provides recognition of how LMD might occur more informally without planning and deliberation. A key issue, however, is how leaders and managers might come to recognize learning opportunities as part of their work. Writers such as Vince and Reynolds (2010) point to the importance of reflection to capture learning from work and events, allowing sense to be made and changes in practice to be considered. Such a process can also become more public, allowing learning to be shared with others. It is probably best to see these two definitions as contrasting poles of a dimension, as shown in Figure 10. 1.

LMD is planned
and deliberate

LMD is recognized
from work and
events

Figure 10.1 *Planned versus recognized LMD*

As a contrasting dimension, it is possible to see how, even in planned LMD programmes, such as a strategy workshop for senior managers, there is also the possibility for informal learning to occur as participants share ideas and catch up with the latest gossip and stories about the business. Equally, some events can be planned to allow learning to emerge. For example, outdoor management development programmes have to be planned to some extent, but much of the learning will need to be recognized through reviews and discussion. Within these definitions, there are a wide range of LMD processes, which we will consider in more detail below.

reflective question   How much of your learning is planned and how much is based on informal recognition?

Strategic LMD

There is a general view that LMD is part of a 'formula for success' for a national economy. However, there are also many detractors of this view (Holmes, 1995b), based on the difficulty of demonstrating how LMD affects the performance of leaders and managers, as well as the overall performance of organizations and nations (Tamkin and Denvir, 2006). Nevertheless, for over 20 years, there have been calls for the nation and organizations to take a more strategic approach to LMD. For example, in 2002, the Council for Excellence in Management and Leadership (CEML; 2002) called for a strategic body to oversee LMD based on dissatisfaction with the quality of leadership and management, and on a mismatch of the demand and supply of LMD opportunities. In organizations, the Handy (1987) and then the Constable and McCormick (1987) reports both pointed to a failure in the UK to prepare and develop managers in comparison with other countries such as Germany and the USA, consequently making the link to the UK's poor productivity.

Much too macho?

A 2010 newspaper report of some Canadian research claimed that 'testosterone-fuelled' young executives who bark orders and throw their weight around, making lives a misery for their staff, actually turn out to make the worst business deals. Apparently, the aggressive model of the ruthless manager, so beloved of TV series, is not very effective, and as such managers are likely to 'pursue those things which give them the most dominance but do not give them the most value' (*Daily Telegraph*, September 10, 2010).

Coming so soon after a series of spectacular cases of mismanagement in the finance sector, this example resonates with a wider critique of the value of much management education. Analyses of management training since the 1980s have repeatedly shown that it is 'only moderately' effective. The MBA remains the staple of management education, but its providers, mainly university business schools, have no way of telling how much, or even if, the MBA contributes to the subsequent performance of the MBA-qualified manager. Among several criticisms of the typical MBA is that it is based on a Western business model and learning style, both of which may be inappropriate when delivered, as many now are, in other societal contexts. Perhaps more significant is the criticism made by Susan Vinnicombe and Val Singh (2003) that the whole ethos of management education is overwhelmingly male. They argue that as men were almost the only managers around when MBA programmes were first designed, and as the majority of business school academics were, and still are, male, it is inevitable that MBAs reflect male priorities and ways of learning.

Female participation rates on MBA programmes are stuck at around the 30 per cent mark. A US study of female MBA students indicated that among the factors they found discouraging were the lack of female role models at leadership levels, the overly competitive culture and the lack of class diversity. Vinnicombe and Singh (2003) argue that there may

also be deeper reasons, to do with the content of MBAs as much as their availability or access to them. They report that women seemed to be turned off by the lack of any ethical debate over the wealth-maximizing rationale that underpins dominant theories of management. They further claim that whereas male learning styles are based on replication of knowledge and analysis of cases, women prefer to start with personal experience and self-analysis, and work collaboratively to understand their wider significance. In the male learning model tutors are 'gurus', but in the female learning model they are guides and facilitators.

Vinnicombe and Singh conclude that women experienced the MBA as something to be survived and, even though this might well prepare them for their subsequent organizational experience, they felt marginalized, which affected their learning.

Stop! Think about the course you are on. Do you think that the way in which it is taught or the values that it stresses are more likely to appeal to men than women? Or the other way round?

Sources and further information: See Vinnicombe and Singh (2003) for the background to this study. For further information, see also Saks et al. (2011).

Note: This was written by Chris Baldry, University of Sterling.

www Visit the companion website at www.palgrave.com/business/bratton5 for bonus HRM in practice features on Business Alliance in Leeds and the Clinical Leadership Competency Framework.

©istockphoto.com/Jacob Wackerhausen

Since then, surveys have shown some improvement in the priority given to LMD (Thomson et al., 2001). The CEML (2002) reported that there had been an increase in management qualifications with significant amounts of money invested in LMD, even though there was lack of focus and dissatisfaction with outcomes. More recently, efforts have been made to show the link between good management practice and performance (Advanced Institute of Management, 2009). For example, the model developed by Tamkin and Denvir (2006), shown as Figure 10.2, suggests business impact and outcomes are based on:

- *Inputs to management capability* – factors to develop management capability, education, ongoing formal and informal learning, and job experience
- *Context* – includes the human resources (HR) environment, the presence and operation of rules, the degree of flexibility managers have, and the devolvement of management responsibility
- *Management practice* – the processes and practices adopted in terms of managing people, structure, processes, strategy and innovation
- *People capability* – skills, capabilities and engagement of employees will all mediate the effect of management practice.

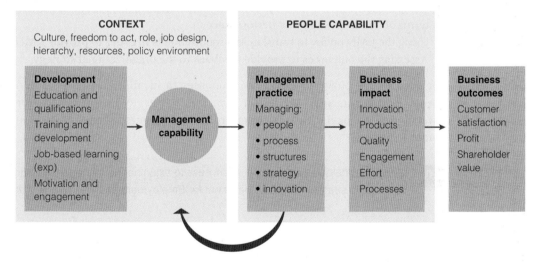

Figure 10.2 *A model of impacts on organizational performance*
Source: Tamkin and Denvir (2006), p. 12

We will have more to consider against each of these factors during this chapter.

HRM web links 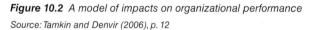 The Advanced Institute of Management was a large management research project that ran during the 2000s. Results from the project can be found at www.aimpractice.com. During the 2000s there has been growing attention to LMD in the public sector. Go to www.nationalcollege.org.uk for the National College for Leadership of Schools and Children's Services, and https://firelearn.fireservicecollege.ac.uk for the Fire Service College.

Strategy and LMD in organizations

In the face of change and turbulence, such as increasing globalization, larger customer demand, technological advances and economic instability, LMD could be seen as a deliberate attempt to implement a strategic response (Brown, 2007). There seem to be two possible purposes for LMD strategies (Chartered Institute of Personnel and Development, 2002):

- To sustain the business by developing leaders and managers with the skills to carry out determined roles
- To advance the business by developing new models in fast-moving sectors and turbulent environments.

The first might be considered to be the orthodox view, reflecting what Garavan et al. (1999b, p. 193) call 'the functional performance rationale' for LMD, implying a causal link between strategy, LMD and performance. This approach involves:

1 Setting the organization's strategy in response to an assessment of changes in the environment
2 Agreeing the response with the various stakeholders and interested parties
3 Using the strategy to provide guidance on the requirements for leaders and managers in terms of numbers, skills and performance
4 Using the LMD policy to translate the requirements in order to provide LMD activities
5 Assessing the outcomes to provide feedback to the organizational strategy.

Included in any policy for LMD are responses to identified weaknesses and improvements for performance, succession planning, values to be promoted (for example, diversity and ecology), new services or products to be pursued and requirements for new leader-managers.

HRM web links **WWW** Go to www.delni.gov.uk/leading-to-success to examine the Management and Leadership strategy for the Department for Employment and Learning in Northern Ireland.

The second purpose of advancing the business by developing new models suggests that LMD can also play a role in *making* strategy as well as *responding* to strategy. This also connects to a recent interest in talent management (see Chapter 6). For example, Tansley et al. (2007b) showed how a number of organizations were developing a 'talent pipeline' for senior positions by strategically identifying staff of high potential and performance for development as leaders and managers.

Allowing LMD to influence strategy formation creates a link between what leaders and managers learn and the organization's future activities. This might require a change in understanding how strategy is made. According to Mintzberg et al. (1998), most approaches to strategy are based on a *prescription* of how strategy should be carried out – this could include what leaders and managers must learn and do. This can be contrasted with a learning approach that considers the value of using ongoing actions and decisions as the source of change. In this way, strategy is said to *emerge*, often in an unplanned way. An LMD strategy would need to include how this can be achieved and also how, as Mintzberg et al. (p. 195) suggest, 'Real learning takes place at the interface of thought and action, as actors reflect on what they have done'.

reflective question How could 'real learning' by you and your friends be achieved and influence strategy in your current work organization or college?

To make a link between learning and strategy is also to recognize that strategy is something people *do*, a form of practice. This can include attending workshops to develop plans using tools such as 'scenarios', which are used to create different versions of the future, and techniques of analysis such SWOT and PESTLE (see Jarzabkowski et al., 2009). It should also include a recognition of how learning is part of leaders' and managers' everyday practice.

According to Brown (2005), a strategic approach to LMD can stimulate strategic change-enhancing capability in strategic management. In addition, if consistency at different levels of leadership and management can be maintained during a strategic initiative, a significant improvement in performance can occur (O'Reilly et al., 2010). There is still, however, little evidence that a strategic approach to LMD is being taken. Part of the reason seems to be a failure to distinguish between future-oriented or strategic skills and general business skills, mainly based on a conservative approach taken by LMD providers who tend to focus on short-term issues (Clarke et al., 2004), and a lack of influence of human resource development (HRD) and LMD at board level. The onset of recession could easily reinforce a conservative approach, but organizations are urged to maintain investment in LMD to ensure their survival (Holbeche, 2008b).

Evidence for LMD

If there are continuing doubts and difficulties in taking a strategic approach to LMD, perhaps one of the reasons is the lack of evidence to show that LMD can work, especially in terms that meet the expectations of senior managers or even managers who undertake LMD. For example, Mabey and Thomson (2000) found differences between HRD managers who provided LMD and managers with MBAs in how far LMD linked to business strategy. Most MBA managers saw little link between the two. However, evidence of what works could be used to form an LMD strategy. For example, based on 'best' practices in organizations, Leskew and Singh (2007) suggest that there need to be:

- A thorough needs assessment
- The selection of a suitable audience
- The design of an appropriate infrastructure
- The design and implementation of an entire learning system
- An evaluation system
- Corresponding actions to reward success and improve on deficiencies.

Within such factors are issues concerned with support for LMD including a positive HR context, composed of planned career structures, succession planning and fast-tracking, all linked to LMD processes and with LMD as a priority. Mabey (2002) suggested that such factors indicate that a long-term view is being taken. Perhaps the most crucial factor is the support given to informal learning and development, often seen by managers as effective. Further work by Mabey (2005) highlighted the crucial links between LMD and organizational measures such as commitment, performance and productivity, as shown in Figure 10.3, in which the thickness of the lines indicates the strength of the links.

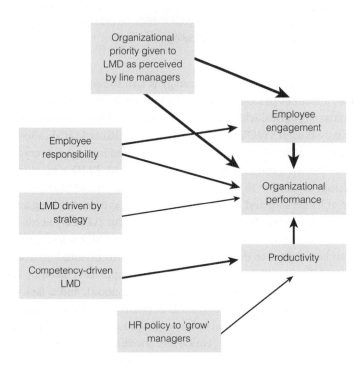

Figure 10.3 *How LMD links to organizational performance*
Source: Mabey (2005)

It can be seen that perceptions are a crucial part of the evidence, so that if managers perceived a priority for LMD on the part of *their own* line managers, who took responsibility for support, it enhanced the link to engagement and performance. Competencies also indicated that a strategic approach was being taken.

Such evidence-based approaches require, according to Hamlin (2010):

- A systematic feedback of the opinions and preferences of managers and leaders and organizations
- Good, critically reflective evaluation data
- Relevant, good-quality empirical research of all kinds including both 'pure' and 'applied' research
- A consensus of recognized professional experts in the field of management and leadership
- Affirmed professional experience that substantiates practice.

Organizations can use such ideas to gather evidence for practice and, reflecting on the findings, to demonstrate the links between LMD and performance. As evidence is gathered, there can, relating to results, be an analysis to consider how improvements can be made, which in turn forms the focus for future LMD.

reflective question   Based on the evidence presented so far, is there a strategic case for LMD?

Implementing LMD

There is growing evidence that an investment in LMD can have an impact on an organization's performance and productivity (Mabey and Ramirez, 2005), although this is unlikely to occur in a straightforward manner. In implementing LMD, there are some key issues to consider, such as:

• What is understood as leadership and management?
• How can leaders and managers be assessed in terms of their development?
• How do leaders and managers learn?
• What activities can be provided for LMD?
• How can LMD activities add value?

As we seek to answer these questions in what follows, keep in mind the dual aspects of the definitions considered earlier, in which the two perspectives of planned processes and recognized opportunities were presented.

Models of leaders and managers

As we have already indicated, there has been an ongoing search to find particular meanings for what leaders and managers are supposed to do and the behaviours they are required to perform as leaders and managers. The search continues to the present day, with new models of an 'excellent' leader or an 'effective' manager readily available. Some models are even presented in terms of being 'scientifically' valid and can be used to measure aspects of a person's personality or behaviour. Not all models can, however, claim scientific credentials.

reflective question

Write down the six most important behaviours that you would expect a good manager to demonstrate. Compare your response with those of three other people. How far do you agree and disagree with each other?

Suffice it to say that many models of leaders and managers have been presented. One distinction can, however, be made between models that are meant apply to all leaders and managers in all situations – referred to as *generic models* – and models that are developed for application in a specific organization – referred to as *organization-specific* models. For example, as part of their work for the CEML, Perren and Burgoyne (2002) presented a model of abilities for generic leaders and managers, shown in Figure 10.4.

Such frameworks are useful for assessing the needs of leaders and managers, and LMD activities can be stimulated by both the frameworks themselves and managers' needs. The precise meanings of each cluster of abilities such as 'Manage resources' still need to be determined, but the terms can be employed in all organizations. In contrast, organization-specific models use the meanings that are understood within an organization and are more specific to a particular context. In many organizations, models of leadership and management are expressed as competencies, which, as we considered in Chapter 8, are descriptions of the behaviours, attributes and skills that people need to perform work effectively, or the outputs to be achieved from such work that can be assessed against performance criteria.

Manage and lead people
- acknowledge and reward others
- assess and recognise people's potential
- build teams
- consult and collaborate
- deal with politics
- delegate work and responsibility
- develop people
- facilitate and chair meetings
- handle a diverse workforce
- know employment rules
- manage conflict situations
- manage level above
- motivate people
- possess patience and tolerate mistakes
- provide feedback
- recruit competent people
- support people
- trust people

Think strategically
- balance agendas
- challenge the status quo and the opposition
- develop industry knowledge
- develop networks
- focus on customer
- set goals
- spot opportunities
- think conceptually and use reflection
- think creatively
- think entrepreneurially
- think globally
- think markets
- think strategically
- think technologically

Lead direction and culture
- create good organisational communication
- create shared vision
- encourage creativity and flexibility
- handle change
- handle risk and ambiguity
- inspire people
- lead by example
- manage public relations
- plan small wins and reinforce

Manage self
- accept responsibility
- demonstrate dependability
- exude enthusiasm
- handle stress and health issues
- manage time
- possess adaptability and flexibility
- possess drive, passion and capacity to work hard
- possess personal ethics and values
- possess self-confidence
- possess spontaneity
- possess stamina and perseverance
- possess tough-mindedness
- provide good instincts and common sense
- strive for consistency of approach
- strive for emotional stability and be emotionally stable
- strive for self-awareness and development

Manage relationships
- bargain, sell and negotiate
- build empathy, relationships and trust
- create bearing and presence
- display assertiveness
- display humour
- listen to people
- present self and ideas

Excellence in management and leadership

Manage activities and quality
- attend to detail
- audit quality
- control and monitor activities
- develop knowledge of business
- develop systems and procedures
- establish priorities
- evaluate progress
- monitor, plan and control projects
- provide practical and technical competence
- solve problems

Manage information
- acquire information
- analyse information
- make plans
- manage accounts and finances
- manage budgets
- take decisions

Manage resources
- allocate resources
- marshal resources
- safeguard assets

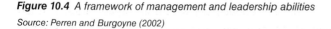

| KEY | ▓ Thinking abilities | ▒ People abilities | ░ Task abilities |

Figure 10.4 *A framework of management and leadership abilities*
Source: Perren and Burgoyne (2002)

For many years, there has been an interest in the behaviours of leaders and managers in relation to high performance. One of the first models dealing with this was presented in the USA by Boyatzis (1982); this consisted of five clusters of competencies, shown as

Figure 10.5. Boyatzis made it clear that competencies alone would not explain performance: it was also necessary to consider the environment and context in which performance took place, as well as the particular requirements of the work. Such limitations have not, however, prevented the development of a large number of competence frameworks for both generic and organization-specific purposes. An example of a generic leadership framework of competencies is presented by Bass and Avolio (2004), whose Multifactor Leadership Questionnaire allows a leader's style to be assessed against four leadership dimensions – transformational leadership, transactional leadership, non-transactional leadership and outcomes of leadership.

Goal and action cluster	Leadership cluster	Human resource cluster	Directing subordinates cluster	Focus on others cluster
• efficiency orientation • proactivity • diagnostic use of concepts	• self-confidence • use of oral presentations • logical thought • conceptualization	• use of socialized power • positive regard • managing group process • accurate self-assessment	• developing others • use of unilateral power • spontaneity	• self-control • perceptual objectivity • stamina and responsibility • concern with close relationships

Figure 10.5 *Boyatzis' competency clusters*
Source: Adapted from Boyatzis (1982)

Another generic model is concerned with defining a set of standards for leaders and managers. In the UK, such a model was developed in 1991 to fit into the Vocational Qualifications framework and, at the time, was said to 'reflect the best practices of management'. Since that time, the model has been revised several times, with the most recent revision in 2008. The model, known as the Management Standards, begins with what is agreed to be the 'key purpose' of management and leadership:

To … Provide direction, gain commitment, facilitate change and achieve results through the efficient, creative and responsible deployment of people and other resources.

Based on this definition of 'key purpose', six functional areas can be identified, as shown in Figure 10.6.

HRM web links WWW — You can find more details about the Management Standards at www.management-standards.org. In particular, check how each functional area is broken down into units of competence, elements of competence, and performance criteria for each element. Standards also underpin the qualifications offered by the Institute for Leadership and Management; for more details, go to www.i-l-m.com/learn-with-ilm/370.aspx.

Whereas generic models can be used by all leaders and managers in any context or to cover a group of professionals who might work in different contexts, organization-specific models are expressed in terms of what is understood to be meaningful in one particular context. They provide clarity for leaders and managers, aligned with business requirements. For example, within one organization in the UK there was a need for more focus on the future, with competencies including 'Delivering the vision' and 'Change and creativity'.

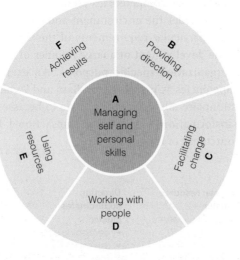

Figure 10.6 *Functional areas of management and leadership standards*
Source: *The Management Standards Centre (available via www.management-standards.org)*

Both generic and organization-specific models of competencies are popular and represent well-supported views of what leaders and managers need to learn. They are therefore the most common approach to assessing and developing leaders and managers, now becoming almost 'ubiquitous' (Bolden and Gosling, 2006, p. 147). The danger here is that the presentation of a framework of competencies can easily become confused with the reality of leading and managing. This warning has not, however, prevented the spread of the idea of competencies to include emotional intelligence (Goleman, 2006) and social and cultural competence (Boyatzis, 2008), despite how difficult these may be to put into practice.

HRM web links Check the Emotional Intelligence quiz at www.haygroup.com/leadershipandtalentondemand/demos/ei_quiz.aspx.

Visit www.palgrave.com.business/bratton5 to read an HRM in practice feature on the Clinical Leadership Competency Framework.

Ever since competencies for leaders and managers appeared, they have met with critical comments. Some of the criticism relates to the vague terms and the use of language that people find difficult to understand, along with a proliferation of paperwork that can shift attention away from the purpose of LMD (Gold et al., 2010b). Perhaps of more concern is the way in which competencies can falsely bring order to what is complex activity. As Lawler (2005) suggests, competencies can minimize the fluid and objective experience of leaders and managers. However, those who control the competence frameworks gain a degree of power over such experience, which can also result in pressure to control performance. As argued by Holmes (1995b), competencies can become the legitimate way to talk about performance, and this can force out alternative ways of talking. Indeed, it is argued that competencies can be use to define leadership and management performance, requiring leaders and managers to align themselves with a particular way of behaving (Salaman and Taylor, 2002).

Assessing the need for LMD

The various models and frameworks of leadership and management can be used to help leaders and managers determine their needs for LMD. This is not, however, an especially straightforward process since it requires an assessment of behaviour and/or performance, which, as we have seen in Chapter 8, requires judgements to be made. Assessment of needs is usually incorporated into a performance management system that allows discussions of performance in the context of the organization's objectives. For example, when the phone company O$_2$ was preparing for its launch in 2002, all senior managers were assessed against a competence framework, resulting in a personal report containing skills gaps against which LMD, supported by coaching, could be provided.

As we also indicated in Chapter 8, judgement in assessment involves feedback. Leaders and managers, like everyone else, will vary in their response to feedback on their performance. Research by Judge et al. (1997) pointed to the importance of key psychological factors such as self-esteem, self-efficacy, locus of control and neuroticism, which affect responses. Some leaders and managers thrive on feedback, and actively seek it, which can play a role in improving their performance. VandeWalle et al. (2000) showed the importance of a manager's learning-goal orientation in seeking feedback that is then used to develop new skills, although contextual factors such as leadership of the organization will play a role too.

reflective question Are you a feedback-seeker? Do you seek feedback to develop new skills, or do you use feedback used to avoid negative judgements?

As we have shown in previous chapters, assessment/development centres, appraisal and multisource feedback can be used to assess performance and determine HRD needs. For leaders and managers, multisource feedback can involve:

- Appraisal by staff – *upward appraisal*
- Appraisal by fellow managers – *peer appraisal*
- Appraisal by the person in charge – *top-down appraisal*
- Appraisal by the manager, and/or staff/peers – *180-degree appraisal*
- Appraisal by the manager, staff and peers – *360-degree appraisal*
- Appraisal by the manager, staff, peers, customers, suppliers and others who are in an interdependent relationship with the manager – *540-degree appraisal*.

Multisource feedback is a demanding approach to LMD, and since it involves feedback from different angles, it needs to be supported (Brutus and Derayeh, 2002), with the results used to set goals for action that are in turn supported by coaching (Luthans and Peterson, 2003). However, all assessments of leaders and managers involve self-appraisal, which inevitably carries face validity but is likely to be distorted by bias and disagreements with the views of others, as we showed in Chapter 8. Upward appraisal can complement self-appraisal and can be viewed positively if it is anonymous and provides constructive feedback (Antonioni, 1994). In addition, where leaders and managers rate themselves more highly than staff rate them, this is unlikely to lead to changes in their behaviour, although some might reduce their own ratings in response to lower staff ratings (Dierendonck et al., 2007). Peer appraisal is more likely to lead to LMD if negative evaluation can be avoided.

Leaders and managers are probably anxious to avoid disturbing relationships with each other, so will be less inclined to give formal feedback on performance; they may, however, do so informally (Peiperl, 2001). Peer appraisal is also likely to be accepted in professional environments such as schools and hospitals (Dupee et al., 2011).

Moving from upward and peer appraisal to 360-degree appraisal provides a more rounded view of performance but requires confidence and trust on the part of leaders and managers since the barrage of feedback received could potentially make the process deeply negative and demoralizing (Gold et al., 2010b). For such reasons, 360-degree appraisal schemes can become unworkable (Fletcher, 1998). The balance of such schemes has to be tilted toward development, and this needs to be made clear to leaders and managers in both words and actions in order to avoid confusion and possible cynicism. Whatever emerges from the process, goals need to be set, LMD undertaken and support provided if performance improvement is to be achieved (Smither et al., 2008). As with any approach to LMD, personal development plans that are meaningful to leaders and managers can be motivating and effective in creating a virtuous process of performance, review and learning (see McCall, 2010).

HRM web links   Go to www.businesslink.gov.uk/bdotg/action/pdp for an online tool to develop a personal development plan.

Approaches to learning in LMD

As in all HRD activities, learning is central, and in LMD the topic of learning has received significant attention from researchers over the last 40 years. One of the reasons for this is that LMD often requires an investment of resources that can easily be wasted if the way in which leaders and managers learn is not considered in the delivery of LMD activities. Gold et al. (2010b) highlight the learning processes that are effective for leaders and managers as one of three aspects that need to be considered for effectiveness in LMD. In addition to this, the meaning of effective behaviour for leaders and managers needs to be identified, and processes developed that will help leaders and managers to become effective.

These aspects of effectiveness in LMD can create difficulties where, for example, people other than the leaders or managers decide what leaders and managers need to learn. Generic or generalized skills or knowledge, for example, can result in problems of transfer of learning (Gilpin-Jackson and Bushe, 2007), or even worse, if leaders and managers see little value in undertaking LMD, referred to by Gold et al. (2010b, p. 115) as 'vicious learning'. To avoid such an effect, it is important to pay attention to what leaders and managers see as relevant in their roles as managers. To ensure this happens, we need to consider leaders and managers as adult learners, working with the principles set by Malcolm Knowles (1998), as follows:

- The learner is largely self-directed but has a conditioned expectation to want to be dependent and to be taught.
- The learner arrives with experience, which in effect means that, with many kinds of learning, adults are themselves a very rich resource for each other, and that there is a wide range of experience in any group.
- Adults are ready to learn when they have a need to perform better in some aspect of their lives.

- For the most part, adults do not learn for the sake of learning – they learn in order to be able to perform a task, solve a problem or live in a more satisfying way.
- Although adults will respond to some external motivators (for example, a better job or a salary increase), the more potent motivators are internal – self-esteem, recognition, greater self-confidence and self-actualization.

reflective question   Knowles referred to such principles of learning as 'andragogy', to contrast with child learning as 'pedagogy'. How much of your learning has been andragogic?

Both andragogy and pedagogy are found in approaches to LMD. Holman (2000) has provided a framework that shows how the approach of the learner is considered in LMD:

- *Academic liberalism* – the pursuit of objective knowledge as principles and theories, through access to expertise via books, seminars and so on.
- *Experiential liberalism* – experience is the source of learning that provides ideas for practice, through reflection on practice.
- *Experiential vocationalism* – profiles of skills and competencies, defined by organizations or an occupational area, which need to be learned for practice.
- *Experiential critical* – leaders and managers, through a questioning of assumptions that underpin their practice, find a degree of 'emancipation' from particular aspects of their lives at work that reflect dominant or powerful forces.

Within the framework, you might be able to identify some of the theories of learning that we considered in Chapter 9. For example, cognitive theories might be more prominent in situations where leaders and managers are required to learn ideas and knowledge presented to them, and behaviour theories when particular skills have to be put into practice and then reinforced through feedback. Experiential learning, especially the models presented by Kolb (1984) and Honey and Mumford (1996) in the UK, have been very influential in LMD. This relates partly to their value in enabling leaders and managers to assess their learning preferences and styles through questionnaires, and to the value of the learning cycle in helping with the design of LMD events.

As we indicated in Chapter 9, there has been some critique of the 'learning style questionnaire'. For example, Coffield et al. (2004) examined 71 learning style instruments and suggested two things: that only two could be recommended for use in higher education, and that nearly all the instruments lacked validation. Reynolds' (1997) main argument against the models is the decontextualization of learning and the prominence given to individuals, which reduces the complexity of a leader or manager's interaction within their context.

Nevertheless, it is still possible to make use of experiential learning in LMD, especially if the social and political features of organizational life can be incorporated (Reynolds, 2009). One approach is to use Kolb's learning cycle as a problem management cycle (Kolb, 1982), shown as Figure 10.7. This portrayal of the learning cycle is interesting and allows a leader or manager to understand how problems are currently managed against preferred approaches to learning. For example, where abstract conceptualization is preferred, the result might be a push for solving problems, maybe at the expense of analysing problems. A low preference for concrete experience could result in low attention to problem-setting, which aims to find and define problems. By combining the two cycles, leaders and managers can give conscious attention to learning and working on a task or problem at work, which we will consider below as forming part of *practice-based learning.*

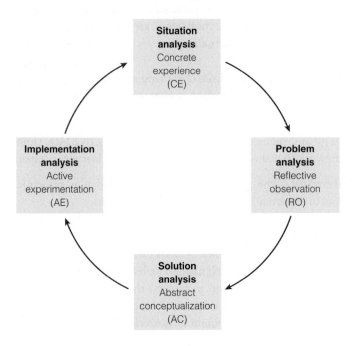

Figure 10.7 *Learning and problem management cycles*
Source: Adapted from Kolb (1982)

Learning in and from practice is connected to Lave and Wenger's (1991) situated learning theory. The key idea is that learning occurs through practice at work, often informally and incidentally. There is a link here to the idea of 'natural learning', as part of an everyday process (Stuart, 1984); this was also identified by Davies and Easterby-Smith (1984) as a crucial source of LMD, especially by dealing with problems and finding new ways of dealing with difficult situations. Situated learning provides a theory to explain these processes by showing how learning occurs within a 'community of practice' where newcomers or 'novices' learn to participate in the community by assisting and learning from more experienced members. Such newcomers remain on the 'periphery' of the community but learn to move from this position by observing others and copying them (Fox, 1997).

HRM web
links   **www**   Learn more about situated learning and its connection to Vygotsky's psychological theory at http://tip.psychology.org/lave.html.

Providing activities for LMD

There has never been a shortage of ideas for LMD. As the CEML (2002) report suggested, there is a large supply of opportunities, but it is 'mixed on quality' and 'confusing' (p. 4). Much of the provision is generic so is less likely to accommodate the specific circumstances of leaders, managers or their organizations. Furthermore, as Bolden (2005) points out, there tends to be an overemphasis on individual development rather than the development of leadership and management capacity. Following Day (2001), especially with reference to leadership development, there can be choice between a focus on individuals or on LMD activities that instead build networks and relationships and allow the sharing of ideas throughout an organization. This view allows more recognition of what Gronn (2008) refers to as hybrid configurations of leadership ranging between the individual as a solo leader to a collective and distributed understanding of leadership. This variation is shown as a dimension in Figure 10.8. This dimension of possible targets for LMD also presents a problem for those appointed as individual leaders because it suggests that influence and power can be exerted throughout an organization (Harris, 2008).

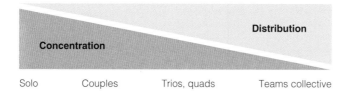

Figure 10.8 *Concentration and distribution in LMD*
Source: Ross et al. (2005), p. 131

HRM web links   Go to www.distributedleadership.org/DLS/Home.html for details of the Distributed Leadership Study in schools in Chicago.

Although the focus of LMD can vary, so too can the approach to LMD, as we have already indicated in Figure 10.1. Based on the two definitions of LMD presented, we can also see how this is supported by different theories of learning, with informal and unplanned learning often occurring. Working with a typology based on that suggested by Rodgers et al. (2003), which combines Figures 10.1 and 10.8, we propose considering some of the main types of LMD provision. The typology is shown as Figure 10.9. A quick search of Google will reveal the vast range of activities available for LMD, from the obvious training course in leadership skills or strategy to the use of drama and Shakespeare for learning. Here, we can only provide brief coverage of some of the key activities indicated by Figure 10.9.

Q1

Training events and courses

These are usually focused on individuals or small groups and teams. Training forms the basis of what most people understand as LMD (Suutari and Viitala, 2008). Events are often based on theories, models and ideas that are presented as 'best practice'. They are often delivered 'off-site', therefore away from the location of practice. We can also include in this section formally organized courses, which may lead to accreditation in the form of a qualification, such as an MBA. In either case, there is usually a clear understanding of the objectives or outcomes to be achieved or assessed. Of course, such a specification can create a gap between what individual leaders and managers *need* and what is *provided* (Antonacopoulou, 1999). Formal qualifications such as MBAs are considered to be too focused on skills of analysis at the expense of implementation (Mintzberg, 2004).

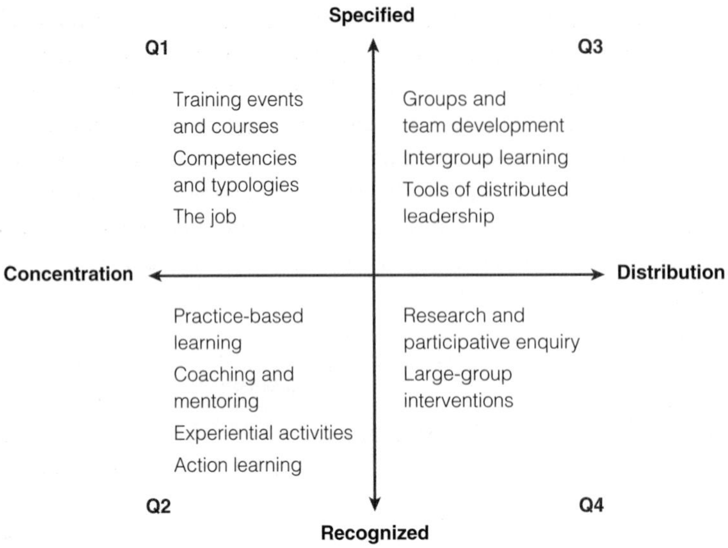

Specified

Q1

Training events
and courses

Competencies
and typologies

The job

Q3

Groups and
team development

Intergroup learning

Tools of distributed
leadership

Concentration ← → Distribution

Practice-based
learning

Coaching and
mentoring

Experiential activities

Action learning

Research and
participative enquiry

Large-group
interventions

Q2

Q4

Recognized

Figure 10.9 *A typology of LMD activities*

Source: Adapted from Rodgers et al. (2003)

Competencies and typologies

LMD events and activities are often based on models of behaviours, skills and so on. There are many such models, such as Belbin's team role inventory (Belbin, 1981) for developing management teams, which are often based on a questionnaire to allow diagnosis or even feedback from others.

reflective question   How do you feel about completing questionnaires to assess your management, leadership, group or team role preferences?

The job

Plans can be made for leaders and managers to learn about the roles they undertake. For example, any change in job or job content or even within the job can provide an opportunity for LMD, although this is not always grasped by leaders and managers. Other planned approaches can include secondment as part of a succession plan (Kur and Bunning, 2002).

Q2

Practice-based learning

While formal moves into and between jobs can provide sources for LMD, it is also clear that many leaders and managers learn informally, perhaps by accident or incidentally through experience and practice (Marsick and Watkins, 1990). Crucially, many opportunities go unnoticed, so leaders and managers need to make such learning more deliberate by reviewing and reflecting on the actions taken (Eraut, 2000b). Learning from work is now considered to be a crucial source of LMD, and recognizing the possibilities for this is seen as a way of questioning assumptions that underpin actions, allowing new thoughts and ideas to emerge (Raelin, 2004). Projects relating to specific tasks or problems are a way of making learning explicit, benefiting both participants and the organization; if accreditation can be gained, they also allow rigour and theoretical contribution to be considered (Rounce et al., 2007).

One of the difficulties of practice-based learning relates to the requirement for recognition, since many leaders and managers learn without being aware that they have learned (Kempster, 2009). For this reason, as suggested above, review and reflection are advocated as ways by which leaders and managers 'can engage more directly and effectively with their worlds' (Sadler-Smith, 2006, p. 185). Reviews and reflection allow a consideration of what has happened in key events, but also act to bring to the surface attitudes and perspectives on meaning, revealing the assumptions being made. Reflection and a subsequent analysis of events that reveals underlying assumptions can be threatening, but is also a way by which leaders and managers can become more critical of their practice and find new ways of taking action (Mezirow, 1990). There are links between practice-based learning and leaders and managers taking responsibility for their own development, usually referred to as self-development (Pedler et al., 2006), and action learning (see below).

reflective question How much time have you taken over the reflective questions in this book, and how beneficial have you found it to reflect on such questions?

Coaching and mentoring

Leaders and managers learn better when they receive the support of others in helping to identify opportunities for learning and reviewing what happened. Much of this is unplanned, and the main learning experience of many leaders and managers seems to be 'being thrown in at the deep end', along with watching others as role models (Watson and Harris, 1999, p. 107). To make learning more explicit, coaching and mentoring are identified as important. As we have already indicated in Chapter 9, coaching has seen significant growth in the UK, and many organizations are seeking to develop coaching cultures. In addition to coaching by line managers, there has for senior managers been the development of *executive coaching*, in which someone outside the organization provides the service. Research suggests that this leads to the formation of more specific goals, more effort to make improvements and better ratings from staff (Smither et al., 2003). Nor does gender seem to make a difference – that is, male managers can be coached by females and vice versa, with the same effect (Gray and Goregaokar, 2010).

HRM web links Learn more about executive coaching at www.execcoach.net and www. theexecutivecoachingforum.com.

Whereas coaching and executive coaching can help leaders and managers learn from everyday issues and their work, *mentoring* is seen as a process for the longer term. It is often informal and is concerned with careers, personal growth and all-round development (Mumford, 1993). Research has shown the success of mentoring for personal development and careers in such contexts as medicine (Sambunjak et al., 2006). However, mentoring does not always work, and it can even lead to negative experiences such as the mentor taking undue credit for the mentee's accomplishments (see Simon and Eby, 2003, for more problems). It is therefore important for both parties in a mentoring relationship to understand what they want. Both parties must be willing to learn (Megginson et al., 2006).

Experiential activities

Drawing on experiential learning theories, activities can be provided to stimulate the involvement of leaders and managers so they can reflect on aspects of their roles, including key features of organizational life that are often left unconsidered (Reynolds and Vince, 2007). Activities can be challenging, which also allows emotions to be revealed, in particular where problems that do not have clear outcomes are set. Such problems provide points of analogy for leaders and managers, who can then, through review and reflection, consider possibilities for work application. Experiential learning is often associated with outdoor management development, focusing on personal and team development. Outdoor management development requires a balance between task completion and the chance to discuss learning and application at work, making use of models such as Kolb's cycle, as suggested above, or Adair's (2005) action-centred leadership model, which considers task needs, individual needs and team needs.

HRM web links **www**
For stories by managers about outdoor management development, go to www.reviewing.co.uk/research/ple_sum.htm. Go to www.johnadair.co.uk for more details on action-centred leadership.

Experiential activities can be extended beyond outdoor management development to include the use of drama (Olivier and Verity, 2008), music, comedy and the arts generally. In addition, sports such as golf, rugby and even falconry have been used as source of experience for learning about leadership and management.

reflective question
Is there a link between learning to play golf and leading at work?

©istockphoto.com/Dirk Freder

Action learning

Leaders and managers form a small group or 'set' of between five and eight participants to work on difficult problems, agreeing to take action and then at subsequent meetings reviewing the learning from the actions taken. Pedler (2008) suggests the process of action learning can help individuals, teams and organizations to deal with change and innovation.

Reg Revans (1982) was the originator of action learning, developing the process in the UK during the 1950s. This was based on the assumption that leaders and managers learn best by working on real problems that are important to them as 'comrades in adversity' (Revans, 1982, p. 636). Participants agree to help each other through questions and discussion that enable possible actions to emerge. The attention to questions in action learning is given prominence in Revan's well-known learning equation of $L = P + Q$, where P is programmed knowledge or answers

Experiential activities such as falconry have been used to enable leaders and managers to learn more about their roles.

already available to deal with problems, and Q is the questioning insight that arises from questions and leads to actions when no one has an answer. By then taking action and reporting learning, leaders and managers can advance their identities (Anderson and Gold, 2009). Action has to be taken beyond the set, requiring interaction between the participant and the situation he or she is trying to influence, referred to by Revans as system gamma.

More recently, others have developed a more critical approach to action learning that makes more explicit the tensions and power dynamics arising from such interactions (Trehan and Pedler, 2009).

HRM web links Go to http://research.mbs.ac.uk/revans-academy for the Revans Academy of Action Learning. Action learning has become a significant LMD activity in Korea; go to http://kala.or.kr/e_home for details.

Q3

Groups, teams and community development

Research on distributed leadership shows the importance of working with groups and teams in order to create alignment between them (Leithwood et al., 2008). There are well-known models of group and team development, and leaders and managers can become more involved as team coaches, a role that helps teams to improve their performance through reflection and dialogue (Clutterbuck, 2007).

Intergroup learning

Groups and teams increasingly need to find ways of collaborating across boundaries, both within and between organizations. Since each group or team can be seen as a figuration of shared leadership, working across boundaries becomes an example of 'co-configuration' (Victor and Boynton, 1998, p. 195). This requires joint training in skills of debate and dialogue to bring to the surface differing values, cultures and disciplines (Tomlinson, 2003).

Tools of distributed leadership

As research into distributed leadership has continued, it has also become more possible to specify how to implement this approach in practice. Much of the research has appeared in schools and colleges, but it is also important for distributed leadership to be recognized in other contexts, especially where staff have greater discretion for making decisions with implications for joint working. It becomes essential to align work practices for change and performance improvement (Heck and Hallinger, 2010).

HRM web links Go to www.nationalcollege.org.uk/index/leadershiplibrary/leadingschools/developing-leadership-in-your-school/distributed-leadership/about-distributed-leadership.htm, where there is a link to resources and tools for distributed leadership.

Q4

Research and participative enquiry

Specified approaches to distributed leadership will only go so far since much of the influence that is exercised as leadership occurs in daily practice that is not easily seen or understood; the effects are likely to be emergent (Spillane et al., 2008). Action-oriented approaches to research and enquiry, to make improvements by involving many others, allow leaders and managers to learn about how influence can be exerted as leadership while seeking to align activities and intervene where necessary. One approach is found in appreciative enquiry (Reed, 2007), a process that reveals how good practice occurs and the values that inform practice. For example, in an inquiry completed at O_2, staff were asked what they liked about working at the company. This was then followed by 10 employees approaching 2000 staff informally to gather more data, which resulted in significant improvements in satisfaction with work, and leadership and management behaviour (Keers, 2007).

Large-group interventions

It is possible for leaders and managers to use large-group interventions to create a momentum for 'whole-systems change'. The outcomes are emergent, and the processes require the engagement and commitment of participants to generate ideas and take action. One approach, for example, is to use open space technology (Owen, 2008) – a conference in which the agenda is set by participants who respond to a key question that is important. The events at the conference emerge from the participants, as do the actions that are agreed.

HRM web links   You can find out a lot more about large-group intervention methods from Martin Leith's online guide at www.largescaleinterventions.com/documents/leiths_guide_to_lgis.pdf, which also covers future search and real-time strategic change. Another method is World Café; try www.theworldcafe.com.

Can LMD activities add value?

Given that significant resources can be devoted to LMD through the activities referred to above, it becomes crucial to show that value has been added. This is especially true in times when there is competition for resources, such as during a recession, and politics is bound to play a role (Kim and Cervero, 2007). Thorpe et al. (2009) argue that evaluation of LMD is straightforward to consider – find what works and what does not, learn the lessons, and then apply the lessons. However, as we have already shown in Chapter 9, evaluation is not an easy process, especially where there is a desire to show a return on investment – something of a holy grail in HRD (Russ-Eft and Preskill, 2005) – and, we would suggest, also when the value added can often be something of an 'act of faith'.

reflective question   Why do you think that evaluation of LMD might be difficult, and value added by LMD activities might be an 'act of faith'?

In Chapter 9, we presented mechanistic ideas of evaluation, usually connected to levels or stages of results, such as the Kirkpatrick (1998) model. This also has strong appeal in LMD, but, as Gold et al. (2010b) suggest, there are also difficulties with such models based on the fact that:

- LMD is more than just attending training courses and needs to include less formal activities
- Leaders and managers often complete and participate in a range of LMD activities, formally and informally, which occur in relation to each other
- Leaders and managers learn in different ways and differ in how they seek activities
- Leadership and management work takes place in different contexts, and this affects how far they can use ideas they learn as part of LMD and change their behaviour.

Issues such as these will impact on decisions relating to the purpose of evaluation of LMD and how techniques of evaluation can be used. Easterby-Smith (1994) suggests that there are four purposes of evaluation for LMD – proving, improving, learning and controlling – and that the choice of purpose is decided on grounds of expediency such as stakeholders' interests. Anderson's (2007) recent consideration of evaluation, for example, gives prominence to the needs of decision-makers so they can assess whether investment in learning is contributing to organizational performance. Thorpe et al. (2009) argue that evaluation of LMD has to be holistic to take account of wider system impacts, but also has to acknowledge the need for data to show evidence of value added. Figure 10.10 shows the key features of this view.

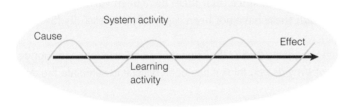

Figure 10.10 *Holistic evaluation*
Source: Thorpe et al. (2009), p. 180

As leaders and managers participate in a range of LMD events, whether formal or informal, the intentions of participants, perhaps as goals and plans, are both used as data and monitored as learning proceeds, perhaps through reviews with a coach or a group of peers. The effects of the system become apparent in terms of how leaders and managers can apply learning, and also in how they might be prevented from being applied due to the factors we identified in Chapter 9 as the learning climate or environment. Evaluation can help leaders and managers prepare to cope with difficulties of applying learning and may also require an understanding of their self-efficacy; this is a concept developed by developmental psychologist Albert Bandura (1977) and concerns people's belief that they can carry out behaviour to achieve certain outcomes. Tams (2008) shows the importance of considering how people think about their ability to perform a task, which could also cover judgements on task completions, what has happened in the past, the responses of others and dealing with negative feedback.

HRM web links 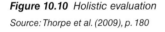 Try a general self-efficacy measurement at http://userpage.fu-berlin.de/~health/selfscal.htm.

Developing leaders and managers in small and medium-sized enterprises

Much of our discussion so far has made little distinction between leadership and management in different contexts and situations. For example, the size and purpose of the organization could be important and have implications for LMD, and we should not assume that the principles of LMD that have been developed for larger organizations can apply in smaller ones (Johnson, 1999).

This complication is important, especially when we consider that most business units in the UK and elsewhere are SMEs. Recent statistics (Department of Business, Innovation and Skills, 2010b) showed that SMEs accounted for 99.9 per cent of 4.8 million private sector enterprises and 60 per cent of all employment in the UK. We should also add that the vast majority of SMEs, some 4.6 million enterprises, have between zero and nine employees and are usually referred to as microenterprises. It should therefore be clear that SMEs as a whole – all enterprises up to 249 employees – must be recognized as sources of wealth and employment for the economy and therefore as a focus for development. For many years, little attention was given to SME development, and SMEs were considered to be marginal to the economy. Recognition of their contribution was, however, provided by the Bolton Report (1971), and since then there have been various efforts to stimulate SME development, although these have not been especially successfully (Storey, 2009).

reflective question David Storey suggests that SMEs cannot be used as a 'panacea' for economic development. Why do you think it has been difficult to stimulate the development of SMEs?

HRM web links Up-to-date figures on SMEs can be found at http://stats.berr.gov.uk/ed/sme.

With so many SMEs, it is not surprising that it becomes difficult to consider this sector as a homogenous entity. There is a wide variety of differences relating to ownership, turnover, market structure and so on. Although the number of employees is a common measure of size, there are bound to be differences between, for example, an engineering company with 100 employees and a firm of lawyers with 70, mostly qualified as solicitors or legal executives. Many SMEs are also owner-managed, possibly with a link to previous generations of family ownership. This can mean that the development or purpose of the organization is closely related to the interests and aspirations of the manager. It also makes the structure of the business more personalized rather than more objective and rationally organized (Gibb and Dyson, 1982). Furthermore, whereas many SME managers seek to grow their business through entrepreneurial behaviour, many others may prefer to give more attention to sustainability to ensure a satisfactory lifestyle (Rodgers, 2010).

LMD in SMEs

Although the terms 'leader' or 'leadership' are not especially recognized in SMEs (Kempster and Cope, 2010), it is important to understand that any learning is closely tied to the interests and aspirations of the managers. It is through the development of managers that a business can advance, but this is likely to occur informally rather than through recognized approaches to LMD (Fuller-Love, 2006). Furthermore, SMEs are less likely to respond to formal initiatives such as Investors in People and vocational qualifications (Matlay, 2004).

Garengo et al. (2005) have shown that managers in SMEs have difficulty finding time to undertake activities that do not relate to immediate concerns. They also use short-term measures of performance, which limit the focus of what they can do. Such measures, especially those which concern immediate revenues and costs, seldom allow time to escape the pressures of everyday business and create 'strategic space' for considering the long-term development of the business and the managers' own learning (Thorpe et al., 2009). This often means that most learning on the part of SME managers happens in the everyday by solving problems, making mistakes, copying others and so on (Beaver et al., 1998; Gibb, 1997). Furthermore, such working is seldom recognized by the managers *as learning*.

Informal learning that is part of working but is hardly recognized as such does have the advantage that is it is an everyday process (Billett, 2000) and therefore natural. If such learning can be recognized, there is potential that it can be enhanced for the benefit of not only the manager, but also the business. These considerations would suggest that the learning theories most suited to SMEs need to be based on Vygotsky's (1978) sociocultural theory, which can also be extended to include Lave and Wenger's (1991) situated learning theory within a community of practice (see Chapter 9). In particular, Vygotsky's concern with action, interaction with others, the achievement of goals and tool mediation allow importance to be placed on LMD practices that occur in the context of the business. This can also include the role of interaction with others in networks that help SME managers to overcome problems (Jones et al., 2010).

One aspect of Vygotsky's theory concerns the process of support from another, through interaction, to try new behaviours. Support needs to consider the manager's current situation in terms of desires and interest and what constitutes an acceptable level of movement from this position. Vygotksy referred to the area of movement as the zone of proximal development, and the value of this consideration is to understand how far a manager can be stretched in trying a new skill. Gold and Thorpe (2008) have shown how understanding LMD in an SME in terms of a manager's zone of proximal development can provide the basis for new capabilities appropriate to new circumstances.

reflective question   Based on these ideas of learning in SMEs, what provision would be most suitable for LMD in SMEs?

LMD provision for SMEs

There is a tendency in LMD in SMEs for provision to be presented ahead of requirement (CEML, 2002), that is for supply to precede demand, and this continues to be a problem, particularly in the UK. The problem is that many managers in SMEs do not have the time to engage in LMD and so avoid offers of provision, even if it is subsidized or offered free of charge. Such managers are considered 'hard to reach' or 'tough nuts to crack' (Devins and Gold, 2000). However, through a process of engagement, it becomes possible to stimulate the demand for LMD and this requires skills of conversation to establish relationships with managers so that they can consider the possibility of help through LMD. SME managers are likely to be suspicious of any approach that might waste their time or require excessive paperwork to gain funding for LMD, so engagement has to overcome such perceptions by relating to the manager's specific requirements (Gold and Thorpe, 2008).

If engagement can be achieved and needs for development articulated, perhaps through a development plan, a number of approaches to LMD can be presented. For example, managers in SMEs often find it useful to discuss problems and learn from other managers (Zhang and Hamilton, 2006). Some managers are prepared to join local networks, and recent evidence has suggested that such networks provide a way for SME managers to invest in their own skills and can also lead to them developing the skills of their staff. Therefore, from a policy perspective, such networks could become a way to support LMD for managers in SMEs (UK Commission for Employment and Skills, 2010). This process could become more formal by establishing action learning sets (Clark et al., 2006; Gibb, 2009) in which a degree of informality is preserved but learning is made more central through the support and challenge of other SME managers who also face problems.

HRM web links For stories about the use of action learning with managers of SMEs, visit www.sfbn-mandl.org.uk/alfl_success_stories.htm.

Visit www.palgrave.com.business/bratton5 to read an HRM in practice feature on Business Alliance in Leeds.

Another possibility for the provision of LMD is some degree of one-to-one support for any issue that is considered to be important and is preventing progress. Such support could be called coaching or mentoring, but in LMD in SMEs the labels are less important than the process of help and support (Devins and Gold, 2000). Both coaching and mentoring are now considered to be crucial processes to support development in SMEs, especially those which have the potential for high growth (Department of Business Innovation, and Skills, 2011). Furthermore, once a coach/mentor gains the confidence of managers, other possibilities can be introduced, such as master classes, seminars, workshops and e-learning resources, all of which can relate to particular requirements. Perhaps one of the most important findings from research in recent years is the concept of 'strategic space' referred to above, allowing managers time away from their day-to-day work so that they can consider new ideas.

The City of Sahali

Setting

The city of Sahali is located in the central interior of British Columbia. Like the rest of the Canadian public sector, the City Council is facing a wave of retirements as the working population ages and the first group of 'baby-boomers' begin to leave the workplace. This year, the largest group of employees in known history of the City gave notice to retire, with increasing numbers of retirements from the higher levels of management being predicted over the next 5 years. Even more problematic, there have been, as a result of recent retirements, major changes in the senior management team, including a new City Mayor, Chief Administrative Officer and Human Resources Director.

©istockphoto.com/Paul Velgos

The problem

There has been a clear need to develop these new leaders, and their future successors, in order to cope with ongoing internal and external demands and tax-payers' expectations. As a result, the City recently made the decision to hire a private consulting firm to develop and provide a customized leadership development training programme called Leading for Excellence. Although the City's unions were in support of the initiative, this was to require a large amount of staff time and financial resources. Based on the needs identified by the City's Human Resources Department, the training programme's curriculum focused on three main areas:

- Module I: Self-management – management roles, values, skills, and time and stress management (2 days)
- Module II: Management of the team – interpersonal communication, coaching and performance management (2 days)
- Module III: Management of the organization – understanding the organization and how to create more interdepartmental collaboration (2 days).

The fourth module, which lasted 1 day, focused on the integration of learning, motivation, learning from peers and creating successful daily habits.

Module participants were divided into departmental groups of either management or union supervisory staff. Their inclusion in the training programme was prompted by recognition of the important role that union supervisors play in implementing HR policies and providing leadership to staff on a daily basis, and a desire to promote unionized staff into management as vacancies became available. Managers or union supervisors attended the first three modules with their group, and joined their counterparts from the same department in the fourth module. The intent was to keep a department's managers and union supervisors apart for the first three modules in order to encourage open and honest discussion.

Shortly after the training programme had been completed, Jennifer Chang, the City's new Human Resources Director, scheduled a meeting with her staff. The first item on the agenda was to discuss how to justify the expenditure for training that was earmarked in the department's budget. At the meeting, Jennifer expressed a concern that evaluating the effectiveness of the training had not been considered when the programme had been designed or developed. Janna McCormick, a junior HR Advisor, was adamant that it was too late. She remarked, 'We don't have a baseline measure prior to the training to compare with changes after the programme was completed.'

Senior HR Advisor, Nathan Cole, disagreed, saying it was still possible. He suggested, 'We can determine whether desired behaviour has been brought back into the workplace by surveying those who work with the participants and who may observe changes in their behaviour. We can also see if there are any organizational changes resulting from this changed

358

behaviour.' Jennifer asked Nathan to submit a proposal on how such an evaluation could be undertaken so that it could be given to senior management staff at their next meeting.

Assignment

Working either alone or in a group, prepare a report drawing on this chapter and other researched material, addressing the following:

1 What challenges does the Human Resources Department face in identifying any changes resulting from the training?

2 What sources could the Human Resources Department draw upon to gather data to evaluate the training's organizational impact?

3 What recommendations would you make in regard to evaluating future leadership training programmes?

Note: This feature was written by Lori Rilkoff, HR Manager at City of Kamloops, BC, Canada, and Jeff Gold.

 Visit the companion website at www.palgrave.com/business/bratton5 for guidelines on writing reports.

summary

- There are differing meanings of leadership and management, both in theory and in practice. It is suggested that both leadership and management occur in practice, but in uncertain and difficult times, leaders tend to be given prominence.
- LMD can be defined as a planned and deliberate process, and also as a process of learning that emerges and has to be recognized.
- There have been concerns in the UK about the quality and quantity of leaders and managers, with recent efforts to show the link between good practice and performance.
- There are different purposes for LMD strategies, including sustaining the business by developing leaders and managers with the right skills, or advancing business by developing new models based on what leaders and managers learn.
- There is evidence that LMD works best when support is given to informal learning and there are perceptions by leaders and managers that learning and development are given priority.
- There are both generic and organization-specific models of leadership and management, expressed as skills, attributes or competencies. Models of leadership and management, especially competencies, have been subjected to critical comment.
- Models and frameworks of leadership and management can be used to help leaders and managers determine their needs for learning and development, but this is not a straightforward process since it requires an assessment of behaviour and/or performance. Many leaders and managers face multisource feedback.
- Leadership and management learning needs to be considered as an adult process that is largely self-directed. Experiential learning is a frequent approach to LMD, but 'natural learning' in a situation of practice is also important.
- There are many LMD activities that focus on individuals and more collective units. Activities can also be specified and pre-set, or recognized and emergent, requiring reflection and review. Generic or generalized skills or knowledge can result in problems with the transfer of learning.
- Evaluation of LMD is often an 'act of faith'. Evaluation needs to consider wider system impacts as well as the collection of data to show evidence of value added. Evaluation can also help leaders and managers prepare to cope with difficulties in applying learning.
- In SMEs, it is important to understand that any learning is closely tied to managers' interests and aspirations. It is through the development of managers that a business can advance, but this is likely to occur informally rather than through recognized approaches to LMD.

vocab checklist for ESL students

- ◀ andragogy (n)
- ◀ fast-track (v), fast-tracking (n)
- ◀ generic (adj)
- ◀ implement (v) (n), implementation (n)
- ◀ learning style (n)
- ◀ manage (v), manager (n), management (n), managerial (adj)
- ◀ mentor (v) (n), mentoring (n)
- ◀ multisource feedback (n)
- ◀ outdoor management development (n)

- ◀ reflect (v), reflection (n), reflective (adj)
- ◀ return on investment (n)
- ◀ transact (v), transaction (n), transactional (adj)
- ◀ transform (v), transformation (n), transformational (adj)
- ◀ typology (n)
- ◀ value-added (adj)
- ◀ zone of proximal development (n)

 Visit www.palgrave.com/business/bratton5 for a link to free definitions of these terms in the Macmillan Dictionary, as well as additional learning resources for ESL students.

review questions

1 How would LMD in an architect's firm differ from that in a financial services organization?

2 What strategy for LMD is needed during a recession?

3 Do competency frameworks provide the best way of assessing and developing leaders and managers?

4 360-degree feedback is 'scary' but 'powerful' for leaders and managers. Discuss.

5 How can reflection for leaders and managers be implemented?

6 How can evaluation of LMD become more than an 'act of faith'?

further reading to improve your mark

Reading these articles and chapters can help you gain a better understanding and potentially a higher grade for your HRM assignment.

- ◀ Much of the writing in LMD presents normative and functionalist views. However, if you would like to consider a variety of alternative understandings or discourses, try C. Mabey and T. Finch-Lees (2008) *Leadership and Management Development*. London: Sage.

- ◀ A more critical view requires a consideration of the political and cultural factors that affect LMD. A good consideration of such factors can be found in G. Salaman and J. Butler, J. (1990) Why managers won't learn. *Management Education and Development*, **21**(3): 183–91.

- ◀ How a programme for managers was disrupted and curtailed by senior managers is explained in H. Höpfl and F. Dawes (1995) 'A whole can of worms!': the contested frontiers of management development and learning. *Personnel Review*, **24**(6): 19–28.

- ◀ As a response to difficulties faced by leaders and managers, they are advised to become critically reflective thinkers. J. Gold, D. Holman and R. Thorpe (2002) The role of argument analysis and story telling in facilitating critical thinking. *Management Learning*, **33**(3): 371–88 shows how managers can analyse their claims within reflective story-telling logs to surface underlying assumptions that can then be critiqued. In addition, E. P. Antonacopoulou (2006) *Introducing Reflexive Critique into the Business Curriculum: Reflections on the Lessons Learned*. London: Advanced Institute of Management shows how critical thinking can be introduced to an MBA programme.

◀ Executive coaching has become a popular but expensive approach to helping leaders learn. An assessment of impact can found in F. Moen and E. Skaalvik (2009) The effect from executive coaching on performance psychology. *International Journal of Evidence Based Coaching and Mentoring*, **7**(2): 31–41.

◀ Women leaders and managers face significant obstacles, and this is considered critically by S. Mavin (2006) Venus envy: problematizing solidarity behaviour and queen bees. *Women in Management Review*, **21**(4): 264–76.

◀ Differing ideas on green management to ensure sustainable development for future generations are explored by A. Marcus and A. Fremeth (2009) Green management matters regardless. *Academy of Management Perspectives*, **23**(4): 17–26.

 Visit www.palgrave.com/business/bratton5 for lots of extra resources to help you get to grips with this chapter, including study tips, HRM skills development guides, summary lecture notes, and more.

part V

the employment relationship

chapter **11**

reward management

objectives

After studying this chapter, you should be able to:

1 Explain the key functions of reward management and evaluate the approach to reward that seeks to align pay systems with an organization's business strategy

2 Explain the manner and extent to which reward influences employees' attitudes and behaviour

3 Define and evaluate different reward systems and structures related to the job, person and performance

4 Describe and evaluate job evaluation as a method for developing a pay system

5 Explain how governments intervene in the pay determination process

6 Explain the paradoxes and tensions in pay systems in relation to managing the employment relationship

introduction

Reward is the centrepiece of the employment relationship as it underscores the fact that the relationship constitutes an economic exchange (Arrowsmith et al., 2010). That is, an employee engages in work-related physical and/or mental activities that benefit the employer in return for some payment or reward. The more prescriptive approaches to reward emphasize the challenges of integrating it into either 'best practice' or 'best fit' models. A controversial issue in reward management is the process and extent to which extrinsic rewards influence employees' attitudes such as commitment (or employee engagement) and behaviour, particularly performance (or productivity). The concept of the psychological contract suggests that any 'incongruence' of expectation concerning the rewards employees receive when they join the organization can lead to a perceived violation of the contract (see, for example, Rousseau and Ho, 2000).

Political ideology, the economy and social factors strongly influence the design of reward systems. The 'new pay agenda' (Heery, 2000), fuelled by neo-liberal ideology and the deregulation of labour markets, has dominated human resources (HR) practices and research for three decades. Reward systems are also shaped by the prevailing societal values and norms, which research suggests are strongly gendered (see, for example, Grimshaw and Rubery, 2010). In addition, pay stokes the incendiary debate over executive pay packages, the 'bonus culture', notions of 'fairness' and social inequality (see, for example, Dawber, 2010).

The main goal of this chapter is to provide a conceptual model for reviewing and understanding key developments in reward management in the UK. This model identifies major reward concepts and processes. The chapter considers the nature of rewards before examining the role of government in reward management. On a more theoretical level, we conclude with a critical analysis of the position of rewards in the prescriptive human resource management (HRM) model, which reveals tensions, contradictions and ethical concerns.

The nature of reward management

In the literature, the term 'compensation' is used as an alternative to 'reward' (Martocchio, 2011). Although both terms are problematic, we consider that the new vocabulary of 'reward management' best captures the 'new pay' paradigm in Britain, which focuses on the employee's market worth, flexibility and performance (Corby et al., 2009). Managers typically define reward as the package of monetary rewards (wages, salaries and benefits) an employee receives, but employees generally define it even more narrowly as just the wage or salary received from the employer for their work. The reward function does not operate in isolation and has major knock-on effects for other HR policies and practices (Martocchio, 2011). To understand the crucial role that reward plays in managing the employment relationship, it is necessary to conceptualize it in its broadest sense.

An organization can provide two broad types of reward: *extrinsic* and *intrinsic*. Extrinsic rewards satisfy an employee's basic needs for survival, security and recognition, and derive from factors associated with the job context. This includes financial payments, working conditions and managerial behaviour. Intrinsic rewards refer to psychological 'enjoyment' and the satisfaction of 'challenge' (Bratton et al., 2010), sometimes called 'psychic income', that a worker derives from her or his paid work. These rewards derive from factors inherent in the way in which the work is designed, that is, the job content (see Chapter 4). Consequently, for our purposes, we will define reward in the following terms:

[Reward refers to a package of monetary, non-monetary and psychological payments that an organization provides for its employees in exchange for a bundle of valued work-related behaviours.]

It is pay that has traditionally been the centrepiece of the reward system.

©istockphoto.com/alan gallyer

This definition draws attention to the multifaceted nature of the employment relationship. The employment contract is generally seen as one involving complex, multiple exchanges. Reward is primarily but not exclusively the exchange of pay and other tangible monetary benefits, and possibly other intangible benefits such as a positive emotion (Kessler, 2007). The mix of extrinsic and intrinsic rewards provided by the employer is termed its *reward system*. The monetary element can be divided into pay, consisting of the employee's wages or salary, and non-pay benefits, including, for example, medical insurance and a pension. Combined pay and non-pay benefits constitute the *payment system*, but it is pay that has traditionally been the centrepiece of the reward system. The management of rewards must meet numerous economic and behavioural objectives (Figure 11.1).

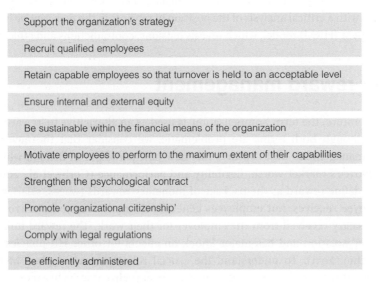

Support the organization's strategy

Recruit qualified employees

Retain capable employees so that turnover is held to an acceptable level

Ensure internal and external equity

Be sustainable within the financial means of the organization

Motivate employees to perform to the maximum extent of their capabilities

Strengthen the psychological contract

Promote 'organizational citizenship'

Comply with legal regulations

Be efficiently administered

Figure 11.1 *Objectives of the reward system*

A reward system consists of the integrated policies, processes, practices and administrative procedures for implementing the system within the framework of the HR strategy. A reward strategy comprises an organization's plan and actions pertaining to the mix and total amount of direct pay (for example, salary) and indirect monetary payments (benefits) paid to various categories of employee. Two key questions pertain to any pay strategy: 'How should monetary payments be paid?' and 'How much should be paid?' The optimal choice ultimately depends on the objectives of the reward system. At one extreme, reward may include direct pay only, and at the other extreme, no pay whatsoever. In terms of the latter, it is easy to think, 'Who works for nothing?', but many voluntary organizations, such as Oxfam, Save the Children and Médicins Sans Frontières rely upon unpaid volunteers.

More controversial perhaps, is unpaid work undertaken as part of the 'Big Society' project advocated by Britain's Prime Minister, David Cameron. The project envisions 'An army of community organizers [who] will recruit and encourage (unpaid) people on the ground to get stuck in to improving neighbourhoods' (Cameron, 2010). Detractors see the project as 'code for a retrenchment in public services' (Gray, 2010, p. 39). In concrete terms, a 'volunteerist' Big Society addresses the problem of delivering public services in an age of austerity by devolving them from waged employees to unpaid community volunteers (Grint and Holt, 2011; Renzetti, 2011), The point here is that the amount of pay (extrinsic) reward needed to hire people will vary depending upon the availability of other (intrinsic) rewards that the organization offers (Long, 2010).

To fully understand the conceptual analysis of the place of rewards within an HR strategy, it is first necessary to recall the nature of the employment relationship, discussed in Chapter 1. We noted there that the way in which workers are rewarded for their work, as part of the wage–effort exchange, is central to the employment relationship. All pay systems contain two elements that are in contradiction with each other:

- *Cooperation* between employee and employer or manager is an essential ingredient of the employment relationship if anything is to be produced. Cooperation is fostered through the logic of financial gain for the worker.
- *Conflict* is engendered through the logic that makes the 'buying' of labour the reward for one group and the cost for the other.

These two features of the employment contract mean that employees and those responsible for reward management have different objectives when it comes to monetary rewards. For most employees, the pay cheque is typically the major source of personal income and hence a critical determinant of an individual's purchasing power, standard of living and social well-being. Employees constantly seek to maximize their pay because of inflation and rising expectations. The organization, on the other hand, is interested in the absolute cost of the rewards because of its bearing on profitability or cost-effectiveness. The importance of this varies with the type of organization. The relative labour costs in a petroleum refinery, for example, are minimal, whereas in healthcare they are substantial.

This fundamental tension underpinning the exchange makes the employment relationship unstable, which, in the context of globalization, or at least the ruthless internationalization of the market economy, is constantly being adjusted. To increase market 'viability', for example, employers attempt to increase performance through pay incentives, or through pay cuts to reduce labour costs. Furthermore, the employees' contribution, or 'effort' itself, is 'a highly unstable phenomenon', and a payment system forms part of an array of managerial strategies to control the contribution or 'effort' of labour (Baldamus, 1961; Watson, 2008). Unsurprisingly therefore, it has been conceded that the satisfactory management of pay is an essential, although not sufficient, condition of the satisfactory management of people (Brown, 1989).

reflective
question Think about the reward system at your most recent job. Did it cause conflict or tension among the workforce? If so, why? What impact did the reward system have on your behaviour in the workplace? Do you believe that it was equitable? Share your experience with members of your class. Of the reward systems described by class members, which appear to generate most conflict, which appear to be most effective or most equitable, and why?

A model of reward management

To help us examine the complexities and principles underpinning the 'new pay agenda', we have developed a pay model that serves as both a framework for analysing reward management and a guide for the chapter (Figure 11.2). The model contains five basic building blocks:

- Strategy
- Reward objectives
- Reward options
- Reward techniques
- Reward competitiveness.

Our model shows first that reward management is linked to an organization's overarching strategic goals. *Strategy* focuses on those reward choices that support the organization's strategic goals. Going back to our discussion on corporate strategy (see Chapter 2), this means that each business strategy – and in this example we used Porter's (1980) typology of cost leadership and differentiation – should be supported by a different HR strategy, including a package of rewards. The underlying premise here is that the design of the reward system should flow from and seek to execute the organization's business strategy – the principle of *strategic pay*.

The *reward objectives* emphasize the linkage between a reward system and employees' attitudes and behaviours. There are three principal objectives that are desired by management – membership behaviour, commitment behaviour and task behaviour – and the reward system can play an essential role in eliciting all three (Long, 2010). Research on reward and attraction suggest that both collective and individual rewards may have positive connotations for potential applicants' 'cultural perceptions, as well as on income expectations' (Kuhn, 2009, p. 1646). Although the reward system is an important consideration when the organization is trying to attract talented people, there is, however, considerable disagreement over the extent to which reward is a determinant of employees' commitment and performance at work. Depending on the writer's perspective, the notion of commitment is discussed in terms of 'organizational citizenship behaviour' (Long, 2010) or 'compliance' and 'control of meaning', psychosocial factors subject to manipulation by management (Thompson and McHugh, 2009). The reward system aims to promote commitment behaviours, but employee commitment is an elusive construct.

As we have noted, the employment relationship is more than just an economic exchange – it embraces also a psychological relationship. The fashionable argument that reward can create, fulfil, change or violate the psychological contract (Rousseau and Ho, 2000) reflects the fact that pay lies at the heart of the employment relationship. So how

HRM in practice 11.1 ➡ 'Duvet days' or 'presenteeism'?

The annual absence and workplace health survey for 2010 from the Confederation of British Industry (CBI) claimed that employee absence cost the UK an estimated £17 billion in 2009, with an average rate of absence of 6.4 days per employee. However, only a third of employers believed that all sickness absence was genuine. Such data underpin the regular accusations in the media about 'sicknote Britain', that British workers are inclined to use sickness absence as an excuse to enjoy a 'duvet day' off work.

Much of this popular discourse fails to distinguish between absence and 'absenteeism': it is the latter term which indicates *voluntary* absence – a deliberate decision to stay away. Absence on its own can be seen as an unlooked-for response to illness or family emergency. In industrial sociology, voluntary absence was traditionally seen as one manifestation of industrial conflict – one of the ways in which an individual worker, with no means of collectively remedying an unfavourable work situation, could balance the wage–effort equation by temporarily absenting him- or herself.

However, as Taylor et al. (2010) have demonstrated, this interpretation may no longer be valid as government and management policies have become more stringent. Since the Statutory Sick Pay Act of 1994, management has been increasingly concerned with minimizing the cost of sickness absence, including sick pay, lost productivity and the cost of cover. The CBI literature emphasizes employee well-being policies and rehabilitation for those on long-term sick leave; case study research, however, indicates that company policies frequently use the 'Bradford factor' calculation, which penalizes multiple short-term sickness absences, and commonly feature return to work interviews following an illness. The result, argue Taylor et al., is that employees are now under pressure to attend work even if they are still ill, for fear of triggering disciplinary action.

©istockphoto.com/Ana Abejon

In their detailed analysis of absence statistics, Taylor et al. demonstrate a series of fallacies behind the popular view of sickness absence. What the CBI terms 'non-genuine' absence accounts for only 12 per cent of the total days lost due to absence, and there is no evidence that 'sickies' are linked to long weekends or major sporting events. Indeed, rates of sickness absence have decreased over the past decade. International comparisons are tricky because of different bases for measurement, but UK sickness absence does not seem to rank particularly highly; where higher, this may have more to do with the British culture of long working hours rather than any predisposition to take time off.

Both government and employer data sets indicate that absence is more likely to occur in larger organizations and among female workers (especially single mothers), the young (short-term absences), older workers (long-term absences) and manual compared with professional grades. When absence figures are adjusted for age, gender and size of the organization, the discrepancy between rates for the public and private sectors virtually disappears. In addition, public sector workers seem more likely to display 'presenteeism' – continuing to work when ill – because of factors such as job insecurity, the lack of cover when absent and a sense of responsibility to service users.

Although managerial desire to reduce voluntary absence is understandable, the question raised by research is whether draconian sickness absence policies can prove counterproductive. Return to work interviews, while ostensibly about helping the employee, may, if conducted in a disciplinary fashion, contribute to a low-trust culture, the opposite of the stated goals of HRM. In addition, workers who continue to work while ill have been shown to contribute to productivity losses greater than those produced by absenteeism.

Stop! Should sickness absence policies give a priority to employee well-being or to cost minimization?

Sources and further information For further information, see Taylor et al. (2010).

Note: This feature was written by Chris Baldry at the University of Stirling.

Visit the companion website at www.palgrave.com/business/bratton5 for a bonus HRM in practice feature on bargaining performance related-pay at Severn Trent Water.

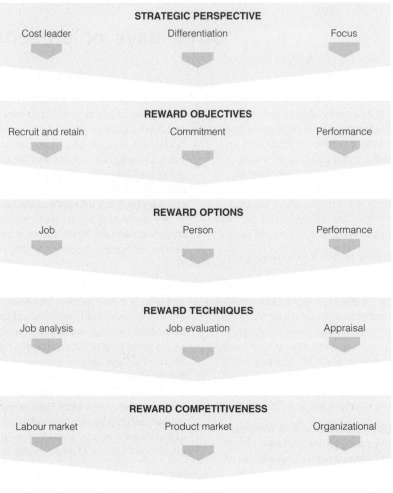

PAY SYSTEM

Figure 11.2 *A model for reward management*

does reward shape the psychological contract? According to Rousseau and Ho (2000), reward signals to workers the behaviour that the organization values. Second, the reward system promotes a particular form of employment relationship 'based on what the compensation system signals, in conjunction with other human resource practices, regarding the attachment between workers and the firm' (Rousseau and Ho, 2000, p. 305). The perceptual and idiosyncratic nature of psychological contracts means that what others have received from the organization does matter: an employee may perceive a breach of contract even if co-workers have received the same monetary reward.

Pay and work motivation

Can money change work behaviours? The differing answers to this question reflect a fundamental tension between economic theories and social psychological theories of motivation. Economics thinking emphasizes that pay incentives can achieve performance goals either by paying above the market rate or, additionally, by offering selective employees large bonuses to spur extra effort ('tournament theory'). In the banking sector before the recent economic crisis, for example, the bonus culture changed behaviour – as the Treasury Committee's report deftly observed, 'A culture of easy reward, illustrated by risky lending of credit and capital' (House of Commons, 2009).

Social psychology makes a very different set of assumptions; it emphasizes that all employees possess a common 'hierarchy of needs' (see, for example, Herzberg et al., 1959; Maslow, 1954) and also highlights the role of cognitive choices in determining work motivation. The most well-known 'process' theories include equity theory (Adams, 1965), expectancy theory (Vroom, 1964) and goal-setting theory (Locke, 1968). These 'process' theories emphasize the role of an employee's cognitive processes, for example the expectation that the assigned work is achievable, in determining her or his level of work behaviour. The sociological concept of the 'self' informs less-known theories that seek to explain and understand the mechanisms by which money may positively affect employee performance. The self-concept theory (Fairholm, 1996; Leonard et al., 1999) posits that an inner source of energy motivates 'non-calculative-based' behaviour in the workplace (Bratton et al., 2010, p. 208).

The primacy of money as a key motivator of worker behaviour is challenged by social psychological and sociological theories. Indeed, some motivation scholars argue that the application of monetary incentives can actually serve to destroy the intrinsic motivation that may otherwise exist in the workplace (Deci et al., 1999). Within the same theoretical genre, an alternative means of motivating worker behaviour is the use of non-cash employee recognition to identify and reinforce desired work behaviours (Long and Shields, 2010). As a motivational tool, non-cash recognition has become a widespread HR practice in Canadian and Australian companies, but although proponents of non-cash recognition urge managers to 'load on the praise', there is no evidence of a 'substitution effect' between non-cash rewards and cash rewards (Long and Shields, 2010, p. 1165).

As most prescriptive HRM/organizational behaviour texts affirm, understanding the nature of the relationship between pay and work behaviour is complex and requires, at the very least, a knowledge of both the individual and the context. From this perspective, it is not surprising to find disagreement over the strength or effectiveness of the reward–performance link. Locke et al. (1980, pp. 379–81) assert that 'Money is the crucial incentive because … it is related to all of man's needs.' In contrast, Pfeffer (1998, p. 112) argues, 'People do work for money – but they work even more for meaning in their lives.' Caruth and Handlogten (2001, p. 4) express the received wisdom of the pay–performance relationship thus:

A compensation system that rewards employees fairly according to efforts expended and results produced creates a motivating work environment.

In the debate on the reward–performance relationship, there is a tendency for prescriptive writers to view workers through a management lens, at the expense of analysing management per se – what managers do and how well they do it. Blinder's (1990, quoted by Kessler, 1995, p. 261) insightful conclusion is particularly helpful in understanding the complexity of the reward–performance relationship: 'Changing the way workers are treated may boost productivity more than changing the way they are paid.' Put another way, creating dignity *at* work (Bolton, 2007) may improve employee work performance more than changing the pay system can.

Reward options are shown in the third box of Figure 11.2. Typically, the design of reward systems hinge on three key contingencies: job, person and performance (Mahoney, 1989).

Payment systems have traditionally been founded on *job-based* pay systems – the level of pay (wage or fixed salary) is assigned to the jobs that employees perform. Jobs of similar value to the organization are assigned to the same pay grades: the higher the value of the job, the higher the pay grade. In establishing the internal value of its jobs, an organization has to consider both external and internal labour market equity (Kessler, 2007). Job-based payment systems are considered to reinforce bureaucratic hierarchical structures, encourage a 'command and control' style of management, and be less compatible with team-based work systems (Guthrie, 2008).

In the second contingency, *person-based* pay systems, pay is assigned to the breadth and/or depth of knowledge, formal qualifications, skills or competencies possessed by an individual employee. Under this type of pay regime, pay enhancements are awarded when employees are certified as having acquired additional knowledge, qualifications or skills that are of value to the organization. Research suggests that person-based pay systems are a 'better fit' with high-involvement work systems (Guthrie, 2008; Lawler, 2000).

Performance-based pay systems tie pay to employees' 'effort' or outputs. These outputs might derive from the contributions of the individual, a team or the collective, providing the basis for different types of pay system (Table 11.1). In broad terms, *individual* pay is paid directly to the individual employee and is based on a commitment of time, energy or a combination of both. *Team* or *group* pay systems have become more prevalent in Europe and North America with the popularity of self-managed teams. *Organizational* pay, such as profit-sharing, has also grown in popularity as a way of motivating employees and gaining employee commitment to customer-driven work cultures (Kersley et al., 2006). Profit-sharing is seen by managers as a way of increasing organizational performance through employee involvement in decision-making (Pendleton, 1997) and stronger employee identification with the business (Long, 2010).

Table 11.1 *Types of employee pay*

Type of reward	Examples	Type of behaviour
Individual rewards	Basic wage Overtime Piece rate Commission Bonuses Merit Paid leave Benefits	*Time*: maintaining work attendance *Energy*: performing tasks *Competence*: completing tasks without errors
Team rewards	Team bonuses Gain-sharing	*Cooperation*: with co-workers
Organizational rewards	Profit-sharing Share ownership Gain-sharing	Commitment to strategic goals

HRM web links   For information on team-based pay, go to http://www.101rewards.com. For more information on profit-related pay and share-ownership schemes in Britain, go to the 2004 Workplace Employee Relations Survey website at www.wers2004.info.

reflective
question

If you are an employer, paying employees only when the desired performance takes place sounds like 'common sense'. Can you think of any circumstances in which individual-based performance pay would be advantageous or disadvantageous for a particular organization?

There is considerable disagreement over the effects of pay on the performance of the individual or group. The argument involves fundamental issues of causality and the HR 'black box' problem (see Chapter 3). That said, different pay systems appear to encourage or reinforce different modes of behaviour. Piecework pay schemes, for example, encourage volume output, while profit-sharing schemes may foster employee loyalty and commitment (Kessler, 2007). Team-based reward systems may facilitate the sharing and creation of tacit knowledge and informal learning among team members and generate more organizational citizenship behaviours (Kim and Gong, 2009). These alternative pay systems, which are explained later in the chapter, offer managers a choice of pay contingencies that best fits their organization.

Reward techniques is the fourth component of our reward model. Job analysis and job evaluation highlight the importance attached to internal labour market equity, that is, the pay relationships between jobs within a single organization. Employees' work motivation is influenced by relative, not absolute, rewards, and they also compare their pay with that of comparable co-workers or 'referent others' (Corby et al., 2009, p. 12). These are typically their own co-workers (internal equity), but this may extend to those doing comparable jobs in other organizations (external equity).

Job analysis refers to the systematic process of collecting and evaluating information about the tasks, responsibilities and context of a specific job. The process informs decision-makers about the major tasks undertaken by the current employee in that role, the outcomes that are expected, and the job's relationships to other jobs in the organizational hierarchy. The basic premise underlying job analysis is that jobs are more likely to be described, differentiated and equitably evaluated if accurate information is available to decision-makers (Milkovitch et al., 2010). *Job evaluation* involves systematically comparing jobs in terms of their relative contributions to the organization's goals. Under job-based pay systems, job evaluation is the most common method used to establish the relative value of different jobs inside the organization, and we will examine job evaluation in more detail below.

The process of *performance appraisal* is used to evaluate employees' performance. From differing perspectives, the practice has come under much critical scrutiny in recent years. Research on work psychology shows that a reliance on 'subjective global ratings' for measuring employee performance is 'notoriously subject to individual supervisory biases and political decisions'; to eradicate the corrosive effects of politics, organizations need to design performance appraisal processes systematically and comprehensively (Kepes et al., 2009, p. 525). Critical scholars argue that the appraisal process is designed to make employees 'known' to managers (Townley, 1994); that it is 'inextricably linked to the contested terrain of control' (Newton and Findlay, 1996, p. 56) over labour input; and that it provides a 'disciplinary matrix' within which to communicate and reinforce organizational values and inculcate employee loyalty, commitment and dependency (Legge, 2005). As such, it is suggested that performance appraisal is an important management tool used to engineer 'shared meaning' and change organizational culture. We examined performance appraisal in Chapter 8.

Reward competitiveness is the fifth component of the model. It draws attention to the importance of external equity and, by implication, why the organization needs to pay 'competitive' labour market rates for a given occupation. So how should an organization position its pay relative to what others are paying? The organization has three options: to be a pay leader, to match the market rate or to lag behind what competitive organizations are paying. Kessler (2007, p. 167) argues that external equity is an 'organizational impera- tive' if it is going to 'win the talent war' of attracting and retaining talented people. Research suggests that reward sends 'signals' to prospective applicants regarding the organization's values and culture, and may affect the composition of the labour force in the form of talent and/or disposition (Guthrie, 2008). Empirical research on how reward influences recruit- ment and retention is, however, limited, and we have much to learn about how, why and when reward influences employees' attraction to an organization (Barber and Bretz, 2000). Reward competitiveness has typically been analysed in terms of three contingencies: labour market, product market and organizational.

Labour market

Managers may typically be heard saying, 'Our pay levels are based upon the market.' Understanding markets requires an analysis of the demand for and supply of labour. Neo- classical labour economists inform us that, in a perfectly 'free' labour market, the pay level of a particular occupation in a certain geographical area is determined by the interaction between the demand and supply of labour. Most markets, including labour, are not, however, free but have what economists call 'imperfections' on both the demand (for example, discrimination) and the supply (for example, membership of a professional body) side. The labour market provides a context for reward management and can set limits within which it operates.

Product market

The degree of competition between producers and the level of the demand for products or services are two key product market factors affecting the ability of the firm to change the prices of its products and services. If prices cannot be changed without negative effects on revenue, the ability of the organization to pay higher rates is constrained. The product market factors set the limits within which the pay level can be established.

Organizational

An organization's reward system is shaped by national employment institutions, national cultural values, labour legislation and the organization's own culture (Corby et al., 2009). In many Western industrialized countries, for example, the floor, or minimum, is set by minimum wage legislation. In addition, reflecting differing countries' cultural values and norms, there is a wide variation in the number of employee vacation days granted.

The figures in Table 11.2 are based on a global survey showing the combined total of the statutory minimum number of days of personal holiday allowance and public holidays. Most Canadian workers, for example, receive a minimum 10 days that employers must grant, plus another 9 days of statutory holidays. The US figure is based on 15 days of personal holiday, but many Americans receive fewer days off as there is no statutory minimum.

HRM **and** globalization

Building a hybrid at Samsung

Globalization is often portrayed as a kind of hydraulic system: ideas and practices from the developed West somehow 'flow' to other parts of the world. According to this model, those on the receiving end of this 'flow' welcome the new practices from the West assuming that their lives and their workplaces will improve as a consequence of new, and improved, ways of doing things.

Of course, the reality is exceptionally more complex than this, and to learn more about the challenges of exporting and importing HR practices, it is helpful to look closely at Samsung's approach to reward management. Widely recognized as a paradigm of success in the global economy, senior executives at Samsung knew that, to stay on top, they would have to think critically about the approaches to HR that had enabled them to succeed in the past. Company chairman Lee Kun-Hee anticipated that Koreans would not necessarily wholeheartedly welcome new management practices from the West. Strongly influenced by Japanese cultural values, Samsung placed considerable emphasis on Confucian respect for one's elders. However, given the choice between Western and Eastern approaches to reward management, Lee Kun-Hee refused to choose one over the other and instead opted for a hybrid approach blending the best of the West and the East.

But endorsing a hybrid ideal is one thing. Implementing it is another. What makes it particularly difficult to introduce new management practices is that the practices already in existence tend to be embedded. For example, promotion on the basis of seniority is part of a cluster of related social practices, and it is difficult to call into question one element of the cluster without calling into question the whole cluster. Obviously, this kind of fundamental cultural challenge would be unacceptable to most Koreans. One of the keys to Kun-Hee's success was his flexible 'trial and error'

approach. In some instances, Kun-Hee was willing to backtrack, to revert to the traditional Korean way when there was significant resistance to the Western way.

Stop! As a young HR graduate, you have an opportunity to spend a year in Korea interning at a company that produces various electronic devices. You are invited to participate in a group discussion in which the 'pros and cons' of seniority- versus merit-based approaches to reward and promotion will be debated. How can you state your pro-merit position without offending the seminar's Korean participants? Can respect for competence and respect for one's elders be reconciled? Are national cultures homogenous? Is it possible that Korea has an indigenous cultural tradition that challenges patriarchal authority and values merit as much as seniority?

Sources and further information: For further information, see Khanna et al. (2011). Sociologist Talcott Parsons offered a classic statement of the notion of clusters of traits in his discussion of pattern variables. To learn more about pattern variables, go to Wikipedia's entry for Parsons and check out the web links at the end of the entry.

Note: This feature was written by David MacLennan at Thompson Rivers University.

©bikeriderlondon/shutterstock.com

In Korea, Samsung takes a hybrid approach to reward management, blending a Western system based around merit with a traditional Eastern respect for seniority.

Table 11.2 Employee statutory minimum holiday entitlement, 2011

Top 5 countries	Days
Brazil	41
Lithuania	41
Finland	40
France	40
Russia	40
UK	**28**
Bottom 5 countries	
Hong Kong	26
Singapore	25
US	25
China	21
Canada	19

Source: Report on Business, The Globe and Mail, February 21, 2011, p. B1.

We will now examine in more detail research evidence on the 'strategic' approach to reward, examine job evaluation and explore changes in pay practices and legislation that have occurred in the UK in recent years.

HRM web links For the latest information on employment income in Britain, go to the National Statistics website at www.statistics.gov.uk. For information on employment income in North America, go to Statistics Canada's website at www.statcan.gc.ca; for the USA, go to the Bureau of Labour Statistics at www.bls.gov; for South Africa, try www.statssa.gov.za; and for Australia, see www.abs.gov.au. To obtain general information on reward management, go to www.worldatwork.org and www.hrreporter.com and click on 'Compensation'.

The strategic pay paradigm

Before the early 1980s, pay in about 80 per cent of UK workplaces was determined by collective bargaining between employers and trade unions representing employee groups. Collective bargaining or joint regulation was widely seen to provide a basis for regulating the fundamental parts of the pay–effort exchange, pay and working time (Brown, 2010). In the context of globalization and the ascendancy of neo-liberal economic thinking, there have emerged since the mid-1980s both competitive pressures and political opportunities to use pay as a tool to deliver strategic goals (Corby et al., 2009). As discussed in Chapter 2, corporate strategy is a definite pattern of behaviours that organizations enact to achieve their goals. As the hierarchy of established goals is translated from one level to the next, the reward for their satisfactory implementation constitutes critical elements of managerial control within the organization. A pay system is therefore a key instrument that can influence each step of the strategy process (Gerhart, 2000).

The 'new pay agenda', with its focus on aligning reward with corporate strategy, caught the *zeitgeist* (Corby et al., 2009): the espoused theory of strategic pay starts with corporate strategy and work design. It is predicated on the notion of 'strategic choice', which involves managers choosing a pay system that is judged through Weberian-style rational deliberation to be the most fitting (Trevor, 2009). Key to the rationalist argument is the assumption that the closer the alignment or 'fit' between the reward system and corporate strategy, the more effective the organization (see, for example, Gomez-Mejia and Balkin, 1992; Lawler, 1990, 1995; Mintzberg et al., 1998; Pfeffer, 1998). The notion of alignment is explained by Pfeffer (1998, p. 99):

The diagnostic framework is premised on the idea of alignment, that is, that an organization does specific things to manage the employment relationship and these practices need to be first, internally consistent or aligned with one another, and second, externally consistent, in the sense that the organization's procedures produce behaviours and competencies required for it to compete successfully given its chosen marketplace and way of differentiating itself in that marketplace.

Let us illustrate the 'strategic' approach to reward with an example involving two organizations with two different corporate strategies and completely different payment systems. Precision Engineering produces high-quality, customized machine tools for the aerospace industry. The manufacturing process is organized around self-managed work teams. Rather than pay an hourly wage rate to the skilled machine operators, which is the industry norm, the company pays a base salary, additional pay being awarded if the workers learn new skills. All employees receive an excellent benefits package and profit-sharing bonuses based on company profits. Labour costs at Precision Engineering are above the industry average. The culture at Precision Engineering encourages informal workplace learning, and, not surprisingly, labour turnover is extremely low.

Seafresh Foods, in contrast, operates a plant that produces fish fingers. The work is organized around a conveyor belt, with workers stationed along the assembly line performing each step in the process, from gutting the fish to packaging. The work requires little training and is monotonous. The process workers at Seafresh Foods are paid an hourly wage rate that is 10 per cent above the minimum wage, and there are no additional payments or benefits. Labour turnover exceeds 100 per cent a year.

reflective question

Think about the business strategy and reward systems at these two companies. How can Precision Engineering compete when it pays above the industry average? And how can Seafresh Foods survive with such a high turnover? Go back to Chapter 2 and look again at the 'integrative model'.

The strategic approach would suggest that, despite the two completely different payment systems at Precision Engineering and Seafresh Foods, both are effective (Long, 2010); each payment system is aligned with the firm's business strategy. Again, using Porter's (1980) typology – differentiation and cost leadership – Precision Engineering is following a differentiation competitive strategy, with a focus on high-quality machine tools. Owing to the complexity of the production process, high-skilled workers are given a considerable amount of autonomy. The reward system (base pay, benefits and pay-for-knowledge)

Performance-related pay

Finding fair and effective ways to pay employees is a big issue in both the private and the public sector. Many organizations use appraisal to drive pay decisions because they want to tie performance to pay, believing that this will motivate people to do their best at work and that it is a fair approach. Money is important to everyone who holds a job, and we all know people who have refused a job because the money is inadequate. However, while money is a powerful force, this does not mean that money alone motivates us every day to put forth our best efforts.

Consider this scenario (Coens and Jenkins, 2002). At 8 am one morning, your manager asks you to work on a project. You and your team work hard on it all day, coming up with some good ideas. Your manager says the next morning that he had handed you the wrong brief (so all your work on the project the previous day has been wasted). What would your reaction be? You would undoubtedly be upset. If work were *only* about money, such incidents might not be an issue. After all, you would be paid for the work you did and the time you spent working on the 'wrong' project. But you would undoubtedly not be happy with the news:

This is because, regardless of money, each of us has a deep desire to do meaningful work. After going through this scenario many people tell about how they took a pay loss to quit jobs that did not allow them to contribute, that seemed like a waste of their time and talent. All of this does not mean that money isn't a motivator. It does however begin to show us the depth of complexity in sorting pay, motivation and work. (Coens and Jenkins, 2002)

A recent UK government-commissioned review advocated a more elaborate system of performance-related pay (PRP) for senior civil servants. Under this system, the best would get the highest pay, and the worst would lose pay. Yet evidence shows that, for jobs which encourage teamwork and collaboration, individually based incentive pay does not work. Some research demonstrates that paying people for doing something actually reduces their other motivation for doing it. Sometimes 'it is hard for economists to understand that human nature is more complex than their models' (Layard, 2011).

However, PRP schemes bring certain problems with them, as evidenced by this quote (Layard, 2011):

The first is demoralisation. It is great to be recognised but hugely discouraging not to be. Research shows that assessment by different assessors often favours different workers – so it is not surprising that feelings of bitter injustice are common. Everyone knows that a system of promotion is essential, but annual performance related pay, which grades colleagues into classes, introduces unnecessary tension. Co-operation not competition should be the dominant ethos.

Stop! To what extent do you agree and disagree with the arguments for and against PRP? Consider other ways in which managers could encourage a highly motivated workforce. To what extent is meaningful work more or less important than incentive? What are the key components of meaningful work?

Sources and further information: See Coens and Jenkins (2002) and Layard (2011) for background to this feature. An interesting debate on PRP can be found in Leopold and Harris (2009), and for an example of PRP, read the article by Samantha Gee, KPMG's Head of Reward (Gee, 2008).

Note: This feature was written by Norma D'Annunzio-Green at Edinburgh Napier University.

 Visit the companion website at www.palgrave.com/business/bratton5 for a bonus HRM in practice feature on bargaining performance related-pay at Severn Trent Water.

therefore supports the 'high-commitment' HR strategy. Is this altruism or good business? Precision Engineering's reward system is good business for the following reasons:

- There is higher productivity resulting from increased functional flexibility.
- A highly skilled and flexible workforce reduces machine downtime and scrap rates.
- The use of self-managed work teams eliminates the amount paid to supervisors and quality control inspectors as team members undertake these tasks for themselves.
- Low turnover means that recruitment and training costs are reduced.

In contrast, Seafresh Foods depends for its survival on following a cost leadership strategy (in which low-cost production is essential). This competitive strategy requires low-skilled employees and little employee commitment because managers exert control using technology (the speed of the assembly line). Labour turnover is high, but unskilled workers are easy to recruit and training costs are low. At Seafresh Foods, the reward system (only a near-minimum wage) supports a 'traditional low-commitment' HR strategy. The business cases for paying a wage rate higher than the market rate, for egalitarian pay structures and for superior benefits to employees is illustrated by a study comparing Costco Wholesale Corporation to its fierce rival Sam's Club, a division of Walmart Stores. For Costco, a wage rate 42 per cent higher than the rate at Sam's Club 'translates into more efficiency' (Guthrie, 2008, p. 344).

The strategic approach has been used as an analytical tool for explaining developments and the factors influencing the choice of reward systems over the last two decades. The economic demands, for example deregulation, privatization and the need for flexibility and innovation, explain why managers chose a payment system based on a combination of individual performance, pay-for-knowledge and profit-sharing to meet the needs of a high-quality manufacturing strategy. As Corby and her colleagues (2009, p. 7) note, one major objective of the 'new pay' paradigm is the 'individualization of reward packages, an objective that fits with a wider social decline in collectivism'. The current literature on the 'new pay agenda' has emphasized the need for organizations to adopt 'good' reward practices that encourage a constellation of attitudes and behaviours meeting the perceived needs of 'post-Fordist' work systems, as illustrated in Table 11.3.

Table 11.3 *Alignment of business strategy, work design and reward practices*

Bureaucratic 'old' job-based pay model	Post-bureaucratic 'strategic' pay model
Base wage or salary	Variable pay
Based on cost of living and labour market	Based on organizational performance
Evenly distributed between employees	Differentiated
Correlated with seniority	Based on individual performance
Based on individual performance	Based on team (unit) and organizational performance
Viewed as a result of behaviour values	Used as a means of communicating

Source: Adapted from Pfeffer (1998)

In the 1990s, the strategic approach to pay framed the more prescriptive HRM writing on reward and influenced managers as they developed their policies. The basic premise of this approach is that the reward system should be aligned to the organization's business strategy. Pay can therefore be a strategic 'lever' to improve organizational performance. As two American reward theorists, Gomez-Mejia and Balkin, explain (1992, p. 4):

The emerging paradigm of the (pay) field is based on a strategic orientation where issues of internal equity and external equity are viewed as secondary to the firm's need to use pay as an essential integrating and signalling mechanism to achieve overarching business objectives.

A reward management survey by the Chartered Institute of Personnel and Development (CIPD; cited by Kessler, 2007, p. 162) reported that, among organizations with a reward strategy, almost 80 per cent indicated that 'supporting business goals' was their principal reward objective (p. 162). In 2010, it was reported that 35 per cent of UK organizations (729 respondents) responding to a CIPD survey had a written reward strategy (CIPD, 2010g). These findings appear to give support to Gomez-Mejia and Balkin's statement.

Variable payment schemes in UK workplaces

Empirical evidence appears to show a growing incidence of the new reward agenda in UK workplaces. A notable feature of the 2004 Workplace Employment Relations Survey (WERS) is the contraction in the number of UK workplaces where pay is set by collective bargaining, from an estimated 60 per cent in 1984 to just 26 per cent in 2004. Parallel with this is the growth of variable pay schemes (VPSs) in UK workplaces (Arrowsmith and Marginson, 2011). WERS data show that the most common form of variable reward is PRP schemes, also known as incentive pay schemes, which are present in 40 per cent of UK workplaces (Table 11.4). PRP systems were more prevalent in the private sector (44 per cent) compared with public sector workplaces (19 per cent). Recent survey data show marked differences in reward practices within sectors by size of organization, by occupation and between the private and public sectors (CIPD, 2006b, 2007b; Corby et al., 2009).

Comparative studies have found a growing use of incentive pay systems that link pay to performance, at both the individual and collective levels, in Britain, and even more so in France, where the institutional regulation of pay and employment relations is stronger (Marsden and Belfield, 2010). Research in banking in Austria, Norway, Spain and the UK has found an extensive use of VPSs in each case and noted that forms of VPS show distinct similarities: 'Seniority systems are in decline; merit pay is almost a universal phenomenon, and bonuses are increasingly important' (Arrowsmith et al., 2010, p. 2736).

In British retail banking, various forms of performance bonus are now 'strongly embedded' as tools to motivate and control employees through pay (Arrowsmith and Marginson, 2011). Various forms of share ownership (21 per cent) and profit-related pay schemes (30 per cent) were reported to be in use across the economy. Since 2001, there have been attempts to re-engineer the architecture of pay determination in the UK public sector. In so doing, there has been a movement from seniority-based progression to pay more explicitly determined by reference to performance results (Perkins and White, 2009). As a measure of the current trend in pay systems, a CIPD reward management survey found that 68 per cent of organizations reported individual performance to be the criterion they used to manage pay progression (CIPD, 2010g).

The interest in variable or contingency pay arrangements can best be understood in terms of the dominant political ideology before the 2008 economic implosion, particularly in North America and Britain. A concerted ideological campaign against automatic annual pay increases and 'artificially inflated' public sector pay by the UK's Thatcher government in the 1980s encouraged a movement towards linking pay to individual performance and

Table 11.4 *VPSs in UK workplaces, 2004*

Type of reward scheme	Percentage of workplaces
Performance-related pay	40
Profit-related payments	30
Employee share ownership payments	21

Source: Data from Kersley et al. (2006, pp. 189–92)

local labour markets (Curnow, 1986; Grimshaw and Rubery, 2010; Pendleton, 1997; Sisson and Storey, 2000). Under the 'new pay' paradigm, the reality for the vast majority of private sector employees in UK workplaces is that pay is set unilaterally by management. This raises concerns for both equity and organizational performance. In the absence of a joint regulation of pay, many individual employees will be unlikely to address problems of inequality and indignity at work. In addition, it is plausible that organizations will be disadvantaged from not hearing the collective employees' 'voice', which might contribute to innovations in the workplace or to successful implementation of HR practices and thence improved performance (Grimshaw and Rubery, 2010).

Criticism of the 'new pay agenda' has revolved around not only its ideological significance, but also the fact that the so-called 'strategic' paradigm has not been universally applied across UK workplaces (Corby et al., 2009; Kessler, 2007). Indeed, the WERS data set suggests that three out of five workplaces had *not* adopted PRP schemes for some employees. Despite the hype surrounding the 'strategic' approach to pay, various studies show that there is in practice evidence of 'rowing back', with workplaces establishing broad-banded pay structures to represent graded pay structures or 'even *de facto* traditional salary structures' (Corby et al., 2009, p. 7).

Kessler (2007) argues that the significance of internal equity has increased more recently in at least three different forms. The first relates to attempts by New Labour governments in the UK to regulate pay at the extremes of the labour market, by implication seeking to encourage organizations to narrow the gap between high- and low-income earners. Research shows that, despite the economic recession, the median total remuneration for top executives in Britain's FTSE 100 companies was almost £3 million in 2010, up 19 per cent from 2009 (Dawber, 2010). Pay inequality remains a legitimate concern for individuals and society, a concern magnified by pervasive media coverage of government bail-outs of some UK retail banks while the top ruling elite within banking sector pay themselves exorbitant salaries and bonus packages.

The second form relates to the pursuit of pay equality, particularly between women and men. Although the last 20 years have seen a slow convergence of the average pay for female and male employees, the gender pay gap in the UK is still obstinately wide 42 years after the passing of the 1970 Equal Pay Act. According to recent research, women in executive positions may have to wait another 98 years, until 2109, for parity in pay (Goodley, 2011). The reasons for the slow convergence of female and male pay are varied and complex, but critical labour market observers have emphasized that 'gender discrimination is strongly entrenched' in UK pay structures (Grimshaw and Rubery, 2010, p. 357).

Finally, related to the issue of 'fair' pay processes, there is an absence of transparency from companies on pay determination and banding. Evidence from surveys suggests that, when designing contingent pay systems, organizations rate the importance of their being 'equitable and consistent' and the ability to differentiate pay for performance well ahead of the principle of aligning pay with corporate strategy.

On the specific notion of strategic pay, the principle of 'fit' commonly cited in the strategic HRM literature is fraught with theoretical and practical difficulties. First, at the theoretical level, rational decision-making, which underpins the pay–strategy link, assumes that managers have perfect knowledge and the cognitive ability to organize and process all relevant information. In practice, decision-makers may not know whether a pay–strategy decision is 'optimal' because they have only imperfect knowledge and limited calculative ability (Trevor, 2009). Second, there is a mechanistic relationship between reward practices and organizational performance, a hypothesis that is based on the assumption that pay practices change employees' attitudes and behaviour in ways that advance organizational goals. This is somewhat at odds with the expanded multicausational approach, which privileges social relations and 'bundles' of HR practices as the key lever (see Chapter 3).

At the practical level, empirical support for strategic pay theory is limited. Kessler (2007) notes how survey data show that only a small proportion – 6 per cent – of organizations responding reported that their pay strategy was 'fully aligned' with their business strategy. Furthermore, the use of a pay-for-performance system to achieve corporate goals is not as straightforward as prescriptive HRM writers suggest. It is plagued by operational difficulties, especially in relation to objective-setting, performance measurement and pay determination. Finally, in practice, a pay system, as a social construct, is invariably subject to social and power pressures and, as such, is inevitably customized and subverted to meet context-specific demands. Recent literature suggests that 'theory is out of step with reality and may represent a largely unattainable ideal in practice' (Trevor, 2009, p. 36).

In reality, decision-makers are able to exercise a *degree* of strategic choice, and work design and organizational factors exert a 'substantial influence' on organizations' pay choices (Marsden and Belfield, 2010). This echoes other studies suggesting that new work systems, defined in terms of flexibility, quality and productivity, explained management's decision to favour 'simplified, aggregate forms of bonus over individual payment-by-results as part of a wider change agenda' (Arrowsmith and Marginson, 2010, p. 309). In the past three decades, there has been a trend towards individualism in reward management and the 'incentivization' of work. The 'new pay' paradigm focuses on paying employees for their individual contributions. Payment by results is widely presumed to entail negative consequences for the regulation of pay by trade unions, but collective bargaining can be reconfigured to embrace it alongside established conventions for negotiating increases in basic pay (Corby et al., 2009; Marginson, 2009). Operational constraints, particularly work systems that emphasize flexible working rather than flexible pay, place limits on the individualization of pay (see, for example, Arrowsmith and Marginson, 2010).

Job evaluation and internal equity

The traditional 'old pay' paradigm emphasized the importance of internal equity, which refers to comparisons between jobs or skill levels inside the organization. Lawler (1990, 1995), an advocate of the 'new pay agenda', notes that reward should not be job- but person-based, such that the position of employees within the pay structure is determined less by the formal job description and more by the skills and performance they bring to that job. Thus, job evaluation, the main technique used to determine the internal value of jobs, is a technique associated with old pay structures developed to meet the needs of bureaucratic Fordist-type organizations. The study by McNabb and Whitfield (2001), for example, notes that that job evaluation might inhibit the development of 'high-involvement' work systems. Not surprisingly, Lawler (1990) speaks strongly against traditional job evaluation and instead advocates 'skill-based pay' (see Heery, 2000). However, contrary to the reward principles proposed by Gomez-Mejia and Balkin (1992), internal equity is still, in the UK at least, a key consideration. Despite its reported death, job evaluation is 'alive and kicking in the public sector, driven in large part by concern about pay for work of equal value' (Corby et al., 2009, p. 8).

Job evaluation is a generic label for a variety of processes used to establish pay structures by systematically comparing jobs in terms of their relative contributions to the organization's overarching goals (Egan, 2004; Milkovitch et al., 2010). It can be defined as:

A systematic process designed to determine the relative worth of jobs within a single work organization.

The goal of job evaluation is to achieve internal equity by determining a hierarchy of jobs that is based on the relative contribution of each job to the organization. This hierarchy is then used to allocate rates of pay to jobs regardless of the employee working in that role. The importance of job evaluation to managers has increased because of equal pay legislation, which requires, either implicitly or explicitly, that gender-neutral job evaluation schemes be adopted and used to determine and compare the value of jobs within the organization.

Job evaluation is often misunderstood, so the following three characteristics of all formal job evaluation methods need to be emphasized:

- The technique is systematic rather than scientific, the process depending on a series of subjective judgements.
- The premise that job evaluation is based on the worth of the job rather than on the worth of the employee in that particular job is fundamental (Risher, 1978; Welbourne and Trevor, 2000).
- The validity of the job evaluation process, or how accurately the method assesses job worth, is suspect (Collins and Muchinsky, 1993).

Studies have suggested that formal job evaluation offers an opportunity for discretionary decision-making, with 'departmental power' thus affecting the outcome (Welbourne and Trevor, 2000). Formal job evaluation can be seen as important in generating a feeling of equity in the workplace (McNabb and Whitfield, 2001) and thus constitutes the foundation of pay equity (Conway, 1987). A political perspective on job evaluation also emphasizes the fact that job evaluation ratings are often gender-biased by, for example, giving a higher weighting to physical demands and continuous service, which tend to favour men, and by the gender linkage of job titles. In one study, for example, evaluators assigned significantly lower ratings to jobs with a female-stereotyped title, such as 'secretary – accounting', than to the same job with a more gender-neutral title, for example 'assistant – accounting' (McShane, 1990).

The job evaluation process itself comprises four steps:

1 Gathering the data
2 Selecting compensable factors
3 Evaluating the job
4 Assigning pay to the job.

Let's look at each of these in turn.

Gathering the job analysis data

Information must be collected via a method of job analysis, and validity should be a guiding principle in this first step. The job analyser must accurately capture all the job's content, as ambiguous, incomplete or inaccurate job descriptions can result in jobs being incorrectly evaluated.

Selecting compensable factors

Compensable factors are the factors the organization chooses to reward through differential pay. The most typical compensable factors are skill, effort, knowledge, responsibility and working conditions.

Evaluating the job

There are four fundamental methods of job evaluation:

- Ranking
- Job-grading
- Factor comparison
- The point method.

The latter is the most commonly used evaluation technique. For comparison purposes, we will provide brief descriptions of the other methods but will focus here on the point method.

In *ranking*, jobs are ordered from the least to the most valued in the organization, this rank order or hierarchy of jobs being based on a subjective evaluation of relative value. In a typical factory, we might finish up with the rank order shown in Table 11.5; in this example, the evaluators have agreed that the job of inspector is the most valued of the six jobs listed. Rates of pay will then reflect this simple hierarchy. This method has a number of advantages: it is simple, fast and inexpensive. The ranking method will be attractive for small organizations and for those with a limited number of jobs. Obvious disadvantages are that it is crude and entirely subjective; the results are therefore difficult to defend, and legal challenges might make the approach costly.

Table 11.5 *Typical job-ranking*

Job title	Rank
1. Forklift driver 2. Machinist 3. Inspector 4. Secretary 5. File clerk 6. Labourer	**Most valued** 1. Inspector 2. Machinist 3. Secretary 4. Forklift driver 5. Labourer 6. File clerk **Least valued**

Job-grading, or job classification, works by placing jobs in a hierarchy or series of job grades. It is decided in advance how many grades of pay will be created, the jobs falling into each grade being based on the degree to which the jobs possess a set of compensable factors. The lowest grade will be defined as containing those jobs that require little skill and are closely supervised. With each successive grade, skills, knowledge and responsibilities increase. Grade A will, for example, include jobs that require no previous experience, are under immediate supervision and need no independent judgement. Grade F, however, will contain jobs that require apprenticeship training under general supervision with some independent judgement. In our example in Table 9.5, the file clerk and the machinist might be slotted into grades A and F, respectively. The advantage of this method is that it is relatively simple, quick and inexpensive. A disadvantage is that complex jobs are difficult to fit into the system as a job may seem to have the characteristics of two or more grades.

Factor comparison evaluates jobs on the basis of a set of compensable factors. Internal jobs are compared with each other across several factors, such as skill, mental effort, responsibility, physical effort and working conditions. For each job, the compensable factors are ranked according to their relative importance in each job. Once each benchmark job has been ranked on each factor, the decision-maker allocates a monetary value to each factor. This is done by deciding how much of the pay rate for each benchmark job is associated with skill requirement, how much with mental effort and so on across all the compensable factors. The main disadvantage of this approach is that it is complex, and translating a factor comparison into actual pay rates is a cumbersome exercise. Because of its complexity, it is used less frequently than the other methods.

The *point method* is the most frequently used of the four techniques. Like the factor comparison method, the point method develops separate scales for each compensable factor in order to establish a hierarchy of jobs, but instead of using monetary values, points are assigned. Each job's relative value, and hence its location in the pay structure, is determined by adding up the points assigned to each compensable factor.

The exercise starts with the allocation of a range of points to each compensable factor. Any number between 1 and 100 points might be assigned to each factor. Next, each of the factors is given a weighting, which is an assessment of how important one factor is in relation to another. In the case of the machinist, for example, if skill is felt to be twice as important as working conditions, it is assigned twice as many points (20 versus 10). The results of the evaluation might look like those displayed in Table 11.6.

The point values allocated to each compensable factor are then added up across factors, allowing jobs to be placed in a hierarchy according to their total point value. In our example, this would mean that the machinist's wage rate would be twice that of the labourer. Such a differential might be unacceptable, but this difficulty can be overcome by tailoring the job evaluation scheme to the organization's pay policy and practical objectives.

The advantage of the point system is that it is relatively stable over time and, because of its comprehensiveness, is more acceptable to interested parties. Its shortcomings include a high administrative cost, which might be too high to justify its use in a small workplace. A variation of the point system is the widely used 'Hay plan', which employs a standard point matrix applicable across organizational and national boundaries. Decision-makers should, however, be aware that, as far as job evaluation is concerned, there is no perfect system because the process involves subjective judgement.

Table 11.6 Point system matrices

Job title	Factor					
	Skill	Mental effort	Responsibility	Physical effort	Working conditions	Total
Forklift driver	10	10	10	10	5	45
Machinist	20	15	17	8	10	70
Inspector	20	20	40	5	5	90
Secretary	20	20	35	5	5	85
File clerk	10	5	5	5	5	30
Labourer	5	2	2	17	9	35

Assigning pay to the job

The final outcome of the evaluation exercise is a hierarchy of jobs in terms of their relative value to the organization. Assigning pay to this hierarchy of jobs is referred to as 'pricing the pay structure', this practice requiring a policy decision on pay structure in the organization.

HRM web
links

www Go to www.statistics.gov.uk (UK New Earnings Survey), www.salariesreview.com, www.bls.gov, www.kpmg.com (KPMG), www.haygroup.com (Hay Management Consultants USA), www.abs.gov.au (Australia) and www.kelly.co.za (South Africa) for published pay surveys.

Establishing pay structure and levels

This section examines two aspects of pay structure: *pay dispersion* and the *basis of the pay level*. Pay structures can range from a relatively flat or 'egalitarian' pay distribution, with limited differences across levels and jobs or positions, to pay distributions that are 'hierarchical', displaying wide differences across levels and positions. Remuneration survey data appear to show a trend towards pay structures that are hierarchical and 'tournament-like' – high remuneration for those at the top of the pay structure to attract a talented pool of employees (Guthrie, 2008). In Britain, the chief executives of FTSE companies are paid 100 times the pay of their average employees (Fletcher, 2010; Wintour et al., 2010). In Canada, the ratio of CEO remuneration to average worker pay has gone from 45 to 1 in 1960 to more than 500 to 1 in 2010. Put another way, 99 per cent of Canadians working full time throughout 2010 earned an average of $45,344, but by 10.33 am on January 2, 2010, the top 1 per cent of Canadian CEOs had already been paid that amount. The evidence on pay dispersion effects is mixed. Although studies suggest that a more 'egalitarian' pay structure will enhance employee cooperation and satisfaction, it is argued that both excessively egalitarian and excessively hierarchical pay structures are 'likely to violate equity theory' (Guthrie, 2008, p. 355).

With respect to pay basis, under traditional job-based pay systems, the pay level for any job reflects its relative and absolute worth. A job's relative worth to the organization is determined by its ranking through the job evaluation process, whereas its absolute worth is influenced by what the labour market pays for similar jobs. In Britain, since the global recession, the issue of pay and the value we assign to it has become particularly divisive (Reeves, 2010).

Table 11.7 UK salaries for selective occupations and CEOs, 2010

Über-salary earners	Tom Albanese, Rio Tinto	£1.42 million
	Stephen Hester, RBS	£1.22 million
	Micheal Geoghegan, HSBC	£1.07 million
	Leslie Van De Walle, Rexam	£762,000
	Simon Wolfson, Next plc	£682,000
Over £40,000	GP	£78,366
	Pilot	£73,281
	MP	£64,766
	Police inspector	£53,937
	Train driver	£40,337
£30,000 – £40,000	Fire officer	£38,744
	Teacher	£34,861
	Coal miner	£37,943
	Midwife	£33,875
	Social worker	£30,422
£20,000 – £30,000	Nurse	£29,431
	Journalist	£29,384
	Plumber	£27,706
	Construction trades	£24,021
	Traffic warden	£20,827
Under £20,000	Secretarial	£19,072
	Care assistant	£16,180
	Sales assistant	£14,065
	Hairdresser	£12,402
	Waiter/waitress	£11,930

Source: Office for National Statistics (2010) and Dawber (2010)

reflective question

Thinking about the average UK wage in relation to the pay for selected occupations, what do the various pay scales suggest about the value we assign to jobs? What is a job worth? Is gender important in valuing jobs?

UK earnings statistics show that, in 2010, the median annual UK wage for full-time employees was £25,948 (or £27,976 for men and £22,828 for women). Ten per cent of full-time workers earned more than £51,168, while 10 per cent earned less than £14,352. The chief executives of FTSE 100 companies, on the other hand, have seen their remuneration quadrupled between 2000 and 2010, while share prices have declined, suggesting that there is a weak link between rewards, performance and shareholder value (Fletcher, 2010). The top five CEOs were paid an average salary of £1.03 million, excluding bonuses. Table 11.7 shows the value we assign to a range of occupations. To answer the question, 'How do organizations assign a pay rate?', most organizations rely on pay surveys of 'benchmark' jobs. The data from these are used to anchor the organization's pay scale, other jobs then being slotted in on the basis of their relative worth to the organization.

Determining the pay level often means combining the results of the job evaluation process (internal equity criteria) and market pay data (external competitiveness criteria) on a graph, as depicted in Figure 11.3. The horizontal axis depicts an internally consistent job structure based on job evaluation, each grade being made up of a number of jobs (A–O) within the organization. The jobs in each category are considered equal for pay purposes – they have about the same number of points. Each grade has its own pay range defining the lower and upper limits of pay for jobs in that grade, and all the jobs within the grade have the same range. Jobs in grade 1 (that is, jobs A, B and C), for example, have lower points and pay range than jobs in grade 2 (D, E and F). The actual minimum and maximum pay rates paid by the organization's competitors are established by survey data. Individual levels of pay within the range may reflect differences in performance or seniority. As depicted, organizations can structure their rate ranges to overlap a little with adjacent ranges so that an employee with experience or seniority might earn more than an entry-level person in the pay grade above.

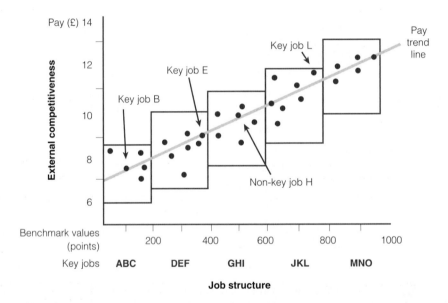

Figure 11.3 *The construction of a pay level*

Each dot on the graph in Figure 11.3 represents the intersection of the going pay rate (the vertical axis), as determined by the pay survey, and the point value (horizontal axis) for a particular benchmark job. Key jobs B, E and L are, for example, worth 100, 375 and 750 points respectively and are paid £7.50, £9.00, and £11.80 an hour. A pay trend line is drawn through the dots, as close to as many points as possible, using a statistical technique called the least squares method. The pay trend line serves as a reference line around which pay structures and rates are established for non-benchmark jobs in the organization.

There are two steps in this process. The first step is to locate the point value for the non-benchmark job on the horizontal axis; the second is to trace the line vertically to the pay trend line and then horizontally to the pay scale. The amount on the vertical axis is then the appropriate pay rate for the non-benchmark job. Non-benchmark job H is, for example, worth 500 points. By tracing a vertical line up to the pay trend line and then horizontally to the vertical pay scale in Figure 11.3, it can be seen that the appropriate pay rate for job H is £10.00 per hour. Thus, both market survey information and job evaluation translate the concepts of external competitiveness and internal equity into pay practices.

Once a pay trend line has been established, management has three choices: to *lead* the competition, to *match* what other organizations are paying or to *lag* behind what competitors are paying their employees – establishing a lag or lead policy by shifting the pay trend line down or up. The least-risk approach is to set the pay level to match that of the competition, although some organizations may set different pay policies for different categories of employee with different skill sets. The company could, for example, adopt a 'lead' policy for critical skills, such as computer design engineers, a 'match' policy for less critical skill sets and a 'lag' policy for jobs that could be easily filled in the local labour market. A variety of pay policies may thus exist within organizations. It was reported that, in 2010, 40 per cent of UK organizations (729 respondents) used market rates (and not a job evaluation database) to determine pay levels (CIPD, 2010g). Thus, although the pay levels within an organization often reflect external competitiveness and internal equity considerations, the decision on the final pay level – the organization's pay policy – will be determined by many factors, including competitive strategy, HR strategy, work and organizational design, and organizational values and norms.

The role of collective bargaining and government in determining pay

In most Western economies, collective bargaining and government drive changes in pay and working conditions. With respect to collective bargaining, it is the framework within which negotiations over pay and working time take place, either at the level of the workplace, at corporate level or at industry level, often involving employer organizations. In practice, the level at which collective bargaining occurs is closely linked to business structures and 'profit centres'. Collective bargaining over pay, working time and conditions is the *raison d'être* of trade unions. For much of the twentieth century and for much of the British workforce, negotiations on pay and employment conditions have been conducted within a framework of collective bargaining. Although collective bargaining is a very complex phenomenon depending on underlying cost structures, strategy and power (see Chapter 12), much of the focus is on bilateral negotiations between the employer and union(s) over the single facet of pay.

Bargaining power is defined as the ability to induce the other party to accept an agreement on one's own terms. The union's bargaining power depends on its ability to inflict costs on the employer while minimizing the costs of any action or stoppage to its members in terms of lost pay and lost jobs. The employer's bargaining power depends on its ability to minimize its costs from the union action while maximizing the cost of the collective action on the union membership. The outcome of pay negotiations will depend upon the parties' relative bargaining power, which in turn depends on complex economic factors such as the firm's product, the firm's technology and the laws governing the industrial relations system (Dau-Schmidt and Ellis, 2009).

In recent years, not unique to the UK, but unlike other member states in the European Union, this framework has collapsed for employees in the private sector (Brown, 2010). In workplaces with 25 or more employees, WERS survey data show that in only 26 per cent establishments did joint regulation determine pay (Kersley et al., 2006, p. 20). This means that pay arrangements for a vast majority of workers in the private sector fall outside the influence of collective bargaining. With only limited legal regulation of employment relations, it is management, not the trade unions, who determine pay for the vast majority of private sector employees, an important factor in explaining the UK's high incidence of low-paid work (Grimshaw and Rubery, 2010, p. 354).

In European member states and North America, government intervention, both directly and indirectly, affects employees' pay. In Britain, the *direct* effect on pay occurs through employment legislation and pay control plans (see Table 1.1 for an outline of the key legislation related to reward management). Given the importance of legal intervention in reward management, the next section reviews the important issues of pay equity and the regulation of low pay.

HRM web links

Go to the following websites to compare employment standards legislation relating to reward: www.hmso.gov.uk/acts.htm provides Acts of Parliament for the UK in full; and http://www.hrsdc.gc.ca/eng/labour/index.shtml gives information on Canadian employment standards and legislation. While there, click on the 'Employment law' button. Are there any major differences in the statutory provision provided by your jurisdiction and that of others?

Equal pay legislation

Gender discrimination in pay systems and practices is a reflection of society's values and norms. As Smith et al. (1982, quoted in Wedderburn, 1986, p. 447) note, 'discriminatory employment practices are a manifestation of prejudicial patterns of behaviour in society generally'. In the new millennium, gender discrimination remains 'strongly entrenched' in UK pay practices (Grimshaw and Rubery, 2010, p. 357).

The gender pay gap is also evident in Australia (Eveline and Todd, 2009) and in the US labour market. For example, in 2011 Walmart Stores Inc., the world's largest retailer, faced a lawsuit alleging that the company 'systematically paid female store workers less than men with similar or less experience and provided them fewer opportunities for promotion' (Zimmerman and Kendall, 2011, p. B10). According to the US Supreme Court brief, the plaintiffs contended that their experiences at Walmart reflected a corporate culture 'rife with gender stereotypes. One long-time Walmart employee said she was told by her manager that her male co-worker received a large pay increase 'because [he] had a family to support'. The US Equal Employment Opportunity Commission supported the plaintiffs' case, but in June 2011, the US Supreme court rejected the case, ruling that the claim

©Gina Sanders /Shutterstock.com

Gender discrimination in pay systems and practices is a reflection of society's values and norms.

against Walmart on behalf of as many as 1.6 million women failed to meet the standard for class action cases (Rushe, 2011).

Pay equity is important to all workers, and thus has implications for satisfaction with the level of pay (Brown, 2001). The concept of pay equity is in conflict with classical economic thinking that pay should be dictated by the forces of the supply and demand of labour (Corby et al., 2009). Equal pay legislation has existed in the UK for over three decades, but its origins can be traced back to 1919 when the International Labour Organization made the concept of equal pay for work of equal value one of its founding principles. Then, in 1951, the International Labour Organization passed Convention 100: 'Each member shall ... ensure the application to all workers of the principle of equal remuneration for men and women workers for work of equal value.'

In 1972, the UK became bound to Article 19 of the EEC's Treaty of Rome, which stated that 'Each member state shall ... maintain the application of the principle that men and women should receive equal pay for equal work.' The Equal Pay Act 1970 inserts into contracts of employment an implied term, the 'equality clause'. This enforces equal terms in the contract of employment for women in the same employment, requiring the elimination of less favourable terms where men and women are employed on similar work and where a job evaluation assessor has rated the work as equivalent in the same employment.

HRM web
links   www   The campaign for equal pay for women was dramatized in the 2010 film, *Made in Dagenham*, directed by Nigel Cole and starring Rita O'Grady. For a preview of the film go to: http://www.guardian.co.uk/film/video/2010/sep/14/made-in-dagenham-clip.

Despite the existence of equal pay legislation in the UK since 1975, the income disparity between men and women is still widely acknowledged. In Britain, in what has been called the 'lost decade' from 1992 to 2002, women's average relative pay improved marginally, from 70.5 per cent to 72 per cent (Grimshaw and Rubery, 2010). The last decade, however, has witnessed a narrowing of the gender pay gap. Relative to full-time male employees, pay for all female employees increased from 78 per cent in 2009 to 80.2 per cent in 2010, the largest movement in the gender pay gap since 1997 (Office for National Statistics, 2011b). The gender–pay dynamics that produce the pay gap are complex and are, as indicated, rooted in societal and organizational conditions and values. In the workplace, there is the feature of a 'masculine logic' (Fletcher, 1999) of effectiveness operating that leads to the undervaluing of many jobs, both full time and part time, that are associated with female labour.

Another related feature causing pay inequality, discussed earlier in this chapter, is gender bias in job evaluation. Finally, pay inequality is shaped by the degree of occupational sex segregation, that is, the gap between the types of job performed by men and those performed by women, which is acknowledged to be an important source of gender discrimination in pay practices (see, for example, Grimshaw and Rubery, 2010; Guy and Newman, 2004). Studies suggest that the percentage of skilled women employed in an occupation is negatively associated with level of pay. Working in an all-male workplace in the private sector reduces pay by 6 per cent, compared with a penalty of 7 per cent in an all-female workplace (Forth and Millward, 2000). 'In sum, being a woman has a negative effect on income', conclude Gattiker and Cohen (1997, p. 523). One labour lawyer has suggested that pay equity will be secured 'only when its justice is adequately understood and practised by men' (Wedderburn, 1986, p. 503).

HRM web
links
Go to the following websites to compare men's and women's pay levels:
www.statistics.gov.uk, www.ilo.org, www.clc.ca, www.tom.quack.net/wagegap.html,
www.statssa.gov.za and www.abs.gov.au. How does pay for women compare with
that for men in your jurisdiction?

In 1982, the European Court held that the UK's Equal Pay Act did not comply with Article 119 of the Treaty of Rome because equal pay was available for work of equal value only when the employer had chosen to conduct a job evaluation study, which a woman could in fact compel her employer to do. Consequently, the Equal Pay Act was amended by the 1983 Equal Pay (Amendment) Regulations. This means that even where there is no 'like work' or non-discriminatory job evaluation, the equality clause entitles a woman to conditions corresponding to those of a man if her work is of 'equal value'. The new Regulations were first tested in the case of *Hayward* v. *Cammell Laird Shipbuilders Ltd* [1987], in which a cook – supported by her trade union and the Equal Opportunities Commission – established her work as being of equal value to that of men working in the shipyard as insulation engineers, painters and joiners. The concept of equal value acknowledges that sex segregation persists in the workplace and that the concomitant undervaluation of 'women's' work is primarily responsible for pay inequality (Conway, 1987). The European Commission further expanded the provision for equal opportunities with the Fourth Medium-Term Community Action Programme on Equal Opportunities, which came into operation on 1 January 1996 (see Singh, 1997).

Regulation of low pay

From 1997, one of New Labour's goals was to address the issue of low-wage work through the introduction in 1999 of a statutory national minimum wage. Between April 1999 and October 2010, the national minimum wage for workers aged 22 years and older increased by 64.7 per cent, from £3.60 to £5.93 (Low Pay Commission, 2011). In the UK, evidence suggests that there are problems of enforcement and of non-compliance with respect to migrant workers in the informal sectors of the economy (Colling, 2010). Pay for workers at the bottom end of the labour market has undoubtedly increased in *absolute* terms, although their *relative* position has barely improved (Colling and Terry, 2010). Over the last two decades, the nature and scope of legal regulation has shifted decisively, going to the crux of the employment relationship. In particular, New Labour's National Minimum Wage Act has extended legal regulation into payment systems. It is now possible to argue that the protection of low-wage employees increasingly relies on legal rights rather than collective bargaining (Dickens and Hall, 2010).

reflective
question
It has been pointed out by some that minimum wage regulations increase the cost of doing business and cause unemployment. What do you think of this argument? Go to www.fraserinstitute.ca and www.clc-ctc.ca for contrasting views on this issue.

Even in those countries which give official support to the notion of 'multiculturalism', employment equity laws in the private sector have failed to deal with low pay resulting from discrimination against visible minorities. It is evident that the 18–24-year-old children of visible minority immigrant parents earn less than their similarly qualified white counterparts. The reasons for this are always complex, but part of it may be that the social networks they inherit from their parents are less likely to lead to 'good', high-paying jobs. In addition, part of the explanation may be plain discrimination. For example, a recent study found that job applicants with English-sounding names were 40 per cent more likely to get a job interview than those with identical CVs and a foreign-sounding name (Friesen, 2011).

reflective question What do you think of this argument? Are high-paying jobs equally accessible by white and visible minorities in your country? Go to http://www.hrmguide.net/canada/diversity/non-anglo.htm and read the study on discrimination in recruitment practices.

Government policies can also directly affect reward management by introducing pay control programmes, which typically aim to maintain low inflation by limiting the size of pay increases. Pay controls, popular in the 1970s, can vary in the broadness of their application and in the stringency of the standard applied. Broadness of application can include all employees, public and private, or focus on one particular group, for example the government's own employees. The standard for allowable pay increases can range from zero to amounts equal to some change in the consumer price index or to a measure of labour productivity. Numerous governments have used a tight control of public sector pay to influence pay trends in their economies. In the 1980s, Britain's Conservative government had an approach to pay-setting in the public sector that was summarised by Norman Lamont, then chief secretary to the Treasury, when he said that the government had used a 'combination of pressures' to 'reproduce the discipline which markets exert in the private sector' (Labour Research Department, 1991).

Finally, the state is involved in developing economic policies that impact *indirectly* upon the pay-setting process. Visible trade union activity on pay equality issues has been part of a wider public social inequality discourse, and it is arguable that legal strategies pursued by Conservative and Labour governments that restrict the right to free collective bargaining indirectly influence pay-setting. Government actions affect both the demand and the supply of labour, and consequently pay levels. Legislation can restrict the supply of labour in an occupation: a statute setting minimum age limits would, for example, restrict the supply of young people. Government action can also affect the demand for labour. It is a major employer and therefore a dominant force in determining pay levels in and beyond the public sector. In the domain of fiscal and monetary policies, significant changes in government expenditure can impact overall consumer demand and the labour market, and thence greatly influence pay determination in both public and private sectors of employment.

Tension and paradox

Let us finish our discussion of reward management by examining some of the tensions and contradictions inherent in pay systems, as well as some ethical issues. At both practical and theoretical levels, reward management has an interlocking set of tensions and paradoxes. For employers, reward is a cost, but for employees, it is typically their only source of income. Each party attempts to secure a pay outcome that, from their position, is more satisfactory. Thus, conflict is structured into the management of pay. Furthermore, pay is subject to contradiction or 'strategic tension', shaped and negotiated through social and power relations rather than straightforward 'rational' processes (Boxall et al., 2008).

In addition to this, reward exhibits the 'overarching tension' between neo-classical economic theories and social psychological theories with regard to the management conundrum of employee motivation (Corby et al., 2009). Economists argue that pay incentives can motivate workers; work psychologists and sociologists argue that workers' needs and social norms have a major influence on work motivation. This tension is documented in workplace research reporting that individually based pay-for-performance schemes can undermine work team effectiveness, and that team-based pay schemes are also imbued with the 'free-rider' problem (Guthrie, 2008). The goal of flexibility obtained through a pay-for-knowledge system might also not be achieved for economic reasons, especially if the high cost of paying for additional skills, which is not directly relevant to increasing productivity, leads to a 'capping' of skill or knowledge acquisition.

The objectives of the 'new pay agenda' are identified in normative models of HRM, including employee commitment and functional flexibility. Managers' attempts to foster worker commitment through variable or contingency pay arrangements might, however, be undermined if pay to superior performers could not be made because of the company's poor financial performance. Disappointment resulting from unfulfilled expectations might be a source of dissatisfaction with the organization, leading to a breach of the psychological contract rather than increased commitment. We should note Beer's et al. (1984) and Pfeffer's (1998) argument that PRP creates tensions that can undermine workers' 'intrinsic motivation'. Furthermore, PRP is prone to the 'twin vices of subjectivity and inconsistency' (Kessler, 1994) and might become discredited in the eyes of subordinates because of perceived 'procedural injustices' caused by subjective and inconsistent appraisals by managers. The literature would suggest that if this occurred, the psychological contract would be breached and employee commitment weakened.

Heery's (2000) criticism of the 'new pay' paradigm is based on its 'ethical deficiencies'. He argues that ethicists should be concerned about new pay practices for two reasons. First, increased employee risk and diminished collective representation are present in reward systems. The trend towards variable pay represents a dramatic growth in 'pay-at-risk' for employees, a characteristic of other 'innovative' management practices such as outsourcing. Employee risk increases as a larger proportion of pay is contingent on individual, team or organizational performance. The link between pay and working time, for instance, which offers more predictable earnings for employees, will be progressively reduced.

The second ethical concern is the decline of collective representation in the effort–reward process. The absence of a strong collective voice in the pay-setting process arguably means that the 'new' pay is 'potentially unjust in both procedural and distributive senses; and that it affords little scope for the exercise of democratic rights by citizens at the place of work' (Heery, 2000, pp. 182–3). One principle of ethical reward management, which could restore some balance towards the interest of the employees, is the use of variable pay as a supplement and not a replacement for a 'fair' base wage or salary.

Finally, we should appreciate the relationship between the choice of payment system and power. The choice of a pay system does not operate in a vacuum, but is dictated by perceptions of power on the part of labour and management. This suggests that we can predict that pay systems will change according to their effectiveness in terms of the relationship of effort to pay and shifts in power. The balance of power is therefore a strategic factor that helps to explain the choice of pay arrangements within any HR strategy.

Ruth has worked across a variety of sectors and industries throughout her career, including several positions as HR Director. Her last role was as Director of HR and Development for Cranfield University, which she left in summer 2011 to move back into consultancy and interim work.

Ruth Altman
Freelance HR practitioner

Her route through HR has been first as an HR generalist working with the business, gaining experience in more specialist areas such as reward, industrial and employee relations, organization development, change management and delivering management development programmes. She then took up more overarching strategic HR roles. More recently, Ruth was a member of the Universities Human Resources Executive and the Higher Education Sector's HR professional body, for which she chaired the annual national conference committee. For the last 2 years, she was also a judge for the sector's marketing and communications initiatives, the Heist Awards.

www Visit www.palgrave.com/business/bratton5 to watch Ruth talking about the challenges of working in a HR department at a university, and how higher university fees will impact on the reward system in universities. Then think about the following questions:

1 How does Ruth explain the development of the psychological contract at work?
2 How are changes in universities affecting HR?
3 How can a HR department really 'add value'?

HRM **as I see it**

Cordaval University

Setting

The Canadian university sector has recently experienced major changes and increasingly faces new challenges of rising tuition fees for students, changing political agendas, squeezed public funding and an unpredictable demand from international students. The increase in student fees has sharpened students' focus on the value they receive from their universities. Running parallel is the entry into the sector of new universities created by rebranding well-established 2-year colleges into 'applied' universities. Globalization has created a booming market in higher education, and, aided by the dissolution of national market borders, international partnerships have developed to create 'superuniversities' with overwhelming competitive advantages over locally or regionally focused institutions.

Located in eastern Canada, Cordaval University, created from an applied university-college, gained university title in 2004. The university employs 400 full-time and 150 part-time teaching staff. The university's student numbers have grown steadily in the past few years, with a current headcount of 25,000 full- and part-time students. The university's core activity is helping students to succeed. The vast majority of students attend the university to improve their career prospects or to change career. Cordaval offers programmes across a comprehensive range of disciplines. The university's strategic plan is to deliver high-quality innovative, flexible programmes both on and off the campus. In setting a course to achieve its new strategic vision, the university has established five strategic goals:

- Helping every career-motivated student to achieve his or her career aspirations
- Consistently delivering academic excellence
- Building the university's track record in applied research
- Developing the capacity to generate income
- Contributing to the cultural and economic prosperity of the region
- Establishing a school of law.

The problem

The Ad Hoc Joint Committee established by the University's Board of Governors, which consisted of representatives from the teaching staff, deans, students' union and HR, chaired by the President, Dr Sara Ferguson, was mandated to develop an action plan to create a school of law (goal 6). This was to consist of a Dean of Law, executive assistant and four teaching faculty, paid a salary scale between $106,360 and $136,905.

At the first meeting, Malcolm O'Reilly, the Human Resource Advisor for Cordaval University, presented data on salary structures from other Canadian universities that were offering law degrees. In closing his presentation, he remarked that while Cordaval's teaching staff was on average paid at levels below those of comparable universities (see the table for Cordaval's salaries), there was insufficient funding to raise academic salaries across the board. This would not change any time soon because:

We can recruit in most disciplines; it's only in law that we anticipate a problem. We have little choice but to create a new higher salary structure for law lecturers that is competitive with the labour market. Funding will not provide sufficient money to maintain equitable pay differences between new law lecturers and current teaching staff.

Bill Warren from the Department of Philosophy, History and Politics forcefully countered:

Arts and social science teaching staff are underpaid relative to other universities, and we are struggling to recruit good people because of this. Paying higher salaries just to law professors will demotivate staff and undermine efforts to develop interdisciplinary degrees.

Dr Michael Peters, from the department of anthropology, geography and sociology, then spoke up:

What is vexing is inequity within the social science school. I have colleagues who routinely, year after year, teach far fewer students than the contract limit. Yet we're all equally responsible for the same standards of teaching, research and service, not to mention pay. It's not hard to think that good teachers and vibrant disciplines are being 'rewarded' with more work. Poor teachers in moribund disciplines are, in a sense, rewarded with more pay.

Dr John Rickman, a professor of English, remarked:

What does annoy me is that I periodically hear justifications of administrative salaries being what they are – exorbitant when compared with teaching salaries – in terms of some wider 'market'. We have to pay this dean this much because that's the 'going rate' at Calgary, but we never hear the same argument when it comes to teaching faculty. What about the rest of us?

Another member of the Ad Hoc Committee, Dr Chris Woodstock, an executive member of the University Teaching Union (UTU) said, 'Michael's and John's views illustrate the position of UTU. A new pay structure only for law professors is very divisive and in the long-term will prove disastrous for employee relations at the university'.

Dr Ferguson then summed up the contributions from around the table. Finally, following extended discussion, it was agreed that John Rickman, Chris Woodstock and Malcolm O'Reilly would draft a discussion paper for the next meeting on what could be done to address the salary problem that existed at Cordaval university.

Assignment

Working in a small group, and role-playing the members of the subcommittee, prepare a report for the Ad Hoc Joint Committee drawing on the material from this chapter, addressing the following:

1 Based on the data collected by the HR Department, what reward problems exist at Cordaval University?
2 Is the proposal from the HR advisor for a differential salary structure favouring law lecturers justifiable?
3 Does the proposal to pay higher salaries to one particular group of teaching staff impact positively or negatively on the strategic plan? Explain your answer.
4 What reward policy would you suggest to the university?

5 How should the university address the problem of disgruntled lecturers who feel underpaid?

Essential reading

Long, R. (2010) Evaluating the market. In *Strategic Compensation* (4th edn) (pp. 333–58). Toronto: Nelson.

Pfeffer, J. and Langton, N. (1993) The effect of wage dispersion on satisfaction, productivity, and working collaboratively: evidence from college and university faculty. *Administrative Science Quarterly*, **38**: 382–407.

Shaw, J. D., Delery, J. E., Jenkins, G. and Gupta, N. (1998) An organizational-level analysis of voluntary and involuntary turnover. *Academy of Management Journal*, **41**: 511–25.

Tien, F. F. and Blackburn, R. (1996) Faculty rank system, research motivation, and faculty research productivity: measure refinement and theory testing. *Journal of Higher Education*, **67**(1): 2–22.

Salary schedules at Cordaval University

Step	Current pay ($)	Academic rank
21	**106,905**	Full professor ceiling
20	104,723	
19	102,541	
18	100,359	
17	**98,178**	Associate professor ceiling
16	95,451	
15	92,723	
14	89,996	
13	87,269	
12	**84,542**	Assistant professor ceiling
11	81,269	
10	78,542	
9	**76,360**	Full professor floor
8	73,176	
7	70,496	
6	67,816	
5	**65,136**	Associate professor floor
4	62,456	
3	59,776	
2	57,095	
1	**54,415**	Assistant professor floor

Note: This case was written by John Bratton.

 Visit the companion website at www.palgrave.com/ business/bratton5 for guidelines on writing reports.

summary

◀ This chapter has emphasized that reward management is central to the effective management of the employment relationship. The pay model we have developed shows that reward is multidimensional, and emphasizes two fundamental policy issues: *internal* and *external equity*.

◀ A reward system is a key mechanism that can influence each step of the strategy process. Although this view has been contested, we explained that the current new pay literature stresses that an 'effective' pay system is one that is aligned with the organization's business strategy.

◀ We discussed why no single best pay system exists. A pay system that may seem highly appropriate in one period, with a particular organization and work design supporting a management strategy, can be highly inappropriate in the next, when the business strategy and organizational design have changed.

◀ We explained that changes in reward systems reflect shifts in management thinking. The adoption of more variable pay systems is ideologically driven to encourage labour flexibility, although there is an apparent lack of consensus on the type of pay system that might encourage behavioural change.

◀ We have also examined how government intervenes both *directly* and *indirectly* in the pay determination process. We examined equal pay, national minimum pay legislation, and how government economic policies impact on pay determination.

◀ We have explored some of the strategic tension in reward systems. Under the logic of political economy, pay systems cannot obviate the contradictory tensions that bedevil employment relations. We also focused on some 'ethical deficiencies' with respect to contingency pay increasing employee risk.

vocab checklist for ESL students

◀ benchmark (v) (n)

◀ collective bargaining (n)

◀ commission (v) (n)

◀ compensate (v), compensation (n), compensable (adj)

◀ equity (n), equitable (adj)

◀ extrinsic (adj)

◀ hierarchy (n), hierarchical (adj)

◀ intangible (adj)

◀ intrinsic (adj)

◀ non-cash recognition (n)

◀ paradox (n), paradoxical (adj), paradoxically (adv)

◀ payment-by-results (n)

◀ performance-related pay (PRP) (n)

◀ piece rate (n)

◀ reward objectives (n)

◀ tangible (adj)

◀ trade unions (n)

◀ variable pay scheme (n)

WWW Visit www.palgrave.com/business/bratton5 for a link to free definitions of these terms in the Macmillan Dictionary, as well as additional learning resources for ESL students.

review questions

1 Explain the statement 'The design of reward systems is contingent upon the organizational context in which they must operate.'

2 Is money the prime driver of employee performance?

3 'New payment systems generate greater employee risk and diminish democratic rights in the workplace.' Discuss.

4 Do incentive-pay schemes have a motivational or a demotivational effect on employees?

5 'Equal pay for women will be secure only when its justice is adequately understood and practised by men' (Wedderburn, 1986). Do you agree or disagree? Discuss.

further reading to improve your mark

Reading these articles and chapters can help you gain a better understanding and potentially a higher grade for your HRM assignment.

◀ Martocchio, J. J. (2011) *Strategic Compensation*. New York: Pearson Prentice-Hall.

◀ Arrowsmith, J. and Marginson, J. (2011) Variable pay and collective bargaining in British retail banking. *British Journal of Industrial Relations*, **49**(1): 54–79.

◀ Kersley, B., Alpin, C., Forth, J., Bryson, A., Bewley, H., Dix, G. and Oxenbridge, S. (2006) The determinants of pay and other terms and conditions. In B. Kersley, C. Alpin, J. Forth, A. Bryson, H. Bewley, G. Dix and S. Oxenbridge (eds) *Inside the Workplace: Findings from the 2004 Workplace Employment Relations Survey* (pp. 178–206). London: Routledge.

◀ Corby, S., Palmer, S. and Lindop, E. (eds) (2009) *Rethinking Reward*. Basingstoke: Palgrave. Read pp. 102–19.

◀ Heery, E. (2000) The new pay: risk and representation at work. In D. Winstanley and J. Woodall (eds) *Ethical Issues in Contemporary Human Resource Management* (pp. 172–88). Basingstoke: Palgrave.

◀ Kessler, I. (2007) Reward choices: strategy and equity. In J. Storey (ed.) *Human Resource Management: A Critical Text* (3rd edn) (pp. 159–76). London: Thomson Learning.

 Visit www.palgrave.com/business/bratton5 for lots of extra resources to help you get to grips with this chapter, including study tips, HRM skills development guides, summary lecture notes, and more.

chapter **12**

industrial relations

objectives

After studying this chapter, you should be able to:

1   Define and describe contemporary trends in industrial relations

2   Describe the core legal principles relating to union–management relations

3   Explain and critically evaluate different types of union–management strategy

4   Explain the pattern of trade union membership and union structure

5   Understand the nature and importance of collective bargaining

6   Critically evaluate the importance of 'partnership' for industrial relations

introduction

A series of 5-day strikes at British Airways in the summer of 2010 (Milmo, 2010a) and recent public-sector strikes over changes to pensions (Grice et al., 2011) have focused attention on strikes and union–management relations. Despite the fact that the number of days lost to strikes is currently running at its lowest since the Great Depression of the 1930s, there has been, unsurprisingly, much public criticism of the strikes. Context, however, is paramount. As one senior trade union official acutely put it: 'no strike in our country could inflict the sort of economic damage which the banks and finance houses have' (Kenny, 2011, p. 30). Less well-known perhaps, was another event in 2010 involving trade unions – the 'Green Growth' conference convened by the UK Trades Union Congress (TUC; 2010).

The central significance of these actions is to remind us that the employment relationship, which human resource management (HRM) seeks to shape and manage, is dynamic in the sense that it involves both collective conflict and cooperation. There is an underlying conflict of interest between employers and workers that emerges during periods of change or crisis. On the other hand, the overwhelming need to develop a sustainable, low-carbon economy, or a cataclysmic event such as the 2011 explosion at Japan's Fukushima nuclear plant, acts on all parties to induce high levels of cooperation.

Since the 1980s, part of the neo-liberal axiomatic idea that markets 'know best' is the notion that trade unions are a matter of irrelevance – dinosaurs from the past. We disagree. Social inequality, human dignity *in* and *at* work, worker physical and mental well-being, and sustainable strategies illustrate the importance of a union voice in the contemporary workplace. Managing people, therefore, has both an individual and collective dimension (see, for example, Kelly, 2005). In this field of study, academics differ over the use of the terms 'industrial relations', 'labour relations' and 'union–management relations' (see Colling and Terry, 2010; Gunderson et al., 2005), but in this chapter we will use the terms interchangeably. In so doing, we focus upon the relationship between management and organized (union) labour, the balance of power between the two parties, and the extent to which the employment relationship is jointly regulated through collective bargaining.

We will begin the chapter by defining industrial relations and the scope of this interdisciplinary field of study. Next we will examine a number of strategic decisions that management must take with regard to trade unions. After providing an overview of the legal context of industrial relations, the chapter will examine trends in UK trade union membership and collective bargaining. Finally, the chapter will turn to the issue of social partnership, 'worker commitment' and an assessment of the unions' response to the HRM agenda.

reflective question It is important to examine your own values and life experiences, and therefore your own perspective on trade unions. Do you think that unions have a role to play in the new knowledge-based economy or are they 'dinosaurs' from a past era?

The nature of industrial relations

As we mentioned above, there is controversy among the academic community over the precise meaning and relevance of the term 'industrial relations'. Traditionally, it was widely accepted that industrial relations was the study of management and union relations, together with collective bargaining, strikes and labour laws affecting the relations between the two parties. This approach has now become outdated. The debate has been strongly influenced by declining union membership, the contraction of collective bargaining and the apparent marginalization of unions, in the modern workplace as well as in the academic community. As Wood (2000, p. 1) notes, the 'lifeblood' of industrial relations – unions and collective bargaining – 'once so central ... seem to have ceased to be of such consuming interest'.

Over the past three decades, the British system of industrial relations has been so radically transformed by a combination of economic, political and social factors as to cause one industrial relations scholar to state, 'It is difficult to believe that such a world existed less than twenty years ago' (Hyman, 1997a, p. 317). Running parallel with (and not unrelated to) these changes has, of course, been the ascendancy of the HRM paradigm. Some critics argue that particular patterns of HRM are inconsistent with the traditional British system of industrial relations, albeit for very different reasons (Godard, 2005; Guest, 1995; Wells, 1993). Others, however, maintain that analytical HRM is not a union-avoidance strategy (Boxall, 2008).

The radical transformation of the British system of industrial relations has not been limited to the UK. In the rest of the European Union (EU), the traditional pattern of industrial relations has also undergone profound modifications in the intervening period. Throughout the enlarged Europe, the drive for competitive advantage has been pursued consistently and universally, and employers have demonstrated determination in remodelling their national industrial relations systems. European employers have, for example, increasingly exercised their prerogative over key business decisions and enhanced management legitimacy, with government help, by popularizing the ideological argument for veneration of the 'marketplace'.

European trade unions have been weakened both numerically and politically, and in general their participation in the collective bargaining process has been marked by retreat and action to defend living standards and working conditions (Baglioni and Crouch, 1991). The response to intensified global competition has not, however, been the same in every EU member state (Morley et al., 2000). Thus, in some respects, the pattern of European industrial relations systems has always sharply diversified, 'a contradictory mix of market liberalization and social regulation', representing a complex interaction between 'Europeanization' and 'Anglicization' forms of employment relations (Hyman, 2010, p. 75.)

In the light of these profound contextual and institutional changes, it has become widely accepted that industrial relations must be reconceptualized and extend its focus beyond traditional issues to a broader concern with all the forces and processes that shape the employment relationship (Colling and Terry, 2010; Gunderson et al., 2005). Moreover, it is acknowledged that any reconceptualization of industrial relations must focus analysis on the three defining features of the employment relationship (Colling and Terry, 2010, pp. 7–8):

- It is *indeterminate*, which derives from the fact that the labour contract involves an exchange for money for a *potential* level of performance;
- *Power* is unequally distributed between the parties; and
- The employment relationship is *dynamic*.

A contemporary industrial relations perspective also acknowledges that the category of 'worker' is itself contested, and that it is necessary to consider the influence of patriarchy, allowing for interests grounded in gender, ethnicity and other identities (Heery, 2009). The principal institutions and processes that encompass the field of study are, moreover, not gender-neutral but reflect 'masculine priorities and privilege' in work organizations (Wajcman, 2000, p. 183).

Understanding why employees join trade unions

Trade unions in the UK have approximately 6.5 million members, which amounts to about one-third of the labour force. In the EU, 1 in 4 employees is a member of a trade union. Significant variations exist between EU members states: in 2010, the EU's four most populated states had different rates of unionization, with Italy at 30 per cent, the UK at 29 per cent, Germany at 27 per cent and France at 9 per cent. In Canada, 4.4 million workers are members of a trade union, and in the USA, the figure in 2010 was 14.7 million. Worldwide, trade unions have approximately 320 million members (Visser, 2003). It is therefore important to understand the decision to join a trade union from an individual employee's perspective.

Workers join unions for a wide variety of reasons (Schnabel, 2003). First, they may be motivated to join a union for *economic* reasons. In a classic study, Sidney and Beatrice Webb (1911) suggested that workers' pursuit of higher wages and improved conditions expressed a basic motive to reduce domination by their employers. Workers may also be motivated to join a union because they feel that economic inequality in society is too high and that the variance between perceived actual and legitimate earnings should be reduced (Checchi et al., 2010). Equity theory posits that workers will engage in social action to the extent that they perceive the situation to be equitable (Bratton et al., 2009).

In addition to economic and equity rationales, employees also join unions because they want to gain a *voice* in decision-making in their workplace. Joining a union may bring workers the benefit of an indirect voice mechanism, which can potentially allow them to improve conditions, resolve irritating problems or address unreasonable workplace behaviour. In a democratic society, workers may make a decision to unionize in order to lobby politicians for political action on work-related or societal improvements. The participation of unions in civil society can also help to bring about the demise of authoritarian regimes. The democratization of Poland, for example, was led by the trade union Solidarity (Frost and Taris, 2005, p. 40).

In a survey of UK workplaces, workers disclosed that they had decided to join a union to improve their pay and conditions and for collective protection against management's actions (Waddington and Whitston, 1997). The findings from workplace surveys in the UK and North America suggest that workers' perceptions of the imbalance of power between 'them' (the management) and 'us' (the workers) necessitates some form of collective voice or representation in the form of a union.

reflective question   What factors make unions relevant today? What factors make them irrelevant? And what do employees want from unions?

Trade unions in action

In a non-unionized workplace, managers have flexibility in designing work, selecting, promoting and training people, and determining rewards and other human resources (HR) practices, but much of this can change when workers join a union. After recognizing the union, representatives from union and management negotiate a collective agreement that spells out the details of the employment relationship that will be jointly determined. This can typically include establishing some control over core HR policies and practices, including rewards, recruitment and selection, training and employee development and health and safety:

- First and foremost, unions seek to control *rewards* and attempt to maximize the pay side of the wage–effort contract.

- In the area of *recruitment and selection*, unions, in some industries at least (for example, construction, film and theatre), have had some control over external recruiting.
- Unions also take an active interest in work-related *learning* and *employee development*, trying to ensure that training opportunities are distributed equitably and that the employer adheres to the principle of maintained earnings during training.
- Perhaps most controversially, the whole practice of *employee performance appraisal* poses challenges to the unions. The central tenet of traditional unionism has been the collectivist culture, namely the insistence on rewards according to the same definite standard and its application in the workplace. Such collectivist goals have resulted in unions strongly resisting all forms of performance appraisal based on individual performance.
- Occupational *health hazards* and environmental pollution disproportionately affect those in the lower social class strata, the working class. Unions have a long history of campaigning and negotiating for the removal of toxic substances and for healthier and safer workplaces.

These examples illustrate that 'control over work relations' (Hyman, 1975, p. 31) is a central feature of industrial relations, which here refers to:

The *relations* between organized employees (represented by a union) and management, the *processes* that regulate the employment contract, the *context* within which a union and an employer interact.

Let us briefly expand on the components of this definition. The '*relations*' between the workforce and management are both economic and social: they are an economic relation because employers buy employees' potential physical and mental abilities, and they are a social relation because, when employees enter into a contract, they agree to comply with the employer's standards and rules. These relationships between the workforce and management may be played out in different arenas – at the workplace level, at industry level and at the national level – where union, employer and government representatives participate in a social dialogue on economic and employment-related issues.

The word '*processes*' refers to collective bargaining, by which unions represent their members' interests through formal negotiations with management representatives. Through collective bargaining, a hierarchy of rules and regulations affecting employment and workplace behaviour is generated, and this is the process that may provide the focal point for studying the *mediating* effects of key variables in the HRM–performance casual chain, often referred to as the 'HR black box' (see Chapter 3).

The third key feature of the definition, '*context*', refers to the economic, legal and political conditions and constraints within which management and union relations take place. Our definition of industrial relations recognizes the fluidity of contexts and the processes of control over the employment relationship. This dynamic mix means that, in a unionized environment, managing the interactions between union and management representatives can be a significant area of HRM activity.

HRM web links   Go to www.eurofound.europa.eu/eiro for information on economic, political and collective bargaining developments in the EU. For information on industrial relations in North America go to www.ilr.cornell.edu, for Australia see http://whirlpool.net.au/wiki/industrial_relations_websites – and click on 'Labour relations'. See also www.cosatu.org.za (South Africa).

HRM **and** globalization

The role of unions in South Africa

For decades, the apartheid policies of South Africa were condemned by nations around the world. Studies of South Africa during this period reveal persistent patterns of inequality, which appeared to have changed little since the early days of colonialism. The reasons for this were obvious. Laws and policies supported by the South African state provided a foundation on which the exploitation of the black African majority could be pursued without sanction. South Africa embodied what Charles Tilly (2008) calls 'categorical inequality', an asymmetrical situation in which the advantages enjoyed by one category of persons are directly related to the disadvantages experienced by another.

All this began to change in the late 1970s and early 1980s. Crucial to the change were penalties imposed on South Africa by the international community. Also important were various forms of social protest, protests that often united groups with different ethnic and racial backgrounds. During this period, unions acted as agents of change. According to Barchiesi (2008, p. 121), the success of unions as change agents may be attributed to three factors: 'their capacity to forge broad social alliances with unwaged sectors …, their ability to put pressure on ruling parties … [and] their internal democratic practices.'

In the postapartheid period, the ability of unions to acts as agents of progressive change has diminished. As elsewhere, integration with the global economic system has gone hand in hand with changing belief systems. There is a trend among some South African politicians to endorse versions of neo-liberalism – the belief that the state's role in society, including in protecting workers and the environment, should be cut back.

When neo-liberalism emerges as the dominant political belief system, corporations and employers are empowered. This due in part to the so-called 'race to the bottom' (see Chapter 15). When one country fails to enforce rules protecting workers, other countries feel compelled to do the same. Unions find themselves in a vulnerable position, as governments move to privatize public services, and corporations threaten to send work 'off shore'

if union demands are too high. In one case discussed by Barchiesi (2008), a third union-weakening strategy is identified: the company supplements its workforce by local outsourcing, hiring workers from a labour brokering agency. These workers are on fixed-term contracts and do not receive medical insurance. Barchiesi concludes that, due in part to this general climate of neo-liberalism and its associated HR practices, union traditions of collective action and democratic practice in South Africa are being eroded.

It is important to note that the vulnerable situation unions find themselves in is not limited to places such as South Africa where restrictions against unions have only recently been lifted. Even in the USA, where unions have been considered to be a legitimate and valuable part of civil society, their very right to exist has been challenged: in Madison, Wisconsin, the governor sought to enact legislation that would all but eliminate unions and collective agreements in the public sector.

Stop! Are you familiar with other situations in which unions have been agents of progressive social change? In the USA, there has been a decline in the percentage of workers enrolled in unions but events in Madison suggest that unions can still play a role in articulating a vision of the just society. Explain.

Sources and further information: See Barchiesi (2008) and Tilly (2008) for more information on this area.

Note: This feature was written by David MacLennan at Thompson Rivers University.

The legal context of industrial relations

Management and union strategies, collective bargaining processes and outcomes (for example, sustainable work systems, pay and working time, skills, equality and dignity, and workplace grievances and disputes) are influenced by economic, political and legal factors. The state, which is normally thought of as comprising the executive, Parliament, the judiciary, the civil service and the police and armed forces, has considerable influence on industrial relations in two major areas: through *legislation* and through *third-party intervention* (as, for example, in the UK, by the Advisory, Conciliation and Arbitration Service – ACAS).

Labour law is an aspect of industrial relations that interacts with the institutions, processes and behaviour of the key actors in the system. As a body of statutes and cases, labour law regulates union organization and governance, and relations between different unions, union recognition by employers, collective bargaining and manifestations of collective workplace conflict, such as strikes, are the main concerns. Whereas individual labour law governs the relations between individual employees and their employer, collective labour law therefore governs the collective aspects of the employment relationship.

When trade unions organized in eighteenth-century Britain, they faced illegality under both criminal and civil law. The Combination Acts of 1799 and 1800 were only part of a battery of more than 40 statutes that criminalized trade union activities. The legal framework for industrial relations activities established between 1870 and 1906 was significantly remodelled by the Conservative governments of the 1980s and 1990s (McIlroy, 1988).

Brought in by the New Labour government, the Employment Relations Act 1999 provides a more supportive statutory framework for union organization and governance and collective bargaining, including provision for statutory union recognition, changed balloting procedures and increased protection for union members when participating in official industrial action (see Selwyn, 2011; Wood and Godard, 1999; Wood et al., 2002). Reviewing trade union rights under the New Labour government, from 1997, Smith and Morton (2006, p. 414) argue that partnership agreements 'entrench employers' power'. They also contend that, to strengthen workers' power, legislation is needed to establish 'a statutory right of trade unions to have access to, and assembly at, the workplace'. Some of the key UK legislative provisions related to industrial relations are shown in Table 12.1.

HRM web links WWW
Go to the following websites to compare collective labour law relating to unions and union–management relations: www.legislation.gov.uk provides the full text of UK Acts of Parliament; www.canadianlabour.ca/home and www.law-lib.utoronto.ca give information on Canadian laws; and www.dol.gov/elaws/aud_gen_emp.asp outlines the US information.

reflective question
In the middle of a recession in which organizations are cutting jobs with alacrity, should trade unions have more or fewer rights?

The impact of EU regulation has also influenced British industrial relations. In 2007, the landmark judgements of the European Court of Justice in the Viking and Laval cases adopted the principle that, irrespective of national law, work stoppages that interfered

Table 12.1 Main UK legislative provisions related to industrial relations, 1980–2004

Act	Date	Coverage
Employment Act	1980	Public funds for union ballots (since repealed) Provision for codes on picketing and closed shop
Employment Act	1982	New definition of a 'trade dispute'
Trade Union Act	1984	Compulsory secret ballots for union positions and before industrial action; otherwise no immunity
Employment Act	1988	Greater control to members of union governance
Employment Act	1990	Abolished the closed shop and immunity in respect of secondary industrial action
Trade Union and Labour (Consolidation) Act	1992	Consolidated all relevant law on unions and labour relations together with ACAS. Code provides for disclosure of information to unions for collective bargaining purposes
Trade Union Reform and Employment Rights Act	1993	Independent scrutineer of union elections given more powers. Voting fully postal
Employment Relations Act	1999	New statutory framework for collective bargaining, including provision of statutory union recognition, changed balloting procedures and increased protection for union members when participating in official industrial action
Employment Relations Act	2004	Union recognition rights for the purpose of conducting collective bargaining. Outlines additional responsibilities of the Central Arbitration Committee to facilitate collective bargaining

with freedom of movement were lawful only if they satisfied a 'proportionality' test (Hyman, 2010, p. 75).

A direct consequence in the UK of ever-complex legal rules regulating strike action was the injunction preventing the airline cabin crew's union Unite calling a strike against British Airways in 2010. The landmark decision by Mr Justice McCombe granted the injunction against the strike, overturning an 81 per cent vote by BA's cabin crew in favour of industrial action. The judge ruled that Unite had not complied with a particularly esoteric point of the 1992 Trade Union and Labour Relations (Consolidation) Act that orders unions to notify not just the result of any secret ballot to all eligible voters, but also the exact breakdown of votes, including spoiled ballot papers, of which there were 11 (Milmo and Pidd, 2010). Reacting to the verdict, the joint general secretaries of Unite, Tony Woodley and Derek Simpson (quoted by Milmo and Pidd, 2010, p. 1), said:

This judgement is an absolute disgrace and will rank as a landmark attack on free trade unionism and the right to take industrial action. Its implication is that it is now all but impossible to take legally protected strike action against an employer who wishes to seek an injunction on even the most trivial grounds.

The traditional attitude of the UK courts is that there is no 'right to strike' in the UK: Parliament has granted unions immunities not rights (as set out in the case *Express Newspapers* v. *McShane*, 1979). The judge in this case, Lord Denning, held that unions had no right 'to break the law or do wrong by inducing people to break contracts ... only immunity if they did'. That view was open to question once UK law incorporated the European Convention on Human Rights through the Human Rights Act 1998. Article 11 of the Convention recognizes a right to freedom of association, which has been

©istockphoto.com/tillsonburg

Although the traditional attitude of the UK courts is that there is no 'right to strike', there is a consensus that some form of a right to strike must be respected if that is really the democratic will of union members.

interpreted as incorporating a right to strike. In *British Airways Plc* v. *Unite Union* (2010), Judge McCombe seemed to resurrect Lord Denning's view.

However, at the Court of Appeal it was held that Unite had complied with the Trade Union and Labour Relations (Consolidation) Act 1992. The Lord Chief Justice described the ballot as having been 'impeccably conducted'. The Court of Appeal did not clarify the argument of whether the right to strike is recognized in the UK as a fundamental human right: 'The judgments of the majority do, however, seem to assume that some form of a right to strike must be respected if that is really the democratic will of union members' (Eady and Motraghi, 2010, p. 1). The effects of the legal strategies – despite promoting 'social partnerships' – pursued by UK Conservative and Labour governments has thus considerably restricted lawful industrial action (Dickens and Hall, 2010).

ACAS, the UK third-party intervention institution, was established in 1974 in order to promote orderly industrial relations and to intervene in those industrial disputes which the government viewed as particularly damaging to the national economy. ACAS is a state mechanism and is funded by the UK government. In 1993, legislation removed ACAS's responsibility for the promotion of collective bargaining. ACAS's role as an arbitrator and mediator is less significant today, given the restrictive legal framework and the decline in official industrial stoppages, but recent ACAS figures reveal that requests for individual conciliation are increasing each year.

HRM web links For information on ACAS, go to www.acas.org.uk.

Management strategies

Management plays a predominant role in constructing collective relations in the workplace, with managers shaping the options and largely determining the outcomes (Hyman, 1997b), and employees and their unions generally reacting to management initiatives. Over the past three decades, studies have investigated how British managers have reorganized the conduct of workplace industrial relations (see, for example, Cully et al., 1999; Kersley et al., 2006).

An industrial relations strategy refers to the plans and policies chosen by management to deal with trade unions (Gospel and Littler, 1983). The idea of choice among alternative industrial relations strategies is closely linked to the concept of 'business strategy' and 'HR strategy'. The debate on globalization, however, has highlighted the increasing global dominance of the neo-liberal, Protestant, Anglo-American model of capitalism in various areas, including union representation (see Jacoby, 2005). The choice of a strategy towards unions is substantially constrained by a number of complex factors, including historical legacies, path dependency, union power and existing bargaining structures (Hyman, 1999; Thompson and Ponak, 2005). The work from the 'varieties of capitalism' literature has also highlighted the importance of culture and national institutions and labour laws that substantially constrain – as well as explain – the choice of an industrial relations strategy.

Although it is simplifying a complex phenomenon, the various strategic alternatives can, for analytical purposes, be classified into four broad industrial relations strategies (Thompson and Ponak, 2005): union acceptance, union resistance, union replacement and union avoidance.

The *union-acceptance* strategy is defined here as a decision by top managers to accept the legitimacy of the union role and, in turn, of collective bargaining as a process for regulating the employment relationship to support their corporate strategy. The reforms during the third-quarter of the twentieth century have been characterized as an industrial relations strategy designed to engender 'a degree of order, regulation and control' (Nichols and Beynon, 1977, p. 129). Survey evidence indicates that, even in the inimical environment of the 1980s, a number of important Japanese companies chose a union-acceptance strategy, albeit in a modified form, to achieve their employment objectives (Bassett, 1987; Wickens, 1987). In Britain, survey data indicate a sharp decline in the adoption of a union-acceptance strategy. In the private sector, for example, the proportion of workplaces adopting a union-acceptance/recognition strategy fell from 48 per cent to 16 per cent (Kersley et al., 2006).

The *union-resistance* strategy describes a decision by senior managers to limit the spread of unionization to other sections of the company's workforce, although they accept the legitimacy of their existing unions. For example, the spread of unionization among administrative staff is discouraged by communicating to this group of employees that improvements in pay and conditions are due to management initiative, not union pressure. Where there is no union present in the establishment, the union-resistance strategy may involve a combination of unlawful and unethical counterunionization actions by employers, including threatening legal action, distributing anti-union literature, using 'union-busting' consultants or victimizing union activists. The study by Heery and Simms (2010, p. 9) give two graphic illustrations of outright anti-union action by employers:

Example 1: There are surveillance cameras at the only entrance of the building. Staff were afraid to even stop and speak to us at the gate. Management had previously sacked the last employee who spoke about getting a union.

Example 2: When we first started the [union] campaign factory-gating, the factory manager, who is Asian, called all the Asian workers together on the shopfloor and told them that he would sack anyone who joined the union. That week, he phoned them all at home and told them again that they would be sacked.

The *union-replacement* strategy means that top management have decided to achieve their strategic goals without any consultation or agreement with trade unions. De-recognition refers to a decision by management to withdraw from collective bargaining in favour of unilateral arrangements for the governance of employment relations. Douglas Smith, then chair of ACAS, said in his 1987 address to the Institute of Personnel Management conference that 'across the spectrum there were now managements whose intention was increasingly to marginalize trade unions'. Several studies provide convincing evidence of de-recognition or substitution practices in Britain (see, for example, Claydon, 1989; Heery and Simms, 2010; Smith and Morton, 1993). The union-replacement scenario describes a case in which a relatively weak union is de-recognized and management install a non-union employee representation arrangement as 'a deliberate attempt to pre-empt the return of a union voice' (Butler, 2009, p. 207).

Among North American industrial relations academics, there is a popular view that Canadian employers are less willing to oppose unionization than are their US counterparts. Bentham's (2002) recent study suggests, however, that this may be a misconception because the vast majority of Canadian workplaces studied 'engaged in actions that can only be characterized as overt and active resistance' to unions (p. 181). Opposition to unions in Canada is illustrated by the actions of McDonalds. In 1998, an outlet of the fast-food giant on the West Coast was the first to be unionized in North America. The union hailed this a major victory. Shortly after, however, the employer mounted a successful legal challenge by asserting that employees 19 years of age and less were 'infants' under the law and could not apply for union membership or be authorized to pay union dues (Thompson and Ponak, 2005, p. 123).

HRM web links WWW For information on how industrial relations strategies in Britain have changed over the past two decades, go to the WERS 2004 website: www.wers2004.info.

Throughout the 1990s, a union-replacement strategy was evident in UK workplaces. Survey results showed that 6 per cent of all established workplaces de-recognized unions between 1990 and 1998 (Millward et al., 2000). Bacon and Storey's (2000) analysis reveals a 'disjuncture between unions and "new" corporate thinking'. One manager (quoted in Bacon and Storey, 2000, p. 412) expressed the new management thinking towards unions like this:

Collectivism via trade unions is something we want to remove ... We are not anti-union; it is just that they are incompatible with our current direction. I think we can win by edict in the current climate and drive through changes against any opposition and hope that in the end people will see there is no choice.

One interesting aspect of Bacon and Storey's study is the evidence suggesting that British management did not take full advantage of its power. Two reasons are given for this. First, the 'heavy threats' to the unions contributed to higher levels of employee dissatisfaction and mistrust of management. This observation can be linked to the importance of the psychological contract. It would appear that the adoption of a union-replacement strategy, particularly during a period of major restructuring and downsizing, can rupture the contract, with subsequent decreases in employees' loyalty and commitment. With this in mind, Bacon and Storey's (2000, p. 423) note that managers were 'reluctant to sacrifice employee trust' is important. The second reason managers did not use their power and push through with de-recognizing the unions was because the very threat of such action alone 'allowed managers to introduce many of the changes they had wanted to drive through' in the workplace (Bacon and Storey, 2000, pp. 413–14). Overall, then, although most managers have an enduring preference for non-union relations (what is referred to as 'unitarism'), pragmatic considerations in these cases deterred the adoption of a union-replacement strategy.

The fourth strategy, *union avoidance,* is defined here as a decision to maintain the status quo of a non-union workforce by pursuing HR policies that give employees a 'voice', such as non-union grievance and disciplinary procedures, employee participation schemes, and various forms of team-based participation (see Chapter 4). The retail giant Marks & Spencer exemplifies the union-avoidance strategy, which was explained like this by the company's CEO, Lord Sieff, in 1981 (quoted by Purcell and Sisson, 1983, p. 114):

Human relations in an industry should cover the problems of the individual at work … the contribution people can make, given encouragement – these are the foundations of an effective policy and a major contribution to a successful operation.

In Britain, Heery and Simms (2010) conclude that, between 1998 and 2004, a period that was relatively favourable to trade unions under a Labour government, there was no single dominant industrial relations strategy – 'support, suppression and substitution' were all evident. However, the research found strong support for a contingency approach affecting strategic choice. The primary contingency at play is path dependency: in establishments where management have no experience of dealing with unions, or the union occupies only a marginal position, 'hostility' to unionization 'is more likely'. Where management has experience of unions and where the unions have an institutional presence, unionization is more likely to be supported (Heery and Simms, 2010, p. 19). Given that the majority of private sector organizations are not unionized, we can assume that the union-avoidance strategy is the most prevalent industrial relations strategy in Britain and North America (Gollan, 2002).

HRM web links   Go to www.ipa-involve.com and www.acas.org.uk for information on how many work organizations in the UK have negotiated partnership agreements.

The significance of this debate for industrial relations strategies is this: the HRM model is not restricted to a 'union-exclusion' environment. Guest (1995) analyses the strategic options in terms of industrial relations that are available to management, the 'new realism' option appearing to illustrate the case of HRM and industrial relations operating in tandem. Within the EU legislative framework, British industrial relations have been 'Europeanized' (Hyman, 2010), and prior to 2008–09 managers were beginning to take a more proactive approach towards union involvement in workplace decision-making. In the tougher conditions of the post-financial meltdown and enthusiasm for downsizing, however, it reminds us that both private and public sector management strategies can and do change depending on the economic and political climate; in addition, different strategies can be applied to different firms within the same industrial sector and to different groups of employee within the same organization. With this caveat in mind, the present recession and the growing globalization of corporate structures will compel senior management to make strategic choices about their business processes and how they will arrange related aspects of HR practices, including industrial relations.

Trade unions

Most students using this textbook will be probably be surprised to learn that, three decades ago, British trade unions were considered to be powerful social institutions that merited close study. Indeed, one scholar referred to trade unions as 'one of the most powerful forces shaping our society' (Clegg, 1976, p. 1). Between 1968 and 1979, trade union membership

BA told to hit union 'where it hurts'

The HRM–trade union debate poses some interesting questions for academics and practitioners alike. For example, can a worker be simultaneously committed to the goals of both the organization and the trade union? How does the HRM concept of 'high employee commitment' present a threat to unions? And can the HRM model function alongside traditional collective bargaining? Depending upon the answers to these, and other, questions, management may choose to deal with trade unions in different ways. Consider this recent industrial relations case (Milmo, 2010b):

> British Airways commissioned an academic consultant who told it to 'force the issue' with the cabin crew union that is leading the strike action against the company by 'hitting the leadership where it hurts '… Union insiders said it amounted to a blueprint for the company's hardline approach to industrial relations. 'It confirms everything that we have argued all along – that this company has a secret union-busting agenda which in the final analysis is the reason why so many passengers are suffering the inconvenience of this dispute … The advice includes recommendations to the airline on:

- *Taking an 'anti-Bassa' [the union] approach*
- *Recognizing 'there is no prospect of … partnership' under the union's current leadership*
- *Seeking help from the TGWU [Transport and General Workers Union], in a 'divide and rule' approach. The document states: 'The management team should agree and express a determination to force the issue with Bassa (union). Some consideration should be given to hitting the leadership of Bassa where it hurts. Ground rules for paid time off for trade union duties are an area which needs to be very closely examined.'*

This chapter identifies four broad industrial relations strategies: union acceptance, union resistance, union replacement and union avoidance. It also examines the concept of 'social partnerships'. For some, social partnerships provide a philosophy based on the employer and union working together to achieve common goals such as fairness and competitiveness (Verma, 1995). Critics, however, argue that partnership can potentially weaken the growth of workplace unionism (Kelly, 1996).

Stop! Having outlined above the broad strategies pursued by organizations, what type of industrial relations strategy is BA following? What are the constraints on management if they introduce non-union worker representation at BA?

Sources and further information: The extract is taken from Dan Milmo's (2010b) article 'BA told to hit union 'where it hurts''. For more information, see also Godard (1997) and Williams et al. (2011).

Note: This feature was written by John Bratton.

©istockphoto.com/mbbirdy

increased by 3.2 million to 13.2 million, and trade union density – the proportion of employees who are in a union – exceeded 50 per cent. The sheer scale of union organization represented a 'decade of exceptional union growth' (Bain and Price, 1983, p. 6).

In contrast, between 1979 and 2000, union membership in Britain dropped sharply: in 1979, 53 per cent of workers were union members, but by 2000, this had fallen to 29 per cent. The 1980s were referred to as the 'decade of non-unionism', and the 1990s as the decade of 'renewal' or 'revitalization' (Heery et al., 2004). The impact of the present global crisis, exacerbated in the UK by a curtailment of government expenditure, may well see a reversal of the recent gains associated with 'union renaissance'. This section examines recent trends in union membership before examining union structure, in the belief that a knowledge of these developments is important for understanding the debate on HRM and unions.

Union membership

The decline in aggregate membership of British trade unions is well documented and is shown in Table 12.2. In 1979, when Margaret Thatcher was first elected Prime Minister of Britain, union membership stood at over 12 million. Since then, membership has fallen by over 5 million, or 43 per cent. From the peak years of 1976–80, union density fell from 55 per cent, to stand at 28 per cent in 2006–11. Union density was higher among women than men – 29.5 per cent compared with 25.2 per cent in 2011.

Table 12.2 *Union membership in the UK, 1971–2011*

5-year annual average	Members (000s)	% of employed
1971–75	11,548 (+1.5)	50.0
1976–80	12,916 (+1.5)	55.9
1981–85	11,350 (–3.5)	49.1
1986–90	10,299 (–1.7)	44.6
1991–95	8,740 (–4.0)	37.8
1996–2000	7,910 (–9.5)	34.2
2003–05	7,772 (–1.7)	33.6
2006–11	7,436 (–4.3)	28.0

Source: Data from Sneade (2001) and the EIRO website

Table 12.3 describes the pattern of union membership across major sectors of the British economy from 1980 to 2011. The union presence at workplace level remained stable in the early 1980s at 73 per cent, but then fell sharply to 64 per cent in 1990, falling to 54 per cent in 1998, and continuing to fall to 28 per cent in 2011. Union presence differed significantly across the broad sectors of the economy. The decline in union presence was most marked in private manufacturing – down from 77 per cent in 1980 to just 42 per cent of workplaces in 1998. Union density in both private manufacturing and services was just 15 per cent in 2011. The trade union presence in public sector workplaces over the three decades fell from 99 per cent in 1980 to 56 per cent in 2011. Furthermore, in both private manufacturing and services, the decline was 'more substantial in small workplaces' and among traditionally 'male-dominated' workplaces (Millward et al., 2000, p. 86).

Table 12.3 Union presence by broad sector, 1980–2011

	Percentages					
	1980	**1984**	**1990**	**1998**	**2004**	**2011**
All establishments	73	73	64	54	34	28
Sector of ownership						
Private manufacturing	77	67	58	42	na	
Private services	50	53	46	35	22[1]	151
Public sector	99	100	99	97	64	56

Note: 1. This figure only refers to the 'private' sector – both manufacturing and services

Source: Adapted with permission from Millward et al. (2000, p. 85) and Kersley et al. (2006, p. 12); 2011 figures are based on the Certification Officer and TUC websites

reflective question Can you think of any environmental factors (for example, new legislation) that might lead workers to join unions? What internal factors (for example, perceived violation of the employment contract) can affect unionization?

HRM web links For further information on union presence in the workplace in different countries, go to the International Labour Organization website (www.ilo.org), and for the figure for EU member states, go to www.eurofound.europa.eu/eiro.

Interpreting union decline

Although the general pattern clearly indicates that union membership and union density in the UK have fallen sharply and continually since 1979, there is a debate over the precise scale of the trend, its cause and its likely duration. Part of the problem is measurement. The key statistic of union density can be measured in nine different ways depending on which of three different data series for potential membership and trade union membership is used (see Kelly and Bailey, 1989).

One influential explanation of variations in the rate of unionization was developed almost 30 years ago by Bain and Price (1983). The central argument here is that variations in union density over time were explained by the business cycle, public policy, the restructuring of work and industry, and, moreover, employer policy. Employer resistance to unions also has a decisive influence on trade union recruitment. Others argue that although employer policy towards unions is a significant influence, effective campaigning by unions can neutralize employer resistance (Bronfenbrenner, 1997).

Although Bain and Price's approach is comprehensive, it is difficult to disentangle the relative importance of each of the determinants in interpreting aggregate union decline in the UK. Within the business cycle framework, it is contended that high levels of unemployment have eroded the constituencies of manual workers, from which unions have traditionally recruited (Disney, 1990; Waddington, 1992). Following the election of a Conservative government in 1979, public policy towards trade unions was overtly hostile. Freeman and Pelletier (1990) estimate that the industrial relations laws of the Thatcher government reduced union density by 1–1.7 percentage points per year from 1980 to 1986. This type of analysis is, however, fraught with problems: it is difficult to disentangle cause and effect when dealing with trade union law (Disney, 1990).

The continual restructuring within the UK economy from manufacturing to service also affects union membership. Running parallel with 'deindustrialization' and the contraction of traditional 'masculine work' is evidence of 'a general withering of enthusiasm' for union representation within continuing workplaces, especially in the private sector, and 'a lack of recruitment among new workplaces in both private and public sectors' (Millward et al., 2000, p. 136). Another significant development is the collapse of compulsory unionism – the 'closed shop' – among non-manual workers (Wright, 1996). This pessimistic scenario is countered by the argument that although the heterogeneity of individual employment contracts and atomized conditions challenges a 'command and control' form of collectivism based on 'mechanical solidarity' (Hyman, 2001), there is space in the contemporary workplace for other conceptions of solidarity around, for example, variegated reward systems, temporal flexibility or work–life balance issues (Doherty, 2009).

Employers' policies will significantly influence workers' support for unionization. If managers are openly hostile or less supportive of unions in their workplace, workers will be more likely to perceive union membership to be an act of 'disloyalty' to the organization and, more importantly, as jeopardizing their employment prospects. As noted, the strategic de-recognition of unions has been associated with the growing adoption of the 'Americanized' HRM model (Brown et al., 1997). Furthermore, the inclusion of the union 'voice' in workplace governance was not part of the management mantra during the 1990s.

With New Labour's 1999 Employment Relations Act, the climate for union recognition became more favourable (Wood et al., 2002). The whole rhetoric of New Labour towards the trade unions, and social partnership in particular, encouraged employers and workers to reassess the benefits of unionization. The analysis of union development over the past three decades emphasizes the interplay between long-term economic developments, the shift towards the service sector, the increasing number of workers on precarious contracts, the adverse political and legal environments and the growing number of firms adopting a union-exclusion strategy.

HRM web links For further information on the union-renaissance report and the latest figures for union recognition agreements, go to the TUC website at www.tuc.org.uk and follow the headings to 'Organization and recruitment'.

Union structure

The word 'structure' in relation to trade unions denotes the 'external shape' of trade unions (Hyman, 1975) or job territories – the areas of the labour market from which the union aims to recruit. There are many variants of union structure within countries, traditionally expressed in terms of the four classic ideal types within British union structures: craft, industrial, general and white-collar unions. In practice, however, these classical union structures have never existed in their true forms (Ebbinghaus and Waddington, 2000). The British contemporary union movement is associated with multi-unionism as craft and general unions cross the boundaries of workplaces and industries (Visser and Waddington, 1996). In addition, technological change has both undermined the traditional craft unions and created new occupations, thus blurring the distinction between manual and non-manual. The wave of union mergers over the past two decades reflects the 'deep crisis' in unionization and has resulted in the formation of 'super-unions' (Ebbinghaus and Waddington, 2000).

UK trade unions recorded a total membership of 7,387,898 in 2009–10. The major unions, with a membership of over 100,000, accounted for 6,290,083 members or 85.1 per cent of the total (Certification Officer, 2010). Table 12.4 illustrates the wave of mergers and amalgamations of TUC-affiliated trade unions since 1979. It shows that the number of trade unions affiliated to the TUC has fallen from 109 to 58, almost entirely as a result of mergers. The three largest unions, with a membership of over, 3,598,000 (Table 12.4), accounted for 55.5 per cent of the TUC union membership. This illustrates a philosophy of 'big is best' to encourage 'natural growth', and an 'industrial logic' (Waddington, 1988) in order to avoid the duplication of administrative costs. In 2007, for example, the union Unite was formed by the merger of Amicus and the TGWU, amid expectations that the new enlarged union would give employees the largest resources in industrial disputes. In explaining merger activity, formal union links to the British Labour Party, what is called a 'political logic', are also influential (Waddington and Whitston, 1994).

Table 12.4 *Largest TUC-affiliated unions, 1979–2011*

| Ranking union (size) | Affiliated membership | | % change 1979–2011 | Website (www) |
| | Membership (000s) | | | |
	1979	2011		
1. UNITE[1]	5,058	1,635	(–)67.6	unitetheunion.org.uk
2. UNISON[2]	1,697	1,362	(–)23.3	unison.org.uk
3. GMB	967	601	(–)37.9	gmb.org.uk
4. USDAW	470	370	(–)29.6	usdaw.org.uk
5. PCS	n.d.	300		pcs.org.uk
6. CWU[3]	197	231	(+)30.9	cwu.org
7. NUT	291	366	(–)17.9	teachers.org.uk
8. NASUWT	124	322	(+)79.8	nasuwt.org.uk
9. UCU	n.d.	119		ucu.org.uk
10. UCATT	320	130	(–)65.6	ucatt.org.uk
Total TUC membership	**12,175**	**6,480**	**(–)46.7**	tuc.org.uk
Number of TUC unions	**109**	**58**	**(–)46.8**	

Notes:
1. Formed by the merger in 2007 of TGWU and Amicus (Amicus having been created by the 2002 merger of the AEEU and MSF)
2. Formed by the merger in 1992 of NALGO, NUPE and COHSE
3. Growth has been caused by merger activity within the communications industry.
n.d., no data

Source: TUC website (2011)

The structure of British trade unions is recognized to be complex, diverse and 'chaotic' – as observed by Hyman (1997a) – and the competitive scramble to seek membership anywhere has created trade union structures that can seem bewildering and incomprehensible. The membership distribution between individual trade unions is skewed. At one extreme, there are a relatively small number of trade unions with a disproportionate share of the total union membership, whereas at the other, there are a large number of unions with very small memberships. As the data in Table 12.4 show, the 10 largest TUC-affiliated unions have a total membership of over 6 million – 85 per cent of all TUC membership.

U nite is a large trade union formed by a merger between two of Britain's leading unions, the TGWU and Amicus. It is a democratic and campaigning union that strives to achieve equality in the workplace for its members, as well as advancing its members' interests politically. Unite is active on a global scale and represents over 3 million members in the UK, Republic of Ireland, North America and the Caribbean.

Ray Fletcher OBE

Director of Personnel and Development, Unite the Union

www.unitetheunion.org

Ray Fletcher worked in personnel in the automobile and building materials industries before moving over to the not-for-profit sector, where he became Executive Director of HR and External Affairs at Remploy. Remploy seeks to provide sustainable employment opportunities for disabled people, and Ray was awarded an OBE in 2004 for his work there. Ray currently works at Unite, where he has been for 6 years. He is a Fellow of the Chartered Institute of Personnel and Development and the Chartered Institute of Marketing, and has 40 years' experience in personnel.

 Visit www.palgrave.com/business/bratton5 to watch Ray talking about trade unions in the contemporary workplace, their contribution to workplace learning, and possibilities for union–green coalitions, and then think about the following questions:

1 According to Ray, in the context of change and restructuring, does the role of HR change?
2 What does Unite do to promote learning at work?
3 Can a balance be found between green policies and the interests of union members?

HRM as I see it

The major structural characteristic of British trade unions in 2011 was the predominance of horizontal or 'conglomerate' unions, that is, large individual unions whose members were distributed over a wide range of different industries. In the past decade, parallel trends of restructuring have become evident among trade unions in other developed capitalist economies (see, for example, Ebbinghaus and Waddington, 2000; Streeck and Visser, 1997; Visser and Waddington, 1996).

HRM web links For further information on union membership, governance, services and policies, go to any of the websites listed in Table 12.4.

Collective bargaining

The previous sections have examined the principal 'actors' in industrial relations: management and the unions. We will now focus our attention on a central activity that regulates the employment relationship for over 6 million UK workers – collective bargaining. In any democratic society, the freedom for workers to bargain collectively is a core human right (Adams, 2006). In Canada, for example, the right to collective bargaining in the workplace is protected by the Charter of Rights. In a landmark judgement in 2007, Chief Justice Beverley McLachlin and Mr Justice Louis LeBel (quoted by Makin, 2007, p. A4) wrote:

⎡ The right to bargain collectively with an employer enhances the human
dignity, liberty and autonomy of workers by giving them the opportunity
to influence the establishment of workplace rules and thereby gain some
⎣ control over a major aspect of their lives, namely their work.

We define collective bargaining here as:

> an institutional system of negotiation in which the making, interpretation and adminis-
> tration of rules, as well as the application of statutory controls affecting the employment
> relationship, are decided within union–management negotiating committees.

Several important points arise from this definition. First, collective bargaining is a
process through which representatives of the union and management *jointly* determine
some of the rules and regulations appertaining to the employment contract. As such,
collective bargaining establishes a form of workplace democracy, which has been well
articulated by Chamberlain and Kuhn (1965, p. 135; quoted in Adams, 2006, p. 17). The
ethical principle underlying the concept of collective bargaining as a process of industrial
governance is that those who are integral to the conduct of the enterprise should have a
voice in decisions of concern to them. Collective bargaining is therefore a correlation of
political democracy.

The second important point is that there are two types of rule: *substantive* and *procedural*. Substantive rules establish terms and conditions of employment, such as pay, working
hours and holidays, whereas procedural rules regulate the way in which substantive rules
are made and interpreted, and indicate how workplace conflicts are to be resolved.

Third, the parties negotiating the collective agreement also *enforce* the agreement.
Unlike, for example, Canada and the USA, the British system of collective bargaining is
perhaps most noted for its lack of legal regulation. Collective agreements are, with a few
exceptions, not regarded as contracts of legal enforcement between the parties (see Davies
and Freedland, 1984).

Collective bargaining structure

The structure of collective bargaining is the framework within which negotiations take
place and defines the scope of the employers and employees covered by the collective
agreement. In Britain, there is no single uniform structure of collective bargaining, the
major structural characteristic of the system being wide variety. Thus, collective bargaining
is conducted at several levels – workplace, corporate or industry.

The term 'multiemployer bargaining' refers to an arrangement whereby a number of
employers reach a central collective agreement on pay and conditions with a trade union(s).
The multiemployer agreement therefore covers all those companies which are signatories
to the agreement. Single-employer bargaining, particularly in large multiplant businesses
(for example, the motor industry), can be either centralized or decentralized. Where a
holding company covers a group of companies, bargaining can be conducted at the level of
the subsidiary companies or below – at the divisional level or at the level of the individual
plant. Some multiplant companies have a single-company agreement applying to all their
plants, whereas other similar companies have a separate agreement at each plant.

In practice, survey evidence shows that collective bargaining structures are closely linked
with business structures and 'profit centres'. Union recognition and collective bargaining

©istockphoto.com/Brasil2

Single-employer bargaining, particularly in large multiplant businesses (for example, the motor industry), can be either centralized or decentralized.

coverage – the percentage of employees whose pay and working conditions are negotiated between a union and their employer – are mutually dependent, and both have been decreasing. This is best charted by considering bargaining over rewards (Brown et al., 2000, 2010). Table 12.5 provides an approximate picture of the changes in the pattern of pay determination since 1984. Based upon survey data, it shows that the proportion of British workplaces (with 25 or more employees) in which collective bargaining was the dominant method of pay determination fell from 60 per cent in 1984 to 26 per cent in 2004.

Subsequent survey results reveal a precipitous decline in national or industry-wide collective bargaining. In 1984, multi-employer agreements featured in 41 per cent of workplaces, whereas by 2004 this figure had contracted to only 7 per cent. Collective bargaining over pay is no longer the norm in Britain, as is evident from Table 12.5. The proportion of all workplaces in which pay was not subject to negotiation increased from 40 per cent in 1984 to 70 per cent in 2004, although the aggregate data mask variations in pay bargaining. The proportion of workers covered by collective agreements broadly reflects the pattern of union density, workers employed in the public sector and in workplaces employing 25 or more individuals being more likely to have their pay determined by collective bargaining (Brown, 2010; Cully et al., 1999; Kersley et al., 2006).

Table 12.5 *Coverage of collective bargaining in Britain, 1984–2004*

	Percentages			
	1984	**1990**	**1998**	**2004**
Collective bargaining	60	42	29	26
Level of negotiations				
Multiemployer bargaining	41	23	13	7
Single-employer, multisite	12	14	12	5
Workplace/establishment	5	4	3	1
Not the result of bargaining	**40**	**58**	**71**	**70**

Source: Millward et al. (2000, p. 186) and Kersley et al. (2006, p. 20). Used with permission

By the early twenty-first century, collective bargaining coverage in the private sector had diminished to no more than 2 workers in 10, offering a 'patchy and highly localised protection to a small and shrinking minority of workers' (Brown and Nash, 2008, p. 102). In the public sector, on the other hand, collective bargaining has continued to be over-whelmingly important for determining rewards. The decline in collective bargaining coverage has meant that, for 7 out of 10 employees, 'the only cushion against the vagaries of an open labour market has been provided by the state' (Brown, 2010, p. 258) through the statutory national minimum wage. The steep decline in collective bargaining coverage appears to be largely confined to the UK. The coverage rate is as high as 70 per cent or more in other EU member states, such as Belgium, Denmark, Finland, France, Italy, The Netherlands and Sweden.

HRM web links 📶 For further information on union membership in the EU, go to the EIRO website, www.eurofound.europa.eu/eiro.

Collective bargaining over pay, effort level and the control of work is the *raison d'être* of trade unionism, but the data underscore how little involved unions are in pay bargaining and other aspects of the employment contract in the twenty-first century. There has been considerable debate over the causes of the sustained collapse in collective bargaining. The contraction of employment in the manufacturing sector, anti-union legislation and Conservative governments' overt hostility to collective bargaining during the 1980s and early 1990s are commonly assumed to have undermined union strength and collective bargaining. Arguably, the 'golden age' of collective bargaining was relatively short-lived – from 1950 to 1960 – since when it has been going downhill.

When pay is bargained across an industry, it removes management's ability to reduce wages unilaterally and compels employers to find some other dimension of the business on which to compete. This has been called 'taking wages out of competition'. However, by focusing on the institutions governing collective bargaining and formal 'rule-making', this mainstream perspective arguably overplays the importance of harmonious union–management relations, and downplays the daily interaction between workers and managers, as the informal 'rules of the game' are negotiated on a day-to-day basis (Krahn et al., 2011, p. 347).

Brown (2010) posits that when product markets were confined to a national economy, there was relative stability in the system of collective bargaining. Its collapse was caused by the destabilizing forces of globalization and privatization, which increased price competition: 'Legislative restraints on trade unions may have accelerated the process, but it was tougher competitive environments that reduced the share of profits that they [the unions] could win for their members' (Brown, 2010, p. 262). Globalization and the collapse of national product markets may have had a profound effect, but they do not fully explain why collective bargaining, as a system of workplace governance, remains relatively stable in other EU member states. The focus on the precipitous decline in union density may obscure other factors underlying the collapse of collective bargaining, for example power. Hyman (1975, p. 26) explained that employment is a power relationship in which conflict is always a likelihood:

In every workplace there exists an invisible frontier of control, reducing some of the formal powers of the employer: a frontier which is defined and redefined in a continuous process of pressure and counter-pressure, conflict and accommodation, overt and tacit struggle.

In the UK, in the post-Thatcher era, the absence of support from the state for trade unions, and a relatively inequitable industrial relations system, thereby minimizing labour's bargaining power, have contributed to the diminishing significance of collective bargaining as a means of regulating the employment relationship (Sullivan, 2010).

HRM web links   The WERS 2004 survey First Findings is available at http://bis.ecgroup.net/ Publications/EmploymentMatters/WorkplaceEmploymentRelationsSurveyWERS/ 051057.aspx. For EU data, see www.eurofound.europa.eu/eiro.

The collective agreement: an overview

The outcome of collective bargaining is a collective agreement (in North America also referred to as a 'contract'). The collective agreement provides for the terms and conditions of employment of those employees covered by the agreement, also specifying the procedure that will govern the relationship between the signatories. In Britain, the terms of the collective agreement are binding in law on the parties if they are incorporated into the individual contract of employment (see Selwyn, 2011, for a legal discussion on incorporation). The content of the collective agreements varies widely. Generally, the greater the level of aggregation, that is, industry-based agreements compared with single-establishment coverage, the fewer the subjects that can be covered in detail.

Collective agreements can be complex and legalistic. Most, however, have some basic similarities, as well as a common structure that underlies their many complexities (Giles and Starkman, 2001). Collective agreements are typically divided into articles (also called clauses or sections). Most include a number of articles that define and regulate the relationship between the union and the employer. All collective agreements contain groups of articles specifying pay rates, hours of work, working arrangements and workload (referred to as 'substantives rules'), as well as guidelines dealing with discipline, grievances, technological change and redundancy (referred to as 'procedural rules'). The collective agreement usually concludes with an article that specifies the duration of the agreement, followed by the signatures of the union and employer representatives.

For management, the formal negotiation of a collective agreement is a critical instrument for rewriting the 'rules' governing the workplace and legitimizes the radical restructuring of work systems. For trade unions, the process of negotiating a collective agreement is an arena for union representatives to become 'embedded' in workplace governance (Findlay et al., 2009). A key determinant of the contents of the agreement is the balance of power between the parties. When the union and the employer have similar evaluations of their relative market and organizational strength, and an awareness of an implicit strike or closure threat, it can lead to a shift in the balance of power being reflected in the collective agreement without the ultimate sanction of a strike or a lockout (Brown, 2010).

HRM web links   For suggestions on how to write a collective agreement, go to the book's website at www.palgrave.com/business/bratton5.

Trade unions and HRM

The existing literature for the most part presents the HRM model as being inconsistent with traditional stereotyped industrial relations systems in Britain and North America. As Adams (1995) points out, the adversarial traditions of Anglo-Saxon industrial relations systems elicit 'low trust' and non-cooperation between labour and management, rather than a propensity towards 'high trust' and cooperation. There is a *prima facie* case that the 'collectivist' traditions of trade unions are at odds with the 'individualistic' goal in the normative HRM model: 'there is no recognition of any broader concept of pluralism within society giving rise to solidaristic collective orientation' (Guest, 1987, p. 519). The HRM model poses a threat to trade unions in at least four ways: individualization of the employment contract, culture management, intensification of work and the undermining of union solidarity through organizational commitment.

First, critics argue that the 'web of rules' that regulates the modern employment relationship is increasingly being established unilaterally by employers rather than through bilateral – collective bargaining – processes. As Bacon and Storey (1993, pp. 9–10) correctly argue, 'Performance-related pay individualizes the employment relationship because it isolates employees and personalizes issues such as design and evaluation of work'. Moreover, performance appraisal severs the link between pay awards and collective action.

Second, the collective logic of trade union representation is challenged by 'strong' corporate cultures (see Chapter 5). Work-based learning programmes, for example, may strengthen support for corporate culture and 'socialize' workers to accept the hegemony of managerial authority, thus undermining workplace unionism (Bratton, 2001; Wells, 1993).

Third, critical workplace scholars have plausibly argued that high-involvement/high-performance work system structures are a sophisticated form of labour intensification (Danford et al., 2008; Thompson and McHugh, 2009). If we accept the tenor of this research, we could argue that new HRM-inspired work initiatives will fulfil a historic role of creating working conditions that encourage rather than weaken workplace unionism. The ability of team-based work systems to mortally weaken workplace unionism depends upon the context in which they are utilized, for example global product competition, and upon the union strategies adopted.

Fourth, the HRM goal of worker commitment is potentially the 'main challenge to the union' (Guest, 1989, p. 43). Team-working regimes often represent attempts to translate multitasking into team 'commitment', mitigating an understanding of how, through attachment to existing practices, workplace union representation and sectional interests workers have their own logic of commitment and resistance (Thompson and McHugh, 2009). The notion of worker commitment implies a social psychological state of deep identification with a work organization and an acceptance of its goals and values (Guest, 1995). The goals of HRM are often understood as seeking to elicit high commitment and thereby cultivate 'proactive' behaviour, with committed workers expending their effort 'beyond contract' for the enterprise (Guest, 1995, p. 113).

The idea of worker commitment as a powerful, cost-effective mechanism of control is a common theme in the critical sociology literature (see, for example, Burawoy, 1979; Edwards, 1979; Friedman, 1977). The rationale behind the goal of worker commitment is explained by the tensions inherent in the capitalist employment relationship. As Lincoln and Kalleberg (1992, pp. 23–4) put it:

The problem of control in organizations is in large measure solved when the commitment of its members is high. Committed workers are self-directed and motivated actors whose inducement to participation and compliance is their moral bond to the organization.

The case for eliciting workers' commitment seems plausible, but literature on the topic suggests that the concept of commitment is problematic. As Guest (1987) argues, the first issue is 'commitment to what?' Writers taking a managerial perspective are interested in commitment to values that drive business strategy, but Guest (1987, 1995) points out that workers can have multiple and perhaps competing commitments to a profession, a career, a craft, a union and a family. Arguably, the higher the level of commitment to a particular set of skills or professional standards, the greater the likelihood of resistance to multiskilling and flexible job designs. The goal of commitment might thus contradict the goal of flexibility.

Closely associated with the debate on HRM and industrial relations is the notion of 'dual commitment'. Theorists have posed the question of whether workers can be simultaneously committed to the goals and values of both the organization and their trade union. Murphy and Olthuis's (1995) study found support for the idea of dual commitment. They reported that 'many workers are attached to both the union and the company and have a type of 'dual commitment' [, and] attachment to the company does not necessarily lessen attachment to the union, and vice versa' (1995, p. 77). The evidence appears to support the hypothesis that dual commitment is possible where the industrial relations climate is characterized as being cooperative and non-adversarial.

The logic of the HRM model is (at least in theory) that workplace unionism will eventually 'wither and die'. This interpretation has been expressed by prominent union leaders: 'In the wrong hands HRM becomes both a sharp weapon to prise workers apart from their union, and a blunt instrument to bully employees' (Monks, 1998, p. xiii). Although a 'strong' corporate culture may aim to encourage workers to identify with their company's ideals rather than with the union collective, the argument that unions and HRM cannot coexist does not appear to be consistent with the empirical evidence (Wood, 1995).

reflective question What is your own perspective on the union–HRM debate? Can unions and HRM coexist in the contemporary workplace?

Union strategies and paradox

The precipitous decline in union density and collective bargaining coverage provides the backcloth for examining very divergent union renewal strategies. At its core, a union renewal strategy seeks to deliver sustainable increases in workplace power for both unions and their members (Simms and Holgate, 2010). In his study of British trade unions, Heery (2005, p. 103) argues that union strategy is not simply a pragmatic adjustment to a changing national business system: 'It is also an expression of internal politics, dialogue and power … [thus] union politics matter'. Efforts by unions to reverse the steep decline of density and bargaining coverage have prompted a body of scholarship on union renewal (see, for example Hickey et al., 2010). It would be misleading to develop a typology of union strategies – one with mutually exclusive categories – but, for our purposes, we have identified two dominant strategic approaches for the renewal of British trade unions: organizing strategy and partnership strategy.

The *organizing strategy* is internally focused and places a renewed emphasis on 'organizing the unorganized'. A sustained attempt is made to recruit those workers outside the traditional white male norm of full-time employment. The strategy includes a change in union priorities, such that they accommodate a more diverse workforce, 'field enlargement' through 'targeted' recruitment campaigns, and 'issue-based' recruiting, for example focusing on 'justice, dignity and respect' issues in the workplace (Heery, 2002, 2004, 2005).

The aim is to establish an effective workplace union organization that can be self-sustaining in terms of recruitment and service to its members. In this, the Employment Relations Act 1999 assisted union recruitment campaigns only 'where unions already have a presence' (Wood et al., 2002, p. 233). Hickey et al. (2010, p. 75) note an interesting paradox: when statutory procedures, rather than 'pure bargaining power', provide for workplace union organization, the disassociation between the two may have a detrimental effect on employees' commitment to the union. An analysis of successful union renewal campaigns shows support for a strategy that combines both 'bottom-up' grassroots activism and 'top-down' leadership-driven strategies tailored to the specific context (Hickey et al., 2010).

The second dominant approach for the renewal of unions is the *social partnership strategy*. This strategy is externally focused, with its emphasis on industrial relations embedded in 'union-friendly' employment law. Central to the argument is the belief that renewal requires trade unions to take advantage of the facilitating effect of employment law and European social policy in order to develop a new form of workplace governance in increasingly complex competitive environments (see, for example, Terry, 2003). The theoretical basis of the approach can be traced back to North American literature on 'strategic partnerships', 'mutual gains' and 'win-win' principles: reciprocal employer–trade union commitments to deliver mutual gains and establish the basis for trust and cooperation to develop high-performance work systems (Betcherman et al., 1994; Kochan et al., 1986; Verma, 1995).

Following the election of New Labour in the UK in 1997, a partnership approach, part of New Labour's broader 'Third Way' philosophy, to industrial relations became increasingly popular and was adopted by some employers. The TUC published *Partners for Progress: New Unionism at the Workplace* (TUC, 1999), which advocated 'pragmatic partnership' agreements between local union representatives and managers. In the context of falling membership, the unions presented themselves to potential members and employers alike as 'facilitators of cooperative collective relationships' that would have mutual economic benefits (Brown, 2000, p. 303).

The term 'partnership' is used in a variety of ways. With this caveat in mind, it is estimated that 248 partnership agreements exist in Britain, covering fewer than 10 per cent of all employees in 2007, which is a significant increase from fewer than 1 per cent in 1997 (Bacon and Samuel, 2009, p. 243). At the *national level*, partnership agreements have emerged as a potentially important mechanism to involve workers in improving public service delivery (Bacon and Samuel, 2009). The notion of partnership can be applied to tripartite discussions between employer and union representatives and the government. For example, addressing the 2010 TUC Green Growth Conference, Frances O'Grady, TUC Deputy General Secretary, outlined a partnership approach: 'We want a mature debate about how we can accelerate progress towards a low-carbon, ecofriendly economy … And we want to work with ministers and with industry to achieve a *just transition* to a greener economy' (O'Grady, 2010).

HRM web links WWW   For further information on trade union strategies for a 'green' economy, go to www.sustainableworkplaces.org.uk.

At *workplace level*, 'partnership' is the term applied to agreements to promote flexibility in working practices in exchange for a union 'voice' and engagement in life-long learning, specifically with the union learning representative (Cassell and Lee, 2009). According to Roche (2009), partnership-related practices gave rise to 'mutual gains' for each of the main stakeholders: employers, employees and unions. Employers appear to gain with respect to organizational commitment, the climate of employment relations and the quality of managerial supervisory relations. Partnership-related practices improved the intrinsic aspects of work, such as work autonomy, job satisfaction and fairness, for employees. The trade unions gain with respect to union commitment, influence and the likelihood of increased membership. The study, however, reported no gains with respect to employees' willingness to accept change, employment security or higher earnings.

An analysis of the partnership agreements signed in Britain between 1990 and 2007 shows that most have only modest objectives and are 'substantially hollow', although they do offer unions increased involvement in management's decisions (Samuel and Bacon, 2010, pp. 443–4). Potentially, partnership agreements can give unions a place at the 'strategy table' by portraying themselves as authoritative partners in economic management (Munro and Rainbird, 2000, p. 225).

reflective question What do you think of workplace partnerships? How does the partnership strategy reframe employment relations? What are the advantages and disadvantages of partnership?

Partnership agreements also have their detractors (see, for example, Bacon and Storey, 2000; Clayton, 1998; Kelly, 1996; O'Dowd and Roche, 2009; Watson et al., 2009). Clayton (1998), for example, remains sceptical about the likelihood of workplace partnership developing as a vehicle for reconstituting trade union power in response to long-term decline. To paraphrase Guest (2001b), UK management is currently driving the bus, and although the unions may be invited along for the ride, they will remain in the passenger seats to offer guidance only; they will not be trusted to do any driving. Kelly (1996, p. 101) argues that, rather than strengthening the unionization process, partnership can potentially 'weaken or inhibit the growth of workplace union organization', and partnership agreements may form part of 'a longer term *non-union* strategy' (Bacon and Storey, 2000, p. 410).

The findings by O'Dowd and Roche (2009) indicate that partnerships may limit union influence or deflect it away from workplace issues traditionally pursued by unions in collective bargaining. Moreover, while there were benefits to management, in terms of improved productivity, employees covered by partnership experienced 'increased job insecurity, work intensification and reduced job autonomy' (O'Dowd and Roche, 2009, p. 36). Similarly, the advent of partnership between the Benefits Agency and the Public and Commercial Services Union benefited the union in terms of consultation rights, but the membership was 'largely untouched' by the arrangement (Martin, 2010, p. 229).

At a more theoretical level, Watson and his colleagues (2009) note that the partnership model is a problematic concept because of its variety of meanings and potential denial of the 'dual nature' of the employment relationship that involves both cooperation *and* conflict (2009, p. 470). An analysis of the characteristics of British corporate governance – a preference for short-term financial performance and the maintenance of shareholder values (Purcell, 1995) – suggests that British business is an infertile environment for social partnership (Heery, 2002).

Table 12.6 *The benefits and costs of a partnership strategy*

	Benefits	Costs
For organizations	• Efficiency gains • Lower absenteeism/turnover • Better union–management relations • Potential for improved performance	• Greater investment in work-related learning and other human resource programmes • Having to share information • Having to share decision-making
For workers	• Access to work-related learning • Potential increased skills • Discretion over the work process	• A need for greater commitment to the firm • Job loss and lower income growth • Greater work intensification and job-related stress
For unions	• Participation in decision-making • Affirmation of an independent voice for workers • Access to information • Improved status	• A move away from job control unionism • Isolation from union members • Union polices work changes • Leaders challenge

Source: Adapted from Betcherman et al. (1994)

In the long run, partnership is likely to be sustained if it holds the promise of real benefits for the employer, employees and unions. The interests of employers and labour are not identical, so an effective approach to partnership must involve acceptable trade-offs, the trade-offs associated with the partnership model shown in Table 12.6. It is hard to disentangle the effects of partnership; with this in mind, the challenge for trade unions is to transcend the polarized positions of outright opposition to partnership and cooperation, and focus on a strategy to extract the potential from partnership without eschewing traditional union-building activities.

The outcome is indeterminate and will depend upon the ongoing interaction between union and management, and, as Heery (2002) concludes, upon whether the 'qualitative' gains (for example, 'voice' and dignity) are not heavily outweighed by 'quantitative' losses (for example, job loss and inequality). The debate on 'union renewal' and 'social partnerships' occurred, of course, before the financial crisis that erupted in 2008 and has continued to reverberate around the globe (Nolan, P., 2011). A key focus of contemporary debate is the destructive contradiction between unsustainable business strategies that destroy the ecosystem and those which partner with the trade union and environmental movements in the quest to achieve a *just* low-carbon, ecofriendly economy.

Partnership arrangements: the end of an era?

Although partnership arrangements had existed prior to the election of the Labour Government in 1997, they were specially promoted from that date. An important element of the Employment Relations Act 1999 was its support for voluntary partnership arrangements to achieve cooperation between employers and trade unions, based on the principal of mutual benefit.

Throughout the 2000s, debates took place between academics as to whether mutual gains were possible, or whether partnership arrangements actually benefited managers. With trade union membership numbers having declined for two decades, partnership arrangements were seen by many trade unions as a potential route for renewal and expansion. This case was made most influentially by Ackers and Payne (1988), who argued that partnerships gave trade unions 'a seat at the table' – a view that trade unions themselves seemed to accept. In contrast, many empirical studies raised questions over whether the trade unions made any significant gains or were pulled instead into cooperation around controversial management change initiatives. Oxenbridge and Brown (2004) encouraged the debate to move away from this static good/bad dichotomy: they described cooperative arrangements as relationships, which could change and develop and should be seen on a continuum from robust to shallow.

The latest policy discussion paper from ACAS (Wright, 2011) suggests that trade unions no longer favour the partnership approach:

This approach assumed that cooperation would produce more efficient working practices and improved financial performance, which firms would then share with employees through better wages and conditions (Terry, 2003: 462–7). The 248

partnership agreements signed between 1990 and 2007 covered around 10 per cent of all workers in Britain (Samuel and Bacon, 2010: 431). A recent study of these agreements found that most were 'substantively hollow', and not instruments for exchanging greater employment security for more flexible working practices, as their proponents intended. Partnership agreements tended to achieve a more modest trade-off of guaranteed union involvement in managerial decisions in return for commitment to work towards the firm's success. As such, partnership agreements were not mechanisms for employer dominance over employee interests, as many had predicted (Samuel and Bacon, 2010). The election of several prominent critics of the partnership approach to union leadership positions in the early 2000s marginalised it as a central renewal strategy, and partnership is unlikely to be re-embraced across the union movement any time soon.

Samuel and Bacon's paper argues that partnership arrangements actually offered few benefits to either employers or trade unions, being largely procedural. This, they say, reflects the UK tradition of voluntary collective bargaining, which has always had a strong procedural element.

Stop! What do you think? Why have both employers and trade unions been so keen on partnerships if the mutual gains are limited? How significant might a change of government be to employers' and unions' attitudes towards partnership? Do we need legislation to force employers and unions to work together?

Sources and further information: See Wright (2011), from which the extract here was taken. See also Ackers and Payne (1988), Oxenbridge and Brown (2004), Samuel and Bacon (2010) and Terry (2003).

Note: This feature was written by Anne Munro at Edinburgh Napier University.

Rama Garment factory

case study

Setting

In the early twentieth century, the rapid expansion of industry and the growth of the working class in India led to an increase of skilled and literate workers who set the stage for unions to flourish in the workplace. The country's first trade union was formed in 1918, followed by the creation of the regulatory India Trades Union Act in 1926.

Nearly 100 years later, only 8 per cent of the 380 million workforce in India today are unionized, with the official number of registered unions estimated to be 50,000. India has among the lowest trade union densities in the Asia-Pacific region, and the rate continues to decline.

©Paulprescott/Dreamstime

Males overwhelmingly represent the majority of trade union membership in the country. The active participation of women in the trade union movement has historically been low, with social, historical, biological and religious constraints creating barriers to the higher paying opportunities that unionized workplaces can offer. Although trade unions were successful in helping to establish the Maternity Benefit Act in 1961, Indian women are still under-represented at all levels of union leadership and decision-making, and their issues have not taken centre stage in union struggles.

One striking exception to trade union membership for women is in the garment industry, a major source of exports for India. More than 80 per cent of the 3 million people who work in the industry are women, and women can make up as many as 70 per cent of total union members. However, despite the presence of unions in the industry, the work is still characterized by long hours, low wages and minimal regulation.

The problem

Twenty-year-old Asha recently arrived in Baddi, an industrial town in northern India, to find work in the garment factory industry. She had followed her cousin Devi, who had fled their rural village several months earlier after failing to find local work that would pay enough to help support her family. Although both women knew the wages in Baddi's garment industry were low, a job in a factory would still pay more than they could earn performing the traditional agricultural or domestic work available to women in their village. Asha's father was severely ill, and her mother was depending on Asha to provide additional money for his medication. The women also wanted to continue their education, a goal that would be highly unlikely if they remained at home.

Devi, who had had some experience as a seamstress, quickly found work in the tailoring section at one of the newer Baddi factories called Rama. She told Asha that the factory management preferred to hire young women, saying that women were more efficient and disciplined than men. Devi managed to get Asha an interview with the supervisor of the factory she worked for.

At the interview, the supervisor talked to Asha about job responsibilities and salary, and then ended the meeting by saying that she should not get involved in any kind of unionism. 'It's unproductive, 'he said. 'You must pay attention only to your work.' Asha nodded and was happy to learn that she was hired for the job, although the money she would earn would still not be enough to pay for all of her father's medical bills.

On her first day on the job, Asha noticed that although there were a few men on the factory floor, the vast majority of her co-workers were women. The work was routine and the hours were long, but Asha was appreciative of the opportunity the factory management had given her. Within her first few weeks, she was able to send home money to help support her parents and buy her father's medicine.

Shortly after Asha had completed her first year at the factory, her father's condition worsened and he required more medication, putting a further strain on the family's finances. Kapil, who had been hired at the same time as Asha, approached her when they began their shift. He told her that he had contacted a trade union leader to start the process of unionizing the workers and asked for her support. 'The union can help improve our working conditions and get us an increment in pay.' Kapil stressed that he needed the women in the factory to get involved as there were far more of them than men. 'We will never become unionized unless the women come forward,' he said. 'It's for their benefit too.' He asked Asha to meet him the next day to work out a strategy to get the other women to support the idea.

When Asha told Devi what Kapil had said, Devi warned Asha about talking to Kapil any further about unions. 'We cannot take this risk as it is the best work option we have. The men are always trying to bring in the union because it is easier for them to find work elsewhere if the factory lets us go. The other women will not cooperate with the men in trying to unionize our workplace.' Later that day, Asha read a notice that management had posted on the factory floor bulletin board warning that other factories in Baddi had been shut down because of unions protesting against work conditions. It also mentioned that management was reviewing possible pay increments, but only if the factory remained non-unionized.

Asha spent that night worrying about how she was going to continue to support her family and wondered if helping Kapil bring in the union was the right thing to do.

(This case study is based on research by Chakravarty, 2007.)

Assignment

Working either alone or in a study group, prepare a report drawing on this chapter and other recommended material addressing the following:

1 How does India's patriarchal society play a role in Asha's situation and for Indian women in general?
2 What type of industrial relations strategy is Rama's management applying? What national features of India's society and economy might be contributing to their choice of strategy?
3 If you were Asha, would you help Kapil bring in the union? Why or why not?

Essential reading

Chakravarty, D. (2007) 'Docile oriental women' and organised labour: a case study of the Indian garment manufacturing industry. *Indian Journal of Gender Studies*, **14**: 439–60.
Gani, A. (1996) Who joins the unions and why? Evidence from India. *International Journal of Manpower*, **17**(6–7): 54.
Mathias, P. and Davis, J. (eds) (1996) *International Trade and British Economic Growth: From the Eighteenth Century to the Present Day*. Oxford: Blackwell.
Mohanty, M. (ed.) (2004) *Class, Caste, Gender: Readings in Indian Government and Politics*. New Dehli: Sage.
Ramaswamy, E. and Schiporst, F. (2000) Human resource management, trade unions and empowerment: two cases from India. *International Journal of Human Resource Management*, **11**(4): 664–80.
Ratnam, V. (2006) *Industrial Relations*. New Dehli: Oxford University Press.
Saraswati, R. and Bagchi, D. (eds) (1993) *Women and Work in South Asia: Regional Patterns and Perspectives*. New York: Routledge.

Note: This feature was written by Lori Rilkoff, HR Manager at City of Kamloops, BC, Canada.

Visit the companion website at www.palgrave.com/business/bratton5 for guidelines on writing reports.

summary

◀ This chapter recognizes that managing work and people in the workplace includes a collective dimension. Research indicates that a union-avoidance strategy is the one most frequently adopted by UK and US companies. We have emphasized that the selection of an industrial relations strategy involves managers considering a number of complex economic, political, legal and historical factors. Given the different conditions, each industrial relations strategy is likely to be unique and display contradictory practices.

◀ We have also examined union membership, structure and collective bargaining and union strategies. In a nutshell, the dramatic reduction in union membership and collective bargaining coverage has led to a shift in power towards management. The argument here is that this shift in power makes it more likely that employers will be tempted to take the short-term 'low road' to profitability that can potentially violate the psychological contract.

◀ Analysing four fundamental factors influencing union–management relations – the state of the labour market, management's strategic capacity, labour's strategic capacity and the legal and political context of union–management relations – we can say that the jury is still out on whether the present economic crisis will accelerate industrial relations trends.

◀ This chapter examined two dominant union strategies: organizing strategy and partnership strategy. We noted that the long-term success of the partnership strategy will depend upon ongoing union–management relations and on whether or not the qualitative gains are heavily outweighed by quantitative losses. We also emphasized the apparent contradiction in the two union strategy alternatives.

vocab checklist for ESL students

◀ arbitrate (v), arbitrator (n), arbitration (n)

◀ collective bargaining (n)

◀ industrial action (n)

◀ industrial relations (n)

◀ labour relations (n)

◀ mediate (v), mediator (n), mediation (n), mediating (adj)

◀ patriarchy (n), patriarchal (adj)

◀ procedural rules (n)

◀ solidarity (n), solidaristic (adj)

◀ strike (v) (n)

◀ substantive rules (n)

◀ unionize (v), unionism (n), union (n), unionization (n)

◀ unite (v), Unitarianism (n)

WWW Visit www.palgrave.com/business/bratton5 for a link to free definitions of these terms in the Macmillan Dictionary, as well as additional learning resources for ESL students.

review questions

1   What is meant by the term 'industrial relations'?

2   Why are industrial relations strategies said to be the result of strategic choices?

3   Why do employees join trade unions? How can contextual factors explain the development of British trade unions?

4   To what extent is collective bargaining in Britain too fragmented to function effectively in an enlarged European market?

5   What contradictions might be found in the twin goals of union renewal and social partnership?

6   Given the present economic crisis, what are the benefits, if any, of a 'social partnership' involving the union movement, environmental movements, employers, and government to develop a sustainable green economy?

further reading to improve your mark

Reading these articles and chapters can help you gain a better understanding and potentially a higher grade for your HRM assignment.

◀ Brown, W. and Nash, D. (2008) What has happening to collective bargaining under New Labour? Interpreting WERS 2004. *Industrial Relations Journal*, **39**(2): 91–103.

◀ Charlwood, A. (2002) Why do non-union employees want to unionize? Evidence from Britain. *British Journal of Industrial Relations*, **40**(3): 463–91.

◀ Butler, P. (2009) Non-union employee representation: exploring the riddle of managerial strategy. *Industrial Relations Journal*, **40**(3): 198–214.

◄ Heery, E. and Simms, M. (2010) Employer responses to union organizing: patterns and effects. *Human Resource Management Journal*, **20**(1): 3–22.

◄ For an insight into the formal negotiation process, see P. Findlay, A. McKinlay, A. Marks and P. Thompson (2009) Collective bargaining and new work regimes: 'too important to be left to bosses'. *Industrial Relations Journal*, **40**(3): 235–51.

◄ Bacon, N. and Samuel, P. (2010) The contents of partnership agreements in Britain 1990–2007. *Work, Employment and Society*, **24**(3): 430–48.

 Visit www.palgrave.com/business/bratton5 for lots of extra resources to help you get to grips with this chapter, including study tips, HRM skills development guides, summary lecture notes, and more.

part V

the employment relationship

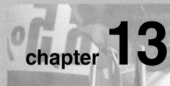

chapter 13

employee relations and involvement

objectives

After studying this chapter, you should be able to:

1 Explain why managers might want to increase employee involvement and participation (EIP) and describe the different dimensions of EIP

2 Appreciate the importance of employee communication in the human resource management paradigm

3 Identify some ethical issues and their relevance to employee relations

4 Describe the major issues relating to sexual harassment in the workplace and the implications for managing employee relations

5 Explain the concepts, values and legal framework that underline the disciplinary process in employment

introduction

As explained in the previous chapter, trade unions have historically provided workers with a 'voice' mechanism for dealing with workplace problems. Exercising the union voice translates into discussing with the employer employment conditions that need to be changed, rather than taking strike action or quitting the job. During the 1980s, a 'new industrial order' emerged in the UK: rather than relying upon the union voice, employers turned more to direct employee voice arrangements (Benson and Brown, 2010; Blyton and Turnbull, 1998; Taras and Kaufman, 2006). Typically, collective union–employer relationships were seen as 'adversarial', and the individual employee–employer relationship was perceived as 'secondary' (Gennard and Judge, 2005). It was during this period that the term 'employee relations' became increasingly used by human resource management (HRM) practitioners, and the term became fashionable among some British academics (Leat, 2007).

Whereas 'industrial relations' addresses the 'collectivist' dimension of the employment relationship, 'employee relations' primarily focuses on the individual aspects of the employer–employee relationship. This interest in non-union forms of employee representation or voice coincides with the decline in membership and influence of trade unions in North America and the UK (Kim et al., 2010). Here, we use the label 'employee relations' to encompass an assortment of human resources (HR) practices that seek to regulate employment relations through effective communications, employee involvement (EI), individual employee rights and grievance-handling and managerial disciplinary action. Although the focus is upon management and managing the employment relationship, these practices provide an opportunity to create and maintain dignity *at* work (Bolton, 2007).

In this chapter, we will explain key issues related to communication in the workplace. We will then go on to explain the terms and the various forms of EI before examining different mechanisms of 'employee voice', such as joint consultative committees (JCCs). Tensions and paradoxes associated with EI, ethical issues, equity and harassment in the workplace are also discussed in some detail before we conclude the chapter with an overview of the process governing employee discipline.

The nature of employee relations

Exactly what constitutes employee relations is not explicable. The term is used in different ways and tends to encompass both collective and individual dimensions, union and non-union relationships. As we noted in Chapter 1, some authors use the terms 'personnel management' and 'human resource management' interchangeably, and for one particular aspect of employment relations, they use 'industrial relations', 'labour relations' and 'employee relations'. Each of these terms has its own particular set of meanings among the academic community.

As we discussed in Chapter 12, 'industrial relations' and 'labour relations' have, for example, been associated with trade unions, adversarial collective bargaining and strikes. As Mabey et al. (1998a, p. 278) comment, each label has 'its own connotations [and] none of them succeed entirely in capturing the essence of the numerous unfolding types of relations associated with work'. Employee relations practices constitute important non-union processes that impact upon the employer–employee relationship. These processes aim to improve both employee voice, itself an imprecise term, and organizational performance. The focus here on non-union models of employee voice should not be interpreted to mean that 'union voice' is unimportant for increasing democracy in the workplace – far from it. Edwards and Sengupta's (2010) evidence highlighting the 'social relations of performance' as a contested arena indicates that employee voice and union voice are important for the achievement of both worker influence and sustainable organizational performance.

Over the past decade, interest in the various aspects of employee voice has grown considerably in Europe and North America (Dundon et al., 2004; Gollan, 2006; Marchington, 2008; Mayrhofer et al., 2000a). For Marchington (2008), employee voice appears to be a vogue term used to describe HR practices designed to permit workers some 'say' in workplace decision-making. Some writers define employee voice in terms of two-way communication between management and employees (Bryson, 2004), whereas others suggest that it is best understood as a complex set of HR practices that are dialectically fashioned by internal management choice on the one hand, and external regulation on the other (Dundon et al., 2004). Processes that provide for employee voice include direct employee involvement and participation (EIP) in workplace decision-making, whether via upward quality control techniques or indirect participative arrangements such as a works council.

It is suggested that allowing employees a bigger voice plays a critical role in constructing a high-involvement workplace and a 'strong' culture that improves 'bottom-line' results for the organization. Taras and Kaufman (2006) rightly observe that management expects the employee voice mechanism to encourage cooperative and productive modes of employment interaction, whereas workers expect that any meaningful employee voice forum will provide a capacity to influence managerial decision-making. EI and employee voice introduces an element of democracy into the workplace. According to Dundon et al. (2004), employee voice can be viewed as:

- A form of contribution to decision-making
- An articulation of individual dissatisfaction (or satisfaction)
- A demonstration of collective organization.

The search for causal links between strategic HRM and organizational performance has elevated the importance of understanding the relationship between employee voice and performance (Boxall and Purcell, 2008). Arguably, employee voice and interpersonal *communication* is the most important work activity, especially in high-involvement work systems, which seek to enlist the creativity, expertise and knowledge of all workers (Danford et al. 2008). The centrality of interpersonal communication is also acknowledged in the 'transformational' leadership literature (Bass and Riggio, 2006; Trethewey, 1997). Murphy (2005), for example, considers that, in order to manage the complexities of current health services, managers must employ a transformational leadership style that empowers staff to be change agents. This can be realized through individual considerations and effective communications.

The antecedents of managerial leadership behaviours, and more recently the focus on 'leader–member exchange' as it applies to the HRM–performance debate (see Chapter 3), underscores the importance of interpersonal communications theories. These emphasize the different ways in which managers communicate the content of a message to their subordinates, and how those ways of communicating affect the quality of the employment relationship. Witherspoon (1997, p. x), a specialist in leadership and communication, argues that 'leadership is to a great extent a communication process'. In our three-dimensional model of management (see Figure 1.2), communication is part of the process of influence by which front-line managers 'personalize' and enact HR practices, which is an element of the HR 'black box'. (See Chapter 3 for an extended discussion on the so-called HR 'black-box'.)

EIP practices are another key dimension of worker voice that is considered to be a key component of high-commitment management and high-involvement work systems workplaces (Cox et al., 2009; Dundon et al., 2004). In Britain, successive Workplace Employee Relations Surveys (WERSs) have documented the growth of EIP initiatives (see, for example, Kersley et al., 2006). The European Works Council (EWC) Directive of 1994 also stimulated interest in the EIP and communications debate (Mayrhofer et al., 2000a). The call for greater worker involvement itself has a long history (see Brannen et al., 1976), but the current interest appears to be associated with the exigencies of knowledge-based work and the need for more open communications and greater transparency in decision-making in order to achieve a competitive advantage. Much of the existing literature characterizes EIP and two-way communications as being 'management rather than union driven' (see, for example, Marchington and Wilkinson, 2000) and part of a sophisticated management strategy designed to increase profitability through more open communications (Gollan, 2006). As such, EIP is closely associated with a high-commitment, high-involvement HR strategy.

The contemporary debate on employee relations practices emphasizes, from a managerialist perspective, the fact that such HR practices fundamentally transform the climate of employee relations because they lead to long-term changes in workers' attitudes and commitment: communication and EIP practices shape 'organizational citizenship'. The obligations that form the core of the psychological contract are shaped by a variety of factors and HR practices, including various forms of workplace communication (Guest, 2008; Guest and Conway, 2002). As Morrison and Robinson (1997, p. 237) argue:

Communication … will help to minimize the 'false consensus effect,' whereby people assume that they share the same perceptions.

Another aspect of the debate, from a critical perspective, is the argument that employee relations initiatives, such as EIP, will, by promoting individual employees rather than employees' collective bodies, deliberately undermine the role of the trade unions and moreover increase managerial control over the labour process (Thompson and McHugh, 2009; Wells, 1993).

In terms of public policy, interest in EIP and partnership deals between unions and management has been encouraged by UK and European Union (EU) legislation, in particular, the 1994 EWC Directive. A set of individual employment *rights* affects the nature of employee relations. The right to be treated fairly and equitably is embedded in UK and EU legislation, which attempts to regulate the behaviour of employers and employees in the workplace. An important aspect of fairness and dignity at work is to allow individual employees to express dissatisfaction about issues that impact on their work experience, and to receive redress for alleged unfair or unreasonable treatment through a formal *grievance* process.

When employee relations practices fail to create, or reinforce, desirable employee behaviours, managers may resort to disciplinary action to encourage compliance with organizational rules and standards. Employee *discipline*, the fourth key dimension in employee relations (Figure 13.1), is the regulation of human activity to produce predictable and effective performance (Torrington, 1998). It ranges from the threat of being dismissed to the subtle persuasions of mentoring. Maintaining discipline is one of managers' central activities. A framework of legal rules and procedures surrounds the disciplinary process to provide a fair and consistent method of dealing with alleged inappropriate or unacceptable behaviour. We will now examine in more detail each of the key dimensions of employee relations.

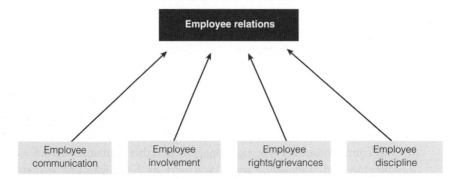

Figure 13.1 *Four important dimensions of employee relations*

The assortment of employer initiatives and HR policies and practices that constitute employee relations – communication, involvement, rights and grievance-handling, discipline – is shown in Figure 13.1. As in other areas of HRM, the ethical dimension of employee relations policy and practice has tended to be downplayed in most HRM texts, where the focus of debate has been on 'best fit' versus 'best HR practices' (Winstanley and Woodall, 2000). Ethical considerations inevitably require managers to reflect on what constitutes ethical employee relations practice in an increasingly globalized and diversified workplace. Empirical data and legal cases continue to reveal in detail problems of discrimination, inequality, harassment and inequitable managerial behaviour.

reflective question Looking at the four key dimensions of employee relations, how can HR practices in each area impact positively and negatively on employee relations? Try to think about your own work experience of 'good' and 'poor' employee relations.

Employee communication

We need to begin with a notion of what is meant by employee communication. One simple definition focuses on information disclosure: 'The systematic provision of information to employees concerning all aspects of their employment and the wider issues relating to the organization in which they work' (Advisory, Conciliation and Arbitration Service, 1987, p. 3). Employee communication involves exchanging information and sharing ideas, feeling and opinions. Meaning is a core concept in communication, and researchers in this field of study define their discipline in complex behavioural and contextual terms. Byers (1997), for example, incorporates three ideas associated with communication – behaviour, meaning and context – and defines communication in the workplace as (p. 4):

Both behaviours and symbols, generated either intentionally or unintentionally, occurring between and among people who assign meaning to them, within an organizational setting.

N orland Managed Services is a provider of hard services-led facilities maintenance and support services in the built environment. It works for national and global organizations to fulfil their building management requirements, its aim being to maintain and enhance its clients' buildings so that those clients can focus on their core business. Among its latest customers are Bloomberg, the O₂ Arena, Scottish Power, Southampton University, Experian and Manchester and Stockport Primary Care Trusts.

Keith Hanlon-Smith has been with Norland since 2006, and has previously worked as HR Manager at Sony DADC and Quantum Business Media, as well as having been Employee Relations Manager at Earls Court Olympia Ltd. He is a member of the HR Professionals Network.

Keith Hanlon-Smith

Employee Relations Director, Norland Managed Services

www.norlandmanagedservices.co.uk

 Visit www.palgrave.com/business/bratton5 to watch Keith talking about employee relations, the employment relationship, and how Norland's HR practices fit with its business strategy, and then think about the following questions:

1   How is HR embedded in the business at Norland Managed Services?
2   What is Keith's view on changes in employee relations?
3   How does Keith think that 'agendas' affect priorities?

HRM **as I see it**

Communication is symbolic, which means that the words managers and workers speak or the gestures they make have no inherent meaning. Symbolic meanings conveyed both verbally and non-verbally only 'gain their significance from an agreed-upon meaning' (Martin and Nakayama, 2000, p. 61).

Downward communication patterns from managers to non-managers need to be explored within the wider context of organizational culture and management practices. Information exchange and the transmission of meaning are the very essence of organizational life. Information about the organization – its production, its products and services, its external environment and its people – is a prerequisite for effective EI in decision-making. A strong advocate of high-involvement work systems, Pfeffer (1998, p. 93), not surprisingly, argues that 'the sharing of information on such things as financial performance, strategy, and operational measures conveys to the organization's people that they are trusted'. Employee communications can be simply viewed as the process by which information is exchanged between a sender and a receiver, but the communication process is complicated by organizational characteristics such as hierarchy and power relations, and by the fact that managers and non-managers all have idiosyncrasies, abilities and biases.

The role of employee communication can be seen in studies of managers and their work. Mintzberg's (1973) ground-breaking study found that managers spend a vast proportion of their working time on interpersonal communications; indeed, he argues that the business of managers is communications. In our discussion of management, communication is an important skill for 'getting things done' (see Figure 1.2). Communication strategies will be determined by the way work is designed; for example, the more the organization relies on knowledge workers and innovation to competitively survive, the more important communications become.

All managers engage in *downward* communication in one form or another, but communication scholars emphasize that, to be effective, employee communication must be a two-way process to give employees the opportunity to participate on a regular basis. Researchers, academics and practitioners have also stressed some key issues related to communications in the workplace (Figure 13.2).

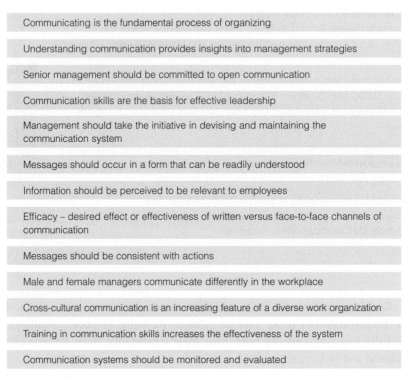

Communicating is the fundamental process of organizing

Understanding communication provides insights into management strategies

Senior management should be committed to open communication

Communication skills are the basis for effective leadership

Management should take the initiative in devising and maintaining the communication system

Messages should occur in a form that can be readily understood

Information should be perceived to be relevant to employees

Efficacy – desired effect or effectiveness of written versus face-to-face channels of communication

Messages should be consistent with actions

Male and female managers communicate differently in the workplace

Cross-cultural communication is an increasing feature of a diverse work organization

Training in communication skills increases the effectiveness of the system

Communication systems should be monitored and evaluated

Figure 13.2 *Key issues related to communication in the workplace*

A communications model

The communications model shown in Figure 13.3 depicts communications in the workplace as a process by which information is exchanged between a sender and a receiver. Employees have three basic methods of transmitting information:

- Verbal
- Non-verbal
- Written.

Verbal communication ranges from a casual conversation between two employees to a formal speech by the managing director. In face-to-face meetings, the meaning of the information being conveyed by the sender can be expressed through gesture or facial expressions, which are referred to as *non-verbal* communication. *Written* communication ranges from a casual email note to a co-worker to an annual report. Social media platforms, including Facebook, Twitter, blogs, LinkedIn, podcasts, YouTube and wikis, are an increasingly popular form of communication within and across organizations for managers under the age of 30 and are revolutionizing business communications (although not without some cost to employee stress; see Chapter 14). The content of any message consists of what is being communicated, and the way in which content is communicated – through the various channels – describes the sender's communication style. In turn, different communication styles, will also, importantly, affect the perception of a message or set of messages.

reflective question   Do you think that new social media systems will improve communication within organizations? Thinking globally, how does this new communications technology impact on international HRM?

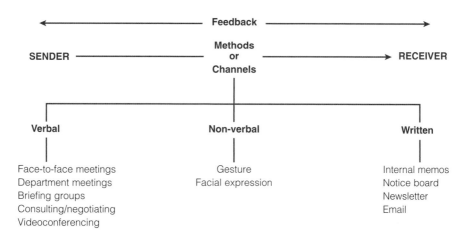

Figure 13.3 *The communications process model*

This interpersonal communications model has its limitations in that it characterizes communication as a linear process and ignores different cultures and subcultures, organizational hierarchies and power relationships (Coates and Pichler, 2011; Rees, 1998; Tan, 1998). People communicate differently depending on their gender, organizational setting and national culture. Language is particularly associated with gender relations and power. In this context, it is argued that written communication is an ideological act in the process of gender redefinition. The interplay of language and power comes through clearly in how Western people use masculine words to signify greater force, significance or value. For instance, the positive word 'seminal', meaning ground-breaking, is derived from the word 'semen or 'male seed'. The positive adjective 'virtuous', meaning morally worthy, is derived from the Latin word *vir*, meaning man. In contrast, the disparaging adjective 'hysterical' comes from the Greek word *hustera*, meaning uterus or womb (Forshaw, 2010).

Ethnographic research shows that most workplaces are predominantly masculine domains with masculine norms of behaviour, which of course includes ways of communicating (see, for example, Coates and Pichler, 2011). Scholars posit that language and gender intersect, and this contributes to different interpretations of meaning in workplace communications. Effective communicators, both female and male, typically draw on a diverse discursive repertoire of social and linguistic practices, ranging from normative 'feminine' to normatively 'masculine' ways of talking (Holmes, 2006). Studies suggest, for example, that male managers tend to be loud, direct, dominant and aggressive. Women, on

Creating union-free workplaces

This chapter examines some of the reasons why management introduces employee voice systems. They may be introduced as a deliberate HR strategy of union avoidance. This is achieved by establishing an employee relations system that emulates a union-based system, as this writer suggests (Knight, 2011, pp. 20–2):

> There is no magic formula for keeping unions at bay … While it is unhealthy to manage in a perpetual state of crisis, driven at all times by a fear of union organizing, it is useful to maintain a healthy respect for that possibility. To avoid this prospect, management should understand the union's sales pitch and bargaining objectives. Then, to the extent possible and always in a manner consistent with the primary objectives of the organization, management should try to replicate much of what the union would promise to employees in an organizing drive – it is difficult for a union to sell something that is already being provided by management. Some of the key aspects of a unionized workplace that non-union workplaces may strive to emulate include:
> - Recognition of service or seniority as a key factor in compensation, vacation entitlement, job security …

- A structured complaints procedure that could double as an employee suggestions procedure that ensures employees have a clearly understood and formal vehicle for reacting to management decisions, including disciplinary decisions
- An effective dispute-resolution mechanism, even if it's simply a clear acknowledgement a manager will make a final decision that will be communicated to the effected employee(s).

One of the proposed management-initiated direct employee voice systems – a structured complaints procedure – is examined in detail in this chapter. Critics tend to be sceptical of employee voice systems because of the shift from a union focus towards an individually oriented focus. Non-unionism avoids the restrictions found in a collective agreement as well as potential intervention of a third party (for example, an arbitrator) in grievance disputes. Other critics of direct employee voice tend to be influenced by Foucauldian theory, which sees such HR practices as making workers' behaviour more manageable (see, for example, Townley, 1994).

Stop! What are the likely benefits for managers of a direct employee voice system in the workplace? Should trade unions be concerned about the introduction of an EI mechanism? If so, why or why not?

Sources and further information: The extract is taken from Jamie Knight's article 'Union-free shops strong in HR' (Knight, 2011). See also Ackers et al. (2005) for more information.

Note: This feature was written by John Bratton.

©Tom Schmucker

(a) ... conveys as ... employees
(b) The Company clearly conveys the mission to its clients
(c) I agree with The Company's overall mission.
(d) I understand how my job aligns with The Company's mission.
(e) I feel like I am a part of The Company.
(f) There is good communication from employees to managers in The Company.
(g) There is good communication from ...agers to employees in ...

the other hand, tend to be more open, self-revealing and polite when they speak, and are superior at decoding non-verbal communication (Aries, 1996). Effective communicators also adroitly select their linguistic practices in response to the interactional context in which communication occurs. Each message may have multiple layers of meaning. Culture, because it shapes our perception of reality, influences communication processes: 'All communities in all places at all times manifest their own view of reality in what they do: The entire culture reflects the contemporary model of reality' (Burke, 1985, quoted in Martin and Nakayama, 2000, p. 62).

These limitations of the linear communication model are particularly significant to international HRM, in which managers have to be aware of, and sensitive to, the cultural situation in which the organization is embedded (see Chapter 15). Arguably, this contextually impoverished model of employee communication needs to be improved upon by sensitivity to cross-cultural norms, as well as to the overall organizational contexts that give rise to the shared meanings through which interpersonal communication occurs.

reflective question Thinking about your own work experience or the experience of a friend, relative or family member, can you think of a situation in which you have perceived differences in communication style between men and women? How important is it to recognize that communication is 'culture-bound'?

HRM web links For more information on electronic business communication, go to www.idm. internet.com/ix and www.writerswrite.com/businesscommunications/links.htm, the latter offering students a wide range of material and practical help with business writing.

For more information on how communication theorists have identified challenges that must be taken into account when designing a communication system, go to www. palgrave.com/business/bratton5.

Direct communication methods

©Jordan Tan/Dreamstime.com

Survey evidence indicates that managers use a variety of methods for communicating directly with their subordinates, including regular meetings, management chain newsletters, notice boards, email, suggestion schemes and employee surveys (see, for example, Kersley et al., 2006). Table 13.1 lists the most frequently discussed direct communication or 'voice' mechanisms, and shows the proportion of workplaces operating such schemes.

A recent survey of workplaces found that close to one-third (30 per cent) of all workplaces operated an employee suggestion scheme.

Table 13.1 *Use of direct communication methods, 1998–2004, by sector ownership*

| | % of all workplaces | | | | | |
| | 1998 | | | 2004 | | |
	Private	Public	All	Private	Public	All
Regular meetings between management and workforce or team briefings	82	96	85	90	97	91
Management chain newsletters	46	75	52	60	81	64
Regular newsletters	35	59	40	41	63	45
Notice boards	–	–	–	72	86	74
Employee surveys[1]	–	–	–	37	66	42
Suggestion schemes[1]	29	35	31	30	30	30
Email[1]	–	–	–	36	48	38
Intranet[1]	–	–	–	31	48	34

Note: [1] No comparable data for 1998
Source: Adapted from Kersley et al. (2006), p. 135

The data show how work design and workplace communications interconnect. The 2004 survey data report the use of work teams in 72 per cent of workplaces. The incidence of workforce meetings or team briefings to transmit information to employees increased in the private sector from 82 to 90 per cent. The issues commonly discussed at these two types of meeting included production issues, planning, training, and health and safety. When there is time for employees to raise questions or make comments, team briefings are considered to be an effective way of increasing the two-way communication flow. Mechanisms designed specifically to elicit information from employees about workplace issues include suggestion schemes and employee surveys. Close to one-third (30 per cent) of all workplaces operated an employee suggestion scheme, and 42 per cent of the respondents reported having conducted an employee attitude survey within the previous 2 years.

HRM web links Further details on the research methods used and outcome of the surveys, including information on how managers communicate with their subordinates, can be found at the website of WERS 2004: see www.bis.gov.uk/policies/employment-matters/research/wers/wers2004 and www.data-archive.ac.uk.

Information disclosed by management

What type of information is communicated through the various communication activities? The kinds of information most likely to be regularly disclosed by managers are staffing plans, the financial position of the workplace and the company, and investment plans (Table 13.2). Since 1998, the incidence of information disclosed on each of these issues, apart from staffing plans, has decreased. Managers in organizations with recognized unions give more information on all topics than do managers in non-unionized workplaces, and UK-owned establishments are less likely than their foreign-owned counterparts to disclose information to their employees (Millward and Stevens, 1986). This is despite evidence indicating that information-sharing is positively related to employee satisfaction and trust in workplace decision-making (Paauwe, 2004).

Table 13.2 Information disclosed by management, 1998–2004, by sector ownership

| | % of all workplaces | | | | | |
| | 1998 | | | 2004 | | |
	Private	Public	All	Private	Public	All
Investment plans	47	59	50	40	50	41
Financial position of workplace	56	82	62	51	76	55
Financial position of company	66	67	66	51	53	51
Staffing plans	55	81	61	61	81	64

Source: Adapted from Kersley et al. (2005), p. 18

Employee involvement and participation

The second key dimension of employee relations is EIP. The term is both problematic and 'loose', covering a range of direct and indirect managerially initiated practices, in unionized and non-unionized workplaces (Cox et al., 2009). A review of the literature reveals that the terms 'employee participation' and 'employee involvement' have different meanings. In essence, employee participation involves workers exerting a countervailing and upward pressure on management control, which need not imply unity of purpose between managers and non-managers. EI is, in contrast, perceived to be a softer form of participation, implying a commonality of interest between employees and management, and stressing that involvement should be directed at the workforce as a whole rather than being restricted to trade union channels. As Guest (1986, p. 687) states: 'involvement is considered to be more flexible and better geared to the goal of securing commitment and shared interest'.

When people talk about participation or involvement, they are reflecting their own attitudes and work experiences, as well as their own hopes for the future. Managers tend to talk about participation when in fact they mean consultation. In this context, consultation, which is explored more fully later in the chapter, usually means a structure for improving communications, either top-down, or upward in the form of problem-solving. When offered consultation, employees, and in unionized workplaces union representatives, tend to believe, however, that they are about to be given participation. Differing expectations among employees will affect their attitude, their propensity to participate and ultimately the success of participation techniques in the organization. A vital first step, if there is to be any meeting of minds, is therefore to create a common language and conceptual model.

Definitions of EIP do not always reflect the range of possibilities available – from having some say over how work is designed and executed to exerting a significant influence over strategic decisions. Strauss maintains that meaningful employee participation in decision-making demands that workers are able to exert influence over their working environment. He defines participation as 'a process which allows employees to exert some influence over their work and the conditions under which they work' (Strauss, 1998, p. 15). If we take the

One of the biases of traditional HR practice is the tendency to see employees as somehow subsumed by their work role rather than being people with a broad range of passions, interests and abilities. This narrow view of the employee goes hand in hand with a narrow view of EI. 'He never asks me about myself, my family or my life outside of work' is a complaint that captures an employee's dismay at not being recognized as a person.

At the other end of the continuum is a workplace where workers are recognized as persons who do have lives and interests outside of work, and sometimes this recognition goes even further. Rather than maintaining the traditional sharp boundary between work and life outside of the workplace, some employers will celebrate a culture that spans both work *and* leisure. Such an approach has the potential to enhance EI and secure high levels of employee identification with the work organization.

Take the case of the Dogfish Head Brewery in Delaware, USA. The company is not shy about its workplace culture, which is in fact very much a part of its 'brand'. A quick glance at the company website illustrates this:

> Dogfish Head? An unconventional company? No way ...

> Okay, so maybe we are a little nuts! We brew strange concoctions of beer, sell silly accessories with our name on it and have our own music group, The Pain Relievaz!

> We like to keep it a little kooky and wacky around the Dogfish joint!

It would be tempting to see this as a simple marketing strategy: the company brands itself a certain way to sell a product (beer) to a niche market. But it seems that the company culture is more than this here. The website also lists a range of activities, mainly related to keeping fit and protecting the environment, that suggest commitment to a 'triple bottom line': people, community and environmental responsibility. Most importantly, many of these activities appear to involve both workers *and* managers. Indeed, Dogfish Head Brewery seems like a

HRM and globalization

A warm welcome to the kooky and the wacky

great place to work if you are particularly green or have a penchant for mountain biking!

Dogfish Head Brewery celebrates its culture – an approach to life that is 'off-centered' but also socially responsible and, it is reasonable to expect, that would enhance work involvement, reducing barriers between employers and employees, and allowing workers to feel comfortable about raising concerns. One could imagine that the spirit of solidarity would improve communication in both formal settings (workplace meetings) and informal settings (the various leisure time activities).

Stop! What if you do not like mountain biking? Might the Dogfish Head approach to EI produce problematic divisions between a group of 'insiders' and a group of 'outsiders'?

What about the global perspective? Is the potential of the Dogfish Head approach limited to countries, like the USA, where egalitarian values are celebrated as part of the national culture? Would the idea of working together and playing together be palatable in countries where traditional hierarchies influence a broad range of everyday interactions?

Sources and further information: For a classic statement on the failure of traditional models of organization to recognize the whole person, see Beetham (1978). For a glimpse of the Dogfish Head Brewery culture, check out their website at http://www.dogfish.com.

Note: This feature was written by David MacLennan at Thompson Rivers University.

literal meaning of the term 'employee participation', the process should provide workers or their representatives with the opportunity to take part in and influence decisions that affect their working lives. As such, an employee participation environment creates an alternative network to traditional hierarchical patterns (Stohl and Cheney, 2001).

There are two types of participation: direct and indirect. The first, *direct*, refers to those forms of participation in which individual employees, albeit often in a very limited way, are given a voice or 'say' in decision-making processes that affect their everyday work routines. Examples of direct EIP include financial involvement, task-based quality-problem-solving participation, and the team-based high-performance work system (HPWS). As a direct form of EIP, financial involvement, which includes profit-related rewards, aims to improve competitiveness by educating employees on the operation of the business. Financial participation initiatives are therefore based on the belief that workers with a financial stake in the enterprise are more likely to be better 'corporate citizens' and work more productively for the company (Marchington, 2001). For a discussion on profit-related rewards, see Chapter 11.

Indirect participation refers to those forms of participation in which representatives or delegates of the main body of employees participate in the decision-making process. Examples of indirect participation include JCCs, works councils and 'worker directors', all forms that are associated with the broader notion of 'industrial democracy' (Bullock, 1977). More recently, as a consequence of the precipitous decline in trade union density – the proportion of employees who are in a union – research has increasingly focused on non-union models of employee representation (Butler, 2009; Marchington, 2008). The WERS data indicates that indirect EI has become less extensive in the period between 1980 and 1998 (Millward et al., 2000).

The plurality of ways in which EIP works gives rise to differing degrees of scope, significance and impact in the workplace. Figure 13.4 provides a framework within which different forms of EIP can be examined and shows the relationship between three constituent elements:

- The *forms* of involvement – direct and indirect
- The *level* of involvement in the organizational hierarchy
- The *degree* of involvement.

Figure 13.4 shows a continuum of EIP from a situation in which employees have no autonomy (for example, a traditionally designed assembly line) to full involvement, in which workers participate in strategic decision-making. Current methods of EIP fall along this continuum.

Research on EIP arrangements in multinational corporations (MNCs) reveals a complex picture. The influence of the structure of corporate strategy and demographic factors in particular, and the method of corporate growth, may account for the variation among MNCs based in any host country. Studies have found that UK-owned MNCs are more likely to have a hybrid arrangement of union and non-union employee representation, consistent with a shift away from union-based employee representation. US-based MNCs have a preference for non-union employee representation and direct forms of employee voice. Nordic-based and Japanese-based MNCs are, however, no more likely to have employee representative structures than their US counterparts. In the main Anglophone countries, there is a trajectory towards non-union employee representation (Marginson et al., 2010). In the EU, EWCs are a common feature of the corporate governance landscape,

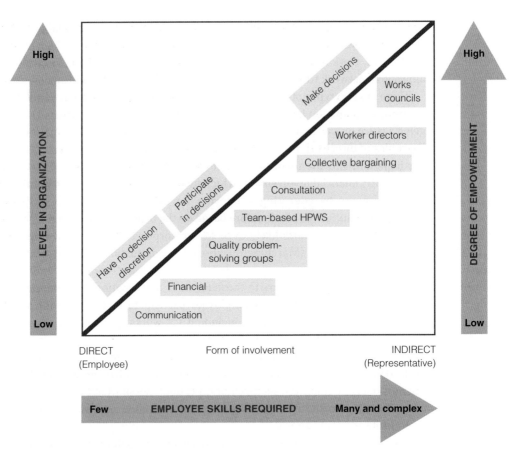

Figure 13.4 *Framework for analysing EI*

although it is outside the scope of this chapter to examine the wider debate on European-style industrial democracy. Indirect EI through the process of collective bargaining was examined in Chapter 12. Before examining forms of EIP in detail, however, let us address the question, 'Why the enthusiasm for EIP?'

HRM web links

For general information on EI schemes, go to www.acas.org.uk (Britain), www.hrdc-drhc.gc.ca (Canada), www.clc-ctc.ca (Canada) or www.dol.gov/_sec/media/reports/dunlop/section2.htm.

reflective question

These different forms of EI need to be understood as part of a HR strategy. Before reading on, review Figure 2.6 and its accompanying text. What is the connection between business strategy, HR strategy and EI? Thinking about the 2012 debate on bankers' bonuses, which forms of EIP would improve transparency and curb excessive executive bonuses?

A general theory of employee involvement

Management has to continually address two interlinked problems – those of control and commitment – with regard to managing the employment relationship. Fox (1985) argues that, faced with the management problem of securing employee compliance, identification and commitment, management has adopted a range of employment strategies including EIP. The current enthusiasm for improved EIP needs to be viewed within the context of changing business and corresponding HR strategies in which the purpose of the latter is to secure EIP support and commitment to HPWSs. The purpose of EIP is to support management's goals either directly through performance improvements, or indirectly through organizational commitment (Marchington, 2001). The commitment–performance link is based on a number of assumptions, the first being that giving workers more autonomy over work tasks will strengthen organizational citizenship. Moreover, it will increase workers' commitment to the organization's goals, which will in turn result in enhanced individual and organizational performance. The involvement–commitment cycle is depicted in Figure 13.5. Lubricating the whole commitment–performance process is a communication style that attempts to build a strong internal culture encouraging initiative, learning, creativity and greater employee identification with the organization.

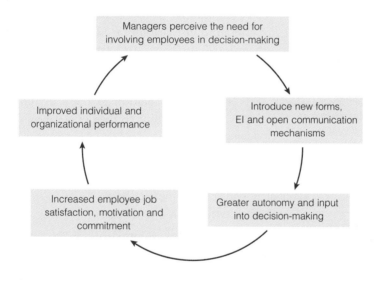

Figure 13.5 *The involvement–commitment cycle*

reflective question What do you think of the assumptions underpinning the involvement–commitment cycle? Can the growth of EI be explained by employer 'needs', or are there other forces determining this employee relations practice?

Management scholars have put forward three main reasons why senior management introduce EIP to allow workers some input or 'voice' in how they do their work (Verma, 1995): *ethical*, *economic* and *behavioural*. The first reason for introducing EIP is derived from an ethical, political and moral base, the argument being that, in a democratic society, workers should have a say in how their workplaces are run when the outcomes of any decisions impact on their lives. EIP therefore presents a socially acceptable management style. The development of EIP will be encouraged because companies generally desire to project 'a socially responsible stance on such issues' (Marchington and Wilding, 1983, p. 32).

The second reason for introducing EIP, championed by the 'model of excellence' school in North America, derives from the utilitarian principle that EIP improves the quality of

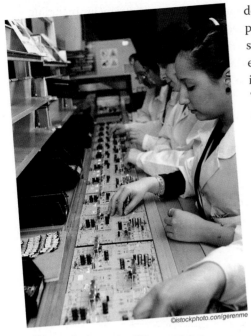

©istockphoto.con/gerenme

Research shows that EIP potentially improves the quality of a decision and its chances of successful implementation on the factory floor.

decision-making and productivity. Research shows that EIP potentially improves the quality of a decision and its chances of successful implementation on the factory floor (see, for example, Marchington, 1982). Similarly, it is asserted that EIP improves productivity and energizes workers (Verma and Taras, 2001), as well as increasing employees' trust in management (Mabey et al., 1998a) and reducing work-related stress (Mackie et al., 2001). Research on the notion of 'embeddedness' in relation to EIP shows that the presence of multiple embedded EIP practices is significantly associated with organizational commitment (Cox et al., 2009). Research on the EIP–performance link of the organization appears to support the theory that giving employees a voice on a range of organizational decisions yields benefits to both the organization and the workforce (Heller et al., 1998).

The third justification for EIP derives from the perennial managerial problems associated with perceived dysfunctional behaviour: resistance to change, strikes, absenteeism and other forms of conflict (Beer et al., 1984; Guest, 1986). EIP is seen as a solution to these dysfunctional human behaviours. According to Beer et al. (1984, p. 53), by introducing EI schemes:

Employers hope that participative mechanisms will create a greater coincidence of interests between employers and employees, thereby increasing trust, reducing the potential for conflict, and increasing the potential for an effective mutual influence process.

Surveys of managers have shown that EIP is typically initiated and operated by management, with the objective of enhancing employee commitment to organizational goals (see Butler, 2009; Marchington, 2001, 2008). Studies have established that the presence of direct-only voice arrangements is more likely to be associated with favourable employee perceptions of the employment relations climate (Pyman et al., 2010). In an interesting study arguing that work remains a significant locus of personal identity, Doherty (2009, p. 97) notes that what provoked most discontent among workers was the belief that they had insufficient 'say or voice' about issues that affected their working lives. Survey analysis reveals a strong association between job characteristics and perceptions of how 'supportive, informative and consultative' management are seen to be with regard to employee well-being and job satisfaction (Wood, 2008, p. 165). The most frequently cited reason for introducing financial participation (for example, profit-sharing schemes) is, for instance, to promote worker identification and commitment (Marchington, 1995, 2001).

In addition, workplace scholars have noted that interest in non-union EIP arrangements coincided with the rise of HRM (Benson and Brown, 2010) and the global decline in union density, while also prompting renewed debates over the need for union voice in the contemporary workplace (Budd et al., 2010). Over the past three decades, research interest has focused on the use of EIP to avert trade union organization or, in North American terminology, 'certification'. As Beer et al. (1984, p. 153) note, 'Some companies introduce participative methods at the shop floor in the hope that a greater congruence of interest will make it less likely that workers will organize.' EIP practices might go hand in hand with changes in an organization's culture away from a collective trade union focus and towards an individual-oriented focus, by promoting a direct relationship between worker and management (Batstone and Gourlay, 1986). As part of a union-avoidance strategy, direct employee voice – a formal complaints and grievance procedure, for example – can 'emulate a unionized workplace' and thus make it 'difficult for a union to sell something that is already being provided by management' (Knight, 2011, p. 22). Other critics of EIP practices tend to be those influenced by Foucauldian theory, who see the processes being used to 'educate' and 'reconstitute the individual', thereby making workers' behaviour and performance more manageable (Townley, 1994).

HRM web links 🌐 For more examples of companies introducing EI practices, go to the websites of the following companies: General Electric (www.ge.com), Walmart (www.walmart.com), IBM (www.ibm.com), ICI (www.akzonobel.com/paints) or a company you are studying. Once there, go to 'Employee participation', 'Communications' or a similar prompt.

Indirect employee participation

Joint consultation is a key type of employee participation (Cregan and Brown, 2010). In its simplest form, joint consultation may take the form of an informal exchange of views between a group of workers and their manager on an incoming piece of machinery or a reorganization of the office. When, however, the size of the organization makes it difficult for workers to access management, a more formal and indirect employee voice network needs to be established. The committee usually includes representatives of management and workers, and in this way differs from collective bargaining because it uses processes of negotiation and agreement between these representatives. The intent is to provide a meeting forum that acts as a channel for employee voice on matters affecting the workplace.

We can develop the difference between joint consultation and collective bargaining further. The difference rests on the idea that both conflict and a common interest are inherent elements of the employment relationship that need to be handled in different ways. Joint consultation is viewed as a means of promoting action when there are no obvious conflicts of interest, whereas collective bargaining is a means of reconciling divergent interests, although we should stress that every aspect of the employment relationship has the potential for conflict.

The balance between joint consultation and collective bargaining will depend upon the power of trade unions. Daniel and Millward (1983, p. 135) found that the existence of JCCs was closely allied to the relative bargaining power of the unions:

> Consultative committees may tend to become an adjunct to the institutes of collective bargaining where workplace trade union organization is well established, but provide an alternative channel of representation where it is weak.

Models of joint consultation

Workplace scholars have put forward two different models of consultation. The *revitalization model* suggests that recent support for consultation has coincided with the increased use of direct EIP approaches by employers. This, it is argued, has the effect, whether planned or not, of undermining union models of collective bargaining and consequently weakening workplace unionism (Batstone, 1984; Edwards, 1985). In contrast, the *marginality model* suggests an increased trivialization and marginalization of joint consultation in the early 1980s, particularly in organizations confronted by deteriorating economic conditions (MacInnes, 1987).

These two models have been challenged because they do not describe the full range of processes that may take place in the consultative arena. Marchington (1987) proposes a third model, the *complementary model*, in which joint consultation complements rather than competes with joint regulation or collective bargaining. The argument is that 'consultation acts as an adjunct to the bargaining machinery' (Marchington, 1987, p. 340). With this model, collective bargaining is used to determine pay and conditions of employment, whereas joint consultation focuses on issues of an integrative nature and helps to improve employment relationships; both processes can provide benefits for employees and the organization. Research has found support for the dual or complementary model, reporting that 'complex consultative structures co-exist with complex collective bargaining arrangements in the public sector in particular' (Millward and Stevens, 1986, p. 143).

Extent of joint consultation

Survey evidence of private sector MNCs in the UK found that the overall proportion of the workplaces with labour–management committees (LMCs) fell between 1984 and 1998 from 34 per cent to 28 per cent (Cully et al., 1998). The WERS 2004 data reveal the extent to which managers normally inform, consult or negotiate with employee representatives (union or non-union) on key aspects of the employment relationship (Table 13.3). In 67 per cent of workplaces, management did not engage with employee representatives on any of the 12 terms and conditions of employment listed. Management were most likely to negotiate over pay with union employee representatives (61 per cent) and non-union employee representatives (18 per cent), and least likely to engage employee representatives with respect to staff selection.

In all cases, the presence of a trade union in the workplace significantly increased the likelihood that managers would engage in some form of joint regulation of the employment relationship. WERS 2004 data appear to corroborate Dundon et al.'s findings that, in the majority of unionized workplaces, joint consultation and collective bargaining operated alongside non-union employee voice channels. Moreover, they found that 'shop stewards appeared more willing than they did a decade ago to participate in such dual representative channels' (Dundon et al., 2004, p. 1160). Other studies show that union membership status has a significant impact on workers' willingness to participate in joint consultation arrangements (Cregan and Brown, 2010). Union members were more willing to participate, 'the more likely they expected the JCC to result in instrumental gains' (p. 344). Importantly, union members were willing to participate in joint consultation arrangements in order to 'build on union-based instrumental gains and to fill the gaps left by collective bargaining' (p. 344).

A contrasting analysis by MacInnes (1985) reminds us that the separation of joint consultation from collective negotiations is often attempted by simply excluding from the negotiating agenda any item that is normally the subject of joint regulation. The result can be the creation of the 'canteen, car park, toilet paper syndrome' and has prompted some observers to characterize the subject matter of JCCs as a 'diet of anodyne trivia and old hat' (pp. 103–4).

Table 13.3 *Incidence of joint regulation of terms and conditions, 2004*

| | % of all workplaces | | | | | |
| | Nothing | | Consult | | Negotiate | |
	Non-union	Union[1]	Non-union	Union	Non-union	Union
Staff selection	78	42	9	23	3	9
Staffing plans	75	33	12	34	3	7
Performance appraisal	75	33	12	33	4	14
Training	75	36	13	31	3	9
Pensions	73	22	6	16	10	36
Equal opportunities	72	22	14	40	5	15
Hours	71	18	8	20	16	53
Holidays	71	19	5	13	15	52
Pay	70	16	5	13	18	61
Health and safety	69	17	17	49	5	15
Grievance procedure	69	15	14	36	9	28
Discipline procedure	69	15	13	35	8	9

Note: [1] Relates to workplaces with recognized trade unions
Source: Adapted from Kersley et al. (2005), p. 22

Although we always have to be careful when making international comparisons – because, for example, researchers define HR practices differently – survey studies show that, across Western Europe between 1997 and 2000, EI practices and downward and upward communication increased by an average of 52 per cent (Mayrhofer et al., 2000a). In Canada, 43 per cent of workplaces reported some form of EI in decision-making (Verma and Taras, 2001). These findings need to be contrasted with more critical studies suggesting that EI in decision-making has not shown any sign of substantive improvement (Thompson and McHugh, 2009).

The structure and operation of joint consultative committees

When choosing a joint consultative structure or developing an existing one, it is necessary to make decisions guided by the organization's goals, philosophy and strategy. Joint consultation requires a high-trust relationship and regular disclosure of information to all participating parties. Managers have to decide how much information will be disclosed, by whom and how. Management's role in a consultative structure is generally to communicate information and be fully involved in the process; anything less than this will result in decisions being made or agreed upon without their knowledge or support. Managers may adopt either of two broad approaches: they can integrate the two processes of consultation and negotiation within the collective bargaining machinery, or they can agree to maintain a separate machinery of joint consultation and regulation:

Three main reasons have been identified for integrating consultative and negotiating machinery:

- Communicating, consulting and negotiating are integrally linked together in the handling of employee relations.

- Union representatives need to be fully involved in the consultative process, if only as a prelude to negotiations.
- As the scope of collective bargaining expands, the issues left are otherwise allocated to what may be viewed as an irrelevant process.

On the other hand, substantive reasons have been cited for establishing separate consultative and collective bargaining structures:

- Separation may help to overcome organizational complexity.
- The fact that collective bargaining deals with substantive or procedural issues, whereas consultation addresses other issues of common interest, forces the two structures apart.
- Regular JCC or LMC meetings and the publication of minutes ensure that joint consultation is accorded a proper place in the organizational system and confirms management's commitment and responsibility to consulting with its employees.

An example of a joint consultation and collective bargaining structure in the public sector is shown in Figure 13.6.

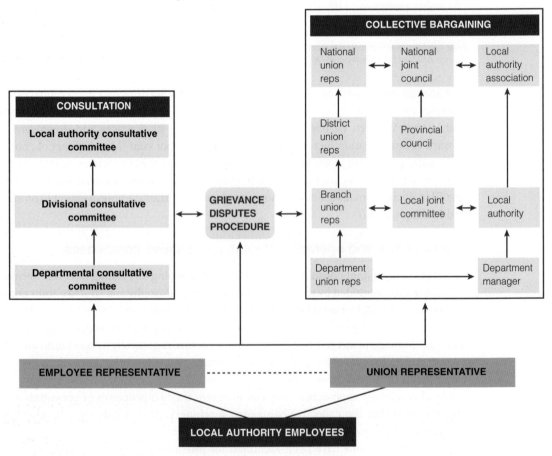

Figure 13.6 *Example of joint consultation and collective bargaining in municipal government*

When there are two sets of arrangements, the terms of reference of the JCC or LMC need to be specified by defining both its subject matter and the nature of its authority. The subject matter may be defined in terms of:

- Excluding from its deliberation anything that is subject to joint regulation, that is, substantive (for example, pay and vacation time) and procedural (for example, discipline and grievance processes) matters
- Enumerating the items that are to be regarded as matters for joint consultation (for example, a corporate plan, HR trends and education and training)
- Items chosen on an ad hoc basis, deciding whether or not an issue should be dealt with in the joint regulation process.

HRM web links WWW

For more information on JCCs, go to the websites of the Advisory, Conciliation and Arbitration Service (ACAS; www.acas.org.uk) and the Trades Union Congress (www.tuc.org.uk). See also www.ccma.org.za (South Africa) and www.airc.gov.au (Australia).

European Works Councils

The German economy – the fifth largest economy in the world and Europe's largest – has made works councils part of its industrial relations landscape since the end of the Second World War. Much of the early research on works councils was focused on German 'co-determination' (*Mitbestimmung*) and worker participation in decision-making, manifested in the Works Constitution Act. EWCs are not the same as LMCs or JCCs: whereas LMCs are voluntary committees, the term 'European Works Council' is used to describe only mandatory consultative committees. Accordingly, works councils can be defined (Frege, 2002, p. 223) as:

Institutionalized bodies of collective worker participation at the workplace level, with specific informatory, consultative and codetermination rights in personnel, social and economic affairs.

Works councils are legally independent of trade unions, and their members are elected in a ballot of all employees rather than just union members. The key functions of EWCs are:

- Establishing two-way communication between employees and management, and union and management
- Maintaining peaceful and cooperative employment relations (as EWCs are not allowed to initiate a stoppage of work)
- Providing training for representatives.

Since the early 1990s, UK managers, trade unions and academics have become more interested in the EWC model, this renewed interest having come about for three principal reasons. First, EU legislation has focused attention on EWCs. As mentioned earlier, the 1994 EWC Directive required organizations employing more than 1000 employees in the EU (excluding the UK) and with at least two establishments in different member states, comprising at least 150 employees (again excluding the UK), to set up works councils. The principal objective of the EWC Directive is to induce organizations across the EU to set up an EWC system for the purpose of informing and consulting employees. In December 1999, the 1994 EWC Directive became law in the UK. To date, agreements between management and unions to establish EWCs have been concluded in over 600 European companies (Gilman and Marginson, 2002). The new EU Directive on Information and

Consultation (2001) is likely to provoke further interest and academic research, especially in member states without a strong EWC tradition (for example, Britain and Ireland).

Second, the decline of union membership in Britain and bargaining power over the past two decades has induced trade union leaders to explore the extension of unions' and workers' rights outside the traditional collective bargaining arena, under the umbrella of EU employee governance law. Third, in the 'transitional economies' of Central Europe, the EWC model has evoked a debate over the conditions for successful implementation of EWCs (Frege, 2002). Although the EWC system is still in its infancy, at least in the UK, EWCs are 'the most prominent, widespread and powerful form of industrial democracy in contemporary capitalist societies' (Frege, 2002, p. 221).

A survey of private sector MNCs in the UK found that 19 per cent operated an EWC (Cully et al., 1998). EWCs have differing degrees of power (Mayrhofer et al., 2000a): in Germany, for example, where EWCs have been a feature of the workplace for decades, employee representatives can resort to the courts to prevent or delay managerial decisions in areas such as changing working practices and dismissals. The range of issues discussed and the degree of legislative support for EWCs would, note Mayrhofer et al. (2000a, p. 226), 'shock US managers brought up on the theories of "manager's right to manage"'. The study by Frege (2002) concluded that there is a lack of research on the determinants of different employment relations, how EWCs work in practice and the specific relation between unions and works councils. Evaluating the existing literature, Frege (2002, p. 241) concludes that 'we know much about the ontology of works councils (what is a works council, what does it do) but much less about the determinants, outcomes and underlying causal relations'.

In terms of links between EWCs and organizational performance, Addison et al. (2000) have also made a contribution to the debate. Using economic data from Germany and Britain, they argue that mandatory indirect participation in decision-making would appear to be associated with higher productivity in workplaces with more than 100 workers and in economies with centralized pay bargaining (for example, Germany). In a recent comparative study of work reorganization in German and US call centres, it was found that institutional supports for collective voice can have a significant influence on the extent of worker control associated with team-based practices. Thus, Germany's stronger employee participation rights provided a 'crucial source of countervailing power in negotiations over work reorganization' (Doellgast, 2010, p. 395).

Employee involvement and paradox

The types of EIP system initiated by management performance contain contradictions and paradoxes. Stohl and Cheney (2001) analyse four main types of EI paradox: structure, agency, identity, and power. They posit that paradox is inherent in EI processes and that these paradoxes set limits that constrain the effectiveness of EI networks.

Organizational *structures* are created to govern EIP, but most EIP arrangements eliminate workers from the most influential network: the executive. Strauss (1998) explains this potential paradox. Direct employee voice mechanisms provide opportunities to make changes only at the margins of managerial decision-making. The 'really important decisions', for example investment in sustainable energy, are made by senior management. Put another way, 'Learn, innovate and voice your opinions as I have planned!'

The idea of *agency* relates to an individual's sense of being and a feeling that she or he can or does make a difference (Giddens, 1984). One paradox of agency references the tensions and contradictions present in HPWSs, in which teams may rely on the active subordination of team members to the will of the team. Thus, 'Do things our way but in a way that is still distinctively your own!'

The paradox of *identity* addresses issues of boundaries, space and the divide between the in-group and the out-group (Stohl and Cheney, 2001). The paradox is linked to the notion of employee commitment. At one level, EI implies commitment to the processes of learning and dialogue. At another level, however, 'commitment is expected to equal agreement' (Stohl and Cheney, 2001, p. 380). In a so-called 'learning organization', the paradox of identity may be expressed as 'Be a self-directed learner to meet organizational priorities.'

The fourth paradox is that of *power*, which centres on issues of access to resources, opportunities for independent voice and the shaping of employee behaviour. Stohl and Cheney (2001, p. 388) provide persuasive evidence of EIP regimes 'getting workers to make decisions that management would have made themselves'. In other words, 'Be an independent thinker, just as I have commanded you!'

Furthermore, contemporary systems of EI also raise ethical concerns. The growing interest in the ethics of EIP might reflect a degree of unease over the shift in power towards employers and management resulting from the decline in trade union influence, the growth of precarious employment, and exorbitant salary increases for corporate executives. Moreover, the paradoxes and contradictions found within the existing EI literature should be no surprise. These mirror the inherent contradiction contained within the employment relationship, that is, the need of management to be able to manage workers as an objectified commodity, but at the same time to call upon the cooperation of employees (Clayton, 2000). As stated elsewhere, it is also a mistake to assume that EIP can serve as an effective alternative to other more robust forms of employee voice based on indirect and independent representation, for example collective bargaining (Heery, 2000). Joint regulation may, in fact, be a prerequisite to nudge managers into more ambitious experiments, for instance in sustainability. These ethical and structured contradictions partly account for the continued scepticism towards EIP on the part of critical workplace researchers (see Thompson and McHugh, 2009). The challenge for both managers and workers is whether creativity and innovation can emerge from these paradoxes.

Employee rights and grievances

The third key dimension of employee relations is the set of individual employment rights and a process to handle individual complaints made to management.

Employee rights

The equality of employee relations is shaped by individual legal rights that protect employees against inequitable behaviour on the part of managers or other co-workers. A fundamental tenet underpinning effective employee relations is that employees must have confidence in management's intention to be fair and equitable. The right to be treated fairly and equitably, with its links to concepts of rights, obligations and 'social justice', has, of course, an ethical dimension (Winstanley and Woodall, 2000) and a 'dignity at work' dimension (Bolton, 2007). Employee rights and dignity at work are closely connected, and indeed 'Employment rights are human rights' (Barber, 2007, p. vii) that form an integral part of a workplace where employees can expect respect, and dignity *in* and *at* work.

As we have explained elsewhere (see, for example, Chapter 1), individual employment rights, embodied in UK and EU legislation, regulate the behaviour of employers and employees. The Sex Discrimination Acts of 1975 and 1986, the Race Relations Act 1976, the Disability Discrimination Act 2005 and the Equality Act 2006, for example, address issues of discrimination and harassment with regard to an employee's gender, disability, ethnicity, race or sexual orientation. To comply with the legislation, HR professionals have developed codes of practice as a guide to better HR practices.

Employee grievances

A key indicator of fairness and dignity in the workplace is the ability of an employee to raise concerns or express dissatisfaction about workplace issues, and receive redress for unfair treatment. A grievance is simply a complaint by an employee that the behaviour of another employee or management has been unfair or damaging to her or him. The formal grievance procedure plays an important role in introducing democracy into the workplace (Craig and Solomon, 1996, p. 334) and is also a form of *direct* employee voice (Marchington, 2008, p. 237). From management's perspective, the formal grievance procedure allows an employee to express dissatisfaction that, if not resolved, can result in unsatisfactory (mis)behaviour (Ackroyd and Thompson, 1999) and performance.

The non-union models of grievance-handling vary widely from one workplace to another and may have fewer than or as many procedural steps as are found in union models; in all instances, the grievance-handling process mirrors the management hierarchy. At a minimum, prescriptive HRM advisors recommend that a grievance workplace policy should:

- Investigate the complaint
- Take appropriate action to resolve the complaint to the mutual satisfaction of the complainant and the management
- Resolve the grievance in a timely manner (see Gennard and Judge, 2005, p. 300).

Employee complaints that require formal grievance management cover a myriad of workplace issues, including undignified or demeaning treatment by front-line managers or other co-workers, workplace bullying and harassment.

Sexual harassment as an employee relations issue

Recent analysis has shown that the negative consequences of sexual harassment and a misogynistic workplace extend beyond individual targets to include co-workers, work groups and whole organizations (Miner-Rubino and Cortina, 2004). As Keith (2000, p. 287) points out, sexual harassment 'poisons the atmosphere in the workplace'. It is an important issue for management, centring as it does on issues of social justice and efficiency. Sexual harassment in the workplace is unlawful, and the courts have increasingly viewed its prevention as the employer's responsibility. The legal concept of 'detriment' is important here. Sexual harassment is a 'detriment' per se; it can lead to an employment-related detriment to the female employee and, as such, has serious implications for management. In 1986, the European Parliament passed a resolution on violence against women, commissioning a report on the dignity of women at work, which led to the adoption of the EU code of practice (Figure 13.7).

The allegations of sexual impropriety against US President Bill Clinton in 1998 and, in 2011, the case of former International Monetary Fund chief Dominique Strauss-Kahn highlighted some of the difficulties seen in cases of sexual harassment in the workplace. The first issue is credibility because there is seldom a witness to support whether the conduct being complained about actually happened. There are, for example, no witnesses to the alleged conduct of Mr Clinton and the White House employee Monica Lewinsky or to the sexual encounter between Mr Strauss-Kahn and the hotel maid, Nafissatou Diallo, a 32-year-old immigrant from Guinea. Credibility and circumstantial evidence are under scrutiny here. Who has more credibility? Is there indirect evidence that might support or dismiss the allegations?

The EU code of practice defines sexual harassment as 'unwanted conduct of a sexual nature' affecting 'the dignity of women and men at work'. It defines harassment as largely subjective, in that it is for the individual to decide whether the conduct is acceptable or offensive.

The code says that member states should take action in the public sector and that employers should be encouraged to:

- issue a policy statement
- communicate it effectively to all employees
- designate someone to provide advice to employees subjected to harassment
- adopt a formal complaints procedure
- treat sexual harassment as a disciplinary offence.

Figure 13.7 *The European code on sexual harassment*

The Clinton case raises another issue that often applies to workplace investigations: the question of containment. In the presidential investigation, the public prosecutor apparently had no interest in limiting the scope of the investigation, but for many HR professionals, containment, in addition to what is legitimate and necessary in terms of conducting the investigation into a complaint of sexual harassment, is also an issue. The aim will be to contain the allegation and limit knowledge about the complaint to those who need to know.

Workplace sexual harassment is 'the most intimate manifestation of employment discrimination faced by women' (Keith, 2000, p. 277), and legal protection against it is complex and sensitive. There is concern expressed by some authors about how women are treated in law (see, for example, Debono, 2001), contending that women are disadvantaged because of a patriarchal or sexist jurisprudence. Debono (2001) found that there are sexist elements to the jurisprudence related to workplace sexual harassment decisions in the UK, the USA and New Zealand. Although the legislation is progressive, it is argued that 'sexist attitudes still remain with those who have the power to use the legislation to compensate the victims' (Debono, 2001, p. 338). Studies tend to emphasize that exposure to workplace sexual harassment impacts negatively on the quality of employee relations and is, moreover, associated with impaired employee well-being and individual and organizational performance (see HRM in practice 13.2).

Employee discipline

So far, we have looked at communication practices, management-initiated EIP and employee rights and grievances. To complete the discussion on employee relations, we must examine a fourth set of HR policies and practices that affect the quality of employee relations: that of *employee discipline*.

When employee voice mechanisms fail to create or reinforce desirable employee attitudes and behaviours, managers may resort to disciplinary action. Indeed, there is evidence that there has been an increased use of formal disciplinary measures since EIP practices were introduced. Mabey et al. (1998a) found a disjuncture between the rhetoric of empowerment and the practical reality of total quality management. Their study found that workers had 'negative perceptions' of total quality management because of a culture incorporating the 'excessive use of disciplinary actions against individuals' (Mabey et al., 1998a, p. 66). In recent years, rates of disciplinary sanctions and dismissals have increased, providing further evidence of the general movement from collective relations towards the individualization of the employment relationship in the UK (Knight and Latreille, 2000).

The modern workplace is pervaded by rules established by management to regulate the behaviour of workers. Indeed, it is argued that obedience underscores the relationship between employer and employee: 'There is certainly nothing more essential to the contractual relation between master and servant than the duty of obedience' (Cairns, 1974, quoted in Wedderburn, 1986, p. 187). Disciplinary practices, ranging from oral warnings to termination of the employment relationship, aim to make workers' behaviour predictable. The employment relationship involves a legal relationship, and for those employers and managers who share a less-than-sophisticated management style known as 'my way or the highway', there is a framework of legal rights regulating the disciplinary process.

The purpose of this section, with supporting companion website material, is modest: to provide an overview of the disciplinary concepts, practices, procedures and statutory rights found in the workplace. UK students and practitioners requiring a detailed knowledge of employment law relating to discipline and dismissal are advised to refer to Selwyn's *Law of Employment* (Selwyn, 2011) or a similar text.

HRM web links [www] Go to the following websites to compare employment standards legislation relating to discipline at work: www.legislation.gov.uk, which provides full texts of UK Acts of Parliament; and www.hrsdc.gc.ca/eng/labour/employment_standards/index.shtml for a comparative study of Canadian employment standards.

Bullying at work: 'My life became a living hell ...'

In 2009, Swansea County Court found Carmarthenshire NHS Trust liable for substantial compensation to Mrs Nanette Bowen, who had been signed off work indefinitely with stress and panic attacks following a 3-year campaign of bullying by her boss. Nanette, an information manager who had worked for the trust for more than 28 years, was not allowed to provide information without her new boss's written consent, had been made to complete a daily form so he could see what she was doing, had her responsibility for hiring staff removed, had been subject to sexual innuendo and aggression, and been banned from attending important meetings (Trades Union Congress, 2009).

Research shows that such a case is anything but unusual. The first national survey of workplace bullying at the end of the 1990s by Hoel and Cooper (2000) surveyed over 5000 employees and managers in 70 different organizations spanning all major sectors of employment. They found that 1 in 10 respondents reported being bullied within the previous 6 months, and that when the reporting period was extended to the previous 5 years, the incidence rose to a quarter of all respondents.

It is important to note that bullying is a long-term situation – a one-off argument does not count as bullying – and that a power imbalance usually makes it difficult for the bullied person to defend themselves. Subsequent surveys typically show that two-thirds of reported cases of bullying involve managers or supervisors as the perpetrators, while a third allege bullying by colleagues or peers (often, however, connected to the presence of a bullying manager). Some researchers have made a further distinction between 'victimization', in which the target of the abusive behaviour is an individual, and 'oppressive work regimes' where everyone is subject to the experience (Hoel and Beale, 2006).

The negative consequences for the organization of a persistent culture of bullying include increases in the rate of sickness absence, lowered productivity arising from lowered morale and commitment, and an increase in labour turnover. This suggests that the effects of

bullying extend further than the victim to create a negative organizational atmosphere that includes those who have been bullied in the past and those who persistently witness bullying behaviour.

Leaving the organization may, however, only be possible when jobs are relatively plentiful: in times of job shortage, workers may feel they have no option but to continue to endure abusive treatment. This suggests that the concept of power imbalance extends to the wider socioeconomic context to include, in the last couple of decades, the unitary nature of HRM; this has seen a subsequent decline in trade union and collective representation in the workplace, and an intensification of managerial control resulting from the recent economic crises and the increased market pressures felt by the private and public sectors alike.

Hoel and Cooper (2000) suggest that management styles need to be analysed in order to achieve the key HRM goals of enhanced employee commitment and engagement. Mangers should move away from 'confrontational' and 'macho' attitudes typical of a US style of management, and instead develop a cooperative style based on personal and professional qualities such as integrity and a regard for the needs of the individual and the group.

Stop! Have you experienced bullying in any job you have had? What did you see as the cause at the time? Why do you think that the incidence of workplace bullying seems to be on the increase?

Sources and further information: See Hoel and Beale (2006) and Hoel and Cooper (2000) for background to this case. Further information can be found in Trades Union Congress (2007).

Note: This feature was written by Chris Baldry at the University of Stirling.

Two-thirds of reported cases of bullying involve managers or supervisors as the perpetrators.

Disciplinary concepts

Discipline can be defined as the process that maintains compliance with employment rules in order to produce a controlled and effective performance. The purpose of discipline in the workplace is threefold:

- *Improvement* – the disciplinary process is seen as one of counselling the disobedient employee back to acceptable behaviour
- *Punishment* – the disciplinary process is seen as being about imposing penalties
- *Deterrent* – the process is seen as educational to deter others.

Corrective discipline refers to management action that follows the infraction of a rule. In North America, the 'hot-stove rule' is used to guide correct discipline. This states that disciplinary action (for example, warnings or suspension from work) should have the same characteristics as the penalty an individual receives from touching a hot stove. These characteristics are that discipline should be, with warning, immediate, consistent and impersonal. Most organizations apply a policy of *progressive discipline*, which means that the employer notifies employees of unacceptable conduct and provides them with an adequate opportunity to correct it.

Disciplinary rules and procedures are designed for promoting orderly employee relations as well as fairness and consistency in the treatment of individuals (Klass, 2009). *Rules* set standards of conduct and performance in the workplace, whereas *procedures* help to ensure that the standards are adhered to and also provide a fair method of dealing with alleged failures to observe them. A disciplinary process typically incorporates the requirements of *natural justice*, which means that employees should be informed in advance of any disciplinary hearing of the alleged misconduct, be given the right to challenge the alleged evidence, have the right to representation and to have witnesses, and be given the right to appeal against any decisions taken by management (Selwyn, 2011).

www For information and guidance on how to manage employee discipline, including ACAS's recommended disciplinary procedures, go to www.palgrave.com/business/bratton5 and look at the text entitled 'Managing employee discipline'.

reflective question Visit the companion website at www.palgrave.com/business/bratton5 and click on 'Managing employee discipline'. What do you think of the ACAS guidelines on disciplinary procedures? How Important is it for an organization's disciplinary process to be seen to be 'equitable'?

case study

Hawthorne Pharmaceuticals

Setting

While most of the Western world is experiencing a decrease in smoking rates, the number of Russian smokers continues to climb. As a result of tobacco companies promoting smoking as part of a 'Western lifestyle' and striving to capitalize on the public's new disposable income after the collapse of the Soviet Union, smoking rates have doubled. One-third of Russia's population smokes, ranking it as the fourth heaviest smoking country in the world, behind Serbia, Greece and Bulgaria. In Moscow, 75 per cent of male children are smokers, trailed only slightly by 65 per cent of the city's girls. Every year, 400,000 people die in Russia from smoking-related diseases.

In the last 20 years, the Russian government has repeatedly proposed legislation banning smoking in workplaces and any other public places, such as on aircraft, trains and municipal transport, as well as in schools, hospitals, cultural institutions and government buildings. Russia is actually falling behind other countries in implementing a smoking ban, which is becoming increasingly common both in Europe and around the world. In March 2004, Ireland became the first EU country to ban smoking in all enclosed places. Since then, a number of other countries have followed suit. The UK's own ban on smoking in public places reduced the effects of passive smoke, which were linked to more than 11,000 deaths every year.

If the legislation is truly put into place this time, the changes will affect not only Russian companies, but also international firms looking to invest in the expanding privatization of the economy. The emerging middle class has produced a potential market of 150 million consumers that lures companies from all over the world hoping to tap into the vast natural resources, advanced technology and skilled workers that Russia has to offer.

The problem

Hawthorne Pharmaceuticals is a global British manufacturer of pharmaceutical, medical device and consumer packaged goods, with 150 subsidiary companies operating in over 32 countries. It recently opened a new operation in Moscow, as part of a strategy to make its mark in the new prosperous Russian economy.

©istockphoto.com/Stepan Popov

The management at Hawthorne Pharmaceuticals were versed in Russian history and understood that workers' attitudes and behaviours had been shaped by 70 years of Communist dictatorship, a centrally planned economic system, and government bureaucracy that had ruled the people's lives. Like most international firms, the management at Hawthorne Pharmaceuticals found Russian workers to be cooperative and compliant, but not risk-takers. Many of the supervisors hired from the local labour pool lacked confidence and drive. Although they followed corporate policies strictly, the employees in turn expected the new company to take care of them and their families.

With the UK having one of the lowest smoking rates in Europe, the management at Hawthorne Pharmaceuticals were surprised at the number of the employees who were smokers – almost 65 per cent. As a company with a focus on health products, one of their first goals was to develop a voluntary tobacco reduction programme, including counselling and nicotine cessation aids, to improve the health of the new staff. Unfortunately, only a small group of workers took advantage of the programme in its first year, and the majority of these were supervisors.

The next step was to implement a smoking ban in the Russian operations. Matthew Duncan, one of the UK managers assigned to the Moscow operation, was given the task of involving employees in the decision. Although it was made clear to all employees that the company president wanted to see the worksites smoke-free regardless of government legislation, only the supervisors were to be given an opportunity to express their positions on the matter.

There were over 100 supervisors, and Matthew was given a short timeframe to present his findings. Although Matthew was free to speak to the supervisors, the company president stressed that he really just wanted to know whether or not the majority of the supervisors favoured the ban. As Matthew had not used any forms of employee communication before, he felt overwhelmed when he began reading about the various methods that could be used. With his deadline approaching, Matthew chose a questionnaire to quickly survey the supervisors.

In the end, the company president was pleased with the outcome. All the supervisors completed the questionnaire and, as expected, an overwhelming majority agreed with the idea of a smoking ban. The rest of the worker population were not asked for their opinions, but a ban was quickly put into place. Faced with no longer being allowed to smoke in their workplace, there was a major increase in the number of employees willing to participate in the company's tobacco reduction programme.

Assignment

Working either alone or in a study group, prepare a report drawing on this chapter and other recommended material which considers the following:

1 Which aspects of the workplace at Hawthorne Pharmaceuticals might have influenced the survey results?
2 What might have been missed by gathering only the supervisors' opinions?
3 What qualities do the Russian workers exhibit that could have influenced the survey results? Why?

Essential reading

Bryman, J. (ed.) (1988) *Doing Research in Organizations*. London: Routledge.
Elenkov, D. (1998) Can American management concepts work in Russia? *California Management Review*, **40**(4): 133–56.
Miller, K. (2009) *Organizational Communication: Approaches and Processes*. Boston: Wadsworth Cengage Learning.
Oppenheim, A. N. (1992) *Questionnaire Design, Interviewing and Attitude Measurement*. London: Pinter Publishers.
Turner, P. (2003) *Organizational Communication: The Role of the HR Professional*. London: Chartered Institute of Personnel and Development.

Note: This feature was written by Lori Rilkoff, HR Manager at City of Kaloomps, BC, Canada.

Visit the companion website at www.palgrave.com/business/bratton5 for a bonus case study on direct 'employee voice' at AppNett Solutions and for guidlines on writing reports.

summary

◀ This chapter has examined four dimensions of employee relations: communications, EI or voice, employee rights and grievances, and discipline. Communicating is the fundamental process of managing people in the workplace. It includes written, verbal and non-verbal communication, which flows downwards, upwards and horizontally in organizations.

◀ EI or 'voice' provides an opportunity for workers to take an active role in the decision-making process within their organization. EIP may be direct or indirect, voluntary or legislated; it may range from a manager simply exchanging information with employees to their complete participation in a major investment decision.

◀ EI can be seen to be a logical development in employee relations to enlist employees' skills and cooperation. Data provide evidence that British managers are adopting EIP techniques. Critics, as discussed, argue, however, that EIP schemes might be used by managers to marginalize the role of unions.

◀ Employee relations are buttressed by a framework of individual legal rights protecting employees against inequitable or inappropriate behaviour by managers or other co-workers. Formal non-union grievance procedures are a form of employee voice, designed to allow employees to articulate dissatisfaction about an issue directly to management. For managers, a grievance process can be seen as a useful mechanism to identify and resolve inappropriate behaviour, such as bullying or harassment.

◄ Employee discipline is the fourth dimension of employee relations examined in this chapter. Discipline practices vary between national legal systems, but to command support among the workforce, to avoid litigation and to avoid violations of the psychological contract, managers should design and apply practices with due regard to the requirements of *natural justice.*

vocab checklist for ESL students

◄ agency (n), agent (n)

◄ bargain (v) (n)

◄ bias (n), biased (adj)

◄ consult (v), consultant (n), consultation (n)

◄ dignity (n), dignified (adj)

◄ disclose (v), disclosure (n)

◄ employee involvement (EI) (n)

◄ employee involvement and participation (EIP) (n)

◄ employee relations (n)

◄ European Works Council (EWC) (n)

◄ ethics (n), ethical (adj)

◄ ethnographer (n), ethnography (n), ethnographic (adj)

◄ grieve (v), grievance (n)

◄ industrial relations (n)

◄ joint consultative committee (JCC) (n)

◄ labour relations (n)

◄ misogynist (n), misogynistic (adj)

◄ sexual harassment (n)

◄ substantiate (v), substantive (adj)

◄ utilize (v), utilitarian (n) (adj)

◄ works council (n)

Visit www.palgrave.com/business/bratton5 for a link to free definitions of these terms in the Macmillan Dictionary, as well as additional learning resources for ESL students.

review questions

1 What are the links between HR strategies and EI and communication practices?

2 Identify and discuss different schemes that the HR department manages in order to improve employee communications.

3 'Employee voice is a central component of HPWSs.' Do you agree or disagree? Discuss.

4 Explain the difference between participation and involvement in the workplace.

5 'Collective voice achieves what the lone voice could never do: it humanizes and civilizes the workplace.' Do you agree or disagree? Why?

6 What is meant by 'sexual discrimination'? Explain why an effective response to incidents of sexual harassment in the workplace is important for the employer and manager.

further reading to improve your mark

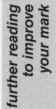

Reading these articles and chapters can help you gain a better understanding and potentially a higher grade for your HRM assignment.

◄ Budd, J., Gollan, P. and Wilinson, A. (2010) New approaches to employee voice and participation in organizations. *Human Relations*, **63**(3): 303–10.

◄ Marchington, M. and Cox, A. (2007) Employee involvement and participation: structures, processes and outcomes. In J. Storey (ed.) *Human Resource Management: A Critical Text* (pp. 177–94). London: Routledge.

◄ Doellgast, V. (2010) Collective voice under decentralized bargaining: a comparative study of work reorganization in US and German call centres. *British Journal of Industrial Relations*, **48**(2): 375–99.

◀ Gollan, P. J. (2006) Editorial: Consultation and non-union employee representation. *Industrial Relations Journal*, **37**(5): 428–37.

◀ Guirdham, M. (2011) *Communicating Across Cultures at Work* (3rd edn). Basingstoke: Palgrave Macmillan.

◀ Hall, M. and Marginson, P. (2005) Trojan horse or paper tigers? Assessing the significance of European Works Councils. In B. Harley, J. Hyman, and P. Thompson (eds) *Participation and Democracy at Work* (pp. 204–21). Basingstoke: Palgrave Macmillan.

◀ Kamenou, N. and Fearfull, A. (2006) Ethnic minority women: a lost voice in HRM. *Human Resource Management Journal*, **16**(2): 154–72.

◀ Marchington, M. (2008) Employee voice systems. In P. Boxall, J. Purcell and P. Wright (eds) *The Oxford Handbook of Human Resource Management* (pp. 231–50). Oxford: OUP.

 Visit www.palgrave.com/business/bratton5 for lots of extra resources to help you get to grips with this chapter, including study tips, HRM skills development guides, summary lecture notes, and more.

part V

the employment
relationship

chapter 14

health and safety management

objectives

After studying this chapter, you should be able to:

1   Explain the benefits of a health and wellness strategy

2   Outline the regulatory framework for workplace health and safety

3   Describe some common hazards in the contemporary workplace

4   Describe the components of a workplace wellness programme

5   Explain the role of trade unions and the influence of the environmental movement in creating sustainable and healthy workplaces and local communities

6   Critique management strategies for health and safety in the workplace

introduction

When TV audiences around the world watched the dramatic rescue of 33 trapped Chilean miners in October 2010, they may have found the news uplifting, but for occupational health and safety (OHS) activists it was a reminder that work can be a life and death experience. Most mornings, we turn the door handle and set off to work in offices, banks, schools, hospitals, universities, construction sites and other workplaces. Most of us assume that we will return home safely at the end of the working day, but many workers unfortunately will not. In 2009–10, 152 British workers lost their lives through a workplace fatality, and a further 233,000 employees suffered a reportable work-related injury, a rate of 840 per 1 million workers (Health and Safety Executive, 2011a).

These data underscore two important realities about work: first, it can be an unhealthy, even deadly, experience; and, second, health and safety in the workplace is all too often mismanaged. Work systems and practices that offer safe and healthy working conditions reduce accidents and help to create dignity *at* work (Bolton, 2007). The World Health Organization (2011) defines 'health' as 'a state of complete physical, mental and social well-being and not merely the absence of disease or infirmity'. According to this definition, managers and, in workplaces where they are organized, trade union representatives are immersed in one of society's greatest challenges – the design and maintenance of sustainable work systems that both support the organization's objectives and provide an environment that is safe and healthy for its workers. Most recently, the industrial pollution of global and local ecosystems has brought into full relief the need for work systems to operate without compromising the health of the local community or destroying the ecosystem.

We will begin this chapter by considering the importance of health and wellness in the management of work and people. After giving a brief overview of the legal framework, we will identify some hazards in the modern workplace. We will then examine the role of trade unions and the influence of the environmental movement in creating sustainable and healthy workplaces and local communities. Finally, we will seek to examine the paradoxes surrounding the issue of health and wellness so that there can be a better understanding of the complexities of the employment relationship.

HRM web links A short film of the rescue of the Chilean miners is available at www.youtube.com/watch?v=XGecqHnN2gQ.

reflective question Who are the stakeholders in health and safety? What are the responsibilities of employers to ensure that work is conducted in a safe and healthy environment? Does the government have a responsibility to (1) employees and (2) the local community to ensure that work systems are safe and sustainable in terms of health? Consider an organization you have worked in. Critically review its health and safety record and training.

Sustainable health, wellness and human resource management

Traditionally, OHS encapsulated quite distinct yet intrinsically related concepts concerned with the identification and control of work-induced ill-health and accidents. Whereas accidents are visible or measurable, not without cause and largely preventable, work-induced ill-health is largely invisible and can develop over a long period of time, as in the case of asbestosis (Cullen, 2002). Although workplace health and safety have long been legitimate areas for regulation, as evidenced by health and safety legislation, occupational safety has typically been given precedence over more general workplace and local community health concerns. The concept of workplace wellness goes beyond the regulation and management of work-related health and safety, to focus on shaping employees' entire lifestyle and well-being. The emerging literature on sustainable business strategies, the 'quadruple bottom line performance' (see Chapter 2), is widening the scope and coverage of 'green' health and safety management. What is important to recognize is that concerns about health and wellness are no longer limited to areas of industrial work. Front-line office workers, managers and professionals are demanding to work in a 'healthy organization', and employers are increasingly acknowledging the adverse economic consequences of employee ill-health.

People living in the locale of industrial polluters – mines, agriculture, chemicals and forestry – and environmental movements are beginning to hold organizations accountable for widespread damage to ecosystems. The instances here are numerous, but well-known examples include the massive oil spill in the Gulf of Mexico in 2010 when BP's wellhead burst, and toxic pollution by the US corporation Union Carbide in Bhopal, India in the 1980s (see Chapter 2). Another case is the industrial poisoning of an entire community's water supply, and subsequent corporate cover-up, by the US Pacific Gas and Electric Company (PG&E) in Hinkley, USA – the legal fight against PG&E was dramatized in the 2000 film *Erin Brockovich*. A most recent example can be found in Western Canada in 2012, where research has shown that oil sand production is responsible for high levels of toxins in the Athabasca watershed. The pollution has been held responsible for rare human cancers diagnosed in residents of Fort Chipewyan (Weber, 2011). In Europe, environmental activists are proposing to the United Nations (UN) that 'ecocide' – the extensive destruction, damage to or loss of ecosystems in a given territory, whether by human agency or by other causes – be declared an international crime against peace (Jowit, 2010).

Such experiences and campaigns have brought into the modern discourse on low-carbon economies a recognition that OHS and the protection of ecosystems form an important subgroup of organizational contingencies affecting corporate strategy. Moreover, they underscore the need to develop a proactive human resource management (HRM) strategy that can contribute to the management of health, wellness and environmental-related risks.

Although there has been a deluge of research on HRM problems and issues, it is unfortunately true, apart from a few notable cases (Nichols, 1997; Taylor and Connelly, 2009), that workplace health and safety is under-researched by workplace scholars, partly because it has entered the HRM discourse in only a marginal way. Rising costs associated with work-induced injuries and ill-health, issues relating to the psychological contract, new laws and growing concerns about protecting ecosystems are important reasons why workplace health, safety and wellness should be part of any introduction to the field of HRM. But there is another important reason why HRM scholars and practitioners need to pay more attention to health and wellness: if strategic HRM means anything, it must encompass the development and promotion of a set of health and wellness policies to protect the organization's most valued asset – its people.

The employer has a legal duty to maintain a healthy and safe workplace, the health and safety function being directly related to key HRM activities such as selection, appraisal, rewards and learning, and development. Health issues and policy can affect the *selection* process in two ways. First, it is safe to assume that, during the recruitment process, potential applicants will be more attracted to an organization that has a reputation for offering a healthy and safe work environment for its employees. Second, the maintenance of a healthy and safe workplace can be facilitated in the selection process by choosing applicants with personality traits that decrease the likelihood of an accident. In the USA, for example, predictors of safety-related behaviours have been used for almost 30 years across a variety of industries. Selection instruments are used to screen out applicants deemed to have 'unsafe' or 'at-risk' personality traits (Ford, 2011). *Appraisal* of a manager's performance that incorporates the safety record of a department or section can also facilitate health and safety. Research suggests that safety management programmes are more effective when the accident rates of their sections are an important criterion of managerial performance.

Safe work behaviour can be encouraged by a *reward* system that ties bonus payments to the safety record of a work group or section. Some organizations also give their employees prizes for safe work behaviour, a good safety record or suggestions for improving health and safety. Training and human resources (HR) development play a critical role in promoting health and safety awareness among employees, and indeed the Health and Safety at Work etc. Act (HASAWA) 1974 requires employers to provide instruction and training to ensure the health and safety of their employees. Studies indicate that safety training for new employees is particularly beneficial because accidents are highest during the early months in a new job.

On the question of the importance of OHS, although economic cost and HR considerations will always be predominant for the organization, the costs of ill-health and work-related accidents are not only borne by the victims, the families and their employers: they are also clearly borne by the tax-payer and public sector services. The healthcare sector, for example, bears the costs of workplace ill-health and accidents. Reliable estimates of the total cost of occupational ill-health and accidents are incomplete, which is perhaps symptomatic of the low priority given to this area of work. The Health and Safety Executive (HSE) has admitted that although occupational diseases kill more people in the UK each year than industrial accidents, there is only limited information on the former. An estimate put the cost to British society for workplace injuries and work-related ill health at £20–31.8 billion in 2001–02 (Georgiou et al., 2009, p. 1039).

HRM web links For further information on the costs of workplace injuries and ill-health, see also Maniv Pathak's 2008 report *The Cost to Employers in Britain of Workplace Injuries and Work Related Ill Health in 2005/06*, which can be found at www.hse.gov.uk/economics/research/injuryill0506.pdf.

The changing approach to workplace health and safety

The traditional approach to OHS is called, the *'careless worker'* model. It is assumed by most employers, the courts and accident prevention bodies that most accidents have resulted from an employee's failure to take safety seriously or protect herself or himself. The implication of this is that work can be made safe simply by changing the behaviour of employees by poster campaigns and accident prevention training. In the past, the attitudes of trade unions often paralleled those of employers and managers.

Early trade union activity tended to focus on basic wage and job security issues rather than safety: trade union representatives used their negotiating skill to 'win' wage increases, and health and safety often came rather low down in their bargaining priorities. If union representatives did include health and safety as part of their activities, it was often so that they could negotiate the payment of 'danger' or 'dirt' money over and above the regular wage rate. According to Eva and Oswald (1981, p. 33), the tendency for union officials was 'to put the onus on to inspectors and government rather than to see OHS as part of the everyday activity of local union representatives'.

Among employees, dangerous and hazardous work systems were accepted as part of the risk of working. Lost fingers and deafness, for example, were viewed as a matter of 'luck' or the 'inevitable' outcome of work. Four decades ago, a major investigation into OHS concluded that 'the most important single reason for accidents at work is apathy' (Robens, 1972, p. 1). So there is a paradox here. When there are major disasters on land, air or sea involving fatalities, society as a whole takes a keen interest, yet society's reaction towards the fact that hundreds of employees die and thousands receive serious injuries every year in the workplace tends to be muted.

The 1972 Robens Report encouraged managers and labour organizations to take greater interest in OHS. Importantly, regulatory bodies and many decision-makers reached a developmental stage in which the careless worker model no longer effectively addressed work-induced ill-health caused by unhealthy and unsustainable work systems. A new approach, the *'shared responsibility'* model, assumes that the best way to reduce levels of occupational accidents and disease relies on the cooperation of both employers and employees, a 'self-generating effort' between 'those who create the risks and those who work with them' (Robens, 1972, p. 7).

The British Trades Union Congress articulated a 'trade union approach' to OHS emphasizing that the basic problem of accidents stemmed from the hazards and risks that were built into the work structure or system. Nichols' (1997) characterized such workplaces as constituting 'potentially injurious structure(s) of vulnerability' (quoted by Taylor and Connelly, 2009, p. 161). Systematic breaches of health and safety legislation, the absence of employee representation, and unilateral mismanagement by managers were the causes of many workplace accidents. The trade union approach, therefore, argued that the way to improve OHS was through union-based employee representation and redesigning organizations and work systems in order to 'remove hazards and risks at source' (Trades Union Congress, 1979, p.10). An HSE document gives support to this approach, stating that most accidents involve an element of failure in control – in other words a failure in managerial skill. A guiding principle when drawing up arrangements for securing health and safety should be that work should, as far as possible, be adapted to people and not vice versa. The trade union view of health and safety, which draws attention to potential hazards in the labour process, is depicted in Figure 14.1.

In an effort to effectively leverage people in order to improve competitiveness and public services, and encourage organizational change (Madsen, 2003), many organizations introduced a wellness model in the 1990s. Wellness is the 'process of living at one's highest possible level as a whole person' (Schafer, 1996, p. 33). It is a general philosophy or holistic approach taken by top management to enhance the overall well-being of the workforce through a combination of voluntary diagnostic and educational health programmes.

Figure 14.1 *A trade union view of workplace health and safety*
Source: Eva and Oswald (1981)

Whereas workplace 'health' manages the tension between organizational goals and employee health, the intrinsically related concept of 'wellness' endeavours to 'improve' emotional, intellectual, physical, social and spiritual health (Madsen, 2003, p. 48).

Just as safety is regulated and typically given primacy over workplace health issues, wellness is far less likely to be monitored and managed than general health in the workplace (Mearns and Hope, 2005). Workplace wellness encourages the view that both the employer and the employee benefit from wellness management activities. A common metaphor to underpin the approach is that of the 'healthy organization' (Haunschild, 2003). The performance argument – that is, that wellness interventions reduce employee absenteeism, improve the bottom line and encourage workers to accept change – provides the ideological basis of wellness management (Haunschild, 2003). A survey of Canadian workplaces reported that 83.4 per cent of employers offered some form of wellness programming (Bentley, 2005).

The importance of health and wellness

There are strong economic, legal, psychological and ethical reasons why managers should take health and safety seriously, and these will be discussed in turn below.

Economic considerations

The Health and Safety Commission (HSC) and the Department of the Environment, Transport and the Regions (2000) document made the 'business case' for health and safety in the workplace. In considering the economics of an unhealthy and unsafe workplace, it is necessary to distinguish between costs falling upon the organization and costs falling upon government-funded bodies such as hospitals. It is not difficult for an organization to calculate the economic costs of a work-related accident. In addition to direct costs related to lost production due to accidents and illness, there are also indirect costs.

The indirect costs can include the overtime payments necessary to make up for lost production, the cost of retaining a replacement employee and the legal cost associated with court hearings in contested cases. The indirect costs of workplace accidents and illnesses also fall on society through the extra need for healthcare provision. The economic costs of work-related accidents, and the techniques for assessing them, require further research (Georgiou et al., 2009).

A safe and healthy work environment, built on sustainable principles, can reduce operating costs and improve organizational effectiveness. It has long been argued that an investment in health and wellness improves worker commitment and performance (Mearns and Hope, 2005). Thus, top management should approach health and wellness as an investment rather than a cost (Dyck, 2002).

Legal considerations

With respect to workplace health and safety, the legal rights of employees can be categorized into two broad categories: *individual* and *collective*. The first source of individual rights evolves from common law. Every employer has a vicarious common law duty to provide a safe working environment for her or his employees. But the primary source of individual rights arises from statute law. In Britain, an example is the HASAWA 1974. Within the European Union (EU), individual rights stemming from directives under Article 189 of the Treaty of Rome are a second important source of legislated protection standards promoting safe working environments.

The main source of collective health and safety rights arises from the negotiated collective agreements between union and management. In current labour law, Canadian, American and New Zealand workers have legal rights to refuse to perform unsafe or unhealthy work (Pye et al., 2001). In 1974, a Royal Commission on the Health and Safety of Workers first articulated the three principal rights of Canadian workers: the right to refuse dangerous work without penalty, the right to participate in identifying and correcting health and safety problems, and the right to know about hazards in the workplace. These three fundamental rights continue to be enshrined in current Canadian legislation (Montgomery and Kelloway, 2002). In the EU and the USA, failure to provide a safe working environment may result in the employer being prosecuted for *corporate manslaughter*. Health and safety legislation is discussed more fully in the next section.

HRM web links   Visit the websites of any of the following OHS organizations for detailed information on health and safety legislation: Britain (www.hse.gov.uk), Canada (www.ccohs.ca), Finland (www.occuphealth.fi), Australia (http://safeworkaustralia.gov.au/Pages/default.aspx), Hong Kong (www.hkosha.org.hk) and Europe (www.osha.eu.int).

Psychological considerations

Apart from economic and legal considerations, a healthy and safe work environment helps to facilitate employee commitment and improve industrial relations. In Beer et al.'s (1984) model of HRM, it is recognized that, going beyond the legal requirement of 'due diligence', a healthy organization can have a strong positive effect on the psychological contract by strengthening employees' commitment, motivation and loyalty (p. 153):

[There is some evidence to indicate that work system design may have
  effects on physical health, mental health, and longevity of life itself.

A survey of UK workplaces found a strong association between worker reports of a 'healthier workplace' and greater experience of HR practices. With respect to work-related stress, a 'healthier workplace' and a more positive state of the psychological contract were associated with lower reported levels of stress (Guest, 2008). At a collective level, it is argued that union–management relations are improved when employers satisfy their employees' health and safety needs. When organizations accept greater responsibility for the health, wellness and safety of their employees, it can change workplace behaviour, and employees may take a less militant stance during wage bargaining if management pays attention to housekeeping.

Ethical considerations

In the area of OHS, can employers raise the ethical stakes? Do employers have a moral responsibility to provide a safe and healthy workplace? Do employers have a moral responsibility to safeguard the local ecosystems and the health of people living close to the business operation? Do employers have a moral responsibility to avoid creating a long-hours culture that brings physical and psychological problems, and leads to a 'vicious cycle' of stress and people losing out on family life (Campbell, 2010; Owen, 2011)?

Sustainable business practices and health are inextricably linked, and health issues have implications for corporate responsibility and managerial ethics. Gewirth (1991) argues that those individuals who contribute to the causation of work-related diseases (for example, asbestosis, lung cancer and exposure to second-hand smoke) and who do so knowingly can be held to be both causally and morally responsible for their action. Doherty and Tyson (2000) argue persuasively that managers are not innocent bystanders with regard to employee health and well-being: their actions – such as the choice of production processes and substances, work speed-up, extra work hours and performance-based pay – have adverse effects on employees' work–life balance, as well as their physical and mental well-being.

A major challenge to managers is clearly to provide a safe and healthy work environment for their employees. Economic and moral reasons dictate such a policy, but, as we have already stated, there is also a pervasive portfolio of legislation, regulations, codes of practice and guidance notes dealing with OHS; in addition, as with other employment law, the HR practitioner has taken on the role of advising managers on the content and legal obligations of this.

Health and safety legislation

The history of occupational safety legislation can be traced back to the Industrial Revolution in the eighteenth century. The pioneering legislation included the 1802 Health and Morals of Apprentices Act, which was designed to curb some of the abuses of child labour. The 1867 Factory Act extended safety laws beyond the textile mills and gave limited coverage to adult male employees. The 1901 Factories and Workshops (Consolidation) Act then remained the governing Act until the Factories Act 1937. The Factories Act 1961 consolidated industrial safety law, establishing minimum standards in factories only for cleanliness, space, temperature, ventilation and lighting, the Offices, Shops and Railway Premises Act 1963 giving similar protection to white-collar workers. Building a statutory framework for OHS has been painfully slow, hindered by consistent opposition from the majority of employers, who have argued that OHS laws would make British industry uncompetitive.

The Robens Report

In the 1960s, when the Labour Party formed the UK government, OHS came under detailed scrutiny. The trade union movement pressed for health and safety legislation to be extended to white-collar workers in hospitals and local government, who were not covered by any of the earlier statutes. The Labour government set up a Committee on Safety and Health at Work, chaired by Lord Robens, to review the whole field and make recommendations. The committee's findings can be summarised thus:

- Despite a wide range of legal regulation, work was continuing to kill, maim and sicken tens of thousands of employees each year. The committee considered that the most important reason for this unacceptable state of affairs was apathy.
- There was too much law. The committee identified 11 major statutes, supported by nearly 500 supplementary statutory instruments. The committee believed that the sheer volume of law had become counterproductive.
- Much of the law was obscure, haphazard and out of date, many laws regulating obsolete production processes. Furthermore, the law was focusing on physical safeguards rather than preventive measures such as training and joint consultation.
- The provision for enforcement of the existing legislation was fragmented and ineffective. The committee felt that the pattern of control was one of 'bewildering complexity'.
- Existing health and safety law ignored a large number of employees: statutes prior to 1974 excluded over 8 million workers in communication, education, hospitals and local government.

The committee therefore made four main proposals to improve OHS:

- The law should be rationalized. A unified framework of legislation should be based upon the employment relationship (rather than on a factory or mine), and all employers involved with work or affected by work activities (except for domestic servants in private homes) would be covered by the new legislation.
- A self-regulating system involving employers, employees and union representatives should be created to encourage organizational decision-makers to design and maintain safe work systems and help employees to take more responsibility for health and safety. The basic concept was to be the employer's duty towards her or his employees – employers being bound to design and maintain safe and healthy systems of work – and the concomitant duty of the employees was to behave in a manner safeguarding their own health and that of their co-workers.
- A new unified statutory framework setting out general principles should be enacted.
- A new unified enforcement agency headed by a national body with overall responsibility should be established and should provide new, stronger powers of sanction.

In 1972, the Robens Committee published its report, and the Conservative government introduced a new Bill in Parliament. Two years later, the Conservatives lost the general election, but in 1974 the Labour government reintroduced a similar Bill, which became the HASAWA 1974, examined in more detail in the next section.

The Health and Safety at Work etc. Act 1974

This Act has been the cornerstone of OHS law for over three decades now. The Act vested trade unions with significant powers related to workplace health and safety matters. As Nichols (1990, p. 366) points out, compared with the 1980s and 90s, the HASAWA was 'a product of a different politics and philosophy'. The complete coverage of this complex Act is outside the scope of this chapter, but we will highlight its salient features so that readers can become familiar with some important principles and terminology. The main duties on employers are contained within Section 2 of the Act (Figure 14.2).

General duties

2. (1) It shall be the duty of every employer to ensure, **so far as is reasonably practicable**, the health, safety and welfare at work of all his employees.

(2) Without prejudice to the generality of an employer's duty under the preceding subsection, the matters to which that duty extends include in particular:

(a) the provision and maintenance of plant and systems of work that are, so far as is reasonably practicable, safe and without risks to health;

(b) arrangements for ensuring, so far as is reasonably practicable, safety and absence of risks to health in connection with the use, handling, storage and transport of articles and substances;

(c) the provision of such information, instruction, training and supervision as is necessary to ensure, so far as is reasonably practicable, the health and safety at work of his employees;

(d) so far as is reasonably practicable as regards any place of work under the employer's control, the maintenance of it in a condition that is safe and without risks to health and the provision and maintenance of means of access to and egress from it that are safe and without such risks;

(e) the provision and maintenance of a working environment for his employees that is, so far as is reasonably practicable, safe, without risks to health, and adequate as regards facilities and arrangements for their welfare at work.

Figure 14.2 The Health and Safety at Work etc. Act 1974, Section 2: Duties on Employers

HRM web links [www] Go to www.hmso.gov.uk/acts.htm for the full text of UK Acts of Parliament.

European Union health and safety legislation

In addition to health and safety legislation from their national governments, employers within EU member countries have EU directives to follow, which adds to the complexity of the situation. EU law affects the health and safety legislation of the UK as it overrides domestic law. The Social Charter (see Appendix A) gives added weight to OHS, stating that workers have the 'right to health protection and safety at the workplace'. EU directives under Article 189 of the Treaty of Rome are also an important source of OHS legislation. These cover a wide range of health and safety issues, such as the use of asbestos, the control of major industrial accident hazards, risk assessment, equipment regulations and the prevention of repetitive strain injuries. Directives are binding, although member states can decide upon the means of giving them legal and administrative effect. In the UK, this is usually in the form of regulations, which are normally published with associated approved codes of practice and guidance notes. Teague and Grahl (1992, p. 136) optimistically argue that the new EU health and safety legislation will 'not be of the "lowest common denominator" type but "maximalist" in nature'.

HRM web links **www**   Visit the websites of any of the following OHS organizations – Australia (www.safetyline.wa.gov.au), Britain (www.hse.gov.uk), Finland (www.occuphealth.fi) or other countries – for more information on how health and safety regulations impact on the design of work and the management of the employment relationship.

At the turn of the new millennium, the UK's New Labour government expressed a commitment to improving OHS. The Revitalising Health and Safety statement, launched by the deputy prime minister and chair of the HSC in 2000, set national targets for improving health and safety performance:

- To reduce the number of working days lost from work-related injury by 30 per cent
- To reduce work-related ill-health by 20 per cent
- To reduce fatalities by 10 per cent by 2010 (HSE, 2001).

Research on health and safety legislation in France and Germany demonstrates, however, the importance of joint safety committees for improving health and safety performance in the workplace (Reilly et al., 1995; Walters, 2004). The implications of OHS legislation for managers and HR professionals are formidable. At executive level in the UK, the 2007 *Corporate Manslaughter and Corporate Homicide Act* establishes organizational liability.

An organization will commit the offence if its activities are managed or organized in such a way that causes death to either employees or members of the public (Lockton, 2010).

As safety experts rightly point out, workplace accidents and ill-health are not without cause, are largely preventable and often arise from failures in control and management (Cullen, 2002). Hazard prevention and control requires managers to undertake risk

©istockphoto.com/Peter Burnett

Research has shown that migrants working in the construction industry are more at risk from accidents in the workplace than non-migrant workers

assessment in order to help the organization decide what health and safety measures need to be implemented. For permanent, unionized, workers, joint consultative health and safety committees potentially have a key role in determining strategic approaches to workplace health and safety. The reality for many casual migrant workers in the UK, however, is that language skills and cost-reducing imperatives are a barrier to health and safety. Research shows that migrants working in the construction industry, built on rules of 'maximum flexibility and profitability', are more at risk than non-migrant workers (Pai, 2010, p. W1).

Legge (2005) notes that the track record of the EU in the area of health and safety has been 'modest', and, particularly during economic recession, has mirrored nineteenth-century discourse on OHS: employers, unions and government agencies have tended to 'back-pedal' and fail to comply with OHS regulations. Similarly, Bain (1997) persuasively argues that, in Europe and the USA, powerful business lobbies and governments have mounted an offensive against health and safety legislation, health regulation being sacrificed on the altar of profit. The source of campaigns for the 'deregulation' of health and environmental safeguards is ideologically driven and can be located in the ascendancy of neo-liberal ideology.

The perceptive reader will have noticed similarities between the argument opposing factory legislation in the nineteenth century and the twenty-first-century debate on the 1997 Kyoto Protocol and the 2011 UN negotiations to establish a new climate accord. Many corporations are opposed to meaningful, legally binding targets on carbon emissions because they would, they argue, make North American industry uncompetitive.

reflective question Henry Ford once said, 'History is bunk.' Consider the debate on global warming; how should the developed nations respond in the post-Kyoto Protocol era? Can the stakeholders – employers, employees, governments and communities – of today learn anything from the history of factory safety legislation in the nineteenth century? What are your views? What role, if any, should organizations and governments play in reducing greenhouse gas emissions?

Workplace health and wellness issues

This section examines several health issues of special concern to today's managers and explains the meaning of workplace wellness.

Health issues

The dynamics of the modern workplace and the changes in the way in which organizations manage employment relations have been linked to numerous health problems. For example, precarious employment, unequal distribution of power, work intensification and role conflicts have all been associated with adverse physiological effects, somatic complaints and psychological stress. This section examines several health and wellness issues: sick building syndrome (SBS), workplace stress, workplace violence, bullying, alcohol abuse, smoking, and acquired immune deficiency syndrome (AIDS).

Sick building syndrome

Interest in the physical aspects of the work building, as a factor affecting employee performance, goes back to at least the 1930s with the Hawthorne experiments in the USA (see Chapter 4). Most recently, the construction of 'closed' office buildings with air-conditioning systems has focused research attention on the working conditions of knowledge workers.

In 1982, SBS was recognized by the World Health Organization as occurring where a cluster of work-related symptoms of unknown cause were significantly more prevalent among the occupants of certain buildings in comparison with others. Researchers have identified numerous symptoms of SBS, including eye/nose/throat irritation, a sensation of dry mucous membranes and skin, skin rash, mental fatigue, headaches, a high frequency of airway infection and cough, nausea, dizziness, hoarseness and wheezing (Bain and Baldry, 1995). The HSC calculated that the staff of 30–50 per cent of newly 'remodelled' buildings in Britain suffered a high incidence of SBS-related illnesses. In Canada, it has been estimated that there are 1800 'sick' buildings affecting 250,000 office workers. Based on such data, the problem of SBS seems to have been 'severely underestimated' (Bain and Baldry, 1995, p. 21), and from the worker well-being perspective, it is a significant problem (Redman et al., 2011, p. 23).

The causes of SBS have been linked to inadequate ventilation, unsuitable lighting and airborne pollutants. Others have focused less on technical explanations and emphasized managerial contingencies. Bain and Baldry (1995) and Bain et al. (1999), for example, propose that, in a context of high energy costs, SBS is related to cost reductions and the intensification of knowledge work. They conclude that 'Changes in the balance of power in the office environment have undoubtedly made it easier for management to gain employee acceptance of much more demanding practices and patterns of work' (Bain and Baldry, 1995, p. 30).

In the SBS debate, air-conditioning is a controversial issue. For managers, air-conditioning represents the ideal way of achieving a stable working environment that helps to improve work performance. For employees and unions, however, air-conditioning is negatively associated with control (Bain and Baldry, 1995), best captured by the competing tensions around who controls the 'open window' (Redman et al., 2011). SBS is negatively associated with job satisfaction and is associated with 'increased management-employment conflict' (Redman et al., 2011, p. 23). SBS is also a 'stressor' and positively associated with emotional exhaustion that can increase labour costs via lower performance and absenteeism. It may in turn undermine the empowerment approach associated with high-commitment work models as managers resort to disciplinary measures to reduce absenteeism or deal with 'open window' control issues.

HRM web links Visit the website www.iea.cc for information on ergonomics, the study of relationships between the physical attributes of workers and their work environment.

Workplace stress

The word 'stress' is now part of the regular vocabulary of managers and other employees. Although a certain degree of stress is normal in life, if stress is repeated or prolonged, individuals experience physical and psychological discomfort. There is widespread recognition that tension and stress have increased in UK workplaces (Green, 2004; Kelliher and Anderson, 2010), and this is supported by evidence of work intensification. The capacity of 'smart' mobile phones, such as the BlackBerry, to create a 24/7, on-demand lifestyle, and to result in the intrusion of work into private life, has been identified by some academics as a potential stressor (Bittman et al., 2009). There is a general consensus that stress and stress-related ill-health can impact negatively on job performance. Figure 14.3 illustrates some common symptoms of stress.

Tension and anxiety	Sleep problems
Anger and aggression	Digestive problems
High blood pressure	Chronic worry
Inability to relax	Irritability and boredom
Excessive alcohol and/or tobacco use	Uncooperative attitudes
Forgetfulness	Increased accidents
Increased absenteeism	Reduced job satisfaction

Figure 14.3 *Typical systems of workplace stress*

HRM web links Go to the websites www.tuc.org.uk/workplace/index.cfm?mins=173&minors=124&majorsubjectID=2, www.hse.gov.uk, www.res.bham.ac.uk/publications/researchpubs/988%20data/OCCHEALT.htm and www.hrreporter.com for more information on workplace stress.

Much research into job-related stress has tended to focus on 'executive burnout' and individuals in the higher echelons of the organizational hierarchy, but stress can affect employees at lower levels too. One US study found that the two most stressful jobs were a manual labourer and a secretary. An early US study reported that the incidence of a first heart attack was 2.5 times greater among skilled manual employees than among senior management grades, the rate in fact increasing the lower the occupational grade (Craig, 1981). In a further report, a US health organization discovered that women in clerical occupations suffered twice the incidence rate of heart disease of all other female employees (Haynes and Feinleils, 1980.

The notion of a work–life balance for employees – the need to balance work and family activities – is a stressor. A 2004 UK survey found a strong association between employee reports of lower levels of work-related stress and a more positive state of the psychological contract and a 'healthier workplace' (Guest, 2008). In addition to the physical and psychological disabilities it causes, occupational stress costs individuals and business considerable sums of money (Coutts, 1998). The HSC has, for example, estimated that workplace stress, depression and anxiety costs the British economy £530 million annually (HSC, 2007).

reflective question Think about a time when you felt under considerable stress. What were the causes of that stress? Could any of the work-related stressors be eliminated or reduced? If not, explain why. Go to www.hse.gov.uk for an example of a stress audit questionnaire.

Juggling work and life

When a long-hours culture is combined with an increase in the proportion of women in the labour force and changes to the pattern of the working day, with many services now being offered on a 24-hour basis, we have a phenomenon that has for two decades been the subject of ongoing academic and policy debates – the so-called work–life balance or work–life boundary.

A few years ago, an editorial in *The Guardian* (*Guardian*, 2005) commented:

> As you hunt for the Easter eggs or visit the garden centre this weekend, spare a thought for the nearly 3 million British workers for whom the Easter break represents a pay cut …. It is a reminder of the peculiarity of the British work culture: compared to the rest of Europe, Britain has fewer bank holidays, takes less holiday and its men work the longest hours.

In the UK, working long hours has traditionally been a way in which workers on a low basic wage could bump up their take-home pay. More recently, there has in addition been a widespread diffusion of *unpaid* overtime. Here, long hours are worked because of more subjective pressures such as not wishing to let the customer or team colleagues down, or wanting to meet management expectations about employee commitment. The result has been that, despite finally signing up to the EU Working Time Directive in 1997, a high proportion of employees in the UK continue to work more than the Directive's maximum of 48 hours a week.

The first policy response to these tensions between work and domestic responsibilities was the promotion of so-called 'family-friendly' employment policies in which employers were encouraged to consider flexible patterns of working to fit in with employees' domestic responsibilities. Since 2003, employees have had the right to request flexible working but, even where this has been practised, it has been only a limited response to perceived imbalance: it focuses only on working parents; it has often been defined in ways that suit the employer's workflow rather than the employees' non-work responsibilities; and it looks only at patterns of working time.

In their examination of call centres and software production, Jeff Hyman and his colleagues (Hyman et al., 2003) made a useful distinction between tangible and intangible work-related incursions into domestic life. The tangible, or quantitative, includes expectations to work overtime, perhaps at short notice and often unpaid, unpredictable shift patterns, and an explicit or implicit expectation to take work home to get the job done. The intangible or qualitative aspect includes exhaustion, feelings of stress and disturbed sleep patterns, and tendencies to worry about work after hours.

Hyman et al. found that, for both groups of 'new' workers, organizational pressures did result in work intruding into non-work areas of employees' lives but, because of the different nature of the labour processes, this was manifested in different ways. For call-centre work, directly reliant on a particular technological system, only managers were likely to take work home with them. For others, spillover was experienced through juggling complex patterns of working hours with domestic responsibilities and aspects of occupationally induced ill-health such as fatigue and stress. For the more autonomous software workers, much of the work was conceptual and less bounded by the actual workplace. Many software workers took work home and thought about work-related problems after hours. Although simple adjustments to starting and finishing times would not in themselves provide an adequate framework for work–life balance, there were fewer intangible extensions of work demands on home life where employees perceived the organization to have a supportive family-friendly culture.

Stop! Has any job you have had ever made your non-work life difficult to manage (for example, part-time work alongside your studies as a student)? Can there even be a satisfactory balance between work and non-work life? What would be the conditions for this to occur?

Sources and further information: For the information quoted in this feature, see *Guardian* (2005) and Hyman et al. (2003). To find out more on work–life balance, see Hogarth et al. (2000) and Houston (2005).

Note: This feature was written by Chris Baldry at the University of Stirling.

 Visit the companion website at www.palgrave.com/business/bratton5 for a bonus HRM in practice feature on workplace bullying.

Causes of workplace stress

Workplace stress occurs when some element of work has a negative impact on an employee's physical and mental well-being. Work overload and unrealistic time deadlines will, for example, put an employee under pressure, and stress may result. Workplace sexual harassment is another source of stress. In addition, occupational stress cannot be separated from personal life: illness in the family or divorce puts an employee under pressure and leads to stress. Researchers have explored the antecedents of workplace stress. Research has investigated *work-related* factors, such as role ambiguity and job design, and *individual* factors, such as debt worries and workplace bullying (Hadikin and O'Driscoll, 2000). The evidence supports the argument that work-related stress is a multifaceted workplace phenomenon caused by multiple social factors.

Work-related factors

A variety of work-related factors – non-permanent employment, role ambiguity, frustration, conflict, job design, harassment and violence – can lead to stress.

Non-permanent employment is associated with mental health and stress. As discussed in Chapter 4, research indicates a growth over the last two decades of non-permanent or 'precarious' employment, although estimates vary by country and by indicators used (see, for example, Vosko, 2000, 2007). Researchers have found strong evidence that precarious employment is associated with poorer employee health outcomes. The association between employment insecurity and stress is explained by the employment relationship characteristics of non-permanent employment, such as uncertainty over work scheduling, keeping levels of performance up and constant evaluation by supervisors. Those experiencing persistent precarious employment self-reported poorer health and stress indicators (Lewchuk et al., 2008).

Retail workers who face the 'eternal conflict' over shift patterns reaffirm that it is not only the 'chattering' middle-class who experience work–life problems (Rigby and O'Brien-Smith, 2010, p. 215). Studies have found a paradoxical outcome of flexible working and work intensification that can, particularly for remote working, be a source of work-related stress (Kelliher and Anderson, 2010). Other findings suggest that as various forms of precarious work increase, there is greater risk to women of predatory sexual harassment as the expectation of future employment diminishes (Chamberlain et al., 2008). It is no surprise, therefore, that research analysis suggests that mental and physical problems associated with work disproportionately affect the working class. There is also little evidence of employee mental well-being and stress being considered a matter of proactive management intervention (Doherty and Tyson, 2000).

Role ambiguity exists when the job is poorly defined, when uncertainty surrounds job expectations and when supervisory staff and their subordinates have different expectations of an employee's responsibilities. Individuals experiencing role ambiguity will be uncertain how their performance will be evaluated and will therefore experience stress.

Frustration, a result of a motivation being blocked to prevent an individual achieving a desired goal, has a major effect. A clerical employee trying to finish a major report before the end of the day is likely to become frustrated by repeated computer breakdowns that prevent the goal being reached. Huczynski and Buchanan (2010) draw on Swedish research to illustrate the frustration of information technology:

Office workers who used to wait happily for hours while folders were retrieved
from filing cabinets now complain when their computer terminals do not give them
instant information on request … Stress arose mainly from computer breakdowns and
telephone calls which interrupted their work. The employees never knew how long
these interruptions would last, and had to watch helplessly while their work piled up.
So they worked rapidly in the mornings in case something stopped them later.

Conflicts, both interpersonal and interteam, are another problem. When employees
with different social experiences, personalities, needs and points of view interact with their
co-workers, disagreements may cause stress.

Job design is a further factor. Jobs that have a limited variety of tasks and low discretion may cause stress. Relevant to work and job design is the 'Whitehall' phenomenon, a
body of research investigating the relationship between grade of employment in the civil
service hierarchy and employee health. Existing research shows a positive association
between grade of employment, coronary heart disease and work-related stress (Marmot
et al., 1978). Contrary to stories about executive burnout, several studies report that the
most stressful jobs are those which combine work intensification and low discretion.
Craig (1981, p. 10) identified job design as a stressor for office workers: 'Countless office
staff work in high bureaucracies which have been described as "honeycombs of depression" … Work that "drives you crazy" because it's so boring.' In the same genre, Mann
and Holdsworth (2003, p. 208) found that 'teleworking' – paid work carried out in a
location where the worker has no personal contact with co-workers – generates significant negative emotions and, overall, 'teleworkers experience more mental ill-health than
office-workers'.

Harassment (both racial and sexual) is another workplace stressor. Racial harassment
can range from racist jokes or verbal abuse to racist graffiti in the workplace or physical
attacks on black or other racial minority employees. No matter how subtle it is, racial
harassment is extremely stressful; it can damage the health of ethnic minority group
employees and presents managers with a major challenge.

Organizational context is a critical determinant of sexual harassment (Chamberlain et
al., 2008). It can take two forms. The first is a hostile environment involving behaviour
that is unwelcome and undesirable or offensive. This kind of sexual harassment includes,
for example, unwanted propositions and sexual innuendo. It can be difficult for an HR
manager to convince employees and other managers to take this kind of sexual harassment seriously as it is often viewed as a 'joke', something to do with 'chatting up' attractive female co-workers or bottom-pinching. Evidence of behaviour that is sufficiently
severe or pervasive to cause changes in the conditions of employment can, however, lead
to a legal case.

The second form of sexual harassment is *quid pro quo* harassment, which is essentially a
kind of sex-for-promotion blackmail. The alleged perpetrator is normally a superior, and
the blackmail is either 'give in to my sexual desires and I'll give you promotion' or 'give in or
your job prospects will suffer'. Both forms of sexual harassment relate to power relationships, harassment typically, but not exclusively, aimed at women by men who occupy positions of power. It is, as one writer put it, 'a new, formal title for an age-old predicament, the
boss-man with anything from a lascivious line of chat, to wandering hands, to explicit
demands for sex as a reward for giving you, the women, work' (Raeburn, 1980).

Individual-related factors

Individual factors causing stress are equally varied and complex; they include financial worries, marital problems, pregnancy, problems with children and the death of a spouse. A record number of mortgages, for example, were foreclosed following the 2008 meltdown, doubtless causing considerable individual stress. A major personal factor that can cause stress among working women is the dual-role syndrome – the additional burden of coping with two jobs: the paid job and the unwaged 'job' at home (cooking, housework, shopping and so on; see Figure 14.4). Craig (1981, p. 18) captures the competing pressures on working mothers like this:

> The pressures on working mothers are enormous. Feeling guilty because you're not an ideal stay-at-home mum … get the breakfasts, get the shopping done, go to the launderette, fetch the kids from school, do the ironing, clean the house. A carefully worked out timetable can be upset and life thrown into chaos when your lunch hour is switched or you're required to do overtime without notice.

Research appears to support the dual-role syndrome as an explanation of work-related stress. A Canadian study among bank employees reported that 22 per cent of respondents said their stress was triggered by balancing family and work (Ross and MacDonald, 1997).

Figure 14.4 Stress caused by the 'dual-role' syndrome
Source: Personnel Management Plus (1992) April

Huczynski and Buchanan (2010) draw attention to research demonstrating a relationship between personality and stress. Individual factors include difficulty in coping with change, a lack of confidence and assertiveness in relationships, and poor stress management. 'Type A' personalities – those individuals who are highly competitive, set high standards, place considerable emphasis on meeting deadlines and are workaholics – tend to have a higher propensity to exhibit symptoms of stress (McShane and Steen, 2010). Examples of work design and individual causes of work-related stress are illustrated in Figure 14.5.

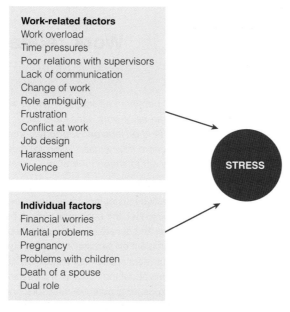

Work-related factors
Work overload
Time pressures
Poor relations with supervisors
Lack of communication
Change of work
Role ambiguity
Frustration
Conflict at work
Job design
Harassment
Violence

STRESS

Individual factors
Financial worries
Marital problems
Pregnancy
Problems with children
Death of a spouse
Dual role

Figure 14.5 *Some causes of work-related stress*

In the HRM canon, work-related stress is underanalysed, the prevailing view being that occupational stress is a personal problem. It is now recognized, however, that work-related stress is a major health problem and that it is a management's responsibility to provide the initiative to eliminate or reduce the causes of work-related stress. At an organizational level, attention to basic work and job design principles can alleviate the conditions that may cause stress. At an individual level, HR professionals have conducted workshops on stress management to help individual employees cope with stress and avoid an overexposure to stress-causing situations. Workshops designed to change lifestyles by promoting healthy eating and fitness, while helping employees to relieve the strains caused by job stress, cannot eliminate the source of the problem. Like other occupational hazards, stress needs to be controlled at source; as discussed above, stress arises from a variety of sources, and it is important for managers to identify priorities and investigate ways of dealing with the problem. Table 14.1 shows some of the specific actions that individual employees, managers and HR practitioners can take to alleviate occupational stress.

Table 14.1 *Action to reduce workplace stress*

Individual strategies	Organizational strategies
Physical exercise	Meeting with employees to discuss the extent of stress
Hobbies	Conduct a survey and inspect the workplace for stress-causing factors
Meditation	Improve job and organizational design
Group discussions	Improve communication
Assertiveness training	Develop a stress policy and monitor its effectiveness
	Train managers to be sensitive to the causes and early symptoms of stress

Work-related stress

The incidence of work-related stress appeared to increase rapidly at the end of the twentieth century, bringing into the spotlight the importance of the health and well-being of employees at work. An extensive research drive followed, attempting to better understand the consequences for individuals (for example, psychological and physical ill-health), for teams (such as conflict between team members) and for organizations (for example, short- and long-term absence). Significant effort was also invested in understanding the work-related causes of stress and the effectiveness of different interventions for preventing, managing and treating it. As a result, plentiful amounts of information and resources are now available for organizations to better manage this aspect of their employees' experience, and the advice given to HR and organizations is fairly consistent. Most advocate a series of linked interventions to manage stress, prioritizing an employee risk assessment of specific work characteristics identified as potentially stressful. Employees are typically asked to rate features of their jobs, such as the amount of control and discretion allowed in their role, usually via questionnaires.

Many of these approaches can genuinely describe themselves as evidence-based, in that they directly link to recent research. Examples are the HSE's Management Standards for Work-related Stress and the toolkits and training courses available specifically for HR practitioners. But, for all this, are these approaches missing something? There are those who think so, as Kevin Daniels, who has researched and written about work-related stress for over a decade describes (2011, p. 33):

The dominant approach to policy and practice in the areas of work stress and well-being has focused on jobs and job redesign, but has evolved to ignore how workers interpret their work and how they act to shape their work.

Recent, and not so recent, research reveals a much more active role for individual employees in shaping how they think, feel and behave at work. It portrays a more complex and dynamic interaction between individuals, for example their personality, coping styles, expectations and motivations, and their work. Individuals make decisions about their choice of jobs and therefore about their exposure to potential stressors; once in the job, they differently interpret its remit, and their coping abilities can influence how they respond to potentially stressful situations. These differences of interpretation can be the result of their personality, abilities and previous experience, and also of the group, organization or national culture they work in.

This brings into question approaches to work-related stress that assume relatively universal relationships between stable, 'bad' work characteristics and related emotional and physical distress, as seen in popular measurements of stress at work. More flexible and employee-centred methods might therefore be needed to generate meaningful insight into employees' experience at work.

Stop! What do you think of the idea of standardized measures of stress at work? What are the advantages of this approach, but what might its limitations be, in light of the discussion above? How might greater sensitivity to the more dynamic interaction between individual, job and organization be achieved?

Sources and further information: For more on Kevin Daniels' research, see Daniels (2006, 2011). For background information, see also Cox et al. (2000), Hagger (2009), Longua et al. (2009) and Rick and Briner (2000).

Note: This feature was written by Chiara Amati at Edinburgh Napier University.

©istockphoto.com/diego cervo

In recent times there has been an increased focus on understanding the causes of work-related stress and its effect on employees.

Workplace violence

For many employees at the front end of service delivery, violence is a critical safety issue. According to the British Crime Statistics, there were during 2009–10 an estimated 677,000 incidents of violence at work, comprising 310,000 assaults and 366,000 threats (Packham, 2011). The HSE describes workplace violence as 'Any incident in which a person is abused, threatened, or assaulted in circumstances relating to their work' (HSE, 2011b). Surveys have found that between 40 and 90 per cent of women suffer some forms of violence and harassment during the course of the working lives. There are three major types of workplace violence:

- *Type 1* – the perpetrator of the violence has no legitimate relationship with the targeted employee and enters the workplace to commit a criminal act (for example, robbery). Retail and service industry employees and taxi drivers are those most exposed to this type of workplace violence.
- *Type 2* – the perpetrator is an employee or former employee of the organization, typically a 'disgruntled employee' who commits a violent act against a co-worker or supervisor for what is perceived to be unfair treatment.
- *Type 3* – the perpetrator is a recipient of a service provided by the targeted employee. Bus drivers, social workers, healthcare providers and teachers are particularly vulnerable to this type of workplace violence.

Montgomery and Kelloway (2002) identify three groups of employee at particular risk of experiencing workplace violence: those who interact with the public; those making decisions that influence other people's lives; and those denying the public a request or a service. Given the growth of the call-centre model for customer service, chronic exposure to 'phone rage' is also a growing problem in some workplaces. Capita UK estimates that the top three triggers of phone rage are:

- The phone not being answered in reasonable time
- The customer feeling processed, or a victim of a faceless corporation
- Standard greetings and pleasantries that do not sound sincere.

Research shows that much of workplace violence goes unrecorded. However, the consequences of workplace violence go beyond immediate physical injury or death. The trauma caused by the violence has negative results for both the individual employee's well-being (that is, in terms of impaired mental and physical health) and the organization (that is, decreased commitment, retention and performance; Montgomery and Kelloway, 2002).

HRM web links The NHS Health Scotland has published the guide *Managing Occupational Violence and Aggression in the Workplace*. Go to the website www.healthscotland.com/uploads/ documents/12251-OccupationalViolenceAndAggressionInTheWorkplace.pdf and/or www.violence-against-women.org for more material on violence in the workplace.

Workplace bullying

Recent research into workplace bullying supports the notion that it is an elusive, complex social phenomenon and, as such, is a significant issue for employee well-being, dignity *at* work (Bolton, 2007), violation of the psychological contract (Parzefall and Salin, 2010) and organizational performance (Branch et al., 2009). The term 'workplace bullying' is often used as an umbrella term to incorporate multiple negative behaviours including, but not limited to, abusive verbal comments, threats, ridicule, unjustified criticism and the spreading of malicious rumours in the workplace. Although it is a form of aggression, some bullying behaviour can be observable, but other instances can be subtle and difficult to observe. The concept has not yet been explored at length in the HRM literature (Parzefall and Salin, 2010).

A definition of workplace bullying needs to incorporate several characteristics. First, workplace bullying is about a personalized attack on one employee by another employee, persistently over a period of time, using behaviours that are emotionally and psychologically punishing. Second, workplace bullying introduces a dynamic into the employment relationship that involves a purposed attempt by one employee to injure another employee's self-esteem, self-confidence and/or reputation, or to undermine their competence to carry out their work duties effectively (Oade, 2009). Third, definitions of workplace bullying emphasize the existence of an imbalance of power between the bully and the recipient (Keashly and Jagatic, 2003). Research has identified a link between economic conditions and bullying, with studies predicting that the threat of job loss is likely to cause an increase in workplace bullying, as is the decline of trade unions and of collective representation (Hirch, 2010).

Although there is little OHS legislation that specifically deals with workplace bullying, in those jurisdictions that have legislation on workplace violence, bullying is often included (Canadian Centre for Occupational Health and Safety, 2001). It may also be addressed in unionized workplaces through collective agreement clauses dealing with harassment. Many organizations choose to address the issue of workplace bullying because it has a detrimental effect on individual and organizational performance. Targeted employees may experience a range of negative effects, including feelings of frustration and/or helplessness, loss of confidence, insomnia and stress-related symptoms. Workplace bullying can affect organizational performance through increased absenteeism, increased turnover, decreased productivity and work motivation. The negative consequences of workplace bullying extend beyond the perpetrator–victim relationship, possibly into 'injustice and psychological contract breach perceptions' (Parzefall and Salin, 2010, p. 774), thereby supporting the notion of a connection between victims' and witnesses' attitudinal change and effective management of the issue.

A workplace policy for bullying should protect the rights and dignity of the targeted individual. The most important component of any workplace prevention programme is commitment on the part of senior management. As noted, the causes of workplace bullying are complex and, as such, a 'one-hat-fits-all' approach is unlikely to address effectively the multiple aspects of the phenomenon. Any effective policy needs to incorporate 'prevention, resolution, and support' (McCarthy et al., 2002, p. 528). The Canadian Centre for Occupational Health and Safety (2001) recommends that a preventive policy on workplace bullying must:

- Be developed by management and employee representatives
- Define workplace bullying in precise, concrete language
- Provide clear examples of inappropriate or unreasonable behaviour
- Precisely state the consequences of making threats or committing acts
- Outline the process by which preventive measures will be developed
- Encourage the reporting of all incidents of workplace bullying
- Make a commitment to provide support services to victims.

Workplace bullying is a significant issue for employee well-being and for achieving dignity *at* work. In conclusion, Aryanne Oade writes, 'Being subject to workplace bullying is among the most horrible workplace experiences you might have' (2009, p. 159). Although it is under-analysed, research shows that workplace bullying can have a detrimental effect upon individual and organizational performance and, consequently, necessitates a response from management and employee representatives, including an effective preventative policy and processes. HR practices designed at helping employee victims of bullying, violence or harassment might include counselling, discipline and assignment to other supervisors (Biron, 2010).

HRM web links Go to the website www.ccohs.ca/oshanswers/psychosocial/bullying.html for a guide to developing a policy on workplace bullying.

Visit the companion website at www.palgrave.com/business/bratton5 for a bonus HRM in practice feature on workplace bullying.

Alcohol abuse

Recent UK research on 'binge-drinking' shows that this social phenomenon has significantly increased in Britain over the last two decades, particularly among women, and is estimated to cost the country £20 billion a year. There is no international agreed definition of binge-drinking, but the Institute of Alcohol Studies (IAS) defines it as the consumption of more than the recommended number of alcoholic drinks in a single drinking session. In 2010, 1 in 4 adults in Britain were reported to be binge-drinkers, and the UK was ranked number one in Europe for alcohol consumption. Data show a narrowing of an alcohol gender gap that has persisted for decades (IAS, 2010). The reported proportion of women binge-drinking increased from 8 per cent to 15 per cent between 1998 and 2006. Over the same period, binge-drinking among men increased only slightly, from 22 to 23 per cent.

According to the IAS, binge-drinking is now so routine that young adults find it difficult to explain why they do it. In a 'culture of intoxication', it is unsurprising that alcohol misuse in the UK accounts for more than 20,000 premature deaths per year. There were 8724 alcohol related deaths in 2007, more than double the 4144 recorded in 1991; in addition, the alcohol-related death rate is on the increase, with 13.4 deaths per 100,000 population in 2006, representing a doubling since 1991 (*Patient*, 2011).

In the context of the workplace, the excessive consumption of alcohol is both a health problem and a job performance problem in every occupational category, be it manual, white collar or managerial. In alcohol abuse, behavioural problems range from tardiness in the early stages to prolonged absenteeism in later ones. The direct and indirect costs of

©istockphoto.com/Paul Velgos

The excessive consumption of alcohol is both a health problem and a job performance problem in every occupational category.

alcohol abuse to employers include the costs of accidents, lower productivity, poor-quality work, bad decisions, absenteeism and managers' lost time in dealing with employees with an alcohol problem.

Employers have been advised to have a written statement of policy regarding alcohol abuse, which can be discussed and agreed with employees and, where applicable, union representatives. The policy should recognize that alcohol abuse is an illness, and it should be supportive rather than punitive or employees will hide their drink problem for as long as possible. The HSE advocates that a policy should encourage any employee who believes that she or he has a drink problem to seek help voluntarily, and should, subject to certain provisions, give the same protection of employment and pension rights as those granted to an employee with problems that are related to other forms of ill-health. Research in Scotland estimated that 20 per cent of employers had a policy to deal with problem drinkers. In addition to preparing a policy, management can devise a procedure for dealing with alcohol abuse; to encourage employees to seek advice, it is suggested that this procedure should be separate from the disciplinary procedure. Finally, the HRM department is advised to establish links with an external voluntary organization to obtain help and develop an employee assistance programme (EAP).

HRM web links   WWW   Go to the website www.drinkaware.co.uk/facts/binge-drinking for factsheets on alcohol consumption and binge-drinking.

Smoking

The tragic death of non-smoker Dana Reeve, the 44-year-old widow of Superman actor Christopher Reeve, in March 2006, highlighted the dangers of both active and passive smoking. It was estimated that, in 2006/07, half of long-term smokers would die prematurely as a result of smoking, half of these in middle age. Passive or 'second-hand' smoking (inhaling other people's smoke) is estimated to kill more than 11,000 people in the UK every year, 600 of whom die from exposure to second-hand smoke in the workplace. It is estimated that, between 1950 and 2000, 6 million Britons and 60 million people worldwide died from tobacco-related diseases (Action on Smoking and Health, 2008).

In many countries, smoking in the workplace is a major problem because active smoking may be a fire hazard or hygiene risk. In addition, the estimated cost attributable to absenteeism and lost productivity associated with active smoking is said to be approximately US$825 per employee per year (Montgomery and Kelloway, 2002). Figure 14.6 shows employers' costs associated with workplace smoking (money that 'goes up in smoke'). Passive smoking in the workplace is also a problem because non-smokers work or live next to or among smokers (in office environments and also in pubs, clubs, aeroplanes, trains and so on) for their full working week, inhaling their smoke and carbon monoxide in large quantities.

A decade ago, the first second-hand smoke case against the USA tobacco industry, filed on behalf of thousands of US-based flight attendants in 1991, resulted in a settlement of US$300 million. Smoking is unlawful in the workplace in the USA, Canada and some EU member states, and the only place where a smoker can jeopardize the health of a non-smoker is at home. In the past, managers in Britain agreed that successful non-smoking policies required consultation with employees and, in a unionized workplace, a joint approach by management and the trade union.

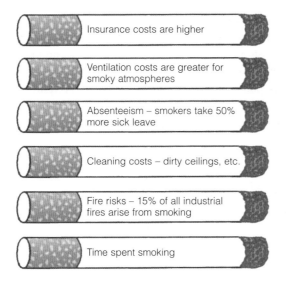

Figure 14.6 *Smoking-related costs*

HRM web
links   WWW   Go to the website www.ash.org.uk for factsheets on smoking statistics: illness and
death. Fact Sheet No. 2 lists both non-lethal illnesses and deaths caused by smoking.

Acquired immune deficiency syndrome

Three decades ago, AIDS became a workplace health and safety issue. It is the most serious disease caused by HIV (the human immunodeficiency virus, or the 'AIDS virus'). HIV impairs the body's defence or immune system and leaves it vulnerable to life-threatening illnesses. One manager with experience of managing the HIV/AIDS problem captured the complexity surrounding the issue: 'I was not trained to manage fear, discrimination, and dying in the workplace' (Smith, 1993). A modern textbook on HRM in the twenty-first century would be incomplete if it contained no reference to HIV/AIDS. In 2002, over 14 million people were estimated to be infected with AIDS in the three continents of Africa, Europe and the Americas.

Human rights legislation impacts on HR policies and practices. In Canada, for example, mandatory testing for HIV/AIDS is regarded as a serious intrusion on individual rights, and employers are prohibited from subjecting job applicants to any type of medical testing for the presence of the HIV/AIDS virus. Furthermore, the employer is obligated to accommodate the needs of an employee with a disability such as HIV/AIDS by, for example, redefining work assignments. The fear of catching HIV can, however, create problems for HR managers. Employees might refuse to work with a person with HIV/AIDS; as one North American HR manager explained in *Business Week* in 1993, 'No matter how sophisticated or educated you are, HIV/AIDS can trigger irrational things in people ... There's a big potential for disruption. It could close a plant down'. A North American chain store manager, one of whose employees developed HIV/AIDS and died, had to call in the Red Cross to explain to distraught employees that HIV/AIDS could not be transmitted through normal contact in the workplace. Six months later, some employees were still refusing to use the drinking fountain or the toilet.

A workplace policy for HIV/AIDS should protect the human rights and dignity of those infected with HIV and those who have AIDS, and should not allow discriminatory action in the provision of services and employment. HIV/AIDS policies and procedures need to be developed through a team approach that includes workers and, if present, trade unions. As with any HRM policy, any policy or programme for HIV/AIDS requires a clear endorsement from top management down if it is going to be successful. The Global Business Coalition (2011) recommends that HIV/AIDS workplace policy should:

- Make an explicit promise for corporate action.
- Commit to confidentiality and non-discrimination for all employees.
- Ensure consistency with appropriate national laws.
- Encourage all employees (regardless of HIV status) to support an inclusive and non-stigmatizing workplace.
- Provide guidance to supervisors and managers.
- Explain to employees living with HIV/AIDS the type of support and care they will receive, so they are more likely to come forward for counselling and testing.
- Help stop the spread of the virus through prevention programmes.
- Make the policy available to all employees, in a format that is easily understood.
- Manage the impact of HIV/AIDS with the ultimate aim of cutting business costs.

HRM web links   Go to www.gbchealth.org for details on HIV/AIDS workplace policies.

It was reported that few North American companies surveyed had a workplace policy for HIV/AIDS and, unsurprisingly, smaller organizations were less likely to have such a policy (Green, 1998). More worrying perhaps is the finding that there is, among employers, a 'declining interest' in HIV/AIDS education in the workplace. In 1997, 18 per cent of US companies surveyed provided HIV/AIDS education for their employees, compared with 28 per cent in 1992 (Green, 1998). Companies that have encountered the problem of managing HIV/AIDS in the workplace have found that it is better to expect a problem and be proactive in educating employees on the issues raised by HIV/AIDS. The chairman of Levi Strauss, Robert Hass, confirms the need for senior management support: '[HIV/AIDS] is frequently viewed as something that the personnel department should take care of, but there has to be support from the top. You can't do it with one flyer' (Smith, 1993). As attitudes and legal considerations change, HIV/AIDS has important implications for HRM policy, programmes and practices.

HRM web links   Visit the following websites for information on AIDS and HRM: UK (www.tht.org.uk), Canada (www.cdnaids.ca), South Africa (www.aidslinkinternational.org) and Australia (www.acsa.org.au).

Workplace wellness

Workplace wellness models typically focus on individual behaviour and the programmes and activities promoting individual behavioural change. Smoking, binge-drinking patterns, poor diet and lack of physical exercise have all been identified as lifestyle problems impacting on the health of the workforce. Here, consistent with the literature, workplace wellness will refer to any voluntary health-improving programme and activity instigated by the employer to effect changes in non-occupational health behaviours. Smoking cessation, personal fitness programmes and EAPs are early examples of workplace health-improvement initiatives. A wide variety of initiatives that fall under the wellness promotion strategy have been instigated in establishments with 500 or more employees, including part or all the following:

- A smoke-free workplace
- Employer-sponsored sports
- Discounted gym facilities
- Health examinations offered to employees
- 'Health fairs' hosted on the premises
- Wellness newsletters
- Smoking cessation incentives
- Weight loss incentives
- Blood pressure and cholesterol testin
- Energy-based therapy seminars
- EAPs.

An EAP provides confidential professional assistance to employees and their families to help resolve problems affecting their personal lives and, in some cases, their job performance. Typically, an EAP provides services such as alcohol and drug abuse, legal, financial, marriage and crisis counselling. These various workplace wellness initiatives tend to operate independently and focus on individual employee goals. Few organizations integrate wellness programmes and initiatives into an overall HR strategy with concrete measures and expected targets (Dyck, 2002). See Chapter 3 for evaluating HR programmes.

reflective question Haunschild (2003) posits that characterizing wellness management merely as a 'healthy' philanthropic act is naive and neglects intended control strategies. Can you think how wellness programmes can act against the interests of the employee?

HRM web links Go to the websites http://wellnessproposals.com/wellness-articles/workplace-wellness-programs-2/, www.healthworks.ca and www.healthworkandwellness.com for more information on workplace wellness. For more information on health and safety representation in Britain over the past two decades, go to the 2004 Workplace Employee Relations Survey website: www.wers2004.info/.

Workplace and community health

Typically, the mainstream analysis of occupational health, safety and wellness management is concerned with the design and maintenance of a work environment that supports the organization's objectives, creates a safe and healthy workplace and promotes the well-being of employees. Less obvious perhaps, but no less substantial, is the connection between sustainable work systems, healthy workplaces, and healthy communities and ecosystems. The adverse effects on the ecosystem of unregulated industrial production were documented in Friedrick Engels' *The Conditions of the Working Class in England* (1845) and

HRM **and** globalization

Food and eating at work: a matter of taste, politics or basic human rights?

Food is fundamental to who we are as human beings. It sustains us biologically, but it is also rich in cultural meaning. Until recently, however, food and eating have received little attention from HR professionals. The success of TV programmes such as Jamie Oliver's *Food Revolution* suggests, however, that this may be about to change. For Oliver, control over food preparation is an empowering process that enables ordinary people to lead healthier lives, even in times of economic hardship.

Others, like journalist and author Michael Pollan, have drawn attention to the emergence of a 'food movement', a loose coalition of groups intent on raising public awareness of the dangers associated with the food industry. In a recent discussion of the food movement, Pollan (2010) writes:

> perhaps the food movement's strongest claim on public attention today is the fact that the American diet of highly processed food laced with added fats and sugars is responsible for the epidemic of chronic diseases that threatens to bankrupt the health care system.

Struggles for change in the food system have met with surprising resistance. The food industry wields considerable economic and political power, and its ties with large work organizations are complex. For a variety of reasons, senior managers may not wish to alter existing agreements with large vendors who provide services to work organizations. Cost is the obvious rationale: companies award contracts to the lowest bidder. Yet short-term savings may divert attention from the long-term negative consequences of their choices.

Stop! How might the challenge of food at work unfold in national settings where local markets have not been penetrated by the fast-food industry and various food service monopolies?

This is a useful exercise in thinking about the challenges of cross-cultural management. First consider one of Jamie Oliver's most important reform initiatives – food services in the state school systems of Great Britain and the USA. This reform has parallels in developing countries where advocates for change see the improvement of school-based food services as a vehicle for social progress.

But what about the private sector? There is very little research on the food and eating policies of private work organizations in developing countries, but it is reasonable to believe that the challenges facing HR professionals may be somewhat different from those faced in developed countries. First, this is because food and eating require time and space, and these do not contribute directly to the production of goods or services. Second, in developed countries, we take for granted that employers will allocate this time and space, but in developing countries struggles to improve the quality of food and eating options at work may be less about resisting the fast-food industry and more about establishing basic standards.

Sources and further information: See Pollan (2010) for more information.

Conduct a web search on the phrase 'food revolution' to find out about the range of Jamie Oliver's contributions to this topic.

Note: This feature was written by David MacLennan at Thompson Rivers University.

While attention has been focused on developing healthy eating in schools, very little research has been carried out on the food and eating policies of private work organizations.

©istockphoto.com/webphotographeer

were the backcloth to Charles Dickens' industrial novel *Hard Times* (1854). Although unsafe and unhealthy workplaces shaped the living conditions of the British urban working class, industrial plants in the new Communist Russia were also a cauldron of appalling pollution, as captured here by Canadian writer, Geoffrey York (2001, p. A1):

> Long before you reach the Russian city, Norilsk announces itself with mounds of dirty blackened snow on the fragile grass of the summer tundra. Then comes the hellish vision of the world's most polluted Arctic metropolis. Looming at the end of the road is a horizon of massive smokestacks ... and thousands of denuded trees as lifeless as blackened matchsticks. Inside malodorous smelters, Russian workers wear respirators as they trudge through the hot suffocating air, heavy with clouds of dust and gases. ... Pollutants from this factory have drifted as far as the Canadian Arctic. Traces of heavy metals have been found in the breast milk of Inuit mothers.

That sustainable work systems, healthy communities and ecosystems are inextricably linked is no better illustrated, perhaps, than by the explosions at the Fukushima nuclear plant in north-eastern Japan in March 2011, which followed a devastating earthquake and tsunami. The Fukushima explosion and fears of a 'meltdown' rank in gravity alongside two previous nuclear accidents in the modern era: Three Mile Island in the USA in 1979, and Chernobyl in the Ukraine in 1986.

Japan's nuclear disaster occurred while writing this new edition of the book and it is too early to judge the full ramifications for the debate on sustainable work systems and environmental regulation. Most obviously, there may develop a 'new and dynamic workplace environmentalism' that is committed to developing the connections between workplace stressors, chemicals, toxins and so on, and the pollution of local and global ecosystems, cancers and ill-health in society at large (Storey, 2004, pp. 443–4). The jobs versus ecosystem dichotomy has often defined the relationship between the OHS/trade union and the environmental movements. But it seems evident that both the goals of a low-carbon sustainable economy and learning from environmental disasters such as the nuclear catastrophe in Japan call for a conceptual rethinking of sustainability and environmental management. From the perspective of management, any alliance between the trade union and environmental movements – a red and green coalition – is both the challenge and the opportunity that face the next generation of HRM managers.

reflective question   Can you think how the 2011 Fukushima explosion will impact on the environmental debate and on 'greening' the workplace?

Paradox in workplace health and wellness

The notion of paradox and ethics that we have discussed in other areas of HRM is also apparent in OHS and wellness. Citing global competition and the need for level playing fields, most employers since the Industrial Revolution have opposed environmental and OHS regulation. The complaints of the corporate elite about the Kyoto Accord are a notable recent example of employer resistance. Arguably, HRM (at least the rhetoric) has raised the ethical stakes over OHS. Yet, despite this claim, the driving force for the majority of employers to provide a safe and healthy working environment has all too often been framed through a 'business case' lens, for example the reduction in sick leave and time lost from accidents. This is especially true for mental well-being, as evidenced by the *Walker* v. *Northumberland* [1994] case (Doherty and Tyson, 2000, p. 103).

At the same time, the trade union movement is far from unified in its interpretation of sustainable and healthy work systems (Storey, 2004). Relations between trade union and environmental movements exist within a complex web of class differences and perceived conflicting interests that often perpetuate the stereotype of 'jobs versus the environment' (Mayer, 2009). Government regulations to reduce carbon emissions, which can act as a limit to economic growth, are therefore perceived as a direct threat to jobs, driving trade unions to align with employers in opposition to governmental environment protection and low-carbon initiatives. The perceived loss of jobs in polluting industries and the low level of eco-literacy among trade union activists can therefore generate tensions related to attempts to develop new sustainable work systems and build union–green coalitions to lobby for healthy workplaces and communities (Mayer, 2009).

Figure 4.7 shows that paradox stems from the multiple consequences of a single management action that seem to conflict with those of another. The abstraction presented in Figure 4.7 can be illuminated using a concrete health and wellness case. Portable computers, cell phones and email have enabled us all to be connected to the Internet and the organization 24 hours a day, 7 days a week. These high-tech instruments have, however, produced adverse results, causing some observers to describe them as 'electronic versions of a ball and chain, keeping us in work mode around the clock' (Drohan, 2000, p. B15). The intended consequence of these high-tech instruments is improved productivity, but the unanticipated consequence of high-tech communications has yielded a major problem of stress and burnout caused by the inability of individuals to maintain a boundary between work and home. This unintended consequence of the high-tech revolution can counteract the positive consequences.

OHS and wellness form an important part of the HRM context, but it is not simply a technical issue of, for example, supplying hard hats and goggles. Above all, OHS underscores the fact that employment relations involve an economic and power relationship. In terms of economics, 'pure market' ideology panders to the shareholder and 'profitability over safety' is favoured (Glasbeek, 1991, p. 196). With regard to power, it is argued (Sass, 1982, p. 52; quoted in Giles and Iain, 1989) that:

> In all technical questions pertaining to workplace health and safety there is the social element. That is … the power relations in production: who tells whom to do what and how fast.

Wellness management also contains a social element. It is arguably about organizations attempting to appropriate the employee's whole body as a matter of surveillance and control (Haunschild, 2003). Using Foucault's power analysis, wellness management represents a process of discipline since activities such as medical screening, fitness programmes and lifestyle counselling are connected to selection, promotion and production processes (Haunschild, 2003; Townley, 1994). It is interesting to note that interest in wellness management increased rapidly in the USA at a time when the regulatory power of the official health and safety agency, the Occupational Safety and Health Administration, had allegedly been curtailed under the Clinton and Bush junior administrations (Cullen, 2002).

Studies undertaken in UK call centres illustrate how economic imperatives impose on health and wellness management. Taylor et al. (2003, p. 452), for example, conclude that highly competitive market conditions compel managers to design workplace norms in which work intensification is 'a habitual and inescapable necessity'. Although the heterogeneity of small firms makes generalization suspect, others have noted that the level of work-induced injuries and ill-health is proportionally worse in small European firms (Walters, 2004). Whereas large establishments are more likely to be regulated and inspected and have worker representatives, small establishments, especially small companies, are less likely to be unionized, and the employment relationship and the design of work are such that health and safety are, 'at best, easily overlooked and at worst deliberately avoided' (Walters, 2004, p. 171).

Most obviously, the economic cost of OHS and wellness is a double-edged sword for the organization. On the one hand, OHS measures that protect employee well-being from physical or chemical hazards can conflict with management's objective of containing production costs. On the other, as we have explained, effective health and wellness interventions can improve the performance of employees and the organization by reducing the cost associated with accidents, disabilities, absenteeism and illness.

To manage the employment relationship effectively, it also needs to be recognized that the employer's perspective on OHS and wellness issues can affect an individual's beliefs, levels of trust and psychological contract (Guest, 2008). Talk of a reciprocal commitment and a psychological contract has a hollow ring for many manual workers: more pressing may be malodorous processes and dangerous work systems. Critical, too, is the ability of global companies to relocate to other parts of the world to avoid stringent health and safety laws and regulations. Creating a level playing field in terms of health and safety legislation within major economic trading blocs may partly ameliorate this problem. Since the passing of the Single European Act in 1987, for example, a company's health and safety policies have been influenced by EU directives and the Social Charter.

Growing public awareness and concern about 'green' and environmental issues have had an effect on OHS and wellness programmes. Organizations have had to become more sensitive to workers' health and general environmental concerns. Manufacturing 'environmentally friendly' products and services, and using ecologically sustainable processes, presents a continuing challenge to all managers in the early twenty-first century. Running parallel with these social developments is the growing demand from powerful business lobbies to 'deregulate' business operations, including dismantling health and safety legislation (Bain, 1997). Deregulation and the growth of outsourcing (Mayhew and Quinlan, 1997) may operate to reduce protection of the organization's 'human assets'. If organizations adopt an HRM model that is 'union-free', it might, given the research evidence (see, for example, James and Walters, 2002; Reilly et al., 1995; Walters, 2004), expose employees to greater work-induced hazards, thereby offering a further paradox in the HRM paradigm. The prioritization of employer, union and government goals may also change following the catastrophic events in Japan in 2011.

The issues of OHS, wellness, risk and the environment are receiving more attention at all levels of organizations. An appreciation of OHS provides a better understanding of managing the employment relationship. The discussion on paradox goes back to basics in reminding us of some of the complexities – economic, legal, social and psychological – and tensions inherent in the employment relationship. The key point is that OHS and wellness policies and practices must, as with other aspects of the HR strategy, be properly integrated in the sense that they are both complementary to and compatible with business strategy.

The City of Kamloops

Setting

In Canada, cities typically provide a range of municipal services, including the police, fire protection, road management, public transit, utility services, land use planning and development, taxation and local economic development (Governance Network, 2002). Local governments provide more jobs than any other level of government in Canada, employing 350,717 people in 1999. In that year, local governments in British Columbia employed approximately 10 per cent of that total (Governance Network, 2002).

In its 2002 study on the Canadian municipal sector and HR entitled *At the Crossroads of Change*, the Federation of Canadian Municipalities (Governance Network, 2002) identified a number of the challenges facing local governments. These included remaining competitive in terms of attracting people and investment in a global economy, considering citizens' demands for approaches to economic development that were environmentally sustainable, and responding to increasingly sophisticated tax-payer expectations relating to accountability and performance. In addition, the transfer of service responsibility from other levels of government and fiscal realities put immense pressure on local governments to review their corporate management. The consideration of innovative and alternative service delivery also created a requirement for organizational change and staff development to meet the needs of local governments in this new environment (Governance Network, 2002).

Kamloops is one of the largest cities in the central interior of British Columbia, Canada, with a city population base of 80,000. The local government, or what is known as the City of Kamloops, has over 500 full-time equivalent employees. Approximately 60 per cent of the staff are represented by the Canadian Union of Public Employees, the rest being divided between firefighters represented by the International Association of Fire Fighters, and management, who are non-unionized. In the previous 2 years, the organization had experienced a major change in its senior management staffing, with a new City Mayor, new Chief Administrative Officer and new Human Resources Director taking over the helm from long-standing incumbents. With its new

Kamloops, BC, Canada.

leadership, the City of Kamloops embarked on a quality improvement initiative labelled Quest for Quality, with the goal of becoming an employer of choice in Canada and improving its capability of facing both external and internal challenges. One of the main objectives of Quest for Quality was to provide employees with the most enjoyable and fulfilling working environment possible and help them to balance this with their home and personal lives.

Shortly after these changes, a disability management programme was also introduced. The programme provided managers with consistent attendance data through bi-weekly payroll reports, showing details on when staff were absent and the status of their leave banks. In addition, training on attendance management and a coaching process were offered to managers to help them deal with staff who had consistently high absenteeism rates. Canadian Union of Public Employees outside workers, such as labourers and equipment operators, historically had higher rates of absenteeism compared with the other employee groups at the City of Kamloops, and emphasis was made, particularly by the Occupational Health and Safety Division, on decreasing the number of days on which these employees missed work.

As a proactive measure within the disability management programme and in line with the Quest for Quality undertaking, the City also implemented a wellness initiative. The human resources department approached wellness as one piece of a healthy workplace approach, which also included developing a safer physical environment and a positive organizational culture. The wellness initiative itself focused on increasing and recognizing staff involvement in both mental and physical health activities, and supporting healthy lifestyles, behaviours and coping skills for employees. As a result, the organization provided two company gyms at the worksite, as well as educational workshops on such topics as nicotine cessation, diabetes and osteoporosis. An EAP providing short-term counselling and health testing for blood sugar level, cholesterol level and bone density were also offered to staff on a regular basis. A walking programme, which supplied staff with pedometers and incentives for individual participation, was used to encourage employees' involvement in physical activity.

The problem

At the monthly meeting of the human resources department, the wellness initiative was item 3 on the agenda. When the issue was reached, the HR Coordinator, Lori Brown, explained how it was expected that, over time, the wellness initiative would contribute to general staff morale. George Brotherton, who had been sceptical about the wellness efforts, said, 'I'm not sure whether the City can continue with this initiative; there are more pressing matters that we must address.' Lori responded that the employees had continually expressed a high level of satisfaction with the wellness events and offerings, and senior management was pleased with the positive feedback they had received about the initiative. The Human Resources Director, who was chairing the meeting, asked Lori whether she could prepare a report for the next meeting to justify the portion of the human resources department's budget that was being spent on the wellness initiative.

Assignment

Working either alone or in a small group, prepare a report drawing on the material from this case study and addressing the following:

1 What challenges does the human resources department face in identifying the contribution that the wellness initiative has provided towards the City's goals?
2 What benefits could the organization see as a result of this wellness initiative?
3 What recommendations would you make with regard to a process for evaluation?

Essential reading

Health Canada (1998) *Influencing Employee Health. Workplace Health System*. Ottawa: Canadian Fitness and Lifestyle Research Institute.
Governance Network (2002) *At the Crossroads of Change: Human Resources and the Municipal Sector*. Ottawa: Federation of Canadian Municipalities.
Go to the City of Kamloops website at www.kamloops.ca.
Visit the Canadian Healthy Workplace Week website at www.healthyworkplacemonth.ca.
To find out about how to implement a healthy workplace go to http://wellnessproposals.com/wellness-articles/workplace-wellness-programs-2/.

Note: This case study was written by Lori Rilkoff, HR Manager at City of Kamloops, BC, Canada.

Visit the companion website at www.palgrave.com/business/bratton5 for guidelines on writing reports.

summary

◀ Employee OHS and wellness should be an important aspect of managing the employment relationship. The issues of low-carbon workplaces and Japan's nuclear disaster provide the context for practitioners to pay more attention than ever before to, and academics to place more research focus on, health and safety in the workplace. This chapter established the importance of workplace health and wellness from an economic, legal, psychological and moral perspective.

◀ As in other aspects of the employment relationship, government legislation and health and safety regulations influence the management of OHS. The HASAWA 1974, for example, requires employers to ensure the health, safety and wellness at work of all employees. Furthermore, in Britain, the HSC has overall responsibility for OHS. EU directives and the Social Charter are an important source of health and safety regulations and counter the 'pure market' ideology.

◀ In this chapter, we have examined some contemporary health issues, such as SBS, workplace stress, alcoholism, smoking, workplace violence, bullying and HIV/AIDS, as well as key elements of a workplace wellness programme.

◀ Trade unions have attempted to secure improvements in OHS through collective bargaining and have pressed for some stringent health and safety legislation. The recent focus on sustainability and 'greening' of the workplace provides a plausible case for a strategic alliance between trade unions and the environmental movement.

◀ Critical analysis of OHS and wellness management draws attention to the fact that employment relations involve an economic and power relationship. Shareholder interests and return on investment may come before workers' health and safety. Wellness management is arguably a distraction because it manages the consequences rather than causes of ill-health.

vocab checklist for ESL students

◀ apathy (n), apathetic (adj)
◀ harass (v), harassment (n)
◀ incentive (n)
◀ legislate (v), legislation (n)
◀ liability (n), liable (adj)
◀ migrant worker (n)
◀ occupational health (n)

◀ paradox (n), paradoxical (adj)
◀ prosecute (v), prosecutor (n), prosecution (n), prosecuted (adj)
◀ regulate (v), regulation (n)
◀ sustain (v), sustainable (adj)
◀ wellness (n), well (adj)

Visit www.palgrave.com/business/bratton5 for a link to free definitions of these terms in the Macmillan Dictionary, as well as additional learning resources for ESL students.

review questions

1 Explain the careless worker model. 'Spending money on a health and wellness programmes is a luxury most small organizations cannot afford.' Build an argument to support this statement, and an argument to negate it.

2 Explain the role of an HRM specialist in providing a safe and healthy environment for employees.

3 Explain the symptoms and causes of job stress and what an organization can do to alleviate them.

4 Explain how an HR professional can justify a workplace wellness programme.

5 'Stress on women both inside and outside the work organization is a huge challenge.' Discuss.

6 What role can the HSE, the trade unions and the environmental movement play in the development of a sustainable and healthy workplace and community?

further reading to improve your mark

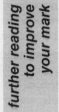

Reading these articles and chapters can help you gain a better understanding and potentially a higher grade for your HRM assignment.

◀ Bain, P. (1997) Human resource malpractice: the deregulation of health and safety at work in the USA and Britain. *Industrial Relations Journal*, **28**(3): 176–91.

◀ Chamberlain, L. J., Crowley, M., Tope, D. and Hodson, R. (2008) Sexual harassment in organizational context. *Work and Occupations*, **35**(3): 262–95.

◀ Parzefall, M. R. and Salin, D. (2010) Perceptions of and reactions to workplace bullying: a social exchange perspective. *Human Relations*, **63**(6): 761–80.

◀ Oade, A. (2009) *Managing Workplace Bullying*. Basingstoke: Palgrave Macmillan.

◀ Loudoun, R. and Johnstone, R. (2009) Occupational health and safety in the modern world of work. In A. Wilkinson, N. Bacon, T. Redman, and S. Snell (eds) *The Sage Handbook of Human Resource Management* (pp. 286–307). London: Sage.

◀ Storey, R. (2004) From the environment to the workplace … and back again? Occupational health and safety activism in Ontario, 1970s–2000+. *Canadian Review of Sociology and Anthropology*, **41**(4): 419–47.

◀ Mayer, B. (2009) *Blue-Green Coalitions: Fighting for Safe Workplaces and Healthy Communities.* Ithaca, NY: Cornell University Press.

◀ Walters, D. (2004) Worker representation and health and safety in small enterprises in Europe. *Industrial Relations Journal*, **35**(2): 169–86.

WWW Visit www.palgrave.com/business/bratton5 for lots of extra resources to help you get to grips with this chapter, including study tips, HRM skills development guides, summary lecture notes, and more.

part VI

the global context of human resource management

499

part VI

the global
context of
human resource
management

chapter **15**

international HRM

objectives

After studying this chapter, you should be able to:

1 Explain how developments in global capitalism affect corporate and human
resources strategies within multinational corporations

2 Describe the difference between strategic international human resource
management (SIHRM) and international human resource management (IHRM)

3 Explain how SIHRM is linked to different global business strategies

4 Outline some key aspects and contemporary issues in IHRM

5 Comment on whether globalization is driving processes of convergence or
divergence in HRM policies and practices

introduction

The mass evacuation of employees from Libya in 2011 focused attention on the reality of managing organizational personnel in a global environment. As antigovernment protests spread to Tripoli, European-based oil companies, such as Royal Dutch Shell PLC and BP, organized flights to evacuate their expat workers or their families from the country (Winfield, 2011). In essence, *international* human resource management (IHRM) refers to all human resources (HR) practices used to manage people in companies operating in more than one country. It can be distinguished from domestic HRM by the fact that core HRM activities have to be culturally sensitive and effective in a cross-cultural, multinational context (French 2010; Scullion and Linehan, 2005). As such, it is different from a related, but separate, field called *comparative* HRM, which identifies and analyses the role of institutions, culture and other societal conditions in understanding differences and similarities in HRM across countries (Bryson and Frege, 2010; Szamosi et al., 2010).

The proliferation of interest in IHRM springs directly from the globalization of markets, international commodity chain configurations (Morris et al., 2009), new 'boundaryless' work organizations and the impact of these changes on national patterns of labour markets and employment relations. Academic interest also stems from neo-liberal-based management theory; that is, the phenomenon of internationalization of HR practices has immense potential to foster a global approach to managing human capital following the paradigmatic Anglo-American model (Farazmand, 2002; Sparrow et al., 2004).

This chapter begins with some developments in global capitalism and how they play out in terms of employment relations and IHRM in global corporations. We identify three alternative theories relating to the impact of global processes on domestic patterns of employment relations. This is followed by an examination of the international aspects of key HR practices in companies operating outside their parent country. We will conclude by examining a pivotal argument in IHRM on whether global capitalism is causing a convergence or a divergence in employment management.

Global capitalism

Globalization seems to define twenty-first century society (Hancke, 2009). The neo-liberal narrative of globalization became infectious in the late twentieth century (Rodrik, 2011; Saul, 2005). Advocates argued with audacity for neo-liberal market economics – an ideology that gives prominence to the role of market forces in maximizing efficiency, believes that privatization sustains economic growth and self-regulation works best, and holds that economic intervention by national governments is ineffective and positively harmful. As a result, the narrative reassured that all societies all around the world would reap the benefits of globalization in the form of higher living standards and the elimination of poverty. Advocates of globalization argued that, in this global era, old national institutions and processes attempting to regulate national economies, national labour markets and national labour standards would be increasingly displaced by the emergence of new transnational institutions and processes.

Traditionally, the employment relationship was strongly influenced by national systems of employment legislation and the cultural contexts in which it operated. A good example here is the use of child labour: in China, for example, a factory called Sturdy Products, in the city of Shenzhen, which makes Disney's best-selling *Cars* toys, uses child labour as young as 14 (Chamberlain, 2011). As the pace of globalization accelerated, however, the notion of a national system of employment relations began to be openly challenged and to appear out of date (Murray, 2005). The range of pressures associated with globalization has, first, enhanced the integration of markets at both the regional (for example, European Union [EU] and North American) and worldwide levels. Second, it has stimulated powerful new markets in Eastern Europe, the People's Republic of China and India. A third economic phenomenon is increased foreign direct investment by multinational corporations (MNCs) and transnational corporations, as well as a cross-border integration of their production and services. Over the last three decades, for example, the number of MNCs has increased eightfold, and foreign direct investment stock has increased 12-fold. These economic indicators reflect 'a reshuffling of total business investment away from domestic to foreign operations, largely through cross-border acquisitions and mergers' (Cooke, 2005, p. 283).

Globalization is arguably about the unfettered pursuit of profit (Hertz, 2002). There is nothing in the logic of profit-making corporations and capital accumulation to keep the manufacture of steel in Sheffield, the Ruhr or Pennsylvania, as many managers and non-managers have discovered (Hobsbawm, 1995). Developments in transport and communication have meant that corporations can increase their profits by relocating their operations beyond their parent country. Higher profits can be realized by transferring their distinctive competencies to foreign markets, by economies of scale and by exploiting location economies (Hill and Jones, 2010). The concept of distinctive competencies, a set of human capabilities unique to a company that give it a competitive advantage in the market, has its roots in resource-based theory (see Chapter 2). MNCs with distinctive competencies can potentially realize higher profits by applying those competencies in foreign markets, where there is no competition or where local competitors lack similar competencies. For example, following the collapse of Soviet Communism, the McDonald's Corporation expanded rapidly in Eastern Europe to exploit its distinctive competencies in managing fast-food operations (Royle, 2005).

reflective question How does the increasing globalization of markets allow MNCs to increase their profit margins?

Higher profits can be realized through economies of scale, which are consistent with the business strategy of low-cost leadership (Porter, 1985). The underlying neo-liberal assumption here is that global corporations that are capable of supplying a global market from a single location are likely to realize economies of scale, and increased profit, more quickly than companies that restrict their marketing to a smaller local economy. Each national (local) economy is embedded within its own social sphere – economic, political, legal and social. Thus, levels of corporate taxation, employment standards and a 'business-friendly' environment can all affect the pursuit of profit. These differences in a country's business climate are known in the language of international management as *economies of location*. In an era of corporate globalization, the portability of capital makes it possible for MNCs to select their production location in an endlessly variable geometry of profit-searching (Castells, 2000). Moreover, the logic of unfettered globalization means that labour-intensive value-added activities migrate from high-wage to low-wage countries, that is, from the rich developed countries such as the USA and Western Europe to poorer developing countries such as Bangladesh.

Typologies of global business strategy

The domain of IHRM connects to issues of significance in the field of global business and the internationalization process (Boxall et al., 2008; Morris et al., 2009). Global business strategies are connected to the generic business-level strategies of cost-leadership and differentiation that were examined in Chapter 2. A useful starting point for understanding global business theories is the model developed by Bartlett and Ghoshal (1989). These two international business theorists suggest that global corporations typically face tension from two types of business pressure. MNCs face, on the one hand, demands for global cost reductions and integration, and, on the other hand, demands for differentiation and local responsiveness. The demand to control costs and integrate has its roots in the classical management theory that there is 'one best way' to manage.

Global companies strive for global efficiency by rationalizing their product lines, standardizing their parts design and integrating their global manufacturing and control systems. The pressures for integration can be high in technologically intensive enterprises or where the product is universal and requires minimal modification to local needs. This typically occurs with goods such as petroleum, steel and chemicals, and is also typical for consumer electronics, for instance mobile phones and personal computers. Demands for integration are also high in industries in which there is excess capacity or in which consumers face low switching costs. For example, the demand for integration has been globally intense in the steel industry, in which differentiation is difficult and price is the main competitive variable (Hill and Jones, 2010).

Countering global strategies and organizational efficiency imperatives are local realities and a need for local responsiveness. Companies have to satisfy consumer tastes and preferences in diverse locations, so competitive advantage may be derived from producing a product or service that is more sensitive to national cultures and local tastes in the host countries where the MNC operates. Culture differentiates one locale from another, and the duality of culture – its pervasiveness yet its uniqueness – impacts on global business strategy (Mintzberg et al., 1998). Pressures to be locally responsive arise from consumer tastes and preferences, differences in the host country's infrastructure and the regulations of the national business environment imposed by the host government. For example, when the Swedish home furnishing company IKEA entered the US market in the 1990s, it offered cut-price standardized products, which had sold well across Europe, based on huge economies of scale. However, IKEA soon found that it had to be responsive to North American tastes and physiques: IKEA's glasses were too small for North American consumers, who tend to add ice to their drinks, and Swedish beds were too narrow for American body sizes (Hill and Jones, 2010).

A second set of demands for local responsiveness arises from differences in the host country's infrastructure. For example, some EU member states use 240-volt

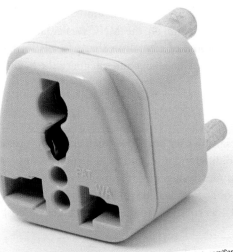

©istockphoto.com/Sam Lee

Differences in the national infrastructure can be a barrier for MNCs.

consumer electric systems, whereas in North America 110-volt systems tend to be standard. Thus, differences in the national infrastructure require MNCs to customize domestic electrical appliances. This diversity in infrastructure has been identified as a barrier to European competitiveness and was behind the Single Europe Act of 1986. The Act aimed to stimulate pan-European trade by harmonizing technical standards governing the production and distribution of goods (Hendry, 1994).

A third set of demands for local responsiveness emanates from nationally based regulatory regimes constructed and maintained by host governments. The regulation of employment relations, consumer products (for example, automobile exhaust emissions), ecological controls and local testing (for example, clinical trials of pharmaceutical products according to domestic standards) may dictate that MNCs be responsive to local conditions. Global corporations can be enticed to relocate by national governments deregulating safety, environmental or employment standards.

The major chemical accident that occurred in Bhopal, India, for example, illustrates the dangers implicit in reducing standards to attract Western investment. A chemical plant owned by the US multinational company Union Carbide engaged in chemical production under conditions that would have been illegal in the USA. On 3 December 1984, the plant experienced a major leak. Within hours, 3000 people were dead, 15,000 more dying in the aftermath. A further 200,000 were seriously injured, and half a million still carry special health cards. Eventually, the MNC paid out just $470 million in compensation (Saul, 2005). More recently, the Indian government gave tax exemptions and deregulated the telecommunications industry in order to increase foreign investment in call centres (Maitra and Sangha, 2005).

Thus, through a wide variety of national or regional policy mechanisms, national governments can effectively shape national business systems and therefore the competitive dynamics within a market (Whitley, 1999). Prahalad and Doz (1987, p. 251) suggest that, because governments influence competitive outcomes, 'MNCs can approach strategy as a process of "negotiation" with host governments'; they call this process 'negotiated strategies'. Overall, MNCs are crucial agents in the transformation of national employment management systems (Marginson and Meardi, 2010). They are widely held to have differing preferences over arrangements for managing the employment relationship: union representation, non-union representation or none at all, direct or indirect forms of employee voice (Marginson et al., 2010). The point we wish to make here is, therefore, that the cost efficiency–responsiveness strategic mix may well depend on the MNC's calculation to exploit cross-national differences, including the model of capitalism that prevails in the host country and that country's political will to protect the planet and safeguard the health and safety of its people.

The integration–responsiveness grid

Local realities are the classic barrier to universal theories of global efficiency. Two pressures – cost efficiencies and rationalization, and differentiation and local responsiveness – form the two dimensions of the integration–responsiveness grid (Figure 15.1). Bartlett and Ghoshal (1989) and Prahalad and Doz (1987) offer four fashionable typologies – global, multidomestic, international and transnational – as solutions to the dual pressure for cost efficiency and responsiveness.

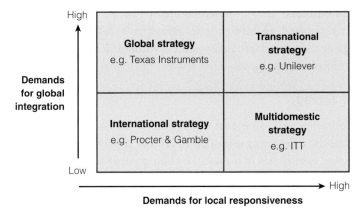

Figure 15.1 *Demands for integration and local responsiveness*
Source: Adapted from Prahalad and Doz (1987) and Bartlett and Ghoshal (1989)

Global strategy

Global corporations that pursue a global strategy focus on increasing profit margins through cost-efficiencies arising from economies of scale and economies of location. These MNCs are pursuing a low-cost leadership strategy. The operations of the MNCs will be concentrated in a few favourable host economies and will tend not to customize their goods to local situations. A global strategy is typically associated with high demands for integration and low demands for local responsiveness (the top-left quadrant of Figure 15.1). Texas Instruments, a company that once dominated the market in pocket calculators and digital watches by focusing persistently on cost reductions and price at the expense of understanding consumers' needs, is an example of an MNC that, until 1982, followed a global strategy (Hill and Jones, 2010).

Multidomestic strategy

Companies pursuing a multidomestic strategy design their operations to maximize local responsiveness. These MNCs tend to customize both their product offering and marketing strategy to different local customer tastes and preferences. A multidomestic company such as ITT developed a 'strategic posture and organizational ability that enables it to be very sensitive and responsive to differences in national environments' (Bartlett and Ghoshal, 1989, p. 14). A multidomestic strategy is typically associated with low demands for integration and high demands for local responsiveness.

International strategy

Global corporations pursuing an international strategy create competitive advantage through a global diffusion of the company's distinctive competencies where its local competitors lack these resources and the capability to integrate and effectively rationalize their value-added activities abroad. An international strategy is typically associated with low demands for integration and low demands for local responsiveness. MNCs pursuing an international strategy tend to centralize their research and development activities in the parent country, but also tend to establish operations in each major national economy in which they do business. The US-based company Procter & Gamble is an example of an MNC that has pursued an international strategy: 'it set up miniature replicas of the domestic organization to adapt P&G products without deviating from the "Procter way"' (Bartlett and Ghoshal, 1989, p. 15).

Transnational strategy

Companies following a transnational strategy strive for competitive advantage worldwide by rationalizing and integrating resources to achieve superior cost efficiencies from economies of scale and economies of location, by being sensitive and capable of responding to local needs, and by sharing knowledge throughout their global operations. In a transnational company, knowledge and distinctive competencies flow to and from each of the company's operations as part of a larger process of 'global learning' that encompasses 'every member of the company' (Bartlett and Ghoshal, 1989, p. 59).

In essence, a transnational company simultaneously achieves low-cost leadership and a competitive advantage in terms of differentiation. The effect is 'a complex configuration of assets and capabilities that are distributed, yet specialized [and] the company integrates the dispersed resources through strong interdependencies ... Such interdependencies may be reciprocal rather than sequential' (Bartlett and Ghoshal, 1989, p. 60). Thus, a world-scale production plant in Mexico may depend on world-scale component plants in Australia, France and South Korea; major sales subsidiaries worldwide may in turn depend on Mexico for their finished products. The transnational's resources and capabilities are represented as an integrated network, a term emphasizing the significant flows of components, products, resources, information and people. Unilever is an example of an MNC that has pursued a transnational strategy, with 17 different and largely decentralized detergent plants in Europe alone.

HRM web links [WWW] Go to the websites of Procter & Gamble UK and Ireland (www.uk.pg.com) and Procter & Gamble USA (www.pg.com/en_US/index.jhtml), ITT (www.itt.com), Unilever (www.unilever.com), Texas Instruments (www.texasinstruments.com) and Hewlett-Packard Co. (www.h-p.com). What is the parent country for these MNCs? How many countries does each MNC operate in?

The integration–responsiveness grid is a simple and impressive model for explaining the strategic choices shaping the strategies and organizational networks of MNCs. Case study research confirms Bartlett and Ghoshal's typology of MNCs that is explained here (see Harzing, 2000; Morris et al., 2009), but we should end this introduction to international business strategies by noting the shift in economic thinking on globalization since the great recession that started in 2008 and by providing a word of caution related to Bartlett and Ghoshal's model.

We should note that, since the financial meltdown in 2008, the theory of 'efficient markets' and the supposedly unmitigated virtues of self-regulation have, unsurprisingly, been severely discredited (see, for example, Nolan, P., 2011; Rodrik, 2011). Long-standing critics of unfettered global capitalism have been joined by mainstream economists in questioning the wisdom of the globalization narrative. Rodrik argues (2011, p. xv) that there has been an extraordinary shift in the intellectual debate. Among dominant mainstream economists, we have, for example, Paul Krugman, the 2008 recipient of the Nobel Prize in Economic Sciences, arguing that trade with low-income economies is no longer too small to have an effect on inequality in rich developed economies, and Larry Summers, former economic advisor to US President Barack Obama, deliberating about the negative impact of a 'race to the bottom' in national regulations and labour standards.

With regard to the integration–responsiveness model, we should note that the typologies proposed by Bartlett and Ghoshal depict a theoretical or 'ideal type' of global strategy that global corporations should strive for if they wish to attain superior performance outcomes. But the evidence suggests that few global companies truly pursue a transnational strategy. Rather, it is far more likely that managing the conflicting pressures for global rationalization and integration (low-cost leadership) and local responsiveness (differentiation) sets the context for IHRM.

International human resource management

As companies increasingly seek to leverage human capital to compete in global markets, academics and practitioners alike have increasingly begun to explore the international potential of strategic HRM. In so doing, they have generally addressed HR policies and practices relating to global and local recruitment and selection, international training and learning, international reward management, performance appraisal and the management of expatriates that define IHRM.

In this section, we will seek to understand the explicit connection between global competition and HRM in MNCs. We will identify three alternative theories relating to the impact of global processes on domestic patterns of employment relations. We will then explain the concepts of strategic IHRM (SIHRM) and critically examine the links between global strategic management and SIHRM and IHRM. Finally, we will look at a model of strategic IHRM first developed by Schuler et al. (1993).

Global capitalism and employment relations

The developments in international capitalism have generated a debate on how globalization impacts on domestic patterns of employment relations. The existing literature identifies three alternative approaches to this: economic, institutionalist and integrated (Bamber et al., 2004).

The *economic* approach follows the classical neo-liberal premise that global business activity has become so interconnected, and that competitive imperatives are so dominant, that they offer little scope for domestic differences in patterns of employment relations. This influential economic approach predicts that international markets operate in accordance with universal principles and will result in a 'convergence' of national employment relations. Economic imperatives will, for example, create 'efficiencies' by driving wages down and eroding employment standards.

The *institutionalist* approach to the impact of globalization contends that global forces are more fluid in their dynamics and more contradictory in their outcome. Moreover, nationally based regulatory institutions form an independent dynamic that structures, controls and legitimates business activities and outcomes. Global trends are mediated by national or local institutional regimes and changed into 'divergent' power struggles over

The effects of globalization can be seen everywhere: few people would question this basic proposition. But when pressed to provide an account of how globalization produces these effects, even the most astute observer may pause. Too often, the particular causal mechanisms of globalization are not specified, and we are left imagining a mysterious force impacting on the world in ways that mere mortals can do little to influence.

HRM and globalization

To move beyond this kind of abstraction, it helps to reflect critically on general claims about globalization. We often encounter the argument that globalization is responsible for the 'race to the bottom', a phrase referring to the fact that, in order to compete with companies in the developing world – or in some cases, with local rivals – managers believe they must reduce costs and opt for traditional low-trust, authoritarian HR practices.

This seems to offer a rather narrow range of options for managers working in more developed economies: they can send work to the developing world, they can import models of compensation and work organization characteristic of the developing world, or they can blend the two low-cost options together. Regardless of which low-cost option is selected, worker compensation and the quality of work are compromised. In this vision of globalization, managers are portrayed as passive agents responding predictably to global forces beyond their control. It implies that if management do not adapt by joining their competitors in this 'race to the bottom', they will be responsible for the failure of their companies. This view, however, is fundamentally flawed.

The reality is in fact more complex. Compare the HR practices of Walmart and Costco. Walmart is the champion of low costs, and this is reflected in its workplace environment (low pay, limited benefits, significant work intensification). However, Walmart's competitor Costco uses a different management model, offering its employees better compensation and a better quality work environment. Judging from the value of Costco stocks, the choice not to participate in 'the race to the bottom' has paid off.

Is 'the race to the bottom' an inevitable consequence of globalization?

A recent study of the airline industry provides a more in-depth analysis. The authors identify a trend towards differentiation in the airline industry in which established airlines have created subsidiaries to compete in the low-cost market. One might expect this to lead to a 'race to the bottom', but while there is some evidence of this, there is a notable exception. 'Go' (part of airline BA) was able to reduce its costs without overly harsh reductions in worker compensation and without sacrificing the quality of the work environment. Go maintained a quality of customer service that made it the preferred choice in this sector of the industry. The authors (Harvey and Turnbull, 2010, pp. 239–40) concluded that:

> the scope for managerial choice in the civil aviation industry should not be underestimated …, nor should the competitive advantage that can be secured from high road employee relations, even when the airline's business strategy might appear position the company in the 'low end' of the market.

Stop! Managers may choose not to participate in the 'race to the bottom'. But how much freedom do they have?

References: See Harvey and Turnbull (2010) for more information. Type the phrase 'race to the bottom' into the search engine Google Scholar to find out what other researchers have said about this important global process.

Note: This feature was written by David MacLennan at Thompson Rivers University.

©istockphoto.com/italia17

particular national employment practices (Hyman, 1999). By highlighting national differences in how societies shape economic and social outcomes, the institutionalist approach emphasizes the variability of market economies and highlights why 'varieties of capitalism' are likely to persist in the future (see, for example, Hall and Soskice, 2009). Furthermore, nationally embedded institutions, for example universities, can confer a comparative competitive advantage, especially in the sphere of innovation.

An *integrated* approach to globalization and national patterns of employment relations has been put forward by Bamber et al. (2004). They suggest that both global economic trends and nationally based institutions are important in structuring national patterns of employment relations. However, because different kinds of market economy are integrated into the global economy in different ways, global economic pressures are likely to be divergent. The integrated approach thus focuses on the effects of global economic developments on the 'interests of different groups of employers, workers and policy-makers within different institutional settings' (Bamber et al., 2004, p. 1483).

IHRM and SIHRM

Before we consider models of SIHRM that have been developed to explain how the HRM function is configured in global companies, it is important to distinguish between IHRM and SIHRM. There are competing definitions of IHRM, although most scholarship in the field has focused on issues associated with the cross-national transfer of expatriates (that is, how to recruit and manage individual managers in international job assignments; see, for example Dowling et al., 2008; Kochan et al., 1992; Shenkar, 1995; Tung, 1988).

Taylor et al. (1996, p. 960) define IHRM as:

The set of distinct activities, functions and processes that are directed at attracting, developing and maintaining an MNC's human resources. It is thus the aggregate of the various HRM systems used to manage people in the MNC, both at home and overseas.

Scullion (2001, p. 288) defines IHRM as the 'HRM issues and problems arising from the internationalization of business, and the HRM strategies, policies and practices which firms pursue in response to the internationalization process'. More recent definitions have extended the term to cover the need to adapt to local contexts, the global coordination of overseas subsidiaries, global knowledge management and global leadership (Scullion and Linehan, 2005).

IHRM tends to celebrate a Western hegemonic culture, one that emphasizes the subordination of domestic culture and domestic employment practices to corporate culture and corporate HRM practices (Boxall, 1995). As such, many contemporary studies of IHRM tend to be seen as a managerial strategic instrument unashamedly connected to the neo-liberalism agenda (Farazmand, 2002). It is the principal discourse of neo-liberalism that provides insights into related debates around labour market rigidities, flexibility, outsourcing, privatization, European integration, shifting macro-economic policy paradigms and international HR practices. IHRM is thus the sum of the various HRM policies and practices used to manage people in companies operating in more than one country.

As we showed in Chapter 2, strategic HRM is the process of explicitly linking the HRM function with the strategic management goals of the organization. Thus, SIHRM is the process of explicitly linking IHRM with the strategy of the global company. In defining SIHRM, we draw on the work of Scullion and Linehan (2005) and Björkman and Stahl

HRM in practice ➡ 15.1

'We are disposable people ...'

n April 2011, the union Unite held a demonstration outside the giant 220-acre Thanet Earth greenhouse complex in Kent, claiming that agency workers were being treated like 'sweatshop labour', denied holiday pay and employed as permanent casual labour with no proper contracts. A migrant worker was reported as saying: 'The agencies have done whatever they want, and Thanet Earth and the supermarkets have let them. When we have asked for our rights we have been told: "You can find another job." We are disposable people to Tesco, Sainsbury's, M&S and the rest.' Thanet Earth, which supplies the major supermarkets with salad produce, refuted the claims, saying that all the agencies supplying its labour had been fully vetted by the Gangmasters Licensing Authority (*Guardian*, April 29, 2011).

This was the latest episode to add to the growing concern over the employment conditions faced by the large number of migrant workers in the UK, particularly in agriculture. The Gangmasters Licensing Authority itself was set up in the aftermath of the death of Chinese shellfish collectors in Morecombe Bay in 2004 with the aim of regulating casual labour agencies and gangmasters. There is, however, evidence that parts of the agriculture sector are still ignoring or undermining minimum labour standards; in October 2010, for example, a group of Romanian children were found picking onions in Worcestershire.

Agriculture has always been characterized by a seasonal use of temporary labour as the agricultural cycle makes it uneconomical to retain a permanent labour force: the use of labour contractors makes achieving numerical flexibility easier for the grower. Rogaly (2008) looked at the increasing use of migrant workers in this sector and concluded that the shift of power away from producers to a small number of powerful retailers had pressured growers to intensify production to compensate for the smaller margins dictated by the supermarkets. This was done through a combination of innovations in growing techniques, manipulation of piecework regimes and innovations in labour control.

Migrants have a strong monetary incentive, and the cutting of piecework rates ensures a higher daily output before the minimum wage equivalent is reached. Growers have preferred non-UK nationals because of their 'work ethic', but these workers form a vulnerable group in the labour market due to factors such as immigration status, a general lack of information and language barriers. Rogaly argues that this vulnerability is used to ensure a compliant labour force. The agencies can exercise power over the workers through being the source of information about jobs, offering transport to the work location and providing credit and, importantly, accommodation. Such workers are more amenable to working irregular hours and may be easier to dispose of when harvesting is over: 'they can easily be turned on and they can easily be turned off', said one grower.

Stop! Should we be prepared to pay more for our food if it guarantees better working conditions for food production workers?

Sources and further information: For background information, see Rogaly (2008) and McKay and Markova (2010).

Note: This feature was written by Chris Baldry at the University of Stirling.

(2006). Schuler et al. (1993, p. 720) define SIHRM as the 'HRM issues, functions and policies and practices that result from the strategic activities of multinational enterprises and that impact the international concerns and goals of those enterprises'. Emphasizing that the study of IHRM is a relatively new area of research, Björkman and Stahl (2006, p. 1) define the field as 'all issues related to the management of people in an international context'. Here SIHRM is defined as:

An array of HR practices and issues related to the management of people that arise from the global competitive activities of MNCs and that explicitly link international HR practices and processes with the worldwide strategic goals of those companies.

SIHRM builds on strategic HRM that aims to connect HRM explicitly with strategic management processes. In so doing, SIHRM recognizes the need to address the tension between the global and the local. This tension is related to balancing global competitiveness (rationalization and integration) and local responsiveness (flexibility) strategies pursued by MNCs while simultaneously leveraging global learning within and across the MNC. As such, SIHRM links 'IHRM explicitly with the strategy and with the MNC' (Scullion and Linehan, 2005, p. 23). This highly dynamic and complex context is the arena of SIHRM.

A model of SIHRM

We have focused so far on some global business strategies and the meaning of IHRM and SIHRM. We will now identify some conceptual models of SIHRM developed to explain IHRM processes and roles, and how external and internal factors impact on HRM in MNCs. Models of SIHRM have been developed by De Cieri and Dowling (1999), Schuler et al. (1993) and Taylor et al. (1996). In Figure 15.2, we present an integrative model that draws primarily from Schuler et al. (1993) and is informed by the work of Bartlett and Ghoshal (1989) and Taylor et al. (1996).

Schuler et al.'s original integrative framework consisted of four core components:

- Exogenous factors
- Endogenous factors
- SIHRM
- The pressures and goals of the MNC.

To this, we have added a fifth component – the corporate SIHRM orientation. The lines and arrows in Figure 15.2 denote the reciprocal relationships between exogenous factors, SIHRM and the pressures and goals of the MNC.

Briefly, *exogenous factors* relate to issues external to the MNC. They include, for example, industry characteristics, the technology available and domestic characteristics such as domestic employment relations. De Cieri and Dowling (1999) argue that exogenous factors exert a direct influence on endogenous factors, SIHRM and the pressures and goals of the MNC. *Endogenous factors* relate to internal organizational issues, such as work design, intraorganizational networks and coordination and control systems.

SIHRM relates to issues of coordination and control, local responsiveness and worldwide learning. It is concerned with 'Developing a fit between exogenous and endogenous factors and balancing the competing demands of global versus local requirements as well as the needs of coordination, control and autonomy' (Schuler et al., 1993, p. 451). *Pressures and goals of the MNC* relate to profitability, the dual demands for cost reductions and local

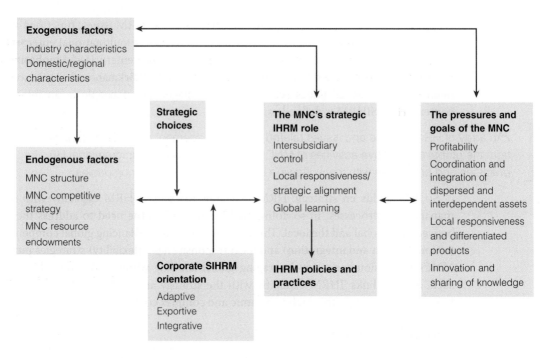

Figure 15.2 *An integrated framework of SIHRM*

Source: Adapted from Schuler et al. (1993), p. 722; Scullion and Linehan (2005), p. 31; Taylor et al. (1996), p. 965; and Bartlett and Ghoshal (1989), p. 67

responsiveness, and the global transfer of innovation. The model suggests that there are reciprocal relationships between exogenous factors, SIHRM and the pressures and goals of the MNC (Scullion and Linehan, 2005). SIHRM is expected to buttress the MNC's global goals. Finally, the corporate *SIHRM orientation* refers to the general philosophy or approach taken by the MNC's top management in designing its total IHRM system.

One of the numerous HRM issues facing MNCs is the extent to which HR practices should be transferred across borders (Stahl and Björkman, 2006, p. 3). Taylor et al. (1996) help to explain why MNCs choose different HRM orientations in different countries by drawing upon the resource-based theory of the firm and resource dependence. Resource-based theory proposes that, in order to provide added value to the organization, the SIHRM system of global affiliates should be built around the company's critical HRM competencies. The resource dependence framework helps to identify those situations in which MNCs will exercise control over their subsidiaries' SIHRM systems. In Figure 15.2, we showed corporate SIHRM orientation impacting on the SIHRM role of MNCs. Taylor et al. propose that the HR strategy of MNCs follows three generic SIHRM orientations: *adaptive, exportive* and *integrative*:

- An *adaptive* SIHRM orientation constructs HRM systems for subsidiaries that reflect the local context. This approach gives more emphasis to differentiation and less to integration. Top managers at corporate head office adopt local HR practices by hiring knowledgeable and competent indigenous HR practitioners.
- An *exportive* SIHRM orientation focuses on replicating in an MNC's overseas affiliates the HR practices used by the corporation in its parent country. This approach gives more emphasis to integration and less to differentiation.

- An *integrative* SIHRM orientation focuses on transferring the 'best' HR policies and practices from any of the company's affiliates worldwide to construct a global HRM system. Taylor et al. contend that the SIHRM orientation of the MNC determines its overall approach to managing the tension between integration and control pressures, and local responsiveness and differentiation pressures. The central theoretical argument of the integrative model is, therefore, that IHRM should be explicitly related to the MNC's global business strategy, and that its changing forms must be understood in relation to the strategic evolution of the MNC (Scullion and Linehan, 2005; Scullion and Starkey, 2000; Taylor et al., 1996).

> **reflective question** 🖧 Go back to Figure 15.1. What type of SIHRM orientation would you expect to find at Texas Instruments, ITT and Unilever? Why?

The integrated model is useful for understanding the link between international business strategy and IHRM in the global corporation, and for identifying a comprehensive range of factors that influence SIHRM in MNCs. However, models are just that: they are a conceptual construct and have been criticized because the alleged direction of the causal relationships within them is uncertain. For example, the argument that exogenous factors exert a direct impact on endogenous factors may privilege external factors as the actor

Huawei is a multinational networking and telecommunications company that provides information and communications technology (ICT) solutions and products to its customers. These solutions and products, including telecom networks, devices and cloud computing, are used in over 140 countries and serve more than a third of the world's population, making the company the largest of its kind in China and the second largest in the world. Huawei is headquartered in Shenzhen in China.

Lesley White is an HR professional with more than 20 years' experience, having started as an HR Assistant. She specialized for 9 years in European Compensation and Benefits, designing reward strategies and associated policies to attract, retain and motivate employees. Her current role covers all areas of HRM, with a key focus on strategy planning and implementation.

 Visit www.palgrave.com/business/bratton5 to watch Lesley talking about the challenges of working in a UK-based HR department for a company headquartered in China, cultural differences in working and management styles, and the place of HR in Huawei's business strategy, and then think about the following questions:

1 What are the key features of working in HR in a global organization, according to Lesley?
2 In Lesley's view, how do Chinese managers respond to directives compared with Europeans, and why?
3 How is information-sharing affected by culture?

Lesley White
Human Resources Director UK and Ireland, Huawei Technologies

www.huawei.com

HRM **as I see it**

when MNCs have actually become global giants that wield titanic political power. Arguably, corporations in fact determine the rules of the game, and governments enforce the rules laid down by others (Hertz, 2002). The MNC is the actor.

Although the framework covers a wide range of relevant issues, the issue of transplanting Western HRM practices and values into culturally diverse domestic environments needs to be researched through a critical lens. Global companies share with their domestic counterparts the intractable problem of managing the employment relationship to reduce the indeterminacy that results from the unspecified nature of the employment contract. If we adopt Townley's (1994) perspective on IHRM, the role of knowledge to render people in the workplace 'governable' is made problematic by the intertwining of highly complex local, regional, national and global cultures (Crane, 1994). It is the *complexity* of operating in different socioculturally diverse environments and employing different national categories of workers, rather than the HR practices as such, which differentiates national and international HRM (Dowling et al., 2008, p. 5).

HRM web links   WWW   For further information on cultural diversity, go to http://www.ethnoconnect.com, www.shrm.org/diversity and www.shrm.org/trends.

The internationalization of HRM practices

The global strategies examined above, in particular the supposed ascendancy of the transnational corporation with global communication networks, has far-reaching implications for the function and practices of IHRM. When leveraging their core HR activities, MNCs must achieve a dynamic balance between the pressures for central control and the pressures for local responsiveness across diverse national locations, intercultural business contexts (Adler, N. J., 2002) and business cultures (Brewster and Bennett, 2010). One important aspect of the internationalization of HRM relates to the 'best practice' versus 'best fit' debate. The former argues for the universal application of certain HR practices, while the latter recognizes the importance of context and societal embeddedness in HRM. It is argued that MNCs in general engage in the straightforward transfer of their own, 'nationally idiosyncratic' HRM policies and practices across borders (Sayim, 2010).

As an independent variable, however, sociocultural embeddedness can have an important influence on the development of IHRM policies and practices and their subsequent effect on global performance (Paauwe and Boselie, 2008, p. 167). Expatriate managers, for example, are required to fit in and be 'legitimated' by the host country nationals (HCNs) but local legitimacy is also dependent on compliance with local norms and mores (Brewster and Bennett, 2010).

In shaping international HR policies and practices, an MNC will need to consider a number of objectives. First, each area of HR activity, like structure and systems, should be consistent with its business strategy, and hence contribute to the MNC's international performance. In sectors such as consumer electronic and clothing – both labour-intensive and prone to intense global competition – HR practices are found to be associated with cost-reduction strategies, narrowly designed jobs, low levels of spending on recruitment, selection and induction, and minimal investment in training. In contrast, MNCs producing sophisticated technical/high value-added products in the same host country are found to employ HR practices associated with Schuler's (1989) 'quality enhancement and innovation' strategies with, for example, high levels of training and employee participation. Although it is not the sole factor, business strategy, which directs commodity chain work configuration, is an important determinant of HR practices (Morris et al., 2009, p. 368).

Second, the array of HR practices needs to recruit, retain, motivate and facilitate the transfer of talented employees internationally. Third, the MNC will want to ensure that the HR practices are equitable and comply with host-country's cultural values (Zhang and Albrecht, 2010) and employment standards. As a whole, the above considerations inevitably raise the potential for countless complexities (Dowling et al., 2008; Varma et al., 2011).

To provide insight into the potential complexities, here we add the dimension of cultural diversity and extend Fombrun et al.'s HRM model to briefly examine the international aspects of recruitment and selection, rewards, training and development, and performance appraisal, as well as the issue of repatriation. Others have noted that cultural diversity represents a variable that poses significant challenges for managing people in an international context. MNCs typically have multicultural workforces made up of employees with a variety of ethnic, racial, religious and cultural values and mores. Indeed, it has been suggested that the central modus operandi of the global company is the creation and effective management of multicultural work teams that represent diversity in competencies, levels of experience, and cultural and language backgrounds (Dowling et al., 2008; Rhinesmith, 1993, quoted in Mabey et al., 1998b, p. 210). A deep sensitivity for cultural diversity implies that researchers and practitioners should attempt to understand the goals and outcomes of HR practices within the wider sociocultural context of societal values and mores.

reflective question

As we have discussed, the global company is characterized by geographical dispersion, demands for rationalization and differentiation, and cultural diversity. When an MNC adopts a global business strategy, what new challenges does it present for managing Fombrun et al.'s four dimensions of recruitment and selection, rewards, training and development, and performance appraisal?

HRM web links

For further information on IHRM issues, policies and practices, go to www.shrmglobal.org, which is the home page of the Society for Human Resources Management.

International recruitment and selection

MNCs do not simply transmit capital: they invariably transmit management 'know-how'. Expatriate managers play a critical role in the transfer of both explicit knowledge and the tacit knowledge of the MNC's practices and management style to the overseas affiliates (Gamble, 2003). As such, international staffing is a crucial aspect of the management of people in the MNC, and is increasingly seen as one of the core HR practices used by global enterprises to control and coordinate their spatially dispersed global operations (Collings and Scullion, 2007).

The use of expatriates to staff vacant positions in subsidiaries in host countries is a widespread practice. In the case of European MNCs, 54 per cent of the managers of their overseas subsidiaries are expatriates, and in North American and Japanese MNCs the pattern is similar, with figures of 51 per cent and 75 per cent, respectively (Bonache and Fernández, 2005, p. 115). It is not surprising, therefore, that in most IHRM publications, recruitment and selection is seen primarily as an issue of expatriate selection. Selection is, however, important beyond simply staffing key technical or managerial positions. Intercultural phenomena suggest that mastering cultural differences may be crucial for successful organizational performance. As such, it is argued that staffing is at the heart of the dilemma of centralization (cost efficiencies) versus decentralization (local responsiveness). The handling of this balance invokes issues of 'ethnocentricity', the belief in the inherent superiority of one's own culture or race, as well as 'managerial empathy' (Torbiörn, 2005).

Much of the IHRM literature on staffing has focused on two alternative categories of recruitment and selection: parent country nationals and HCNs (Tung, 1998). Drawing from these two pools of potential employees seems logical in global recruiting as they mirror the wider dilemma of central versus de-central or local, in that the choice is whether to transfer the dominant norms of the MNC's national culture or make use of those of the local culture. In theory, a varied sociocultural context requires a selective use of parent country nationals and HCNs across staffing decisions. In practice, however, expatriate selection appears to be more a matter of 'good luck than good management' (Anderson, 2005, p. 580). In addition, because the locus of decision-making is embedded in the local culture and norms where the MNC's corporate office is located, expatriate staff at the company's head office may have little idea what culturally derived expectations are needed to 'fit' the local context (Gamble, 2003). Moreover, informal ad hoc selection practices may be frequent, and decisions of intercultural reach may frequently be affected by illogical or irrational elements such as ethnocentrism, ignorance and stereotyping (Torbiörn, 2005).

In 1911, the feminist activist Clara Zetkin founded International Women's Day. A century later, research shows that, despite women's increased presence in Western organizational hierarchies, the number of female expatriates remains only a fraction of those in senior management positions, and 'only in rare circumstances' are female managers offered global assignments (Linehan, 2005, p. 197). The low number of women chosen for global assignments provides evidence that staffing decisions in MNCs may often be irrational and sometimes discriminatory. In all capitalist countries, it is argued, men control economic and political power – management is consequently androcentric.

Numerous studies (see, for example, Adler, 1984, 1994; Caligiuri and Tung, 1999; Linehan, 2000, 2005; Punnett et al., 1992; Taylor and Napier, 1996) point to stereotypical perceptions of women's managerial abilities and business acumen, traditional attitudes towards women's family roles, the need to accommodate dual-career couples, and general discrimination against women as major social barriers to women expanding their career horizons through access to global management positions. Countering one myth, studies by Adler (1987) and Taylor and Napier (1996) found that there were no significant differences between male and female expatriates in their business performance, even in male-dominated cultures such as South Korea and Japan. As in all HR practices, an MNC will, in developing a recruitment and selection policy, need to understand the role of cultural values as a contributor to its strategic development (Zhang and Albrecht, 2010).

reflective question

The term 'glass border' describes the irrational assumptions held by parent country senior management about the suitability of female managers for overseas appointments. To what extent is gender still relevant as a criterion for selecting female expatriates? If gender is still relevant, what can be done to promote equal opportunity for female managers to undertake international assignments?

International rewards

Reward management (salary, allowances and incentive bonuses) generally needs to support overall business strategy in order to attract, retain and motivate needed employees (see Chapter 11). Managing international rewards requires that managers responsible for implementing HR policies and practices are familiar with a range of other issues, including the HCNs, the host country's employment law, national labour relations, the availability of particular allowances or benefits, and currency fluctuations in particular host countries. Even within the 'scant' international reward literature, much of the focus has been on reward management for expatriates and far less on other categories of workers, such as host country and third-country nationals (Mahajan, 2011).

Although the issue of generous remuneration packages for globally mobile corporate elites has become part of the public discourse on what constitutes 'responsible capitalism', most of the reward literature deals with technical rather than strategic or ethical issues of rewards, that is, with how to design effective remuneration packages for expatriates (Bonache and Fernández, 2005). Part of that technical discussion includes deciding which currency it is beneficial to pay rewards in so that, in terms of tax efficiency, the outcome motivates the expatriate. Bonache and Fernández (2005) present a theory-based approach to expatriate rewards based on the costs and benefits. They suggest that when salary and non-salary costs (for example, training) are taken into account, and in certain circumstances (for example, the need to exploit company-specific knowledge), expatriates can be a cost-effective solution. Other studies provide evidence that effective performance management requires expatriates to know whether and how their performance in their overseas assignment is linked to pay and the next step in their career (Tahvanainen and Suutari, 2005).

In terms of strategic issues, limited evidence suggests that international rewards systems that are not aligned with the values and beliefs of the local host country cause negative outcomes for the MNC. Negative effects in terms of the organization arise, when, without reasonable justification, expatriates' reward significantly exceeds those rewards paid to their local colleagues. This internal inequity can cause HCNs to withhold technical and social support to expatriates. Research also suggests that pay systems that are aligned with the host country's values and beliefs and are perceived to be fair and socially responsive to HCNs are likely to render positive outcomes such as 'extra-role behaviour' and support for expatriates (Mahajan, 2011).

Cross-cultural research draws attention to the salience of national culture as an enduring set of beliefs that shape employees' behaviour. These beliefs shape the attitudes of HCNs, including whether a pay system is perceived as fair and locally responsive. In developing an international reward policy, an MNC will need to include the HCNs' perspective. According to Mahajan, a 'cultural alignment' pay system will be more acceptable to HNCs than ethnocentric reward policies 'as it increases perceived status similarity and reduces intergroup conflict between expatriates and HCNs [and] will facilitate adjustment of expatriates and favourably impact overall effectiveness of [MNCs]' (2011, p. 131). While there is evidence of 'strong "pull" factors' for the transfer of contemporary reward practices to HCNs (Sayim, 2010), the need to elicit HCN's voluntary cooperation and knowledge-sharing with expatriates makes international reward management inevitably complex.

International training and development

The transnational strategy focuses attention on the issue of 'best fit' between an MNC's global business strategy and training interventions. Within the global integration versus host country responsiveness framework, the notion of strategic alignment suggests that international training and development will vary and take one of three forms: centralized, synergistic or local (Caligiuri et al., 2005). Evidence suggests that MNCs pursuing a global strategy will tend to place greater emphasis on training rather than development. The general objective of the training interventions will be to provide managers and key technical personnel with the competencies needed to transfer the distinctive competencies and organizational culture successfully from the parent headquarters to the subsidiaries. MNCs pursuing a multidomestic strategy tend to transfer almost all their HR practices to the host country subsidiaries. Local managers at the affiliate make decisions on the types of training intervention required. MNCs pursuing a transnational strategy clearly require the most complex training and development strategy. The transnational strategy requires that managers be recruited from a worldwide pool of employees, regardless of nationality.

Prescriptive HRM advisors tend to view training intervention as a strategic instrument to nurture a 'strong' culture, or what Bartlett and Ghoshal (1989, p. 175) call the 'global glue' that counterbalances the centrifugal forces of decentralized operations and processes. A particular focus in this area has been the predeparture training of expatriates to be 'interculturally competent', which refers to the ability of the effective manager to have both 'communicative competence' – that is, to communicate both verbally and non-verbally with HCNs – and 'cognitive competence', which avoids the use of crude stereotypes to judge people (see, for example, Mabey et al., 1998b). According to Caligiuri et al. (2005, p. 76), training interventions in the transnational MNC aim to help managers 'to work, think and behave synergistically across borders with people from diverse cultural backgrounds'. Irrespective of business strategy, training and development interventions in MNCs typically include cross-cultural training and competencies associated with global leadership. Table 15.1 summarises these interventions and their respective goals. (See Chapter 9 for a further discussion on learning and development.)

International performance appraisal

As we discussed in Chapter 8, performance appraisal has become a key feature of the employment relationship. The desire to control and predict an employee's current and potential performance has resulted in both national and global firms developing integrated performance appraisal systems. In keeping with the critical perspective of HRM, some have argued that the diffusion of performance appraisal systems is associated with low trade union density (Brown and Heywood, 2005), and is indicative of increasing employer attempts to individualize the employment relationship; this will cause greater risk by, foremost, increasing the proportion of pay that is contingent on assessments of individual, group or organizational performance (Heery, 2000). Appraisal systems have also been critiqued on the grounds that they weaken trade union influence over pay determination (see, for example, Gunnigle et al., 1998). Here, we will consider questions of 'why' and 'how' related to international performance appraisal.

Sparrow et al. (2004) argue that five interrelated organizational 'drivers' – core business cost efficiencies, information exchange, building a global presence, global learning and localized decision-making – are together creating an obvious logic of being as effective as possible

Table 15.1 *Examples of training and development interventions in MNCs*

Training and development initiatives	Goals
Cross-cultural orientation (predeparture)	Comfortably live and work in host country
Cross-cultural training (in-country)	Increase cross-cultural adjustment
Diversity training	Increase ability to understand and appreciate multiple cultural perspectives
Language training	Fluency in another language
Traditional education in international management	Increase international business acumen and knowledge
Individualized coaching or mentoring on cultural experiences	Build cultural awareness; work on cultural 'blind spots'; develop competencies for becoming an effective global leader
Immersion cultural experiences	Build extensive understanding of the local culture and increase ability to understand and appreciate multiple cultural perspectives
Cross-border global teams with debriefing	Learn skills to be a better leader (or team member) with multiple cultures involved in the team
Global meetings with debriefing or coaching	Learn skills to conduct a better meeting when multiple cultures are involved in the meeting
International assignment rotations with debriefing or coaching	Develop a deep appreciation for the challenges of working in another culture; increase global leadership competence

Source: Caligiuri et al. (2005), p. 77

across the organization's whole international operations, as well as creating a need for the cross-national transfer of better HR practices such as performance appraisal. Notably, performance appraisal is the favoured way to ensure that strategic employee competencies, employee behaviour and motivation are performed effectively in the host country.

In Eastern Europe, following the collapse of the Soviet Union in 1991, the 'Washington Consensus' dominated the ideology of most newly elected governments. This was the ideology of wide-scale privatization, deregulation and free markets, all promoted by the International Monetary Fund and the World Bank. The new dominant ideology and the orientation towards the EU urged Eastern European managers into new roles requiring increased autonomy and performance appraisal (Koubek and Brewster, 1995; Prokopenko, 1994). According to Shibata (2002), in Asia, when the Japanese 'bubble economy' collapsed in the 1990s, Japanese companies began to be attracted to the performance appraisal systems that had long been found in North American business organizations. Chou's (2005) study examines the implementation of performance appraisal in the civil service in China in the 1990s. It is suggested that changes occurred to improve personnel practices and government capacity in both central and local government.

How far does performance appraisal in an international context resemble the Anglo-American model and practice? Performance appraisal is a political activity. It is about gathering relevant information on an employee's competencies and behaviour; about making judgements on a subordinate's work effort, the level of reward and career paths; about motivation (being inspired by positive appraisal) – and in some cases it involves termination of employment. To perform successfully in a host country, a manager requires technical skills, interpersonal skills, adaptability and cultural sensitivity. Expatriate performance in an international context is, however, affected by volatility in the international environment (for example, fluctuating currency exchange rates), which is outside the expatriate's scope of control, and by cultural and political factors inside the host country (for example, acts of terrorism).

The complexity of the task is compounded by differences in societal values. For example, Chou (2005) found that Anglo-Saxon-style performance appraisal was undermined in China because of the collectivist, relationship-oriented or 'Communist neo-traditionalism' sociopolitical culture. The study found that many managers 'manipulated appraisal results' and refrained from rating subordinates' performance as 'unsatisfactory' because of the importance placed on a 'reciprocal relationship and organizational harmony' (Chou, 2005, p. 54). The evidence suggests that the internationalization of performance appraisal demands sensitivity to different cultural and sociopolitical experiences. This section also illustrates that the cross-national transfer of Anglo-Saxon HR practices for selection, rewards, training and appraisal will require some degree of cultural sensitivity, as well as consultation with HCNs about local suitability (Mabey et al., 1998b).

HRM web links Further information on Geert Hofstede's work on *Culture's Consequences* can be found at www.vectorstudy.com. In addition, for a summary and critique of Hofstede's work, go to http://geert-hofstede.international-business-center.com/mcsweeney.shtml.

reflective question If you were an expatriate, how would you feel about returning to your old position in the company after 5 years working at one of the company's overseas subsidiaries? Can you think of any problems you would encounter on your return to your parent country and company?

Repatriation

Much of the early research on IHRM focuses on expatriates returning to the parent company – repatriation. The foremost reason for a premature return or an ineffective international assignment is a failure of the expatriate and his or her family to adapt to the new setting (Fischlmayr and Kollinger, 2010). In the context of strategic IHRM discussed in this chapter, managing expatriates or 'flex-patriates' (Mayerhofer et al., 2004) returning to the parent company may be the least of the challenges facing a global manager, as our opening chapter statement on events in the Middle East testifies. Nonetheless, for many MNCs, the failure to repatriate managers successfully has caused many expatriates to resign from the company owing to what has been termed re-entry shock.

The complexity of the repatriation problem varies from individual to individual. Linehan and Mayrhofer (2005) point out that a violation of the psychological contract may lead to a negative psychological reaction to repatriation. Anecdotal and empirical evidence of re-entry shock indicates that loss of autonomy, loss of status and loss of career opportunities, together with problems of family members readjusting to the parent culture, are often relevant (Adler, 1994; Brewster and Scullion, 1997; Dowling et al., 1999; Fischlmayr and Kollinger, 2010; Linehan and Mayrhofer, 2005; Mayerhofer et al., 2004; Suutari and Brewster, 2003). Recent expatriate research has shown that HR managers need to develop a formal and informal mentorship system to help expatriates cope with social isolation abroad and assist in balancing expatriate work–life relationships. This is especially the case for female expatriates, given the fact that they in general invest more time in family activities (Fischlmayr and Kollinger, 2010). Even before the attacks on the World Trade Center in New York in 2001 and the revolts in North Africa in 2011, MNCs had begun to experience difficulty attracting managers to accept overseas assignments. The security issue will be an additional contributing factor in this reluctance to go abroad.

The convergence/divergence debate

A common theme in the comparative HRM literature has been 'convergence' and 'divergence' in HR practices, resulting from globalization, in different regions of the world. Historically, orthodox economists have held the belief that unfettered flows of international trade would allow rich and poor economies eventually to converge to similar levels of per capita income, as capital investment would migrate from developed economies, where it would be abundant and returns limited, to developing economies, where capital would be scarce and returns higher. This convergence process should also, according to prevailing management wisdom, result in a convergence of national business environments, including HR practices, towards homogeneity. The power of capital from the parent country, and the weakness and 'receptiveness' of the subordinate host country both underscore notions of how globalization creates uniformity in national business patterns (Rowley and Bae, 2002).

The major challenge to a universal vision of order, equilibrium and convergence arises from local rationalities, local realities, local ideologies and local culture (Clegg et al., 1999; Whitley, 1999). Evidence of continued diversity in local or national patterns of economic activity and employment relations has contributed to the notion of 'varieties of capitalism' (see Hall and Soskice, 2001; Hancke, 2009). Within the 'varieties of capitalism' literature, academics have highlighted the importance of national culture, national economic and political conditions, institutions and historical legacies that substantially shape employment relations (Bryson and Frege, 2010). For Whitley (1999, p. 3), although the global economy continues to be more interconnected, 'societies with different institutional arrangements will continue to develop and reproduce varied systems of economic organization with different economic and social capabilities in particular industries and sectors'.

We therefore go back to a key question in comparative HRM, that of convergence. Is there evidence of convergence in the different trajectories of HR practices within Europe towards a 'European model' of HRM? Drawing upon the data from a 3-year survey of 14 European countries, Chris Brewster, an authoritative observer of European HRM, puts forward the notion of a new 'European HRM model' that recognizes state and trade union involvement in the regulation of the employment relationship. Brewster contends that the European HRM model has a greater potential for 'partnership' between labour and management because, in most EU states, 'the unions are not seen, and do not see themselves, as "adversaries"' (Brewster, 1995, p. 323). The universal 'best practice' model is sustained by Gould-Williams and Mohamed's (2011) recent comparative study of the effects of 'best practice' HRM in Malaysia. Measuring employee perceptions of HR practice in Malaysian local government organizations, the data evince both positive and negative effects of a 'bundle' of HR practices, which 'supports the universal thesis' (p. 671). Others, however, have persuasively argued that, with the existence of distinct national contexts and cross-cultural differences, the notion of the 'universalist' assumption that Anglo-American HRM techniques are directly transferable is wrong (Elenkov, 1998).

Japanese CEO breaks stereotype by firing 14,000 staff

Japan's business system is the most advanced of those in the Asia-Pacific countries reviewed here. Research into traditional HR practices has usually emphasized six characteristics of Japanese employment relations: recruitment and selection, training, the lifetime employment contract, seniority-based rewards, the consensus decision-making process and enterprise trade unionism. The traditional Japanese approach HR so eulogized by Western managers is, of course, a simplistic and sanitized version of reality, as this report helps to illustrate:

Tomoyo Nonaka blew into Sanyo Electrical Co. as the space-cadet chief executive, a former TV anchorwoman with no management experience but lots of rhetoric about listening to the Earth. Yet the New Age CEO's first act atop the troubled electronics giant smacks of Old Age realism: Sanyo will cut 15 per cent of its workforce of 14,000 jobs. Ms. Nonaka, 50, one of the most off-the-wall CEO choices in Japanese corporate history, cloaked the layoffs and factory closings in her trademark mystical language. 'Sanyo will become the company that will listen to the Earth's voice and will please the Earth instead of polluting it,' she said. Ms. Nonaka said the restructuring plan, described by Sanyo as 'Think Gaia' – a reference to the Greek goddess of the Earth – would include greater focus on 'ecological co-existence solutions.' The company also unveiled four programs to realize its new vision: Sanyo Blue Planet, Sanyo Genesis III, Sanyo Harmonious Society, and Sanyo Product Circulation. Observers say Ms. Nonaka's move this year from outside director to Sanyo's CEO is an extreme case of the current appetite for fresh faces to shake up Japan's underperforming companies, instead of the usual line-up of middle-aged Japanese men.

Critical workplace scholars have challenged different aspects of the Japanese HRM model, particularly in the context of globalized capitalism. Relevant here is Whittaker's (1990) study that notes that one of the 'pillars' of Japanese employment – 'lifetime employment' – is highly selective and, where it does exist, excludes part-time, short-term or peripheral workers. Others have noted that, since the 1997 financial crisis, Japanese companies have found it difficult to maintain lifetime employment security and the *nenko* automatic pay increase system (see, for example, Benson, 1996). HRM is universal in the sense that every employer has to manage, in some way, people. However, the practice of HRM varies within and across borders.

Stop! Is this case an example of the destructive 'strategic tension' between global corporations that promote the 'low road' to profitability? Does it provide evidence of the persistence of capitalist employment relations or of a 'convergence' HRM practices? Is there evidence of HRM models converging and, if so, towards which model?

Sources and further information: The extract is taken from Gordon Pitts' article 'CEO's harmonious-society plan? Fire 14,000 staff' (Pitts, 2005). For an analysis of the 2007–08 financial meltdown and its impact on employment relations, see the article 'Money, markets, meltdown' (Nolan, P., 2011).

Note: This feature was written by John Bratton.

©istockphoto.com/Nikada

In the same vein, Clark and Pugh (2000) argue that, despite economic pressures towards convergence, strikingly resilient differences in cultural and institutional contexts produce divergent employment relationships. For example, the 'feminine' culture of The Netherlands encourages the antipathy of Dutch workers toward 'hard' HRM, whereas 'Sweden's strong collectivist culture counters the development of an individualistic orientation to the employment relationship' (Clark and Pugh, 2000, p. 96). Following on from the notion of diversity in national business systems, more reflective observers are increasingly acknowledging that the issues of convergence and divergence in European HRM need 'more careful nuance than has been the case hitherto', and European national institutional patterns are so variable that 'no common model is likely to emerge in the foreseeable future' (Brewster, 2001, p. 268). Thus, cross-national research suggests that national conceptions of better HRM practices remain dominant (Sparrow et al., 2004).

Similarly, studies suggest that there is a considerable divergence of HR practices in Asian economies. Prominent HRM academic Malcolm Warner speaks of a process of 'soft convergence' towards Western-style HR practices in Asia-Pacific economies (Warner, 2002). Paik et al.'s (1996) findings provide strong support for the divergence hypothesis even among the Chinese culture-based countries of Hong Kong, Singapore and Taiwan. Contrary to the convergence hypothesis underpinning globalization, the idea that 'best' HR practices have 'universal' application is untenable when the HRM phenomenon embodies a different national institutional profile and cultural milieu. In the world's third largest economy, China, there have been noteworthy shifts away from the 'iron rice bowl' system to a more 'market-responsive' system of employment relations. Yet, as Hassard et al. (2004) conclude, this is somewhat removed from the HRM ideal-type model. At best, it is argued, globalization may be causing an increasing degree of 'relative convergence' across 'regional clusters' such as China, South Korea and Japan, resulting from globally driven market forces (Rowley et al., 2004). This relative convergence, however, 'is not necessarily towards some *sui generis* model of Asian HRM' (Warner, 2004, p. 620).

Inherent in controversies surrounding the notion of a 'European model' or an 'Asian model' of HRM are questions of the limitations and value of cross-national generalizations in HRM (Hyman, 1994). The theory of a universal model of HRM (which often is interpreted as meaning an Anglo-American model of HRM) is challenged by national rationalities, national institutional settings and national, regional and local cultures. HRM varies between countries, by sector, by size and by ownership of the work organization.

Does globalization bring into being a convergence of HR practices? To address this conundrum, we have drawn on Rowley and Bae's (2002) model (Figure 15.3). The two dimensions in Rowley and Bae's framework are the unit of analysis – *country* versus *organization* – and the foci – *practices* versus *people*. Changes in HR practices within the organization are mediated by environmental changes and universal 'best practices'. However, the framework draws attention to 'gaps' between universalism versus national culture, and HR practices newly adopted versus the organizational culture or the 'shared mindset' of people in the workplace. For example, the change from a regulated to a more market-driven form of capitalism in China, India and Singapore with greater flexibility and unemployment would provide a cultural shock for the nationals of these countries.

Different national institutional systems, which comprise laws, frames of reference and core values and norms, can explain 'divergence' between the parent and host local establishments. Brewster (2001) makes a strong case that the likelihood of a common HRM model emerging in the foreseeable future is remote because the idiosyncratic national

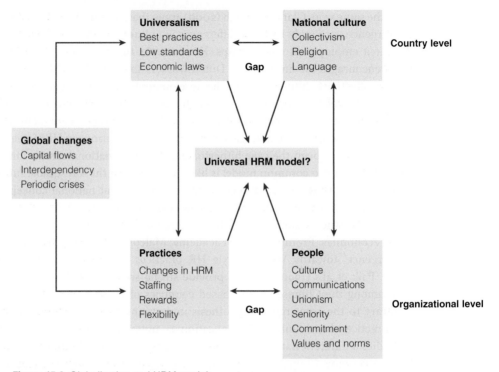

Figure 15.3 *Globalization and HRM models*
Source: *Adapted from Rowley and Bae (2002), p. 543*

institutional settings are so variable in HNCs. Sanford Jacoby (2005) argues the case for a persistence of varieties of capitalism and employment management practices. In Japan, for example, institutions are more closely embedded in social relations and shared social values than they are in the USA. Consequently, institutional change to facilitate movements towards US-inspired market-oriented HR practices and employment management has been slow in Japan.

Similarly, Rowley and Bae (2002) engage in the convergence/divergence debate by pointing out the gap between changes in HR practices and what they call the 'shared mindset' of managers and workers. Successful transfer, it is argued, depends upon two processes:

- The '*implementation*' of the HR practices, whereby workers in the recipient organization change their observable behaviours in respect of the transferred practice
- The '*internalization*' of the HR practices, whereby people fully accept and approve the practices.

The gaps therefore reflect a failure to inculcate HR practices with embedded core 'values'. Thus, 'even if there are "best practices", they would not bring positive effects until people fully accepted and approved them,' assert Rowley and Bae (2002, p. 544).

A further challenge to convergence is the significant cultural and subcultural differences in the way in which people communicate. According to Guirdham (2011), these differences include, but are not limited to, communication styles, non-verbal communication, communication rules, politeness and conversation constraints. For example, one communication style or trait is assertiveness – putting forward one's own rights without hampering other individuals' rights – which has been advocated in Western societies as a way for women and members of visible minorities to communicate, especially with people who are inclined to 'put them down'. Assertiveness is culturally specific, and what is assertive and acceptable in one society is aggressive and unacceptable in another (Guirdham, 2011).

Limited evidence exists that explores the importance of the social and communication support that HCNs may provide to expatriates. Without HCN support, a social schism within the MNC may be created because the expatriate manager is deaf in the HCNs' language and blind in their culture. As social 'outsiders', expatriates may find it difficult to understand the unit's organizational culture (see Chapter 5). Thus, business stories about the unit's 'ways of doing' get lost in translation, organizational rituals and values lose their resonance, and narratives flounder, without deep respect for language, the symbolic web we call culture.

Sparrow et al. (2004) note that there is no reason why some aspects of employment relations and HR practices could not exhibit signs of convergence (decentralized collective bargaining), whereas others would show signs of divergence (trade union density). The gaps between the 'universal' logic of change and HR practices and embedded national business systems problematize any grand narrative on the conversion to either European or Asian models of HRM and their efficacy. Reflecting on the status of women in the developing countries on the 100-year anniversary of International Women's Day, Stephanie Nolan (Nolan, S., 2011) reminds us of the silent majority of the world's women who remain mired in the struggle for the most basic human rights. Moreover, proponents of the notion of the 'universal logic' of change should understand the position of the majority of women in the developing world, where 'There is a universality to sexual harassment, to sexual violence, to the struggle for reproductive rights' (Nolan, S., 2011, p. A14).

With regard to the debate over convergence versus divergence in HRM, the universality phenomenon is by its very nature complex and the 'stream' of evidence exploring the transferability of HR practices from one societal context to another is inconclusive. Chris Brewster captured the inconclusiveness when he summarised the convergence/divergence debate and concluded (2007, p. 212):

Those looking to defend one position or another can easily find evidence to support their case. Thus, there do seem to be trends ... that are widespread, even if they do not seem to be diminishing the differences between the countries in the way they manage their HRM.

Understanding the disjuncture between universal theory and idiosyncratic national institutions and cultures becomes a key competency of the global manager. Although the debate remains equivocal, we can be more confident in affirming that the study of IHRM is no longer a marginal area of interest. Increasingly, as the globalization of world markets continues apace, global managers will be expected to undertake overseas assignments, and IHRM and comparative HRM research will be an important resource for training expatriate managers (Budhwar and Boyne, 2004).

For students of HRM, the highly dynamic, complex and political nature of the global–local issue affirms the need for an international network of academics to undertake intensive collaborative research. The lessons for managers of recent comparative HRM research are to avoid generalizations of trends towards convergence or continued diversity, and to adopt a more nuanced cross-cultural approach to managing people. This approach needs to abandon the 'global template' (Rowley et al., 2004, p. 930) and recognize that the highly complex processes of managing people across borders frequently contains elements of both convergence and national diversity, as well as being shaped by the contingent requirements of management's 'strategic choice' (Quintanilla and Ferner, 2003).

ICAN

Setting

ICAN, established in 1972 in Finland by Vesa Stroh, has experienced considerable growth since Finland joined the EU in the 1990s, to become one of the largest manufacturers of home furnishings in the EU. The parent company is located in Tampere and employs 1750 employees made up of skilled and semi-skilled workers. Two hundred and thirty employees work in design and development and other highly skilled areas. All the employees belong to one trade union. The company has a profit-sharing scheme and an excellent pension scheme.

Since 1972, ICAN has sold a basic range of typically 'Scandinavian' home furnishings in six stores, only one of which – in Helsinki – is inside Finland. The company remains primarily production-oriented, its Finnish management and design group deciding what it is going to manufacture in the most cost-effective way and then how it will sell it to the European homeowner, often with very little market research outside Finland. The company has emphasized its Finnish roots in its European advertising, including the adoption of the colours blue and white, from the Finnish national flag, for its retail outlets and advertising material.

The foundation of ICAN's success has been to offer consumers good value for money, distinctive branding and a good network of suppliers. A supplier for ICAN gains long-term contracts and leased equipment from the company. In return, ICAN demands an exclusive contract and low prices. ICAN's expatriate managers seconded to the subsidiary standardize products and integrate production to gain maximum savings on the final products at a low cost. ICAN sells its avant-garde furniture to customers as self-assembly kits. In this way, the company reaps economies of scale from the large production runs. In 2000, only 13 per cent of its sales were generated in Finland, the balance coming from Germany (33 per cent), Sweden (22 per cent), The Netherlands (11 per cent) and the UK (21 per cent). This strategy allows ICAN to match its competitors on quality but undercut them by up to 30 per cent on price, while maintaining an after-tax return on sales of around 7 per cent.

The problem

In 2010, ICAN decided to establish a factory in Montreal and two retail stores in Canada, followed by

ICAN sells its avant-garde furniture to customers as self-assembly kits.

six in the USA. The Canadian subsidiary was built on a green-field site on the east side of Montreal and employed 320 employees by the end of 2011. Informed that trade union density in Canada was well below that of Finland, expatriate managers were told that unionization was a 'non-issue' and that the company's profit-sharing scheme, similar to the Finnish scheme, would ensure employee loyalty and commitment. The production side of the business was meeting output targets. Preliminary reports, however, indicated that the new North American retail stores were not meeting sales and profit targets as planned. Finnish home furnishings, which sold well in Western Europe, clashed with Canadian and US tastes and sometimes physiques. In addition, the new Canadian factory was experiencing quality control problems and some challenges in managing the workforce.

Vesa Engeström, the factory manager, called a meeting of the Canadian management team. Yrjö Alvesson, an experienced Finnish marketing manager, gave the first presentation to the assembled ICAN managers. He explained that sales had not reached expected targets because the standard furniture did not meet North American tastes and preferences. He said, for example, 'Our Finnish kitchen cupboards are too narrow to take large dinner plates needed for pizza. And our beds are too narrow for American preferences.'

Christian Poikela, the HR manager at the Canadian subsidiary, explained that some of the Canadian managers resented the degree of control exerted over how they managed their units. In addition, he had heard through various managers and supervisors that some employees had been overheard talking about 'bringing in a union' to achieve higher wages. Jonathan Pyrch, one of three Canadian-born and Canadian-educated managers present at the meeting, interjected at this point and said, 'The union isn't the problem; it's poor communications. Many staff can't understand the expatriate managers! I've heard that shop-floor supervisors leave their encounters with Finnish managers feeling frustrated by their inability to understand and relate to them.' Poikela also said that shop-floor staff were reluctant to work at weekends. 'The fact that Quebec, like the other provinces in Canada, has its own labour relations statutes makes dealing with Canadian unions more difficult and frustrating, especially if we open a factory in Calgary,'

he added. What legal rights do unions have in this province, asked Engeström? 'I'm unsure, but I'll investigate', replied Poikela.

Assignment

Given the pressures facing ICAN in the marketplace, prepare a written report to Christian Poikela:

1 Explaining how ICAN can be both competitive and locally responsive, and detailing why ICAN's SIHRM orientation should be linked to its international business strategy and what this would mean for the role of the HRM department at ICAN's Canadian subsidiary
2 Explaining the types of competency you feel the managers at the Canadian subsidiary need, and whether expatriate or local managers can supply these competencies.

Note: This case was written by John Bratton.

WWW Visit the companion website at www.palgrave.com/business/bratton5 for guidelines on writing reports.

---

summary

◀ In this chapter, we explored how global corporations typically face tension from two types of business pressure: on the one hand, pressures for global cost reductions and rationalization, and on the other hand, demands for differentiation and local responsiveness.

◀ We also discussed how IHRM is closely tied to international business strategies and briefly explained four fashionable business strategies – global, multidomestic, international and transnational – as solutions to the dual pressure for cost-efficiencies and responsiveness.

◀ The chapter explained that the driving force behind the growth of interest in SIHRM and IHRM is the resurgence of neo-liberalism and the growth in global markets. Critics argue that globalization has created the new international division of labour, causing the transfer from old industrialized regions of high-wage manufacturing jobs to low-wage developing economies.

◀ An integrative model explored how IHRM should be explicitly linked to the global business strategy of the MNC and how its changing forms must be understood in relation to the strategic evolution of the MNC.

◀ We discussed how the cross-national transfer of Anglo-Saxon HR practices will require some degree of cultural sensitivity, as well as consultation with HCNs about local suitability.

◀ We discussed how variations in national regulatory systems, the labour markets and cultural and polyethnic contexts are likely to constrain or shape any tendency towards 'convergence' or a 'universal' model of 'better' HR practice. The sheer variation of capitalist economies and cultures makes claims for convergence both simplistic and problematic.

◀ Finally, in this chapter, it has been easier to formulate questions than answers, and we have taken the easier rather than the more difficult route. Yet there is value in asking questions. Questions can stimulate reflection and increase our understanding of IHRM. Our object here has been to do both.

vocab checklist for ESL students

◀ adaptive orientation (n)

◀ centralize (v), centralization (n), central (adj)

◀ converge (v), convergence (n)

◀ differentiate (v), differentiation (n), different (adj)

◀ diverge (v), divergence (n)

◀ endogenous (adj)

◀ exogenous (adj)

◀ expatriate (v), expatriate (n)

◀ exportive orientation (n)

◀ global capitalism (n)

◀ globalize (v), globalization (n), global (adj)

◀ host country national (HCN) (n)

◀ integrative orientation (n)

◀ interdepend (v), interdependence (n), interdependent (adj)

◀ internationalize (v), internationalization (n), international (adj)

◀ multidomestic strategy (n)

◀ neo-liberal (adj), neo-liberalism (n)

◀ repatriate (v), repatriate (n), repatriation (n)

◀ strategic international human resource management (SIHRM) (n)

◀ transnationalize (v), transnationalization (n), transnational (adj)

Visit www.palgrave.com/business/bratton5 for a link to free definitions of these terms in the Macmillan Dictionary, as well as additional learning resources for ESL students.

review questions

1 What is meant by SIHRM and IHRM?

2 Explain how MNCs address the tension between the dual imperatives of global integration and local responsiveness.

3 Discuss how differences in national institutional systems influence a corporation's decision to locate its profit-making operations.

4 Explain how a need for rationalization and standardization over foreign operations varies with the business strategy and distinctive competencies of an MNC.

5 How, if at all, can studying anthropology help us understand the highly dynamic and complex nature of IHRM?

further reading to improve your mark

Reading these articles and chapters can help you gain a better understanding and potentially a higher grade for your HRM assignment.

◀ For an introduction to the issues of globalization, see B. Hancke (ed.) (2009) *Debating Varieties of Capitalism: A Reader*. Oxford: OUP.

◀ For more specialized texts in IHRM, refer to P. J. Dowling, M. Festing and D. Engle Allen (2008) *International Human Resource Management* (5th edn). London: Thomson Learning.

◀ G. K. Stahl and I. Björkman (eds) (2006) *Handbook of Research in International Human Resource Management*. Cheltenham: Edward Elgar.

◀ H. Scullion and M. Linehan (2005) *International Human Resource Management. A Critical Text* (2nd edn). Basingstoke: Palgrave Macmillan.

◀ A. Farazmand (2002) Privatization and globalization: a critical analysis with implications for public management education and training. *International Review of Administrative Sciences*, 68: 355–71, is an interesting analysis of globalization, with particular reference to privation and its impact on management and host countries.

further reading to improve your mark

◀ Ashish Mahajan's (2011) article, Host country national's reactions to expatriate pay policies: making a case for a cultural alignment pay model. *International Journal of Human Resource Management*, **22**(1): 121–37, examines global pay systems.

◀ Morris, J., Wilkinson, B. and J. Gamble's (2009) article, Strategic international human resource management or the 'bottom line'? The case of electronics and garments commodity chains in China. *International Journal of Human Resource Management*, **20**(2): 348–71, argues that HR practices in MNCs can best be understood in the context of worldwide commodity chains. Arguably, much of the case for cultural alignment can be made for other HR practices.

◀ Brewster, C. (2007) HRM: the comparative dimension. In John Storey (ed.) *Human Resource Management: A Critical Text* (3rd edn) (pp. 197–214). London: Thompson Learning. This chapter examines the pivotal argument in IHRM of whether there is a convergence of management practices. It underscores idiosyncratic national institutional settings and the need to separate out policy from practice.

 Visit www.palgrave.com/business/bratton5 for lots of extra resources to help you get to grips with this chapter, including study tips, HRM skills development guides, summary lecture notes, and more.

chapter **16**

recession, sustainability, trust: the crisis in HRM

objectives

After studying this chapter, you should be able to:

1 Describe the different ways in which the preceding chapters relate to one another

2 Judge the professional standing of those practising human resource management (HRM)

3 Understand the post-crisis debate on HRM and pedagogy

4 Explain the need for a critical analytical approach to studying HRM

introduction

For nearly three decades, the term 'human resource management' (HRM) has been used to frame issues related to managing the employment relationship, and frequently as a contrast to 'personnel management'. We started this journey into contemporary HRM by examining its history and examining some of the theoretical models used in its study. It was acknowledged that all activity concerning employer–employee relations, whether termed HRM or personnel management, involves cooperation and conflict, creativity and indeterminacy, and contradiction and paradox.

In Part I of the book, we emphasized that the mainstream HRM discourse views the workforce as the most important asset for generating value, increasingly through the creation of knowledge, which gives organizations either a potential, sustainable competitive advantage or superior services. We pointed out that, starting from this premise, the decisions and practices of HRM impact on strategic goals and need to be integrated into the organization's strategy. We examined the pressure to evaluate the contribution of HRM and the growing body of research that seeks to measure the HRM–performance relationship.

In Part II, we emphasized that a range of external and internal contextual factors impact on and shape the design of work and work systems, including pressure to create more sustainable work practices and reduce workplaces' carbon footprints. In Parts III and IV, we examined and evaluated a range of human resources (HR) practices used to attract, develop and maximize the inherent potential of the workforce, including their leaders and managers. In Part V, we described and evaluated HR practices that seek to motivate, to secure commitment and compliance, to promote safe and healthier workplaces, and to address the collective aspects of employment relations. Finally, in Part VI, we examined how HRM has become the favoured discourse to frame developments in globalized employment and HR practices.

The purpose of this final chapter is to reflect on the major landmarks visited along this journey, to consider why a practice perspective on HRM is needed, and to explore how HRM education can become more relevant by advancing critical reflective pedagogy.

Post-crisis recession and sustainability

In the words of that memorable Bob Dylan ballad, 'The times they are a-changin''. Since 1994, when the first edition of *Human Resource Management: Theory and Practice* was published, the pace and magnitude of change in the world seems to have been phenomenal. The first half-decade of the new millennium was marked by unsettling events and crises: the attack on the World Trade Center in New York, fraudulent accounting practices, the dot-com collapse and the invasion of Iraq. By the end of the decade, we witnessed a banking crisis that triggered a global economic recession. As in the Great Depression of 1929–33, the epicentre of this financial and economic earthquake, the biggest for generations, was the USA. Although there were early warnings from the US subprime mortgage crisis in September 2007, the financial bubbles on the stock markets of the USA and the UK began to burst in 2008, and the effects are still vibrating in southern member states of the European Union and worldwide. The cyclical boom of 1992–2007 was built on the speculative real-estate market that was itself lubricated by subprime mortgages, high levels of personal indebtedness and self-deluding optimism.

The quintessential corporate executives of the 1990s were trumped as visionaries, leaders who could think 'outside the box' and were not averse to risk-taking. Today, financial bail-outs of banks by US and UK governments and record indebtedness have sapped public trust in corporate leadership, caused speculation that the City's overtly 'macho culture' encourages unrestrained risk-taking (Rigby and Parker, 2011), and raised serious questions about the way in which society as a whole is organized and about changed expectations of the role of government. Cumulatively, recent events have shown that, in times of crisis, capitalism depends on society, which is why the language among social elites in the City of London and New York of 'too big to fail' simply means 'so big that they can depend on society (that is, tax-payers) to prop them up when they topple' (Patel, 2009, p. 19).

©istockphoto.com/Alvin Burrows

Too big to fail? London's financial district, Canary Wharf, has become an iconic image of a risk-taking corporate mentality.

French President Nicolas Sarkozy's call for the 'moralization' of the capitalist system perhaps best captured the new political consensus (Bratton et al., 2010). At least the moment was a powerful rhetorical symbol of the intellectual and political failure of the Anglo-Saxon market fundamentalism version of capitalism, characterized by far-reaching deregulation and the 'hollowing-out' of government responsibilities and services. Currently, most of the world's developed economies are in an economic abyss and, and, with talk of a 'double-dip' recession (Elliott, 2011; Milne, 2011) and 'jobless recovery', the current economic slump is by far the worst since 1945.

As if that were not enough, as we write this new edition, we have seen the equivalent of the 1917 Russian Revolution as pro-democracy revolts have swept across Tunisia, Egypt, Yemen, Libya, Bahrain and Syria – the Arab Spring. And against this backdrop of economic and political change, with lingering worries over debt restructuring in southern Europe, we witnessed in 2011 a devastating earthquake and tsunami followed by a nuclear disaster in Japan equivalent to the worst nuclear catastrophes in modern times that had occurred in Three Mile Island, USA, and Chernobyl, Ukraine. Mainstream analysis of occupational health and safety is concerned with the design and maintenance of a work environment that supports the organization's objectives and promotes the well-being of employees. Less obvious perhaps, but no less substantial, is the connection between sustainable work systems, healthy workplaces, and healthy communities and ecosystems. That sustainable work systems, healthy communities and ecosystems are inextricably linked is no better illustrated than by the explosions at the Fukushima nuclear plant in north-eastern Japan.

It is too early to judge the full ramifications of the discourse on 'greening' the economy, sustainable work systems and 'green' HRM. Most obviously, a new alliance may develop between workplace trade unionism and community environmentalism, an alliance that is committed to developing collective insight into the connections between unsustainable workplace practices, the degradation of local and global ecosystems, and cancers and ill-health in society at large. Jobs versus ecosystem survival has often framed debates between the trade union and environmental movements. But it seems evident that both the goals of a low-carbon sustainable economy and the nuclear catastrophe in Japan require a conceptual rethinking of sustainability and environmental management (Mayer, 2009; Storey, 2004).

As we have explained in several chapters, environmental destruction has become a major concern for all humankind, and sustainability is an opportunity for new ventures and employment. In Chapter 2, we discussed how a transformation towards a 'green' economy means that three things must happen: society needs to do things more efficiently in order to waste less; it needs to pollute less; and it needs to start valuing natural resources and our ecosystems in terms of their true contribution to the economy. Orthodox economics treats ecosystems as a means to an end, capital accumulation, and therefore in economic terms they are without value, and get used and abused in a way that does not sustain the economy. In essence, a green economy means that society finds ways to 'uncouple our economic growth from the way we consume and pollute' (Steiner, 2011). In the face of accelerating globalization and shifting economic and environmental realities, a coherent vision for a sustainable economy is not optional, but whether leaders and managers are capable of responding remains to be seen (Haden et al., 2009).

The immediacy of current events can easily distract us from more persistent trends in employment management. Work configurations and employment practices cannot be uncoupled from national and global contexts. Thus, although the monumental failure of management in a deregulated system has put some aspects of business and management practices into a sharper relief and under scrutiny, the core attributes of work and how the employment relationship is managed remain unchanged. The attributes have been there since the era of globalization – the 1990s – and we examined them in previous editions: the growth of non-standard or precarious employment, downsizing, the decline in trade union power and influence, inequity, deregulation and consequential work intensification.

We emphasized in the fourth edition that employers and managers operate within a wider institutional, cultural and social context, and that changing business and manage-ment practices requires a fundamental change in organizational context and culture. With regard to reports of highly unethical behaviour, the solution does not lie in removing 'a few bad apples' but in changing the way organizations are regulated by government, changing the way managers are compensated, and changing the values that ultimately prevail in society. And, of course, with regard to environmental destruction, of funda-mental significance is the essential irrationality of capitalism's pursuit of profit, which subordinates everything to orthodox 'growth'. Terry Eagleton writes in his *Why Marx Was Right* (2011) that the two great threats to human survival are military and environmental. In the future, they are increasingly likely to converge as conflicts over finite resources escalate into military conflicts.

We believe that the solution to the economic and environmental problems caused by the Anglo-Saxon economic model lies in fundamental changes to the system. Indeed, few serious mainstream public policy analysts hold the US up as a role model (Simpson, 2011). This is not, however, to underestimate the management roots of the global crisis. North American and UK business schools are partly to blame for the global crisis and are complicit in environmental destruction. For the most part, they have been uncritical advo-cates and 'cheer-leaders' of the 'neo-liberal' Anglo-Saxon model, and they ultimately have a responsibility for educating a new cadre of managers who can help to change the system. Moreover, the discredited neo-liberal economic consensus has proven to be a recipe for social injustice and environmental disaster.

With regard to the former, as we noted in Chapter 11, the gender pay gap is still obsti-nately wide, and the 'new pay' agenda and the 'bonus culture' have contributed to pay inequality in society. The thesis that mainstream HRM is complicit in social injustice is illustrated by Terry Eagleton's (2011) acute observation that executives bemoan their annual bonuses falling below a million pounds, while one-third of children in Britain today lives below the poverty line. We hope to make a modest contribution to developing the type of learning that will make workplaces more effective in a variety of ways – more efficient, more ecologically sustainable, more satisfying, more equitable – and perhaps even help to forge more democratic workplaces through increased employee voice in the future. Through understanding that there is a crisis in HRM, we hope to contribute to a transformative pedagogy and learning.

The profession of HRM and trust

Professional recognition is highly valued in Western economies, and throughout the twentieth century, the number of people engaged in professional work has steadily increased. In the UK, for example, in 2000, we saw the creation of the Chartered Institute of Personnel and Development (CIPD), following an earlier merger between the Institute of Training and Development and the Institute of Personnel Management. The merger reflected an attempt to enhance the status of practitioners and espouse an approach to managing the employment relationship that we would call HRM. In addition, since 2003, professional status has been enhanced by individual members being awarded 'chartered' CIPD membership.

In Chapter 1, we discussed the change from 'personnel' to 'HRM'. To some, this change represented the use of a new label and emphasized the limited and piecemeal diffusion of the HRM style, with only islands of innovation in HRM. For others, the changes represented a transformation of how people could and should be managed at work. This set of perspectives emphasized strategic integration and the HR professional as a member of the senior management team, strategic planning and proactive management. It is the latter image that the CIPD seeks to promote, but what are the key elements of professional work and status? How do HR professionals match such requirements, and, after trumpeting the rhetoric 'People are our greatest asset', how is the current deep recession affecting issues of trust and the status of HRM?

According to Dietrich and Roberts (1997), the starting point for professional work is the existence of clients facing complex issues and problems related to decision-making complexity where such clients are 'incapable of pre-thinking all the issues involved with a decision because of the complexities involved' (p. 16). This provides for the economic bases of professionalism. Through their possession of specialist knowledge and skills, which is based on a particular kind of education and training, professionals make claims that they will help their clients to tackle and solve the problems they face. Continuing and successful practice allows a profession to acquire certain privileges that enhance its status and power. So how does HRM stack up?

In terms of representing a profession, HRM and its professional association, the CIPD, have clearly made significant advances in both the extent of influence of some of the main ideas and the size of the CIPD's membership. There remain, however, some interesting issues to consider with respect to HRM's professional status. For example, although the HRM profession may have made advances against others groups who lack professional status, there are still significant variations in status and authority within the professions, with those in HRM frequently finding their voices downgraded against those of other professionals such as accountants and lawyers. Abbott (1988, p. 9) has argued that the control of a profession 'lies in control of the abstractions that generate the practical techniques' and that:

Only a knowledge system governed by abstractions can redefine its problems and tasks, defend them from interlopers, and seize new problems.

What, then, is the nature of the abstractions in HRM?

Here it is useful to draw on the distinction made by Halliday (1987) between professionals who have technical authority relating to expertise in performing challenging tasks and providing specialized knowledge, and those with moral authority relating to the specification of norms that guide behaviour. It is argued that the 'exercise of moral authority in the name of expertise' is based on professional knowledge that is 'normative', with the consequence that 'its potential breadth of influence' is greater (p. 40). Thus, in many organizations, it is frequently those professions which provide moral authority that gain most influence and whose voices will be heard and proceed to dominate, for example corporate finance and law, even though their words are often disguised as technical advice. Crucially, however, others feel that they should acknowledge and accept such advice.

In contrast, HRM professionals in many organizations are less likely to command authority because they do not have sole control over the sources of professional knowledge and may rely on technical authority. HRM has sought to establish its status on semi-scientific grounds – often by resorting to a never-ending search for the latest techniques. However, because the profession does not have control over the sources of a unifying body of scientific knowledge and certifiable skills that would serve to define the differential distribution of power, HR expertise can be challenged by others inside the organization, thereby undermining both the professionalization and power of HR practitioners. In such a situation, HR practitioners face ongoing professional precariousness (Caldwell, 2001; Jacoby, 2004). In order to advance, HRM needs to develop the normative basis of its professional knowledge to provide a source of moral authority. The crucial issue here is whether HRM is moving in this direction given the perceived crisis in HRM.

The crisis in HRM

The crisis in HRM is occurring at two levels: internal and external. The internal crisis in the HRM field stems from the ambiguity and lingering doubts surrounding the empirical evidence of a causal path between HRM and performance. The second tier of crisis in HRM, the external, results from the post-crisis context and the subsequent impact on trust and the standing of HRM.

What we are calling here the internal crisis focuses around the question, 'Does HRM work?' This is more than a matter of polemics. Evidence that *better* HR practices can indeed contribute to the organization's performance, or in the private sector 'the bottom line', has fundamental implications for whether or not an organization should invest in HR interventions as well as for the HR profession itself. In Chapter 3, we examined the methodology and theory underpinning the research on the HRM–performance relationship, as well as assessing some of the evidence. First, at the level of practice, do those individuals with 'human resources' in their job title do anything different from personnel managers that might be considered an enhancement or a progression? Second, is there anything emerging contextually or theoretically that might help HR managers to improve their status in strategic discussions? Third, what is the experience of those on the receiving end of HR practices, that is, the employees and managers?

To start to answer these questions, let us first consider the use of different job titles. Specialist practitioners who are more qualified also accompany the growth in the number of organizations using 'human resources' within a job title, and have a greater involvement in the design of plans and situations in which employee development is more likely to feature in strategic plans. HRM is associated with more sophisticated practices such as personality testing, reward design, the use of attitude surveys, off-the-job training, union–management negotiations and conflict resolution. Thus, the difference between 'HR' and 'personnel' does seem to matter, and HR specialists have more credibility as professionals if these competences are demonstrated (Hoque and Noon, 2001).

Over the last decade, the route to demonstrating competencies has been principally through the business partner model of HRM, advocated by David Ulrich in the USA (1998) and developed into a recipe for adding value in HRM (Ulrich and Brockbank, 2005); this in turn has provided the basis for a model of business-focused transformation in HRM (Ulrich et al., 2009). Although Ulrich's original presentation suggested four roles for HR as strategic partner, change agent, administrative expert and employee champion, most interest has been directed at the first two roles, which together create a business partner role. This leaves the idea of employee champion, which involves attention to the well-being of staff, to line managers. However, research suggests that this is likely to become imbalanced, with most HR focus being on business issues, with the consequent neglect of staff issues (Francis and Keegan, 2006; Hope-Hailey et al., 2005). Furthermore, from the limited research on business partnering, it would seem that only limited success has been achieved due to the failure of HR managers to develop the appropriate skills needed for business, divisions among HR staff and a loss of trust by employees in HR (Griffin et al., 2009).

Moving to the second question above, the fact that part of the credibility for professionalism in HR might be concerned with an involvement in strategic planning will hearten many advocates of an HRM approach. Indeed, since its first appearance in the USA in the 1980s, the importance of a strategic connection and integration of key HR activities with strategy has been the distinguishing feature of mainstream HRM (Purcell, 2001). Since that time, a large body of research, as we examined in Chapter 3, appears to demonstrate that such a connection improves an organization's performance. For Delbridge and Keenoy (2010, p. 804), uncovering the connection between HR practices and performance is an 'ill-fated project'. However, such research is important in two ways with respect to the stature of HRM professionalism. First, the research that demonstrates a positive association between strategic HRM and organizational performance adds to a body of theoretical knowledge that provides the foundation for professional status. Second, such knowledge forms a repertoire of ideas and activities that serve to persuade others of the legitimacy of HRM.

To the extent that empirical evidence can demonstrate positive effects on organizational performance derived from strategic HR practices, HRM professionals are able to make claims about the efficacy of their involvement in strategic decision-making on the basis of their expertise, and from such expertise flows authority and status (Middlehurst and Kennie, 1997) – and the voice of HRM *should* be heard. However, it is widely acknowledged that the challenge of measuring the contribution of HR practices is somewhat mysterious and not always convincing. This is the internal crisis in HRM – demonstrating the causal path between HR practices and performance.

The CIPD as the professional body for HRM in the UK has sought to provide possible solutions to the conundrums faced by practitioners through its Shaping the Future research programme, with a focus on sustainable organizational performance (CIPD, 2011). Based on a case study methodology, the research was completed in six UK organizations from both the public and private sectors. At the same time, an online network of over 10,000 people was able to consider the issues as they emerged. Not surprisingly, the purpose of the research has been to inform practice, resulting in a list of themes for sustained organizational performance, such as leadership, shared purpose, engagement, assessment and evaluation, agility and capacity-building. These inform 10 'insights' that are considered to be 'unique' (p. 8) and are meant to inform practice. These include (CIPD, 2011, p. 12):

- The organization change response needs to be truly agile and enduring, not a knee-jerk reaction that quickly dissipates
- Collaborative leadership brings sustainability, so don't default to directive and driven when the going gets tough
- Truly understanding employees' locus of engagement can avoid the risk of over-attachment and underperformance.

Our view of these findings is that, like much of the research previously conducted by professional bodies in the people professions, the outcomes might move too quickly towards a generalization to other organizations that were not part of the research. What is particularly interesting about the research is that it was conducted in a collaborative fashion over 2 years, using action research; in our view, this gives significant attention to the development of practical knowledge in a cyclical process of research and action-taking based on what is of concern to the participants who are involved in the process (see Reason and Bradbury, 2001). However, we doubt that others can take advantage of the research without participating in their own projects. We also suspect that the participation of employees in such projects might be limited. To be fair to the CIPD (2011) research, the authors do provide a set of provocative questions against each insight. For example, the insight of 'understanding locus of engagement' referred to above carries the following questions (CIPD, 2011, p. 44):

- How meaningful is your measure of engagement?
- Have you got a handle on employees' locus of engagement? Are they engaged with their team, their customers, their line manager, their organization or something else?
- Don't be seduced by statistics: do you pay attention to the nuances when action planning?

reflective question How could HR professionals use such questions to set up their own action research process? You might want to check Jean McNiff's booklet on action research at www. jeanmcniff.com/ar-booklet.asp.

In recent years, claims that there is a strong association between HRM and organizational performance have been contested. Recent reviews of the current literature have identified that there are still serious gaps in our understanding with respect to what constitutes core 'HR practices' to be 'bundled', how these HR practices operate as a coherent, synergistic cluster, and the causal ordering of the variables involved in the HRM–performance relationship (Purcell and Kinnie, 2008). Furthermore, although it has been accepted that the HRM–performance linkage is positive, there are considerable gaps in our understanding with regard to 'other' causal mechanisms and mediating variables – the metaphorical HR 'black box' stage between HR practices and performance. In other words, there is ambiguity regarding 'what exactly leads to what' (Gerhart, 2005). Moreover, the analysis of the HRM–performance relationship within a 'contingent framework' – which proposes that HR practices influence performance in relation to contingent factors such as union–management relations (Edwards and Sengupta, 2010) – reminds us that positivist generalizations of the HRM–performance relationship are inappropriate.

Particularly galling for the HRM canon is the growing recognition that the HRM–performance relationship is better conceptualized as a complex, interdependent and mutually reinforcing causal mechanism. Conceptualizing the causal chain as a relational construct draws attention to the importance of power in the employer–employee relationship, and identifies first-line managers as key agents of change and potential champions (or spoilers) of HR policies, practices and programmes. It also draws attention to the importance of knowledge-based leadership among front-line employees rather than the traditional focus on traits and 'transformative' leaders. As the literature highlights, if the workplace is recognized as an arena of complex reciprocal human relations that are embedded in an organizational culture and national culture, strategic HRM is more appropriately configured not simply as a 'toolbox' from which a set of practices can deterministically improve performance, but rather as planned practices that *might* be enacted as envisioned. Thus, the existing literature calls for a more inclusive research agenda, one that is context-sensitive, and a wider definition of HRM that includes organizational culture, leadership and ethics.

As we have explained in the text, the employment relationship is shaped by national systems of employment legislation and the cultural contexts in which they operate. The widespread demonstrations in France in spring 2006 against precarious employment – '*Non à la Précarité!*' – and the general strikes in Greece and elsewhere in 2011 against government economic (mis)management affirm the centrality of societal effects on HR practices. If we are to understand the nature of employment management, we need to understand the social relations and the dynamics of the society in which it is embedded. Put another way, management and society are conjoined.

Owing to the pace and extended scope of globalization processes, the notion of embeddedness has become a universally accepted truth in critical HRM research. Longitudinal, more culturally informed and 'societal effects' studies of 'better practice' HRM are increasingly acknowledging that the universal application of 'better practice' needs more careful nuancing than has been the case hitherto, and that national conceptions of better HRM practices remain dominant (see, for example, Brewster, 2001; Jacoby, 2004; Sparrow et al., 2004). Contrary to the convergence hypothesis underpinning globalization, the idea that 'best' HR practices have 'universal' application is untenable when the HRM phenomenon is embedded in different national

John Bratton

This banner displayed by the Occupy Edinburgh group speaks to a widespread disillusionment with unregulated financial capitalism. Critical HRM contextualizes HR practices within the prevailing capitalist society.

institutional profiles with shared social values that are distinct from those in the US or UK. Different national institutional networks, which comprise laws, frames of reference, core values, communication styles and norms, can explain the 'divergence' between parent and host local companies, as can the disjuncture between 'best' HR practices and the 'shared mindset' of stakeholders.

Modelling the HRM–performance relationship becomes problematic when best practice and employment management are transferred to and embedded in a different social milieu. Moreover, given that potential conflict and active cooperation are both inherent in the employment relationship, together with differences in relative power, the capability of managers to create processes by which legitimate differences in stakeholder interests can be reconciled will determine the efficacy of HR practices. This is especially important given the multifaceted reality of corporate capitalism and the requirements of a public service sector in the context of significant budget reductions (see, for example, Dobbin, 2005; Konzelmann, 2005; Sako, 2005). Therefore, if researchers and HR practitioners wish to demonstrate the contribution of HRM to organizational performance, there is a need for more case study research that takes account of the 'societal effects' on HR practices as they are transplanted around the globe and translated locally into workable social relations.

Let us turn now to rhetoric and reality. One is an appealing but elusive favourite of consultants and prescriptive academics who legitimatize corporate management behaviour. The other is actual employee experiences of work and managerial actions, which are not always fulfilling and are often stressful. People who have spent some time in the contemporary workplace know that prescriptive HRM textbooks do not always reflect what reality is really like. Your feelings about what is real are nurtured by things you learn when you have employment experience. Appealing though studies of the HRM–performance relationship may be, the growing discrepancy between mainstream HRM theory and practice – the rhetoric and the reality – creates the second tier of crisis in HRM, the external, which arises from the economic crisis causing large-scale downsizing, this then impacting on trust and on the moral position of HRM professionals. The Oxford Dictionary says that if you 'trust' someone, you believe that they are honest and sincere and will not deliberately do anything to harm you. It has long been argued that employees' perceptions of trustworthiness are strongly influenced through HRM policies and practices. However, HRM often sits uncomfortably between the crucial economic exigencies of the organization and employees' needs. HRM professionals are therefore often tasked with designing and applying practices that have negative and trust-reducing 'outcomes' on employees.

A variety of studies have examined trust-reducing HRM practices. Mabey et al. (1998a), in a collection of case studies, argued that the voice of such recipients had been under-represented. And, as reviewed in previous chapters, 'progressive' HRM has been associated with work intensification (see, for example, Godard, 2004). Mabey et al. (1998a, p. 237) concluded that, 'many of [HRM's] prized goals … remain unproven at best, and unfulfilled at worst'. David Guest (1999) also sought to evaluate employees' experiences of HR practices, partly in response to criticisms from writers such as Karen Legge. His data suggested that progressive HR practices were consistent with positive outcomes such as feelings of fair treatment, although he acknowledged the limitations of survey data. As Nichols et al. (2002) observe, employee satisfaction surveys, claiming to reveal either positive or negative views of the work situation, are rating not simply management practices, but also how workers perceive their own work situation relative to their local economic position, constraints and opportunities: everything cannot be reduced to management techniques.

Our final point on trust-reducing outcomes concerns the problem of shareholder value-driven capitalism and corporate leadership and rewards. Although some have suggested that the greatest challenge facing HRM professionals is an internal issue – demonstrating to and convincing other managers that HR activities do contribute significantly to organizational goals – we would also agree with those observers who suggest that internal issues revolving around the use of stock options for chief executives, and rewards contingent upon meeting 'hard' short-term financial targets, are trust-reducing and serve to undermine HRM (Armstrong, 1987; Legge, 1995; Sisson and Storey, 2000; Storey, 1995b, 2001). In the aftermath of accounting-related scandals in some US and Italian companies, stock option abuses, self-obsessed CEOs and other nefarious activities, this issue is even more pressing. A resource-based approach to sustainable competitive advantage, one requiring a high-skilled, learning-orientated, high-performance workplace, is a long-term investment strategy (see Jacoby, 2004). As long as chief executives are either unable – due to shareholder pressures – or unwilling to invest in people because they have to meet short-term financial targets or wish to maximize their own inflated rewards from share options, there will still be limitations on the development and diffusion of high-performance practices designed to elicit employee cooperation and long-term commitment, and with it the ability to leverage human knowledge, creativity and skills.

In the context of a radically different economic environment and post-crisis critical reflection on management education, there is, we would suggest, a need to study more closely *how* and *why*, even in organizations that espouse HRM, there seem to be consistent barriers to progress that reinforce a lower status for HRM. Here, we advocate a move towards a practice perspective in HRM. Furthermore, the debate on 'reflexive critique' opens a window of opportunity to make this a transformative moment for raising the question of what constitutes critical, analytical HRM. Here, we advocate a move well beyond Ulrich et al.'s (2009) business-driven HR transformation towards what we call a transformative HRM pedagogy.

Towards a practice perspective in HRM

What do we mean when we advocate a practice perspective, and why do we do this? In recent years, in a number of management fields, partly in response to difficulty and contradiction in the research findings, there has been a growing interest in what happens in practice, that is, in the everyday processes and actions that occur. For example, there appears to be a thriving interest in how strategy is made and carried out in organizations, with the focus on activities that occur on a daily basis relating to strategic outcomes (see Jarzabkowsksi and Spee, 2009). In leadership, there is growing interest in how influence is exerted in practice and distributed throughout an organization, rather than being seen as the prerogative of a single individual (see, for example, Spillane, 2006). In workplace learning, increasing attention has been given to how learning occurs and how knowledge is constructed in practice (see, for example, Gold et al., 2007; Jakupec, 2000).

One of the appeals of a practice perspective in HRM is how the concern shifts from what is advocated by prescriptive HRM specialists through policies and procedures to what is actually done or not done, as the case may be. A practice perspective considers 'the conditions of intelligibility' (see Schatzki, 2001, p. 1) of organizational life and the taking of action. It also considers the conditions of emotional intelligence: a self-perceived ability to identify, appraise and control emotions in oneself, other employees and work teams. This inevitably requires access to the various organizational agents who are deemed to have responsibility for or are required to respond to HR interventions. Thus, a practice perspective implies a multivoiced approach to researching organizational life, and the methods employed in such studies have to take account of this feature. It is no use simply asking HR managers for their opinions – instead it is the practice that needs to be accessed.

Why is a practice perspective needed? As has been indicated above, the HRM project has had only partial success. Certainly, in some organizations, considerable research energy has been devoted to demonstrating how HR practices can engender high-performance working and high employee commitment. This is not, however, the case in most organizations, and repeated efforts to persuade such organizations of the need to follow in this direction seem to have fallen on deaf ears or have failed to meet expectations.

More troublesome, perhaps, is the fact that the mainstream HRM paradigm appears to be what *large* progressive work organizations do – or ought to do – with little relevance for understanding what is happening to work and employment management inside small and medium-sized enterprises (Delbridge and Keenoy, 2010). The reasons for this are multiple. First, research design tends to favour data collection in large organizations. Bratton (1992, p. 15) noted 'selection bias' and a tendency for 'the 'better-managed' and more 'successful' organizations to allow outside researchers to enter and conduct employee interviews. Another reason is often due to embedded cultural and historical factors that are manifest in daily interactions but often not fully appreciated by those present. For example, high-skill work is a key feature of the high-commitment ideal, yet there is a persistence of low-skill working that is accepted as the way to do work and little awareness that this may be holding back progress, or how and why this may be the case. Many other facets of HR practice may also face the same fate. The practice perspective is so necessary as it can reveal the apparent contradictions and tensions between what is stated and what is done under the heading of HRM.

At this point, we need to review what we have said about the nature of the employment relationship and address a number of issues that will help us to speculate on the future of HRM, while at the same time providing the reader with some analytical 'tools' for critically studying the HRM literature. Although transformation is a defining feature of modernity – from agriculture to manufacturing industries to service industries to the digital and low-carbon economy – the core characteristic of the capitalist employment relationship has not changed. As we first discussed in Chapter 1, a set of tensions revolves around the buying and selling of human resources and the indeterminate nature of workers' physical or intellectual 'efforts' in the labour process. In other words, the 'pay–effort bargain' is inherently conflict-prone because workers still predominantly seek to 'maximize' and employers to 'minimize' pay. The leverage of human knowledge and skill to generate value is in turn mediated by structural antagonistic employment relations and technological and organizational change, whereas the accumulation of profit is mediated by product markets and global competition. These sets of complex relationships create patterns of conflict, accommodation and cooperation, and engender persistence in employment relations; they also cause minor and fundamental change.

Another feature of the employment relationship emphasized throughout this text relates to the notion of paradox. We do not wish to rehearse all the arguments from the previous chapters but will instead cite a few examples: employee selection processes designed to

©istockphoto.com/Michael Fuller

It often seems like managers have to walk a tightrope between controlling employees in order to maximize productivity and empowering them to facilitate creativity and motivation.

identify individuals possessing 'team' traits while espousing the need for 'independent' and critical thinkers; work regimes that call for critical reflexivity, creativity and experimentation while insisting that workers maintain a 'zero defects' record; employee participation schemes to enhance productivity but exclude the voice of the very people whom the scheme is supposed to empower; learning organizations claiming to emancipate workers yet maintaining an electronic surveillance of operating procedures – computer-controlled autonomy (see, for example, Bratton, 1992); reward systems that link pay and promotion to individual performance yet expect people to collaborate and share their knowledge and information with co-workers.

Managers often appear to be caught between two contradictory imperatives: regulating human endeavours too tightly undermines workers' leverage potential, whereas empowering workers undermines management control. We have assumed that paradox is inherent in organizational structures and HR practices. By illustrating and explaining how various paradoxes in HRM are produced and reproduced, we hope to encourage a greater understanding of and sensitivity towards managing the employment relationship in the future.

In addition, we wish to draw attention to the need for an understanding of historical trajectories in our study of HRM (Bratton et al., 2003). Earlier chapters have emphasized the historical development of HRM and its current practices, which reaffirm Storey's (2001, p. 6) argument that HRM emerged in the 1980s as 'a historically-situated phenomenon'. Whatever the claims of academics and practitioners to apparently 'new' HR practices, most have deep historical roots: whether it is the 'discovery' of the importance of informal learning in the discourse on competitive advantage (recognized in the apprenticeship system of the Middle Ages); the 'discovery' that contract workers are less committed to the organization than permanent workers (well understood and documented by Niccolò Machiavelli in his book *The Prince*, written in 1513); the 'discovery' of the 'virtual' organization without face-to-face human activity, with people working at home and connected through electronic networks (resembling key structural elements of the preindustrial 'putting-out' system); the 'discovery' that 'social partnerships' are advantageous to management faced with uncertainty in product markets and global competition (as researched by the *Committee of Inquiry on Industrial Democracy*, chaired by Lord Bullock in 1977); or the 'discovery' that the nature of paid work itself is a key variable that influences whether organizations choose different 'hard' or 'soft' HRM employment strategies (as argued extensively in the 1970s industrial relations literature; see, for example, Friedman, 1977).

Thus, most of the important practices that make up the 'new' HRM phenomenon are not all that new, and HRM is therefore a product of a set of complex forces at a particular point in the history of Western capitalism. In a field of management so variable and divergent, HRM cannot be understood in the context of simplistic linear models that expunge old practices and substitute new ones. Developments in HRM over the past 25 years may thus be seen as 'innovative' and as evidence of change, but at the same time, when viewed through a historical lens, there is a realization of déjà vu.

Finally, we need to emphasize one of the main features of our treatment of HRM throughout the book, first discussed in Chapter 1: the need to understand the importance of differing 'standpoints' in management theory. The two standpoints we have presented in this book are *mainstream* (functionalist) on the one hand, and *critical* on the other. An understanding that all aspects of managing the employment relationship can be investigated and interpreted from these different standpoints is an important analytical 'tool' for evaluating the diverse range of HRM literature and how differing standpoints produce contradictory claims and conclusions related to HRM. In this context, it will be legitimate to examine the growth of call centres from either the 'new economy' or the 'electronic sweatshop' perspective. A sensitivity to differing theoretical approaches to researching HRM therefore contributes to our ability to identify and understand the roots of the apparent tensions, contradictions and paradoxes that pervade much of the literature on and experiences relating to HR practices. We need to develop a deep and context-informed understanding of HRM which can also play a vital part in the development of theory that is relevant to practice (Tsoukas and Sandberg, 2011).

Towards critical HRM pedagogy

In *Adult Education as Vocation* (1991, p. 101), Michael Collins quotes French writer Victor Hugo:

> The true division of humanity is between those who live in light and those who live in darkness. Our aim must be to diminish the number of the latter and increase the number of the former. That is why we demand education and knowledge.

This section is inspired by these thoughtful words.

Some argue that the 2008 banking crisis, which saw the implosion of two main UK banks together with the ensuing economic collapse and sovereign indebtedness, was in large part attributable to a small groups of elite leaders within Scottish banking (see for example, Kerr and Robinson, 2011). Others, however, argue that the banking crisis was a general failure of regulation in most Western states stemming from the deregulation philosophy that, in the case of the UK, led to 'light-touch' bank rules (see, for example, Ignatieff, 2011; Stiglitz, 2010). As Currie et al. (2010) deftly observe, every cloud has a silver lining. The crisis and the post-crisis recession have generated a process of critical soul-searching among academics responsible for teaching the disgraced bankers and financiers who have caused the crisis. Editing a special edition of the *British Journal of Management*, Graeme Currie and his colleagues (2010) have provided a timely review of what others have considered to be 'a fundamental intellectual failure' to subject neo-liberal inspired business models to critical analysis. Citing *The Economist* (2009), 'This has been a year of sackcloth and ashes for the world's business schools', they posit that prior to the banking collapse, North American and European business schools were, on the whole, narrow-minded and uncritical (Currie et al., 2010, p. 1).

The conventional wisdom of the cause of the current 'Great Depression' is that it is a financial crisis or a management crisis, but, arguably, at the core, it is a crisis in higher education, or to be more specific a crisis in management education. For years, North

American and European business schools have been teaching an excessively quantitative, socially detached style of management that has uncritically accepted the unstated assumptions and values of neo-liberalism. There has been a cascade of neglect. That business schools are complicit in the current economic crisis by largely disregarding more critical pedagogy is perhaps best illustrated by the new ritual in many business schools, including Harvard, of MBA students signing the equivalent of the medical profession's Hippocratic Oath (Currie, et al., 2010).

As the public discourse continues on how to respond to the economic recession and environmental destruction, what society expects of universities, and indeed business schools, may be about to change. In this post-crisis period, we should champion application of the knowledge and skills derived from the various fields in the human sciences. In this spirit, HRM students, as Tony Watson suggests, need to be exposed to what, 53 years ago, C. Wright Mills (1959/2000) called the 'sociological imagination' – the ability to connect local and personal problems to larger macro and global forces.

The relevance and value of the notion of the sociological imagination for understanding the catastrophic 2008 financial meltdown is illustrated by Gillian Tett's (2009) searing narrative of how the world of complex finance and credit derivatives spiralled out of the control of regulators, politicians and even the bankers themselves. In *Fool's Gold,* the author follows one group of bankers through a period of 'product innovation'. She argues that finance is presented as a string of mathematical equations and only understood by a tiny elite. She notes, however, as other have, that the economic models used by the bankers did not give enough emphasis to all the 'human issues'. Tett confides to her readers that she used to keep quiet about her 'strange' academic background as a trained social anthropologist. But she makes a plausible case (2009, p. 298) that:

The finance world's lack of interest in wider matters cuts to the very heart of what has gone wrong. What social anthropology teaches is that nothing in society ever exists in a vacuum or in isolation. Holistic analysis that tries to link different parts of a social structure is crucial, be that in respect to wedding rituals or trading floors. Anthropology also instils a sense of scepticism about official rhetoric. In most societies, elites try to maintain their power not simply by garnering wealth, but by dominating the mainstream ideologies, both in terms of what is said, and also what is not discussed. Social 'silences' serve to maintain power structures in ways that participants often barely understand, let alone plan.

In essence, politicians, regulators, bankers and journalists failed to employ what Gillian Tett calls 'holistic thought', or American sociologist C. Wright Mills called the 'sociological imagination' – a holistic approach that analyses personal or local problems collectively and, often challenges social elites, with full understanding that these problems are linked to wider macro and global structures.

Michael Collins writes, in *Adult Education as Vocation* (1991, p. 118), that transformative pedagogy 'needs to be informed by a theory of justice and social theories of action with which its practitioners can engage'. In sharp contrast to mainstream management education, a critical pedagogy would take it as self-evident that the practice of management can only be understood in the context of the wider social, economic, political and cultural factors that influence or determine organizational life and practices (Adler et al., 2007; Alvesson, 2008; Delbridge and Keenoy, 2010; Watson, 2010). In addition, a critical HRM education is a transformative force in society in that it sees the main task for academics as being to challenge all taken-for-granted, received or conventional assumptions about labour management practices, to ask hard-hitting questions on power and inequality, to seek multicausality, and to encourage critical reflection on workplace issues and their place within both their societal and their global contexts. Furthermore, from the view of a transformative pedagogy, critical HRM education and pedagogy privileges a concern with influencing HR policy and practice on the one hand, and purposively seeking ways to create a more equitable, dignified and sustainable workplace on the other. If these shared commitments coalesce, critical HRM pedagogy would evade complicity with prevailing forms of mismanagement, social injustice and environmental degradation.

The notion of critical reflexivity calls for sustained analysis and the unmasking through pedagogical activities of a world of structural inequalities, indeterminacy, indignities and often tyranny – workplace life as it is. Paraphrasing Noam Chomsky, the main task for HRM intellectuals is to try to be attuned to these realities, to try to understand, to research what, why and how HR factors contribute to organizational performance but, additionally, to extend the analysis to largely excluded voices and employees' responses to HR practices. As we discussed in Chapter 3, to sidestep or play down the reality of structural inequalities and worker experiences is to falsify workplace life and impoverish the notion of analytical HRM.

Final comment

Your journey through some theories and practices of HRM is now drawing to a close. Throughout this book, we have emphasized diversity in both the theory and the practices, and endeavoured to make the field more transparent and relevant through national and global vignettes, web-based sources and case studies. In addition, through the use of reflective questions and features that encourage critical thinking, we have encouraged independent thought and critical inquiry. The time has now come to reflect on what you have learned from this journey.

Adult education scholars emphasize the need for *reflexivity* as a critical component of the learning process. Reflexivity is like using a mirror to help us to look back on our actions and thought processes, and reflective learning occurs where we have experiences and then step back from them to evaluate the learning we have experienced. There are several ways of carrying out reflexivity. One approach is systematically to go back through all that you have learned so far. Another approach, however, is to look at the additional reading listed at the end of each chapter. Other sources of information, particularly material that tends to differ from the approach taken in this textbook, provide mirrors for us and allow us to look at topics from another perspective. Furthermore, other people – friends, relatives and co-workers – also provide mirrors for us, allowing us to understand HRM from another perspective, so talk to other people about the topics covered in *Human Resource Management: Theory and Practice.*

Finally, your own experience of work is excellent material for reflexivity and can provide insightful information on and an understanding of HRM theory and practice. To help you start the reflexivity process, go back to the beginning of each chapter and consider whether you have personally achieved the major learning objectives.

the European Union Social Charter

The Social Charter was adopted by all member states, except the UK, in December 1989. The Social Charter is not a legal text. It is a statement of principles by which governments agree to abide. They will be required each year to present a report on how they are implementing the Charter. Its aim is to highlight the importance of the social dimension of the single market in achieving social as well as economic cohesion in the European Community.

The preamble of the Social Charter gives added weight to other international obligations such as International Labour Organization conventions. The preamble also includes a commitment to combat every form of discrimination, including discrimination on grounds of sex, colour, race, opinions and belief.

Summary of the rights set out in the Social Charter:

1 Freedom of movement throughout the Community with equal treatment in access to employment, working conditions and social protection.
2 Freedom to choose and engage in an occupation, which shall be fairly remunerated.
3 Improvement of living and working conditions, especially for part-time and temporary workers, and rights to weekly rest periods and annual paid leave.
4 Right to adequate social protection.
5 Right to freedom of association and collective bargaining.
6 Right to access to lifelong vocational training, without discrimination on grounds of nationality.
7 Right of equal treatment of men and women, especially in access to employment, pay, working conditions, education and training and career development.
8 Right to information, consultation and participation for employees, particularly in conditions of technological change, restructuring, redundancies, and for transfrontier workers.
9 Right to health protection and safety at the workplace including training, information, consultation and participation for employees.
10 Rights of children and adolescents, including a minimum working age.
11 Right for the elderly to have a decent standard of living on retirement.
12 Right of people with disabilities to programmes to help them in social and professional life.

bibliography

Aaltio-Marjosola, I., and Mills, A. J. (Eds) (2002). *Gender, Identity and the Culture of Organizations*. London: Routledge.

Abbott, A. (1988) *The System of Professions*. Chicago, IL: University of Chicago Press.

Abbott, A. (2009) Organizations and the Chicago School. In P. Adler (ed.) *Oxford Handbook of Sociology and Organization Studies: Classical Foundations*. (pp. 399–420). Oxford: Oxford University Press.

Abraham, S. E., Karns, L. A., Shaw, K. and Mena, M. A. (2001) Managerial competencies and the managerial appraisal process. *Journal of Management Development*, **20**(10): 842–52.

Accounting for People Task Force (2003) *Report of the Accounting for People Task Force*. London: Department for Trade and Industry.

Ackers, S. and Payne, J. (1988) British trade unions and social partnership: rhetoric, reality and strategy. *International Journal of Human Resource Management*, **9**(3): 529–50.

Ackers, P., Marchington, M., Wilkinson, A. and Dundon, T. (2005) Partnership and voice, with or without trade unions: changing UK management approaches to organizational participation. In M. Stuart and M. Martinez (eds) *Partnership and Modernisation in Employment Relations*. London: Routledge.

Ackroyd, S. and Crowdy, P. A. (1990) Can culture be managed? Working with 'raw' material: the case of the English slaughtermen. *Personnel Review*, **19**(5): 3–13.

Ackroyd, S. and Thompson, P. (1999) *Organizational Misbehaviour*. Thousand Oaks, CA: Sage.

Action on Smoking and Health (2008) 'Fact Sheet: Smoking Statistics: Illness and Death'. November. Available at: www.ash.org.uk.

Adair, J. (2005) *Effective Leadership Development*. London: Chartered Institute of Personnel and Development.

Adams, J. S. (1965) Inequality in social exchange. In L. Berkowitz (ed.) *Advances in Experimental Social Psychology* (pp. 267–99). New York: Academic Press.

Adams, R. J. (1995) Canadian industrial relations in comparative perspective. In M. Gunderson and A. Ponak (eds) *Union–Management Relations in Canada* (3rd edn) (pp. 495–526). Don Mills, Ontario: Addison-Wesley.

Adams, R. J. (2006) *Labour Left Out*. Ottawa: Canadian Centre for Policy Alternatives.

Adamson, S. J., Doherty, N. and Viney, C. (1998) The meanings of career revisited: implications for theory and practice. *British Journal of Management*, **9**(4): 251–9.

Addison, J., Siebert, W., Wagner, J. and Wei, X. (2000) Worker participation and firm performance. *British Journal of Industrial Relations*, **38**(1): 7–48.

Adler, L. (2002) *Hire With Your Head*. Chichester: John Wiley & Sons.

Adler, N. J. (1984) Women do not want international careers: and other myths about international management. *Organizational Dynamics*, **13**: 66–79.

Adler, N. J. (1987) Pacific basin managers: a gaijin, not a woman. *Human Resource Management*, **26**(2): 169–92.

Adler, N. J. (1994) Competitive frontiers: women managing across borders. In N. J. Adler and D. N. Izraeli (eds) *Competitive Frontiers: Women Managers in a Global Economy* (pp. 22–40). Oxford: Blackwell.

Adler, N. J. (2002) Global managers: no longer men alone. *International Journal of Human Resource Management*, **13**(5): 743–60.

Adler, N. J. and Gundersen, A. (2008) *International Dimensions of Organizational Behavior* (5th edn). Mason, OH: Thomson/South-Western.

Adler, P., Forbes, L. and Willmott, H. (2007) Critical management studies: premises, practices, problems and prospects. *Annals of the Academy of Management*, **1**: 119–80.

Advanced Institute of Management (2009) *Closing the UK's Productivity Gap: The Latest Research Evidence*. London: AIM.

Advisory, Conciliation and Arbitration Service (1987) *Working Together: The Way Forward*. Leeds: ACAS.

Agashae, Z. and Bratton, J. (2001) Leader–follower dynamics: developing a learning organization. *Journal of Workplace Learning*, **13**(3): 89–102.

Aguinis, H. (2009) *Performance Management* (2nd edn). Upper Saddle River, NJ: Pearson Prentice-Hall.

Ahlstrand, B. W. (1990) *The Quest for Productivity*. Cambridge: Cambridge University Press.

Akerjordet, K. and Severinsson, E. (2009) Emotional intelligence. Part 1: The development of scales and psychometric testing. *Nursing and Health Sciences*, **11**: 58–63.

Albizu, E. and Olazaran, M. (2006) BPR implementation in Europe: the adaptation of a management concept. *New Technology, Work and Employment*, **21**(1): 43–58.

Alimo-Metcalfe, B. and Alban-Metcalfe, J. (2005) Leadership: time for a new direction. *Leadership*, **1**(1): 51–71.

Alis, D., Karsten, L., and Leopold, J. (2006) From gods to goddesses. *Time and Society*, **15**(1): 81–104.

Allen, M. R. and Wright, P (2008) Strategic management and HRM. In P. Boxall, J. Purcell and P. Wright (eds) *The Oxford Handbook of Human Resource Management* (pp. 88–107). Oxford: Oxford University Press.

Allinson, C. W. and Hayes, J. (1996) *The Cognitive Style Index: A Measure of Intuition-Analysis for Organizational Research. Journal of Management Studies*, **33**(1): 119–35.

Alvesson, M. (1996) *Communication, Power and Organization*. Berlin: Walter de Gruyter.

Alvesson, M. (2002) *Understanding Organizational Culture*. London: Sage.

Alvesson, M. (2008) The future of critical management management studies. In D. Barry and H. Hansen (eds) *Handbook of the New and Emerging in Management and Organizational Studies* (pp. 1–26). London: Sage.

Alvesson, M. and Willmott, H. (1996) *Making Sense of Management: A Critical Analysis*. London: Sage.

Alvesson, M. and Willmott, H. (eds) (2003) *Studying Management Critically*. London: Sage.

Amiti, M. and Wei, S.-J. (2009) Service offshoring and productivity: evidence from the US. *World Economy*, **32**(2): 203–23.

Anderson, B. A. (2005) Expatriate selection: good management or good luck? *International Journal of Human Resource Management*, **16**(4): 567–83.

Anderson, C., Keltner, D. and John, O. P. (2003). Emotional convergence between people over time. *Journal of Personality and Social Psychology*, **84**, 1054–68.

Anderson, J. (ed.) (1981) *Cognitive Skills and their Acquisition*. Hillsdale, NJ: Laurence Erlbaum.

Anderson, L. and Gold, J. (2009) Conversations outside the comfort zone: identity formation in SME manager action learning. *Action Learning: Research and Practice*, **6**(3): 229–42.

Anderson, N. and Witvliet, C. (2008) Fairness reactions to personnel selection methods: an international comparison between the Netherlands, the United States, France, Spain, Portugal, and Singapore. *International Journal of Selection and Assessment*, **16**(1): 1–13.

Anderson, V. (2007) *The Value of Learning: A New Model of Value and Evaluation*. London: Chartered Institute of Personnel and Development.

Anderson, V., Rayner, C. and Schyns, B. (2009) *Coaching at the Sharp End: The Role of Line Managers in Coaching at Work*. London: Chartered Institute of Personnel and Development.

Andolšek, D. M. and Štebe, J. (2005) Devolution or (de) centralization of HRM function in European organizations. *International Journal of Human Resource Management*, **16**(3): 311–29.

Anseel, F. and Lievens, F. (2009) The mediating role of feedback acceptance in the relationship between feedback and attitudinal and performance outcomes. *International Journal of Selection and Assessment*, **17**(4): 362–75.

Anseel, F., Lievens, F. and Levy, P. (2007) A self-motives perspective on feedback-seeking behavior: linking organizational behavior and social psychology research. *International Journal of Management Reviews*, **9**(3): 211–36.

Antonacopoulou, E. P. (1999) Training does not imply learning: the individual perspective. *International Journal of Training and Development*, **3**(1): 14–23.

Antonacopoulou, E. P. (2006) *Introducing Reflexive Critique into the Business Curriculum: Reflections on the Lessons Learned*. London: Advanced Institute of Management.

Antonacopoulou, E., Ferdinand, J., Graca, M. and Easterby-Smith, M. (2005) *Dynamic Capabilities and Organizational Learning: Socio-political Tensions in Organizational Renewal*. AIM Working Paper Series. London: Advanced Institute of Management.

Antonioni, D. (1994) The effects of feedback accountability on upward appraisal ratings. *Personnel Psychology*, **47**(2): 349–56.

Appelbaum, E. and Batt, R. (1994) *The New America Workplace: Transforming Systems in the United States*. Ithaca, NY: ICR/Cornell University Press.

Appelbaum, S. H. and Donna, M. (2000) The realistic downsizing preview: a management intervention in the prevention of survivor syndrome. Part I. *Career Development International*, **5**(7): 333–50.

Apprenticeship Task Force (2005) *Apprenticeships Task Force – Final Report*. London: Apprenticeships Task Force.

Argyris, C. and Schön D. A. (1978) *Organizational Learning: A Theory of Action Perspective*. London: Addison Wesley.

Aries, E. (1996) *Men and Women in Interaction: Reconsidering the Differences*. New York: Oxford University Press.

Armson, G. and Whiteley, A. (2010) Employees' and managers' accounts of interactive workplace learning: a grounded theory of 'complex integrative learning'. *Journal of Workplace Learning*, **22**(7): 409–27.

Armstrong, J. (1987) Human resource management: a case of the emperor's new clothes? *Personnel Management*, **19**(8): 30–5.

Armstrong, M. and Baron, A. (2004) *Managing Performance* (2nd edn). London: Chartered Institute of Personnel and Development.

Arrowsmith, J. and Marginson, P. (2010) The decline of incentive pay in British manufacturing. *Industrial Relations Journal*, **41**(4): 289–311.

Arrowsmith, J. and Marginson, P. (2011) Variable pay and collective bargaining in British retail banking. *British Journal of Industrial Relations*, **49**(1): 54–79.

Arrowsmith, J., Nicholaisen, H., Bechter, B. and Nonell, R. (2010) The management of variable pay in European banks. *International Journal of Human Resource Management*, **21**(15): 2716–40.

Arshad, R. and Sparrow, P. (2010) Downsizing and survivor reactions in Malaysia: modelling antecedents and outcomes of psychological contract violations. *International Journal of Human Resource Management*, **21**(11): 1793–815.

Arthur, J. (1994) Effects of human resources systems on manufacturing performance and turnover. *Academy of Management Journal*, **37**, 670–87.

Arthur, M. B. and Rousseau, D. M. (eds) (2000) *The Boundaryless Career*. Oxford: Oxford University Press.

Arvey, R. D. and Campion, J. E. (1982) The employment interview: a summary and review of recent research. *Personnel Psychology*, **35**, 281–322.

Ashkanasy, N. M. , Broadfoot, L. E. and Falkus, S. (2000) Questionnaire measures of organizational culture. In N. M. Ashkanasy, C. P. M. Wilderom and M.

F. Peterson (eds) *Handbook of Organizational Culture and Climate* (pp. 131–45).Thousand Oaks, CA: Sage.

Ashkanasy, N., Zerbe, W. J. and Hartel, C. E. (2002) *Managing Emotions in the Workplace*. Armonk, NY: M. E. Sharpe.

Ashman, I. and Winstanley, D. (2006) The ethics of organizational commitment. *Business Ethics: A European Review*, **15**(2): 142–53.

Ashton, D. and Sung, J. (2002) *Supporting Workplace Learning for High Performance Working*. Geneva: International Labour Organization.

Asmuß, B. (2008) Performance appraisal interviews. *Journal of Business Communication*, **45**(4): 408–29.

Atkinson, C. and Hall, L. (2009) The role of gender in varying forms of flexible working. *Gender, Work and Organization*, **16**(6): 650–66.

Atkinson, J. S. (1984) Manpower strategies for flexible organizations. *Personnel Management*, August: 28–31.

Atkinson, J. S. and Meager, N. (1985) Introduction and summary of main findings. In J. S. Atkinson and N. Meager, *Changing Work Patterns* (pp. 2–11). London: National Economic Development Office.

Atwater, L. E., Waldman, D. A., Atwater, D. and Cartier, P. (2000) An upward feedback field experiment: supervisors' cynicism, reactions and commitment to subordinates. *Personnel Psychology*, **53**(2): 275–97.

Babbie, E. and Benaquisto, L. (2010) *Fundamentals of Social Research* (2nd edn). Toronto, Ontario: Nelson.

Bach, S. D. (2002) Public-sector employment relations reforms under Labour: muddling through on modernization? *British Journal of Industrial Relations*, **40**(2): 319–39.

Bach, S. (2010) Managed migration? Nurse recruitment and the consequences of state policy. *Industrial Relations Journal*, **41**(3): 249–66.

Bacon, N. and Blyton, P. (2003)The impact of teamwork on skills: employee perceptions of who gains and who loses. *Human Resource Management Journal*, **13**(2): 13–29.

Bacon, N. and Samuel, P. (2009) Partnership agreement adoption and survival in the British private and public sectors. *Work, Employment and Society*, **23**(2): 231–48.

Bacon, N. and Samuel, P. (2010) The contents of partnership agreements in Britain 1990–2007. *Work, Employment and Society*, **24**(3): 430–48.

Bacon, N. and Storey, J. (1993) Individualization of the employment relationship and the implications for trade unions. *Employee Relations*, **15**(1): 5–17.

Bacon, N. and Storey, J. (2000) New employee relations strategies in Britain: towards individualism or partnership? *British Journal of Industrial Relations*, **38**(3): 407–27.

Baglioni, G. and Crouch, C. (1991) *European Industrial Relations: The Challenge of Flexibility*. London: Sage.

Bain, G. S. and Price, R. (1983) Union growth: determinants, and density. In G. S. Bain (ed.) *Industrial Relations in Britain* (pp. 3–33). Oxford: Blackwell.

Bain, P. (1997) Human resource malpractice: the deregulation of health and safety at work in the USA and Britain. *Industrial Relations Journal*, **28**(3): 176–91.

Bain, P. and Baldry, C. (1995) Sickness and control in the office – the sick building syndrome. *New Technology, Work and Employment*, **10**(1): 19–31.

Bain, P. and Taylor, P. (2000) Entrapped by the electronic panopticon? Worker resistance in the call centre. *New Technology, Work and Employment*, **15**(1): 2–18.

Bain, P., Taylor, P. and Baldry, C. (1999) Sick building syndrome and the industrial relations of occupational health. *International Journal of Employment Studies*, **7**(1): 125–48.

Bain, P., Watson, A., Mulvey, G., Taylor, P. and Gall, G. (2002) Taylorism, targets and the pursuit of quantity and quality by call centre management. *New Technology, Work and Employment*, **17**(3): 154–69.

Balain, S. and Sparrow, P. (2009) *Engaged to Perform: A New Perspective on Employee Engagement*. White Paper 09/04. Lancaster: Lancaster University Management School.

Baldamus, W. (1961) *Efficiency and Effort: An Analysis of Industrial Administration*. London: Tavistock.

Baldry, C., Bain, P., Taylor, P. and Hyman, J. (2007) *The Meaning of Work in the New Economy*. Basingstoke: Palgrave.

Baldwin, T. T. and Ford, J. K. (1988) Transfer of training: a review and directions for future research. *Personnel Psychology*, **41**: 63–105.

Ball, B. (1997) Career management competences – the individual perspective. *Career Development International*, **2**(2): 74–9.

Ball, K. (2001) The use of human resource information systems: a survey. *Personnel Review*, **30**(6): 677–93.

Ballantyne, I. and Povah, N. (2004) *Assessment and Development Centres*. Gower: Aldershot.

Bamber, G., Ryan, S. and Wailes, N. (2004) Globalization, employment relations and human indicators in ten developed market economies: international data sets. *International Journal of Human Resource Ma*nagement, **15**(8): 1481–516.

Bamberger, P. and Meshoulam, I. (2000) *Human Resource Management Strategy*. Thousand Oaks, CA: Sage.

Bamberger, P. and Phillips, B. (1991) Organizational environment and business strategy: parallel versus conflicting influences on human resource strategy in the pharmaceutical industry. *Human Resource Management*, **30**, 153–82.

Bandura, A. (1977) *Social Learning Theory*. Upper Saddle River, NJ: Prentice-Hall.

Bandura, A. (1986) *Social Foundations of Thought and Action*. Englewood Cliffs, NJ: Prentice Hall.

Barber, A. E. (1998) *Recruiting Employees: Individual and Organizational Perspectives*. Thousand Oaks, CA: Sage.

Barber, A. E. and Bretz, R. (2000) Compensation, attraction and retention. In S. Rynes and B. Gerhart (eds) *Compensation in Organizations: Current Research and Practice* (pp. 32–60). San Francisco, CA: Jossey-Bass.

Barber, B. (2007) Foreword. In S. Bolton (ed.) *Dimensions of Dignity at Work* (pp. viii–x). Amsterdam: Elsevier.

Barchiesi, F. (2008) Wage labour, precarious employment, and social inclusion in the making of South Africa's postpartheid transition. *African Studies Review*, **51**(2): 119–42.

Barclay, J. (1999) Employee selection: a question of structure. *Personnel Review*, **28**(1/2): 134–51.

Barclay, J. (2001) Improving selection interviews with structure: organisations' use of 'behavioural' interviews. *Personnel Review*, **30**(1): 81–101.

Barlow, G. (1989) Deficiencies and the perpetuation of power: latent functions in management appraisal. *Journal of Management Studies*, **26**(5): 499–517.

Barner, R. and Higgens, J. (2007) Understanding implicit models that guide the coaching process. *Journal of Management Development*, **26**(2): 148–58.

Barnes, C. (1996) What next? Disability, the 1995 Disability Discrimination Act and the Campaign for Peoples' Rights. Text of the Walter Lessing Lecture, presented at the National Skill Bureau for Disabled Students, Annual Conference, Leeds, March 2.

Barney, J. B. (1991) Firm resources and sustained competitive advantage. *Journal of Management*, **17**(1): 99–120.

Barney, J., Wright, M. and Ketchen, D. J. (2001) The resource-based view of the firm: ten years after 1991. *Journal of Management*, **27**: 625–41.

Baron, A. (2009) *Performance Management: A Discussion Paper*. London: Chartered Institute of Personnel and Development.

Bartholomew, D. J. (1971) The statistical approach to manpower planning. *Statistician*, **20**: 3–26.

Bartlett, C. A. and Ghoshal, S. (1989) *Managing across Borders: The Transnational Solution*. Boston, MA: Harvard Business School Press.

Baruch, Y. (2004) Transforming careers: from linear to multidirectional career paths. *Career Development International*, **9**(1): 58–73.

Bass, B. M. and Avolio, B. J. (1990) *Multifactor Leadership Questionnaire*. Palo Alto, CA: Consulting Psychologists Press.

Bass, B. M. and Avolio, B. J. (2004). *The Multifactor Leadership Questionnaire (Form 5X)*. Palo Alto, CA: Mind Garden.

Bass, B. M. and Riggio, R. (2006) *Transformational Leadership* (2nd edn). Mahwah, NJ: Lawrence Erlbaum.

Bassett, P. (1987) *Strike Free: New Industrial Relations in Britain*. London: Papermac.

Bate, P. (1995) *Strategies for Cultural Change*. Oxford: Butterworth-Heineman.

Batstone, E. (1984) *Working Order*. Oxford: Blackwell.

Batstone, E. and Gourlay, S. (1986) *Unions, Unemployment and Innovation*. Oxford: Blackwell.

Battisti, M., Fraccaroli, F., Fasol, R. and Depolo, M. (2007). Psychological contract and quality of organizational life: an empirical study on workers at a rest home. *Industrial Relations*, **62**, 664–88.

Bauer, T. N., Truxillo, D. M., Sanchez, R. J., Craig, J. M., Ferrera, P. and Campion, M. A. (2001) Applicant reactions to selection: development of the selection procedural justice scale (SPJS). *Personnel Psychology*, **54**(2): 387–421.

BBC News (2011) 'Fewer new Scottish teachers find permanent jobs', June 15, 2011. Available at: www.bbc.news/uk-scotland-13773708 (accessed November 30, 2011).

BBC News Magazine (2011) 'Home working: why can't everyone telework?' Available at: www.bbc.co.uk/news/magazine-11879241.

Beard, C. and Rees, S. (2000) Green teams and the management of environmental change in a UK county council. *Environmental Management and Health*, **11**(1): 27–38.

Beatty, R. W., Huselid, M. A. and Schneier, C. E. (2003) The new HR metrics: scoring on the business scorecard. *Organizational Dynamics*, **32**(2): 107–21.

Beaver, G., Lashley, C. and Stewart, J. (1998) Management development. In R. Thomas (ed.) *The Management of Small Tourism and Hospitality Firms* (pp. 156–73). London: Cassell.

Beck, U. (2000) *The Brave New World of Work*. Cambridge: Polity Press.

Becker, B. and Gerhart, B. (1996) The impact of HRM on organizational performance: progress and prospects. *Academy of Management Journal*, **39**: 779–801.

Becker, B., Huselid, M. A. and Ulrich, D. (2001) *The HR Scorecard: Linking People, Strategy and Performance*. Boston, MA: Harvard Business Publishing.

Beckett, D. (2000) Making workplace learning explicit: an epistemology of practice for the whole person. *Westminster Studies in Education*, **23**: 41–53.

Beckett, D. and Hager, P. (2002) *Life, Work and Learning: Practice in Postmodernity*. London: Routledge.

Becton, J. B. and Field, H. S. (2009) Cutural differences in organizational citizenship behaviour: a comparison between Chinese and American employees. *International Journal of Human Resource Management*, **20**(8): 1651–69.

Becton, J. B., Matthews, M. C., Hartley, D. L and Whitaker, D. H. (2009) Using biodata to predict turnover, organizational commitment and job performance in healthcare. *International Journal of Selection and Assessment*, **17**(2):190–202.

Beer, M., Spector, B., Lawrence, P. R., Quin Mills, D. and Walton, R. E. (1984) *Managing Human Assets*. New York: Free Press.

Beetham, D. (1978) *Bureaucracy*. Minneapolis: University of Minnesota Press.

Belbin, M. (1981) *Management Teams*. London: Heinemann.

Bell, D. (1989) Why manpower planning is back in vogue. *Personnel Management*, July: 40–3.

Bell, E., Taylor, R. and Thorpe, R. (2002) Organisational differentiation through badging: Investors in People and the value of the sign. *Journal of Management Studies*, **39**(8): 1071–85.

Bell, E., Taylor, R. and Hoque, K. (2004) *Workplace Training and the High Skills Vision: Where Does Investors in People Fit?* SKOPE Research Paper No. 45. Warwick: Warwick University, Centre for Skills, Knowledge and Organisational Performance.

Bendal, S. E., Bottomley, C. R. and Cleverly, P. M. (1998) Building a new proposition for staff at NatWest UK. In P. Sparrow and M. Marchington (eds) *Human Resource Management: The New Agenda* (pp. 90–105). London: Financial Times/Pitman.

Bennis, W. and Nanus, B. (1985) *Leaders*. New York: Harper & Row.

Benschop, Y and Doorewaard, H. (1998) Covered by equality. The gender subtext of organizations. *Organization Studies*, **19**(5): 787–805.

Benson, J. (1996) Management strategy and labour flexibility in Japanese manufacturing enterprises. *Human Resource Management Journal*, **6**(2): 44–57.

Benson, J. and Brown, M. (2010) Employee voice: does union membership matter? *Human Resource Management Journal*, **20**(1): 80–99.

Bentham, K. (2002) Employer resistance to union certification: a case study of eight Canadian jurisdictions. *Relations Industrielles/Industrial Relations*, **57**(1): 159–87.

Bentley, K. (2005) A healthy workplace: more than 'lunch and learns'. *Network*, July: 13–16.

Berger, P. L. (1963) *Invitation to Sociology*. New York: Anchor Books.

Bergsteiner, H., Avery, G. C. and Neumann, R. (2010) Kolb's experiential learning model: critique from a modeling perspective. *Studies in Continuing Education*, **32**(1): 29–46.

Bertua, C., Anderson, N. and Salgado, J. (2005) The predictive validity of cognitive ability tests: a UK meta-analysis. *Journal of Occupational and Organizational Psychology*, **78**, 387–409.

Betcherman, G., McMullen, K., Leckie, N. and Caron, C. (1994) *The Canadian Workplace in Transition*. Queen's University, Kingston, Ontario: IRC Press.

Beynon, H. (1984) *Working for Ford*. Harmondsworth: Penguin.

Bierma, L. L. (2009) Critiquing HRD's dominant masculine rationality and evaluating its impact. *Human Resource Development Review*, **8**(1): 68–96.

Bierma, L. L. (2010) Resisting HRD's resistance to diversity. *Journal of European Industrial Training*, **34**(6): 565–76.

Billett, S. (2000) Guided learning at work. *Journal of Workplace Learning*, **12**(7): 272–85.

Billett, S. (2001) Learning through work: workplace learning affordances and individual engagement. *Journal of Workplace Learning*, **13**(5): 209–15.

Billett, S. (2006) Constituting the workplace curriculum. *Journal of Curriculum Studies*, **38**(1): 31–48.

Birdthistle, N. and Fleming, P. (2005) Creating a learning organization within the family business: an Irish perspective. *Journal of European Industrial Training*, **29**(9): 730–50.

Biron, M. (2010) Negative reciprocity and the association between perceived organizational ethical values and organizational deviance. *Human Relations*, **63**(6): 875–97.

Bittman, M., Brown, J. and Wajcman, J. (2009) The mobile phone, perpetual contact and time pressure. *Work, Employment and Society*, **23**(4): 673–91.

Björkman, I. and Stahl, G.K. (2006) International human resource management research: an introduction to the field. In G. K. Stahl and I. Björkman (eds) *Handbook of Research in International Human Resource Management* (pp. 1–14). Cheltenham: Edward Elgar.

Blinder, A. (ed.) (1990) *Paying for Productivity*. Washington, DC: Brooking Institute.

Bloom, N., Conway, N., Mole, K., Möslein, K., Neely, A. and Frost, C. (2004) *Solving the Skills Gap*. London: Advanced Institute of Management Research.

Blyton, P. and Turnbull, P. (1998) *The Dynamic of Employee Relations* (2nd edn). Basingstoke: Palgrave Macmillan.

Bohle, P., Willaby, H., Quinlan, M. and McNamara, M. (2011) Flexible work in call centres: working hours, work-life conflict and health, *Applied Ergonomics*, **42**(2): 219–24.

Bolden, R. (2005) *What Is Leadership Development?* Exeter: Leadership South West.

Bolden, R. and Gosling, J. (2006) Leadership competencies: time to change the tune? *Leadership*, **2**(2): 147–63.

Bolton, J. (1971) *Report of the Committee of Inquiry on Small Firms*. London: HMSO.

Bolton, S. C. (2005) *Emotion Management in the Workplace*. Basingstoke: Palgrave Macmillan.

Bolton, S. C. (ed.) (2007) *Dimensions of Dignity at Work*. Amsterdam: Elsevier.

Bolton, S. C. (2009) Getting to the heart of the emotional labour process: a reply to Brook. *Work, Employment and Society* **23**(3): 549–60.

Bolton, S. C. (2010) *Old Ambiguities and New Developments: Exploring the Emotional Labour Process*. In P. Thompson, and C. Smith, C. (eds) Working *Life* (pp. 205–22). Basingstoke: Palgrave Macmillan.

Bolton, S. C. and Houlihan, M. (eds) (2007) *Searching for the Human in Human Resource Management: Theory, Practice and Contexts*. Basingstoke: Palgrave Macmillan.

Bolton, S. C. and Houlihan, M. (eds) (2009) *Work Matters*. Basingstoke: Palgrave Macmillan.

Bonache, J. and Fernández, Z. V. (2005) International compensation: costs and benefits of international assignments. In H. Scullion and M. Linehan (eds) *International Human Resource Management* (pp. 114–30). Basingstoke: Palgrave Macmillan.

Bonk, C. J. and Graham, C. R. (2006) *The Handbook of Blended Learning: Global Perspectives, Local Designs*. San-Francisco: Jossey-Bass.

Bonney, C. (2010) Correlation and Causality. In E. Babbie and L. Benaquisto (eds) *Fundamentals of Social Research* (2nd edn) (pp. 86–7). Toronto, Ontario: Nelson.

Boon, C., Paauwe, J., Boselie, P. and Den Hartog, D. (2009) Institutional pressures and HRM: developing institutional fit. *Personnel Review*, **38**(5): 492–508.

Boselie, P. (2010) *Strategic Human Resource Management: A Balanced Approach*. London: McGraw-Hill.

Boselie, P., Dietz, G. and Boon, C. (2005) Commonalities and contradictions in HRM and performance research. *Human Resource Management Journal*, **15**(3): 67–94.

Bosquet, M. (1980) The meaning of job enrichment. In T. Nichols (ed.) *Capital and Labour* (pp. 370–80). Glasgow: Fontana.

Boud, D. and Garrick, J. (eds) (1999) *Understanding Learning at Work*. London: Routledge.

Boudreau, J. and Ramstad, P. (2009) *Beyond HR: The New Science of Human Capital*. Boston, MA: HBR Press.

Bourne, M. and Franco-Santos, M. (2010) *Investors in People, Management Capabilities and Performance*. Berkhamstead: Cranfield University.

Bouskila-Yam, O. and Kluger, A. (2011) Strength-based performance appraisal and goal setting. *Human Resource Management Review*, 21: 137–42.

Bowen, D. E. and Ostroff, C. (2004) Understanding HRM–firm performance linkages: the role of the 'strength' of the HRM system. *Academy of Management Review*, **29**(2): 203–21.

Boxall, P. F. (1992) Strategic human resource management: beginnings of a new theoretical sophistication? *Human Resource Management Journal*, **2**(3): 60–79.

Boxall, P. F. (1995) Building the theory of comparative HRM. *Human Resource Management Journal*, **5**(5): 5–17.

Boxall, P. F. (2003) HR strategy and competitive advantage in the service sector. *Human Resource Management Journal*, **13**(3): 5–20.

Boxall, P. (2008) The goals of HRM. In P. Boxall, J. Purcell and P. Wright (eds) *The Oxford Handbook of Human Resource Management* (pp. 48–67). Oxford: Oxford University Press.

Boxall, P. and Macky, K. (2009) Research and theory on high-performance work systems: progressing the high-involvement stream. *Human Resource Management Journal*, **19**(1): 3–23.

Boxall, P. F. and Purcell, J. (2003) *Strategy and Human Resource Management*. Basingstoke: Palgrave Macmillan.

Boxall, P. and Purcell, J. (2008) *Strategy and Human Resource Management*, (2nd edn). New York: Palgrave Macmillan.

Boxall, P., Purcell, J. and Wright, P. (2008) Human resource management: scope, analysis and significance. In Boxall, J. Purcell, and P. Wright (eds) *The Oxford Handbook of Human Resource Management* (pp. 1–16). Oxford: Oxford University Press.

Boyatzis, R. (1982) *The Competent Manager: A Model for Effective Performance*. New York: John Wiley & Sons.

Boyatzis, R. (2008) Competencies in the 21st century. *Journal of Management Development*, **27**(1): 5–12.

Boyatzis, R. E., Smith, M. L. and Blaize, N. (2006) Developing sustainable leaders through coaching and compassion. *Academy of Management Learning and Education*, **5**(1): 8–24.

Boyce, M. (1997) Organizational story and storytelling: a critical review. *Journal of Organizational Change Management*, **9**(5): 5–26.

Boydell, T. H. (1976) *Guide to the Identification of Training Needs* (2nd edn). London: BACIE.

Brady, P. W., Meade, A. W., Michael, J. J. and Fleenor, J. W. (2009) Internet recruiting: effects of website content features on viewers' perceptions of organizational culture. *International Journal of Selection and Assessment*, **17**(1): 19–34.

Brady, T. and Davies, A. (2004) Building project capabilities: from exploratory to exploitive learning. *Organization Studies*, **25**(9): 1601–21.

Bramley, P. (1989) Effective training. *Journal of European Industrial Training*, **13**(7): 2–33.

Branch, S., Ramsey, S. and Barker, M. (2009) Workplace bullying. In T. Redman and A. Wilkinson (eds) *Contemporary Human Resource Management* (3rd edn) (pp. 517–41). London: Prentice Hall.

Brannen, P., Batstone, E., Fatchett, D. and White, P. (1976) *The Worker Directors*. London: Hutchinson.

Brannie, M. (2008) Graduate recruitment and selection in the UK. *Career Development International*, **13**(6): 497–513.

Bratton, A. J. (2009) HRM Practices and Environmental Management: An Exploratory Case Study of a UK City Council. Unpublished MSc dissertation, University of Edinburgh.

Bratton, J. (1992) *Japanization at Work: Managerial Studies for the 1990s*. Basingstoke: Palgrave Macmillan.

Bratton, J. (1999) 'Gaps in the workplace learning paradigm: labour flexibility and job design', paper presented at the 1st International Conference on Researching Work and Learning, University of Leeds, UK.

Bratton, J. (2001) Why workers are reluctant learners: the case of the Canadian pulp and paper industry. *Journal of Workplace Learning*, **13**(7/8): 333–43.

Bratton, J. (2005) Work redesign and learning at work: a win–win game? In E. Poikela (ed.) *Osaaminen ja Kokemus – työ, oppiminen ja kasvatus*. Tampere, Finland: Tampere University Press.

Bratton, J. and Garrett-Petts, W. (2008) Art and workplace learning: innovation, and the economic development of Canadian small cities. In D. Livingstone, K. Mirchandani and P. Sawchuk (eds) *The Future of Lifelong Learning and Work: Critical Perspectives*. Rotterdam: Sense Publishers.

Bratton, J., Helm-Mills, J., Pyrch, T. and Sawchuk, P. (2003) *Workplace Learning: A Critical Introduction*. Toronto, Ontario: Garamond Press.

Bratton, J., Grint, K. and Nelson, D. (2004a) *Organizational Leadership*. Mason, OH: Thomson/South-Western.

Bratton, J., Helm-Mills, J., Pyrch, T. and Sawchuk, P. (2004b) *Workplace Learning: A Critical Introduction*. Toronto, Ontario: Garamond Press.

Bratton, J. Denham, D. and Deutschmann, L. (2009)

Capitalism and Classical Sociological Theory. Toronto, Ontario: University of Toronto Press.

Bratton, J., Sawchuk, P., Forshaw, C,. Callinan, M. and Corbett, M. (2010) *Work and Organizational Behaviour* (2nd edn). London: Palgrave Macmillan.

Braverman, H. (1974) *Labour and Monopoly Capital*. New York: Monthly Review Press.

Brewis, J. and Linstead, S. (2000) *Sex, Work and Sex Work: Eroticizing Organization*. London: Routledge.

Brewster, C. (1995) Towards a 'European model' of human resource management. *Journal of International Business Studies*, First Quarter: 1–21.

Brewster, C. (2001) HRM: 'the comparative dimension'. In J. Storey (ed.) *Human Resource Management: A Critical Text* (pp. 255–71). London: Thompson Learning.

Brewster, C. (2007) HRM: the comparative dimension. In J. Storey (ed.) *Human Resource Management: A Critical Text* (3rd edn) (pp. 197–214). London: Thompson Learning.

Brewster, C. and Bennett, C. V. (2010) Perceptions of business cultures in eastern Europe and their implications for international HRM. *International Journal of Human Resource Management*, **21**(14): 2568–88.

Brewster, C. and Scullion H. (1997) A review and an agenda for expatriate HRM. *Human Resource Management Journal*, **7**(3): 32–41.

Brewster, C., Carey, L., Grobler, P., Holland, P. and Warnich, S. (2008) *Contemporary Issues in Human Resource Management*. Cape Town, South Africa: Oxford University Press.

Brindle, D. (2010) Embrace the grey workforce, scheme urges employers. *The Guardian*, June 5, p. W2.

Brint, S. (2006) *Schools and Societies*. Stanford, CA: Stanford Social Sciences.

Broadbridge, A., Maxwell, G. A. and Ogden, S. M. (2009) Selling retailing to Generation Y graduates: recruitment challenges and opportunities. *International Review of Retail, Distribution and Consumer Research*, 19(4): 405–20.

Bronfenbrenner, K. (1997) The role of union strategies in NLRB certification elections. *Industrial and Labor Relations Review*, 50(2): 195–212.

Brook, P. (2009) In critical defence of 'emotional labour': refuting Bolton's critique of Hochschild's concept. *Work, Employment and Society*, **23**(3): 531–48.

Brown, A. (2005) Implementing performance management in England's primary schools. *International Journal of Productivity and Performance Management*, **54**(5/6): 468–81.

Brown, B., Hanson, M., Liverman, D. and Merideth, R. (1987) Global sustainability: towards a definition. *Environmental Management*, **11**(6): 713–19.

Brown, D., Caldwell, R., White, K., Atkinson, H., Tansley, T., Goodge, P. and Emmott, M. (2004). *Business Partnering: A New Direction for HR*. London: CIPD.

Brown, J. S. and Duguid, P. (1991) Organizational learning and communities-of-practice: toward a unified view of working, learning and innovation. *Organization Science*, **2**(1): 40–7.

Brown, M. (2001) Unequal pay, unequal responses? Pay referents and their implications for pay level satisfaction. *Journal of Management Studies*, **38**(6): 879–96.

Brown, M. B. (1984) *Models of Political Economy*. London: Penguin.

Brown, M. and Heywood, J. (2005) Performance appraisal systems: determinants and change. *British Journal of Industrial Relations*, **43**(4): 659–79.

Brown, M., Hyatt, D. and Benson, J. (2010) Consequences of the performance appraisal experience. *Personnel Review*, **39**(3): 375–96.

Brown, P. (2007) Strategic management development. In R. Hill and J. Stewart (eds) *Management Development, Perspectives from Research and Practice* (pp. 40–59). London: Routledge.

Brown, W. (1988) The employment relationship in sociological theory. In D. Gallie (ed.) *Employment in Britain* (pp. 33–66). Oxford: Blackwell.

Brown, W. (1989) Managing remuneration. In K. Sisson (ed.) *Personnel Management in Britain* (pp. 249–70). Oxford: Blackwell.

Brown, W. (2000) Putting partnership into practice in Britain. *British Journal of Industrial Relations*, **38**(2): 299–316.

Brown, W. (2010) Negotiation and collective bargaining. In T. Colling and M. Terry (eds) *Industrial Relations: Theory and Practice* (3rd edn) (pp. 253–74). Chichester: John Wiley & Sons.

Brown, W. and Nash, D. (2008) What has happening to collective bargaining under New Labour? Interpreting WERS 2004. *Industrial Relations Journal*, **39**(2): 91–103.

Brown, W., Deakin, S. and Ryan, P. (1997) The effects of British industrial relations legislation. *National Institute Economic Review*, **161**: 69–83.

Brown, W., Deakin, S., Nash, D. and Oxenbridge, S. (2000) The employment contract: from collective procedures to individual rights. *British Journal of Industrial Relations*, **38**(4): 611–29.

Browning, V. and Edgar, F. (2004) Reactions to HRM: an employee perspective from South Africa and New Zealand. *Journal of Management and Organization*, **10**(2): 1–13.

Brutus, S. and Derayeh, M. (2002) Multi-source assessment programs in organizations: an insider's perspective, *Human Resource Development Quarterly*, **13**, 187–201.

Bryant, S. (2000) At home on the electronic frontier: work, gender and the information highway. *New Technology, Work and Employment*, **15**(1): 19–33.

Bryman, A., Teevan, J. and Bell, E. (2009) *Social Research Methods*. Don Mills, Ontario: Oxford University Press.

Bryman, J. (ed.) (1988) *Doing Research in Organizations*. London: Routledge.

Bryson, A. (2004) Management responsiveness to union and nonunion worker voice in Britain. *Industrial Relations*, **43**(1): 213–41.

Bryson, A. and Frege, C. (2010) The importance of comparative workplace employment relations studies. *British Journal of Industrial Relations*, **48**(2): 231–4.

Bryson, A., Gomez, R., Kretschmer, T. and Willman, P. (2007) The diffusion of workplace voice and high-commitment human resource management practices in Britain, 1984–1998. *Industrial and Corporate Change*, **16**(3): 395–426.

Buchanan, D. A. (1997) The limitations and opportunities of business process re-engineering in a politicized organizational climate. *Human Relations*, **50**(1): 51–72.

Buckingham, G. (2000) Same indifference. *People Management*, **6**(4): 44–6.

Buckley, R. and Caple, J. (2007) *The Theory and Practice of Training* (5th edn). London: Kogan Page.

Budd, J., Gollan, P. and Wilinson, A. (2010) New approaches to employee voice and participation in organizations. *Human Relations*, **63**(3): 303–10.

Budhwar, P. S. and Boyne, G. (2004) Human resource management in the Indian public and private sectors: an empirical comparison. *International Journal of Human Resource Management*, **15**(2): 346–70.

Budhwar, P. and Yaw, D. (2001) *Human Resource Management in Developing Countries*. London: Routledge.

Budhwar, P., Verma, A., Malhotra, N. and Mukherjee, A. (2009) Insights into the Indian call centre industry: can internal marketing help tackle high employee turnover. *Journal of Services Marketing*, **23**(5): 351–62.

Bullock, Lord (1977) *Report of the Committee of Inquiry on Industrial Democracy*. Cmnd 6706. London: HMSO.

Burawoy, M. (1979) *Manufacturing Consent: Changes in the Labour Process Under Monopoly Capitalism*. Chicago, IL: Chicago University Press.

Burgoyne, J., Hirsh, W. and Williams, S. (2004) *The Development of Leadership and Management Capability and its Contribution to Performance: The Evidence, the Prospects and the Research Need*. Report No. 560. London: Department for Education and Skills.

Burke, J. (1985) *The Day the Universe Changed*. Boston, MA: Little, Brown.

Burke, W. (2011) *Organizational Change: Theory and Practice*. Los Angeles, CA: Sage.

Burkett, H. (2005) ROI on a shoestring: evaluation strategies for resource-constrained environments or ROI on a shoestring. *Industrial and Commercial Training*, **37**(2): 97–105.

Buruma, I. (2011) Political aftershock: public trust breakdown. *Globe and Mail*, April 8, p. A15.

Butler, A. B. and Skattebo, A. L. (2004) What is acceptable for women may not be for men: the effect of family conflicts with work on job performance ratings. *Journal of Occupational and Organizational Psychology*, **77**: 553–64.

Butler, P. (2009) Non-union employee representation: exploring the riddle of management strategy. *Industrial Relations Journal*, **40**(3): 198–214.

Butwell, J. (2006) Group supervision for coaches: is it worthwhile? A study of the process in a major professional organization. *International Journal of Evidence Based Coaching and Mentoring*, **4**(2): 43–53.

Buyens, D. and De Vos, A. (2001) Perceptions of the value of HR function. *Human Resource Management Journal*, **11**(3): 70–89.

Byers, P. Y. (ed.) (1997) *Organizational Communication: Theory and Behavior*. Boston: Allyn & Bacon.

Cabanero-Johnson, P. and Berge, Z. (2009) Digital natives: back to the future of microworlds in a corporate learning organization. *Learning Organization*, **16**(4): 290–7.

Cabinet Office (2007) *Social Enterprise Action Plan: Scaling New Heights*. London: Cabinet Office.

Cable, D. M. and Parsons, C. K. (2001) Socialization tactics and person–organization fit. *Personnel Psychology*, **54**(1): 1–23.

Caers, R. and Castelyns, V. (2010) LinkedIn and Facebook in Belgium: the influences and biases of social network sites in recruitment and selection procedures. *Social Science Computer Review*, **29**(4): 437–48.

Caldwell, R. (2001) Champions, adaptors, consultants and synergists: the new change agents in HRM. *Human Resource Management Journal*, **11**(3): 39–52.

Caligiuri, P. M. and Tung, R. (1999) Comparing the success of male and female expatriates IToma V.S.-based company. *International Journal of Human Resource Management*, **10**(5): 763–82.

Caligiuri, P. M., Lazarova, M. and Tarique, L. (2005) Training, learning and development in multinational organizations. In H. Scullion and M. Linehan (eds) *International Human Resource Management* (pp. 71–90). Basingstoke: Palgrave Macmillan.

Callaghan, G. and Thompson, P. (2001) Edwards revisited: technical control and worker agency in call centres. *Economic and Industrial Democracy*, **22**: 13–37.

Cameron, D. (2010) What's the big idea about the Big Society? *The Observer*, April 18, p. 34.

Campbell, D. (2010) The binge working culture is taking its toll. *The Observer*, May 16, 37.

Campbell, D. J. and Lee, C. (1988) Self-appraisal in performance evaluation. *Academy of Management Review*, **13**(2): 3–8.

Campion, M. A., Palmer, D. K. and Campion, J. E. (1997) A review of structure in the selection interview. *Personnel Psychology*, **50**: 655–702.

Canadian Centre for Occupational Health and safety (2001) 'Violence in the Workplace Prevention Guide'. Available at: www.ccohs.ca/oshanswer/psychosocial/bullying.html.

Cappelli, P. (2001) Making the most of on-line recruiting. *Harvard Business Review*, **79**, 139–46.

Cappelli, P. (2009) A supply chain approach to workforce planning. *Organizational Dynamics*, **38**(1): 8–15.

Cappelli, P. and Singh, H. (1992) Integrating strategic human resources and strategic management. In D. Lewin, O. S. Mitchell and P. Sherer (eds) *Research Frontiers in Industrial Relations and Human Resources* (pp. 165–92). Madison, WI: Industrial Relations Research Association.

Carless, S. A. (2005) Person–job fit versus person–organization fit as predictors of organizational attraction and job acceptance intentions: a longitudinal study. *Journal of Occupational and Organizational Psychology*, **78**: 411–29.

Carlsson, M. and Rooth, D. (2008) *Is it Your Foreign Name or Foreign Qualifications? An Experimental Study of Ethnic Discrimination in Hiring*. IZA Discussion Paper No. 3810. Bonn: Institute for the Study of Labor.

Carrick, P. and Williams, R. (1999) Development centres – a review of assumptions. *Human Resource Management Journal*, **9**(2): 77–92.

Carroll, W.K. (2004) *Corporate Power in a Globalizing World: A Study of Elite Social Organization*. Don Mills, Ontario: Oxford University Press.

Carter, B., Danford, A., Howcroft, D., Richardson, H., Smith, A. and Taylor, P. (2011) 'All they lack is a chain': lean and the new performance management in the British Civil Service. *New Technology Work and Employment*, **26**(2): 83–97.

Caruth, D. and Handlogten, G. (2001) *Managing Compensation: A Handbook for the Perplexed*. Westport, CT: Quorum.

Casella, A. and Hanaki, N. (2008) Information channels in labor markets: on the resilience of referral hiring. *Journal of Economic Behavior and Organization*, **66**, 492–513.

Cassell, C. and Lee, B. (2009) Trade union representatives: progressing partnerships? *Work, Employment and Society*, **23**(2): 213–30.

Casserley, T. and Critchley, B. (2010) Sustainable leadership: perennial philosophy. *People Management*, August 12: 20–4.

Castells, M. (1996) *The Rise of the Network Society*. Oxford: Blackwell.

Castells, M. (2000) Information technology and global capitalism. In W. Hutton and A. Giddens (eds) *On the Edge: Living with Global Capitalism* (pp. 52–74). London: Cape.

Caulkin, S. (2001) The time is now. *People Management*, **7**(17): 32–4.

Cawley, B. D., Keeping, L. M. and Levy, P. E. (1998) Participation in the performance appraisal process and employee reactions: a meta-analytic review of field investigations. *Journal of Applied Psychology*, **83**(4): 615–33.

Ceci, S. and Williams, W. (2000) Smart bomb. *People Management*, **6**(17): 32–6.

Certification Officer (2010) 'Annual report, 2009–10'. Available at: www.certoffice.org (accessed March 29, 2011).

Chakravarty, D. (2007) 'Docile oriental women' and organised labour: a case study of the Indian garment manufacturing industry. *Indian Journal of Gender Studies*, **14**, 439–60.

Chamberlain, G. (2011) Disney factory faces probe into sweatshop suicide claims. *The Observer*, August 28, p. 17.

Chamberlain, L. J., Crowley, M., Tope, D. and Hodson, R. (2008) Sexual harassment in organizational context. *Work and Occupations*, **35**(3): 262–95.

Chamberlain, N. and Kuhn, J. (1965) *Collective Bargaining* (2nd edn). New York: McGraw-Hill.

Champy, J. (1996) *Reengineering Management: The Mandate for New Leadership*. New York: HarperCollins.

Chandler, A. (1962) *Strategy and Structure*. Cambridge, MA: MIT Press.

Chang, T., Liao, J. and Xinyan, W. (2008) The effect of team-based performance appraisal on knowledge sharing: constructing and verifying an influencing model. *International Journal of Data Analysis Techniques and Strategies*, **1**(2): 153–72.

Chapman, D. and Zweig, D. (2005) Developing a nomological network for interview structure: antecedents and consequences of the structured selection interview. *Personnel Psychology*, **58**: 673–702.

Charlwood, A. (2002) Why do non-union employees

want to unionize? Evidence from Britain. *British Journal of Industrial Relations*, **40**(3): 463–91.

Charmaz, K. (2000) Grounded theory: objectivist and constructivist methods. In N. Denzin and Y. Lincoln (eds) *Handbook of Qualitative Research* (2nd edn) (pp. 509–35). Thousand Oaks, CA: Sage.

Chartered Institute of Personnel and Development (2002) *Developing Managers for Business Performance*. London: CIPD.

Chartered Institute of Personnel and Development (2003) *Managing Careers Survey*. London: CIPD.

Chartered Institute of Personnel and Development (2005a) *Human Capital Reporting: An Internal Perspective*. London: CIPD.

Chartered Institute of Personnel and Development (2005b) *Recruitment, Retention and Turnover*. London: CIPD.

Chartered Institute of Personnel and Development (2005c) *Training and Development*. London: CIPD.

Chartered Institute of Personnel and Development (2006a) *Offshoring and the Role of HR*. London: CIPD.

Chartered Institute of Personnel and Development (2006b) *Reward Management Annual Survey Report 2006*. London, UK: Chartered CIPD.

Chartered Institute of Personnel and Development (2007a) *Diversity in Business*. London: CIPD.

Chartered Institute of Personnel and Development (2007b) *Reward Management Annual Survey Report 2007*. London, UK: CIPD.

Chartered Institute of Personnel and Development (2008) *Learning and Development Survey*. London: CIPD.

Chartered Institute of Personnel and Development (2009a) *Fighting Back Through Talent Innovation*. London: CIPD.

Chartered Institute of Personnel and Development (2009b) *Performance Management in Action*. London: CIPD.

Chartered Institute of Personnel and Development (2009c) *Learning and Development Survey*. London: CIPD.

Chartered Institute of Personnel and Development (2010a) *The Talent Perspective. What Does It Feel Like To Be Talent-Managed?* London: CIPD.

Chartered Institute of Personnel and Development (2010b) *Opening Up Talent For Business Success*. London: CIPD.

Chartered Institute of Personnel and Development (2010c) *Resourcing and Talent Planning*. London: CIPD.

Chartered Institute of Personnel and Development (2010d) 'Competency and competency frameworks'. Available at: www.cipd.co.uk/subjects/perfmangmt/ competnces/comptfrmwk.htm (accessed January 12, 2011).

Chartered Institute of Personnel and Development (2010e) *Learning and Talent Development*. London: CIPD.

Chartered Institute of Personnel and Development (2010f) *Next Generation HR*. London: CIPD.

Chartered Institute of Personnel and Development (2010g) *Reward Management Annual Survey Report 2010*. London: CIPD.

Chartered Institute of Personnel and Development (2011) *Sustainable Organisation Performance*. London: CIPD.

Chatzitheochari, S. and Arber, S. (2009) Lack of sleep, work and long hours culture: evidence from the UK Time Use Survey. *Work, Employment and Society*, **23**(1): 30–48.

Checchi, D., Visser, J. and van de Werfhorst, H. (2010) Inequality and union membership: the influence of relative earnings and inequality attitudes. *British Journal of Industrial Relations*, **48**(1): 84–108.

Chen, T., Wu, P. and Leung, K. (2011) Individual performance appraisal and appraisee reactions to workgroups. *Personnel Review*, **40**(1): 87–105.

Chen, Y.-S. (2011) Green organizational identity: sources and consequence. *Management Decision*, **49**(3): 384–404.

Chiaburu, D. and Tekleab, A. (2005) Individual and contextual influences on multiple dimensions of training effectiveness. *Journal of European Industrial Training*, **29**(8): 604–26.

Child, J. (1972) Organizational structure, environment and performance: the role of strategic choice. *Sociology*, **6**(1): 331–50.

Chomsky, N. (1999) *Profit over People*. New York: Seven Stories Press.

Chou, B. K. (2005) Implementing the reform of performance appraisal in China's civil service. *China Information*, **19**(1): 39–65.

Chuai, X., Preece, D. and Iles, P. (2008) Is talent management just 'old wine in new bottles'? *Management Research News*, **31**(12): 901–11.

Clark, J., Thorpe, R., Anderson, L. and Gold, J. (2006) It's all action, it's all learning: action learning in SMEs. *Journal of European Industrial Training*, **30**(6): 441–55.

Clark, T. and Pugh, D. (2000) Similarities and differences in European conceptions of human resource management. *International Studies of Management and Organizations*, **29**(4): 84–100.

Clarke, M., Butcher, D. and Bailey, C. (2004) Strategically aligned leadership development. In J. Storey (ed.) *Leadership in Organizations* (pp. 271–92). London: Routledge.

Clarke, N. (2003) The politics of training needs analysis. *Journal of Workplace Learning*, **15**(4): 141–53.

Clarke, N. (2004) HRD and the challenges of assessing learning in the workplace. *International Journal of Training and Development*, **8**(2): 140–56.

Claydon, T. (1989) Union de-recognition in Britain in the 1980s. *British Journal of Industrial Relations*, **27**(2): 214–24.

Clayton, T. (1998) Problematizing partnerships: the prospects for a cooperative bargaining agenda. In P. Sparrow and M. Marchington (eds) *Human Resource Management: The New Agenda* (pp. 180–92). London: Financial Times Management.

Clayton, T. (2000) Employee participation and involvement. In D. Winstanley and J. Woodall (eds) *Ethical Issues in Contemporary Human Resource Management* (pp. 208–23). Basingstoke: Palgrave Macmillan.

Cleary, P. (2010) Human Resource Accounting. In D. McGuire and K. M. Jorgensen (eds) *Human Resource Development* (pp. 44–54). London, Sage.

Clegg, H. (1976) *Trade Unionism Under Collective Bargaining*. Oxford: Blackwell.

Clegg, S. R. (1990) *Modern Organizations: Organization Studies in the Postmodern World*. London: Sage.

Clegg, S. R. and Hardy, C. (eds) (1999) *Studying Organizations: Theory and Method*. London: Sage.

Clegg, S., Hardy, C., and Nord, W. (eds) (1999) *Managing Organizations: Current Issues*. Thousand Oaks, CA: Sage.

Cloke, K. and Goldsmith, J. (2002) *The End of Management and the Rise of Organizational Democracy*. San Francisco, CA: Jossey-Bass.

Clutterbuck, D. (2007) *Coaching the Team at Work*. London: Nicholas Brealey.

Clutterbuck, D. and Megginson, D. (2005a) *Making Coaching Work: Creating a Coaching Culture*. London: Chartered Institute of Personnel and Development.

Clutterbuck, D. and Megginson, D. (2005b) How to create a coaching culture. *People Management*, 21 April: 44–5.

Coates, D. (1975) *The Labour Party and the Struggle for Socialism*. Cambridge: Polity Press.

Coates, J. and Pichler, P. (eds) (2011) *Language and Gender: A Reader* (2nd edn). Chichester: Wiley-Blackwell.

Coens, T. and Jenkins, M. (2002) *Abolishing Performance Appraisals*. San Francisco, CA: Berrett-Koehler.

Coffield, F., Moseley, D., Hall, E. and Ecclestone, K. (2004) *Learning Styles and Pedagogy in Post-16 Learning: A Systematic and Critical Review*. Wiltshire: Learning and Skills Research Centre.

Cohen, E. (2010) *CSR for HR: A Necessary Partnership for Advancing Responsible Business Practices*. Sheffield: Greenleaf Publishing.

Cohen, W. and Levinthal, D. (1990) Absorptive capacity: a new perspective on learning and innovation. *Administrative Science Quarterly*, **35**: 128–52.

Coleman, S. and Keep, E. (2001) 'Background literature review for PIU project on workforce development'. Available at: www.cabinet-office.gov.uk/innovation/2001/workforce/literaturereview.pdf.

Colling, T. (1995) Experiencing turbulence: competition, strategic choice and the management of human resources in British Airways. *Human Resource Management*, **5**(5): 18–32.

Colling, T. (2005) Managing human resources in the networked organization. In S. Bach (ed.) *Managing Human Resources* (pp. 90–112). Oxford: Blackwell.

Colling, T. (2010) Legal institutions and the regulation of workplaces. In T. Colling and M. Terry (eds) *Industrial Relations: Theory and Practice* (3rd edn) (pp. 323–46). Chichester, John Wiley & Sons.

Colling, T. and Terry, M. (eds) (2010) Work, the employment relationship and the field of industrial relations. In T. Colling and M. Terry (eds) *Industrial Relations: Theory and Practice* (3rd edn) (pp. 3–25). Chichester: John Wiley & Sons.

Collings, D. and Mellahi, K. (2009) Strategic talent management: A review and research agenda. *Human Resource Management Review*, **19**(4): 304–13.

Collings, D. G. and Scullion, H. (2007) Global staffing and multinational enterprise. In J. Storey (ed.) *Human Resource management: A Critical Text* (3rd edn) (pp. 215–31). London: Thomson Learning.

Collings, D. G., Demirbag, M., Mellahi, K. and Tatoglu, E. (2010) Strategic orientation, human resource management practices and organizational outcomes: evidence from Turkey. *International Journal of Human Resource Management*, **21**(14): 2589–613.

Collins, C. and Han, J. (2004) Exploring applicant pool quantity and quality: the effects of early recruitment strategies, corporate advertising and firm reputation. *Personnel Psychology*, **57**: 685–717.

Collins, H. M. (2001) Tacit knowledge, trust, and the Q of sapphire. *Social Studies of Science*, **31**(1): 71–85.

Collins, J. M. and Muchinsky, P. M. (1993) An assessment of the construct validity of three job evaluation methods: a field experiment. *Academy of Management Journal*, **36**, 895–904.

Collins, M. (1991) *Adult Education as Vocation*. London: Routledge.

Colthart, I., Cameron, N., McKinstry, B. and Blaney, D. (2008) What do doctors really think about the relevance and impact of GP appraisal 3 years on? A survey of Scottish GPs. *British Journal of General Practice*, **58**: 82–7.

Confederation of British Industry (2008) *Talent Not*

Tokenism: The Business Benefits of Workforce Diversity. London: CBI/TUC/EHRC.

Conley, H. (2008) The nightmare of temporary work: a comment on Fevre. *Work, Employment and Society*, **22**(4): 731–36.

Connelly, S. and Ruarck, G. (2010) Leadership style and activating potential moderators of the relationships among leader emotional displays and outcomes. *Leadership Quarterly*, **21**: 745–64.

Connerley, M. L., Carlson, K. D. and Mecham, R. L. (2003) Evidence of differences in applicant pool quality. *Personnel Review*, **32**(1): 22–39.

Constable, J. and McCormick, R. (1987) *The Making of British Managers*. London: BIM/CBI.

Contractor, F. J., Kumar, V., Kundu, S. K. and Pedersen, T. (2010) Reconceptualizing the firm in a world of outsourcing and offshoring: the organizational and geographical relocation of high-value company functions. *Journal of Management Studies*, **47**(8): 1417–33.

Conway, H. E. (1987) *Equal Pay for Work of Equal Value Legislation in Canada: An Analysis*. Ottawa: Studies in Social Policy.

Cook, J. and Crossman, A. (2004) Satisfaction with performance appraisal systems. *Journal of Managerial Psychology*, **19**(5): 526–41.

Cook, M. (1994) *Personnel Selection and Productivity*. Chichester: John Wiley & Sons.

Cooke, F. L. (2000) *Human Resource Strategy to Improve Organisational Performance: A Route for British Firms?* Working Paper No. 9. Economic and Social Research Council Future of Work Programme. Swindon: ESRC.

Cooke, W. N. (2005) Exercising power in a prisoner's dilemma: transnational collective bargaining in an era of corporate globalization? *Industrial Relations Journal*, **36**(4): 283–302.

Coopey, J. (1996) Crucial gaps in the 'learning organization'. In K. Starkey (ed.) *How Organizations Learn* (pp. 348–67). London: International Thomson Business.

Corby, S., Palmer, S. and Lindop, E. (eds) (2009) *Rethinking Reward*. Basingstoke: Palgrave Macmillan.

Cordery, J. and Parker, S. K. (2008) Work Organization. In P. Boxall, J. Purcell and Wright, P. (eds) *The Oxford Handbook of Human Resource Management* (pp. 187–209). Oxford: Oxford University Press.

Coriat, B. (1980) The restructuring of the assembly line: a new economy of time and control. *Capital and Class*, (11): 34–43.

Council for Excellence in Management and Leadership (2002) *Managers and Leaders: Raising Our Game*. London: CEML.

Coutts, J. (1998) Workplace stress more prevalent than illness, injury. *Globe and Mail*, April 8, 1998.

Cowling, A. and Walters, M. (1990) Manpower planning – where are we today? *Personnel Review*, **19**(3): 3–8.

Cox, A., Marchington, M. and Suter, J. (2009) Employee involvement and participation: developing the concept of institutional embeddedness using WERS2004. *International Journal of Human Resource Management*, **20**(10): 2150–68.

Cox, T., Griffiths, A., Barlowe, C., Randall, R., Thomson, L. and Rial-Gonzalez, E. (2000) Organizational interventions for work stress: a risk management approach. HSE Contract Research Report. London: HSE.

Coyle-Shapiro, J. A.-M., Shore, L., Taylor, M. S. and Tetrick, L. (2005) *The Employment Relationship*. Oxford: Oxford University Press.

Craig, A. W. J. and Solomon, N. (1996) *The System of Industrial Relations in Canada* (5th edn). Scarborough, Ontario: Prentice-Hall.

Craig, M. (1981) *Office Worker's Survival Handbook*. London: BSSR.

Crane, A. (1995) Rhetoric and reality in the greening of organizational culture. *Greener Management International*, **12**: 49–62.

Crane, D. (ed.) (1994) *The Sociology of Culture*. Cambridge, MA: Blackwell.

Cregan, C. and Brown, M. (2010) The influence of union membership status on workers' willingness to participate in joint consultation. *Human Relations*, **63**(3): 331–48.

Cross, B. and Travaglione, A. (2004) The times they are a-changing: who will stay and who will go in a downsizing organization? *Personnel Review*, **33**(3): 275–90.

Crossan, M. M. (1999) An organizational learning framework: from intuition to institution. *Academy of Management Review*, **24**(3): 522–38.

Crossan, M., Lane, H. and White, R. (1999) An organizational learning framework: from intuition to institution. *Academy of Management Review*, **24**: 522–37.

Crouch, C. (1982) *The Politics of Industrial Relations* (2nd edn). London: Fontana.

Cullen, L. (2002) *A Job To Die for: Why so Many Americans Are Killed, Injured or Made Ill at Work and What To Do About It*. Monroe, ME: Common Courage Press.

Cully, M., O'Reilly, A., Woodland, S. and Dix, G. (1998) 'The 1998 Workplace Employee Relations Survey, first findings'. Available at: www.dti.gov.uk/emar.

Cully, M., Woodland, S., O'Reilly, A. and Dix, G. (1999) *Britain at Work*. London: Routledge.

Cunningham, S., Ryan, Y., Stedman, L., Bagdon, K.,

Flew, T. and Coaldrake, P. (2000) *The Business of Borderless Education*. Canberra: Department of Education, Training and Youth Affairs.

Curnow, B. (1986) The creative approach to pay. *Personnel Management*, October: 32–6.

Currie, G., Knights, D. and Sgtarkey, K. (2010) Introduction: a post-crisis critical reflection on business schools. *British Journal of Management*, 21: 1–5.

Curson, J. (2006) Crystal-ball gazing: planning the medical workforce. *British Journal of Hospital Medicine*, 67(8): 1141–7.

Curson, J. A., Dell, M. E., Wilson, R. A., Bosworth, D. L. and Baldauf, B. (2010) Who does workforce planning well? *International Journal of Health Care Quality Assurance*, 23(1): 110–19.

Czerny, A. (2004) Not so quick and easy. *People Management*, 26 February: 14–15.

Daft, R. (2010) *Organizational Theory and Design* (10th edn). Mason, OH: South-Western.

Dai, G. and DeMeuse, K. P. (2007) *A review of onboarding research*. White Paper. Los Angeles, CA: Korn/Ferry International.

Dalen, L. H., Stanton, N. A. and Roberts, A. D. (2001) Faking personality questionnaires in personnel selection. *Journal of Management Development*, 20(8): 729–41.

Danford, A., Richardson, M., Stewart, P., Tailby, S. and Upchurch, M. (2008) Partnership, high performance work systems and quality of working life. *New Technology, Work and Employment*, 23(3): 151–66.

Daniel, W. W. and Millward, N. (1983) *Workplace Industrial Relations in Britain*. London: Heinemann.

Daniels, C. (2004) 50 best companies for minorities. *Fortune*, 149(13): 136–42.

Daniels, K. (2006) Rethinking job characteristics in work stress research. *Human Relations*, 59(3): 267–90.

Daniels, K. (2011) Stress and well-being are still issues and something still needs to be done: or why agency and interpretation are important for policy and practice. In G.P. Hodgkinson and J. K. Ford (eds) *International Review of Industrial and Organizational Psychology*, No. 26 (pp. 1–46). New York: John Wiley & Sons.

Daniels, K. and Macdonald, L. (2005) *Equality, Diversity and Discrimination*. London: Chartered Institute of Personnel and Development.

Datta, D., Guthrie, J., Basuil, D. and Pandey, A. (2010) Causes and effects of employee downsizing: a review and synthesis. *Journal of Management*, 36(1): 281–348.

Dau-Schmidt, K. G. and Ellis, B. (2009) The relative bargaining power of employers and unions in the global information age: a comparative analysis of the United States and Japan. *International and Comparative Law Review*, 20(1): 1–19.

Davidson, M. J. and Cooper, C. L. (1992) *Shattering the Glass Ceiling*. London: Paul Chapman.

Davies, H. (2002) Understanding organizational culture in reforming the National Health Service. *Royal Society of Medicine Journal*, 95(3): 140–2.

Davies, J. and Easterby-Smith, M. (1984) Learning and developing from managerial work experiences. *Journal of Management Studies*, 21(2): 168–83.

Davies, P., Freeedland, M. (1994) *Labour Law: Text and Materials*. London: Weidenfeld & Nicolson.

Dawber, A. (2010) We're all in it together? Company bosses enjoy £500,000 pay increases. *The Independent*, August 11, p. 6.

Dawson, M. (2005) Costa's 'filter' gets the right employees. *Human Resource Management International Digest*, 13(4): 21–2.

Day, D. (2001) Leadership development: a review in context. *Leadership Quarterly*, 11(4): 581–613.

Dayan, K., Fox, S. and Kasten, R. (2008) The preliminary employment interview as a predictor of assessment center outcomes. *International Journal of Selection and Assessment*, 16(2): 102–11.

Deal, T. E. and Kennedy, A. A. (1982) *Organization Cultures: The Rites and Rituals of Organization Life*. New York: Addison-Wesley

Dean, D. and Liff, S. (2010) Equality and diversity: the ultimate industrial relations concern. In T. Colling and M. Terry (eds) *Industrial Relations Theory and Practice* (3rd edn) (pp. 422–46). Chichester: John Wiley & Sons.

Debono, J. (2001) Sexual harassment in employment: an examination of decisions looking for evidence of a sexist jurisprudence. *New Zealand Journal of Industrial Relations*, 26(3): 329–40.

Deci, E. L., Koestner, R. and Ryan, R. M. (1999) A meta-analytic review of experiments examining the effects of extrinsic rewards on intrinsic motivation. *Psychological Bulletin*, 125(6): 627–68.

De Cieri, H. (2008) Transnational firms and cultural diversity. In P. Boxall, J. Purcell and P. Wright (eds) *The Oxford Handbook of Human Resource Management* (pp. 509–29). Oxford: Oxford University Press.

De Cieri, H. and Dowling, P. (1999) Strategic human resource management in multinational enterprises: theoretical and empirical developments. In P. Wright, L. Dyer, J. Boudreau and G. Milkovich (eds) *Research in Personnel and Human Resource Management* (pp. 305–27). Stanford, CT: JA Press.

Deery, S. and Kinnie, N. (2004) *Call Centres and Human Resource Management: A Cross-national Perspective*. Basingstoke: Palgrave Macmillan.

Delaney, J. T. and Goddard, J. (2001). An industrial relations perspective on the high-performance paradigm. *Human Resource Management Review*, **11**: 395–429.

Delaney, J. T. and Huselid, M. A. (1996) The impact of HRM practices on perceptions of organizational performance. *Academy of Management Journal*, **39**(4): 949–69.

Delbridge, R. and Keenoy, T. (2010) Beyond managerialism? *International Journal of Human Resource Management*, **21**(6): 799–817.

Delbridge, R. and Turnbull, T. (1992) Human resource maximization: the management of labour under JIT system. In P. Blyton and P. Turnbull (eds) *Reassessing Human Resource Management* (pp. 56–73). London: Sage.

Delery, J. (1998) Issues of fit in strategic human resource management: implications for research. *Human Resource Management Review*, **8**(3): 289–309.

Delery, J. and Doty, H. (1996) Modes of theorizing in strategic human resource management: tests of universalistic, contingency and configurational performance predictions. *Academy of Management Journal*, **39**: 802–35.

Delery, J. and Shaw, J. (2001) The strategic management of people in work organizations: review, synthesis and extension. *Research in Personnel and Human Resources Management*, **20**: 165–97.

De Menezes, L. and Wood, S. (2006) The reality of flexible work systems in Britain. *International Journal of Human Resource Management*, **17**(1): 106–38.

Den Hartog, D. N. and Verburg, R. M. (2004) High performance work systems, organizational culture and firm effectiveness. *Human Resource Management Journal*, **14**(1): 55–78.

DeNisi, A. and Kluger, A. (2000) Feedback effectiveness: can 360-degree appraisal be improved? *Academy of Management Executive*, **14**(1): 129–39.

Denzin, N. and Lincoln, Y. (2005) *Handbook of Qualitative Research* (3rd edn). Thousand Oaks, CA: Sage.

Department for Business, Innovation and Skills (2010a) *Skills for Sustainable Growth*, London: Department for Business, Innovation and Skills.

Department for Business, Innovation and Skills (2010b) *Small and Medium-sized Enterprise (SME) Statistics for the UK and Regions 2009*. London: Department of Business Innovation and Skills.

Department for Business, Innovation and Skills (2011) *Helping Small Firms Start, Grow and Prosper*. London: Department of Business Innovation and Skills.

Department for Education and Employment (1991) *Education and Training for the 21st Century*. White Paper. Sheffield: DfEE.

Department for Education and Employment (1998) *The Learning Age: A Renaissance for a New Britain*. Green Paper. Sheffield: DfEE.

Department for Education and Skills (2003) *21st Century Skills – Realising our Potential: Individuals, Employers, Nation*. London: DfES.

Department for Education and Skills (2005) *Skills: Getting on in Business, Getting on at Work*. London: DfES.

Department of Employment (1974) *Company Manpower Planning*. Manpower Papers No. 1. London: HMSO.

Department of Innovation, Universities and Skills (2007) *World Class Skills: Implementing the Leitch Review of Skills in England*. London; DIUS.

Department of Trade and Industry (2004) *The UK Contact Centre Industry: A Study*. London: DTI.

Department of Trade and Industry (2005a) *People, Strategy and Performance: Results from the Second Work and Enterprise Business Survey*. London: DTI.

Department of Trade and Industry (2005b) *Inside the Workplace: First Findings from the 2004 Workplace Employment Relations Survey* (WERS 2004). London: DTI.

Des, G. G. and Shaw, J. D. (2001) Voluntary turnover, social capital and organizational performance. *Academy of Management Review*, **26**: 446–56.

Despres, C. and Hiltrop, J. (1995) Human resource management in the knowledge age: current practice and perspectives on the future. *Employee Relations*, **17**(1): 9–23.

Devanna, M. A., Fombrun, C. J. and Tichy, N. M. (1984) A framework for strategic human resource management. In C. J. Fombrun, N. M. Tichy and M. A. Devanna (eds) *Strategic Human Resource Management* (pp. 3–18). New York: John Wiley & Sons.

Devins, D. and Gold, J. (2000) 'Cracking the tough nuts': mentoring and coaching managers of small firms, *Career Development International*, **5**(4/5): 250–5.

De Vos, A. and Soens, N. (2008) Protean attitude and career success: the mediating role of self-management. *Journal of Vocational Behavior*, **73**: 449–56.

Dex, S. (1988) Gender and the labour market. In D. Gallie (ed.) *Employment in Britain* (pp. 281–309). Oxford: Blackwell.

Dickens C. (1854/1995) *Hard Times*. London: Penguin.

Dickens, C. (1859/1952) *A Tale of Two Cities*. London: HarperCollins.

Dickens, L. (1998) What HRM means for gender equality. *Human Resource Management Journal*, **8**(1): 23–45.

Dickens, L. and Hall, M. (2010) The changing legal framework of employment relations. In T. Colling and

M. Terry (eds) *Industrial Relations: Theory and Practice* (3rd edn) (pp. 298–322); Chichester: John Wiley & Sons.

Diefendorff, J., Richard, E., Erin, R. M. and Croyle, M. H. (2006) Are emotional display rules formal job requirements? Examination of employee and supervisor perceptions. *Journal of Occupational and Organisational Psychology*, **79**(2): 273–98.

Diekma, A. B. and Eagly, A. H. (2000) Stereotypes as dynamic constructs: women and men of the past, present, and future. *Personality and Social Psychology Bulletin*, **26**: 1171–88.

Dierendonck, D., Haynes,C., Borrill, C. and Stride, C. (2007) Effects of upward feedback on leadership behaviour toward subordinates. *Journal of Management Development*, **26**(3): 228–38.

Dietrich, M. and Roberts, J. (1997) Beyond the economics of professionalism. In J. Broadbent, M. Dietrich and J. Roberts (eds) *The End of the Professions?* (pp. 14–33). London: Routledge.

Disney, R. (1990) Explanations of the decline in trade union density in Britain: an appraisal. *British Journal of Industrial Relations*, **28**(2): 165–77.

Dixon, N. (1994) *The Organizational Learning Cycle: How We Can Learn Collectively*. Maidenhead: McGraw-Hill.

Dobbin, F. (2005) Is globalization making us all the same? *British Journal of Industrial Relations*, **43**(4): 569–76.

Docherty, P., Kira, M. and Shani, A..B (2009) *Creating Sustainable Work Systems* (2nd edn). London: Routledge.

Doellgast, V. (2010) Collective voice under decentralized bargaining: a comparative study of work reorganization in US and German call centres. *British Journal of Industrial Relations*, **48**(2): 375–99.

Doherty, M. (2009) When the working day is through: the end of work as identity? *Work, Employment and Society*, **23**(1): 84–101.

Doherty, N. and Tyson, S. (2000) HRM and employee well-being: raising the ethical stakes. In D. Winstanley and J. Woodall (eds) *Ethical Issues in Contemporary Human Resource Management* (pp. 102–115). Basingstoke: Palgrave.

Donaldson, T. and Preston, L. E. (1995) The stakeholder theory of the corporation: concepts, evidence and implications. *Academy of Management Review*, **20**(1): 15–19.

Donkin, R. (2010) *The Future of Work*. Basingstoke: Palgrave Macmillan.

Donnelly, E. (1987) The training model: time for a change. *Industrial and Commercial Training*, May/June: 3–6.

Donovan, Lord (1968) *Royal Commission on Trade Unions Employers' Association*. Cmnd 3623. London: HMSO.

Dore, R. (1973) *British Factory, Japanese Factory*. London: Allen & Unwin.

Dowling, P. J., Welch, D. and Schuler, R. (1999) *International Journal of Human Resource Management: Managing People in the International Context* (3rd edn). Cincinatti, OH: South-Western.

Dowling, P. J., Festing, M., and Engle Allen, D. (2008) *International Human Resource Management* (5th edn). London: Thomson Learning.

Down, S. and Smith, D. (1998) It pays to be nice to people. *Personnel Review*, **27**(2): 143–55.

Drew, G. (2009) A '360' degree view for individual leadership development. *Journal of Management Development*, **28**(7): 581–92.

Drohan, M. (2000) Technology comes with a price: stress and depression. *Globe and Mail*, October 11, p. B15.

Drucker, P. F. (1993) *Post-capitalist Society*. London: Butterworth Heinemann.

du Gay, P. (1996) *Consumption and Identity at Work*. London: Sage.

Dulewicz, V. and Higgs, M. (2000) Emotional intelligence: a review and evaluation. *Journal of Managerial Psychology*, **15**(4): 341–72.

Dundon, T., Wilkinson, A., Marchington, M. and Ackers, P. (2004) The meaning and purpose of employee voice. *International Journal of Human Resource Management*, **15**(6): 1149–70.

Dunphy, D. C. Griffiths, A. and Benn, S(2003) *Organizational Change for Corporate Sustainability: Understanding Organizational Change*. London: Routledge.

Dupee, J. M., Ernst, N. P. and Caslin, K. E. (2011) Does multisource feedback influence performance appraisal satisfaction? *Nursing Management*, **42**(3): 12–16.

Durkheim, E. (1933/1997) *The Division of Labor in Society*. New York: Free Press.

Duxbury, L. and Higgins, C. (2002) Telework: a primer for the millennium introduction. In Cooper, C. L. and Burke, R. J. (eds) *The New World of Work: Challenges and Opportunities* (pp. 157–200). Oxford: Blackwell.

Dweck, C. (2008) *Mindset: The New Psychology of Success*. New York: Ballantine.

Dwelly, T. and Bennion, Y. (2003) *Time To Go Home: Embracing the Home-working Revolution*. London: Work Foundation.

Dyck, D. E. (2002) *Disability Management: Theory, Strategy and Industrial Practice* (2nd edn). Markham, Ontario: Butterworths.

Eady, J. and Motraghi, N. (2010) United action. *New Law*

Journal, 160 (7423). Available at: www.newlawjournal. co.uk (accessed March 26, 2011).

Eagleton, T. (1983) *Literary Theory: An Introduction*. Minneapolis: University of Minnesota Press.

Eagleton, T. (2011) *Why Marx Was Right*. New Haven: Yale University Press.

Eagly, A. (1987) Sex differences in social behavior: a social-role interpretation. Hillsdale, NJ: Lawrence Erlbaum.

Easterby-Smith, M. (1994) *Evaluating Management Development, Training and Education* (2nd edn). Aldershot: Gower.

Easterby-Smith, M. and Prieto, I. (2008) Dynamic capabilities and knowledge management: an integrative role for learning? *British Journal of Management*, **19**(3): 235–49.

Easterby-Smith, M., Snell, R. and Gherardi, S. (1998) Organizational learning: diverging communities of practice. *Management Learning*, **29**(3): 259–72.

Easterby-Smith, M., Burgoyne, J. and Araujo, L. (eds) (1999) *Organizational Learning and the Learning Organization*. London: Sage.

Ebbinghaus, B. and Waddington, J. (2000) United Kingdom/Great Britain. In B. Ebbinghaus and J. Visser (eds) *The Societies of Europe: Trade Unions in Western Europe Since 1945* (pp. 705–56). Basingstoke: Palgrave Macmillan.

Edgell, S. (2012) *The Sociology of Work* (2nd edn) London: Sage.

Edvinsson, L. and Malone, M. S. (1997) *Intellectual Capital*. London: Piatkus.

Edwards, J. (2000) Technological discontinuity and workforce size: an argument for selective downsizing. *International Journal of Organizational Analysis*, **8**(3): 290–308.

Edwards, P. K. (1985) *Managing Labour Relations Through the Recession*. Warwick: Industrial Relations Research Unit, University of Warwick.

Edwards, P. K. (1986) *Conflict at Work: A Materialist Analysis of Workplace Relations*. Oxford: Blackwell.

Edwards, P. K. (1995) The employment relationship. In P. K. Edwards (ed.) *Industrial relations: Theory and Practice in Britain*. Oxford: Blackwell.

Edwards, P. and Sengupta, S. (2010) Industrial relations and economic performance. In T. Colling and M. Terry (eds) *Industrial Relations: Theory and Practice* (3rd edn) (pp. 378–97). Chichester: John Wiley & Sons.

Edwards, P. and Wajcman, J. (2005) *The Politics of Working Life*. Oxford: Oxford Universtiy Press.

Edwards, P. and Wright, M. (2001) High involvement work systems and performance outcomes: the strength of variable, contingent and context bound relationships. *International Journal of Human Resource Management*, **124**: 568–85.

Edwards, P. K., Geary, J. and Sisson, K. (2001) Employee invovement in the workplace: transformative, exploitative or limited and controlled? In J. Bélanger, G. Murray and P.-A. Lapointe (eds) *Work and Employment Relations in the High Performance Workplace*. London: Cassell/Mansell.

Edwards, P., Belanger, J., and Wright, M. (2002) The social relations of productivity. *Relations Industrielles/ Industrial Relations*, **57**(2): 309–28.

Edwards, R. (1979) *Contested Terrain: The Transformation of the Workplace in the Twentieth Century*. London: Heinemann.

Egan, J. (2004) Putting job evaluation to work: tips from the front line. *IRS Employment Review*, (792): 8–15.

Eisenhardt, K. M. (1989) Agency theory: an assessment and review. *Academy of Management Review*, **14**: 57–74.

Elenkov, D. (1998) Can American management concepts work in Russia?: a cross-cultural comparative study. *California Management Review*, **40**(4): 133–56.

Elger, T. and Smith, C. (1994) *Global Japanization?* London: Routledge.

Elias, P. and Purcell, K. (2003) *Measuring Change in the Graduate Labour Market*. Research Paper No. 1. Bristol: Employment Studies Research Institute.

Elkington, J. (1998) Enter the triple bottom line. In A. Henriques and J. Richardson (eds) *The Triple Bottom Line: Does it All Add Up?* (pp. 1–16). London: Earthscan.

Ellinger, A. and Bostrom, R. (2002) An examination of managers' beliefs about their roles as facilitators of learning. *Management Learning*, **33**(2): 147–79.

Elliott, L. (2011) Double-dip recession fears see 49bn wiped off shares. *The Guardian*, September 6, p. 1.

Engels, F. (1845/1973) *The Conditions of the Working Class in England*. Moscow: Progress Publishers.

Enhert, I. (2009) Sustainability and human resource management: reasoning and applications on corporate websites. *European Journal of International Management*, **3**(4): 419–38.

Equality and Human Rights Commission (2011) *Sex and Power 2011*. London: EHRC.

Eraut, M. (2000a) Non-formal learning and tacit knowledge in professional work. *British Journal of Educational Psychology*, **70**: 113–36.

Eraut, M. (2000b) Non-formal learning, implicit learning and tacit knowledge in professional work. In F. Coffield (ed.) *The Necessity of Informal Learning* (pp. 12–31). Bristol: Policy Press.

Etzioni, A. (1988) *The Moral Dimension*. New York: Free Press.

European Commission (2008) *Restructuring in Europe*. Brussels: European Commission.

Eva, D. and Oswald, R. (1981) *Health and Safety at Work*. London: Pan Original.

Evans, A. L. and Lorange, P. (1989) The two logics behind human resource management. In P. Evans, Y. Doz and A. Laurent (eds) *Human Resource Management in International Firms: Change, Globalization, Innovation* (pp. 144–62). Basingstoke: Palgrave Macmillan.

Evans, J. A., Kunda, G. and Barley, S. A. (2004) Beach time, bridge time, and billable hours: the temporal structure of technical contracting. *Administrative Science Quarterly*, **49**: 1–38.

Eveline, J. and Todd, P. (2009) Gender mainstreaming: the answer to the gender pay gap? *Gender, Work and Organization*, **16** (5): 536–58.

Evered, R. D. and Selman, J. C. (1989) Coaching and the art of management. *Organizational Dynamics*, Autumn: 16–32.

Exworthy, M. and Halford S. (eds) (1999) *Professionals and the New Managerialism in the Public Sector*. Buckingham: Open University Press.

Fairholm, G. W. (1996) Spiritual leadership: fulfilling whole-self needs at work. *Leadership and Organizational Development*, **17**(5): 11–17.

Farazmand, A. (2002) Privatization and globalization: a critical analysis with implications for public management education and training. *International Review of Administrative Sciences*, **68**: 355–71.

Farndale, E., Hope-Hailey, V. and Kelliher, C. (2011) High commitment performance management: the roles of justice and trust. *Personnel Review*, **40**(1): 5–23.

Farrell, A. and Hart, M. (1998) What does sustainability really mean? The search for useful indicators. *Environment*, **40**(9): 4–31.

Farrell, D. (2005) Offshoring: value creation through economic change. *Journal of Management Studies*, **42**(3): 675–83.

Fayol, H. (1949) *Administration Industrielle et Générale/ General and Industrial Management*. London: Pitman.

Felstead, A. and Jewson, N. (1999) Flexible labour and non-standard employment: an agenda of issues. In A. Felstead and N. Jewson (eds) *Global Trends in Flexible Labour* (pp. 1–20). Basingstoke: Palgrave Macmillan.

Felstead, A., Jewson, N., Phizacklea, A. and Walters, S. (2002) Opportunities to work at home in the context of work–life balance. *Human Resource Management Journal*, **12**(1): 54–76.

Feltham, R. (1992) Using competencies in selection and recruitment. In S. Boam and P. Sparrow (eds) *Designing and Achieving Competency*. (pp. 89–103). Maidenhead: McGraw-Hill.

Ferguson, K. L. and Reio, T.G. (2010) Human resource management systems and firm performance. *Journal of Management Development*, **29**(5): 471–94.

Fernandez, E., Junquera, B., and Ordiz, M. (2003) Organizational culture and human resources in the environmental issue. *International Journal of Human Resource Management*, **14**(4): 634–56.

Findlay, P., McKinlay, A., Marks, A. and Thompson, P. (2000) Flexible when it suits them: the use and abuse of teamwork skills. In S. Procter and F. Mueller (eds) *Teamworking* (pp. 222–43). Basingstoke: Palgrave Macmillan.

Findlay, P., McKinlay, A., Marks, A. and Thompson, P. (2009) Collective bargaining and new work regimes: 'too important to be left to bosses'. *Industrial Relations Journal*, **40**(3): 235–51.

Finegold, D. and Soskice, D. (1988) The failure of training in Britain: analysis and prescription. *Oxford Review of Economic Policy*, **4**(3): 21–53.

Fineman, S. (1996) Emotional subtexts in corporate greening, *Organizational Studies*, **17**(3): 479–500.

Fineman, S. (2003) *Understanding Emotion at Work*. London: Sage.

Fischlmayr, I. and Kollinger, I. (2010) Work-life balance – a neglected issue among Austrian female expatriates. *International Journal of Human Resource Management*, **21**(4): 455–87.

Fitz-enz, J. (2000) *The ROI of Human Capital*. New York: AMACOM.

Fitz-enz, J. and Davison, B. (2002) *How to Measure Human Resources Management* (3rd edn). New York: McGraw-Hill.

Fitzgerald, A. and Teal, G. (2004) Health reforms, professional identity and occupational sub-cultures: the changing interprofessional relations between doctors and nurses. *Contemporary Nurse*, **16**: 9–19.

Flamholz, E. (1985) *Human Resource Accounting*. Los Angeles, CA: Jossey-Bass.

Flanagan, J. C. (1954) The critical incident technique. *Psychological Bulletin*, **51**(4): 327–59.

Flecker, J. and Meil, P. (2010) Organizational restructuring and emerging service value chains: implications for work and employment. *Work, Employment and Society*, **24**(4): 680–98.

Fletcher, C. (1998) Circular argument. *People Management*, October 1: 46–9.

Fletcher, C. (2004) *Appraisal and Feedback: Making Performance Review Work* (3rd edn). London: Chartered Institute of Personnel and Development.

Fletcher, J. K. (1999) *Disappearing Acts: Gender, Power and Relational Practices at Work*. Cambridge, MA: MIT Press.

Fletcher, N. (2010) Executive pay quadrupled while share prices fell. *The Guardian*, July 5, p. 22.

Flood, P. Mkamwa, T., O'Regan, C., Guthrie, J. P., Liu,

W., Armstrong, C. and MacCurtain, S. (2008) *New Models of High Performance Work Systems: The Business Case for Strategic HRM, Partnership and Diversity and Equality Systems*. Dublin: NCPP and Equality Authority.

Florida, R. (1996) Lean and green: the move to environmentally conscious manufacturing. *California Management Review*, **39**(1): 80–105.

Foley, G. (2001) *Strategic Learning: Understanding and Facilitating Organizational Change*. Sidney: Centre for Popular Education.

Fombrun, C. J., Tichy, N. M. and Devanna, M. A. (eds) (1984) *Strategic Human Resource Management*. New York: John Wiley & Sons.

Ford, G. (2011) The link between personality and human error: using assments to hire safety-minded employees. *PeopleTalk*, **16**(1): 16–18.

Ford, J., Tomlinson,, J., Sommerlad, H. and Gold, J. (2009) "'Just don't call it diversity': Developing a programme for the business case for diversity in west yorkshire", paper presented at the HRD conference, Newcastle-upon-Tyne.

Forde, C., Stuart, M., Gardiner, J., Greenwood, I., MacKenzie, R. and Perett, R. (2008) *Socially Responsible Restructuring in an Era of Mass Layoffs*. CERIC Working Paper No. 5. Leeds: Leeds University.

Forshaw, C. (2010) Communications. In Bratton, J., Sawchuk, P., Forshaw, C., Callinan, M. and Corbett, M. (eds) *Work and Organizational Behaviour* (2nd edn) (pp. 383–406). Basingstoke: Palgrave Macmillan.

Forth, J. and Millward, N. (2000) *The Determinants of Pay Levels and Fringe Benefit Provision in Britain*. NIESR Discussion Paper No. 171. London: National Institute of Economic and Social Research.

Fosket, J. and Mamo, L. (2009) *Living Green*. Vancouver, British Columbia: New Society Publishers.

Foster, C. and Harris, L. (2005) Easy to say, difficult to do: diversity management in retail. *Human Resource Management Journal*, **15**(3): 4–17.

Fox, A. (1974) *Beyond Contract: Work, Power and Trust Relations*. London: Faber.

Fox, A. (1985) *Man Mismanagement* (2nd edn). London: Hutchinson.

Fox, S. (1997) From management education and development to the study of management learning. In J. Burgoyne and M. Reynolds (eds) *Management Learning* (pp. 21–37). London: Sage.

Francis, H. and Keegan, A. (2005) Slippery slope. *People Management*, June 30: 26–31.

Francis, H. and Keegan, A. (2006) The changing face of HRM: in search of balance. *Human Resource Management Journal*, **16**(3): 231–49.

Francis, H. and Reddington (2012) Employer branding and organisational effectiveness. In Francis, H., Holbeche, L. and Reddington, R. (eds) *People and Organisational Development: A New Agenda for Organisational Effectiveness*. London: Chartered Institute of Personnel and Development.

Fredrickson, B. L. and Losada, M. F. (2005) Positive affect and the complex dynamics of human flourishing. *American Psychologist*, **60**(7): 678–86.

Freeland, C. (2011) Revolutions spawned in economic despair. *Globe and Mail*, March 4, p. B2.

Freeman, R. B. and Lazear, E. P. (1995) An economic analysis of works councils. In J. Rogers and W. Streeck (eds) *Works Councils: Consultation, Representation and Cooperation in Industrial Relations* (pp. 27–50). Chicago, IL: University of Chicago Press.

Freeman, R. B. and Pelletier, J. (1990) The impact of industrial relations legislation on British union density. *British Journal of Industrial Relations*, **28**(2): 141–64.

Frege, C. M. (2002) A critical assessment of the theoretical and empirical research on works councils. *British Journal of Industrial Relations*, **40**(2): 221–48.

French, R. (2010) *Cross-Cultural Management in Work Organizations* (2nd edn). London: Chartered Institute of Personnel and Development.

Fried, Y., Cummings, A., and Oldham, G. R. (1998) Job design. In M. Poole and M. Warner (eds) *The IEBM Handbook of Human Resource Management* (pp. 532–43). London: International Thomson Business Press.

Friedman, A. (1977) *Industry and Labour: Class Struggle at Work and Monopoly Capitalism*. London: Macmillan.

Friedrich, T. L., Vessey, W. B., Schuelke, M. J., Ruark, G. A. and Mumford, M. D. (2009) A framework for understanding collective leadership: the selective utilization of leader and team expertise within networks. *Leadership Quarterly*, **20**: 933–58.

Friesen, J. (2011) Wage gap wider for children of immigrants. *Globe and Mail*, February 26, p. A15.

Fröbel, P. and Marchington, M. (2005) Teamworking structures and worker perceptions: a cross-national study in pharmaceuticals. *International Journal of Human Resource Management*, **16**(2): 256–76.

Frost, A. and Taris, D.(2005) Understanding the unionization decision. In M. Gunderson, A. Ponak and D. Taras (eds) *Union-Management Relations in Canada* (5th edn) (pp. 23–57). Toronto, Ontario: Pearson.

Fulford, R. (1999) *The Triumph of Narrative*. Toronto, Ontario: Anansi.

Fuller, A. and Unwin, L. (2003) Fostering workplace

learning: looking through the lens of apprenticeship. *European Educational Research Journal*, **2**(1): 41–55.

Fuller, A., Ashton, D., Felstead, A., Unwin, L., Walters, S. and Quinn, M. (2003) *The Impact of Informal Learning at Work on Business Productivity*. London: Department of Trade and Industry.

Fuller, L. and Smith, V. (1991) Consumers' reports: management by customers in a changing economy. *Work, Employment and Society*, **5**(1): 1–16.

Fuller-Love, N. (2006) Management development in small firms. *International Journal of Management Reviews*, **8**(3):175–90.

Furnham, A. (2004) Performance management systems. *European Business Journal*, **16**(2): 83–94.

Furnham, A. (2008) HR professionals' beliefs about, and knowledge of, assessment techniques and psychometric tests. *International Journal of Selection and Assessment*, **16**(3): 300–5.

Fyfe, J. (1986) Putting people back into the manpower planning equation. *Personnel Management*, October: 64–9.

Gabriel, Y. (1995) The unmanaged organization: stories, fantasies and subjectivity. *Organizational Studies*, **16**(3): 477–501.

Gagnon, S. and Cornelius, N. (2000) Re-examining workplace equality: the capabilities approach. *Human Resource Management Journal*, **10**(4): 68–87.

Gahan, P. and Abeysekera, L. (2009) What shapes an individual's work values? An integrated model of the relationship between work values, national culture and self-construal. *International Journal of Human Resource Management*, **20**(1): 126–47.

Gamble, J. (2003) Transferring human resource practices from the United Kingdom to China: the limits and potential for convergence. *International Journal of Human Resource Management*, **14**(3): 369–87.

Gani, A. (1996) Who joins the unions and why? Evidence from India. *International Journal of Manpower*, **17**(6–7): 54.

Garavan, T. N. (1997) The learning organization: a review and an evaluation. *Learning Organization*, **4**(1): 18–29.

Garavan, T. (2007) A strategic perspective on human resource development. *Advances in Developing Human Resources*, **9**(1): 11–30.

Garavan, T. and McCarthy, A. (2007) Multi-source feedback and management. In Hill, R. and Stewart, J. (eds) *Management Development Perspectives from Research and Practice*. London: Routledge.

Garavan, T. and McGuire, D. (2010) Human resource development and society: human resource development's role in embedding corporate social responsibility, sustainability, and ethics in organizations. *Advances in Developing Human Resources*, **12**(5): 487–507.

Garavan, T. N., Heraty, N. and Barnicle, B. (1999a) Human resource development: current issues, priorities and dilemmas. *Journal of European Industrial Training*, **23**(4/5): 169–79.

Garavan, T., Barnicle, B. and O'Suulleabhain, F. (1999b) Management development: contemporary trends, issues and strategies. *Journal of European Industrial Training*, **23**(4/5):191–207.

Garavan, T. N., Morley, M., Gunnigle, P. and Collins, E. (2001) Human capital accumulation: the role of human resource development. *Journal of European Industrial Training*, **25**(2–4): 48–68.

Garavan, T., Heraty, N., Rock, A., and Dalton, E. (2010) Conceptualizing the behavioral barriers to CRS and CS in organizations: a typology of HRD interventions. *Advances in Developing Human Resources*, **12**(5): 587–613.

Garengo, P., Biazzo, S., and Bititci, U. (2005) Performance measurement systems in SMEs: a review for a research agenda. *International Journal of Management Reviews*, **7**(1): 25–47.

Garrick, J. (1998) *Informal Learning in the Workplace*. London: Routledge.

Garrick, J. (1999) The dominant discourses of learning at work. In D. Boud and J. Garrick (eds) *Understanding Learning at Work* (pp. 216–29). London: Routledge.

Garvey, B. and Williamson, B. (2002) *Beyond Knowledge Management*. Harlow: Pearson Education.

Garvey, R., Stokes, P. and Megginson, D. (2009) *Coaching and Mentoring: Theory and Practice*. London: Sage.

Gascó, J. L., Llopis, J. and González, M. (2004) The use of information technology in training human resources. *Journal of European Industrial Training*, **28**(5): 370–82.

Gattiker, U. E. and Cohen, A. (1997) Gender-based wage differences. *Relations Industrielles/Industrial Relations*, **52**(3): 507–29.

Gault, J., Leach, E. and Duey, M. (2010) Effects of business internships on job marketability: the employers' perspective. *Education and Training*, **52**(1): 76–88.

Geary, J. F. and Dobbins, A. (2001) Teamworking: a new dynamic in pursuit of management control. *Human Resource Management Journal*, **11**(1): 3–23.

Gee, S. (2008) Bang on target. *People Management*, February 8. Available at: www.peoplemanagement. co.uk/pm/articles/2008/02/bangontarget.htm (accessed February 17, 2012).

Geertz, C. (1973) Thick description: toward an

interpretive view of culture. In *The Interpretation of Cultures* (pp. 3–32). New York: Basic Books.

Gennard, J. and Judge, G. (2005) *Employee Relations* (4th edn). London: Chartered Institute of Personnel and Development.

Georgiou, S., Thomson, M., Richardson-Owen, A., and Edwards, H. (2009) The costs of workplace injuries and work-related ill health in the UK. *Ege Academic Review*. Available at: http://eab.ege.edu.tr/pdf/9_3/C9-53-M13 pdf.

Gereffi, G. and Christian, M. (2009) The impacts of Wal-Mart: the rise and consequences of the world's dominant retailer. *Annual Review of Sociology*, **35**: 573–91.

Gerhart, B. (2000) Compensation strategy and organizational performance. In S. Rynes and B. Gerhart (eds) *Compensation in Organizations: Current Research and Practice* (pp. 151–94). San Francisco, CA: Jossey-Bass.

Gerhart, B. (2005) Human resources and business performance: findings, unanswered questions, and an alternative approach. *Management Revue*, **16**(2): 174–85.

Gerhart, B. (2008) Modelling HRM and performance linkages. In P. Boxall, J. Purcell and P. Wright (eds) *The Oxford Handbook of Human Resource Management* (pp. 552–80). Oxford: Oxford University Press.

Gewirth, A. (1991) Human rights and the prevention of cancer. In D. Poff and W. Waluchow (eds) *Business Ethics in Canada* (2nd edn) (pp. 205–15). Scarborough, Ontario: Prentice Hall.

Giacalone, R. A., Jurkiewicz, C. and Deckop, J. (2008) On ethics and social responsibility: the impact of materialism, post-materialism, and hope. *Human Relations*, **61**(4): 483–514.

Giambatista, R. C., Rowe, W. G. and Riaz, S. (2005) Nothing succeeds like succession: a critical review of leader succession literature since 1994. *Leadership Quarterly*, **16**: 963–91.

Gibb, A. A. (1997) Small firms training and competitiveness: building on the small business as a learning organisation. *International Small Business Journal*, **15**(3): 13–29.

Gibb, A. A. (2009) Meeting the development needs of owner managed small enterprise: a discussion of the centrality of action learning. *Action Learning: Research and Practice*, **6**(3): 209–27.

Gibb, A. A and Dyson, J. (1982) *Stimulating the Growth of Owner Manager Firms*. Research Paper. Durham: Durham University Business School.

Gibb, S. (2003) Line manager involvement in learning and development: small beer or big deal? *Employee Relations*, **25**(3): 281–93.

Gibb, S. (2008) *Human Resource Development: Process, Practices and Perspectives* (2nd edn). Basingstoke: Palgrave Macmillan.

Giddens, A. (1984) *The Constitution of Society*. Berkeley, CA: University of California Press.

Giddens, A. (1990) *The Consequences of Modernity*. Cambridge: Polity Press.

Giddens, A. (2009) *Sociology* (6th edn). Cambridge: Polity Press.

Giddens, A. and Hutton, W. (2000) In conversation. In W. Hutton and A. Giddens (eds) *On the Edge: Living with Global Capitalism* (pp. 1–51). London: Jonathan Cape.

Giles, A. and Iain, H. (1989) The collective agreement. In J. Anderson, M. Gunderson and A. Ponak (eds) *Union–Management Relations in Canada* (2nd edn). Don Mills, Ontario: Addison-Wesley.

Giles, A. and Starkman, A. (2001) The collective agreement. In M. Gunderson, A. Ponack and D. Taras (eds) *Union–Management Relations in Canada* (4th edn) (pp. 272–313). Toronto, Ontario: Addison-Wesley Longman.

Gillani, B. B. (2003) *Learning Theories and the Design of E-Learning Environments*. Lanham, MD: University Press of America.

Gillespie, R. (1998) Mayo, George Elton. In M. Poole and M. Warner (eds) *The IEBM Handbook of Human Resource Management* (pp. 905–9). London: International Thomson Business Press.

Gilliland, S. W. (1993) The perceived fairness of selection systems: An organizational justice perspective, *Academy of Management Review*, **18**: 694–734.

Gilman, M. and Marginson, P. (2002) Negotiating European Works Councils: contours of constrained choice. *Industrial Relations Journal*, **33**(1): 36–51.

Gilmore, S. (2010) WikiLeaks just made the world more repressive. *Globe and Mail*, November 30, p. A19.

Gilpin-Jackson, Y. and Bushe, G. R.(2007) Leadership development training transfer: a case study of post-training determinants. *Journal of Management Development*, **26**(10): 980–1004.

Glasbeek, H. (1991) The worker as a victim. In D. Poff and W. Waluchow (eds) *Business Ethics in Canada* (2nd edn) (pp. 199–204). Scarborough, Ontario: Prentice Hall.

Global Business Coalition (GBC) 'Fighting HIV/AIDS in the workplace: a company management guide'. Available at: www.gbcimpact.org/HIVWorkplace.

Godard, J. (1991) The progressive HRM paradigm: a theoretical and empirical re-examination. *Relations Industrielles/Industrial Relations*, **46**(2): 378–99.

Godard, J. (1997) Managerial strategies, labour and employment relations and the state: the Canadian case and beyond. *British Journal of Industrial Relations*, **35** (3): 399–426.

Godard, J. (2004) A critical assessment of the high-performance paradigm. *British Journal of Industrial Relations*, **42**(2): 349–78.

Godard, J. (2005) *Industrial Relations: The Economy and Society* (3rd edn). Concord, Ontario: Captus Press.

Goffman, E. (1959) *The Presentation of Self in Everyday Life*. New York: Doubleday Anchor.

Goffman, E. (1961) *Asylums: Essays on the Social Situation of Mental Patients and Other Inmates*. New York: Doubleday Anchor.

Goffman, E. (1967) *Interaction Ritual: Essays on Face-to-Face Behavior*. New York: Doubleday Anchor.

Gold, J. and Smith, V. (2003) Advances toward a learning movement: translations at work. *Human Resource Development International*, **6**(2): 139–52.

Gold, J. and Stewart, J. (2011) Theorising in HRD. *Journal of European Industrial Training*, **35**(3): 196–8.

Gold, J. and Thorpe, R. (2008) 'Training, it's a load of crap!': the story of the hairdresser and his 'suit'. *Human Resource Development International*, 11(4): 385–99.

Gold, J. and Thorpe, R. (2010) Leadership and management development in SMEs. In J. Gold, R. Thorpe and A. Mumford (eds) *The Gower Handbook of Leadership and Management Development*. Aldershot: Gower.

Gold, J., Holman, D. and Thorpe, R. (2002) The role of argument analysis and story telling in facilitating critical thinking. *Management Learning*, **33**(3): 371–88.

Gold, J., Rodgers, H. and Smith, V. (2003) What is the future for the human resource development professional? A UK perspective. *Human Resource Development International*, **6**(4): 437–455.

Gold, J., Thorpe, R., Woodall, J. and Sadler-Smith, E. (2007) Continuing professional development in the legal profession: a practice-based learning. *Management Learning*, **38**(2): 235–50.

Gold, J. , Holden, R., Griggs, V. and Kyriakidou, N. (2010a) Workplace learning and knowledge management. In Gold, J., Holden, R., Iles, P., Stewart, S. and Beardwell, J. (eds) *Human Resource Development: Theory and Practice* (pp. 194–215). Basingstoke: Palgrave Macmillan.

Gold, J., Thorpe, R. and Mumford, A. (2010b) *Leadership and Management Development*. London: Chartered Institute of Personnel and Development.

Gold, J., Wadsworth, B., Kaye, D. and Dawson, C. (2010c) 'Coaching as bricolage', paper presented at the HRD in Europe Conference, Pecs, Hungary.

Golden, T., Veiga, J. and Dino, R. (2008) The impact of professional isolation on teleworker job performance and turnover intentions: does time spent teleworking, interacting face-to-face, or having access to communication-enhancing technology matter? *Journal of Applied Psychology*, **93**(6): 1412–21.

Goldthorpe, J. H., Lockwood, D., Bechhofer, F. and Platt, J. (1968) *The Affluent Worker: Industrial Attitudes and Behaviour*. Cambridge: Cambridge University Press.

Goleman, D. (2006) *Emotional Intelligence* (10th anniversary edition). London: Bantam.

Gollan, P. J. (2002) So what's the news? Management strategies towards non-union employee representation at News International. *Industrial Relations Journal*, **33**(4): 316–31.

Gollan, P. J. (2006) Editorial: Consultation and non-union employee representation. *Industrial Relations Journal*, **37**(5): 428–37.

Gomez-Mejia, L. and Balkin, D. (1992) *Compensation, Organizational Strategy, and Firm Performance*. Cincinnati, OH: South-Western.

Goodley, S. (2011) Equal pay coming for female bosses ... in 98 years' time. *The Guardian*, August, 31, p. 1.

Goodstein, E. S. (1999) *Economics of the Environment*. Englewood Cliffs, NJ: Prentice Hall.

Google (2012) 'Top 10 reasons to work at Google'. Available at: www.google.co.uk/jobs/reasons.html.

Gorz, A. (1982) *Farewell to the Working Class*. London: Pluto.

Gospel, H. F. and Littler, C. R. (eds) (1983) *Managerial Strategies and Industrial Relations*. London: Heinemann.

Gould, A. (2010) Working at McDonalds: some redeeming features of McJobs. *Work, Employment and Society*, **24**(4): 780–802.

Gould-Williams, J. and Mohamed, R. B. (2011) A comparative study of the effects of 'best practice' HRM on worker outcomes in Malaysia and England local government. *International Journal of Human Resource Management*, **21**(5): 653–75.

Gourlay, S. (2006) Towards conceptual clarity for 'tacit knowledge': a review of empirical studies. *Knowledge Management Research and Practice*, **4**(1):60–9.

Governance Network (2002) *At the Crossroads of Change: Human Resources and the Municipal Sector*. Ottawa: Federation of Canadian Municipalities.

Grant, R. (2010) *Contemporary Strategic Analysis* (7th edn). Chichester: John Wiley & Sons.

Grant, T. (2011) Fears of a 'lost generation'. *Globe and Mail*, February 4, p. B3.

Gratton, L. (2000) A real step change. *People Management*, **6**(6): 26–30.

Gray, D. E. (2010) *Business Coaching for Managers and Organizations – Working with Coaches that Make the Difference*. Amherst, MA: HRD Press.

Gray, D. E. and Goregaokar, H. (2010) Choosing an executive coach: the influence of gender on the coach-coachee matching process. *Management Learning*, **41**(5): 525–44.

Gray, J. (2010) Very good one for the party's bigoted tendency. *The Guardian*, May 8, p. 39.

Green, F. (2004) Why has work effort become more intense?' *Industrial Relations* **43**: 709–41.

Green, F., Machin, S. and Wilkinson, D. (1998) Trade unions and training practices in British workplaces. *Industrial and Labour Relations Review*, **52**(2): 179–95.

Green, F., Ashton, D. N., James, D. and Sung, J. (1999) The role of the state in skill formation: evidence from the Republic of Korea, Singapore and Taiwan. *Oxford Review of Economic Policy*, **15**(1): 82–96.

Green, F., Mayhew, K. and Molloy, E. (2003) *Employer Perspectives Survey*. Warwick University: Centre for Skills, Knowledge and Organisational Performance.

Green, J. (1998) Employers learn to live with AIDS. *HR Magazine*, **43**(2): 62–7.

Greenhaus, J. H., Callanan, G. A. and Godshalk, V. M. (2010) *Career Management* (4th edn). Thousand Oaks, CA: Sage.

Gregory, A. and Milner, S. (2009) Editorial: Work–life balance: a matter of choice? *Gender, Work and Organization*, **16**(1): 1–13.

Grey, C. (2005) *Studying Organizations*. London: Sage.

Grey, C. and Mitev, N. (1995) Reengineering organizations: a critical appraisal. *Personnel Review*, **24**(1): 6–18.

Grice, A., Garner, R. and Morrison, S. (2011) Britain takes sides. *The Independent*, June 29, pp. 1–3.

Griffin, E., Finney, L., Hennessy, J. and Boury, D. (2009) *Maximising the Value of HR Business Partnering*. Horsham: Roffey Park.

Grimshaw, D. and Rubery, J. (2010) Pay and working time: shifting contours of the employment relationship. In T. Colling and M. Terry (eds) *Industrial Relations Theory and Practice* (3rd edn) (pp. 347–77). Chichester: John Wiley & Sons.

Grint, K. (2001) *The Arts of Leadership*. Oxford: Oxford University Press.

Grint, K. (2005) *Leadership: Limits and Possibilities*. Basingstoke: Palgrave Macmillan.

Grint, K. and Holt, C. (2011) Leading questions: If 'Total place', 'Big Society' and local leadership are the answers: what's the question? *Leadership*, **7**(1): 85–98.

Grint, K. and Willcocks, L. (1995) Business process re-engineering in theory and practice: business paradise regained? *New Technology, Work and Employment*, **10**(2): 99–108.

Grobler, P. and Warnich, S. (2005) *Human Resource Management in South Africa*. Hampshire: Thomson Learning.

Gröjer, J.-E. and Johanson, U. (1998) Current development in human resource accounting and costing. *Accounting, Auditing and Accountability*, **11**(4): 495–505.

Gronn, P. (2008) The future of distributed leadership. *Journal of Educational Administration*, **46**(2): 141–58.

Grote, R. (1996) *The Complete Guide to Performance Appraisal*. New York: American Management Association.

Groysberg, B. (2010) *Chasing Stars: The Myth of Talent and the Portability of Performance*. Princeton, NJ: Princeton University Press.

Groysberg, B., Nanda, A. and Nohria, N. (2004) The risky business of hiring stars. *Harvard Business Review*, **82**(5): 93–100.

Grugulis, I. (2002) *Skill and Qualification: The Contribution of NVQs to Raising Skill Levels*. SKOPE Research Paper No. 36. Warwick University: Centre for Skills, Knowledge and Organisational Performance.

Grugulis, I., Vincent, S. and Hebson, G. (2003) The rise of the 'network organization' and the decline of discretion. *Human Resource Management Journal*, **13**(2): 45–59.

Grund, C. and Sliwka, D. (2009) The anatomy of performance appraisals in Germany. *International Journal of Human Resource Management*, **20**(10): 2049–65.

Grzeda, M. M. (1999) Re-conceptualizing career change: a career development perspective. *Career Development International*, **4**(6): 305–11.

Guardian (2005) Women come off worse. *The Guardian*, April 10. Available at: www.guardian.co.uk/news/2004/apr/10/leadersandreply.mainsection.

Guba, E. G. and Lincoln, Y. S. (1989) *Fourth Generation Evaluation*. London: Sage.

Gubbins, C. and Garavan, T. (2009) Understanding the HRD Role in MNCs: the imperatives of social capital and networking. *Human Resource Development Review* **8**. 245–75.

Guest, D. E. (1986) Worker participation and personnel policy in the UK: some case studies. *International Labour Review*, **125**(6): 406–27.

Guest, D. E. (1987) Human resource management and industrial relations. *Journal of Management Studies*, **24**(5): 503–21.

Guest, D. E. (1989) HRM: implications for industrial relations. In J. Storey (ed.) *New Perspectives on Human Resource Management* (pp. 41–55). London: Routledge.

Guest, D. E. (1990) Human resource management and the American dream. *Journal of Management Studies*, **27**(4): 377–97.

Guest, D. E. (1995) Human resource management, trade unions and industrial relations. In J. Storey (ed.) *Human Resource Management: A Critical Text* (pp. 110–41). London: Routledge.

Guest, D. E. (1997) Human resource management and performance: a review and research agenda. *International Journal of Human Resource Management*, **8**(3): 263–76.

Guest, D. E. (1998) Beyond HRM: commitment and the contract culture. In P. Sparrow and M. Marchington (eds) *Human Resource Management: The New Agenda* (pp. 37–51). London: Financial Times/ Pitman.

Guest, D. E. (1999) Human resource management – the workers' verdict. *Human Resource Management Journal*, **9**(3): 5–25.

Guest, D. E. (2000) Piece by piece. *People Management*, **6**(15): 26–30.

Guest, D. (2001a) Human resource management: when reality confronts theory. *International Journal of Human Resource Management*, **12**: 1092–106.

Guest, D. E. (2001b) Industrial relations and human resource management. In J. Storey (ed.) *Human Resource Management: A Critical Text* (2nd edn) (pp. 96–113). London: Thomson Learning.

Guest, D. (2008) HRM and the worker: towards a new psychological contract? In P. Boxall, J. Purcell and P. Wright (eds) *The Oxford Handbook of Human Resource Management* (pp. 128–46) Oxford: Oxford University Press.

Guest, D. (2011) Human resource management and performance: still searching for some answers. *Human Resource Management Journal*, **21**(1): 3–13.

Guest, D. E. and Conway, N. (2002) Communicating the psychological contract: an employer perspective. *Human Resource Management Journal*, **12**(2): 22–38.

Guest, D. and Conway, N. (2004) *Employee Well-being and the Psychological Contract: A Report for the CIPD*. London: Chartered Institute of Personnel and Development.

Guest, D. and King, Z. (2004) Power, innovation and problem solving: the personnel managers' three steps to heaven? *Journal of Management Studies*, **41**(3): 401–23.

Guest, D. E., Davey, K. and Patch, A. (1998) *The Impact of New Forms of Employment Contract on Motivation and Innovation*. London: Economic and Social Research Council.

Guest, D. E., Michie, J., Conway, N. and Meehan, M. (2003) Human resource management and corporate performance in the UK. *British Journal of Industrial Relations*, **41**(2) 291–314.

Guirdham, M. (2011) *Communicating Across Cultures at Work* (3rd edn). Basingstoke: Palgrave Macmillan.

Gunderson, M. Ponak, A. and Taras, D. (eds) (2005) *Union–Management Relations in Canada* (5th edn). Toronto, Ontario: Pearson.

Gunnigle, P., Turner, T. and D'Art, D. (1998) Counterpoising collectivism: performance-related pay and industrial relations in greenfield sites. *British Journal of Industrial Relations*, **36**(4): 565–79.

Guthrie, J. P. (2008) Remuneration: pay effects on work. In P. Boxall, J. Purcell and P. Wright (eds) *The Oxford Handbook of Human Resource Management* (pp. 344–63). Oxford: Oxford University Press.

Guthrie, J. P., Flood, P., Liu, W. and MacCurtain, S. (2009) High performance work systems in Ireland: human resource and organizational outcomes. *International Journal of Human Resource Management*, **20**(1): 112–25.

Guy, M. E. and Newman, M. (2004) Women's jobs, men's jobs: sex segregation and emotional labor. *Public Administration Review*, **64**(3): 289–98.

Hackman, J. R. and Oldham, G. R. (1980) *Work Redesign*. New York: Addison-Wesley.

Haden, S. S. P, Oyler, J. D. and Humphreys, J. H. (2009) Historical, practical, and theoretical perspectives on green management. *Management Decision*, **47**(7): 1041–55.

Hadikin, R. and O'Driscoll, M. (2000) *The Bullying Culture: Causes, Effect, Harm Reduction*. Melbourne: Books for Midwives.

Hagger, M. (2009) Personality, individual differences, stress and health. *Stress and Health: Journal of the International Society for the Investigation of Stress*, **25**(5): 381–6.

Hales, C. P. (1986) What do managers do? A critical review of the evidence. *Journal of Management Studies*, **23**(1): 88–115.

Hall, D. T. (2002) *Careers In and Out of Organizations*. Thousand Oaks, CA: Sage.

Hall, M. and Marginson, P. (2005) Trojan horse and paper tigers. Assessing the significance of European Works Councils. In B. Harley, J. Hyman and P. Thompson (eds) *Participation and Democracy at Work* (pp. 204–21). Basingstoke: Palgrave Macmillan.

Hall, P. and Soskice, D. (2001) *Varieties of Capitalism*. Oxford: Oxford University Press.

Hall, P. A. and Soskice, D. (2009) An introduction to varieties of capitalism. In B. Hancke (ed.) *Debating Varieties of Capitalism: A Reader* (pp. 21–74). Oxford: Oxford University Press.

Halliday, T. C. (1987) *Beyond Monopoly: Lawyers, State Crises and Professional Empowerment*. Chicago, IL: University of Chicago Press.

Halman, F. and Fletcher, C. (2000) The impact of development centre participation and the role of individual differences in changing self-assessments.

Journal of Occupational and Organizational Psychology, **73**: 423–42.

Hamlin, B. (2010). Evidence-based leadership and management development. In J. Gold, R. Thorpe and A. Mumford (eds) *Gower Handbook of Leadership and Management Development*. Aldershot: Gower.

Hammer, M. (1997) *Beyond Reengineering*. New York: HarperCollins.

Hammer, M. and Champy, J. (1993) *Reengineering the Corporation*. London: Nicholas Brealey.

Hancke, B. (2009) (ed.) *Debating Varieties of Capitalism: A Reader*. Oxford: Oxford University Press.

Handy, C. (1987) *The Making of Managers*. London: NEDO.

Handy, L., Devine, M. and Heath, L. (1996) *360° Feedback: Unguided Missile or Powerful Weapon?* Berkhamsted: Ashridge Management Research Group.

Hansen, M. T., Mors, M. L. and Løvas, B. (2005) Knowledge sharing in organizations: multiple networks, multiple phases. *Academy of Management Journal*, **48**(5): 776–93.

Harding, K. (2003) A leap of faith. *Globe and Mail*, January 8, p. C1.

Harland, C., Knight, L., Lamming, R. and Walker, H. (2005) Outsourcing: assessing the risks and benefits for organisations, sectors and nations. *International Journal of Operations and Production Management*, **25**(9): 831–50.

Harley, B., Sargent, L. and Allen, B. (2010) Employee responses to 'high performance work system' practices. *Work, Employment and Society*, **24**(4): 740–60.

Harper, S. C. (1983) A developmental approach to performance appraisal. *Business Horizons*, September/October: 68–74.

Harri-Augstein, S. and Webb, I. M. (1995) *Learning To Change*. Maidenhead: McGraw-Hill.

Harrington, B., McLoughlin, K. and Riddell, D. (1998) Business process re-engineering in the public sector: a case study of the Contributions Agency. *New Technology, Work and Employment*, **13**(1): 43–50.

Harris, A. (2008) Distributed leadership: according to the evidence. *Journal of Educational Administration*, **46**(2): 172–88.

Harris, L. C. and Crane, A. (2002) The greening of organizational culture: management views on the depth, degree and diffusion of change. *Journal of Organizational Management*, **15**(3): 214–34.

Harris, M. M. (1989) Reconsidering the employment interview: a review of recent literature and suggestions for future research. *Personnel Psychology*, **42**: 691–726.

Harter, J., Schmidt, F., and Haynes, T. (2002) Business unit level relationships between employee satisfaction, employee engagement and business outcomes: a meta analysis. *Journal of Applied Psychology*, **87**(2): 268–79.

Harvey, D. (1994) *The Conditions of Postmodernity: An Enquiry into the Origins of Cultural Change*. Oxford: Blackwell.

Harvey, G. and Turnbull, P. (2010) On the Go: walking the high road at a low cost airline. *International Journal of Human Resource Management*, **21**(2): 230–41.

Harzing, A. W. (2000) An empirical analysis and extension of the Bartlett and Ghoshal typology of multinational companies. *Journal of International Business Studies*, **31**(1): 101–20.

Hassard, J. and Parker, M. (1993) *Postmodernism and Organizations*. London: Sage.

Hassard, J., Morris, J. and Sheehan, J. (2004) The 'third way': the future of work and organization in a 'corporatized' Chinese economy. *International Journal of Human Resource Management*, **15**(2): 314–30.

Hatry, H. P. (2010) Looking into the crystal ball: performance management over the next decade. *Public Administration Review*, **70**(Suppl. 1): s208–11.

Hau Siu Chow, I. and Liu, S. S. (2009) The effect of aligning organizational culture and business strategy with HR systems on firm performance in Chinese enterprises. *International Journal of Human Resource Management*, **20**(11): 2292–310.

Haunschild, A. (2003) Humanization through discipline? Foucault and the goodness of employee health programmes. *Journal of Critical Postmodern Organization Science*, **2**(3): 46–59.

Hausknecht, J., Day, D. and Thomas, S. (2004) Applicant reactions to selection procedures: an updated model and meta-analysis. *Personnel Psychology*, **57**: 639–83.

Haynes, S. G. and Feinleils, M. (1980) Women, word and coronary heart disease: prospective findings from the Framingham Heart Study. *American Journal of Public Health* **70**(2): 133–41.

Health Canada (1998) *Influencing Employee Health*. Workplace Health System. Ottawa: Canadian Fitness and Lifestyle Research Institute.

Healthcare Commission (2009) *Investigation into Mid Staffordshire NHS Foundation Trust*. London: Healthcare Commission.

Health and Safety Commission and Department of the Environment, Transport and the Regions (2000) *Revitalizing Health and Safety*. Strategy Statement. London: DETR.

Health and Safety Executive (2001) 'Heath and safety statistics, 2000/2001'. Available at: www.hse.gov.uk/statistics/2001.

Health and Safety Executive (2007) 'Workplace stress costs Great Britain in excess of 530 million'. Available at: www.hse.gov.uk/press/2007/c07021.htm.

Health and Safety Executive (2011a) 'Health and Safety Executive annual report'. Available at: www.hse.gov. uk/ (accessed March 9, 2011).

Health and Safety Executive (2011b) 'Statistics on violence at work'. Available at: www.hse.govt.uk/violence.

Heathfield, S. (2007) Performance appraisals don't work – what does? *Journal for Quality and Participation*, Spring: 6–9.

Heck, R. and Hallinger, P. (2010) Testing a longitudinal model of distributed leadership effects on school improvement. *Leadership Quarterly*, **21**(5): 867–85.

Heckscher, C. and Donnelon, A. (eds) (1994) *The Post-bureacratic Organization*. Thousand Oaks, CA: Sage.

Heery, E. (2000) The new pay: risk and representation at work. In D. Winstanley and J. Woodall (eds) *Ethical Issues in Contemporary Human Resource Management* (pp. 172–88). Basingstoke: Palgrave.

Heery, E. (2002) Partnership versus organizing: alternative futures for British trade unionism. *Industrial Relations Journal*, **33**(1): 20–35.

Heery, E. (2004) The trade union response to agency labour in Britain. *Industrial Relations Journal*, **35**(5): 434–50.

Heery, E. (2005) Sources of change in trade unions. *Work, Employment and Society*, **19**(1): 91–106.

Heery, E. (2009) The representation gap and the future of worker representation. *Industrial Relations Journal*, **40**(4): 324–36.

Heery, E. and Simms, M. (2010) Employer responses to union organizing: patterns and effects. *Human Resource Management Journal*, **20**(1): 3–22.

Heery, E., Conley, H., Delridge, R., Simms, M. and Stewart, P. (2004) Trade union responses to non-standard work. In G. Healy, E. Heery, P. Taylor and W. Brown (eds) *The Future of Worker Representation* (pp. 127–50). Basingstoke: Palgrave Macmillan.

Heller, F., Pusic, E., Strauss, G. and Wilpert, B. (1998) *Organizational Participation: Myth and Reality*. Oxford: Oxford University Press.

Hendry, C. (1994) The single European market and the HRM response. In P. Kirkbride (ed.) *Human Resource Management in Europe* (pp. 93–113). London: Routledge.

Hendry, C. and Pettigrew, A. (1990) Human resource management: an agenda for the 1990s. *International Journal of Human Resource Management*, **1**(1): 17–44.

Henkens, K., Remery, C. and Schippers, J. (2005) Recruiting personnel in a tight labour market: an analysis of employers' behaviour. *International Journal of Manpower*, **26**(5): 421–33.

Herod, A., Rainnie, A. and McGrath-Champ, S. (2007) Working space: why incorporating the geographical is central to theorizing work and employment practices, *Work, Employment and Society*, **21**(2): 247–64.

Herriot, P., Manning, W. E. G. and Kidd, J. M. (1997) The content of the psychological contract. *British Journal of Management*, **8**(2): 151–62.

Hertz, N. (2002) *The Silent Takeover: Global Capitalism and the Death of Democracy*. London: Arrow.

Herzberg, F., Mansner, B. and Snyderman, B. (1959) *The Motivation to Work* (2nd edn). New York: Wiley.

Heyes, J. (2000) Workplace industrial relations and training. In H. Rainbird (ed.) *Training in the Workplace* (pp. 148–68). Basingstoke: Palgrave Macmillan.

Heyes, J. and Nolan, P. (2010) State, capital and labour relations in crisis. In T. Colling and M. Terry (eds) *Industrial Relations: Theory and Practice* (3rd edn) (pp. 106–24). Chichester: John Wiley & Sons.

Heywood, J. S., Siebert, W. S., and Wei, X. (2010) Work–life balance: promises made and promises kept. *International Journal of Human Resource Management*, **21**(11): 1976–95.

Hickey, R., Kuruvilla, S. and Lakhani, T. (2010) No panacea for success: member activism, organizing and union renewal. *British Journal of Industrial Relations*, **48**(1): 53–83.

Hijzen, A. and Venn, D. (2011) *The Role of Short-time Work Schemes During the 2008–09 Recession*. OECD Social, Employment and Migration Working Paper No. 115. Brussels: OECD Publishing.

Hilbrecht, M., Shaw, S., Johnson, L. C. and Andrey, J. (2008) 'I'm home for the kids': contradictory implications for work–life balance of teleworking mothers. *Gender, Work and Organization*, **15**(5): 454–76.

Hill, C. and Jones, G. (2010) *Strategic Management Theory: An Integrated Approach* (9th edn). Mason, OH: South-Western.

Hirch, A. (2010) Bullying in the workplace on the rise. *The Guardian*, January 4. Available at: www.guardian.co.uk/money/2010/jan/04/bully-workplace-recession (accessed March 15, 2011).

Hirsh, W. and Jackson, C. (1997) *Strategies for Career Development: Promise, Practice and Pretence*. Report No. 305. Brighton: Institute for Employment Studies.

Hirsh, W. and Tamkin, P. (2005) *Planning Training for your Business*. Report No. 422. Brighton: Institute of Employment Studies.

Hitt, M., Bierman, L., Shimizu, K., and Kochhar, R. (2001) Direct and moderating effects of human capital on strategy and performance in professional service firms: a resource-based view perspective. *Academy of Management Journal*, **44**(1): 13–28.

HM Treasury Committee (2010) *Treasury Committee Report on Women in The City*. London: TSO.

Hobsbawm, E. (1995) *Age of Extremes*. London: Abacus.

Hochschild, A. R. (1983) *The Managed Heart: Commercialization of Human Feeling*. Berkeley, CA: University of California Press.

Hodgkinson, G.P. and Clarke, I. (2007) Exploring the cognitive significance of organizational strategizing: a dual-process framework and research agenda. *Human Relations*, **60**, 243–55.

Hodson, R. (2001) *Dignity at Work*. Cambridge: Cambridge University Press.

Hoel, H. and Beale, D. (2006) Workplace bullying, psychological perspectives and industrial relations: towards a contextualised and interdisciplinary approach. *British Journal of Industrial Relations*, **44**(2): 239–62.

Hoel, H. and Cooper, C. (2000) *Destructive Conflict and Bullying at Work*. Manchester: Manchester School of Management, UMIST.

Hofman, A. and Hofman, T. (2010) Why are senior woman so rare in finance? *Financial Times*, May 20. Available at: http://www.ft.com/cms/s/0/69ca3d46-6444-11df-8618-00144feab49a.html#axzz1me1HjsY0 (accessed February 17, 2012).

Hofstede, G. Hofstede, Gert Jan and Minkov, M. (2010) *Cultures and Organizations: Soft-ware of the mind* (3rd edn). London: McGraw-Hill.

Hogarth, T., Hasluck, C. and Pierre, G. (2000) *Work–Life Balance 2000: Baseline Study of Work–Life Balance Practices in Great Britain*. Summary Report. London: DfEE.

Hogarth, T., Hasluck, C., Pierre, G., Winterbotham, M. and Vivien, D. (2001) *Work–Life Balance 2000: Results from the Baseline Study*. Department for Education and Employment Research Report No. 249. London: DfEE.

Holbeche, L. (1999) *Aligning Human Resources and Business Strategy*. Oxford: Butterworth Heinemann.

Holbeche, L. (2008a) Developing leaders for uncertain times. *Impact*, (23): 6–9.

Holbeche, L. (2008b) The leadership paradox. *Futures*, (1): 2–4.

Hollenbeck, J. (2000) A structural approach to external and internal person–team fit. *Applied Psychology: An International Review*, **49**(3): 534–49.

Holman, D. (2000) Contemporary models of management education in the UK, *Management Learning*, **31**(2): 197–217.

Holman, D., Pavlica, K. and Thorpe, R. (1997)

Rethinking Kolb's theory of experiential learning in management education: the contribution of social constructionism and activity theory. *Management Learning*, **28**(2): 135–48.

Holman, D., Batt. R. and Holtgrewe, U. (2007) 'The Global Call Centre Report: international perspectives on management and employment'. Available at: www.ilr.cornell.edu/globalcallcenter (accessed December 1, 2010).

Holmes, C. and Mayhew, K. (2010) *Are UK Labour Markets Polarising?* SKOPE Research Paper No. 97. Warwick: Warwick University, Centre for Skills, Knowledge and Organisational Performance.

Holmes, J. (2006) *Gender Talk at Work*. Oxford: Blackwell.

Holmes, L. (1995a) 'The making of real managers: ideology, identity and management development'. Available at: www.re-skill.org.uk/relskill/realmgr.htm (accessed April 14, 2011).

Holmes, L. (1995b) HRM and the irresistible rise of the discourse of competence. *Personnel Review*, **24**(4): 34–49.

Holton, E. F., Bates, R. A., Booker, A. I. and Yamkovenko, V. B. (2007) Convergent and divergent validity of the learning transfer system inventory. *Human Resource Development Quarterly*, **18**(3): 385–419.

Hom, P. W., Griffeth, R. W., Palich, L. E. and Bracker, J. S. (1999) Revisiting met expectations as a reason why realistic job previews work. *Personnel Psychology*, **52**(1): 1–16.

Home Office (2003) *Diversity Matters*. London: Home Office.

Honey, P. and Mumford, A. (1996) *Manual of Learning Styles* (3rd edn). Maidenhead: Honey Publications.

Honeyball, S. (2010) *Honeyball and Bower's Textbook on Employment Law* (11th edn). Oxford: Oxford University Press.

Hoogvelt, A. (2001) *Globalization and the Postcolonian World* (2nd edn). Basingstoke: Palgrave Macmillan.

Hope-Hailey, V., Farndale, E. and Truss, C. (2005) The HR department's role in organizational performance. *Human Resource Management Journal*, **15**(3): 49–66.

Höpfl, H. and Dawes, F. (1995) 'A whole can of worms!': the contested frontiers of management development and learning. *Personnel Review*, **24**(6): 19–28.

Hoque, K. (1999) Human resource management and performance in the UK hotel industry. *British Journal of Industrial Relations*, **37**(3): 419–43.

Hoque, K. (2003) All in all, it's just another plaque on the wall: the incidence and impact of the Investors In People standard. *Journal of Management Studies*, **40**(2): 543–71.

Hoque, K. and Noon, M. (2001) Counting angels: a

comparison of personnel and HR specialists. *Human Resource Management Journal*, **11**(3): 5–22.

Hoque, K., Taylor, S. and Bell, E. (2005) Investors in People: market-led voluntarism in vocational education and training. *British Journal of Industrial Relations*, **43**(1): 135–53.

House of Commons (2009) 'Treasury – Ninth Report, Banking crisis: reforming corporate governance and pay in the City', May. Available at: www.publications. parliament.uk/pa/cm200809/cmselect/cmtreasy/519/51902.htm.

House of Commons Transport Committee (2008) *The Opening of Heathrow Terminal 5*. London: TSO.

Houston, D. M. (ed.) (2005) *Work–Life Balance in the 21st Century*. Basingstoke: Palgrave Macmillan.

Howe, C.L., Auflick, P. and Freiberger, G. (2011) Upward evaluation at the Arizona Health Sciences Library. *Journal of the Medical Library Association*, **99**(1): 91–4.

Huczynski, A. and Buchanan, D. A. (2010) *Organizational Behaviour* (7th edn). Harlow: Pearson Education.

Huffcutt, A. I., Weekly, J. A., Wiesner, W. H., DeGrout, T. G. and Jones, C. (2001) Comparison of situational and behavior description interview questions for higher-level positions. *Personnel Psychology*, **54**(3): 619–44.

Hughes, E. C. (1945) Dilemmas and contradictions of status. *American Journal of Sociology*, **50**(5): 353–9.

Hughes, J. (1990) *The Philosophy of Social Research* (2nd edn). Harlow: Longman.

Hui, C. and Graen, G. (1997) Guanxi and professional leadership in contemporary Sino-American joint ventures in mainland China. *Leadership Quarterly*, **8**(4): 451–65.

Hume, D. (1748/2007) *An Enquiry Concerning Human Understanding* (P. Millican, ed.). Oxford: Oxford University Press.

Hurley-Hanson, A. and Giannantonio, C. (2008) 'Human resource information systems in crises', paper presented at Academy of Strategic Management Conference, Tunica.

Huselid, M. A. (1995) The impact of HRM practices on turnover, productivity, and corporate financial performance. *Academy of Management Journal*, **38**(3): 635–72.

Huselid, M. A., Beatty, R. W. and Becker, B. E. (2005) A players or A positions? The strategic logic of workforce management. *Harvard Business Review*, **83**(12): 110–17.

Hutchinson, S. and Purcell, J. (2010) Managing ward managers for roles in HRM in the NHS: overworked and under resourced. *Human Resource Management Journal*, **20**(4): 357–74.

Hutchinson, S., Purcell, J. and Kinnie, N. (2000)

Evolving high commitment management and the experience of the RAC call centre. *Human Resource Management Journal*, **10**(1): 63–78.

Huws, U. (1997) Teleworking: *Guidelines for Good Practice*. Report No. 329. Brighton: Institute for Employment Studies.

Hyman, J., Baldry, C., Scholarios, D. and Bunzel, F. (2003) Work–life imbalance in call centres and software development. *British Journal of Industrial Relations*, 41(2): 215–39.

Hyman, R. (1975) *Industrial Relations: A Marxist Introduction*. Basingstoke: Palgrave Macmillan.

Hyman, R. (1987) Trade unions and the law: papering over the cracks? *Capital and Class*, (31): 43–63.

Hyman, R. (1989) *The Political Economy of Industrial Relations*. Basingstoke: Palgrave Macmillan.

Hyman, R. (1994) Industrial relations in Western Europe: an era of ambiguity? *Industrial Relations Journal*, **33**(1): 1–24.

Hyman, R. (1997a) The future of employee representation. *British Journal of Industrial Relations*, **35**(3): 309–36.

Hyman, R. (1997b) Editorial. *European Journal of Industrial Relations*, **3**(1): 5–6.

Hyman, R. (1999) National industrial relations systems and transnational challenges: an essay review. *European Journal of Industrial Relations*, **5**(1): 89–110.

Hyman, R. (2001) *Understanding European Trade Unionism*. London: Sage.

Hyman, R. (2010) British industrial relations: the European dimension. In T. Colling and M. Terry (eds) *Industrial Relations: Theory and Practice* (3rd edn) (pp. 54–79). Chichester: John Wiley & Sons.

Hyman, R. and Brough, I. (1975) *Social Values and Industrial Relations*. Oxford: Blackwell.

Hynie, M., Jensen, K., Johnny, M., Wedlock, J. and Phipps, D. (2011) Student internships bridge research to real world problems. *Education and Training*, **53**(1): 45–56.

Ichniowski, C., Kochan, T., Levine, D., Olson, C. and Strauss, G. (1996) What works at work: overview and assessment. *Industrial Relations*, **35**(3): 299–333.

Ichniowski, C., Shaw, K. and Prennushi, G. (1997) The effects of human resource management on productivity: a case study of steel finishing lines. *American Economic Review*, **87**(3): 291–313.

Ignatieff, M. (2011) Crisis of faith. *Globe and Mail*, September 10, pp. F1–3.

Iles, P. and Preece, D. (2010) Talent management and career development. In Gold, J., Thorpe, R. and Mumford, A. (eds) *Gower Handbook of Leadership and Management Development* (pp. 243–60). Aldershot: Gower Press.

Iles, P. and Salaman, G. (1995) Recruitment, selection

and assessment. In Storey, J. (ed.) *Human Resource Management* (pp. 203–33). London: Routledge.

Ilgen, D. R., Fisher, C. D. and Taylor, M. S. (1979) Consequences of individual feedback on behavior in organizations. *Journal of Applied Psychology*, **64**(4): 349–71.

Immen, W. (2011) Duking it out with bad managers. *Globe and Mail*, January 21, p. B14.

Incomes Data Services (2003) *Pay and Conditions in UK Call Centres*. London: IDS.

Incomes Data Services (2010) *Talent management. HR studies*. No. 918. London: IDS.

Industrial Relations Services (2001) *Competency Frameworks in UK Organisations*. London: IRS.

Industrial Relations Services (2003a) Sharpening up recruitment and selection with competencies. *IRS Employment Review*, **782**: 42–9.

Industrial Relations Services (2003b) Performance management; policy and practice. *Employment Trends*, **781**: 12–19.

Institute of Alcohol Studies (2010) 'Binge drinking: nature, prevalence and causes'. Available at: www.ias. org.uk/resources/factsheets/binge drinking.pdf.

International Labour Organization (2000) 'High performance working: research project overview'. Available at: www.ilo.org/public/english/employment/ skills/training/casest/overivew.htm (accessed May 2, 2002).

Jabbour, C. J. C. (2011) How green are HRM practices, organizational culture, learning and teamwork? A Brazilian study. *Industrial and Commercial Training*, **43**(2): 98–105.

Jabbour, C. J. C., Santos, F. C. A., and Nagano, S. M. (2010) Contributions of HRM throughout the stages of environmental management: methodological triangulation applied to companies in Brazil. *International Journal of Human Resource Management*, **21**(7): 1049–89.

Jackson, C. (1996) *Understanding Psychological Testing*. Leicester: BPS Books.

Jackson, D. J. R., Stillman, J. A. and Englert, P. (2010) Task-based assessment centers: empirical support for a systems model. *International Journal of Selection and Assessment*, **18**(2): 141–54.

Jackson, L. (2010) Enterprise resource planning systems: revolutionizing lodging human resources management. *Worldwide Hospitality and Tourism Themes*, **2**(1): 20–9.

Jackson, S. E. and Schuler, R. S. (1995) Understanding human resource management in the context of organizations and their environments. In M. R. Rosenzweig and L. W. Porter (eds) *Annual Review of Psychology*, **46**: 237–64.

Jacoby, S.M. (2004) *Employing Bureaucracy: Managers,* Unions, and the Transformation of Work in the 20th Century. London: Taylor & Francis.

Jacoby, S. M. (2005) *The Embedded Corporation: Corporate Governance and Employment Relations in Japan and the United States*. Princeton, NJ: Princeton University Press.

Jaffee, D. (2001) *Organization Theory: Tension and Change*. Boston: McGraw-Hill.

Jakupec, V. (2000) The politics of flexible learning: opportunities and challenges in a global world. In V. Jakupec and J. Garrick (eds) *Flexible Learning, Human Resource and Organisational Development* (pp. 67–84). London: Routledge.

Jamali, D., Sidani, Y. and Zouein, C. (2009) The learning organization: tracking progress in a developing country. *Learning Organization*, **16**(2): 103–21.

James, P. and Walters, D. (2002) Worker representation in health and safety: options for regulatory reform. *Industrial Relations Journal*, **33**(2): 141–56.

James, S. (2010) *What is apprenticeship?* Issues Paper No. 22. Oxford: SKOPE, Oxford University.

Jameson, F. (1991) *Postmodernism, or The Cultural Logic of Late Capitalism*, London: Verso.

Jang, B. (2011) Air Canada to launch cut-rate carrier. *Globe and Mail*, April 12, pp. B1, B4.

Jansen, B. and Jansen, K. (2005) Using the web to look for work. *Internet Research*, **15**(1): 49–66.

Janssens, M. and Steyaert, C. (2009) HRM and performance: a plea for reflexivity in HRM studies. *Journal of Management Studies*, **46**(1): 143–55.

Jarzabkowsksi, P. and Spee, A. P. (2009) Strategy-as-practice: a review and future directions for the field. *International Journal of Management Reviews*, **11**(1): 69–95.

Jarzabkowski, P., Giulietti, M. and Oliveira, B. (2009) *Building a Strategy Toolkit: Lessons from Business*. London: Advanced Institute of Management.

Jewson, N. and Mason, D. (1986) The theory and practice of equal opportunities policies: liberal and radical approaches. *Sociological Review*, **34**(2): 307–34.

Johanson, U. (1999) Why the concept of human resource costing and accounting does not work. *Personnel Review*, **28**(1/2): 91–107.

Johanson, U. and Nilson, M. (1996) *Human Resource Costing and Accounting and Organisational Learning*. Report No. 1995:1. Stockholm: Personnel Economics Institute.

Johnson, G., Scholes, K. and Whittington, R. (2005) *Exploring Corporate Strategy: Text and Cases* (8th edn). Harlow: Pearson Education.

Johnson, M. and Senges, M. (2010) Learning to be a programmer in a complex organization. *Journal of Workplace Learning*, **22**(3): 180–94.

Johnson, S. (1999) *Skills Issues in Small and Medium*

Sized Enterprises, National Skills Task Force Research Paper No. 13. Nottingham: DfEE.

Jones, A., Visser, F., Coats, D., Bevan, S. and McVerry, A. (2007) *Transforming Work*. London: Work Foundation.

Jones, G. (ed.) (2011) *Current Research in Sustainability*. Prahan: Tilde University Press.

Jones, O., Macpherson, A. and Thorpe, R. (2010) Learning in owner-managed small firms: mediating artefacts and strategic space. *Entrepreneurship and Regional Development*, **22**(7): 649–73.

Jones, V. (2009) *The Green Collar Economy*. New York: HarperCollins.

Jowit, J. (2010) British lawyer wants UN to declare 'ecocide' a crime. *The Guardian*, April 10, p. 21.

Judge, T. A. and Cable, D. M. (1997) Applicant personality, organizational culture and organization attraction. *Personnel Psychology*, **50**: 359–94.

Judge, T. A., Locke, E. A. and Durham, C. C. (1997) The dispositional causes of job satisfaction: a core evaluation approach. *Research in Organizational Behaviour*, **19**: 151–88.

Kagaari, J. R. K., Munene, J. C. and Ntayi, J. M. (2010) Performance management practices, information and communication technology (ICT) adoption and managed performance. *Quality Assurance in Education*, **18**(2): 106–25.

Kalleberg, A. L. and Moody, J. W. (1994) Human resource management and organizational performance. *American Behavioral Science*, **37**(7): 948–62.

Kamenou, N. and Fearfull, A. (2006) Ethnic minority women: a lost voice in HRM. *Human Resource Management Journal*, **16**(2): 154–72.

Kamoche, K. (1996) Strategic human resource management within a resource-capability view of the firm. *Journal of Management Studies*, **22**(2): 213–33.

Kamoche, K., Debrah, Y. A., Horwitz, F. M. and Muuka, G. N. (2004) *Managing Human Resource Management in Africa*. London: Routledge.

Kanuka, H. and Kelland, J. (2008) Has e-learning delivered on its promises? Expert opinion on the impact of e-learning in higher education. *Canadian Journal of Higher Education*, **38**(1): 45–65.

Kaplan, R. and Norton, D. (2000) *The Strategy-focused Organization: How Balanced Scorecard Companies Thrive in the New Business Environment*. Boston, MA: Harvard Business School Press.

Kärreman, D. and Alvesson, M. (2009) Resistaing resistance: counter-resistance, consent and compliance in a consulting firm. *Human Relations*, **62**(8): 1115–44.

Keashly, L. and Jagatic, K. (2003) By any other name: American perspectives on workplace bullying. In S. Einarsen, H. Hoel, D. Zapf and C. Cooper (eds) *Bullying and Emotional Abuse in the Workplace:*

International Perspectives in Research and Practice (pp. 31–61). London: Taylor and Francis.

Keegan, A. and Francis, H. (2010) Practitioner talk: the changing textscape of HRM and emergence of HR business partnership. *International Journal of Human Resource Management*, **21**(6): 873–98.

Keenan, G. (2011a) Sales gains give hope for Detroit Three. *Globe and Mail*, January 5, p. B1.

Keenan, G. (2011b) Honda, Toyota extend production cuts. *Globe and Mail*, April 9, p. B8.

Keenoy, T. (1990) Human resource management: rhetoric, reality and contradiction. *International Journal of Human Resource Management*, **1**(3): 363–84.

Keenoy, T. and Anthony, P. (1992) HRM: metaphor, meaning and morality. In P. Blyton and P. Turnbull (eds) *Reassessing Human Resource Management* (pp. 233–55). London: Sage.

Keep, E. (1999) *Employer Attitudes Towards Adult Learning*. Skills Task Force Research Paper No. 15. London: Department for Education and Employment.

Keep, E. (2004) Trapped on the low road? *Adults Learning*, February: 16–17.

Keep, E. and Mayhew, K. (2010) Moving beyond skills as a social and economic panacea. *Work Employment and Society*, **24**(3): 565–77.

Keep, E., Mayhew, K. and Payne, J. (2006) From skills revolution to productivity miracle: not as easy as it sounds? *Oxford Review of Economic Policy*, **22**(4): 539–59.

Keers, C. (2007) Using appreciative inquiry to measure employee engagement. *Strategic HR Review*, **2**(6): 10–11.

Keith, M. (2000) Sexual harassment case law under the Employment Contracts Act 1991. *New Zealand Journal of Industrial Relations*, **25**(3): 277–89.

Kelliher, C. and Anderson, D. (2008) For better or for worse? An analysis of how flexible working practices influence employees' perceptions of job quality. *International Journal of Human Resource Management*, **19**(3): 421–33.

Kelliher, C. and Anderson, D. (2010) Doing more with less? Flexible working practices and the intensification of work. *Human Relations*, **63**(1): 83–106.

Kelly, J. E. (1985) Management's redesign of work: labour process, labour markets and product markets. In D. Knights, H. Willmott and D. Collinson (eds) *Job Design: Critical Perspectives on the Labour Process* (pp. 30–51). Aldershot: Gower.

Kelly, J. E. (1996) Union militancy and social partnership. In P. Ackers, C. Smith and P. Smith (eds) *The New Workplace and Trade Unionism* (pp. 77–91). London: Routledge.

Kelly, J. E. (2005) Industrial relations approaches to the

employment relationship. In J. A.-M. Coyle-Shapiro, L. Shore, S. Taylor and L. Tetrick (eds) *The Employment Relationship: Examining Psychological and Contextual Perspectives* (pp. 48–64). Oxford: Oxford University Press.

Kelly, J. E. and Bailey, R. (1989) Research note: British trade union membership, density and decline in the 1980s. *Industrial Relations Journal*, **20**(1): 54–61.

Kempster, S. (2009) *How Managers Have Learnt To Lead*. Basingstoke: Palgrave Macmillan.

Kempster, S. and Cope, J. (2010) Learning to lead in the entrepreneurial context. *International Journal of Entrepreneurial Behaviour and Research*, **16**(1): 5–34.

Kennedy, V. (2010) 'Role of HR in catalyzing CSR policy to practice', January 10. Available at: www.articlesbase.com/human-resources-articles/role-of-hr-in-catalyzing-csr-policy-to-practice-1801505.html (accessed November 2011).

Kennerley, M. and Neely, A. (2002) A framework of the factors affecting the evolution of performance measurement systems. *International Journal of Operations and Production Management*, **22**: 1222–45.

Kenny, P. (2011) Quoted in the Editorial. *The Guardian*, June 7, 2011, p. 30.

Kepes, S., Delery, J., and Gupta, N. (2009) Contingencies in the effects of pay range on organizational effectiveness. *Personnel Psychology*, **62**, 497–531.

Kerr, R. and Robinson, S. (2011) Leadership as an elite field: Scottish banking leaders and the crisis of 2007–2009. *Leadership*, **7**(2): 151–73.

Kersley, B., Alpin, C., Forth, J., Bryson, A., Bewley, H., Dix, G. and Oxenbridge, S. (2005) *Inside the Workplace: First Findings from the 2004 Workplace Employment Relations Survey (WERS 2004)*. London: DTI/ESRC/ACAS/PSI.

Kersley, B., Alpin, C., Forth, J., Bryson, A., Bewley, H., Dix, G. and Oxenbridge, S. (2006) *Inside the Workplace: Findings from the 2004 Workplace Employment Relations Survey*. London: Routledge.

Kessels, J. W. M. (2001) Learning in organisations: a corporate curriculum for the knowledge economy. *Futures*, **33**(6): 497–506.

Kessler, I. (1994) Performance pay. In K. Sisson (ed.) *Personnel Management* (2nd edn). Oxford: Blackwell.

Kessler, I. (1995) Reward systems. In J. Storey (ed.) *Human Resource Management: A Critical Text* (pp. 254–79). London: Routledge.

Kessler, I. (2007) Reward choices: strategy and equity. In John Storey (ed.) *Human Resource Management: A Critical Text* (3rd edn) (pp. 159–76) London: Thomson Learning.

Kettley, P. (1997) *Personal Feedback: Cases in Point*. Report No. 326. Brighton: Institute for Employment Studies.

Kettley, P. and Reilly, P. (2003) *e-HR: An Introduction*. Report No. 398. Brighton: Institute of Employment Studies.

Khanna, T., Song, J. and Lee, K. (2011) The paradox of Samsung's rise. *Harvard Business Review*, **89**(7/8): 142–7.

Khapova, S. N. Arthur, M. B. and Wilderom, C.P.M (2007) The subjective career in the knowledge economy. In H. Gunz and M. Peiperl (eds) *Handbook of Career Studies* (pp. 114–30). Thousand Oaks, CA: Sage.

Kidwell, R. and Fish, A. (2007) High-performance human resource practices in Australian family businesses: preliminary evidence from the wine industry. *International Entrepreneurship and Management Journal*, **3**(1): 1–14.

Kim, H. and Cervero, R. M. (2007) How power relations structure the evaluation process for HRD programmes. *Human Resource Development International*, **10**(1): 5–20.

Kim, H. and Gong, Y. (2009) The roles of tacit knowledge and OCB in the relationship between group-based pay and firm performance. *Human Resource Management Journal*, **19**(2): 120–39.

Kim, J., MacDuffie, J.P. and Pil, F. (2010) Employee voice and organizational performance: team versus representative influence. *Human Relations*, **63**(3): 371–94.

Kinnie, N. J. and Arthurs, A. J. (1996) Personnel specialists' advanced use of information technology. *Personnel Review*, **25**(3): 3–19.

Kinnie, N., Hutchinson, S., Purcell, J., Rayton, B. and Swart, J. (2005) Satisfaction with HR practices and commitment to the organization: why one size does not fit all. *Human Resource Management Journal*, **15**(4): 9–29.

Kirkpatrick, D.L. (1998) *Evaluating Training Programs* (2nd edn). San Francisco, CA: Berrett-Koehler.

Kirton, G. and Greene, A. (2000) *The Dynamics of Managing Diversity*. Oxford: Butterworth Heinemann.

Kirton, G. and Greene, A.-M. (2010) *The Dynamics of Managing Diversity: A Critical Approach* (3rd edn). Oxford: Butterworth-Heinemann.

Klass, B. S. (2009) Discipline and grievances. In A. Wilkinson, N. Bacon, T. Redman and S. Snell (eds) *The Sage Handbook of Human Resource Management* (pp. 322–35) London: Sage.

Klass, B., Gainey, T., McClendon, J. and Yang, H. (2005) Professional employer organizations and their impact on client satisfaction with human resource outcomes: a field study of human resource outsourcing in small and medium enterprises. *Journal of Management*, **31**(2): 234–54.

Klein, N. (2000) *No Logo*. London: Flamingo.

Klein, N. (2007) *The Shock Doctrine*, Toronto, Ontario: Vintage Canada.

Kline, J. (2010) *Ethics for International Business: Decision-Making in a Global Political Economy*. New York: Routledge.

Kluger, A. N. and DeNisi, A. S. (1996) The effects of feedback interventions on performance: a historical review, a metaanalysis, and a preliminary feedback intervention theory. *Psychological Bulletin*, **119**: 254–84.

Kluger, A. N. and Nir, D. (2009) The feedforward interview. *Human Resource Management Review*, **20**: 235–46.

Knight, J. (2011) Union-free shops strong in HR. *Canadian HR Reporter*, February 28: 20–2.

Knight, K. and Latreille, P. (2000) Discipline, dismissals and complaints to employment tribunals. *British Journal of Industrial Relations*, **38**(4): 533–55.

Knights, A. and Poppleton, A. (2008) *Developing Coaching Capability in Organisations*. London: Chartered Institute of Personnel and Development.

Knights, D. and Willmott, H. (eds) (1986) *Gender and the Labour Process*. Aldershot: Gower.

Knowles, M. (1998) *The Adult Learner* (5th edn). Houston, TX: Gulf Publishing.

Knox, S. and Freeman, C. (2006) Measuring and managing employer brand image in the service industry. *Journal of Marketing Management*, **22**(7–8): 695–717.

Kochan, T. (2008) Social legitimacy of the HRM profession: a US perspective. In P. Boxall, J. Purcell and P. Wright. *The Oxford Handbook of Human Resource Management* (pp. 599–619). Oxford: Oxford University Press.

Kochan, T. A. and Barocci, T. (1985) *Human Resource Management and Industrial Relations*. Glenview, IL: Scott, Foresman.

Kochan, T. E., Katz, H. and McKersie, R. (1986) *The Transformation of American Industrial Relations*. New York: Basic Books.

Kochan, T. E., Batt, R. and Dyer, L. (1992) International human resource studies: a framework for future research. In D. Lewlin, O. Mitchell and P. Sterer (eds) *Research Frontiers – Industrial Relations and Human Resources* (pp. 309–37). Madison, WI: Industrial Relations Association, University of Wisconsin.

Kolb, D. (1982) Problem management: learning from experience. In S. Srivastva (ed.) *The Executive Mind* (Ch. 5). San Francisco, CA: Jossey-Bass.

Kolb, D. A. (1984) *Experiential Learning*. Englewood Cliffs, NJ: Prentice Hall.

Koleva, P., Rodet-Kroichvili, N., David, P. and Marasova, J. (2010) Is corporate social responsibility the privilege of developed market economies? Some evidence from Central and Eastern Europe. *International Journal of Human Resource Management*, **21**(2): 274–93.

Kolk, N., Born, M. and van den Flier, H. (2003) The transparent assessment centre: the effects of revealing dimensions to candidates. *Applied Psychology: An International Review*, **52**(4): 648–68.

Konzelmann, S. (2005) Varieties of capitalism: production and market relations in the USA and Japan. *British Journal of Industrial Relations*, **43**(4): 593–603.

Konzelmann, S., Conway, N., Trenberth, L. and Wilkinson, F. (2006) Corporate governance and human resource management. *British Journal of Industrial Relations*, **44**(3): 541–67.

Korczynski, M. (2002) *Human Resource Management in Service Work*. Basingstoke: Palgrave Macmillan.

Kotter, J. P. (1982) *The General Managers*. New York: Free Press.

Kotter, J. (1996) *Leading Change*. Boston, MA: Harvard Business.

Koubek, J. and Brewster, C. (1995) Human resource management in turbulent times: HRM in the Czech Republic. *International Journal of Human Resource Management*, **6**(2): 223–47.

KPMG (1996) *Learning Organisation Benchmarking Survey*. London: KPMG.

Kraaijenbrink, J., Spender, J-C. and Groen, A. (2010) The resource-based view: a review and assessment of its critiques. *Journal of Management*, **36**(1): 349–72.

Krahn, H., Lowe, G., and Hughes, K. (2011) *Work, Industry, and Canadian Society* (6th edn). Toronto, Ontario: Nelson Education.

Kristof, A. L. (1996) Person–organization fit: an integrative review of its conceptualizations, measurement, and implications. *Personnel Psychology*, **49**: 1–49.

Kuhn, K. M. (2009) Compensation as a signal of organizational culture: the effects of advertising individual or collective incentives. *International Journal of Human Resource Management*, **20**(7): 1634–48.

Kur, E. and Bunning, R. (2002) Assuring corporate leadership for the future. *Journal of Management Development*, **21**(9/10): 761–79.

Kuttner, R. (2000) The role of governments in the global economy. In W. Hutton and A. Giddens (eds) *On the Edge: Living with Global Capitalism* (pp. 147–63). London: Jonathan Cape.

Kydd, B. and Oppenheim, L. (1990) Using human resource management to enhance competitiveness:

lessons from four excellent companies. *Human Resource Management Journal*, **29**(2): 145–66.

Labour Research Department (1991) *Future Uncertain for Public Sector Pay. Bargaining Report*. London: Labour Research Department.

Lance, C.E. (2008). Why assessment centers do not work the way they are supposed to. *Industrial and Organizational Psychology: Perspectives on Science and Practice*, **1**: 84–97.

Lash, M. L. (2010) *Intensive Culture: Social Theory, Religion and Contemporary Capitalism*. London: Sage.

Laszlo, E. (2009) *WorldShift 2012*. Toronto, Ontario: McArthur & Co.

Latham, G. P., Saari, L. M., Pursell, E. D. and Campion, M. A. (1980) The situational interview. *Journal of Applied Psychology*, **65**: 422–7.

Lave, J. and Wenger, E. (1991) *Situated Learning. Legitimate Peripheral Participation*. Cambridge: Cambridge University Press.

Lawler, E. E. (1990) *Strategic Pay: Aligning Organizational Strategies and Pay Systems*. San Francisco, CA: Jossey-Bass.

Lawler, E. E. (1995) The new pay: a strategic approach. *Compensation and Benefits Review*, July–August: 64–54.

Lawler, E. (2000) *Rewarding Excellence*. San Francisco, CA: Jossey-Bass.

Lawler, J. (2005) The essence of leadership? Existentialism and leadership. *Leadership*, **1**(2): 215–31.

Lawrence, T. B., Mauws, M. K., Dyck, B. and Kleysen, R. F. (2005) The politics of organizational learning: integrating power into the 4I framework. *Academy of Management Review*, **30**(1): 180–91.

Layard, R. (2011) 'The case against performance-related pay', April 17. Available at: www.ft.com/cms/s/0/f2d347bc-6917-11e0-9040-00144feab49a.html#axzz1me1HjsY0 (accessed February 17, 2011).

Learning and Skills Council (2008) 'World-class comparisons research'. Available at: http://readingroom.lsc.gov.uk/lsc/National/world-class_comparisons-final_report-Sept2008.pdf (accessed March 16, 2011).

Leat, M. (2007) *Exploring Employee Relations* (2nd edn). Oxford: Butterworth-Heinemann.

Lee, B. and Cassell, C. (2004) A study of accountability in work-based learning: the learning representative initiative in the UK. *Management*, **8**: 171–81.

Lee, M. (2004) A refusal to define HRD. In M. Lee, J. Stewart and J. Woodall (eds) *New Frontiers in HRD* (pp. 27–40). London: Routledge.

Legge, K. (1989) Human resource management: a critical analysis. In J. Storey (ed.) *New Perspectives on Human Resource Management* (pp. 21–36). London: Routledge.

Legge, K. (1995) *Human Resource Management: Rhetorics and Realities*. Basingstoke: Macmillan.

Legge, K. (2001) Silver bullet or spent round? Assessing the meaning of the 'high commitment'/performance relationship. In J. Storey (ed.) *Human Resource Management* (pp. 21–36). London: Thomson Learning.

Legge, K. (2005) *Human Resource Management: Rhetorics and Realities* (anniversary edn). Basingstoke: Palgrave Macmillan.

Legge, K. (2007) Networked organizations and the negation of HRM? In J. Storey (ed.) *Human Resource Management: A Critical Text* (3rd edn) (pp. 39–56). London: Thomson Learning.

Leigh, D., Evans R. and Mahmood, M. (2010) Killer chemicals and greased palms – the deadly 'end game' for leaded petrol. *The Guardian*, July 1, pp. 1, 15

Leitch, S. (2006) *Prosperity For All in the Global Economy – World Class Skills*. London: HM Treasury.

Leithwood, K., Mascall, B. and Strauss, T. (eds) (2008) *Distributed Leadership According to the Evidence*. London: Routledge.

Leonard, N. H., Beauvais, L. L. and Scholl, R. W. (1999) Work motivation: the incorporation of self-concept-based processes. *Human Relations*, **52**(8): 969–98.

Leopold, J. and Harris, L. (2009) *The Strategic Managing of Human Resources*. Harlow: Pearson.

Lepak, D. P. and Snell, S. A. (1999) The strategic management of human capital: determinants and implications of different relationships. *Academy of Management Review*, **24**(1): 1–18.

Leskew, S. and Singh, P. (2007) Leadership development: learning from best practices. *Leadership and Organization Development Journal*, **28**(5): 444–64.

Levashina, J. and Campion, M. A. (2006) A model of faking likelihood in the employment interview. *International Journal of Selection and Assessment*, **14**: 299–316.

Levinson, H. (1970) Management by whose objectives? *Harvard Business Review*, July/August: 125–34.

Levy, D. L. (2005) Offshoring in the new global political economy. *Journal of Management Studies*, **42**(3): 685–93.

Lewchuk, W., Clarke, M. and de Wolf, A. (2008) Working without commitments: precarious employment and health. *Work, Employment and Society*, **22**(3): 387–406.

Lewin, A., Massini, S. and Peeters, C. (2009) Why are companies offshoring innovation? The emerging global race for talent. *Journal of International Business Studies*, **40**: 901–25.

Lewin, K. (1951) *Field Theory in Social Science*, New York: Harper.

Lewis, J. P. (2000) The *Project Manager's Desk Reference: A Comprehensive Guide To Project Planning, Scheduling, Evaluation, and System*. New York: McGraw Hill.

Lewis, P., Ryan, P. and Gospel, H. (2008) A hard sell? The prospects for apprenticeship in British retailing. *Human Resource Management Journal*, **18**(1): 3–19.

Lewis, R. E. and Heckman, R. J. (2006) Talent management: a critical review. *Human Resource Management Review*, **16**(2): 139–54.

Li, L. C., Grimshaw, J. C., Nielsen, C., Judd, M., Coyte, P. C. and Graham, I. (2009) Use of communities of practice in business and health care sectors: a systematic review. *Implementation Science*. Available at: www.implementationscience.com/content/pdf/1748-5908-4-27.pdf (accessed March 14, 2011).

Liden, R. C., Bauer, T. N. and Erdogan, B. (2005) The role of leader-member exchange in the dynamic relationship between employer and employee: implications for employee socialization, leaders, and organizations. In J. A.-M. Coyle-Shapiro, L. Shore, M. Taylor and L. Tetrick (eds) *The Employment Relationship* (pp. 226–50). Oxford: Oxford University Press.

Lievens, F. and Harris, M. M. (2003) Research on internet recruiting and testing: current status and future directions. In C. L. Cooper and I. T. Robertson (eds) *International Review of Industrial and Organizational Psychology*, **16**: 131–65.

Liff, S. (1997a) Constructing HR information systems. *Human Resource Management Journal*, **7**(2): 18–31.

Liff, S. (1997b) Two routes to managing diversity: individual differences or social group characteristics. *Employee Relations*, **19**(1): 11–26.

Liff, S. (2000) Manpower or human resource planning – what's in a name? In S. Bach and K. Sisson (eds) *Personnel Management* (3rd edn) (pp. 93–110). Blackwell: Oxford.

Lincoln, J. and Kalleberg, A. (1992) *Culture Control and Commitment*. Cambridge: Cambridge University Press.

Lindkvist, L. (2004) Governing project-based firms: promoting market-like processes within hierarchies. *Journal of Management and Governance*, **8**: 3–25.

Linehan, M. (2000) *Senior Female International Managers: Why so Few?* Aldershot: Ashgate.

Linehan, M. (2005) Women in international management. In H. Scullion and M. Linehan (eds) *International Human Resource Management* (pp. 181–201). Basingstoke: Palgrave Macmillan.

Linehan, M. and Mayrhofer, W. (2005) International careers and repatriation. In H. Scullion and M. Linehan (eds) *International Human Resource Management* (pp. 131–55). Basingstoke: Palgrave Macmillan.

Linnenluecke, M. and Griffiths, A. (2010) Corporate sustainability and organizational culture. *Journal of World Business* **45**: 357–66.

Linstead, S. and Grafton Small, R. (1992) Corporate strategy and corporate culture: the view from the checkout. *Personnel Review*, **19**(4): 9–15.

Linstead, S., Fulop, L., and Lilley, S. (2009) *Management and Organization: A Critical Text* (2nd edn). Basingstoke: Palgrave Macmillan.

Lips-Wiersma, M. and Hall, D. T. (2007) Organizational career development is not dead: a case study on managing the new career during organizational change. *Journal of Organizational Behavior*, **28**: 771–92.

Littler, C. R. (1982) *The Development of the Labour Process in Capitalist Societies*. London: Heinemann.

Littler, C. R. and Salaman, G. (1984) *Class at Work: The Design, Allocation and Control of Jobs*. London: Batsford.

Littler, C. R., Wiesner, R. and Dunford, R. (2003) The dynamics of de-layering: changing management structures in three countries. *Journal of Management Studies*, **40**(2): 225–56.

Lloyd, C. and Payne, J. (2004) *Just Another Bandwagon? A Critical Look at the Role of the High Performance Workplace as Vehicle for the UK High Skills Project*. SKOPE Research Paper No. 49. Warwick: ESRC Research Centre on Skills, Knowledge and Organisational Performance.

Locke, E. A. (1968) Towards a theory of task motivation and incentives. *Organizational Behavior and Human Performance*, **3**: 152–89.

Locke, E. A., Feren, D. B., McCaleb, V., Shaw, K. and Denny, A. (1980) The relative effectiveness of four methods of motivating employee performance. In K. D. Duncan, M. Gruneberg and D. Wallis (eds) *Changes in Working Life* (pp. 363–83). London: John Wiley & Sons.

Locke, G. and Latham, E. (2009) Has goal setting gone wild, or have its attackers abandoned good scholarship? *Academy of Management*, February: 17–23.

Lockton, D. J. (2010) *Employment Law* (7th edn). Basingstoke: Palgrave Macmillan.

Long, R. (2010) Evaluating the market. In *Strategic Compensation* (4th edn) (pp. 333–58). Toronto, Ontario: Nelson.

Long, R. J. and Shields, J. (2010) From pay to praise? Non-cash employee recognition in Canadian and Australian firms. *International Journal of Human Resource Management*, **21**(8): 1145–72.

Longua, J., DeHart, T., Tennen, H. and Armeli, S. (2009) Personality moderates the interaction between positive and negative daily events predicting negative affect and stress. *Journal of Research in Personality*, **43**(4): 547–55.

Lorbiecki, A. and Jack, G. (2000) Critical turns in the evolution of diversity management. *British Journal of Management*, **11**: S17–31.

Loudoun, R. and Johnstone, R. (2009) Occupational health and safety in the modern world of work. In A. Wilkinson, N. Bacon, T. Redman, and S. Snell (eds) *The Sage Handbook of Human Resource Management* (pp. 286–307). London: Sage.

Low Pay Commission (2011) *National Minimum Wage*. Report Cm 8023, London: HMSO. Also available at: www.lowpay.gov.uk/lowpay/report/pdf/Revised_Report_PDF_with_April_date.pdf (accessed January 2011).

Luthans, F. and Peterson, S. J. (2003) 360-degree feedback with systematic coaching: empirical analysis suggests a winning combination. *Human Resource Management*, **42**: 243–56.

Lyon, P. and Glover, I. (1998) Divestment or investment? The contradictions of HRM in relation to older employees. *Human Resource Management Journal*, **8**(1): 56–68.

Mabey, C. (2002) Mapping management development practice. *Journal of Management Studies*, **39**(8): 1139–60.

Mabey, C. (2005) *Management Development Works: The Evidence*. London. Chartered Management Institute.

Mabey, C. and Finch-Lees, T. (2008) *Leadership and Management Development*. London: Sage.

Mabey, C. and Ramirez, M. (2005) Does management development improve organizational productivity? A six-country analysis of European firms, *International Journal of Human Resource Management*, **16**(7): 1067–82.

Mabey, C. and Thomson, A. (2000) The determinants of management development. *British Journal of Management*, **11**, Special Issue: 3–16.

Mabey, C., Skinner, D. and Clark, D. (eds) (1998a) *Experiencing Human Resource Management*. London: Sage.

Mabey, C., Salaman, G. and Storey, J. (eds) (1998b) *Human Resource Management: A Strategic Introduction*. Oxford: Blackwell.

McBride, J. (2008) The limits of high performance work systems in unionized craft-based work settings. *Work, Employment and Society*, **23**(3): 213–28.

McCall, M. (2010) Recasting leadership development. *Industrial and Organizational Psychology*, **3**(1): 3–19.

McCarthy, A. M. and Garavan, T. N. (2001) 360°

feedback processes: performance improvement and employee career development. *Journal of European Industrial Training*, **25**(1): 5–32.

McCarthy, A. and Garavan, T. (2007) Understanding acceptance of multisource feedback for management development. *Personnel Review*, **36**(6): 903–17.

McCarthy, J. and Goffin, R. (2004) Measuring job interview anxiety: beyond weak knees and sweaty palms. *Personnel Psychology*, **57**: 607–37.

McCarthy, P., Henderson, M., Sheehan, M. and Barker, M. (2002) Workplace bullying: its management and prevention. In *Australian Master OHS and Environmental Guide 2003* (pp. 519–49). Sydney: CCH Australia.

McCarthy, S. (2010) Business urged to keep on eco-track. *Globe and Mail*, November 24, p. B4.

McCormack, B. (2000) Workplace learning: a unifying concept. *Human Resource Development International*, **3**(3): 397–404.

McCracken, M. and Wallace, M. (2000) Towards a redefinition of strategic HRD. *Journal of European Industrial Training*, **24**(5): 281–90.

McCrone, D. (2001) *Understanding Scotland*. London: Routledge.

McCulloch, M. and Turban, D. (2007) Using person–organization fit to select employees for high-turnover jobs. *International Journal of Selection and Assessment*, **15**(1): 63–71.

McCullum, S. and O'Donnell, D. (2009) Social capital and leadership development. *Leadership and Organization Development Journal*, **30**(2): 152–66.

McDonald, P., Brown, K. and Bradley, L. (2005) Explanations for the provision utilisation gap in work–life policy. *Women in Management Review*, **20**(1): 37–55.

MacDuffie, J. P. (1995) Human resource bundles and manufacturing performance: organizational logic and flexible production systems in the world of auto industry. *Industrial and Labor Relations Review*, **48**: 197–221.

McGoldrick, J. and Stewart, J. (1996) The HRM–HRD nexus. In J. McGoldrick and J. Stewart (eds) *Human Resource Development* (pp. 9–27). London: Pitman Publishing.

McGoldrick, J., Stewart, J. and Watson, S. (2001) Theorizing human resource development. *Human Resource Development International*, **4**(3): 343–56.

McGregor, D. (1957) An uneasy look at performance appraisal. *Harvard Business Review*, **35**(3): 89–94.

McGregor, D. (1960) *The Human Side of Enterprise*. New York: McGraw-Hill.

McGuire, D. (2011) Foundations of human resource development. In McGuire, D. and Jorgenson, K. (eds)

Human Resource Development (pp. 1–11). London: Sage.

McHenry, R. (1997) Tried and tested. *People Management*, January 23: 32–7.

Machin, S. and Vignoles, A. (2001) *The Economic Benefits of Training to the Individual, the Firm and the Economy: The Key Issues*. London: Centre for the Economics of Education.

McIlroy, J. (1988) *Trade Unions in Britain Today*. Manchester: Manchester University Press.

MacInnes, J. (1985) Conjuring up consultation. *British Journal of Industrial Relations*, **23**(1): 93–113.

MacInnes, J. (1987) *Thatcherism at Work*. Milton Keynes: Open University Press.

McInnis, K. J., Meyer, J. P. and Feldman, S. (2009) Psychological contracts and their implications for commitment: a feature-based approach. *Journal of Vocational Behavior*, **74**: 165–80.

Macionis, J. and Gerber, L. M. (2011) *Sociology* (7th Canadian edn). Toronto, Ontario: Pearson.

McKay, S. and Markova, E. (2010) The operation and management of agency workers in conditions of vulnerability. *Industrial Relations Journal*, **41**(5): 446–60.

McKenna, S., Richardson, J. and Manroop, L. (2011) Alternative paradigms and the study and practice of performance management and evaluation. *Human Resource Management Review*, **21**(2): 148–57.

Mackie, K. S., Holahan, C. and Gottlieb, N. (2001) Employee involvement management practices, work stress, and depression in employees of a human services residential care facility. *Human Relations*, **54**(8): 1065–92.

McKie, L., Hogg, G., Airey, L., Backett-Milburn, K., and Rew, Z. (2009) Autonomy, control and job advancement. *Work, Employment and Society*, **23**(4): 789–96.

McKinlay, A. (2002) The limits of knowledge management. *New Technology Work and Employment*, **17**(2): 76–88.

McKinlay, A. and Taylor, P. (1998) Through the looking glass: Foucault and the politics of production. In A. McKinlay and K. Starkey (eds) *Foucault, Management and Organizational Theory* (pp. 173–90). London: Sage.

Macky, K. and Boxall, P. (2007) The relationship between 'high-performance work practices' and employee attitudes: an investigation of additive and interaction effects. *International Journal of Human Resource Management*, **18**(4): 537.

Maclagan, P. (2008) Organizations and responsibility: a critical overview. *Systems Research and Behavioral Science*, **25**(3): 371–81.

McLean, G. N. (2004) National human resource development: what in the world is it? *Advances in Developing Human Resources*, **6**(3): 269–75.

Macleod, D. and Clarke, N. (2009) *Engaging for Success: Enhancing Performance Through Engagement*. London: Department of Business.

McLoughlin, I. and Clark, J. (1988) *Technological Change at Work*. Milton Keynes: Open University Press.

McMillan-Capehart, A. (2005) A configurational framework for diversity: socialization and culture. *Personnel Review*, **34**(4): 488–503.

McNabb, R. and Whitfield, K. (1997) Unions, flexibility, teamworking and financial performance. *Organisation Studies*, **18**(5): 821–38.

McNabb, R. and Whitfield, K. (2001) Job evaluation and high performance work practices: compatible or conflictual? *Journal of Management Studies*, **38**(2): 293–312.

Macpherson, W. (1999) *The Stephen Lawrence Inquiry*. London: Stationery Office.

McShane, S. L. (1990) Two tests of direct gender bias in job evaluation ratings. *Journal of Occupational Psychology*, **63**: 129–40.

McShane, S. L. and Steen, S. (2010) *Canadian Organizational Behaviour* (7th ed.) Toronto, Ontario: McGraw-Hill.

McSweeney, B. (2002) Hofstede's model of national cultural differences and their consequences: a triumph of faith – a failure of analysis. *Human Relations*, **55**(1): 89–118.

Madsen, S. R. (2003) Wellness in the workplace: preparing employees for change. *Organization Development Journal*, **21**(1): 46–55.

Mahajan, A. (2011) Host country national's reactions to expatriate pay policies: making a case for a cultural alignment model. *International Journal of Human Resource Management*, **22**(1): 121–37.

Mahoney, T. (1989) Multiple pay contingencies: strategic design of compensation. *Human Resource Management*, **28**(3): 337–47.

Main, P., Curtis, A., Pitts, J. and Irish, B. (2009) A 'mutually agreed statement of learning' in general practice trainer appraisal: the place of peer appraisal by experienced course members. *Education for Primary Care*, **20**(2): 104–10.

Maitra, S. and Sangha, J. (2005) Intersecting realities: young women and call centre work in India and Canada. *Women and Environments*, Spring/Summer: 40–2.

Mäkelä, K., Björkman, I. and Ehrnrooth, M. (2010) How do MNCs establish their talent pools? Influences on individuals' likelihood of being labeled as talent. *Journal of World Business*, **45**(2): 134–42.

Makin, K. (2007) Collective bargaining is a right, top court rules. *Globe and Mail*, June 9, p. A4.

Mallon, M. and Walton, S. (2005) Career and learning: the ins and the outs of it. *Personnel Review*, **34**(4): 468–87.

Manji, I. (2010) How complex the culture of fear. *Globe and Mail*, November 26, p. A21.

Mankin, D. P. (2001) A model for human resource development. *Human Resource Development International*, **4**(1): 65–85.

Mann, D. (2011) *Understanding Society* (2nd edn). Don Mills, Ontario: Oxford University Press.

Mann, S. and Holdsworth, L. (2003) The psychological impact of teleworking: stress, emotion and health. *New Technology, Work and Employment*, **1**(3): 196–211.

Mannion, E. and Whittaker, P. (1996) European Passenger Services Ltd – assessment centres for recruitment and development. *Career Development International*, **1**(6): 12–16.

Marchington, M. (1982) *Managing Industrial Relations*. Maidenhead: McGraw-Hill.

Marchington, M. (1987) A review and critique of research on developments in joint consultation. *British Journal of Industrial Relations*, **25**(3): 339–52.

Marchington, M. (1995) Involvement and participation. In J. Storey (ed.) *Human Resource Management: A Critical Text* (pp. 280–305). London: Routledge.

Marchington, M. (2001) Employee involvement. In J. Storey (ed.) *Human Resource Management: A Critical Text* (pp. 232–52). London: Thomson Learning.

Marchington, M. (2008) Employee voice systems. In P. Boxall, J. Purcell and P. Wright (eds) *The Oxford Handbook of Human Resource Management* (pp. 231–50). Oxford: Oxford University Press.

Marchington, M. and Cox, A. (2007) Employee involvement and participation: structures, processes and outcomes. In J. Storey (ed.) *Human Resource Management: A Critical Text* (pp. 177–94). London: Routledge.

Marchington, M. and Grugulis, I. (2000) 'Best practice' human resource management: perfect opportunity or dangerous illusion? *International Journal of Human Resource Management*, **11**(6): 1104–24.

Marchington, M. and Wilding, P. (1983) Employee involvement inaction? *Personnel Management*, December: 73–82.

Marchington, M. and Wilkinson, A. (2000) Direct participation. In S. Bach and K. Sisson (eds) *Personnel Management: A Comprehensive Guide to Theory and Practice* (Ch. 14). Oxford: Blackwell.

Marchington, M., Grimshaw, D., Rubery, J. and Willmott, H. (eds) (2005) *Fragmenting Work: Blurring Organizational Boundaries and Disordering Hierarchies*. Oxford: Oxford University Press.

Marcus, A. and Fremeth, A. (2009) Green management

matters regardless. *Academy of Management Perspectives*, **23**(4): 17–26.

Marginson, P. (2009) Performance pay and collective bargaining: a complex relationship. In S. Corby, S. Palmer and E. Lindop (eds) *Rethinking Reward* (pp. 102–19) Basingstoke: Palgrave Macmillan.

Marginson, P. and Meardi, G. (2010) Multinational companies: transforming national industrial relations? In T. Colling and M. Terry (eds) *Industrial Relations: Theory and Practice* (3rd edn) (pp. 207–30). Chichester: John Wiley & Sons.

Marginson, P., Edwards, P. Edwards, T., Ferner, A. and Tregaskis, O. (2010) Employee representation and consultative voice in multinational companies operating in Britain. *British Journal of Industrial Relations*, **48** (1): 151–80.

Marmot, M. G., Rose, G., Shipley, M. and Hamilton, P. J. (1978) Employment grade and coronary heart disease in British civil servants. *Journal of Epidemiology and Community Health*, **32**(4): 244–9.

Marsden, D. and Belfield, R. (2010) Institutions and the management of human resources: incentive pay systems in France and Great Britain. *British Journal of Industrial Relations*, **48**(2): 235–83.

Marsick, V. and Watkins, K. (1990) *Informal and Incidental Learning in the Workplace*. London: Routledge.

Marsick, V. and Watkins, K. E. (1999) Envisioning new organisations for learning. In D. Boud and J. Garrick (eds) *Understanding Learning at Work* (pp. 199–215). London: Routledge.

Marsick, V. J. and Watkins, K. (2001) Informal and incidental learning. *New Directions for Adult and Continuing Education*, **89**: 25–34.

Martin, D. (2010) The removal of workplace partnership in the UK Civil service: a trade union perspective. *Industrial Relations Journal*, **41**(3): 218–32.

Martin, G., Reddington, M. and Kneafsey, M. B. (2009a) *Web 2.0 and Human Resource Management: Groundswell or Hype?* Research into Practice Report. London: Chartered Institute of Personnel and Development.

Martin, G., Reddington, M., Kheafsey, M. B. and Sloman, M. (2009b) Scenarios and strategies for Web 2.0. *Education and Training*, **51**(5/6): 370–80.

Martin, J. (1992) *Cultures in Organizations: Three Perspectives*. New York: Oxford University Press.

Martin, J. (2002) *Organizational Culture: Mapping the Terrain*. Thousand Oaks, CA: Sage.

Martin, J. and Frost, P. (1996) The organizational culture war games: a struggle for intellectual dominance. In S. R. Clegg, C. Hardy and W. R. Nord (eds) *Handbook of Organizational Studies* (pp. 599–621). London: Sage.

Martin, J. N. and Nakayama, T. K. (2000) *Intercultural Communications in Context* (2nd edn). Mountain View, CA: Mayfield.

Martin, J. and Siehl, C. (1983) Organizational culture and counterculture: an uneasy symbiosis. *Organizational Dynamics*, **122**: 52–65.

Martin, P. and Pope, J. (2008) Competency-based interviewing – has it gone too far? *Industrial and Commercial Training*, **40**(2): 81–6.

Martín-Tapia, I., Aragón-Correa, J.A. and Guthrie, J. (2009) High performance work systems and export performance. *International Journal of Human Resource Management*, **20**(3): 633–53.

Martocchio, J. J. (2011) *Strategic Compensation*. New York: Pearson, Prentice-Hall.

Marx, K. and Engels, F. (1998) *The German Ideology*. New York: Prometheus Books.

Maslow, A. (1954) *Motivation and Personality*. New York: Harper & Row.

Mason, R., Power, S., Parker-Swift, J. and Baker, E. (2009) 360-degree appraisal: a simple pragmatic solution. *Clinical Governance: An International Journal*, **14**(4): 295–300.

Mathew, J. and Ogbonna, E. (2009) Organizational culture and commitment: a study of an Indian software organization. *International Journal of Human Resource Management*, **20**(3): 654–75.

Mathias, P. and Davis, J. (eds) (1996) *International Trade and British Economic Growth: From the Eighteenth Century to the Present Day*. Oxford: Blackwell.

Matlay, H. (2004) Contemporary training initiatives in Britain: a small business perspective. *Journal of Small Business and Enterprise Development*, **11**(4): 504–13.

Matthews, J. M. and Candy, P. (1999) New dimensions in the dynamics of learning and knowledge. In D. Boud and J. Garrick (eds) *Understanding Learning at Work* (pp. 47–64) London: Routledge.

Mavin, S. (2006) Venus envy: problematizing solidarity behaviour and queen bees. *Women in Management Review*, **21**(4): 264–76.

Mayer, B. (1996) *Blue-Green Coalitions: Fighting for Safe Workplaces and Healthy Communities*. Ithaca, NY: Cornell University Press.

Mayer, B. (2009) *Blue-Green Coalitions: Fighting for Safe Workplaces and Healthy Communities*. Ithaca, NY: Cornell University Press.

Mayerhofer, H., Hartmann, L., Michelitsch-Riedl, G. and Kollinger, I. (2004) Flexpatriate assignments: a neglected issue in global staffing. *International Journal of Human Resource Management*, **15**(8): 1371–89.

Mayfield, M., Mayfield, J. and Lunce, S. (2003) Human resource information systems: a review and model development. *Advances in Competitiveness Research*, **11**(1): 139–51.

Mayhew, C. and Quinlan, M. (1997) Subcontracting and occupational health and safety in the residential building industry. *Industrial Relations Journal*, **28**(3): 192–205.

Mayo, A. (2002) A thorough evaluation. *People Management*, **8**(7): 36–9.

Mayo, A. (2004) *Creating a Learning and Development Strategy*. London: Chartered Institute of Personnel and Development.

Mayrhofer, W., Brewster, C., Morley, M. and Gunnigle, P. (2000a) Communication, consultation and the HRM debate. In C. Brewster, W. Mayrhofer and M. Morley (eds) *New Challenges for European Human Resource Management* (pp. 222–44). Basingstoke: Palgrave Macmillan.

Mayrhofer, W., Brewster, C. and Morley, M. (2000b) The concept of strategic european human resource management. In C. Brewster, W. Mayrhofer and M. Morley (eds) *New Challenges for European Human Resource Management* (pp. 3–37). London: Macmillan.

Mearns, K. and Hope, L. (2005) *Health and Well-being in the Offshore Environment: The Management of Personal Health*. Research Report No. 305, London: Health and Safety Executive.

Meek, L. (1992) Organizational culture: origins and weaknesses. In G. Salaman (ed.) *Human Resources Strategies* (pp. 198–229). London: Sage.

Megginson, D. and Pedler, M. (1992) *Self Development*. Maidenhead: McGraw-Hill.

Megginson, D., Clutterbuck, D., Garvey, B., Stokes, P. and Garrett-Harris, R. (2006) *Mentoring in Action* (2nd edn). London: Kogan Page.

Melchers, K. G., Kleinmann, M. and Prinz, M. A. (2010) Do assessors have too much on their plates? The effects of simultaneously rating multiple assessment center candidates on rating quality. *International Journal of Selection and Assessment*, **18**(3): 329–41.

Mellahi, K. and Wilkinson, A. (2010) Slash and burn or nip and tuck? Downsizing, innovation and human resources. *International Journal of Human Resource Management*, **21**(13): 2291–305.

Metcalfe, B. D. (2010) Leadership and diversity development. In Gold, J., Thorpe, R. and Mumford, A. (eds) *Gower Handbook of Leadership and Management Development* (pp. 151–73). Aldershot: Gower Publishing.

Meyer, H. H., Kay, E. and French, J. R. P. (1965) Split roles in performance appraisal. *Harvard Business Review*, **43**: 123–29.

Mezirow, J. (1990) *Fostering Critical Reflection in Adulthood*. San Francisco, CA: Jossey-Bass.

Mezirow, J. (1991) *Transformative Dimensions of Adult Learning*. San Francisco, CA: Jossey-Bass.

Michaels, E., Handfiled-Jones, H. and Axelrod, B. (2001) *The War for Talent*. Boston, MA: Harvard Business School Press.

Michie, J. and Sheehan-Quinn, M. (2001) Labour market flexibility: human resource management and corporate performance. *British Journal of Management*, **12**(4): 287–305.

Mićić, P. (2010) Developing leaders as futures thinkers. In J. Gold, R. Thorpe and A. Mumford (eds) *The Gower Handbook of Leadership and Management Developmen* (p. 547–66). Aldershot: Gower.

Middlehurst, R. and Kennie, T. (1997) Leading professionals: towards new concepts of professionalism. In J. Broadbent, M. Dietrich and J. Roberts (eds) *The End of the Professions?* (pp. 50–68). London: Routledge.

Miles, R. and Snow, C. (1984) Designing strategic human resources systems. *Organizational Dynamics*, Summer: 36–52.

Milkovitch, G., Newman, J. and Cole, N. (2010) *Compensation* (3rd Canadian edn). New York: McGraw-Hill.

Miller, K. (2009) *Organizational Communication: Approaches and Processes*. Boston: Wadsworth Cengage Learning.

Miller, L., Rankin, N. and Neathey, F. (2001) *Competency Frameworks in UK Organizations*. London: Chartered Institute of Personnel and Development.

Miller, P. (1987) Strategic industrial relations and human resource management – distinction, definition and recognition. *Journal of Management Studies*, **24**(4): 347–61.

Mills, C. Wright (1959/2000) *The Sociological Imagination*. Oxford: Oxford University Press.

Millward, N. and Stevens, M. (1986) *British Workplace Industrial Relations 1980–1984*. Aldershot: Gower.

Millward, N., Bryson, A. and Forth, J. (2000) *All Change at Work: British Employee Relations 1980–1998*. London: Routledge.

Milmo, D. (2010a) Will BA row keep union flags flying. *The Guardian*, June 5, p. 45.

Milmo, D. (2010b) BA told to hit union `where it hurts'. *The Guardian*, March 27, pp. 1–2.

Milmo, D. and Pidd, H. (2010) Union cries foul after court blocks BA cabin crew strike. *The Guardian*, May 18, p. 1.

Milne, R. (2011) Bond yields and stocks plummet as fears mount of impending recession. *Financial Times*, 19 August, p. 1.

Miner-Rubino, K. and Cortina, L. M. (2004) Working in a context of hostility towards women: implications for employees' well-being. *Journal of Occupational Health Psychology*, **9**(2): 107–22.

Mintzberg, H. (1973) *The Nature of Managerial Work*. London: Harper & Row.

Mintzberg, H. (1978) Patterns in strategy formation. *Management Science*, **24**(9): 934–48.

Mintzberg, H. (1987) Crafting strategy. *Harvard Business Review*, July/August: 66–75.

Mintzberg, H. (1989) *Mintzberg on Management*. New York: Collier/Hamilton.

Mintzberg, H. (1990) The design school: reconsidering the basic premises of strategic management. *Strategic Management Journal*, **11**: 171–95.

Mintzberg, H. (2004) *Managers Not MBA's: A Hard Look at the Soft Practices of Managing and Management Development*. San Francisco, CA: Berrett-Koehler.

Mintzberg, H. (2009) America's monumental failure of management. *Globe and Mail*, March 16, p. A11.

Mintzberg, H., Ahlstrand, B. and Lampel, J. (1998) *Strategic Safari: A Guided Tour Through the Wilds of Strategic Management*. New York: Free Press.

Moen, F. and Skaalvik, E. (2009) The effect from executive coaching on performance psychology. *International Journal of Evidence Based Coaching and Mentoring*, **7**(2): 31–41.

Mohanty, M. (ed.) (2004) *Class, Caste, Gender: Readings in Indian Government and Politics*. New Dehli: Sage Publications.

Mone, E., Eisinger, C., Guggenheim, K., Price, B. and Stine, C. (2011) Performance management at the wheel: driving employee engagement in organizations. *Journal of Business and Psychology*, **26**(2): 205–12.

Monks, J. (1998) Foreword. In C. Mabey, Skinner, D. and D. Clark (eds) *Experiencing Human Resource Management*. London: Sage.

Monks, K. and McMackin, J. (2001) Designing and aligning an HR system. *Human Resource Management Journal*, **11**(2): 57–72.

Montgomery, J. and Kelloway, K. (2002) *Management of Occupational Health and Safety* (2nd edn). Scarborough, Ontario: Nelson Thomson Learning.

Mooney, T. and Brinkerhoff, R. (2008) *Courageous Training: Bold Actions for Business Results*. San Francisco, CA: Berett-Koehler.

Morgan, G. (1997) *Images of Organization*. London: Sage.

Morgan, P. I. and Ogbonna, E. (2008) Subcultural dynamics in transformation: a multi-perspective study of healthcare professionals. *Human Relations*, **61**(1): 39–65.

Morgeson, F. P., Campion, M. A, Dipboye, R. L., Hollenbeck, J. R., Murphy, K. and Schmitt, N. (2007a) Reconsidering the use of personality tests in personnel selection contexts. *Personnel Psychology*, **60**, 683–729.

Morgeson, F. P., Campion, M. A, Dipboye, R. L., Hollenbeck, J, R., Murphy, K. and Schmitt, N. (2007b) Are we getting fooled again? Coming to terms with limitations in the use of personality tests for personnel selection. *Personnel Psychology*, **60**: 1029–49.

Morley, M., Brewster, C., Gunnigle, P. and Mayrhofer, W. (2000) Evaluating change in European industrial relations: research evidence on trends at organizational level. In C. Brewster, W. Mayrhofer and M. Morley (eds) *New Challenges for European Human Resource Management* (pp. 199–221). New York: St Martin's Press.

Morrell, K. M., Loan-Clarke, J. and Wilkinson, A. J. (2001) Unweaving leaving: the use of models in the management of employee turnover. *International Journal of Management Reviews*, **3**(1): 219–44.

Morrell, K. M., Loan-Clarke, J. and Wilkinson, A. J. (2004) Organisational change and employee turnover. *Personnel Review*, **33**(2): 161–73.

Morris, J. Wilkinson, B., and Gamble, J. (2009) Strategic international human resource management or the 'bottom line'? The case of electronics and garments commodity chains in China. *International Journal of Human Resource Management*, **20**(2): 348–71.

Morrison, E. W. and Robinson, S. L. (1997) When employees feel betrayed: a model of how psychological contract violation develops. *Academy of Management Review*, **22**(1): 226–56.

Moynagh, M. and Worsley, R. (2005) *Working in the Twenty-first Century*. Leeds: ESRC Future of Work Programme.

Mudambi, S. M. and Tallman, S. (2010) Make, buy or ally? Theoretical perspectives on knowledge process outsourcing through alliances. *Journal of Management Studies*, **47**(8): 1434–56.

Mullen, A. (2010) *Degrees of Inequality: Culture, Class and Gender in American Higher Education*. Baltimore, MD: Johns Hopkins University Press.

Mumford, A. (1993) *How Managers Can Develop Managers*. Aldershot: Gower.

Munro, A. and Rainbird, H. (2000) The new unionism and the new bargaining agenda: UNISON–employer partnerships on workplace learning in Britain. *British Journal of Industrial Relations*, **38**(2): 223–40.

Munro-Fraser, J. (1971) *Psychology: General, Industrial, Social*. London: Pitman.

Murphy, C. and Olthuis, D. (1995) The impact of work reorganization on employee attitudes towards work, the company and the union. In C. Schenk and J. Anderson (eds) *Re-shaping Work: Union Responses to Technological Change* (pp. 76–102). Toronto, Ontario: Ontario Federation of Labour.

Murphy, L. (2005) Transformational leadership: a cascading chain reaction. *Journal of Nursing Management*, **13**: 128–36.

Murray, G. (2005) Like a phoenix? Sources of renewal in the organized study of work and employment. *Selected Papers from the XLIth Annual CIRA Conference* (pp. 11–21). Concord, Ontario: Captus Press.

Mwita, J. I. (2000) Performance management model. *International Journal of Public Sector Management*, **13**(1): 19–37.

Nadler, L. and Nadler, Z. (1989) *Developing Human Resources*. San Francisco, CA: Jossey-Bass.

National Employers Skills Survey (2009) *Employers Skills Survey: Main Report*. London: UK Commission for Employment and Skills.

National Skills Task Force (1998) *Towards a National Skills Agenda*. London: Department for Education and Employment.

Neely, A. (2007) *Business Performance Measurement*. Cambridge: Cambridge University Press.

Newell, S. (2005) Recruitment and selection. In S. Bach (ed.) *Managing Human Resources* (pp. 115–47). Oxford: Blackwell.

Newell, S., Robertson, M., Scarbrough, H. and Swan, J. (2002) *Managing Knowledge Work*. Basingstoke: Palgrave Macmillan.

Newton, T. and Findlay, P. (1996) Playing God? The performance of appraisal. *Human Resource Management Journal*, **6**(3): 42–58.

Nichols, T. (1986) *The British Worker Question: A New Look at Workers and Productivity in Manufacturing*. London: Routledge & Kegan Paul.

Nichols, T. (1990) Industrial safety in Britain and the 1974 Health and Safety at Work Act: the case of manufacturing. *International Journal of the Sociology of Law*, **18**: 371–42.

Nichols, T. (1997) *The Sociology of Industrial Injury*. London: Mansell Publishing.

Nichols, T. and Beynon, H. (1977) *Living with Capitalism: Class Relations and the Modern Factory*. London: Routledge & Kegan Paul.

Nichols, T., Sugur, N. and Demir, E. (2002) Globalized management and local labour: the case of the white-goods industry in Turkey. *Industrial Relations Journal*, **33**(1): 68–85.

Nijholt, J. and Benders, J. (2010) Measuring the prevalence of self-managing teams: taking account of defining characteristics. *Work, Employment and Society*, **24**(2): 375–85.

Nikolaou, I. and Judge, T. (2007) Fairness reactions to personnel selection techniques in Greece: the role of core self-evaluations. *International Journal of Selection and Assessment*, **15**(2): 206–19.

Nixon, D. (2009) 'I can't put a smiley face on': working-class masculinity, emotional labour and service work in the 'new economy'. *Gender, Work and Organization*, **16**(3): 300–22.

Noble, C. (1997) International comparisons of training policies. *Human Resource Management Journal*, **7**(1): 5–18.

Nolan, P. (2011) Money, markets, meltdown: the 21st-century crisis of labour. *Industrial Relations Journal*, **42**(1): 2–17.

Nolan, S. (2011) In much of the world, gains in rights elude a silenced majority. *Globe and Mail*, March 8, pp. A1, A14.

Nonaka, I., Toyama, R. and Nagata, A. (2000a) A firm as a knowledge creating entity: a new perspective on the theory of the firm. *Industrial and Corporate Change*, **9**(1): 1–20.

Nonaka, I., Toyama, R. and Konno, N. (2000b) SECI, Ba and leadership: a unified model of dynamic knowledge creation. *Long Range Planning*, **33**: 5–34.

Nopo, H. (2011) The Inter-American Development Bank presents … pushing for progress. Women, work, and gender roles in Latin America. *Harvard International Review*, Summer: 78–83.

Oade, A. (2009) *Managing Workplace Bullying*, Basingstoke: Palgrave Macmillan.

Oates, A. (1996) Industrial relations and the environment in the UK. In W. Wehrmeyer (ed.) *Greening People: Human Resources and Environmental Management* (pp. 117–40) Sheffield: Greenleaf Publishing.

O'Connor, J. (1996) The second contradiction of capitalism. In T. Benton (ed.) *The Greening of Marxism* (pp. 197–221). New York: Guilford Press.

O'Donoghue, J. and Maguire, T. (2005) The individual learner, employability and the workplace. *Journal of European Industrial Training*, **29**(6): 436–46.

O'Dowd, J. and Roche, W. K. (2009) Partnership structures and agendas and managers' assessments of stakeholder outcomes. *Industrial Relations Journal*, **40**(1): 17–39.

Office for National Statistics (2010) 2010 'Annual survey of hours and earnings'. Available at: www.ons.gov.uk/ons/rel/ashe/annual-survey-of-hours-and-earnings/2010-results/index.html.

Office for National Statistics (2011a) Available at: www.statistics.gov.uk (accessed February 4, 2011).

Office for National Statistics (2011b) 'Gender pay gap falls below 10 per cent in 2011', November 23. Available at: www.ons.gov.uk/ons/rel/mro/news-release/annual-survey-of-hours-and-earnings-2011/ashe-2011-nr.html (accessed January 12).

Ogbonna, E. (1993) Managing organizational culture: fantasy or reality. *Human Resource Management Journal*, **3**(2): 211–36.

Ogbonna, E. and Harris, L. C. (2006) Organizational culture in the age of the internet: an exploratory study. *New Technology, Work and Employment*, **21**(2): 162–75.

O'Grady, F. (2010) 'Keynote address to TUC green Growth Conference', October 13. Available at: www.tuc.org.uk/social/tuc-18662-f0.cfm (accessed October 15, 2010).

Oliver, N. and Wilkinson, B. (1988) *The Japanization of British Industry*. Oxford: Blackwell.

Olivier, R. and Verity, J. (2008) Rehearsing tomorrow's leaders: the potential of mythodrama. *Business Strategy Series*, **9**(3): 138–43.

Ones, D. S., Dilchert, S., Viswesvaran, C. and Judge T. A. (2007) In support of personality assessment in organizational settings. *Personnel Psychology*, **60**: 995–1027.

Oppenheim, A. N. (1992) *Questionnaire Design, Interviewing and Attitude Measurement*. London: Pinter Publishers.

Ordanini, A. and Silvestri, G. (2008) Recruitment and selection services: efficiency and competitive reasons in the outsourcing of HR practices. *International Journal of Human Resource Management*, **19**(2): 372–91.

O'Reilly, C. and Tushman, M. (2004) The ambidextrous organization. *Harvard Business Review*, April: 74–81.

O'Reilly, C., Caldwell, D. F., Chatman, J. A., Lapiz, M. and Self, W. (2010) How leadership matters: the effects of leaders' alignment on strategy implementation. *Leadership Quarterly*, **21**(1): 104–13.

Organization for Economic Co-operation and Development (1996) *The Knowledge-based Economy*. Paris: OECD.

Örtenblad, A. (2002) Organizational learning: a radical perspective. *International Journal of Management Reviews*, **4**(1): 87–100.

Örtenblad, A. (2004) The learning organization: towards an integrated model. *Learning Organization*, **11**(2): 129–44.

Ostroff, C., and Bowen, D. (2000) Moving HR to a higher level: HR practices and organizational effectiveness. In K. Klein and S. Kozlowski (eds) *Multilevel Theory, Research and Methods in Organizations: Foundations, Extensions and New Directions*. San Francisco, CA: Jossey-Bass.

Ouchi, W. (1979) A conceptual framework for the design of organizational control mechanisms. *Management Science*, **25**(9): 833–48.

Ouchi, W. G. (1980) Markets, bureaucracies, and clans. *Administrative Science Quarterly*, **25**(1): 129–41.

Ouchi, W. (1981) *Theory Z: How American Companies Can Meet the Japanese Challenge*. Reading, MA: Addison-Wesley.

Owen, H. (2008) *Open Space Technology: A User's Guide* (3rd edn). San Francisco, CA: Berrett-Koehler.

Owen, J. (2011) Families feel the pressure as slump takes its tool. *The Independent*, October 9. Available at: www.independent.co.uk/health-and-families (accessed January 8, 2012)

Oxenbridge, S. and Brown, W. (2004) A poisoned chalice? Trade union representatives in partnership and co-operative employer–union relationships. In G. Healy, E. Heery, P. Taylor and W. Brown (eds) *The Future of Worker Representation* (pp. 187–206). Basingstoke: Palgrave Macmillan.

Paauwe, J. (2004) *HRM and Performance: Achieving Long-Term Viability*. New York: Oxford University Press.

Paauwe, J. and Boselie, P. (2003) Challenging 'strategic HRM' and the relevance of the institutional setting. *Human Resource Management Journal*, **13**(3): 56–70.

Paauwe, J. and Boselie, P. (2008) HRM and social embeddedness. In P. Boxall, J. Purcell and P. Wright (eds) *The Oxford Handbook of Human Resource Management* (pp. 166–84). Oxford: Oxford University Press.

Packham, C. (2011) *Violence at Work: Findings from the 2009–10 British Crime Survey*. London: Health and Safety Executive.

Pai, H.-H. (2010) The safety catch: migrant construction workers risk their lives because they fear for their jobs and status. *The Guardian*, April 4, p. W1.

Paik, Y., Vance, C. and Stage, H. (1996) The extent of divergence in human resource practice across three Chinese national cultures: Hong Kong, Taiwan and Singapore. *Human Resource Management Journal*, **6**(2): 20–31.

Parker, B. and Caine, D. (1996) Holonic modelling: human resource planning and the two faces of Janus. *International Journal of Manpower*, **17**(8): 30–45.

Parker, J., Mars, L., Ransome, P. and Stanworth, H. (2003) *Social Theory: A Basic Tool Kit*. Basingstoke: Palgrave Macmillan.

Parker, M. (2000) *Organizational Culture and Identity*. London: Sage.

Parker, P., Hall, D. T. and Kram, K. E. (2008) Peer coaching: a relational process for accelerating career learning. *Academy of Management Learning and Education*, **7**(4): 487–503.

Parker, S. and Wall, T. (1998). *Job and Work Design: Organizing Work to Promote Well-being and Effectiveness*. Thousand Oaks, CA: Sage.

Parry, E. and Tyson, S. (2008) An analysis of the use and success of online recruitment methods in the UK. *Human Resource Management Journal*, **18**(3): 257–74.

Parry, E. and Wilson, H. (2009) Factors influencing the adoption of online recruitment. *Personnel Review*, **38**(6): 655–73.

Parsons, D. (2010) Medical-workforce planning: an art or science? *Human Resource Management International Digest*, **18**(5): 36–8.

Parsons, T. (1951) *The Social System*. Glencoe, IL: Free Press.

Parzefall, M.-R. and Salin, D. (2010) Perceptions of and reactions to workplace bullying: a social exchange perspective. *Human Relations*, **63**(6): 761–80.

Patel, R. (2009) *The Value of Nothing*. Toronto, Ontario: HarperCollins.

Patient (2011) Binge drinking. Available at: patient.co.uk/doctor/alcohol-related-problems.htm.

Paton, R., Peters, G., Storey, J. and Taylor, S. (2007) *Handbook of Corporate University Development: Managing Strategic Learning Initiatives in Public and Private Domains*. Aldershot: Gower.

Patterson, M. G., West, M. A., Lawthon, R. and Nickell, S. (1997) *Impact of People Management Practices on Business Performance*. London: Institute of Personnel and Development.

Patterson, M. G., West, M. A., and Wall, T. D. (2004) Integrated manufacturing, empowerment and company performance. *Journal of Organizational Behavior*, **25** (4): 641–65.

Patterson, M., Rick, J., Wood, S., Carroll, C., Balain, S. and Booth, A. (2010) Systematic review of the links between human resource management practices and performance. *Health Technology Assessment*, **14**(51).

Payne, J. (2008) Sector skills councils and employer engagement – delivering the 'employer-led' skills agenda in England. *Journal of Education and Work*, **21**(2): 93–113.

Payne, S. C., Horner, M. T., Boswell, W. R., Schroeder, A. N. and Stine-Cheyne, K. J. (2009) Comparison of online and traditional performance appraisal systems. *Journal of Managerial Psychology*, **24**(6): 526–44.

Pedler, M. (2008) *Action Learning for Managers*. Aldershot: Gower.

Pedler, M., Boydell, T. and Burgoyne, J. (1988) *The Learning Company Project Report*. Sheffield: Manpower Services Commission.

Pedler, M., Burgoyne, J. and Boydell, T. (1991) *The Learning Company: A Strategy for Sustainable Development*. Maidenhead: McGraw-Hill.

Pedler, M., Burgoyne, J. and Boydell, T. (2006) *A Manager's Guide to Self-Development* (5th edn). Maidenhead, McGraw-Hill.

Peiperl, M. A. (2001) Best practice: Getting 360-degree feedback right. *Harvard Business Review*, January: 142–7.

Pelletier, K. L. (2010) Leader toxicity: an empirical investigation of toxic behavior and rhetoric. *Leadership*, **6**(4): 373–89.

Peña, I. and Villasalero, M. (2010) Business strategy, human resource systems, and organizational performance in the Spanish banking industry. *International Journal of Human Resource Management*, **21**(15): 2864–88.

Pendleton, A. (1997) What impact has privatization had on pay and employment? *Relations Industrielles/Industrial Relations*, **52**(3): 554–82.

Pennell, K. (2010) The role of flexible job descriptions in succession management. *Library Management*, **31**(4/5): 279–90.

Penrose, E. T. (1959) *The Theory of the Growth of the Firm*. Oxford: Blackwell.

Peritz, I. and Friesen, J. (2010) Multiculturalism's magic number. *Globe and Mail*, October 2, pp. A14–15.

Perkins, S. and White, G. (2009) Modernising pay in the UK public services: trends and implications. *Human Resource Management Journal*, **20**(3): 244–57.

Perren, L. and Burgoyne, J. (2002) *Management and Leadership Abilities: An analysis of Texts, Testimony and Practice*. London: Council for Excellence in Management and Leadership.

Peters, T. and Waterman, R. (1982) *In Search of Excellence*. New York: Harper & Row.

Pettijohn, L. S., Parker, S., Pettijohn, C. E. and Kent, J. L. (2001) Performance appraisals: usage, criteria and observations. *Journal of Management Development*, **20**(9): 754–71.

Pfeffer, J. (1994) *Competitive Advantage Through People: Understanding the Power of the Workforce*. Boston, MA: Houghton Mifflin.

Pfeffer, J. (1998) *The Human Equation*. Boston, MA: Harvard Business School Press.

Pfeffer, J. (2005) Changing mental models: HR's most important task. *Human Resource Management*, **44**(2): 123–8.

Pfeffer, J. and Langton, N. (1993) The effect of wage dispersion on satisfaction, productivity, and working collaboratively: evidence from college and university faculty. *Administrative Science Quarterly*, **38**: 382–407.

Phillips, J. J. (1996a) *Accountability in Human Resource Management*. Houston, TX: Gulf Publishing.

Phillips, J. (1996b) Measuring the ROI: the fifth level of evaluation. *Technical and Skills Training*, April: 10–13.

Phillips, J. (2005) Measuring up. *People Management*, April 7: 42–3.

Phillips, J. M. (1998) Effects of realistic job previews on multiple organizational outcomes: a meta-analysis. *Academy of Management Journal*, **41**(6): 673–90.

Philips, L. (2007) Go green now to combat climate change. *People Management*, August 23.

Phillips, P. and Phillips, E. (1993) *Women and Work: Inequality in the Canadian Labour Market*. Toronto, Ontario: Lorimer.

Phillips, R. (1995) Coaching for higher performance. *Executive Development*, **8**(7): 5–7.

Pickard, J. (1997) Vacational qualifications. *People Management*, 10 July: 26–31.

Pickard, J. (2001) When push comes to shove. *People Management*, **7**(23): 30–5.

Pil, F. K. and Macduffie, J. P. (1996) The adoption of high-involvement work practices. *Industrial Relations: A Journal of Economy and Society*, **35**(3): 423–55.

Pilch, T. (2000) *Dynamic Reporting for a Dynamic Economy*. London: Academy of Enterprise.

Pilch, T. (2006) *Diversity and Economy*. London: Smith Institute.

Piore, M. and Sabel, C. (1984) *The Second Industrial Divide*. New York: Basic Books.

Piotrowski, C. and Armstrong, T. (2006) Current recruitment and selection practices: a national survey of Fortune 1000 firms. *North American Journal of Psychology*, December: 488–93.

Pitcher, G. (2008) Backlash against human resource management partner model as managers question results. *Personnel Today*, September 17. Available at www.personneltoday.com/articles/2008/01/28/44126.

Pitts, G. (2005) CEO's harmonious-society plan? Fire 14,000 staff. *Globe and Mail*, July 6, p. A1.

Plachy, R. J. (1987) Writing job descriptions that get results. *Personnel*, October: 56–63.

Platt, L. (1997) Employee work–life balance: the competitive advantage. In F. Hesselbein, M. Goldsmith and R. Beckhard (eds) *The Drucker Foundation, the Organization of the Future* (Chapter 32). San Francisco, CA: Jossey-Bass.

Polanyi, M. (1967) *The Tacit Dimension*. Garden City, NY: Doubleday.

Pollan, M. (2010) 'Food movement, rising', June. *New York Review of Books* Available at: www.nybooks.com/articles/archives/2010/jun/10/food-movement-rising/?pagination=false.

Pollard, E. and Hillage, J. (2001) *Exploring e-Learning*. Report No. 376. Brighton: Institute for Employment Studies.

Pollert, A. (1988) Dismantling flexibility. *Capital and Class*, (34): 42–75.

Pollert, A. (1991) *Farewell to Flexibility?* Oxford: Blackwell.

Pollitt, C. (2000) Is the emperor in his new underwear?: an analysis of the impacts of public management reform. *Public Management*, **2**(2): 181–99.

Pollitt, D. (2005) E-recruitment gets the Nike tick of approval. *Human Resource Management International Digest*, **13**(2): 33–5.

Pollitt, D. (2007) Software solves problem of global succession planning at Friesland Foods. *Human Resource Management International Digest*, **15**(6): 21–23.

Pollitt, D. (2008) Online recruitment connects 3 with top talent. *Human Resource Management International Digest*, **16**(4): 25–6.

Poon, J. (2004) Effects of performance appraisal politics on job satisfaction and turnover intention. *Personnel Review*, **33**(3): 322–34.

Porter, M. (1980) *Competitive Strategy*. New York: Free Press.

Porter, M. (1985) *Competitive Advantage: Creating and Sustaining Superior Performance*. New York: Free Press.

Posthuma, R., Morgeson, F. and Campion, M. (2002) Beyond employment interview validity: a comprehensive narrative review of recent research and trends over time. *Personnel Psychology*, **55**: 1–82.

Potosky, D. and Bobko, P. (2004) Selection testing via the internet: practical considerations and exploratory empirical findings. *Personnel Psychology*, **57**: 1003–34.

Prahalad, C. K. and Doz, Y. L. (1987) *The Multinational Mission: Balancing Local Demands and Global Vision*. New York: Free Press.

Premack, S. L. and Wanous, J. P. (1985) A meta-analysis of realistic job preview experiments. *Journal of Applied Psychology*, **70**(4): 706–19.

Preskill, H. (2008) Evaluation's second act: a spotlight on learning. *American Journal of Evaluation*, **29**(2): 127–38.

Procter, S. (2006) Organizations and organized systems: from direct control to flexibility. In S. Ackroyd, R. Batt, P. Thompson, and Tolbert, P. (eds) *The Oxford Handbook of Work and Organization* (pp. 462–84). Oxford: Oxford University Press.

Procter, S. and Mueller, F. (eds) (2000) *Teamworking*. Basingstoke: Palgrave Macmillan.

Proença, M. T. and de Oliveira, E. T. (2009) From normative to tacit knowledge: CVs analysis in personnel selection. *Employee Relations*, **31**(4): 427–47.

Prokopenko, J. (1994) The transition to a market economy and its implications for HRM in Eastern Europe. In P. S. Kirkbride (ed.) *Human Resource Management in Europe* (pp. 147–63). London: Routledge.

Prowse, P. and Prowse, J. (2010) Whatever happened to human resource management performance? *International Journal of Productivity and Performance Management*, **59**(2): 145–62.

Pulakos, E. D. and Schmitt, N. (1995) Experienced-based and situational questions: studies of validity. *Personnel Psychology*, **48**: 289–309.

Pulignano, V. and Stewart, P. (2006) Bureaucracy transcended? New patterns of employment regulation and labour contol in the international automotive industry. *New Technology, Work and Employment*, **21**(2): 90–106.

Pun, K. F. and White, A. S. (2005) A performance measurement paradigm for integrating strategy formulation: a review of systems and frameworks. *International Journal of Management Reviews*, **7**(1): 49–71.

Punnett, B., Crocker, O. and Stevens, M. (1992) The challenge for women expatriates and spouses: some empirical evidence. *International Journal of Human Resource Management*, **3**(3): 585–92.

Pupo, N.J. and Thomas, M.P. (2010) *Interrogating the New Economy*. Toronto, Ontario: University of Toronto Press.

Purcell, J. (1989) The impact of corporate strategy on human resource management. In J. Storey (ed.) *New Perspectives on Human Resource Management* (pp. 67–91). London: Routledge.

Purcell, J. (1995) Corporate strategy and its link with human resource management strategy. In J. Storey (ed.) *Human Resource Management: A Critical Text* (pp. 63–86). London: Routledge.

Purcell, J. (1999) Best practice and best fit: chimera or cul-de-sac? *Human Resource Management Journal*, **9**(3): 26–41.

Purcell, J. (2001) The meaning of strategy in human resource management: a critical text. In J. Storey (ed.) *Human Resource Management* (pp. 59–77). London: Thomson Learning.

Purcell, J. and Ahlstrand, B. (1994) *Human Resource Management in the Multi-divisional Company*. Oxford: Oxford University Press.

Purcell, J., and Hutchinson, S. (2007) Front-line managers as agents in the HRM-performance causal chain: theory, analysis and evidence. *Human Resource Management Journal*, **17**(1): 3–20.

Purcell, J. and Kinnie, N. (2008) HRM and business performance. In P. Boxall, J. Purcell and P. Wright (eds) *The Oxford Handbook of Human Resource Management* (pp. 533–51). Oxford: Oxford University Press.

Purcell, J. and Sisson, K. (1983) Strategies and practices in the management of industrial relations. In G. Bain (ed.) *Industrial Relations in Britain* (pp. 95–120). Oxford: Blackwell.

Purcell, J., Kinnie, N., Swart, J., Rayton, B. and Hutchinson, S. (2009) *People Management and Performance*. London: Routledge.

Pye, M., Cullinane, J. and Harcourt, M. (2001) The right to refuse unsafe work in New Zealand. *New Zealand Journal of Industrial Relations*, **26**(2): 199–216.

Pyman, A., Holland, P., Teicher, J. and Cooper, B. (2010) Industrial relations climate, employee voice and managerial attitudes to unions: an Australian study. *British Journal of Industrial Relations*, **48**(2): 460–80.

Quaddus, M. A. and Siddique, M. A. B. (eds) (2011) *Handbook of Corporate Sustainability*. Cheltenham: Edward Elgar.

Quah, D. (1997) Weightless economy packs a heavy punch. *The Independent on Sunday*, May 18, p. 4.

Quintanilla, J. and Ferner, A. (2003) Multinationals and human resource management: between global convergence and national identity. *International Journal of Human Resource Management*, **14**(3): 363–8.

Race for Opportunity (2008) *Race to the Top*. London: RfO.

Raeburn, A. (1980) *Cosmopolitan*. August. Quoted in Craig, M. (1981) *Office Worker's Survival Handbook* (p. 19). London: BSSR.

Raelin, J. (2004) Don't bother putting the leadership into people. *Academy of Management Executive*, **18**(3): 131–5.

Ramaswamy, E. and Schiporst, F. (2000) Human resource management, trade unions and empowerment: two cases from India. *International Journal of Human Resource Management*, **11**(4): 664–80.

Ramsay, H., Scholarios, D. and Harley, B. (2000) Employees and high-performance work systems: testing inside the black box. *British Journal of Industrial Relations*, **38**(4): 501–31.

Randell, G. (1994) Employee appraisal. In K. Sisson (ed.) *Personnel Management* (pp. 221–52). Oxford: Blackwell.

Randers, J. (2008) Global collapse – fact or fiction? *Futures*, **40**: 853–64.

Rao, A. S.(2007) Effectiveness of performance management systems: an empirical study in Indian companies. *International Journal of Human Resource Management*, **18**(10): 1812–40.

Rarick, C. A. and Baxter, G. (1986) Behaviourally anchored rating scales (bars): an effective performance appraisal approach. *SAM Advanced Management Journal*, Winter: 36–9.

Ratnam, V. (2006) *Industrial Relations*. New Dehli: Oxford University Press.

Ray, C.A. (1986) Corporate culture: the last frontier of control? *Journal of Management Studies*, **23**(3): 287–97.

Ready, D. and Conger, J. (2007) Make your company a talent factory. *Harvard Business Review*, **85**(6): 68–77.

Reason, P. and Bradbury, H. (eds) (2001) *The SAGE Handbook of Action Research. Participative Inquiry and Practice*. London: Sage.

Rebelo, T. M. and Gomes, A. (2011) Conditioning factors of an organizational learning culture. *Journal of Workplace Learning*, **23**(3): 173–94.

Redman, T., Snape, E., Thompson, D. and Ka-Ching Yan, F. (2000) Performance appraisal in an NHS hospital. *Human Resource Management Journal*, **10**(1): 48–62.

Redman, T., Hamilton, P., Mallock, H., and Kleymann, B. (2011) Working here makes me sick! The consequences of sick building syndrome. *Human Resource Management Journal*, **21**(1): 14–27.

Reed, J. (2007) *Appreciative Inquiry*. London, Sage.

Rees, T. (1998) *Mainstreaming Equality in the European Union: Education, Training and Labour Market Policies*. London: Routledge.

Rees, W. E. (1995) More jobs, less damage: a framework for sustainability, growth and employment. *Alternatives*, **21**(4): 24–30.

Reeves, R. (2010) What are you worth? *The Observer Magazine*, April 25, pp 43–56.

Reilly, B., Paci, P. and Holl, P. (1995) Unions, safety committees and workplace injuries. *British Journal of Industrial Relations*, **33**(2): 275–87.

Reilly, P. (2005) Get the best from knowledge workers. *People Management*, **29**(September): 52–3.

Reilly, P., Tamkin, P. and Broughton, A. (2007) *The Changing HR Function: Transforming HR?* London: Chartered Institute of Personnel and Development.

Remler, D. K. and Van Ryzin, G. G. (2011) *Research Methods in Practice: Strategies for Description and Causation*. Los Angeles, CA: Sage.

Renwick, D., Redman, T. and Maguire, S. (2008) *Green HRM: A Review, Process Model, and Research Agenda*. Discussion Paper Series No. 2008.01 April. Sheffield: University of Sheffield Management School.

Renzetti, E. (2011) The Big Society. *Globe and Mail*, February 12, pp. F1, 6–7.

Revans, R. (1982) *The Origins and Growth of Action Learning*. Bromley: Chartwell-Bratt.

Reynolds, M. (1997) Learning styles: a critique. *Management Learning*, **28**(2): 115–33.

Reynolds, M. (2009) Wild frontiers – reflections on experiential learning. *Management Learning*, **40**(4): 387–92.

Reynolds, M. and Vince, R. (2007) Introduction. In M. Reynolds and R. Vince (eds) *Handbook of Experiential Learning and Management Education* (pp.1–18). Oxford: Oxford University Press.

Riach, P. A. and Rich, J. (2002) Field experiments of discrimination in the market place. *Economic Journal*, **112**(483): 480–518.

Richard, P., Devinney, T., Yip, G. and Johnson, G. (2009) Measuring organizational performance: towards methodological best practice. *Journal of Management*, **35**(3): 718–804.

Richardson, J., McBey, K. and McKenna, S. (2008) Integrating realistic job previews and realistic living conditions previews. *Personnel Review*, **37**(5): 490–508.

Richbell, S. (2001) Trends and emerging values in human resource management. *International Journal of Manpower*, **22**(3): 261–8.

Rick, J. and Briner, R. (2000) Psychosocial risk assessment: problems and prospects. *Occupational Medicine*, **50**: 310–14.

Rifkin, J. (1996) *The End of Work*. New York: Tarcher/ Putnam Press.

Rigby, E. and Parker, G. (2011) City boards 'need women' to fight culture of macho men. *Financial Times*, September 6, p. 2.

Rigby, M. and O'Brien-Smith, F. (2010) Trade union interventions in work–life balance. *Work, Employment and Society*, **24**(2): 203–20.

Rigg, C., Stewart, J. and Trehan, K. (2007) *Critical Human Resource Development: Beyond Orthodoxy*. Harlow, FT/Prentice Hall.

Risher, H. (1978) Job evaluation: mystical or statistical. *Personnel*, **55**: 23–36.

Ritzer, G. (2000) *The McDonalization of Society* (New Century edn). Thousand Oaks, CA: Pine Forge Press.

Ritzer, G. (2004) *The McDonalization of Society*. (Revised New Century edn). Thousand Oaks, CA: Pine Forge Press.

Robbins, S. P. (1989) *Organizational Behavior* (4th edn). London: Prentice Hall.

Robens, Lord (1972) *Safety and Health at Work*. Cmnd 5034. London: HMSO.

Roberts, G. (1997) *Recuitment and Selection*. London: Institute of Personnel and Development.

Roberts, J. (2006) Limits to communities of practice. *Journal of Management Studies*, **43**(3): 623–39.

Robertson, I. T., Baron, H., Gibbons, P., MacIver, R. and Nyfield, G. (2000) Conscientiousness and managerial performance. *Journal of Occupational and Organizational Psychology*, **73**(2): 171–81.

Robinson, S. (2010) Leadership ethics. In J. Gold, R. Thorpe and A. Mumford (eds) *Handbook of Leadership and Management Development* (pp. 175–96). Aldershot: Gower.

Roche, W. K. (2009) Who gains from workplace partnership? *International Journal of Human Resource Management*, **20**(1): 1–33.

Rodger, A. (1970) *The Seven Point Plan* (3rd edn). London: NFER.

Rodgers, C. (2010) Sustainable entrepreneurship in SMEs: a case study analysis. *Corporate Social Responsibility and Environmental Management*, **17**(3): 125–32.

Rodgers, H., Frearson, M., Gold, J. and Holden, R. (2003) *International Comparator Contexts: The Leading Learning Project*. London: Learning and Skill Research Centre.

Rodrik, D. (2011) *The Globalization Paradox*. New York: Norton.

Roethlisberger, F. J. and Dickson, W. J. (1939). *Management and the Worker*. Cambridge, MA: Harvard University Press.

Rogaly, B. (2008) Intensification of workplace regimes in British horticulture: the role of migrant workers. *Population, Space and Place*, **14**: 497–510.

Rohrbach, D. (2007) The development of knowledge societies in 19 OECD countries between 1970 and 2002. *Social Science Information*, **46**(4): 655–89.

Rose, M. (1988) *Industrial Behaviour*. London: Penguin.

Rose, M. (2000) Target practice. *People Management*, **6**(23): 44–5.

Rose, N. (1999) *Governing the Soul: The Shaping of the Private Self* (2nd edn). London: Sage.

Ross, I. and MacDonald, G. (1997) Scars from stress cut deep in workplace. *Globe and Mail*, October 9, p. B16.

Ross, L., Rix, M. and Gold, J. (2005) Learning distributed leadership. Part 1. *Industrial and Commercial Training*, **37**(3): 130–7.

Rossett, A. (2002) *The ASTD E-Learning Handbook*. New York: McGraw-Hill.

Rothwell, W. J. (2011) Replacement planning: a starting point for succession planning and talent management. *International Journal of Training and Development*, **15**(1): 87–99.

Rounce, K., Scarfe, A. and Garnett, J. (2007) A work-based learning approach to developing leadership for senior health and social care professionals. *Education and Training*, **49**(3): 218–26.

Rousseau, D. M. (1995) *Psychological Contracts in Organizations: Understanding Written and Unwritten Agreements*. Thousand Oaks, CA: Sage.

Rousseau, D. M. and Ho, V. T. (2000) Psychological contract issues in compensation. In S. L. Rynes and B. Gerhart (eds) *Compensation in Organizations: Current Research and Practice* (pp. 273–310). San Francisco, CA: Jossey-Bass.

Rowley, C. and Bae, J. (2002) Globalization and transformation of human resource management in South Korea. *International Journal of Human Resource Management*, **13**(3): 522–49.

Rowley, C., Benson, J. and Warner, M. (2004) Towards an Asian model of human resource management? A comparative analysis of China, Japan and South Korea. *International Journal of Human Resource Management*, **14**(4): 917–33.

Royle, T. (2005) The union recognition dispute at McDonald's Moscow food-processing factory. *Industrial Relations Journal*, **36**(4): 318–32.

Rubery, J. (1996) The labour market outlook and the outlook for labour market anaysis. In R. Crompton, D. Gallie and K. Purcell (eds) *Changing Forms of Employment Organization, Skills and Gender*. London: Routledge.

Rubery, J. Earnshaw, J., Marchington, M., Cooke, F. L. and Vincent, S. (2002) Changing organizational forms and the employment relationship. *Journal of Management Studies*, **39**(5): 645–72.

Rubin, J. (2009) *Why Your World Is About to Get a Whole Lot Smaller*. Toronto, Ontario: Vintage Canada.

Rucci, A. J., Kirn, S. P. and Quinn, R. T. (1998) *Harvard Business Review*, January–February: 82–97.

Rushe, D. (2011) Victory for Walmart as huge sex bias case is thrown out. *The Guardian*, June 21, 2011, p. 20.

Russ-Eft, D. and Preskill, H. (2005) In search of the holy grail: return on investment evaluation in human resource development. *Advances in Developing Human Resources*, **7**(1): 71–85.

Russell, B. (2008) Call centres: a decade of research. *International Journal of Management Reviews*, **10**(3): 195–219.

Ryan, J. C. and Tipu, S. A. (2009) An instrument for the self-appraisal of scientific research performance. *International Journal of Productivity and Performance Management*, **58**(7): 632–44.

Sackett, P. and Lievens, F. (2008) Personnel selection. *Annual Review of Psychology*, **59**: 419–50.

Sadler-Smith, E. (2006) *Learning and Development for Managers*. Oxford: Blackwell.

Sako, M. (2005) Does embeddedness imply limits to within-country diversity? *British Journal of Industrial Relations*, **43**(4): 585–92.

Sako, K. and Tierney, A. (2005) *Sustainability of Business Service Outsourcing: The Case of Human Resource Outsourcing (HRO)*. AIM Working Paper. London: Advanced Institute of Management.

Saks, A. M. (2000) *Research, Measurement, and Evaluation of Human Sources*. Scarborough, Ontario: Nelson/Thompson Learning.

Saks, A., Tamkin, P. and Lewis, P. (2011) Editorial – management training and development. *International Journal of Training and Development*, **15**(3): 179–83.

Salaman, G. and J. Butler, J. (1990) Why managers won't learn. *Management Education and Development*, **21**(3): 183–91.

Salaman, G. and Taylor, S. (2002) 'Competency's consequences: changing the character of managerial work', paper presented at the Critical Management Studies Seminar at the ESRC Workshop on Managerial Work, Cambridge, June.

Salgado, J. F. (1997) The five factor model of personality and job performance in the European Community. *Journal of Applied Psychology*, **82**(1): 30–43.

Sambrook, S. (2008) Critical HRD: a concept analysis. *Personnel Review*, **38**(1): 61–73.

Sambrook, S. and Stewart, J. (2005) A critical review of researching human resource development: the case of a pan-European project. In C. Elliott and S. Turnbull (eds) *Critical Thinking in Human Resource Development* (pp. 67–84). London: Routledge.

Sambunjak, D., Straus, S. and Marušić, A. (2006) Mentoring in academic medicine. *Journal of the American Medical Association*, **296**(9):1103–15.

Samuel, P. and Bacon, N. (2010) The contents of partnership agreements in Britain 1990–2007. *Work, Employment and Society*, **24**(3): 430–48.

Sánchez, M. P., Elena, S. and Castrillo, R. (2009) Intellectual capital dynamics in universities: a reporting model. *Journal of Intellectual Capital*, **10**(2): 307–24.

Saraswati, R. and Bagchi, D. (eds) (1993) *Women and Work in South Asia: Regional Patterns and Perspectives*. New York: Routledge.

Sarkis, J., Gonzalez-Torre, P. and Adenso-Diaz, B. (2010) Stakeholder pressure and the adoption of environmental practices: the mediating effect of training. *Journal of Operations Management*, **28**: 163–76.

Sass, R. (1982) Safety and self-respect. *Policy Options*, July–August: 17–21.

Saul, J. R. (2005) *The Collapse of Globalism*. Toronto, Ontario: Viking.

Saul, J. R. (2008) *A Fair Country*. Toronto, Ontario: Viking.

Saunders, D. (2010) Just watch us. *Globe and Mail*, December 18, p. F4.

Saunders, J. and Hunter, I. (2007) *Human Resource Outsourcing: Solutions, Suppliers, Key Processes and the Current Market*. London: Orion Partners.

Sayer, A. (2000) *Realism and Social Science*. London: Sage.

Sayer, A. (2005) *The Moral Significance of Class*. Cambridge: Cambridge University Press.

Sayer, D. (1991) *Capitalism and Modernity: Excursus on Marx and Weber*. London: Routledge.

Sayim, K. Z. (2010) Pushed or pulled? Transfer of reward management polcies in MNCs. *International Journal of Human Resource Management*, **21**(14): 2631–58.

Scarbrough, H. (2000) The HR implications of supply chain relationships. *Human Resource Management Journal*, **10**(1): 5–17.

Scarbrough, H. and Swan, J. (2001) Explaining the

diffusion of knowledge management: the role of fashion. *British Journal of Management*, **12**(1): 3–12.

Schafer, D. (1996) *Stress Management for Wellness* (3rd edn). Chico, CA: Harcourt Brace.

Schatzki, T. R (2001) Introduction. In T. R. Schatzki, K. Knorr Cetina and E. Von Savigny (eds) *The Practice Turn in Contemporary Theory* (pp. 1–14). London: Routledge.

Schein, E. (2010) *Organizational Culture and Leadership* (4th edn). San Francisco, CA: Jossey-Bass.

Schilling, J. and Kluge, A. (2009) Barriers to organizational learning: an integration of theory and research. *International Journal of Management Reviews*, **11**: 337–60.

Schmidt, F. L. (2002) The role of general cognitive ability and job performance: why there cannot be a debate. *Human Performance*, **15**: 187–210.

Schnabel, C. (2003) Determinants of trade union membership. In J. T. Addison and C. Schnabel (eds) *International handbook of Trade Unions* (pp. 13–43). Cheltenham: Edward Elgar.

Schneider, B. (1987) The people make the place. *Personnel Psychology*, **40**: 437–53.

Schneider, B. (1999) Research in the workplace: whose knowledge is it anyway? In *Conference Proceedings, How to Keep Your Intellectual Capital* (pp. 56–71). Calgary: University of Calgary.

Schneider, B. (2000). The psychological life of organizations. In N. Ashkanasy, C. Wilderon and M. Peterson (eds) *Handbook of Organizational Culture and Climate* (pp. xvii–xxi). Thousand Oaks, CA: Sage.

Schneider, R. (2001) Variety performance. *People Management*, **7**(9): 26–31.

Schön, D. A. (1983) *The Reflective Practitioner: How Professionals Think in Action*. London: Maurice Temple Smith.

Schuler, R. S. (1989) Strategic human resource management and industrial relations. *Human Relations*, **42**(2): 157–84.

Schuler, R. S. (1992) Strategic human resource management: linking people with the strategic needs of the business. *Organizational Dynamics*, **21**: 18–31.

Schuler, R. S. and Jackson, S. (1987) Linking competitive strategies and human resource management practices. *Academy of Management Executive*, **1**(3): 209–13.

Schuler, R., Dowling, P. and De Cieri, H. (1993) An integrative framework of strategic international human resource management. *Journal of Management*, **19**(2): 419–59.

Schuler, R. S., Jackson, S. and Storey, J. (2001) HRM and its links with strategic management. In J. Storey (ed.) *Human Resource Management: A Critical Text* (2nd edn) (pp. 114–30). London: Thompson Learning.

Schultz, H. (with Gordon, J.) (2011) *Onward: How Starbucks Fought for its Life Without Losing its Soul*. Chichester: John Wiley & Sons.

Schultz, T. W. (1981) *Investing in People: The Economics of Population Quality*. Berkeley, CA: University of California Press.

Scott, B. and Revis, S. (2008) Talent management in hospitality: graduate career success and strategies. *International Journal of Contemporary Hospitality Management*, **20**(7): 781–91.

Scott, M. (1998) *Value Drivers*. Chichester: John Wiley & Sons.

Scott, S. G. and Einstein, W. O. (2001) Strategic performance appraisal in team-based organizations: one size does not fit all. *Academy of Management Executive*, **15**(2): 107–16.

Scott-Dixon, K. (2004) *Doing IT: Women Working in Information Technology*. Toronto, Ontario: Sumach Press.

Scullion, H. (2001) International human resource management. In J. Storey (ed.) *Human Resource Management: A Critical Text* (2nd edn) (pp. 288–313). London: Thompson Learning.

Scullion, H. and Linehan, M. (eds) (2005) *International Human Resource Management: A Critical Text* (2nd edn). Basingstoke: Palgrave Macmillan.

Scullion, H. and Starkey, K. (2000) The changing role of the corporate human resource function in the international firm. *International Journal of Human Resource Management*, **11**(6): 1061–81.

Sealy, R., Vinnicombe, S. and Singh, V. (2008) *The 2008 Female FTSE Report: A decade of delay*. Cranfield: Cranfield School of Management.

Séguin, R. (2010) Quebec labour, student groups unite to fight to right. *Globe and Mail*, November 6, p. A16.

Self, D. R., Armenakis, A. A., and Schraeder, M. (2007) Organizational change content, process, and context: a simultaneous analysis of employee reactions. *Journal of Change Management*, **7**: 211–29.

Sellen, A. and Harper, R. (2002) *The Myth of the Paperless Office*. Cambridge, MA: Massachusetts Institute of Technology.

Selwyn, N. M. (2004) *Selwyn's Law of Employment* (15th edn). London: Butterworths.

Selwyn, N. M. (2011) *Selwyn's Law of Employment* (16th edn). London: Butterworths.

Selznick, P. (1957) *Leadership and Administration*. New York: Harper & Row.

Senge, P. (1990) *The Fifth Discipline*. New York: Doubleday.

Sennett, R. (1998) *The Corrosion of Character*. New York: Norton.

Sennett, R. (2004) *Respect: The Formation of Character in an Age of Inequality*. London: Penguin.

Sewell, G. (1998) The discipline of teams: the control of team-based industrial work through electronic and peer surveillance. *Administrative Science Quarterly*, **43**: 397–428.

Sewell, G. (2005) Doing what comes naturally? Why we need a practical ethics of teamwork. *International Journal of Human Resource Management*, **16**(2): 202–18.

Sewell, G. and Wilkinson, B. (1992) Someone to watch over me: surveillance, discipline and the just in time labour process. *Sociology*, **26**(2): 271–89.

Shane, J. M. (2010) Performance management in police agencies: a conceptual framework. *Policing: An International Journal of Police Strategies and Management*, **33**(1): 6–29.

Shaw, J. D., Delery, J. E., Jenkins, G. and Gupta, N. (1998) An organizational level analysis of voluntary and involuntary turnover. *Academy of Management Journal*, **41**: 511–25.

Shaw, J. D., Duffy, M. K., Johnson, J. L. and Lockhart, D. E. (2005) Turnover, social capital losses and performance. *Academy of Management Journal*, **48**(4): 594–606.

Sheffield, J. and Coleshill, P. (2001) Developing best value in a Scottish local authority. *Measuring Business Excellence*, **5**(2): 31–8.

Shenkar, O. (1995) *Global Perspectives on Human Resource Management*. Englewood Cliffs, NJ: Prentice Hall.

Shibata, H. (2002) Wage and performance appraisal systems in flux: a Japan–United States comparison. *Industrial Relations*, **41**(4): 629–52.

Shrivastava, P. (2011) Why is sustainability important to business today? *Report on Business*, January: 3–5.

Siebert, W. S. and Zubanov, N. (2009) Searching for the optimal level of employee turnover: a study of a large U.K. retail organization. *Academy of Management Journal*, **52**(2): 294–313.

Sillup, G. P and Klimberg, R. (2010) Assessing the ethics of implementing performance appraisal systems. *Journal of Management Development*, **29**(1): 38–55.

Simms, M. and Holgate, J. (2010) Organising for what? Where is the debate on the politics of organizing? *Work, Employment and Society*, **24**(1): 157–68.

Simon, S. and Eby, L. (2003) A typology of negative mentoring experiences: a multidimensional scaling study, *Human Relations*, **56**(9): 1083–106.

Simosi, M. and Xenikou, A. (2010) The role of organizational culture in the relationship between leadership and organizational commitment: an empirical study in a Greek organization. *International Journal of Human Resource Management*, **21**(10): 1598–616.

Simpson, J. (2011) Trading partner, sure thing; economic model, no thanks. *Globe and Mail*, September 7, p. A15.

Singh, R. (1997) Equal opportunities for men and women in the EU: a commentary. *Industrial Relations*, **28**(1): 68–71.

Singh, V. (2002) *Managing Diversity for Strategic Advantage*. London: Council for Excellence in Management and Leadership.

Sisson, K. and Storey, J. (2000) *The Realities of Human Resource Management: Managing the Employment Relationship*. Buckingham, Oxford University Press.

Skivenes, M. and Trygstad, S. (2010) When whistle-blowing works: the Norwegian case. *Human Relations*, **63**(7): 1071–97.

Sklair, L. (2002) *Globalization: Capitalism and its Alternatives* (3rd edn). New York: Oxford University Press.

Slapper, G. and S. Tombs (1999) *Corporate Crime*. Essex: Longman.

Sloman, M. (2005) *Training to Learning*. London: Chartered Institute of Personnel and Development.

Sloman, M. and Reynolds, J. (2002) 'Developing the e-learning community', paper presented to the Third Conference on Human Resource Development: Research and Practice Across Europe, Edinburgh, January.

Smethurst, S. (2004) The allure of online. *People Management*, 29 July: 38–40.

Smircich, L. (1983) Concepts of culture and organizational analysis. *Administrative Science Quarterly*, **28**(3): 339–58.

Smith, A. (1776/1982) *The Wealth of Nations*. Harmondsworth: Penguin.

Smith, A. R. (1980) *Corporate Manpower Planning*. London: Gower Press.

Smith, C., Valesechhi, R., Muller, F. and Gabe, J. (2008) Knowledge and the discourse of labour process transformation. *Work, Employment and Society*, **22**(4): 581–99.

Smith, L. (1993) Quoted in: Managing AIDS: how one boss struggled to cope. *Business Week*, February 1: 48.

Smith, P. and Morton, G. (1993) Union exclusion and the decollectivization of industrial relations in contemporary Britain. *British Journal of Industrial Relations*, **31**(1): 97–114.

Smith, P. and Morton, G. (2006) Nine years of New Labour: neoliberalism and workers' rights. *British Journal of Industrial Relations*, **44**(3): 401–20.

Smith, S. M. (2009) Investors in People: the chicken and the egg: HR specialists should be cautious about claims for the standard. *Human Resource Management International Digest*, **17**(1): 38–9.

Smither, J., Reilly, R., Millsap, R., Pearlman, K. and Stoffey, R. (1993) Applicant reactions to selection procedures. *Personnel Psychology*, **46**: 49–76.

Smither, J., London, M., Flautt, R., Vargas, Y. and Kucine, I. (2003) Can working with an executive coach improve multi-source feedback ratings over time? A quasi-experimental field study. *Personnel Psychology*, **56**(1): 23–44.

Smither, J., London, M. and Reilly, R. (2005) Does performance improve following multisource feedback? A theoretical model, meta-analysis, and review of empirical findings. *Personnel Psychology*, **58**: 33–66.

Smither, J. W., Brett, J. F. and Atwater, L. E. (2008) What do leaders recall about their multisource feedback? *Journal of Leadership and Organizational Studies*, **14**(3): 202–18.

Sneade, A. (2001) Trade union membership 1999–2000: an analysis of data from the certification officer, and The Labour Force Survey. *Labour Market Trends*, September: 433–41.

Snell, S. A. (1992) Control theory in strategic human resource management: the mediating effect of administrative information. *Academy of Management Journal*, **35**: 292–327.

Snell, S. A., Youndt, M. A. and Wright, P. M. (1996) Establishing a framework for research in strategic human resource management: merging source theory and organizational learning. *Research in Personnel and Human Resources Management*, **14**: 61–90.

Soltani, E., ven der Meer, R. and Williams, T. (2005) A contrast of HRM and TQM approaches to performance management: some evidence. *British Journal of Management*, **16**(3): 211–30.

Sparrow, P. (2007) Globalization of HR at function level: four UK-based case studies of the international recruitment and selection process. *International Journal of Human Resource Management*, **18**(5): 845–67.

Sparrow, P. (2008) Performance management in the UK. In A. Varma, P. S. Budwar and A. Denisi (eds) *Performance Management Systems: A Global Perspective* (pp. 131–46). Abingdon: Routledge.

Sparrow, P., Brewster, C. and Harris, H. (2004) *Globalizing Human Resource Management*. London: Routledge.

Spender, J.-C. (2008) Organizational learning and knowledge management: whence and whither? *Management Learning*, **39**(2): 159–76.

Spillane, J. (2006) *Distributed Leadership*. San Francisco, CA: Jossey-Bass.

Spillane, J. P., Camburn, E. M., Pustejovsky, J. Pareja, A. S. and Lewis, G. (2008) Taking a distributed perspective. *Journal of Educational Administration*, **46**(2): 189–213.

Spitzmüller, C., Neumann, E., Spitzmüller, M., Rubino, C., Keeton, K., Sutton, M. T. and Manzey, D. (2008) Assessing the influence of psychosocial and career mentoring on organizational attractiveness. *International Journal of Selection and Assessment*, **16**(4): 403–15.

Spychalski, A. C., Quiñones, M. A., Gaugler, B. B. and Pohley, K. (1997) A survey of assessment center practices in the United States. *Personnel Psychology*, **50**, 71–90.

Squires, G. (2001) Mangement as a professional discipline. *Journal of Management Studies*, **38**(4): 473–87.

Stahl, G. K. and Björkman, I. (eds) (2006) *Handbook of Research in International Human Resource Management*. Cheltenham: Edward Elgar.

Stanton, P. and Nankervis, A. (2011) Linking strategic HRM, performance management and organizational effectiveness: perceptions of managers in Singapore. *Asia Pacific Business Review*, **17**(1): 67–84.

Stanworth, C. (2000) Flexible working patterns. In D. Winstanley and J. Woodall (eds) *Ethical Issues in Contemporary Human Resource Management* (pp. 137–55). Basingstoke: Palgrave Macmillan.

Stavrou, E., Brewster, C., and Charalambous, C. (2010) Human resource management and firm performance in Europe through the lens of business systems: best fit, best practice or both? *International Journal of Human Resource Management*, **21**(7): 933–62.

Steiner, A. (2011) 'The interview – Achim Steiner: Ontario and the green economy'. Available at: www.tvo.org/cfmx/tvoorg/theagenda/index.cfm?page_id=7&bpn=109158&bpn_segment_id=10072&ts=2011-05-10%2020:00:00.0 (accessed May 17, 2011).

Sternberg, R. J. and Horvath, J. A. (eds) (1999) *Tacit Knowledge in Professional Practice: Researcher and Practitioner Perspectives*. Mahwah, NJ: Lawrence Erlbaum.

Stewart, H. (2009) Economists tell Queen how they failed to see the recession coming. *The Observer*, July 27, p. 1.

Stewart, J. (2007) The ethics of HRD. In C. Rigg, J. Stewart and K. Trehan (eds) *Critical Human Resource Development: Beyond Orthodoxy* (pp. 59–78), Harlow: Prentice Hall.

Stewart, J. (2010) E-learning for managers and leaders. In J. Gold, R. Thorpe and A. Mumford (eds) *The Gower Handbook of Leadership and Management Development* (pp. 441–56). Aldershot: Gower.

Stewart, P. and Danford, A. (2008) Editorial: Union strategies and worker engagement with new forms of work and employment. *New Technology, Work and Employment*, **23**(3): 146–50.

Stewart, R. (1975) *Contrasts in Management*. Maidenhead: McGraw-Hill.

Stiglitz, J. E. (2010) Contagion, liberalization, and the optimal structure of globalization. *Journal of Globalization and Development*, **1**(2): Article 2.

Stober, D. and Grant A. M. (eds) (2008) *Evidence-Based Coaching Handbook*. New York: John Wiley & Sons.

Stohl, C. and Cheney, G. (2001) Participatory processes/paradoxical practices. *Management Communications Quarterly*, **14**(3): 349–407.

Stoner, J. S. and Gallagher, V. C. (2010) Who cares? The role of job involvement in psychological contract violation. *Journal of Applied Social Psychology*, 40(6): 1490–514.

Storey, J. (1983) *Managerial Prerogative and the Question of Control*. London: Routledge & Kegan Paul.

Storey, J. (ed.) (1989) *New Perspectives on Human Resource Management*. London: Routledge.

Storey, J. (1992) *Developments in the Management of Human Resources*. Oxford: Blackwell.

Storey, J. (1995a) Human resource management: still marching on or marching out? In J. Storey (ed.) *Human Resource Management: A Critical Text* (pp. 3–32). London: Routledge.

Storey, J. (ed.) (1995b) *Human Resource Management: A Critical Text*. London: Routledge.

Storey, J. (2001) Human resource management today: an assessment. In J. Storey (ed.) *Human Resource Management: A Critical Text* (2nd edn) (pp. 3–20). London: Thompson Learning.

Storey, R. (2004) From the environment to the workplace … and back again? Occupational health and safety activism in Ontario, 1970s–2000+. *Canadian Review of Sociology and Anthropology*, 41(4): 419–47.

Storey, J. (ed.) (2007) Human resource management today: an assessment. In J. Storey (ed.) *Human Resource Management: A Critical Text* (pp. 3–20). London: Thompson Learning.

Storey, J. (2008) What is strategic HRM? In J. Storey (ed.) *Human Resource Management: A Critical Text* (3rd edn) (pp. 59–78). London: Thompson Learning.

Storey, D. J. (2009) *Small Firms in Regional Economic Development*. Cambridge: Cambridge University Press.

Storey, J., Cressey, P., Morris, T. and Wilkinson, A. (1997) Changing employment practices in UK banking: case studies. *Personnel Review*, **26**(1): 24–42.

Strauss, G. (1998) An overview. In F. Heller, E. Pusic, G. Strauss and B. Wilpert (eds) *Organizational Participation: Myth and Reality* (pp. 8–39). Oxford: Oxford University Press.

Strebler, M., Robinson, D. and Heron, P. (1997) *Getting the Best Out of Your Competencies*. Report No. 334. Brighton: Institute for Employment Studies.

Stredwick, J. and Ellis, S. (2005) *Flexible Working* (2nd edn). London: Chartered Institute of Personnel and Development.

Streeck, W. (1987) The uncertainties of management in the management of uncertainty. *Work, Employment and Society*, **1**: 281–308.

Streeck, W. and Visser, J. (1997) The rise of the conglomerate union. *European Journal of Industrial Relations*, **3**(3): 305–32.

Stuart, M., Cook, H., Cutter, J., and Winterton, J. (2010) *Assessing the Impact of Union Learning and the Union Learning Fund: Union and Employer Perspectives*. Leeds: Leeds University Business School.

Stuart, R. (1984) Towards re-establishing naturalism in management training and development. *Industrial and Commercial Training*, July/August: 19–21.

Sturges, J., Conway, N. and Liefooghe, A. (2010) Organizational support, individual attributes, and the practice of career self-management behavior. *Group and Organization Management*, **35**(1):108–41.

Su, S., Baird, K. and Blair, B. (2009) Employee organizational commitment: the influence of cultural and organizational factors in the Australian manufacturing industry. *International Journal of Human Resource Management*, **20**(12): 2494–516.

Sullivan, R. (2010) Labour market or labour movement? The union density bias as barrier to labour renewal. *Work, Employment and Society*, **24**(1): 145–56.

Sullivan, S. and Arthur, M. (2006) The evolution of the boundaryless career concept: examining physical and psychological mobility. *Journal of Vocational Behavior*, **69**: 19–29.

Sullivan, S. E., Forret, M. L., Mainiero, L. A. and Terjesen, S. (2007) What motivates entrepreneurs? An exploratory study of the kaleidoscope career model and entrepreneurship. *Journal of Applied Management and Entrepreneurship*, **12**: 4–19.

Sullivan, S. E., Forret, M. L., Carraher, S. M. and Mainiero, L. A. (2009) Using the kaleidoscope career model to examine generational differences in work attitudes. *Career Development International*, **14**(3): 284–302.

Sumner, J. (2005) *Sustainability and the Civil Commons: Rural Communities in the Age of Globalization*. Toronto, Ontario: University of Toronto Press.

Sumner, J. (2007) *Sustainability and the Civil Commons*. Toronto, Ontario: University of Toronto Press.

Sun, P. and Anderson, M. (2010) An examination of the

relationship between absorptive capacity and organizational learning, and a proposed integration. *International Journal of Management Reviews*, **12**(2): 130–50.

Sung, J. and Ashton, D. (2005) *High Performance Work Practices: Linking Strategy and Skills to Performance Outcomes*. London: Department of Trade and Industry/Chartered Institute of Personnel and Development.

Suutari, V. and Brewster, C. (2003) Repatriation: empirical evidence from a longitudinal study of careers and expectations among Finnish expatriates. *International Journal of Human Resource Management*, **14**(7): 1132–51.

Suutari, V. and Viitala, R. (2008) Management development of senior executives: methods and their effectiveness. *Personnel Review*, **37**(4): 375–92.

Sveiby, K. E. (1997) *The New Organizational Wealth: Managing and Measuring Organizational Wealth*. San Francisco, CA: Berrett-Koehler.

Swanson, R. A. (2001) HRD and its underlying theory. *Human Resource Development International*, **4**(3): 299–312.

Swedberg, R. (2005) *The Max Weber Dictionary: Keywords and Central Concepts*. Stanford: Stanford University Press.

Swinburne, P. (2001) How to use feedback to improve performance. *People Management*, **7**(11): 46–7.

Sydow, J., Lindkvist, L. and DeFillippi, R. (2004) Project-base organizations, embeddedness and repositories of knowledge: editorial. *Organization Studies*, **25**(9): 1475–89.

Sylva, H. and Mol, S. (2009) E-Recruitment: a study into applicant perceptions of an online application system. *International Journal of Selection and Assessment*, **17**(3): 311–22.

Szamosi, L. T., Wilkinson, A., Wood, G. and Psychogios, A. (2010) Developments in HRM in south-eastern Europe. *International Journal of Human Resource Management*, **21**(14): 2521–8.

Tahvanainen, M. and Suutari, V. (2005) Expatriate performance management in MNCs. In H. Scullion and M. Linehan (eds) *International Human Resource Management* (pp. 91–113). Basingstoke: Palgrave Macmillan.

Tal, B. (2007) Booming job market and disappointing economy: explaining the disconnect. *Canadian Employment Quality Index, Economics and Strategy*. February 1. Available at: www.cibcwm.com/research.

Tamkin, P. and Denvir, A. (2006) *Strengthening the UK Evidence Base on Leadership and Management Capability*, London: Department of Trade and Industry.

Tamkin, P., Barber, L. and Dench, S. (1997) *From Admin to Strategy: The Changing Face of the HR Function*.

Report No. 32. Brighton: Institute for Employment Studies.

Tamkin, P., Aston, J., Cummings, J., Hooker, H., Pollard, E., Rick, J. et al. (2002) *A Review of Training in Racism Awareness and Valuing Cultural Diversity*. Brighton: Institute of Employment Studies.

Tamkin, P., Giles, L., Campbell, M. and Hillage, J. (2004) *Skills Pay: The Contribution of Skills to Business Success*. Brighton: Institute for Employment Studies.

Tamkin, P., Cowling, M. and Hunt, W. (2008) *People and the Bottom Line*. Brighton: Institute of Employment Studies.

Tams, S. (2008) Constructing self-efficacy at work: a person-centered perspective. *Personnel Review*, **37**(2): 165–83.

Tan, J.-S. (1998) Communication, cross-cultural. In M. Poole and M. Warner (eds) *Handbook of Human Resource Management* (pp. 492–97). London: Thomson Business.

Tansley, C., Turner, P. and Foster, C. (2007a) *Talent: Strategy, Management, Measurement. Research into Practice*. London: Chartered Institute of Personnel and Development.

Tansley, C., Turner, P., Foster, C., Harris, L., Stewert, J. and Sempik, A. (2007b) *Talent Strategy, Management and Measurement*. London: Chartered Institute of Personnel and Development.

Taras, D. and Kaufman, B. (2006) Non-union employee representation in North America: diversity, controversy and uncertain future. *Industrial Relations Journal*, **37**(5): 513–42.

Taskin, L. and Edwards, P. (2007) The possibilities and limits of telework in a bureaucratic environment: lessons from the public sector. *New Technology, Work and Employment*, **22**(3): 195–207.

Tatli, A., Mulholland, G., Ozbilgin, M. and Worman, D. (2007) *Managing Diversity in Practice: Supporting Business Goals*. London: Chartered Institute of Personnel and Development.

Taylor, F. (1911) *Principles of Scientific Management*. New York: Harper.

Taylor, H. (1991) The systematic training model: corn circles in search of a spaceship? *Management Education and Development*, **22**(4): 258–78.

Taylor, P. (2010) The globalization of service work: analysing the transnational call centre value chain. In P. Thompson and C. Smith (eds) *Working Life* (pp. 244–68). Basingstoke: Palgrave Macmillan.

Taylor, P. and Bain, P. (1998) An assembly line in the head: the call centre labour process. *Industrial Relations Journal*, **30**(2): 101–17.

Taylor, P. and Bain, P. (2005) Indian calling to the far away towns. *Work, Employment and Society*, **19**(2): 261–82.

Taylor, P. and Connelly, L. (2009) Before the disaster:

health and safety and working conditions at a plastic factory. *Work, Employment and Society*, **23**(1): 160–8.

Taylor, P., Baldry, C., Bain, P. and Ellis, V. (2003) A unique working environment: health, sickness and absence management in UK call centres. *Work, Employment and Society*, **17**(3): 435–58.

Taylor, P., Cunningham, I., Newsome, K. and Scholarios, D. (2010) 'Too scared to go sick' – reformulating the research agenda on sickness absence. *Industrial Relations Journal*, **41**(4): 270–88.

Taylor, R. (2002) *Britain's World of Work – Myths and Realities*. Swindon: Economic and Social Research Council.

Taylor, S. (1998) *Employee Resourcing*. London: Institute of Personnel Development.

Taylor, S. and Bright, D. S. (2011) Open-mindedness and defensiveness in multisource feedback processes: a conceptual framework. *Journal of Applied Behavioral Science*, **47**: 432–60.

Taylor, S. and Napier, N. (1996) Working in Japan: lessons from women expatriates. *Sloan Management Review*, **37**: 125–44.

Taylor, S., Beechler, S. and Napier, N. (1996) Toward an integrative model of strategic international human resource management. *Academy of Management Review*, **21**(4): 959–85.

Teague, P. and Grahl, J. (1992) *Industrial Relations and European Integration*. London: Lawrence & Wishart.

Teece, D., Pisano, G. and Shuen, A. (1997) Dynamic capabilities and strategic management. *Strategic Management Journal*, **18**(7):509–33.

Templer, A. J. and Cawsey, T. F. (1999) Rethinking career development in an era portfolio careers. *Career Development International*, **4**(2): 70–6.

Templer, K. J., Tay, C. and Chandrasekar, N. A. (2006) Motivational cultural intelligence, realistic job preview, realistic living conditions preview, and cross-cultural adjustment. *Group and Organization Management*, **31**(1): 154–73.

Temporal, P. (1978) The nature of non-contrived learning and its implications for management development. *Management Education and Development*, **9**: 20–3.

Terpstra, D. E. and Rozelle, E. J. (1993) The relationship of staffing practices to organizational level measures of performance. *Personnel Psychology*, **46**: 27–48.

Terry, M. (2003) Can partnership reverse the decline in of british trade unions? *Work, Employment and Society*, **17**(3): 459–72.

Tett, G. (2009) *Fool's Gold: How Unrestrained Greed Corrupted a Dream, Shattered Global Markets and Unleashed a Catastrophe*. London: Little, Brown.

Thompson, E. P. (1967) Time, work-discipline, and industrial capitalism. *Past and Present*, **38** (December): 56–97.

Thompson, M. and Ponak, A. (2005) The management of industrial relations. In M. Gunderson, A. Ponak and Taras, D. (eds) *Union–Management Relations in Canada* (5th edn) (pp. 112–33) Toronto, Ontario: Pearson.

Thompson, P. (1989) *The Nature of Work* (2nd edn). Basingstoke: Palgrave Macmillan.

Thompson, P. (1993) Postmodernism: fatal distraction. In J. Hassard and M. Parker (eds) *Postmodernism and Organizations* (pp. 183–203). London: Sage.

Thompson, P. and B. Harley, B. (2008) HRM and the worker: labour process perspectives. In P. Boxall, J. Purcell and P. Wright (eds) *The Oxford Handbook of Human Resource Management* (pp. 147–65). Oxford: Oxford University Press.

Thompson P. and McHugh, D. (2009) *Work Organisations: A Critical Approach* (4th edn). Basingstoke: Palgrave Macmillan.

Thompson, P. and Smith, C. (2010) (eds) *Working Life*. Basingstoke: Palgrave Macmillan.

Thompson, P. and van den Broek, D. (2010) Managerial control and workplace regimes. *Work, Employment and Society*, **24**(3): 1–12.

Thompson, P. and Warhurst, C. (eds) (1998) *Workplaces of the Future*. Basingstoke: Palgrave Macmillan.

Thomson, A., Mabey, C., Storey, J., Gray, C. and Iles, P. (2001) *Changing Patterns of Management Development*. Oxford: Blackwell.

Thomson, N. and Millar, C. (2001) The role of slack in transforming organizations. *International Studies of Management and Organization*, **31**(2): 65–83.

Thornhill, A., Saunders, M. N. K. and Stead, J. (1997) Downsizing, delayering – but where's the commitment. *Personnel Review*, **26**(1): 81–98.

Thornton, G. and Gibbons, A. (2009) Validity of assessment centers for personnel selection. *Human Resource Management Review*, **19**(3): 69–187.

Thorpe, R., Gold, J., Anderson, L., Burgoyne, J., Wilkinson, D. and Malby, R. (2009) *Towards Leaderful Communities in the North of England* (2nd edn). Cork: Oaktree Press.

Thorpe, R., Gold, J. and Lawler, J. (2011) Distributed leadership: the current position. *International Journal of Management Reviews* (in press).

Thursfield, D. (2000) *Post-Fordism and Skill*. Aldershot: Ashgate.

Thurston, P. W. and McNall, L. (2010) Justice perceptions of performance appraisal practices. *Journal of Managerial Psychology*, **25**(3): 201–28.

Tien, F. F. and Blackburn, R. (1996) Faculty rank system, research motivation, and faculty research productivity: measure refinement and theory testing. *Journal of Higher Education*, **67**(1): 2–22.

Tietze, S. (2002) When 'work' comes 'home': coping

strategies of teleworkers and their families. *Journal of Business Ethics*, **41**, 385–96.

Tilly, C. (2008) *Democracy*. Cambridge: Cambridge University Press.

Tomlinson, K. (2003) *Effective Interagency Working: A Review of the Literature and Examples from Practice*. LGA Research Report No. 40. Slough: NFER.

Ton, Z. and Huckman, R. S. (2008) Managing the impact of employee turnover on performance: the role of process conformance. *Organization Science*, **19**(1): 56–68.

Toplis, J., Dulvicz, V. and Fletcher, C. (2005) *Psychological Testing* (4th edn). London: Chartered Institute of Personnel and Development.

Torbiörn, I. (2005) Staffing policies and practices in European MNCs: strategic sophistication, culture-bound policies or ad hoc reactivity? In H. Scullion and M. Linehan (eds) *International Human Resource Management* (pp. 47–68). Basingstoke: Palgrave Macmillan.

Torres, R. T., Preskill, H., and Piontek, M. E. (2005) *Evaluation Strategies for Communicating and Reporting: Enhancing Learning in Organizations*. Thousand Oaks, CA: Sage.

Torrington, D. (1998) Discipline and dismissals. In M. Poole and M. Warner (eds) *The Handbook of Human Resource Management* (pp. 498–506). London: International Thomson Business Press.

Tosey, P. (2010) Neuro-linguistic programming for leaders and managers. In J. Gold, R. Thorpe and A. Mumford (eds) *The Gower Handbook of Leadership and Management Development* (pp. 313–30). Aldershot: Gower.

Toulson, P. K. and Dewe, P. (2004) HR accounting as a measurement tool. *Human Resource Management Journal*, **14**(2): 75–90.

Townley, B. (1993) Performance appraisal and the emergence of management. *Journal of Management Studies*, **30**(2): 221–38.

Townley, B. (1994) *Reframing Human Resource Managment*. London: Sage

Trades Union Congress (1979) *The Safety Rep and Union Organization*. London: TUC Education.

Trades Union Congress (1999) *Partners for Progress: New Unionism in the Workplace*. London: TUC.

Trades Union Congress (2007) *Bullying at Work: Guidance for Safety Representatives*. London: Trades Union Congress.

Trades Union Congress (2009) Bullying boss blamed for breakdown. *Risks*, 396.

Trades Union Congress (2010) 'TUC Green Growth Conference'. Available at: www.tuc.org.uk/social/tuc.

Trapp, R. (2005) The mirror has two faces. *People Management*, 19 May: 40–2.

Travaglione, A., and Cross, B. (2006) Diminishing the social network in organizations: does there need to be such a phenomenon as "survivor syndrome" after downsizing? *Strategic Change*, **15**: 1–13.

Travis, A. (2011) Probation officers spend 75% of time on red tape, report finds. *The Guardian*, July 27, p. 7.

Trehan, K. and Pedler, M. (2009) Animating critical action learning: process-based leadership and management development. *Action Learning: Research and Practice*, **6**(1): 35–49.

Tremblay, D.-G. (2003) Telework: a new mode of gendered segmentation? Results from a study in Canada. *Canadian Journal of Communication*, **28**(4): 461–78.

Trethewey, A. (1997) Organizational culture. In P. Y. Byers (ed.) *Organizational Communication: Theory and Behavior* (pp. 203–34). Boston: Allyn & Bacon.

Trevor, J. (2009) Can pay be strategic?' In S. Corby, S. Palmer and E. Lindop (eds) *Rethinking Reward* (pp. 21–40). Basingstoke: Palgrave Macmillan.

Truss, C. (2001) Complexities and controversies in linking HRM with organizational outcomes. *Journal of Management Studies*, **38**(8): 1121–49.

Tseng, C.-C. and McLean, G. (2008) Strategic HRD practices as key factors in organizational learning. *Journal of European Industrial Training*, **32**(6): 418–32.

Tsoukas, H. (2000) Knowledge as action, organization as theory. *Emergence*, **2**(4): 104–12.

Tsoukas, H. and Sandberg, J. (2011) Grasping the logic of practice: theorizing through practical rationality, *Academy of Management Review*, **36**(2): 338–60.

Tucker, R. C. (1978) *The Marx–Engels Reader*. New York: Norton.

Tulip, S. (2004) Hired education. *People Management*, September 30: 46–9.

Tung, R. (1988) *The New Expatriates*. Boston, MA: Ballinger.

Tung, R. (1998) A contingency framework for selection and training of expatriates revisited. *Human Resource Management Review*, **98**(8): 23–38.

Turner, G. (1996) Human resource accounting – whim or wisdom? *Journal of Human Resource Costing and Accounting*, **1**(1): 63–73.

Turner, P. (2003) *Organizational Communication: The Role of the HR Professional*. London: Chartered Institute of Personnel and Development.

Tushman, M. and O'Reilly, C. (1996) Ambidextrous organizations: managing evolutionary and revolutionary change. *California Management Review*, **38**(4): 8–30.

Tyler, M. and Wilkinson, A. (2007) The tyranny of corporate slenderness: 'corporate anorexia' as a metaphor for our age. *Work, Employment and Society*, **21**(3): 537–49.

Tyson, S. (1995) *Human Resource Strategy*. London: Pitman.

Tziner, A., Joanis, C. and Murphy, K. R. (2000) A comparison of three methods of performance appraisal with regard to goal properties, goal perception and ratee satisfaction. *Group and Organization Management*, **25**(2): 175–90.

UK Commission for Employment and Skills (2009) *Ambition 2020, World Class Skills and Jobs for the UK*. London: UKCES.

UK Commission for Employment and Skills (2010) *Developing Leadership and Management Skills through Employer Networks*. London: UKCES.

UK Commission for Employment and Skills (2011) *Skills for Jobs: Today and Tomorrow*: London: UKCES.

Ulrich, D. (1997) Human resource champions. *The Next Agenda for Adding Value and Delivering Results*. Boston, MA: Harvard Business School Press.

Ulrich, D. (1998) A new mandate for human resources. *Harvard Business Review*, **76**: 124–34.

Ulrich, D. and Beatty, R. W. (2001) From partner to players. *Human Resource Management*, **40**(4): 293–307.

Ulrich, D. and Brockbank, W. (2005*) The HR Value Proposition*. Boston, MA: Harvard Business School Press.

Ulrich, D., Alenn, J., Brockbank, W., Younger, J. and Nyman, M. (2009) *HR Transformation: Building Human Resources From the Outside In*. New York: McGraw-Hill.

Ulrich, L. and Trumbo, D. (1965) The selection interview since 1949. *Psychological Bulletin*, **63**: 100–16.

Vallas, S., Finlay, W. and Wharton, A. (2009) *The Sociology of Work*. New York: Oxford University Press.

Van den Brink, M., Brouns, M. and Waslander, D. (2006) Does excellence have a gender? *Employee Relations*, **28**(6): 523–39.

Vanderklippe, N. (2011) Keystone faces 'last stand'. *Globe and Mail*, September 26, p. B1.

VandeWalle, D., Ganesan, S., Challagalla, G. N. and Brown, S. P. (2000) An integrated model of feedback-seeking behavior: disposition, context and cognition. *Journal of Applied Psychology*, **85**(6): 96–103.

Van Dierendonck, D., Haynes, C., Borrill, C. and Stride, C. (2007) Effects of upward feedback on leadership behaviour toward subordinates. *Journal of Management Development*, **26**(3): 228–38.

van Vijfeijken, H., Kleingeld, A., van Tuijl, H., Algera, J. and Thierry, H. (2002) Task complexity and task, goal, and reward interdependence in group performance management: a prescriptive model. *European Journal of Work and Organizational Psychology*, **11**(3): 363–83.

Varma, A. and Pichler, S.and Budhwar, P. (2011) The relationship between expatriate job level and host country national categorization: an investigation in the UK. *International Journal of Human Resource Management*, **22**(1): 103–20.

Verma, A. (1995) Employee involvement in the workplace. In M. Gunderson and A. Ponak (eds) *Union–Management Relations in Canada* (3rd edn) (pp. 281–308). Don Mills, Ontario: Addison-Wesley.

Verma, A. and Taras, D. (2001) Employee involvement in the workplace. In M. Gunderson, A. Ponak and D. Taras (eds) *Union–Management Relations in Canada* (4th edn) (pp. 447–85). Don Mills, Ontario: Addison-Wesley.

Verma, S. and Dewe, P. (2008) Valuing human resources: perceptions and practices in UK organisations. *Journal of Human Resource Costing and Accounting*, **12**(2): 102–23.

Victor, B. and Boynton, A. (1998) *Invented Here: Maximizing Your Organization's Internal Growth and Profitability*. Boston: Harvard Business School Press.

Vidal, J. (2011) U.S. target EU members over stand on genetically modified crops. *Globe and Mail*, January 1, p. A11.

Vilela, B. B., Gonzalez, J. A. V. Ferrin, P. F. and Araujo, M. L (2007) Impression management tactics and affective context: influence on sales performance appraisal. *European Journal of Marketing*, **41**(5/6): 624–39.

Vince, R. and Reynolds, M. (2010) Leading reflection: developing the relationship between leadership and reflection. In J. Gold, R. Thorpe and A. Mumford (eds) *The Gower Handbook of Leadership and Management Development* (pp. 331–46). Aldershot: Gower Press.

Vinnicombe, S. and Singh, V. (2003) Women-only management training – an essential part of women's leadership development. *Journal of Change Management*, **3**(4): 294–306.

Visser, J. (2003) Unions and unionism around the world. In J. T. Addison and C. Schnabel (eds) *International Handbook of Trade Unions* (pp. 366–414). Cheltenham: Edward Elgar.

Visser, J. and Waddington, J. (1996) Industrialization and politics: a century of union structural developments in three European countries. *European Journal of Industrial Relations*, **2**(1): 21–53.

Von Krogh, G. (2003) Knowledge sharing and the communal resources. In M. Easterby-Smith and M. A. Lyles (eds) *The Blackwell Handbook of Organizational Learning and Knowledge Management* (pp. 372–92). Oxford: Blackwell.

Vosko, L. (2000) *Temporary Work: The Gendered Rise of a Precarious Employment Relationship*. Toronto, Ontario: University of Toronto Press.

Vosko, L. F. (2007) Gendered labour market insecurities: manifestations of precarious employment in different locations. In V. Shalla and W. Clement (eds) *Work in Tumultuous Times: Critical Perspectives* (pp. 52–97). Montreal: McGill-Queen's University Press.

Vroom, V. H. (1964) *Work and Motivation*. New York: John Wiley & Sons.

Vygotsky, L. S. (1978) *Mind and Society: The Development of Higher Mental Process*. Cambridge, MA: Harvard University Press.

Waddington, J. (1988) Business unionism and fragmentation within the TUC. *Capital and Class*, (36): 7–15.

Waddington, J. (1992) Trade union membership in Britain, 1980–1987: unemployment and restructuring. *British Journal of Industrial Relations*, **30**(2): 7–15.

Waddington, J. and Whitston, C. (1994) The politics of restructuring: trade unions on the defensive in Britain since 1979. *Relations Industrielles/Industrial Relations*, **49**(4): 794–817.

Waddington, J. and Whitston, C. (1997) Why do people join unions in a period of membership decline? *British Journal of Industrial Relations*, **35**(4): 515–46.

Wagner, R. F. (1949) The employment interview: a critical summary. *Personnel Psychology*, **2**: 17–46.

Wajcman, J. (1998) *Managing Like a Man*. University Park, PA: Pennsylvania State University Press.

Wajcman, J. (2000) Feminism facing industrial relations in Britain. *British Journal of Industrial Relations*, **38**(2): 183–201.

Wall, T. D. and Clegg, C. W. (1998). Job design. In C. L. Cooper and C. Argyris (eds) *The Concise Blackwell Encyclopedia of Management* (pp. 337–9). Oxford: Blackwell.

Wall, T. D. and Wood, S. J. (2005) The romance of human resource management and business performance, and the case for the big science. *Human Relations*, **58**(4): 429–61.

Walters, D. (2004) Worker representation and health and safety in small enterprises in Europe. *Industrial Relations Journal*, **35**(2): 169–86.

Walton, J. (2005) Would the real corporate university please stand up. *Journal of European Industrial Training*, **29**(1): 7–20.

Walton, R. (1985) From control to commitment in the workplace. *Harvard Business Review*, March/April: 77–84.

Wang, G. (2008) National HRD: a new paradigm or reinvention of the wheel. *Journal European Industrial Training*, **32**(4): 303–16.

Warhurst, C., Eikhof, D. R. and Haunschild, A. (2008) *Work Less, Live More? Critical Analysis of the Work– Life Boundary*. Basingstoke: Palgrave Macmillan.

Warner, M. (2002) Globalization, labour markets and human resources in Asia-Pacific economies: an overview. *International Journal of Human Resource Management*, **13**(3): 384–98.

Warner, M. (2004) Human resource management in China revisited: introduction. *International Journal of Human Resource Management*, **15**(4): 617–34.

Warr, P. (2008) Work values: some demographic and cultural correlates. *Journal of Occupational and Organizational Psychology*, **81**: 751–75.

Watkins, K. E. and Marsick, V. J. (1996) *Dimensions of the Learning Organization Questionnaire (DLOQ)*. Warwick, RI: Partners for the Learning Organization.

Watson, S. and Harmel-Law, A. (2010) Exploring the contribution of workplace learning to an HRD strategy in the Scottish legal profession. *Journal of European Industrial Training*, **34**(1): 7–22.

Watson, T. (1986) *Management, Organization and Employment Strategy*. London: Routledge & Kegan Paul.

Watson, T. (1994) Recruitment and selection. In Sisson, K. (ed.) *Personnel Management* (pp. 185–252). Oxford: Blackwell.

Watson, T. (1999) Human resourcing strategies. In J. Leopold, L. Harris and T. Watson (eds) *Strategic Human Resourcing* (pp. 17–38). London: Pitman.

Watson, T. (2003) *Sociology, Work and Industry* (4th edn). London: Routledge.

Watson, T. (2004) HRM and critical social sciences. *Journal of Management Studies*, **41**(3): 447–67.

Watson, T. (2007) HRM, ethical irrationality, and the limits of ethical action. In A. Pinnington, R. Macklin and T. Campbell (eds) *Human Resource Management. Ethics and Employment* (pp. 223–36). Oxford: Oxford University Press.

Watson, T. J. (2008) *Sociology, Work and Industry*. London: Routledge.

Watson, T. J. (2010) Critical social science, pragmatism and the realities of HRM. *International Journal of Human Resource Management Studies*, **21**(6): 915–31.

Watson, T. and Harris, P. (1999) *The Emergent Manager*. London: Sage.

Watson, T. J. Leopold, J., and Watling, D. (2009) Strategic choice in patterns of employment relationships. In J. Leopold and L. Harris (eds) *The Strategic Management of Human Resources* (2nd edn) (pp. 442–72). Harlow: Prentice Hall.

Watts, J. J. (2009) Leaders of men: women 'managing' in construction. *Work Employment and Society*, **23**(3): 512–30.

Weale, S. (2000) Law: is it safe to speak out? It's a year since the new legislation was passed to protect whistleblowers at work. Sally asks if it's working. *The Guardian*, July 3, p. 8.

Webb, S. and Webb, B. (1911) *Industrial Democracy*. London: Longmans.

Weber, B. (2011) Oil sands polluting Alberta watersheds, panel reports. *Globe and Mail*, March 10, p. A5.

Weber, M. (1903–1917/1949) *The Methodology of the Social Sciences* (eds E. Shils and H. Finch). New York: Free Press.

Weber, M. (1904–05/2002) *The Protestant Ethic and the Spirit of Capitalism*, London: Penguin.

Weber, M. (1922/1968) *Economy and Society*. New York: Bedminster.

Wedderburn, Lord (1986) *The Worker and the Law* (3rd edn). Harmondsworth: Penguin.

Wehrmeyer, W. (1996) *Greening People: Human Resources and Environmental Management*. Sheffield: Greenleaf Publishing.

Wei, L.-Q. and Lau, C.-M. (2010) High performance work systems and performance: the role of adaptive capability. *Human Relations*, **63**(10): 1487–511.

Wei, L.-Q., Liu, J. and Herndon, N. C. (2011) SHRM and product innovation: testing the moderating effects of organizational culture and structure in Chinese firms. *International Journal of Human Resource Management*, **22**(1): 19–33.

Weichman, D. and Ryan, A. (2003) Reactions to computerized testing in selection contexts. *International Journal of Selection and Assessment*, **11**: 215–29.

Weick, K. E. (2001) *Making Sense of the Organization*. Oxford: Blackwell.

Weick, K. and Westley, F. (1996) Organizational learning: affirming an oxymoron. In S. Clegg, C. Hardy and W. Nord (eds) *Handbook of Organization Studies* (pp. 190–208). London: Sage.

Welbourne, T. and Trevor, C. (2000) The roles of departmental and position power in job evaluation. *Academy of Management Journal*, **43**(4): 761–71.

Weldy, T. G. (2009) Learning organization and transfer: strategies for improving performance. *Learning Organization*, **16**(1): 58–68.

Weldy, T. G. and Gillis, W. E. (2010) The learning organization: variations at different organizational levels. *Learning Organization*, **17**(5): 455–70.

Wells, D. (1993) Are strong unions compatible with the new model of human resource management? *Relations Industrielles/Industrial Relations*, **48**(1): 56–84.

Wells, G. (1999) *Dialogic Inquiry: Towards a Sociocultural Practice and Theory of Education*. New York: Cambridge University Press.

Wenger, E. C. and Snyder, W. M. (2000) Communities of practice: the organizational frontier. *Harvard Business Review*, January–February: 139–45.

Wente, M. (2011) The nest bubble to burst may be yours. *Globe and Mail*, March 12, p. F9.

Western, S. (2008) *Leadership: A Critical Text*. London: Sage.

Westley, F. and Mintzberg, H. (2007) Visionary leadership and strategic management. *Strategic Management Journal*, **10**(1): 17–32.

Wheatley, M. (1994) *Leadership and the New Science*. San Francisco, CA: Berrett-Koehler.

Wheelen, T. and Hunger, J. (1995) *Strategic Management and Business Policy* (5th edn). New York: Addison-Wesley.

Wheeler, A. R., Buckley, M. R., Halbesleben, J. R., Brouer, B. and Ferris, G. R. (2005) The elusive criterion of fit revisited: toward an integrative theory of multidimensional fit. *Research in Personnel and Human Resources Management*, **24**: 265–304.

Whelan, E. and Carcary, M. (2011) Integrating talent and knowledge management: where are the benefits? *Journal of Knowledge Management*, **15**(4): 675–87.

Whiddett, S. and Hollyforde, K. (2003) *A Practical Guide to Competencies*. London: Chartered Institute of Personnel and Development.

Whitley, R. (1999) *Divergent Capitalism: The Social Structuring and Change of Business Systems*. Oxford: Oxford University Press.

Whitmore, J. (2002) *Coaching For Performance: Growing People, Performance and Purpose* (3rd edn). London: Nicholas Brealey Publishing.

Whittaker, D. H. (1990) *Managing Innovation: A Study of British and Japanese Factories*. Cambridge: Cambridge University Press.

Whittaker, S. and Marchington, M. (2003) Devolving HR responsibilities to the line: threat, opportunity or partnership? *Employee Relations*, **36**(3): 245–61.

Whittington, R. (1993) *What is Strategy and Does it Matter?* London: Routledge.

Wickens, P. (1987) *The Road to Nissan*. London: Palgrave Macmillan.

Widget Finn (2010) 'Best Workplaces 2010'. Barinnga Partners, UK's Best Workplaces, May. Available at: www.greatplacetowork.co.uk.

Wiggins, J. S. (ed.) (1996) *The Five-factor Model of Personality*. New York: Guildford Publications.

Wilk, S. and Cappelli, P. (2003) Understanding the determinants of employer use of selection methods. *Personnel Psychology*, **57**: 103–24.

Williams, R. (1976) *Keywords: A Vocabulary of Culture and Society*. New York: Oxford University Press.

Williams, R. (1983) *Keywords*. New York: Oxford University Press.

Williams, S. (1999) Policy failure in education and training: the introduction of National Vocational Qualifications (1986–1990). *Education and Training*, **41**(5): 216–26.

Williams, S., Abbott, B. and Heery, E. (2011) Non-union,

worker representation through civil society organizations: evidence from the United Kingdom. *Industrial Relations Journal*, **42**(1): 69–85.

Willmott, H. (1984) Images and ideals of managerial work. *Journal of Management Studies*, **21**(3): 349–68.

Willmott, H. (1993) 'Strength is ignorance: freedom is slavery': managing culture in modern organizations. *Journal of Management Studies*, **30**(4): 515–52.

Willmott, H. (1995) The odd couple?: re-engineering business processes; managing human relations. *New Technology, Work and Employment*, **10**(2): 89–97.

Wilkinson, R. and Pickett, K. (2010) *The Spirit Level: Why Equality is Better for Everyone*. London: Penguin.

Wilson, J. P. and Western, S. (2000) Performance appraisal: an obstacle to training and development. *Journal of European Industrial Training*, **24**(7): 384–90.

Wilson, K. and Jones, R. (2008) Reducing job-irrelevant bias in performance appraisals: compliance and beyond. *Journal of General Management*, **34**(2): 57–70.

Wilson, R. and Hogarth, T. (2003) *Tackling the Low Skills Equilibrium: A Review of Issues and Some New Evidence*. London: Department of Trade and Industry.

Winfield, N. (2011) 'EU, oil companies begin Libya evacuations', February 21. Available at: www.chron.com/disp/story.mpl (accessed March 3).

Winstanley, D. and Woodall, J. (eds) (2000) *Ethical Issues in Contemporary Human Resource Management*. Basingstoke: Palgrave Macmillan.

Winstanley, D. and Stuart-Smith, K. (1996) Policing performance: the ethics of performance management. *Personnel Review*, **25**(6): 66–84.

Wintour, P., Stratton, A. and Treanor, J. (2010) Cable attacks 'nauseating businessmen'. *The Guardian*, April 10, p. 1.

Witherspoon, P. D. (1997) *Communicating Leadership*. Boston: Allyn & Bacon.

Witz, A. (1986) Patriarchy and the labour market: occupational control strategies and the medical division of labour. In D. Knights and H. Willmott (eds) *Gender and the Labour Process* (pp. 14–35). Aldershot: Gower.

Wolf, A. (2011) *Review of Vocational Education*. London: Department of Education.

Womack, J., Jones, D. and Roos, D. (1990) *The Machine that Changed the World*. New York: Rawson Associates.

Wood, I., Rodgers, H. and Gold, J. (2004) 'Picturing prejudice: learning to see diversity', paper presented at the Fifth HRD Conference, Limerick University, May.

Wood, S. (1995) The four pillars of HRM: are they

connected? *Human Resource Management Journal*, **5**(5): 49–59.

Wood, S. (2000) The BJIR and industrial relations in the new millennium. *British Journal of Industrial Relations*, **38**(1): 1–5.

Wood, S. (2008) Job characteristics, employee voice and well-being in Britain. *Industrial Relations Journal*, **39**(2): 153–68.

Wood, S. and Godard, J. (1999) The statutory union recognition procedure in the Employment Relations Bill: a comparative analysis. *British Journal of Industrial Relations*, **37**(2): 203–44.

Wood, S., Moore, S. and Willman, P. (2002) Third time lucky for statutory recognition in the UK. *Industrial Relations Journal*, **33**(3): 215–33.

Wood, S., Holman, D. and Stride, C. (2006) Human resource management and performance in UK call centres. *British Journal of Industrial Relations*, **44**(1): 99–124.

Woodall, J. (2001) Editorial. *Human Resource Development International*, **4**(3): 287–90.

Woodall, J., Scott-Jackson, W., Newham, T. and Gurney, M. (2009) Making the decision to outsource human resources. *Personnel Review*, **38**, (3):236–52.

Woodruffe, C. (2000) *Development and Assessment Centres* (3rd edn). London: Chartered Institute of Personnel and Development.

World Health Organization (2011) www.who.int/about/definition (accessed March 9, 2011).

Wright, C. (2011) 'What role for trade unions in future workplace relations?' ACAS Future of Workplace Relations discussion paper series. Available at: www.acas.org.uk.

Wright, M. (1996) The collapse of compulsory unionism? Collective organization in highly unionized British companies, 1979–1991. *British Journal of Industrial Relations*, **34**(4): 497–513.

Wright, P. M. and Boswell, W. R. (2002) Desegregating HRM: a review and synthesis of micro and macro human resource management research. *Journal of Management*, **28**(3): 247–76.

Wright, P. and Gardner, T. (2003) The human resource–firm performance relationship. Methodological and theoretical challenges. In D. Holman, T. Hall, C. Clegg, P. Sparrow, and A. Howard (eds) *The New Workplace: A Guide to the Human Impact of Modern Work Practices* (pp. 311–29). London: John Wiley & Sons.

Wright, P. M. and McMahan, C. G. (1992) Theoretical perspectives for strategic human resource management. *Journal of Management*, **18**: 295–319.

Wright, P. and Snell, S. (1998) Towards a unifying framework for exploring fit and flexibility in strategic human resource management. *Academy of Management Review*, **23**(4): 756–72.

Wright, P. M., Gardner, T. M. and Moynihan, L. M. (2003) The impact of HR practices on the performance of business units. *Human Resource Management Journal*, **13**(3): 21–36.

Yakabuski, K. (2008) The kindness of corporations. Report on business. *Globe and Mail*, July–August: 66–71.

Yammarino, F. J. and Atwater, L. E. (1997) Implications of self–other rating agreement for human resources management. *Organizational Dynamics*, **25**(4): 35–44.

Yang, B., Watkins, K. E. and Marsick, V. J. (2004) The construct of the learning organization: dimensions, measurement, and validation. *Human Resource Development Quarterly*, **15**(1): 31–5.

Yanow, D. (2000) Seeing organizational learning: a 'cultural' view. *Organization*, **7**(2): 247–68.

Yanow, D. (2004) Translating local knowledge at organizational peripheries. *British Journal of Management*, **15**(1): 9–25.

Yap, M. and Konrad, A. (2009) Gender and racial differentials in promotions: is there a sticky floor, a mid-level bottleneck, or a class ceiling? *Relations Industrielle/Industrial relations*, **64**(4): 593–620.

York, G. (2001) Russian city ravaging Arctic land. *Globe and Mail*, July 25, p. A1.

Youndt, M. A., Snell, S. A., Dean, J. W. and Lepak, D. P. (1996) Human resource management, manufacturing strategy and firm performance. *Academy of Management Journal*, **39**: 836–66.

Yu, G. and Park, J. (2006) The effect of downsizing on the financial performance and employee productivity of Korean firms. *International Journal of Manpower*, **27**: 230–50.

Yu, K.-H. and Levy, F. (2010) Offshoring professional services: institutions and professional control. *British Journal of Industrial Relations*. **48**(4): 758–83.

Yukl, G. (2005) *Leadership in Organizations* (6th edn). Englewood Cliffs, NJ: Prentice Hall.

Zhang, J. and Hamilton, E. (2006) 'Entrepreneurial learning through peer networks: a process model', paper presented at the British Academy of Management conference in Belfast' September.

Zhang, Y. and Albrecht, C. (2010) The role of cultural values on a firm's strategic human resource management development: a comparative study of Spanish firms in China. *International Journal of Human Resource Management*, **21**(11): 1911–30.

Zhang, Y. and Begley, T. M. (2011) Perceived organizational climate, knowledge transfer and innovation in China-based research and development companies. *International Journal of Human Resource Management*, **22**(1): 34–56.

Zimmerman, A. and Kendall, B. (2011) Wal-Mart gears up for sex-discrimination case. *Globe and Mail*, March 11, p. B10.

subject index

Page numbers marked with an asterisk (*) denote website addresses on those pages
HRM stands for human resource management